Great Britain, the Dominions and the Transformation of the British Empire, 1907–1931

The relations of Great Britain and its Dominions significantly influenced the development of the British Empire in the late 19th and the first third of the 20th century. The mutual attitude to the constitutional issues that Dominion and British leaders have continually discussed at Colonial and Imperial Conferences respectively was one of the main aspects forming the links between the mother country and the autonomous overseas territories. This volume therefore focuses on the key period when the importance of the Dominions not only increased within the Empire itself, but also in the sphere of the international relations, and the Dominions gained the opportunity to influence the forming of the Imperial foreign policy. During the first third of the 20th century, the British Empire gradually transformed into the British Commonwealth of Nations, in which the importance of Dominions excelled. The work is based on the study of unreleased sources from British archives, a large number of published documents and extensive relevant literature.

Jaroslav Valkoun is an assistant professor of general history at the Department of Historical Sciences, University of West Bohemia, Pilsen, and the Department of Global History, Charles University, Prague.

Routledge Studies in Modern British History

White-Collar Crime in Late Nineteenth and Early Twentieth-Century Britain
John Benson

Transport and Its Place in History
Making the Connections
Edited by David Turner

The Independent Labour Party 1914–1939
The Political and Cultural History of a Socialist Party
Keith Laybourn

Sport and the Home Front
Wartime Britain at Play, 1939–45
Matthew Taylor

Weather, Migration and the Scottish Diaspora
Leaving the Cold Country
Graeme Morton

Science, Utility and British Naval Technology, 1793–1815
Samuel Bentham and the Royal Dockyards
Roger Morriss

Credit and Power
The Paradox at the Heart of the British National Debt
Simon Sherratt

The Casino and Society in Britain
Seamus Murphy

Great Britain, the Dominions and the Transformation of the British Empire, 1907–1931
The Road to the Statute of Westminster
Jaroslav Valkoun

The Discourse of Repatriation in Britain, 1845–2016
A Political and Social History
Daniel Renshaw

The Devil and the Victorians
Supernatural Evil in Nineteenth-Century English Culture
Sarah Bartels

Lord Dufferin, Ireland and the British Empire, c. 1820–1900
Rule by the Best?
Annie Tindley

For more information about this series, please visit: https://www.routledge.com/history/series/RSMBH

Great Britain, the Dominions and the Transformation of the British Empire, 1907–1931
The Road to the Statute of Westminster

Jaroslav Valkoun

NEW YORK AND LONDON

First published 2021
by Routledge
52 Vanderbilt Avenue, New York, NY 10017

and by Routledge
2 Park Square, Milton Park, Abingdon, Oxon, OX14 4RN

Routledge is an imprint of the Taylor & Francis Group, an informa business

© 2021 Jaroslav Valkoun

The right of Jaroslav Valkoun to be identified as author of this work has been asserted in accordance with sections 77 and 78 of the Copyright, Designs and Patents Act 1988.

All rights reserved. No part of this book may be reprinted or reproduced or utilised in any form or by any electronic, mechanical, or other means, now known or hereafter invented, including photocopying and recording, or in any information storage or retrieval system, without permission in writing from the publishers.

Trademark notice: Product or corporate names may be trademarks or registered trademarks, and are used only for identification and explanation without intent to infringe.

Published in Czech as *Na cestě k Westminsterskému statutu: Velká Británie, dominia a proměna Britského impéria v letech 1907–1931* by Univerzita Karlova v Praze, Filozofická fakulta, 2015

Library of Congress Cataloging-in-Publication Data
Names: Valkoun, Jaroslav, 1983- author.
Title: Great Britain, the Dominions and the transformation of the British Empire, 1907-1931 : the road to the statute of Westminster / Jaroslav Valkoun.
Description: New York, NY : Routledge, 2021. | Series: Routledge studies in modern British history | Includes bibliographical references and index.
Subjects: LCSH: Great Britain--Colonies--History--20th century. | Commonwealth countries--History--20th century. | Great Britain--History--Edward VII, 1901-1910. | Great Britain--History--George V, 1910-1936. | Great Britain--Foreign relations--1901-1936.
Classification: LCC DA16 .V35 2021 (print) | LCC DA16 (ebook) | DDC 909/.09712410821--dc23
LC record available at https://lccn.loc.gov/2020049724
LC ebook record available at https://lccn.loc.gov/2020049725

ISBN: 978-0-367-65447-4 (hbk)
ISBN: 978-1-003-12947-9 (ebk)

Typeset in Sabon
by SPi Global, India

Contents

List of Abbreviations   vi

Introduction   1

1   The British Empire, or Commonwealth?   13

2   Great Britain and Its Dominions Before the First World War   27

3   The Empire During the War and Post-War Period   87

4   The New Constitutional Status for the Dominions?   173

5   The Road to the Statute of Westminster   235

Conclusion   279

Bibliography   284
Author Index   329
Subject Index   334

Abbreviations

ADM	Admiralty Papers
AP	Amery Papers
APD	Commonwealth of Australia, Parliamentary Debates
BD	British Documents on the Origins of the War
BDEEP	British Documents on the End of Empire
BL	The British Library
BLO	Bodleian Library
BP	Balfour Papers
BT	Board of Trade Papers
CAB	Cabinet Office Papers
CAC	Churchill Archives Centre
CCP	Cecil of Chelwood Papers
CO	Colonial Office Papers
CP	Curtis Papers
CPD	Canada, Parliamentary Debates
CUL	Cambridge University Library
DBFP	Documents on British Foreign Policy
DCER	Documents on Canadian External Relations
DÉ	Dáil Éireann
DIFP	Documents on Irish Foreign Policy
DO	Dominion Office Papers
FO	Foreign Office Papers
FRUS	Papers Relating to the Foreign Relations of the United States
HMSO	His Majesty's Stationery Office
HoC	House of Commons
HoL	House of Lords
HoR	House of Representatives
HP	Hankey Papers
IPD	Ireland, Parliamentary Debates
LCO	Lord Chancellor's Office

PD	United Kingdom, Parliamentary Debates
PREM	Prime Minister's Office Papers
PRO	Public Record Office Papers
SP	Smuts Papers
TNA	The National Archives

Introduction

The passing of the Statute of Westminster in 1931 is an important milestone in the history of the British Empire. Just as the First World War marks the end of the "long 19th century", so 1931 represents a watershed moment for the British Empire. It signifies the end of one era of relations between the mother country and its Dominions, i.e. the *de facto* "white" settlements, with a complex Imperial structure beginning the gradual transformation into the Commonwealth, or officially the Commonwealth of Nations. Despite the fact that the statute represented an almost "revolutionary transformation" in the status of the Dominions, everything ran smoothly without major complications. Many contemporaries held the opinion that the British Commonwealth represented a kind of "living organism" with a more natural internal ability to adjust to new external and internal factors than other empires bound by rigid rules had.[1] The Secretary of State for the Colonies and Dominions of many years, Leopold Stennett Amery, had a similar perspective on the essence of Britain's Commonwealth of Nations:

> The essential characteristic of an organism, as contrasted with a mechanical structure, is that there is vitality in all its parts, mutual cooperation between them, and above all a general purpose to maintain its existence, whether centralised or diffused through the whole organism.[2]

Since there were no legal or constitutional obstacles to prevent changes in the "organism", there was a slow, perhaps overly lengthy, but natural process during which individual states transformed themselves into the British Commonwealth. This transformation had a natural genesis in the gradual changes and transformations in relations towards the mother country. Within the Commonwealth, actually one of the oldest international associations of states still existing today, the level of mutual obligations has always played an important role, because all the different members of the British Commonwealth of Nations have not always had the same status. Time has shown that the constitutional status of Dominions was the most important issue.

Although the term "Dominion status" first appeared in 1867, it wasn't until the end of the First World War that it was in common use within the Imperial structure. For decades, coming up with a precise definition was an objective for many British and Dominion politicians and statesmen. The term was originally used mainly to give a summary of the various privileges which the Crown gradually awarded to its overseas autonomous governments, which over time moved towards full state sovereignty alongside membership of Britain's Commonwealth of Nations. The causes of this process are to be found in past centuries in which colonial administrators collected experience of state administration. Critics of the British Empire's constitutional development very frequently noted that Dominion status had not been defined or otherwise codified. In contrast, its defenders argued that it was constantly developing and as such could not be codified in legislation, and in fact it would be inadvisable to do so, as this could suppress its "natural" development. Imperialism theoreticians determined that the secession of the thirteen North American colonies had taught the valuable lesson that overly strict laws did not allow one to effectively overcome unanticipated challenges which one might encounter in the overseas possessions.[3]

No part of the history of the British Commonwealth of Nations can be perceived from the perspective of the overseas territories alone, or exclusively on the basis of the opinions of the mother country. Although Dominion status allowed the Self-Governing Colonies to attain "virtual" freedom in decisions about local matters, the Dominions did not have an effect on the Empire's direction as a whole, since its representatives did not sit in Westminster and were not involved in the operation of British ministries, and as such were unable to make decisions on key matters of imperial foreign policy. Over time, however, Dominion representatives came to the impression that the level of constitutional relations was not entirely satisfactory.

The end of the First World War represented the beginning of a new era in the history of the British Empire, which was transformed into a regular international community, raising the importance of the overseas autonomous territories. In the end, this was an ambivalent process. On the one hand, the Commonwealth continued to symbolise unity, and on the other hand there was a relaxation in previously close relations between the English-speaking population and the mother country which had lasted two centuries, leading in some countries to emancipation and a desire for independence from Britain.

This monograph looks not just at the roles of significant Dominion representatives in constitutional matters determining the development of the British Commonwealth of Nations, but also the roles of leading British politicians and interest groups formulating attitudes towards the Empire.

Overseas prime ministers in particular had a unique influence on relations with the mother country. They generally had "first hand" information and in many cases had bonds of friendship with British politicians, or at least personal contact with them, through which they were able to influence the opinions of the British people, and vice versa. In regard to Dominion prime ministers, I have focused on analysing the Commonwealth from three perspectives: (1) the perspective of the leading representatives of its countries, (2) the perspective of statesmen responsible for the "smooth running" of the British Empire, and (3) the perspective of representatives of domestic parliaments to which they were responsible.

Naturally, one cannot investigate the status of Dominions purely on the basis of personal or political stances, decisions and the constitutional measures taken by Dominion and British statesmen and politicians at Colonial (Imperial) Conferences, especially in the period following the First World War, and on the basis of an analysis of the communication method within the Empire and the implementation and direction of Imperial foreign policy in which some sided with the British course, others took the opposite approach. Frequently, the Dominions did not act as "one large partner" to the mother country speaking the same language and with the same interest; each Dominion built up relations to London individually. As such, levels of willingness of Commonwealth members to co-operate varied greatly.

Although relations between the Dominions and the mother country were full of imperial symbolism, aspects which formed them were frequently difficult to define. Despite all this, autonomy, equal status and obligations to the Crown inherently bound them to the mother country. Although matters of fundamental importance to the Empire were mostly decided upon during Colonial and Imperial Conference meetings, or sometimes "only" in London, for various reasons Dominion prime ministers frequently came up against limits which arose from the specific status of individual Dominions and which had to reflect local public opinion. As such, the composition of local parliaments often had a significant impact on the stance of overseas politicians in dealing with various imperial matters. Nevertheless, Dominion prime ministers made no commitments at conferences which their governments or local legislature would not have approved.

The question arises indirectly from this as to whether initiative in constitutional matters came from the overseas statesmen or British representatives, or whether the British Colonial Office, or the Dominion Office, were able to effectively respond to the emancipation of the overseas autonomous territories and the demands they made. Despite the fact that the economic aspects of relations between the Dominions and the mother country played an important role over the period investigated here and that these were frequently discussed, especially at Imperial Conferences, crucially they did not affect the constitutional issue. As such, in order to ensure an acceptable scope, this work will not focus in great detail on this aspect.

This monograph is divided into five chapters. The first of these is an analysis of terminological genesis, defining and explaining the co-existence of the terms "British Empire" and "Commonwealth" from the end of the 19th century until 1931. In this regard, I have also posited the question of whether both terms can be considered equivalents, or rather synonyms. In the other parts of the work, I have taken a chronological approach in my analysis of the issue. The second chapter, included to give a more comprehensive overview of the complex relationships within the Empire, looks at the shaping of constitutional relations between the mother country and the Dominions prior to the First World War, between 1887 and 1914. In individual subchapters, I have considered issues related to the existence of Self-Governing Colonies, the forming of the first Dominions, the (lack of) success of Colonial Conferences, and last but not least also academic and political discussions on various concepts for the future organisational structure of the British Empire. At the same time, I have analysed the gradual creation and institutionalisation of the system of Imperial Conferences and its "competition" with the Imperial Defence Committee on the final say on the form of relations between the mother country and Dominions and on the "primacy" of the Imperial institutions. Nor have I neglected an analysis of the positions of leading British and Dominion representatives within the narrower Imperial union, including in particular Leopold Stennett Amery and Lionel George Curtis, and Imperial organisations, of which the most important and most influential was the Round Table Movement.

The book's third chapter analyses developments between 1914 and 1921, i.e. the period from the outbreak of the First World War to the signing of the December 1921 Anglo-Irish Agreement which ended one stage in relations between the overseas governments and London. In this chapter, I have focused on analysing the influence of war and post-war events on the transformation of constitutional relationships between the Dominions and the mother country. The British Empire was experiencing its greatest test of cohesion since the first Dominions were formed. As such, the first section of the chapter looks in particular at the co-ordination of war efforts using the newly established Imperial War Cabinet and constitutional matters which culminated in adoption of the key Resolution IX at the Imperial War Conference in 1917. In subsequent sections, I have posited the question of whether the Great War affected the status of Dominions towards the mother country and foreign countries outwardly, and if so, whether this change was temporary or permanent. For this reason, I have thoroughly analysed the political measures, dealings and positions of British and Dominion statesmen at the Paris Peace Conference and in post-war constitutional discussions. In this section, I have looked at the positions of British and Dominion leaders, the most significant of whom were Leopold Amery and Jan Christiaan (Christian) Smuts. Since the level of involvement in making decisions on the direction of Imperial foreign policy was one of the key causes of conflict between overseas and London politicians which led to demands for constitutional changes, I have also analysed the position of Dominions in regard to the extension of the Anglo-Japanese Alliance and the course of the naval disarmament conference in Washington. Another important section of this chapter is an analysis of the circumstances which led to the acceptance of Ireland's Dominion status and which caused confusion over what the actual definition of Dominion status was within the Empire's structure.

The fourth chapter is an analysis of the period from 1922 until the end of 1925, i.e. from the Chanak Crisis until the conclusion of the Rhineland Pact. In individual sections, I have focused on the issues regarding to what extent Dominions influenced Imperial foreign policy using the example of key events such as the Chanak incident, the Lausanne Conference, the so-called Halibut Treaty, the Imperial Conference in 1923, the Article X of the Covenant of the League of Nations,[4] the Geneva Protocol, the Locarno Treaties and how these were reflected in matters of the Dominions' constitutional status. In regard to the arrival of Leopold Amery as Secretary of State for the Colonies, who began a new stage in constitutional relations between the Dominions and the mother country, I have also analysed the transferral of Dominion affairs out of Britain's Colonial Office and the establishment of a separate office for the Dominions.

In the final, fifth, chapter I have analysed events from 1926 to 1931, i.e. the period from the adoption of the Balfour Declaration until adoption of the Statute of Westminster. I have paid particular attention to the disputes between Canadian Prime Minister William Lyon Mackenzie King and the Canadian Governor-General, Lord Byng, and political changes in the Union of South Africa, which affected the agenda at the key 1926 Imperial Conference, in which a constitutional declaration was issued defining Dominions' status within the Empire. I have also analysed the impacts of the final report of the Inter-Imperial Relations Committee and its legislative installation within the Statute of Westminster. In the context of the Balfour Declaration, I have posited the fundamental question of whether from a constitutional perspective it dealt with the existing disputes between the Dominions and the mother country.

During the research phase, a significant complication for me was the fact that although there is a large amount of sources and academic publications on the topic, none have been produced over the last half century which have directly focused on the constitutional issue. The key sources for my research of relations between the Dominions and Great Britain are located in the National Archives in Kew, London. These archives have a large amount of materials and documents not just on relations within the British Empire, but also on constitutional matters, the genesis of which my monograph focuses on. Over the course of my research, I focused on a number of key collections which cannot be disregarded in any study of relations between the mother country and the overseas autonomous territories.

In particular, these sources include the Colonial Office Papers. I made particular use of files CO 323 and CO 537 containing general official and confidential correspondence between the department and overseas representatives, and CO 885 and CO 886 including confidential documents related to the international status of Dominions and Self-Governing Colonies in regard to third countries and the agenda of Colonial and Imperial Conferences. I also made use of the Dominion Office Papers, of which I mainly studied files DO 35 and DO 117 focused on official correspondence between the Dominion Office and overseas governments, and DO 114 and DO 121 containing confidential documents and correspondence with British Governors-General, or governors and British representatives in regard to the political situation within the Dominions. Series DO 127 looks at adoption of the Statute of Westminster.

The second main group of archive material I exploited in my research comprised the British government's Cabinet Office Papers. In my research, I worked mainly from files CAB 1, CAB 2, CAB 5, CAB 17 and CAB 34, containing documents focused on Imperial defence and co-operation within the Committee of Imperial Defence, and CAB 21 looking at the circumstances of the establishment of the Anglo-Irish Agreement of 1921. I also studied file CAB 23, which contains minutes and conclusions of British cabinet meetings, and CAB 24, including memoranda the government worked on. Both collections are an important source for analysing government positions on Imperial policy implementation. I also worked with archival records focused on minutes, conclusions and memoranda from meetings of British Empire delegates at international conferences such as the Paris Peace Conference (CAB 29) and the Washington Disarmament Conference (CAB 30). Last but not least, I then analysed the minutes, conclusions and memoranda of meetings of British and Dominion statesmen at Imperial and Imperial War Conferences which are stored in the archive under file numbers CAB 32 and CAB 37.

At the National Archives in Kew, I partly worked on collections of the Admiralty Papers (ADM 1) and the Board of Trade Papers (BT 11) looking at certain sub-aspects of the Washington Disarmament Conference, with the Lord Chancellor's Office Papers (LCO 2) containing material on the Statute of Westminster, with material in the Public Record Office (PRO 30/30) including some of Lord Milner's papers, and with the Foreign Office Papers (FO 372 and FO 800) containing correspondence on matters of Imperial foreign policy.

Over the course of my research, I also focused my attention on the study of archival records from the estates of major British and Dominion politicians and statesmen. First of all, these involve the Cambridge University Library archives which include some correspondence between

South African General and Prime Minister Jan Christiaan Smuts (Add. MS 7917) and the Gillette family. I also undertook research in the Churchill Archives Centre at Cambridge University's Churchill College, which includes the papers of Britain's Secretary of State for the Colonies and Dominions, Leopold Stennett Amery, and Cabinet and Committee of Imperial Defence Secretary, Sir Maurice Hankey. The collections relating to Amery (AMEL 1, AMEL 2, AMEL 3 and AMEL 5) mainly contain official and personal correspondence with British and Dominion statesmen, politicians and leading representatives of society. Of Sir Maurice Hankey's estate, I studied files HNKY 7, HNKY 24 and HNKY 27, looking at the activities of the Imperial Conferences and Imperial Defence Committee, the Paris Peace Conference and correspondence with General Smuts. I also undertook archival research in the British Library, which contains the estate of Lord Balfour and Viscount Cecil of Chelwood. In my studies, I particularly focused on their correspondence with the Committee of Imperial Defence (Add MS 49698), with members of the British cabinet (Add MS 49734, Add MS 49775) and with Maurice Hankey (Add MS 49704) and on Imperial foreign policy (Add MS 49748, Add MS 51102). At the same time, also interesting are the Lionel Curtis Papers in the Bodleian Library at University of Oxford.

Of published sources, I used documents from Britain's House of Commons, in particular government publication papers (Command Papers) C., Cd. and Cmd. series, containing published minutes, conclusions and correspondence on Colonial and Imperial Conference matters, Imperial foreign and defence policy and international conferences and conventions. I also analysed transcripts of relevant debates in British and Dominion parliaments (so-called Hansard).

Of published source series, I used *British Documents on the Origins of the War, 1898–1914*,[5] *Documents on British Foreign Policy 1919–1939*,[6] *British Documents on the End of Empire*,[7] *Documents on Canadian External Relations*,[8] *Papers Relating to the Foreign Relations of the United States*[9] and *Documents on Irish Foreign Policy*[10] in my research, these containing important documents (telegrams, memoranda, notes) from Britain's Foreign Office, Colonial and Dominion Office, Governors-General, or Governors in Dominions and individual British embassies. I also worked on the following series of published sources: *Documents and Speeches on British Commonwealth Affairs 1931–1952*,[11] *The Development of Dominion Status, 1900–1936*,[12] *Selected Speeches and Documents on British Colonial Policy, 1763–1917*,[13] *Speeches and Documents on the British Dominions, 1918–1931*,[14] *The Colonial and Imperial Conferences from 1887 to 1937*,[15] focused on the Empire and containing a lot of material (telegrams, minutes and conclusions of parliamentary and conference meetings, treaties, government directives, newspaper articles) on relations between the Dominions and the mother country.

A number of collections of correspondence and speeches of important British and Dominion politicians are focused on constitutional relationships, such as Stanley Baldwin (*Our Inheritance: Speeches and Addresses*),[16] Lord Rosebery (*Lord Rosebery's Speeches [1874–1896]*),[17] Joseph Chamberlain (*Mr. Chamberlain's Speeches; Foreign & Colonial Speeches*),[18] South Africa's General Smuts (*Selections from the Smuts Papers; War-time Speeches*)[19] and Alfred Milner (*The Nation and the Empire*).[20] In my studies, newspapers and magazines were also an important source, if very frequently affected by the period and with subjective bias for one or the other side. Despite this, they were a very important source for certain events and negotiations. I focused in particular on the press of the time published in Britain and in the Dominions – *The New Zealand Herald, Nation and Athenaeum, Spectator, New Statesman, Evening Post, The Press, Barron's, The Sydney Morning Herald* and the *Auckland Star*.

A great number of memoirs, diaries and autobiographies of various British and Dominion figures look at constitutional relations between the Dominions and Great Britain, and these are an important source for understanding the complexity of Britain's Imperial structure. First of all, one must note the diaries and memoirs of Britain's Secretary of State for the Colonies and Dominions, Leopold Amery,[21] the memoirs of Canadian Prime Minister Sir Robert Laird Borden,[22] the autobiography of advocate of the idea of the League of Nations, Viscount Cecil of Chelwood,[23] the diaries of his American colleague, David Hunter Miller,[24] and the memoirs of British Prime Minister David Lloyd George.[25]

In recent decades, academic work has only briefly touched on constitutional affairs within the British Empire, because political, economic, cultural and social complications accompanying the process of decolonisation have "overshadowed" relations between the "white" Dominions and the mother country. I consider the monograph by Australian historian Hessel Duncan Hall[26] to be a fundamental work still not bettered in terms of the scope of the issue looked at. In contrast to other authors, Hall did not favour either advocates of centralisation (federalisation) or advocates of decentralisation (autonomy) of the Empire, instead supporting Smuts's idea of a general declaration of constitutional rights which was partially implemented in 1926.[27] Another key work in studying this field is that of Leopold Amery,[28] someone who promoted the principle of independence and equality between Britain and the Dominions under the condition of inseparable link to the Crown, and who was considered a leading expert on matters of Empire.

Naturally, one cannot neglect the prolific historian Arthur Berriedale Keith,[29] either, whose expert authority often overshadowed British representatives, and who, as an eyewitness observer of the British Empire's constitutional development, focused intensively in his works on relations between the mother country and the overseas autonomous territories.

While Keith was more an advocate of the autonomous position, Lionel Curtis's publications[30] are the work of an apologist for the federalist form of Imperial structure. Another important historian was Australian Sir William Keith Hancock,[31] who was renowned as General Smuts's biographer and who based his works on the concept of the British Empire as a kind of autonomous experiment which was constitutionally developing in a natural manner.[32] I consider the publications of somewhat controversial Irish historian Nicholas Mansergh[33] to be classics today, and in terms of the scope of sources used, they remain of very high quality. Mansergh was critical in his assessment of the fact that the Irish Free State acquired Dominion status, which resulted in a weakening of relationships within the Commonwealth. Other important authors include John Edward Kendle,[34] who focused on constitutional matters and the structure of the Imperial organisation during the period of the first Colonial and Imperial Conferences prior to 1914, and Philip Wigley,[35] who looked at British-Canadian relations between 1917 and 1926.

Naturally, in analysing the British Empire's constitutional development, I have not neglected works of Czech provenance. Czech historiography has generally only touched on the topic I have researched. Magdalena Fiřtová[36] dealt with Canadian history and Jan Frank[37] touched on British-Irish relations in the 20th century, while Lukáš Novotný looked at Britain and its relations with the Dominions and their collective security system in the 1920s,[38] Tomáš Bosák focused on the analysis of federalisation concepts[39] and Martin Šubrt looked at the Canadian policy and the Chanak Crisis (the Chanak Incident).[40]

The final part of an introduction is a fitting place to give thanks. Firstly, I would like to thank my wonderful wife Lucie, in particular for her undoubted superhuman patience and support over the time I wrote this book. At the same time, I would like to thank the University of West Bohemia in Pilsen for its support via the research project SGS-2018-047 British-Dominion Relations, 1907–1931.

Notes

1. Hall, Hessel Duncan, *Commonwealth: A History of the British Commonwealth of Nations*, London: Von Nostrand Reinhold Co, 1971, IX.
2. Rau, Benegal Narsinga, Sir, *India's Constitution in the Making*, Bombay: Orient Longmans, 1963, 358–359.
3. Baring, Evelyn, *Political and Literary Essays, 1908–1913*, London: Macmillan, 1913, 22.
4. This section, which deals with the Article X of the Covenant of the League of Nations, is partially based on the article Valkoun, Jaroslav – Urban, Martin, "Kanada ve Společnosti národů a její postoj k článku 10 Paktu Společnosti národů", *Acta Historica Universitatis Silesianae Opaviensis* 11, 2018, 69–80.
5. Gooch, George Peabody – Temperley, Harold (Eds.), *British Documents on the Origins of the War, 1898–1914* [hereafter *BD*]: *Anglo-German Tension: Armaments and Negotiation*, 1907–12, Vol. 6, London: HMSO, 1930.

6 Butler, Rohan – Bury, J. P. T. – Lambert, M. E. (Eds.), *Documents on British Foreign Policy 1919–1939* [hereafter *DBFP*], 1st Series, Vols. 6, 14, London: HMSO, 1956–1966.
7 Ashton, S. R. – Stockwell, S. E. (Eds.), *British Documents on the End of Empire* [hereafter *BDEEP*]: *Imperial Policy and Colonial Practice, 1925–45*, Series A, Vol. 1, London: HMSO, 1997.
8 MacKay, R. A. (Ed.), *Documents on Canadian External Relations* [hereafter *DCER*]: *The Paris Peace Conference of 1919*, Vol. 2, Ottawa: Queen's Printer, 1969; Clark, Lowell C. (Ed.), *Documents on Canadian External Relations* [hereafter *DCER*]: *1919–1925*, Vol. 3, Ottawa: Information Canada, 1970.
9 United States Department of State, *Papers Relating to the Foreign Relations of the United States* [hereafter *FRUS*], *1920–1925*, Washington: Government Printing Office, 1936–1940.
10 Crowe, Catriona – Fanning, Ronan – Kennedy, Michael et al. (Eds.), *Documents on Irish Foreign Policy* [hereafter *DIFP*]: *The Anglo-Irish Treaty December 1920–December 1921*, https://www.difp.ie/documents/1921treaty.pdf; cit. 2018-10-28.
11 Mansergh, Nicholas (Ed.), *Documents and Speeches on British Commonwealth Affairs 1931–1952*, Vol. 1, London: Oxford University Press, 1953.
12 Dawson, Robert MacGregor (Ed.), *The Development of Dominion Status, 1900–1936*, London: Frank Cass & Co, 1965.
13 Keith, Arthur Berriedale (Ed.), *Selected Speeches and Documents on British Colonial Policy, 1763–1917*, Vol. 2, London: Oxford University Press, 1933.
14 Keith, Arthur Berriedale (Ed.), *Speeches and Documents on the British Dominions, 1918–1931: From Self-government to National Sovereignty*, Oxford: Oxford University Press, 1948.
15 Ollivier, Maurice (Ed.), *The Colonial and Imperial Conferences from 1887 to 1937*, 3 Vols., Ottawa: Queen's Printer, 1954.
16 Baldwin, Stanley, *Our Inheritance: Speeches and Addresses*, London: Hodder & Stoughton, 1928.
17 Beeman, Neville (Ed.), *Lord Rosebery's Speeches (1874–1896)*, London: N. Beeman, 1896.
18 Boyd, Charles W. (Ed.), *Mr. Chamberlain's Speeches*, 2 Vols., London: Constable, 1914; Chamberlain, Joseph, *Foreign & Colonial Speeches*, London: G. Routledge, 1897.
19 Hancock, William Keith – Poel, Jean van der (Eds.), *Selections from the Smuts Papers*, Vols. 2–5, Cambridge: Cambridge University Press 1966; Smuts, Jan Christian, *War-time Speeches: A Compilation of Public Utterances in Great Britain*, London: Hodder & Stoughton, 1917.
20 Milner, Alfred, *The Nation and the Empire: Being a Collection of Speeches and Addresses*, London: Constable, 1913.
21 Amery, Leopold Stennett, *My Political Life: England before the Storm, 1896–1914*, Vol. 1, London: Hutchinson, 1953; Amery, Leopold Stennett, *My Political Life: War and Peace 1914–1929*, Vol. 2, London: Hutchinson, 1953; Barnes, John – Nicholson, David (eds.), *The Leo Amery Diaries: 1869–1929*, Vol. 2, London: Hutchinson, 1980.
22 Borden, Robert Laird, Sir, *Canada in the Commonwealth: From Conflict to Co-operation*, Oxford: Clarendon Press, 1929.
23 Cecil, Robert Gascoyne, *A Great Experiment: An Autobiography*, London: Jonathan Cape, 1941.
24 Miller, David Hunter, *My Diary at the Conference of Paris with Documents* 4, New York: [s. n.], 1924.

25 Lloyd George, David, *The Truth about the Peace Treaties*, 2 Vols., London: Victor Gollancz, 1938; Lloyd George, David, *War Memoirs*, 2 Vols., London: Odhams Press, 1938.
26 Hall, Hessel Duncan, *The British Commonwealth of Nations: A Study of Its Past and Future Development*, London: Methuen, 1920; Hall, Hessel Duncan, *The Government of the British Commonwealth of Nations*, London: Labour Party, 1922; Hall, Hessel Duncan, *Commonwealth: A History of the British Commonwealth of Nations*, London: Von Nostrand Reinhold Co, 1971.
27 McIntyre, W. David, "Clio and Britannia's Lost Dream: Historians and the British Commonwealth of Nations in the First Half of the 20th Century", *The Round Table* 93, No. 376, 2004, 521–522.
28 Amery, Leopold Stennett, *The Problem of the Army*, London: Edward Arnold, 1903; Amery, Leopold Stennett, *Union and Strength: A Series of Papers on Imperial Questions*, London: Edward Arnold, 1912; Amery, Leopold Stennett, *Thoughts on the Constitution*, London: Oxford University Press, 1964; Amery, Leopold Stennett, "Some Aspects of the Imperial Conference", *Journal of the Royal Institute of International Affairs* 6, No. 1, 1927, 2–24; Amery, Leopold Stennett, "Some Practical Steps towards an Imperial Constitution", *United Empire: The Royal Colonial Institute Journal* 1, No. 7, 1910, 487–509.
29 Keith, Arthur Berriedale, *Imperial Unity and the Dominions*, Oxford: Clarendon Press, 1916; Keith, Arthur Berriedale, *Responsible Government in the Dominions*, 3 Vols., Oxford: Oxford University Press, 1912; Keith, Arthur Berriedale, *War Government of the British Dominions*, Oxford: Clarendon Press, 1921.
30 Curtis, Lionel, *The Problem of the Commonwealth*, London: Macmillan, 1916.
31 Hancock, William Keith, *Smuts: The Sanguine Years, 1870–1919*, Vol. 1, Cambridge: Cambridge University Press, 1962; Hancock, William Keith, *Smuts: The Fields of Force, 1919–1950i*, Vol. 2, Cambridge: Cambridge University Press, 1968; Hancock, William Keith, *Survey of British Commonwealth Affairs: Problems of Nationality 1918–1936*, Vol. 1, London: Oxford University Press, 1937.
32 See Hancock, William Keith, "Empire, Commonwealth, Cosmos and His Own Place: The Smutsian Philosophy", *The Round Table* 60, No. 240, 1970, 443–448; McIntyre, *Clio*, 525.
33 Mansergh, Nicholas, *Survey of British Commonwealth Affairs: Problems of External Policy 1931–1939*, London: Oxford University Press, 1952; Mansergh, Nicholas, *The Commonwealth Experience*, London: Weidenfeld & Nicolson, 1969; Mansergh, Nicholas, *The Commonwealth Experience: From British to Multiracial Commonwealth*, Vol. 2, London: Macmillan, 1982; Mansergh, Nicholas, *The Commonwealth of the Nation: Studies in British Commonwealth Relations*, London: Royal Institute of International Affairs, 1948; Mansergh, Nicholas, *The Unresolved Question: The Anglo-Irish Settlement and Its Undoing 1912–72*, New Haven – London: Yale University Press, 1991.
34 Kendle, John Edward, *The Colonial and Imperial Conferences 1887–1911: A Study in Imperial Organizations*, London: Longmans 1967; Kendle, John Edward, *The Round Table Movement and Imperial Union*, Toronto: University of Toronto Press, 1975.
35 Wigley, Philip, *Canada and the Transition to Commonwealth: British-Canadian Relations, 1917–1926*, Cambridge: Cambridge University Press, 1977.

36 Fiřtová, Magdalena, *Kanada*, Praha: Libri, 2014.
37 Frank, Jan, *Irsko*, Praha: Libri, 2006.
38 Novotný, Lukáš – Kodet, Roman, *Velká Británie a konference v Locarnu: Příspěvek ke studiu kolektivní bezpečnosti ve 20. letech 20. století*, Plzeň: Západočeská univerzita v Plzni, 2013; Novotný, Lukáš, "Der Sinowjew Brief", *Prague Papers on the History of International Relations*, 2006, 201–227; Novotný, Lukáš, "Die Britischen Dominions und der Vertrag von Locarno: Der Prüfstein für eine einheitliche Außenpolitik des Empire in der Zwischenkriegszeit", *Jahrbuch für Europäische Überseegeschichte* 10, 2010, 163–188; Novotný, Lukáš, "Konzervativní vláda Stanleyho Baldwina a její odmítnutí Ženevského protokolu: Příspěvek k pokusům o vytvoření kolektivní bezpečnosti ve dvacátých letech 20. století", *Dvacáté století*, 2006, 117–153; Novotný, Lukáš, "On the Journey to the Rhineland Pact: Contribution to the Study of British Perception of the Problem of Collective Security in the 1920's", *Öt kontinens: Az Új- és Jelenkori Egyetemes Történeti Tanszék közleményei / Cinq Continents: Les cahiers du Département d'Histoire moderne et contemporaine*, No. 1, 2009, 369–383; Novotný, Lukáš, "Postoj britských dominií k Locarnskému paktu", *Acta Fakulty filozofické Západočeské univerzity v Plzni* 3, No. 2, 2011; Novotný, Lukáš, "Velká Británie a konference v Locarnu", *Moderní dějiny: Sborník k dějinám 19. a 20. století* 18, No. 2, 2010; Novotný, Lukáš, "Zinověvův dopis a Campbellův případ: Příspěvek ke zkoumání působnosti první labouristické vlády", *Historický obzor* 18, No. 9/10, 2007, 218–226 .
39 Bosák, Tomáš, "Britské federalistické koncepce a pojetí Evropy v éře „skvělé izolace"", *Mezinárodní vztahy* 45, No. 1, 2010, 77–98.
40 Šubrt, Martin, "Kanada a Chanacká krize", *Historica Olomucensia* 56, 2019, 199–214.

1 The British Empire, or Commonwealth?

The term "Empire" is frequently used in contemporary historiography. In terms of Britain, the word "Empire" began to be used under the reign of Tudor monarch Henry VIII, and it was used to describe the Kingdom of England, and was meant to characterise Britain's independence, full sovereignty and freedom from the Holy Roman Empire.[1] It was used even more during the Elizabethan era in connection with overseas expeditions.[2] The beginnings of the word "Commonwealth", or "Common Wealth", date back to the 15th century. Although over time it acquired a number of basic meanings,[3] it is most commonly used as a term for a political nation or state. Despite the fact that the term "Commonwealth" was often linked with Republican ideas as a result of the Cromwell period, it was frequently used until the 18th century in addition to the term "British Empire", which predominantly described the Crown possessions.[4] Over the course of the 19th century, it came up against new terms such as "nation" and "state", and as such somewhat faded into the background for some time. Its use was revived in 1901 when the Australian Self-Governing Colonies obtained Dominion status, and the Commonwealth of Australia was formed.[5] The term "Commonwealth" was a cumbersome one for non-English-speaking nations and difficult to translate into other languages.[6]

Although both terms existed in parallel for centuries, the attempt at encapsulating the constitutional transformation of the British possessions was in a certain manner reflected in the more common use of the new phrase of "Commonwealth", rather than the traditional term of "British Empire". Archibald Philip Primrose, 5th Earl of Rosebery, was one of the first British politicians to use the term, although he did not consider the term "Commonwealth" to be a synonym for "Empire". In January 1884, in a speech focused on the status of the self-governing Australian states within the Empire, he uttered the sentence, "there is no need for any nation, however great, leaving the Empire, because the Empire is a commonwealth of nations",[7] although he did not perceive the term Commonwealth of Nations as analogous to the British Empire.[8] The Liberal leader indirectly confirmed this fact in November 1900 when he said in a speech to Glasgow University students that "there is no convenient synonym ... which as adequately expresses a number of states of vast size under a single sovereign", and as such "the word 'Empire' represents to us our history, our tradition, our race".[9] So although he did not perceive the term "Commonwealth of Nations" as synonymous with the British Empire, he at least contributed to its generalisation within the "white" Self-Governing Colonies. Other leading Liberals prioritised the use of the term "Commonwealth" meaning a confederation of states (Dominions and Crown colonies), and some were not hesitant to claim that "all that has made this Commonwealth great and strong is the work of Liberalism".[10]

During the final decades of the 19th century, it became ever more apparent in regard to the growing number of Self-Governing Colonies that the term "Empire" did not sufficiently characterise the newly established relations between the mother country and these Self-Governing Colonies, which no longer felt they were mere "colonies" under imperial domination. The sometimes-used phrase "Britain and her colonies" also seemed inappropriate in the context of the Empire's development because it represented an inappropriate simplification of the diversity and complexity of the relations within it.[11] British essayist and historian Sir John Robert Seeley, for example, held the opinion that, "the word Empire seems too military and despotic to suit the relation of a mother-country to colonies".[12] In contrast, George Bernard Shaw wrote a very interesting idea in 1900:

> It should be hardly necessary to say here that the words Empire, Imperial, Imperialist, and so forth, are pure claptraps, used by educated people merely to avoid dictionary quibbles, and by uneducated people in ignorance of their ancient meaning. What the colonies are driving at is a Commonwealth; and that is what the English citizen means, too, by the Empire, when he means anything at all.[13]

Shaw perceived the term "Commonwealth" as a community which was formed voluntarily and on the basis of shared interests. In contrast to that, the word "Imperialism" for him symbolised the forced subjugation of other nations.[14] Historian of the time James Stanley Little held a similar stance in regard to the future focus of the Empire: "the Commonwealth of English peoples would be a far more appropriate name for a confederacy of England and her colonies, than a title in which the word Empire [appears]".[15]

Over time, it was shown that the term "Commonwealth" gave an impression of freer relations with the mother country amongst overseas politicians compared to the term "Empire", which evoked feelings of inferior status compared to London.[16] When in 1897 Joseph Chamberlain introduced his proposal for establishment of an Imperial Council, and when in 1905 Alfred Lyttelton announced his intention to run a permanent committee, Cape Colony politician John Xavier Merriman was vigorous in joining in the debate.[17] He proposed in August 1905 that:

> now the word "Empire", which is a perfectly correct one to use as regards the relation of England to India, and to other communities which do not enjoy representative institutions, is clearly not a proper description of the self-governing communities ... [for which] "Commonwealth" and not "Empire" more nearly expresses the sort of relation [with the mother country].[18]

South African politician Viscount Alfred Milner, was also consistent in accepting the need for change. In March 1905 in Johannesburg, he stated: "The word Empire, the word Imperial, are, in some respects, unfortunate. They suggest domination, ascendancy, the rule of a superior state over vassal states."[19] British journalist Richard Jebb also called on Great Britain to stop looking at the Self-Governing Colonies and Dominions as a mere part of the Empire as it had done in times past, and instead to now respect the development of these nations.[20] Ellis Thomas Powell and Ben H. Morgan of the Royal Colonial Institute were also of the opinion that the term "Empire" was imprecise and confusing.[21] In January 1906, Joseph Chamberlain spoke in a similar vein and stressed the fact that the "white" colonies were no longer dictated to by Britain because, "they are self-governing nations [and] they are sister-States".[22]

Compared to other empires, the British Empire was marked out not just by its high level of self-confidence, but also its deep faith in the internal democratic process, symbolised by the considerable number of positions held on individual issues.[23] In regard to the Boer War, the opinions of a smaller group of liberals and radicals who were termed the Little Englanders and who rejected words such as Empire and Imperialism came to the forefront. In their eyes, such terms represented racial dominance, militarism and imperial supremacy. Advocates of this group on the one hand were critical towards the proposed plans of the Imperial federation, and on the other hand were positive in their reflections on changes in the Self-Governing Colonies focusing on national independence.[24] Sir Henry Campbell-Bannerman, who was one of the most significant Little Englanders, spoke in May 1900 of the anticipated federal structure of the Australian Self-Governing Colonies and said that he believed the most appropriate term for the Empire's future form was the British Commonwealth.[25]

When New Zealand and Newfoundland acquired Dominion status in 1907,[26] the issue of the Dominions' status within the British Empire became a particularly topical one, and as such, Alfred Milner returned to the topic. In June 1908, he came to the opinion that there was a "contrast between the self-governing communities of European blood, ... and the communities of coloured race," and thus he reasoned that the Empire was deeply divided into two parts – the "self-governing Empire" and the "dependent Empire".[27] Milner accepted, as John X. Merriman had previously, that there were two groups within the Empire, each with a different relationship to the mother country. Despite all this, however, there was no drop-off in Imperial enthusiasm amongst Dominion politicians in particular, and as such, in 1911 the Australian Prime Minister had no qualms in describing the status of Dominions within the Empire as such: "We are a family of nations."[28] Editor of *The Round Table* journal Philip Kerr, later Lord Lothian, held a similar opinion, seeing the Empire in a positive light because, "the Dominions ... have become strong daughter-nations instead of separate peoples".[29]

At the start of the 20th century, there was no longer any dispute in debate about the nature of the British Empire that the term "Empire" was not just an inaccurate characterisation of the relations of the "white" Self-Governing Colonies, but it also reduced their self-esteem and national pride because it aligned them with other territories with a subordinate colonial status. As such, a change in the Empire's organisational structure was necessary. Although British imperialists admitted that the word "Empire" did not express the essence of the territories sufficiently precisely, they nevertheless found it difficult to accept that the term had "earned" certain negative connotations, mainly due to the course of the Boer War.[30] The term "Commonwealth", symbolising freedom and equality, thus began to take firmer hold, while the term "Empire", linked to subordination and inequality, seemed evermore an anachronism.[31] Sir Albert Frederick Pollard realised this, and as such, in 1909 he attempted to implement a kind of hybrid phrase in response to the rise of nationalism within the Dominions – the "Empire of the British Nations".[32] Although by 1910 the word "Commonwealth" had become so common that authors were willing to use it in the titles of books,[33] leading British advocate of federalisation Lionel George Curtis was not entirely convinced and thus proposed adopting the name of the "Britannic Realms" in place of what was previously described as the "British Empire".[34] A year later, he had accepted the term "Commonwealth" which had in the interim period become a notional driver for new imperial federalisation concepts within the Round Table Movement.[35] In contrast to the federalists, advocates of autonomist concepts of Imperial unity began to side with the consistent use of the phrase "Britannic Commonwealth".[36]

Despite the fact that the term "Commonwealth" had begun to be commonly used even before the First World War broke out, it became especially popular during the years of war, when the word "Empire" elicited certain unfortunate reminiscences on a number of negative factors of Imperial policy (such as expansionism, racial superiority, militarism and aggression towards neighbours). In the context of the events of the Great War, the blame for which was generally placed on the German Empire, there was an analogous association for the term "Empire" such that negative associations such as betrayal of progress and civilisational ideals, etc., began to outweigh positive associations. At the same time, some British imperialists were upset at how the "innocent" imperialist rhetoric often found in pre-war publications took form in the difficult times of war.[37] Philip Kerr, for example, was shocked at the danger of "German imperialism", whose essence he did not hesitate to compare to "the shortest examination of the history of Ireland", and added: "This War, if it has done nothing else, has burnt out of our national consciousness any taint it may have had of militarism or Prussian Imperialism."[38]

Once from a certain perspective the term "Empire" had acquired a pejorative connotation during the First World War, and the term "Commonwealth" had begun to be used ever more frequently as a viable alternative, the question arose as to whether the term fully corresponded to the outlook of how the relationships or status of nations within it would operate in future, or whether this would have to be specified. Groups of advocates and opponents of the Empire, federalists and autonomists, continued to work on previous efforts at promoting the use of the expressions which they considered most exactly characterised the nature of the British Empire. This led to the publication during the war of many books explaining the genesis of imperial relationships, and these defended the use of various terms such as "Imperial Commonwealth", "Britannic Commonwealth", "Commonwealth of Nations" or "British Commonwealth of Nations".[39]

Leading British and Dominion statesmen were more cautious at an official level and for a long time kept up the use of the tried-and-tested term "British Empire", although the impact of the war could not be overlooked. British Prime Minister David Lloyd George thought that the war had transformed the Empire into "a great and effective democratic commonwealth of nations".[40] Some historians are of the opinion that acceptance of the term "Commonwealth" led to the incorporation of multi-national aspects within the imperial structure.[41]

Progress was made during the 1917 Imperial War Conference. On 16 April, on the ninth day of discussions, Canadian Prime Minister Sir Robert Laird Borden first used the term "Imperial Commonwealth of United Nations" in a debate on constitutional matters. This term was advocated by ardent supporters of the Empire. His New Zealand opposite number, William Ferguson Massey, however, supported the term "United Nations of the Empire".[42] "Imperial Commonwealth" represented a kind of hybrid expression combining the older term "Empire" with the newer "Commonwealth".[43]

South African General Jan Christian Smuts, for whom the issue of the British Empire was a burden yet a fascination at the same time, went even further. He personally approved the fact that the British Empire was generally based on liberal principles, freedom and equality. However, he did not see this problem of terminology as mere conception or simple labelling. As such, in contrast to Borden, he showed no hesitation in speaking of the "British Commonwealth", which he perceived in a wider context, and thus he rejected the idea of federation because Empire did not describe one state, but rather a system of states.[44] The "British Commonwealth of Nations" was more than a mere name, because it was an historical idea.[45] In contrast, Amery believed the term "United Nations of the British Empire", which appeared similar to the concept of the United States of America, did not precisely express the international and constitutional status of the self-governing territories.[46] In October 1918, however, Leo Amery no longer took such a critical position, even admitting that in certain regards it suited the post-war freer nature of the Commonwealth.[47]

Since the Imperial Conference participants had promised to focus on constitutional relations between the different parts of the Empire following the end of the First World War, and discussions had come round to recognising the Dominions as autonomous parts of the Empire, Smuts gave a speech on 15 May 1917 in which he stated:

> The British Empire is much more than a State. [I] think the very expression "Empire" is misleading, because it makes people think as if we are one single entity, one unity. ... We are not an Empire. Germany is an Empire, so was Rome, and so is India, but we are a system of nations, a community of states and of nations far greater than any empire which has ever existed ... to this community of nations, I prefer to call the British Commonwealth of Nations.[48]

Smuts's speech had a significant impact on the debate on the Empire's course and aroused substantial interest from British historian Alfred Eckhard Zimmern, who subsequently subjected the phrase and word combination to detailed analysis.[49] The significance of Zimmern's analysis in discussion of the Empire's constitutional transformation lies in particular in the fact that it looked at its development in the context of the principle "trends" and events in global politics.[50]

Although Smuts was not the first to use the term "British Commonwealth of Nations" publicly,[51] he was undoubtedly responsible for its gaining wider attention, and over time this caused him to be referred to as the "founder of the British Commonwealth".[52] When the next Imperial War Conference took place in June 1918, although Smuts in his introductory speech repeatedly described the "British Empire" at an institutional level as the "British Commonwealth of Nations", Canada's Prime Minister Borden continued to stubbornly refer to the "Imperial Commonwealth", or sometimes the "British Commonwealth".[53] Over time, Smuts became the leading promoter or so-called "pioneer" of the term "British Commonwealth of Nations" and he strived to ensure it was adopted at an official level. In 1920 he achieved partial success when the British Labour Party was the first to officially identify with the concept of the Commonwealth in its programme.[54] At the same time, he was against any kind of federalist solutions. To begin with, however, he was unable to ensure that "British Commonwealth of Nations" became a term used officially.[55]

A planned Constitutional Conference was to take place in 1921. Then-Secretary of State for the Colonies, Lord Milner, however, said that it was not yet an appropriate time to begin negotiations between the mother country and the Dominions, because he thought there were more pressing problems to deal with. He was also of the opinion that constitutional matters had to be discussed within the framework of existing institutions, and not "merely" by adoption of an imperial constitution.[56] During the conference, at which New Zealand Prime Minister Massey in particular spoke against the term "Commonwealth of Nations", constitutional matters were sidelined.[57] Although there was no discussion held on constitutional matters, in an unofficial 1921 memorandum on constitutional issues within the Empire, Smuts advocated the adoption of the phrase because he was of the unwavering opinion that the Self-Governing Colonies had transformed the Empire into a community of free and equal sister nations best characterised by the term "British Commonwealth of Nations".[58] The phrase "British Commonwealth of Nations" was first used officially in the text of the December 1921 Anglo-Irish Treaty.[59] Nevertheless, its omission of the term "British Empire" was heavily criticised in Britain's House of Commons.[60]

The end of the First World War has been shown to mark a symbolic transition from the legacy of the past – the British Empire – to the new political structure – the Commonwealth.[61] Over time, this transition was also reflected in the use of a new hybrid term, the "Empire-Commonwealth", used to attempt to fairly capture the essence of both terms.[62] Many contemporaries were of the opinion that, "the British Empire of to-day [1926] is not the British Empire of 1914".[63] In 1919, Lord Alfred Milner boldly declared that equal partnership between Great Britain and its Dominions represented the only option for the British Empire's future continuity. According to him, equality was to be reflected in formal and institutional affairs, without impacting Imperial unity.[64]

Although during the 1920s the phrases "British Commonwealth of Nations" and "British Empire" were often used at an official level as alternative terms or direct equivalents,[65] many politicians continued to observe the older terminology, and occasionally this caused ambiguity in the perception of the status of autonomous parts of the Empire and the mother country. In 1923, for example, when the United States underwent the ratification process for the Canadian-American fishing treaty, Secretary of State Charles Evans Hughes asked the British ambassador in Washington, Sir Auckland Geddes, what significance the phrase "any other part of Great Britain" had in the treaty.[66] Geddes ruled out the idea that in the context of the treaty it was another indirect name for the Canadian Dominion, and gave the interesting interpretation that the resolution "intended to refer exclusively to the geographical entity properly known as Great Britain, namely, England, Scotland and Wales, or is Great Britain, in the mind of the framers of the resolution, intended to be synonymous with the term 'British Empire'".[67] In the end, Hughes more or less accepted this argument and came to the conclusion that it was a synonymous phrase.[68]

During the 1926 Imperial Conference, the complicated terminological essence of the British Empire was aptly described by the South African Prime Minister, General James Barry Munnik Hertzog: "we must see ... the will to live in the Empire, as a Commonwealth of Free Nations".[69] In terms of imperial phraseology, the Balfour Declaration of 1926 is a well-balanced text. In contrast to future developments, the term "British Empire" was still used as a general term for the political unit, because "no other term, indeed, would be appropriate to the totality of autonomous states, dependencies, colonies, protectorates, mandated territories, feudatories, and allies which are comprehended with the orbit of our polity". Nevertheless, the relationships of certain autonomous members formed a political system whose character matched the term "Commonwealth" better.[70]

Despite all this, General Hertzog described a certain difference between the terms "British Empire" and "British Commonwealth of Nations". In December 1926 in Pretoria, he declared that both terms "contemplate no more than two different groupings of the countries and peoples under the British Crown" with a different level of shared obligations towards it. According to the South African Prime Minister, "Commonwealth of Nations" was an equivalent to the free connections between Great Britain and its Dominions, symbolised by the Crown, while "British Empire" was a generic term which included not just the Dominions and the mother country, but also India, Rhodesia and the other countries of the Empire which were not explicitly states within the Commonwealth.[71] In 1927, unofficial Canadian adviser in foreign policy matters Professor Oscar Douglas Skelton declared that in terms of international status, "the best solution ... was to interpret the British Empire as 'a geographical and popular term'". The Balfour Declaration did not mark the end of the use of the term "Empire"; instead it marked the end of one phase of its use – from Empire "was born Commonwealth".[72]

Although there were debates on the substance of these terms and the fact that "British Commonwealth of Nations" should differentiate self-governing territories from dependent ones, it remained fairly difficult to precisely define how they differed. As such, Britain's Dominion Office issued a memorandum in January 1930 which was designed once and for all to define the differences between the two terms. "British Empire" was to be used for the geographical limitations of the Empire, while "British Commonwealth of Nations" was to be used as a political designation of various parts of the Empire. Thus, British Commonwealth of Nations represented individual autonomous nations within the Empire which had representatives at Imperial Conferences. From that moment, the role of the mother country changed, now perceived with its colonial Empire comprising a number of territories with differing levels of dependence on London as merely one member of the British Commonwealth of Nations. At the same time, it was anticipated that in the event of any future emancipation of any of the dependent territories, the number of nations within the British Commonwealth would also grow.[73] Despite this effort at precise terminological definition, some confusion still occasionally occurred.[74]

A complication arose when it became necessary to include India within the system. During the Imperial War Conference in 1917, its special, even privileged, position had been recognised within the Empire, and Resolution IX even awarded it the same right as the Dominions had to have a say on the future direction of the country in foreign policy matters and to be able to hold discussions on all matters with an imperial aspect.[75] Although its representatives participated separately in Imperial Conferences, India did not acquire Dominion status during the 1920s.[76] The 1926 Imperial Conference merely affirmed its special status within the Empire.[77] For this reason, its status as a member of the British Commonwealth of Nations was viewed in a specific manner due to its constitutional position.[78]

"British Commonwealth of Nations" referred to the idea of equality and free co-operation, which represented the foundations of this new group of states. Thus, "British Empire" moved from autonomy to equal status of Dominions, as affirmed in the 1926 Balfour Declaration.[79] The 1931 Statute of Westminster confirmed its conclusions and stressed that "the Crown is the symbol of free association of the members of the British Commonwealth of Nations".[80] Conservative advocates of the form of Empire continued steadfastly to use the word "Empire", with their peers often referring to them as "blockheads".[81] In contrast, other politicians and journalists were insistent in promoting various models of the "Commonwealth" term, which became definitively established after the Second World War, which had resulted in the term "Empire" being naturally forgotten.[82]

Notes

1 Cf. Koebner, Richard, *Empire*, New York: Cambridge University Press, 1961, 55; Lucas, Charles, *Greater Rome and Greater Britain*, Oxford: Clarendon Press, 1912, 8–9.

2 See Parry, Glyn, "John Dee and the Elizabethan British Empire in Its European Context", *The Historical Journal* 49, No. 3, 2006, 643–675.
3 Among these meanings were (1) public welfare, (2) an independent group of people forming a political nation or state, (3) a country whose power comes from the people, (4) in English history, the Republican government from the execution of Charles I to the restoration of the monarchy, (5) in North America, the official term for Massachusetts, Pennsylvania, Virginia and Kentucky, (6) the name of the Commonwealth of Australia from 1901, and (7) a group of people linked by common interest. Mehrotra, S. R., "On the Use of the Term 'Commonwealth'", *Journal of Commonwealth Political Studies* 2, No. 1, 1963, 1–2.
4 Cf. Adams, James Truslow, "On the Term 'British Empire'", *The American Historical Review* 27, No. 3, 1922, 485–489; Hancock, William Keith, *Survey of British Commonwealth Affairs: Problems of Nationality 1918–1936*, Vol. 1, London: Oxford University Press, 1937, 56.
5 Barton, G. B. (Ed.), *The Draft Bill to Constitute the Commonwealth of Australia, As Adopted by the Convention of 1891*, Sydney: N.S.W., 1891, 9–11.
6 Amery, Leopold Stennett, *My Political Life: War and Peace 1914–1929*, Vol. 2, London: Hutchinson, 1953, 390.
7 Crewe-Milnes, Robert Offley Ashburton, *Lord Rosebery*, Vol. 1, London: John Murray, 1931, 186.
8 Mehrotra, 3.
9 Crewe-Milnes, Robert Offley Ashburton, *Questions of Empire*, New York: Arthur L. Humphreys, 1901, 8.
10 Hammond, J. L., "Colonial and Foreign Policy", in: Hammond, J. L. – Hirst, Francis W. – Murray, Gilbert, *Liberalism and the Empire*, London: R. Brimley Johnson, 1900, 207.
11 Romancov, Michael, "Commonwealth – vznik a vývoj", in: Šanc, David – Ženíšek, Marek, *Commonwealth: Z perspektivy politické vědy*, Plzeň: Aleš Čeněk, 2008, 13.
12 See more cf. Burroughs, Peter, "John Robert Seeley and British Imperial History", *The Journal of Imperial and Commonwealth History* 1, No. 2, 1973, 191–211; Seeley, John Robert, Sir, *The Expansion of England: Two Courses of Lectures*, London: Macmillan and Co, 1883, 37.
13 Shaw, George Bernard (Ed.), *Fabianism and Empire: A Manifesto by the Fabian Society*, London: G. Richards, 1900, 49–50.
14 Hirst, Francis W., "Imperialism and Finance", in: Hammond, J. L. – Hirst, Francis W. – Murray, Gilbert, *Liberalism and the Empire*, London: R. Brimley Johnson, 1900, 72–74.
15 Little, James Stanley, *Progress of the British Empire in the Century*, Toronto: Linscott Publishing Co., 1903, 100.
16 Koebner, Richard – Schmidt, H. D., *Imperialism: The Story and Significance of a Political Word, 1840–1960*, Cambridge: Cambridge University Press, 1964, 233.
17 Merriman did not consider the term "British Empire" to be ideal, and as such consistently used the term "British Commonwealth". See Merriman to Smuts, Stellenbosch, 4 June 1904, in: Hancock, William Keith – Poel, Jean van der (Eds.), *Selections from the Smuts Papers: June 1902 – May 1910*, Vol. 2, Cambridge: Cambridge University Press, 1966, Doc. Vol. 3, No. 48, 171.
18 Quotation according to Mehrotra, 4–5.
19 Alfred Milner, Johannesburg, 31 March 1905, in: Milner, Alfred, *The Nation and the Empire: Being a Collection of Speeches and Addresses*, London: Constable, 1913, 90.

20 Jebb, Richard, *Studies in Colonial Nationalism*, London: Edward Arnold, 1905, 272–273.
21 Reese, Trevor R., *The History of the Royal Commonwealth Society 1868–1968*, London: Oxford University Press, 1968, 175.
22 Ewart, John Skirving, *The Kingdom Papers*, Vol. 1, Ottawa: [s. n.], 1912, 8.
23 Jebb, *Studies*, 88.
24 Smith, Goldwin, *Commonwealth or Empire: A Bystander's View of the Question*, New York: Macmillan Co, 1902, 19, 63–64, 79–81.
25 Mehrotra, 9.
26 See more in Fieldhouse, David Kenneth, "Autochthonous Elements in the Evolution of Dominion Status: The Case of New Zealand", *Journal of Commonwealth Political Studies* 1, No. 2, 1962, 85–111.
27 Alfred Milner, *The Two Empires*, Royal Colonial Institute, 16 June 1908, in: Milner, *The Nation*, 290–291.
28 Cd. 5745, *Dominions No. 7: Imperial Conference, 1911: Minutes of Proceedings of the Imperial Conference, 1911*, London: HMSO, 1911, 98.
29 Kerr, Philip Henry – Kerr, A. C., *The Growth of the British Empire*, London: Longmans & Co, 1911, 202.
30 Cf. Amery, Julian, *The Life of Joseph Chamberlain, 1901–1903: At the Height of His Power*, Vol. 4, London: Macmillan, 1951, 414; Crewe-Milnes, *Questions*, 8; Jose, Arthur Wilberforce, *The Growth of the Empire: A Handbook to the History of Greater Britain*, London: John Murray, 1901, 1; Spender, John Alfred, *The Life of the Right Hon. Sir Henry Campbell-Bannerman*, London: Hodder & Stoughton, 1923, 332–351.
31 Hancock, 60.
32 Pollard, Albert Frederick, *The British Empire: Its Past, Its Present, and Its Future*, London: League of the Empire, 1909, viii.
33 E.g. Enock, Charles Reginald, *An Imperial Commonwealth: Being a Discussion of the Conditions and Possibilities Underlying the Unity of the British Empire, and a Plan for the Greater Conservation, Development, and Enjoyment of Its Resources in the Interests of the British People, and for the Advancement of Their Civilization*, London: Grant Richards, 1910.
34 Mehrotra, 8.
35 Ibid., 10.
36 See more in Jebb, Richard, *The Britannic Question: A Survey of Alternatives*, London: Longmans & Co, 1913, 15–16, 81, 180, 189, 228, 240, 247, 252–253.
37 Cf. Kerr, Philip Henry, "Commonwealth and Empire", Newton, Arthur Percival (Ed.), *The Empire and the Future: A Series of Imperial Studies Lectures Delivered in the University of London, King's College*, London: Macmillan, 1916, 72–76; Elliott, William Yandell, *The New British Empire*, New York: McGraw-Hill Book Co, 1932, 7–8; Mehrotra, 10; Zimmern, Alfred Eckhard, "German Culture and British Commonwealth", in: Seton-Watson, Robert William et al., *The War and Democracy*, London: Macmillan, 1915, 348–383.
38 Kerr, *Commonwealth*, 75–76.
39 See more in Curtis, Lionel (Ed.), *The Commonwealth of Nations: An Inquiry into the Nature of Citizenship in the British Empire, and into the Mutual Relations of the Several Communities Thereof*, Part 1, London: Macmillan, 1916; Curtis, Lionel, *The Problem of the Commonwealth*, London: Macmillan, 1916, 127–247; Pollard, Albert Frederick, *The Commonwealth at War*, London: Longmans & Co, 1917; Jan Christian Smuts, *The British Commonwealth of Nations*, Royal Gallery at the House of Lords, London, 15 May 1917, in: Smuts, Jan Christian, *War-time Speeches: A Compilation*

24 The British Empire, or Commonwealth?

    of Public Utterances in Great Britain, London: Hodder & Stoughton, 1917, 25–38.
40 Lloyd George, David, *War Memoirs*, Vol. 1, London: Odhams Press, 1938, 1052.
41 Baker, Andrew, "Divided Sovereignty: Empire and Nation in the Making of Modern Britain", *International Politics* 46, No. 6, 2009, 696.
42 Cf. Cd. 8566, *The Imperial War Conference, 1917: Extracts from Minutes of Proceedings and Papers Laid before the Conference*, London: HMSO, 1917, 41; Hall, Hessel Duncan, *Commonwealth: A History of the British Commonwealth of Nations*, London: Von Nostrand Reinhold Co, 1971, 191.
43 This was a certain compromise between William Massey and Joseph Ward advocating the retention of the current "Empire" designation, and Robert Borden and Jan Christian Smuts, preferring the term "Commonwealth". Hall, *Commonwealth*, 179.
44 Cd. 8566, 46–48.
45 Hall, *Commonwealth*, 181.
46 L. S. Amery to Smuts, Chelsea, 15 May 1917, in: Hancock, William Keith – Poel, Jean van der (Eds.), *Selections from the Smuts Papers: June 1910 – November 1918*, Vol. 3, Cambridge: Cambridge University Press, 1966, Doc. Vol. 15, No. 5, 517.
47 University of Cambridge: Churchill College: Churchill Archives Centre (hereafter CAC), Amery Papers (hereafter AP, AMEL 2/1/1, L. S. A[mery] to Balfour, 27 October 1918, [1].
48 Cf. "General Smuts", *Spectator*, No. 4638, 19 May 1917, 557–558; Smuts, Jan Christian, *The British Commonwealth of Nations: A Speech Made by General Smuts on May 15th, 1917*, London: Hodder & Stoughton, 1917, 5–6; Smuts, *War-time Speeches*, 31–32.
49 Zimmern, Alfred Eckhard, "The Commonwealth Today", Bailey, Sydney Dawson (Ed.), *Parliamentary Government in the Commonwealth*, London: Hansard Society, 1951, 10–11.
50 Miller, John Donald Bruce, "The Commonwealth and World Order: The Zimmern Vision and After", *The Journal of Imperial and Commonwealth History* 8, No. 1, 1979, 160.
51 Zimmern, *German Culture*, 370–371.
52 Brookes, Edgar H., "A Far-seeing International Statesman", Friedlander, Zelda (Ed.), *Jan Smuts Remembered: A Centennial Tribute*, London: Allan Wingate, 1970, 21.
53 Cd. 9177, *The Imperial War Conference, 1918: Extracts from Minutes of Proceedings and Papers Laid before the Conference*, London: HMSO, 1918, 15, 18, 65.
54 For more on Labour's position on Imperial matters: Hall, Hessel Duncan, *The Government of the British Commonwealth of Nations*, London: Labour Party, 1922.
55 While concluding the Paris peace treaties and negotiating the Covenant of the League of Nations, the term "British Empire" continued to be used. Hall, *Commonwealth*, 193.
56 Milner to Lloyd George, 8 October 1920, in: Gollin, Alfred Manuel, *Proconsul in Politics: A Study of Lord Milner in Opposition and in Power*, London: Anthony Blond, 1964, 596.
57 Cmd. 1474, *Conference of the Prime Ministers and Representatives of the United Kingdom, the Dominions and India, Held in June, July, and August 1921: Summary of Proceedings and Documents*, London: HMSO, 1921, 28.

58 Cd. 8566, 47–48; The National Archives (hereafter TNA), Dominion Office (hereafter DO) 117/33, D. 11047, Memorandum by General Smuts on the Constitutional Relations, [June 1921], 6.
59 For the Irish, the term "British Commonwealth" symbolized a greater degree of freedom and independence and was therefore widely used over the rigid term "British Empire". Cf. Cmd. 1560, *Articles of Agreement for a Treaty between Great Britain and Ireland*, London: HMSO, 1921, 3; Keith, Arthur Berriedale (Ed.), *Speeches and Documents on the British Dominions, 1918–1931: From Self-government to National Sovereignty*, Oxford: Oxford University Press, 1948, 77; McIntyre, W. David, *The Commonwealth of Nations: Origins and Impact, 1869–1971*, Minneapolis: University of Minnesota Press, 1977, 185.
60 United Kingdom, *Parliamentary Debates* (hereafter *PD*), *House of Commons* (hereafter *HoC*), 5th Series, Vol. 28, 27 November 1922, 327–387.
61 "Empire or Commonwealth?", *Spectator* 147, No. 5396, 28 November 1931, 723.
62 Cf. Brown, Robert Craig – Cook, Ramsay, *Canada 1896–1921: A Nation Transformed*, Toronto: McClelland and Stewart, 1974, 275; *The Cambridge History of the British Empire: The Empire-Commonwealth 1870–1919*, Vol. 3, Cambridge: Cambridge University Press, 1967.
63 Zimmern, Alfred Eckhard, *The Third British Empire: Being a Course of Lectures Delivered at Columbia University New York*, London: Humphrey Milford, 1926, 2.
64 Cf. Hancock, *Survey of British*, 52; Thompson, J. Lee, *A Wider Patriotism: Alfred Milner and the British Empire*, London: Routledge, 2007, 171, 182.
65 See more cf. Cmd. 2768, *Imperial Conference, 1926: Summary of Proceedings*, London: HMSO, 1926, 59–60; CAC, AP, AMEL 1/3/40, [Alfred Milner], *The British Commonwealth*, Sheldonian Theatre, Oxford, 1 August 1919, 118–128.
66 Allin, Caphas Daniel, "Canada's Treaty Making Power", *Michigan Law Review* 24, No. 3, 1926, 251; The Secretary of State [Hughes] to the British Ambassador (Geddes), Washington, 5 March 1923, in: *FRUS*, 1923, Vol. 1, Washington: Government Printing Office, 1938, 471.
67 Cf. Secretary of State of United States [Hughes] to Ambassador [Geddes], Washington, 4 April 1923, in: *DCER*, Encl. No. 2 [to] Doc. No. 234, 660; The British Ambassador (Geddes) to the Secretary of State [Hughes], Washington, 28 March 1923, in: *FRUS*, 1923, Vol. 1, 471–472.
68 Secretary of State [Hughes] to the British Ambassador (Geddes), Washington, 4 April 1923, in: *FRUS*, 1923, Vol. 1, 472.
69 Cmd. 2769, *Imperial Conference, 1926: Appendices to the Summary of Proceedings*, London: HMSO, 1927, 24–25.
70 Amery, Leopold Stennett, *Thoughts on the Constitution*, London: Oxford University Press, 1964, 130–131.
71 TNA, CO 886/10/4, D. 384/27, Extracts from a Speech Made by General Hertzog, Pretoria, 20 December 1926, Doc. No. 144, 140 [489].
72 Hall, *Commonwealth*, 647.
73 TNA, DO 114/32, D. 15815/29, "British Empire" and "British Commonwealth of Nations": Memorandum, Doc. No. 321, January 1930, 259.
74 TNA, DO 35/538/5, Inter-Imperial Relations: Phraseology, January 1930, [1–6].
75 Cd. 8566, 5.
76 Although Dominion status did not have any explicit definition, it was not anticipated that in future it would expand to include the self-governing colonies

(South Rhodesia, Malta, etc.) or separate members of the Commonwealth of Nations (India) in any form either automatically or over time. As time progressed, the term Dominion status began to symbolise a member of the British Commonwealth of Nations which was separately represented at Imperial Conferences with full autonomy and a democratic form of government. TNA, DO 114/32, D. 15815/29, "British Empire" and "British Commonwealth of Nations": Memorandum, Doc. No. 321, January 1930, 260.
77 Cmd. 2768, 15.
78 TNA, DO 114/32, D. 15815/29, "British Empire" and "British Commonwealth of Nations": Memorandum, Doc. No. 321, January 1930, 260.
79 Mansergh, Nicholas, *Survey of British Commonwealth Affairs: Problems of External Policy 1931–1939*, London: Oxford University Press, 1952, 4.
80 Keith, Arthur Berriedale (Ed.), *Speeches and Documents on the British Dominions, 1918–1931: From Self-government to National Sovereignty*, Oxford: Oxford University Press, 1948, 303; TNA, Lord Chancellor's Office (hereafter LCO) 2/1190, [22 Geo. 5.], Statute of Westminster: A Bill [November 1931], 1.
81 Hancock, 58.
82 Mehrotra, 12.

2 Great Britain and Its Dominions Before the First World War

2.1 The Self-Governing Colonies, the First Dominions and the Colonial Conferences Period

Canada, the oldest Dominion, had many old ties binding it to Great Britain, in contrast to the other "white" overseas settlements. It was also heavily influenced by its proximity to the United States, and the coexistence of its francophone and anglophone population. For Australia and New Zealand, their great distance from the British Isles played an important role, alongside the fact that these territories were settled by an almost exclusively British population which was closer to London in many regards than other Dominions were. South Africa was different from other autonomous territories in two aspects. Historical developments had meant that two "white" nations had participated in settlement, i.e. the British and the Boers (Afrikaners). They each had such a different culture that there were military clashes between them; in addition, the native population outnumbered the "white" settlers. There were numerous differences between the Empire's different nations: in geographic conditions or specificities, in political, economic and social development, in the composition of the population, never mind the many external circumstances forming the history of one or the other territory. As such, one can say that there was no such thing as a "typical Dominion"; each Dominion was a unique territory.[1]

The growing economic importance of the overseas possessions, dominated by the "white" settlements,[2] and the rapid development of communication methods[3] led to more intensive relations with the mother country, and greater emphasis placed on regular discussion, consultation and co-ordination of foreign policy measures and defence strategies. The original set-up of London politicians meeting with representatives of overseas territories only on exceptional occasions thus appeared to be insufficient. The British political elite's increasing interest in colonial issues saw, for example, the establishment of the Royal Colonial Institute in 1868.[4]

Relations between the Self-Governing Colonies, which implemented the principle of responsible government, and the mother country were based on long-term loyalty which was neither contractual nor limited in time.[5] When the Self-Governing Colonies came together to form the Dominion of Canada, it was an important event which had a significant impact on mutual relations, one impact being that the London government began reflecting the potential separatist tendency more boldly, which until then it had not countenanced in its overseas possessions.[6] Establishment of the Dominion also led to the acceptance of the general idea that although Canada represented an integral part of the Empire, it *de jure* could not and *de facto* did not need to have its own diplomatic mission, and as such Britain's Foreign Secretary continued to make decisions on the level of Canadian representatives' involvement in foreign policy.[7]

Originally, Dominion status mainly served as a way of giving a name summarising the various types of privileges the Crown had gradually awarded the autonomous governments. In this regard, a mainly academic debate on the future organisational structure of the British Empire was provoked over the final three decades of the 19th century. Advocates of the Empire realised that the rapid development of the Self-Governing Colonies, which was leading towards the acquisition of Dominion status, would lead to the gradual independence of these nations, and thus they presented a number of plans involving some kind of imperial federation which were designed to inhibit these secessionist tendencies. Also related to this was the Imperialists' attempt at finding a representative name which would best characterise the new formation.[8] Over time, over 150 different plans were discussed, which promoted the expansion of the Westminster parliament by representatives of the colonies, or the adoption of a federal constitution in line with the American model, with an Imperial parliament. Although most of them seemed difficult to implement, or even impossible, the proposal of setting up a Council of Advice comprising representatives of the mother country and the colonies won the greatest number of proponents.[9]

Establishment of the Imperial Federation League in July 1884 served on the one hand to bring together all the diverse federative proposals and debates on the future of the Empire focused on the creation of a centralised political structure within its framework, and on the other hand resulted in an organisation in which Imperialists were able to showcase the idea of federalisation.[10] From its beginning, the federalists endeavoured to "reunite the diffuse parts of the same nation",[11] and as such they focused above all on the Self-Governing Colonies; India remained outside their focus for the meantime.[12] Although the League supported a number of leading British and colonial politicians, it was not always able to ensure the success of its goals.[13] It did nevertheless contribute significantly to the convening of the first Colonial Conference,[14] which was held from 4 April to 9 May 1887 and was chaired by Secretary of State for the Colonies Sir Henry Thurstan Holland, later 1st Viscount Knutsford.[15] Although the original plan was for just the three prime ministers of the Self-Governing Colonies to meet, the involvement of governors and other colonial and London representatives in Queen Victoria's golden jubilee celebrations was used to hold joint informal meetings symbolising unity and co-operation.[16]

Originally, defence and postal and telegraph connections were subjects for discussion, but over the course of the meeting participants also discussed other topical issues, including matters of economics and trade. Issues related to the imperial structure, or to the issue of setting up a political federation, were not discussed with the former Secretary of State for the Colonies, Edward Stanhope, having excluded them from the programme since he did not consider them a topical issue. In contrast to his successor Holland, Stanhope did not ascribe great importance to the conference, and as such insisted it be purely consultative in nature.[17] The Prime Minister, the Marquess of Salisbury, held a similar opinion, and he had no qualms in describing the considerations as great aspirations more suitable for future discussions; he too did not particularly favour extensive changes in regard to the self-governing parts of the Empire.[18] During discussion on customs tariffs, however, Cape politician Jan Hendrick Hofmeyr did mention an Imperial federation in regard to a proposal for establishment of a fiscal parliament which would have similar power and political weight as an "Imperial parliament".[19] Although London cabinet members removed the issue of an Imperial federation from the points of discussion at the conference, it was a unique example of co-operation within the Empire at that time.

Despite the fact that the League's main objective of establishing an Imperial federation was not achieved in 1887, their members spent the subsequent decade in quite fruitful debate over the "ideal" form for an Imperial federation.[20] Eventually, four main groupings were formed within the League, each striving for: (1) establishment of a standard political federation; (2) establishment of a Council of Advice where the colonies' voice could be heard; (3) union through defence commitments, and (4) a trading union on the basis of preference or free trade rules. Over time, advocates of a trading union gained the upper hand.[21]

The League suffered a failure in 1893 when it submitted a proposal to the Liberal government on the federalisation of the Empire. From the very beginning, Secretary of State for the Colonies George Robinson, 1st Marquess of Ripon, opposed them, and he was later joined by Prime Minister William Ewart Gladstone and the other government members, as they feared accepting a narrower union would mean abandoning the principle of free trade. In addition, they rejected the proposal that the matter be discussed at the upcoming Colonial Conference, greatly shaking the basic principles upon which the League was founded. As such, the League ceased operation at the end of 1893.[22] Although a number of smaller groups with similar objectives were subsequently set up, implementing a plan for federalisation of the Empire had in practice lost strong and organised support.[23]

The next Colonial Conference, which took place from 28 June to 9 July 1894 in Ottawa, Canada, contributed little to discussions on Empire federalisation, one reason being that it could hardly be considered a regular forum for all self-governing parts of the Empire – the meeting had been organised by the Canadian government, not the British Colonial Office.[24] Since the points for discussion were dominated by matters regarding the Pacific region, such as linking the Australian and North American continents with a submarine cable, it was mainly representatives of the Australian Self-Governing Colonies and Canada who took part in discussions.[25] One fact that can be termed a success is that, for the first time, delegates proposed a principle of Imperial preference, and the rule that one colony should have one vote in decisions.[26]

It should also be noted that at the time there were no close contacts between the Self-Governing Colonies and the Dominion of Canada, or they were at least rare; the autonomous territories were focused mainly on relations with the mother country, and they did not show particular interest in the other British overseas possessions.[27] All contact took place through the British capital, which played the role of mediator. As the importance of the Self-Governing Colonies grew, so the self-confidence of overseas statesmen also grew. The exceptional status of these autonomous territories arose not just from their economic status, but also from the fact that Dominion status was seldom granted; as such the overseas territories perceived it as a kind of reward from the mother country. Over time, however, this "elite club" of nations came to realise that mutual co-operation might be more advantageous if the mother country adopted, or at least took account of, their opinion. Although the beginnings of regular co-operation between the Self-Governing Colonies and Dominions date back to the period of the 1902 Colonial Conference, more intensive communication became commonplace in later years.[28]

In the second half of the 1890s, Britain's Secretary of State for the Colonies from July 1895, Joseph Chamberlain, took the initiative. Chamberlain had strived for many years for closer links between the Self-Governing Colonies and the mother country, because he recognised the dynamic development of mutual relations and the potential of autonomous overseas possessions. However, this would mean acknowledging the Self-Governing Colonies and Dominions as important parts of the British Empire.[29] He was very pragmatic in his view of other colonial territories and accepted that without Imperial assistance, no rapid progress could be expected.[30] Chamberlain was fully aware of the evident and latent complications that there were and that could emerge over time, as he knew that this was a long-term matter that couldn't be rushed. He nevertheless had no qualms in developing a plan for a closer union right from his first days. To begin with, he preferred the idea of establishing a kind of imperial customs union or trade union rather than some form of defensive grouping on the basis of agreed defence commitments. In regard to establishing an imperial customs union with the Self-Governing Colonies and Dominions, he proposed that the parties involved could form an Imperial Council.[31] This permanently sitting Council would have legislative and executive powers and a trade function, and would also represent a kind of Imperial parliament for a federalised Empire.[32]

The first Conference's success increased the confidence of the Australian Self-Governing Colonies, in particular in the meaningfulness of such meetings. Australian nationalists surprisingly welcomed endeavours at federalising the Empire, because they saw in it the opportunity to gain a certain level of independence within it.[33] The situation was similar in Canada, with the Canadian Imperial Federation League, intensifying its campaign. Canada also attempted to secure regular Colonial Conferences so that in the interim, the continuity of points discussed could be maintained if possible.[34]

In 1897, when the British Empire was celebrating Queen Victoria's Diamond Jubilee and it seemed nothing was impossible for the British nation, another Colonial Conference was held. Similarly to ten years' previously, colonial and Dominion statesmen received, in addition to invitations to the festivities linked to the Jubilee, an invitation to inform discussions with London representatives on a number of issues of Imperial significance.[35] On 24 June 1897, the prime ministers of the Self-Governing Colonies and Dominions[36] met with Chamberlain, who introduced a range of topics within the memorandum which included as well as dominating political relations, defence, economic and trading matters, and also issues linked to the use of submarine cables and the application of immigration laws. Chamberlain stated that discussion had been opened on contemporary and future relations between various parts of the Empire. He also noted the well-known fact that closer links or some form of natural Imperial federation between the self-governing territories and the mother country would undoubtedly bring trade and economic benefits to all those involved. Neither did he neglect to emphasise the necessity of improving the method of consultation in matters which affected the whole Empire.[37]

Over the course of the London meeting in 1897, the British press paid most attention to Canada's Liberal Prime Minister, Sir Wilfrid Laurier, whose popularity had risen significantly thanks to the aforementioned conference in Ottawa. Britain's *Daily Mail* made no bones about declaring him a solid pro-Imperial "politician of our New World [who] has been recognized as the equal of the great men of the Old Country".[38] Although Laurier was not seeking a change in political ties within the Empire, during discussions on constitutional arrangements, he offered partial support to smaller Pacific Self-Governing Colonies who wanted change.[39]

When in 1897 Chamberlain put forward without further explanation the idea of constitutional reform through establishment of a Council of the Empire,[40] British Prime Minister Salisbury did not offer his support. At the time, it was generally thought that relations between Great Britain and the autonomous territories were satisfactory.[41] Chamberlain had advocated the establishment of an Imperial Council, or Council of the Empire, which would aim for closer co-operation in defence and trade relations for many years. Although he had never given a precise description of his idea for an Imperial Council, it is clear that he was thinking not of carrying out any kind of wide-ranging constitutional changes, but rather of setting up a kind of advisory body. Because there was no official Imperial constitution, the Imperial Council, comprising leading representatives of the mother country and the self-governing nations, would informally assume this role and alongside Great Britain constitute the Empire.[42]

Most of the overseas prime ministers, however, were emphatically against establishing any additional body holding a similar weight to the Colonial Conferences, because they feared it would overly impinge upon the recently established system. Ideas of establishing an Imperial Cabinet did not arouse great enthusiasm, either. Representatives of Britain's Colonial Office, Tasmania and New Zealand, however, expressed interest in the original proposal for establishment of an Imperial Council, which in time they began to promote.[43] Another advocate of an Imperial Council was New Zealand Prime Minister Richard John Seddon, who even tried to convince his colleagues to support the proposal during the conference, because he thought that it would mean the opinion of the Self-Governing Colonies and the Dominion of Canada would be adequately represented in matters of defence, foreign policy and trade.[44] Discussion of an Imperial Council confirmed the long-term trend that the system of Conferences within the British Empire had firmly bedded down and represented a generally recognised forum for discussion of Imperial matters.

During the meeting, all prime ministers taking part unanimously endorsed the resolution that a conference on matters of general interest between them and Great Britain representatives should be held regularly, and that geographically close Self-Governing Colonies were ready to create a joint union in the near future. In regard to an evaluation of political relations between the United Kingdom and the self-governing territories, however, they were unable to come to agreement. Prime Ministers of New Zealand, Richard Seddon, and of Tasmania, Sir Edward Braddon, in contrast to the others, were of the opinion that political relations were satisfactory. Their stance arose from the position that mutual relations should be more formal. The overseas prime ministers realised that rapid population growth in their countries meant the time was ripe for Self-Governing Colonies and Dominions to make decisions on, or at least influence, Imperial affairs which fundamentally affected them to a greater extent, just as the mother country did. Although most prime ministers expressed willingness to contribute funding to the implementation of Imperial policies, and had even unofficially agreed to it, no approval of any form of Imperial federation occurred.[45] Opinions on the essence of Imperial reforms were so diverse, due to the large number of conference participants, that further deliberations would not have made sense if the Australian and South African Self-Governing Colonies did not federalise.[46]

The previously relatively calm discussion on the British Empire's future political form was interrupted by the Boer War, which helped to bring together the Self-Governing Colonies and Dominion of Canada with the mother country, and which further opened a new phase in discussions on federalisation of the Empire. In March 1900 in response to the conflict taking place and the involvement of the overseas autonomous territories, Chamberlain put more flesh on the bones of the previously not particularly clear concept of an Imperial Council. He anticipated that the body would permanently sit in London and that it would mainly advise the Secretary of State for the Colonies. Due to the state of war, it was no surprise that matters of Imperial defence were to be the institution's principle task. However, establishment of an Imperial Council collapsed in 1900 due to the fact that Chamberlain remained unable to convince Salisbury of his proposal, with Salisbury inflexibly of the opinion that although a closer Imperial union was essential, this should be implemented sometime in the future or through natural development. Nor did it help that the governments in Canada and Australia were highly sceptical or even dismissive of the idea.[47]

Although Chamberlain did not succeed with his plans at this time, he remained fairly optimistic. His charisma and authority had a significant impact on relations between Dominion prime ministers and British representatives at the turn of the 20th century, and this significantly contributed to the gradual reshaping of the British Empire into the Commonwealth. It can also be said that another important factor in the transition from Empire to Commonwealth of Nations was the change in Royal title[48] following Edward VII's ascension to the throne, with King of the British Dominions being added to his title.[49] The purpose of this change was to give more precise expression of the Dominions' newly forming constitutional position. There was no need to undertake any change or clarifications in the case of India, because since 1876 India had had a special place within the Empire. Modification of the title was indirectly indicated in the change in the King's role as head of this wider "family of nations",[50] in which, "the King is no longer merely King of Great Britain and Ireland and of a few dependencies ... he is now the greatest constitutional bond uniting together in a single Empire communities of free men".[51]

In 1902, for the occasion of Edward VII's coronation, another Colonial Conference took place, its participants dealing with a similar agenda to that in 1897. In contrast to before, not just overseas prime ministers took part in the confidential discussions, but also a number of ministers whose departments the issues discussed related to.[52] During his opening speech to the delegates, Chamberlain referred to the wave of Imperial solidarity which had arisen during the war with the Boers. Impressed by this event and the then general Imperial enthusiasm for reorganisation of the Empire, it seemed that the time was right for these issues, and as such he again proposed establishment of an Imperial Council which in contrast to before would have executive and legislative power rather than operating as an advisory body. According to Chamberlain, it would help to build closer ties between the mother country and the self-governing territories, while also affirming Imperial unity, which he thought of as a kind of voluntary political federation without formal commitments. The Imperial Council, where all issues with an Imperial dimension would be discussed, would serve to bring together this informal group.[53] Although Chamberlain's resubmission of his plan for establishing an Imperial Council was above all a response to events in southern Africa, it was also to a certain extent a response to the demand of Canada's Liberal leader, Sir Wilfrid Laurier, who in 1900 had declared in the Ottawa parliament: "If you want our help, you must call us to your councils." His words indirectly affirmed a long-term trend that Dominion statesmen and some Self-Governing Colonies were ready to assist Great Britain at moments of difficulty in exchange for corresponding influence in Imperial foreign and defence policy.[54]

Although the conference had begun promisingly, advocates of a close union were to be disappointed, with prime ministers avoiding more substantial discussion on political relations with the mother country.[55] Chamberlain's plan for establishing an Imperial Council was just one of many emerging at the time whose authors theorised over the future form of the Empire.[56] Besides the system of Colonial Conferences, Chamberlain's project probably represented the most realistic vision for a "rival" Imperial institution. Its rejection paradoxically meant that advocates of holding the conferences as fora in which the voice of the Dominions and Self-Governing Colonies could be heard were strengthened. The significance of Chamberlain's proposal for constitutional development was in the fact that his Imperial Council was to a certain extent the first attempt at a notional transition from Empire to Commonwealth, i.e. from a geographically defined territory to a clearly organised political structure. Although over the years, Chamberlain's position had evolved as a result of external events (in particular the Boer War) with certain changes in particular areas, in general he still held the opinion that establishment of the Dominions had opened up a new chapter in the history of the British Empire, because the Dominions represented equal partners which had to be incorporated within the Imperial structure in a corresponding manner. In 1897, Chamberlain had spoken only of "sister nations",[57] but three years later he was speaking of "a great federation of sister-nations that we call the British Empire".[58] In June 1902 in an address at a dinner held by the Imperial South African Association, he declared his belief in the Canadian, Australian and South African nations, "because I believed that the strength of the Empire is in the brotherhood of nations come from the same stock".[59] In January 1903 he referred to "the group of free nations gathered round the mother country".[60] Viscount Alfred Milner held a similar position, believing that the British Empire represented, "a group of sister nations spread throughout the world".[61]

Over time, a number of relatively isolated events led to the fact that the Colonial Conferences began to form a distinct system or institution with its own rules, agenda and constitutional composition. At the same time, its importance grew because it was no longer just the prime ministers of the Self-Governing Colonies who attended alongside other important representatives of the Crown such as Governors, or Governors-General, and the British Secretary of State for the Colonies, but also relevant British ministers and senior civil servants. This fact was confirmed when conference participants in 1902 adopted an importance resolution on political relations and modifying previous rules of conduct. From then on, discussion between overseas prime ministers and Britain's Secretary of State for the Colonies in regard to relations between the mother country, Dominions and Self-Governing Colonies was to take place regularly, at least once every four years. The previous practice of the meeting representing merely a kind of marginal affair held during key Imperial events came to an end, while the delegates' demand of 1897 was met. At any time when exceptional problems or issues emerged which needed to be dealt with immediately, the resolution allowed for the calling of a special conference on the issue; the regular meeting was then to take place no earlier than in three years.[62]

It isn't easy with hindsight to assess the 1902 Colonial Conference. Its peculiarity is in the fact that in contrast to previous sessions, a representative of India was able to participate in selected discussions, his presence approved by Joseph Chamberlain on the basis of a request from the India Secretary, Lord George Francis Hamilton. This meant that an Indian delegate took part in future conferences.[63] Despite all the effort and energy Chamberlain expended on the conference, he experienced a number of disappointments. Not only was he unable to ensure closer political union, but discussions of matters of trade and defence did not come to any transformative conclusions either. Since he perceived customs tariffs as a new symbol of constitutional relations and a crucial condition for the effective operation of political union between the mother country, the Dominions and the Self-Governing Colonies, he decided in October 1903 to resign as Colonial Secretary and focus on securing tariff reforms.[64]

Following the rejection of Chamberlain's plan to establish an Imperial Council, most proponents of a closer union decided to support the system of Colonial Conferences through various Imperial organisations.[65] Eventually, the so-called Pollock Committee, chaired by founder and renowned lawyer Sir Frederick Pollock, 3rd Baronet Pollock, rose to the fore. The committee, comprised partly from members of the Imperial Federation (Defence) Committee which had split from the Imperial Federation League in 1893, first met as a discussion club in early 1903 and it aspired to investigate various options for Imperial co-operation and eventual transformations in Imperial structures.[66] Over three years, the group had grown to such a size that its members included not just academic theoreticians and lawyers, but also a number of politicians, economists and civil servants. The Pollock Committee submitted a plan to establish an Imperial Organisation, having an Imperial Advisory Committee with a permanent secretariat.[67] The proposal also rejected the establishment of an Imperial federation, instead supporting principles of co-operation based on Colonial Conferences. For this reason, the Pollock Committee sought the more effective and formal development of this forum.[68]

Pollock's plan to establish an Imperial Organisation built on previous efforts at forming a permanent advisory body for Imperial affairs. In particular, it was a response to Bernard Henry Holland's proposal, published in early 1901, and the recommended creation of an Imperial Council which would meet regularly once every two to three years in London.[69] It was also a successor to a broader plan which was formulated on 9 June 1903 by Liberal politician Richard Burdon Haldane, later 1st Viscount Haldane, in the Royal Colonial Institute. On the one hand, it warned against the precipitous forming of an Imperial union, and on the other hand recommended coming up with a new unwritten constitutional form which would serve as an advisory body to the Crown in Imperial matters. Along the model of the already operating Imperial Defence Committee, Pollock proposed creating a similar representative body, the so-called Cabinet of Empire, comprising the Prime Minister and Secretaries of State for Foreign Affairs and the Colonies.[70] In December 1903, another member of the Pollock Committee, New Zealand statesman and historian William Pember Reeves, responded to Haldane's speech, submitting a proposal that an Imperial Council be established which would be a small, compact, centralised body comprising prime ministers and ministers for the Colonies from Canada, Australia, New Zealand and the Cape Colony, to meet once every two years and having an advisory role.[71]

When the principle of regular Colonial Conferences was adopted in 1902, it surprisingly aroused mixed feelings amongst overseas statesmen. The Self-Governing Colonies and Dominions thought they had acquired an effective form of representation, but they were also faced with the question of how Imperial matters were going to be dealt with in the period between the two Conferences; the next standard meeting was not due to take place until 1906. As such, Britain's Colonial Office was particularly interested in the Pollock Committee's proposals at the end of 1904, because they provided a partial solution to their unanticipated problem.[72] British Secretary of State for the Colonies Alfred Lyttelton adopted a number of Pollock Committee ideas and began preparing a fundamental reform of the system of Colonial Conferences.[73] In early 1905, he had managed to acquire the support of British Prime Minister Sir Arthur James Balfour, later 1st Earl of Balfour, who expressed a certain level of reticence over use of the term "Imperial Conference".[74]

Internal debate of Lyttelton's concept took place from January to April 1905 at the Colonial Office, with a number of modifications made to it in regard to the status of the Prime Minister and Secretaries of State for the Colonies and India. Further progress in the matter occurred on 20 April 1905 when Lyttelton sent the Governors of the Self-Governing Colonies and the Governor-General of the Dominions a circular about the future organisation of Colonial Conferences and a proposal of how they should proceed during periods when the Conferences were not sitting. Lyttelton supported the idea of establishment of an Imperial Council which his predecessor Chamberlain had previously come up with, and the related transformation of the system of Colonial Conferences into an Imperial forum – an Imperial Council. According to Lyttelton's proposal, the London cabinet wanted to know the opinion of the overseas governments on Imperial matters of a civilian nature, and as such the permanent Imperial Council was to comprise the British Secretary of State for the Colonies representing His Majesty's Government, the representative of India and the prime ministers of the self-governing territories or, if they were not present, their named representatives. Similarly, during the 1902 Colonial Conference, for selected specialist matters, consultation with relevant department ministers was also permitted. Lyttelton did not preclude future regular Conferences changing the composition of the Imperial Council, and as such he deliberately did not propose a precise definition of the competencies of the Council, considering that, "the history of Anglo-Saxon institutions, such as Parliament or the Cabinet system, seems to show that an institution may often be wisely left to develop," so that it could adapt flexibly to circumstances.[75]

At times the prime ministers of the autonomous overseas territories were unable to participate in the London meetings due to being occupied with domestic matters, Alfred Lyttelton proposed establishing a Permanent Commission in which skilled and competent representatives of the British government, Self-Governing Colonies and Dominions would sit equally. The Commission would have an office in central London available to it with a corresponding number of administrative workers and a secretary who would have the same power as the Conference secretary when the Imperial Council sat, and who would be responsible for the smooth course of co-operation between the Commission and the Council. In terms of composition, Lyttelton's institution was probably most similar to the

Imperial Defence Committee's civilian option. Lyttelton made the assurance that the Commission would help to speed up communication and that certain important issues could be discussed in advance there. Since it was meant to be a consultative and advisory body, Lyttelton did not anticipate that it would replace the Colonial Office. He was aware that it was a relatively new idea, and as such he acknowledged that the commission should be established for just one year in this form, and that subsequently, in the summer of 1906, its usefulness and success would be evaluated.[76]

Lyttelton's proposal was mostly well-received, although over the course of 1905 some prime ministers suggested significant changes in the Imperial Council,[77] or at least subjected it to thorough examination. Canadian representatives in particular did not consider the Council, which the Colonial Conferences were to transform into, as a sufficiently representative political body, and they thus advocated accepting a new system – Imperial Conferences. They were also sceptical of the idea of a permanent commission, which they perceived as a threat to the independence of the established responsible governments.[78] Canada was more supportive of a form of Empire as advocated by Richard Jebb than by Frederick Pollock. Although both were proponents of a closer form of union, they differed in the methods by which to achieve this. Jebb was convinced that a united Empire could co-exist with the idea of national independence, and therefore he did not believe that establishment of an Imperial Council was the ideal way to improve the organisation of Imperial relationships. According to Jebb, the prime ministers of the self-governing territories should have the final say in the system of Colonial Conferences, each vote being of equal weight. He suggested for the period between two conferences that overseas governments should be represented in London, for example, through High Commissioners who would ensure prime ministers were sufficiently informed in issues of Imperial foreign policy and other matters.[79]

Discussion between Britain's Colonial Secretary, Alfred Lyttelton, and the governors of the Self-Governing Colonies came in the second half of 1905 to two principal conclusions: (1) the Conference was moved to 1907 because the Prime Ministers of Australia and New Zealand were unable to attend on the original dates due to important domestic matters; and (2) at Canada's request, debate on making the Colonial Conference system organisation more effective was postponed until the standard Conference.[80] Postponement of the meeting also suited Britain's Colonial Office, newly led by Liberal politician Victor Bruce, 9th Earl of Elgin, from December 1905. Since Bruce was not an advocate of a formal Imperial union, he took a sceptical position towards the Pollock Committee plans. Due to the exchange of opinions taking place between the Colonial Office and representatives of the Self-Governing Colonies and Dominions, however, he included Lyttelton's proposals as one of the topics for discussion at Conference meetings.[81]

From February 1906, intensive preparations began at Britain's Colonial Office and amongst overseas representatives for the one-month Conference in spring 1907. The agenda was to be dominated by matters around the Imperial Council and the future status of the system of Colonial Conferences, preferential trade, defence, emigration and the granting of citizenship.[82] The preparations demonstrated, however, that Britain's Colonial Office and the individual Self-Governing Colonies and Dominions attached different levels of importance to certain issues. The Australian government, for example, agreed with the idea of setting up an Imperial Council in an almost identical form to that proposed by Lyttelton.[83] The New Zealand cabinet also supported the idea, because they saw it as a great opportunity for the Empire, facilitating communication in Imperial matters.[84] In contrast, the Cape Colony linked the operation of an Imperial Council with the issue of Imperial defence.[85] Canadian Prime Minister Wilfrid Laurier was notorious for his distrust of the proposed Imperial body.[86] Canada had sought the reshaping of the Colonial Conferences into a full-fledged Imperial system for many years, in which cabinet ministers would sit as equal participants and not just the prime ministers of the Dominions and Self-Governing Colonies, or the *ad hoc* invitation of cabinet members without the status of regular participants. However, Lord Elgin did not favour this form and as such referred to the conclusion of the 1902 Colonial Conference in which it was stated that the Secretary of State for the Colonies and Prime Ministers of the Self-Governing Colonies and Dominions were to take part in Conference discussions.[87]

After Australia and New Zealand had expressed their support for certain points in Lyttelton's original plan, the Pollock Committee repeatedly entered discussions on the Imperial Council. In March 1907, it presented a new plan which categorically rejected replacing the Conference system with another Imperial body, suggesting instead that a new more precise term be adopted – an Imperial Conference.[88] Between 1903 and 1907, the Pollock Committee played an important role, managing to arouse wider interest in the issue of an Imperial union and the Conference system, and also forcing Colonial Office officials to reassess their position on the status of Self-Governing Colonies and the natural transformation of constitutional relations within the Empire.[89] The first months of 1907 were also marked by greater activity by other proponents of an Imperial union, including Lord Alfred Milner,[90] Leopold Stennett Amery, Geoffrey Drage and Richard Jebb. Jebb in particular wrote expansively on the issue in a number of articles in the *Morning Post*, in which he campaigned for the establishment of a permanent system of Conferences which would also have an independent secretariat, and he persistently proposed that High Commissioners in London should have the same status as foreign ambassadors.[91] Leo Amery noted that concessions had to be made in order to counter the growing separatist tendencies in the overseas possessions, and as such the British government should look at them as equal partners in foreign policy. Amery saw the principle of equality as a fundamental prerequisite for a united Empire, and therefore sought more intensive mutual communication, which he perceived as one way to achieve this. He also advocated for more frequent consultation during regular conferences, and in the interim period through a permanent secretariat, whose establishment he believed represented a great benefit in improving constitutional relationships within the Empire.[92]

The year 1907 was a certain turning point, with debate on the form and status of Colonial Conferences which had become a distinct system since 1902 reaching a head. The new search for an appropriate definition and conceptual description of the British Empire at the start of the 20th century was related to the "official" creation of new nations (Dominions) which wanted to preserve their separate identity rather than be subject to some political centralised structure.[93] Many Dominion and British statesmen perceived these changes as a turning point, with a new "family of nations" being created. Canadian Prime Minister Laurier, for example, compared the British Empire to a "galaxy of independent nations".[94] He also hoped that "We are reaching the day when our parliament will claim co-equal rights with the British parliament and when the only ties binding us together will be a common flag and a common crown."[95]

The final Colonial Conference took place from 15 April to 14 May 1907. This fifteenth meeting was dominated by the issue of the future organisation of the system of Conferences and its significance within Imperial relationships, in particular from the perspective of the Self-Governing Colonies and Dominions, as well as issues linked to defence and commercial relationships, of which preferential trade was a significant factor.[96] The first four Colonial Conferences had focused on clarifying basic principles and approaches. From 1902 the provision applied that it was a meeting between representatives of autonomous parts of the Empire and British representatives, and that each government held one vote. Discussions were to be purely consultative, informal and private in nature. Although relevant ministers of the Self-Governing Colonies and Dominions were able to be invited to meetings under certain circumstances, they were not regular members and as such did not have the right to vote for final resolutions. India was represented by Sir James Mackay, later 1st Earl of Inchcape, in a kind of "observer" role within the British delegation, naturally without the ability to take part in final voting. Over the course of the meeting, Canadian Prime Minister Laurier, who had advocated an expansion of national representatives to include ministers for many years, managed to overcome the dissent of Lord Elgin, who then agreed to the participation of other ministers.[97]

The main section of debate on the future organisation of Conferences occurred during initial meetings, in which two opposing positions – Canadian and Australian – on reorganisation of the Empire came up against each other. Canadian Prime Minister Laurier feared the Conference might become a forum in which the subordinate position of the Self-Governing Colonies and Dominions towards the mother country could stand out. As such, he responded on 15 April 1907 to the introductory speech by British Prime Minister Sir Henry Campbell-Bannerman who spoke about the essence of British Empire cohesion involving "freedom and independence" and declared that he did not see the Conferences as merely a simple meeting of the prime ministers of the self-governing territories and the British Secretary of States for the Colonies, but rather in particular as "a Conference between the Imperial Government and the Governments of the Self-Governing Colonies of England".[98] Since he was also an opponent of introducing any kind of centralising elements to the Imperial structure, he was stubbornly against establishing a separate Imperial secretariat. He was unexpectedly supported in his stance by conservatives at the Colonial Office, who feared a loss of influence in Imperial affairs as a result of the establishment of an "independent" secretariat.[99]

Laurier's Australian opposite number Alfred Deakin saw clear evidence in the meetings between the British government and the governments of the Self-Governing Colonies and Dominions of the equal status of these overseas parts of the Empire.[100] Although he was a leading defender of Colonial nationalism like Laurier, he did not *a priori* rule out its coexistence with Imperial ties or commitments; his concept of Empire was based on the principle of a partnership of free nations. Furthermore, he had been significantly influenced by the Pollock Committee proposals.[101] In contrast to the Canadian Prime Minister, Deakin believed that establishing a permanent secretariat would maintain and increase the prestige of the system of Conferences during periods when meetings were not held, that it would reduce the influence of the British Colonial Office, and thus its push for centralisation, and that it would help to achieve equality with the mother country for the self-governing territories.[102]

The formation of an advisory body and the future name for the Conference were two further proposals which the prime ministers focused on intensively. The Prime Ministers of the Australian Dominion and the Self-Governing Colonies of New Zealand and the Cape Colony proposed the creation of a permanent body which would replace the Conferences. Lord Elgin realised that the changing Empire required a new means of communication with its self-governing territories, and as such, in March 1907, he submitted a reorganisation plan to the British government which he envisaged would strengthen Imperial unity. He proposed that the three principal overseas regions – North America, the South Pacific and southern Africa – be represented in London by High Commissioners, who would be members of the House of Lords, meaning that the London government could consult them through the Secretary of States for the Colonies on issues related to the overseas territories. The British cabinet nonetheless rejected Elgin's proposal because it did not want to set up an independently assembled body which might threaten Britain's position in Imperial foreign policy. Despite this, however, Elgin's proposal was discussed at the Conference on 17 April 1907.[103]

It was clear from the start that the overseas prime ministers would not be united. Prime Ministers Alfred Deakin of Australia, Sir Joseph George Ward, later 1st Baronet of Wellington, of New Zealand, and Doctor Sir Leander Starr Jameson, later 1st Baronet, of the Cape Colony identified with much of Elgin's proposal, while their Canadian counterpart Sir Wilfrid Laurier, a fundamental opponent of all attempts at creating a central governing body of any form, was against it.[104] Since the system of Conferences until that time had attained its own constitutional structure, the Canadian Prime Minister submitted a counterproposal which aimed to define a new name for the system. The title "Imperial Conference", which was thought to better characterise the agenda discussed during meetings, represented a certain form of compromise between proponents and opponents of an Imperial Council.[105]

Subsequently dealt with was the issue around establishing an Imperial secretariat, as advocated by Australian Prime Minister Deakin in particular, supported by Ward of New Zealand and Jameson of the Cape Colony, against Laurier and the Transvaal Colony's Louis Botha. The idea of setting up a permanent secretariat meant two factors in Imperial thinking of the time which were difficult to reconcile coming together, i.e. the effective independence of Dominions and Self-Governing Colonies at the expense of Britain's Colonial Office, and also real influence in decision-making in Imperial matters. Alfred Deakin, influenced by Pollock Committee ideas and the content of Lyttelton's circular, wanted a secretariat which would serve as an independent body to prepare agendas at Conferences, through which Dominions and the Great Britain government would communicate on foreign policy issues directly without the mediation of the Colonial Office, responsible only to the British Prime Minister. In contrast, the Canadian Prime Minister, strongly supported by his Transvaal opposite number, was uncompromisingly against establishing an independent secretariat because he feared it might restrict Canadian autonomy, and because he considered the Colonial Office to be the ideal institute for communication with the Self-Governing Colonies and Dominions.[106]

The failure of Deakin's plan was a significant disappointment for leading Empire supporters, including Leopold Stennett Amery,[107] Alfred Milner[108] and Richard Jebb.[109] Although they had not managed to set up an independent permanent Secretariat, the overseas prime ministers had managed to agree on a compromise establishing its modified form. A permanent Secretariat was to be available during the period between two Conferences, run by Britain's Colonial Office, and with a purely consultative nature whose principal task was in preparing future Conferences, including communication with the self-governing territories. At the same time, one needs to stress the fact that this small institution remained outside the cabinet's direct influence.[110] Besides critics, there were also positive responses. In Canada in particular, establishment of a small Secretariat represented an acceptable compromise which allowed two years of discussion aroused by Lyttelton's circular to come to an end. Canadian Conservative Sir George Eulas Foster, for example, considered the set-up to be beneficial, allowing the system of Conferences to be more effective.[111]

Approval of the small Imperial Secretariat, or sometimes also the Imperial Conference Secretariat, forced the Secretary of State for the Colonies, Lord Elgin, to listen to the proposals of his Permanent Under-Secretary of State, Sir Francis John Hopwood, later 1st Baron Southborough, on reorganising the Colonial Office.[112] Elgin was categorically against any kind of independence, even financial, for the Secretariat, and as such he assured the Chancellor of the Exchequer that the reallocating of competencies within the Office would require no extra funds, and the newly established department would continue to represent an integral part of the Colonial Office. The reorganisation was officially completed on 1 December 1907, when three departments were set up: (1) for the Dominions; (2) for the Crown Colonies; and (3) for legal and general affairs. In contrast to the March plan which Elgin had submitted to the government, its scope was no longer based on geographical areas but rather now reflected the level of dependence on the mother country.[113] The position of the Imperial Secretariat and the status of the gradually emerging Dominion Department were rather vague to begin with, and as such, in September 1907, Elgin decided to clarify the situation. He informed the Dominions that the Secretariat was linked to the Dominion Department by a personal secretary, who was also a formal member, although he carried out different duties.[114]

The Colonial Conference also helped to create the Dominion Department, set up on 1 December 1907. In subsequent years, this focused mainly on preparing the agenda for future Conferences, run by Britain's Colonial Office. To begin with, the small department with just nine officials had to overcome a number of difficulties, the most significant of which was unexpected criticism from the Colonial Office that the staff of the Dominion Department did not have much personal experience of the Dominions, and as such had to overly rely on reports from British representatives there, and as such they were unable to grasp the true essence of Dominion issues. In fact, the Dominion Department played an important role in discussions on the future form of the Empire, whether with advocates of centralisation, decentralisation or federalisation, or with nationalists in the Dominions.[115]

The final Colonial Conference of 1907 can be considered as marking a notional transition from the British Empire to the Commonwealth, because it changed the previous principles of Colonial Conferences, and because it approved an important resolution modifying constitutional relations and setting a number of rules for the holding of future Imperial Conferences: (1) meetings were to be held once every four years at the latest; (2) the Prime Minister of Great Britain was to chair it by virtue of his title, with the Colonial Secretary chairing it in the event of his absence; (3) only Dominion prime ministers were to be Conference members; (4) at most two ministers from each government were able to take part in each meeting; (5) each country held just one vote and (6) if needed, a Conference could be called for a special purpose.[116] The conclusions of the 1907 Colonial Conference, in terms of participating countries, not just confirmed the conventional practice but also precluded India and other dependent territories from having a voice at the forum in future, thus creating an imaginary barrier preventing such territories from having greater involvement within the British Empire.[117] The term "Dominion", which was first used to characterise the Crown's relationship of possession to Virginia (the Old Dominion), now began to express the idea of constitutional equality between the Self-Governing Colonies and the United Kingdom.[118] In 1907, the number of Dominions increased to four with the addition of Newfoundland and New Zealand.

The Colonial (Imperial) Conference signified a place for the Dominions where they could freely present their positions on current issues, mainly in regard to defence and foreign policy, and express themselves in confidential discussions on the future direction of the British Empire. Despite differing opinions on points under discussion, in vitally important matters such as defence, there was broad consensus. Although at first sight it might appear that Colonial (Imperial) Conferences were solely dominated by matters of a political, constitutional and defence nature, various other issues affecting the everyday life of citizens were also frequently discussed. The Dominions took particular interest in discussions on Imperial Preference,[119] which they perceived not just as an economic benefit, but also as a clear unifying bond within the Empire. Imperial politician Leopold Stennett Amery, for example, was of the opinion that, "for Dominion statesmen Imperial Preference was, first and foremost, a constitutional issue, the obvious and primary method of asserting Imperial unity".[120] Amery believed that Imperial Preference was an issue for the Empire alone.[121] The former Secretary of State for the Colonies Joseph Chamberlain was even convinced that, "the only possible path towards closer imperial unity lay in commercial preference".[122] The Colonial Conferences, held between 1887 and 1907, laid the path for the development of closer co-operation between politicians, institutes and citizens within the British Empire and for the gradual transformation of the Empire into the Commonwealth.

2.2 The Imperial Conferences System, 1907–1911

The failures which accompanied the promotion of the Pollock Committee proposals heralded a decline in the influence of the Pollock "reformers" in Imperial matters.[123] The reform plans of other groupings began to come to the fore,[124] with leading advocates of Imperial union, Alfred Milner and Leopold Amery, gradually taking centre stage. Travelling to Dominions and Self-Governing Colonies, they spoke in favour of effective changes in the Empire's organisation, in particular in terms of expanding the Secretariat's level of independence from the British Colonial Office, and establishing a special ministry for Dominion affairs. Since an Imperial Conference was being prepared for 1911, they aimed to "fill the vacuum" at a time when the Secretariat was tied down by rules and formalities, and to make use of personal contacts and connections to influence the planned agenda in the field of Imperial affairs.[125] Since Canada had not taken a particularly positive stance at the 1907 Colonial Conference, in particular in regard to Deakin's proposals, Amery and Milner focused on Canadian representatives, as they thought convincing them of the need for an Imperial Union was the "key" to success. In autumn 1908, Milner in particular tried through a number of talks he gave for smaller pro-Imperial groupings such as the Canadian Club, founded by his friend, well-known Toronto journalist and stockbroker Arthur James Glazebrook, in order to promote Imperial ideas, influential members of which went on to form a local division of the Round Table Movement in 1909, to convince Canada of the general necessity of more intensive links between the Dominions and the mother country.[126]

Amery and Milner's activities between 1909 and 1911 were part of the Round Table Movement's wider endeavours, a group considered with hindsight the best organised and most influential grouping advocating Imperial union and the idea that Dominions should administer their own foreign affairs independently. The movement's beginnings dated back to the period when Lord Milner and his successor William Palmer, 2nd Earl of Selborne, held the post of High Commissioner in South Africa and were surrounded by young capable Oxford graduates who helped them as administrative assistants.[127] Some of the most important of these were Lionel George Curtis; George Geoffrey Dawson; Philip Henry Kerr, the future 11th Marquess of Lothian, who was Editor in Chief of the pro-Imperial journal *The Round Table*; and to an extent also Leopold Stennett Amery.[128] Critics, however, frequently referred to Milner's colleagues using the not particularly grand term of Milner's Kindergarten.[129] Milner was a key figure, because he sketched out a vision, "constructively and imperially to galvanize the nation and the Empire".[130] Nevertheless, his view of an Imperial union placed little emphasis on economic links between the mother country and the overseas self-governing territories.[131]

Members of the so-called Milner's Kindergarten represented the core of the Round Table Movement, which was officially created in early September 1909 in Plas Newydd in the Lord Anglesey's country seat, and which set for itself two main goals: (1) to support the system of Conferences, which it considered a fundamental aspect in the Empire's permanent stability; and (2) to promote Imperial union.[132] Over the years however, the Movement came up against various obstacles, in particular Dominion nationalism.[133] To begin with, it seemed that the nationalist position of representatives of individual Dominions might speed up the process of deepening Imperial unity, but following the 1911 Imperial Conference, this did not seem realistic. In the end, the Movement decided to support the more realistic idea that the Empire could also form a united block on the basis of free political and economic co-operation.[134]

Over time, a group of historians was formed, including Richard Jebb, John Wesley Dafoe and John Skirving Ewart, who set themselves up as conceptual opponents of Round Table Movement members and presented their own vision of the Empire's future.[135] Radical British Labour members and socialists also had their perspective on the form of relationships within the Empire. Although Fabian members focused more on the issue of economic ties between the mother country and its possessions,[136] some of them prior to 1914 identified with Milner's unionist position. Radical members of the Labour Party in particular were proponents of free trade, opponents of conscription and colonial supremacy and supporters of the Indian emancipation movement and solidarity amongst workers within the Empire.[137]

Lionel Curtis, who was a leading figure in the Round Table Movement, expended unusual efforts in matters of Imperial federation.[138] Curtis was also renowned for undertaking almost "missionary" journeys across the Empire to convince local politicians to adopt the issue of Imperial Union.[139] To begin with, he set himself the task of analysing the differing position of the Dominions to the Empire and selecting the most topical issue out of it. Since he identified with Amery and Milner's position that Canada's stance was most important, he worked on a document in early 1910 called the Memorandum on Canada and the British Empire, also known as the Green Memorandum,[140] which was critical of Dominions' previous "lukewarm" position on Imperial matters, and he subsequently distributed it as a private document during his journeys across the Empire. In it, Curtis expressed the opinion that there should be a closer alignment between Dominions and the mother country, especially in matters of defence and foreign policy, through establishment of an Imperial Government and an Imperial Federal Parliament.[141]

During his journeys to the Pacific Dominions, New Zealand and the Commonwealth of Australia, in August 1910,[142] Curtis formulated the so-called Curtis Memorandum at the request of New Zealand Governor John Dickson-Poynder, 1st Baron Islington. Its central idea was again focused on the idea of firm Imperial unity and a rejection of the idea of mutual co-operation on a voluntary basis. At the same time, Curtis proposed that Britain's Colonial Office be transformed into an Imperial Office, within which the Dominion Department would be separated from the Crown Colonies division. According to Curtis, the Secretariat set up at the Colonial Conference in 1907 was to be run by four High Commissioners, who would better co-operate with the Foreign and War Offices and His Majesty's Government.[143]

At roughly the same time Curtis was travelling across the British Pacific territories, other Round Table Movement members produced a number of internal memoranda in which they expressed their positions on the system of Conferences, the establishment of a Dominion Office and the Secretariat. The most comprehensive perspective was given by Leopold Amery, who had returned in March 1908 to England from South Africa. The so-called Amery Memorandum focused in particular on the equal status of all self-governing parts of the Empire.[144] He had long been interested in the idea of removing Dominion affairs from the competencies of the Colonial Office, and therefore proposed its reform. He planned that the Colonial Office's Dominion Department be allocated a separate Office for Imperial Affairs which would comprise a Dominion Department looking at relations between the London government and Dominion cabinets, and a Secretariat which would focus on preparations for Imperial Conferences. For this reason, a minister responsible for Imperial affairs would be named for each Dominion government who was to be assisted by the High Commissioner.[145]

Although Amery's memorandum generally matched Curtis's for Baron Islington in many points, the two were produced independently. They are similar in terminology and positions because, in February and March 1910, both men discussed South African and Imperial affairs together.[146] They both called for the establishment of an independent Dominion Department and of a Ministry for Dominions in every Dominion government, although they did not agree in the status of the Secretariat and in the task of the High Commissioners. Amery's memorandum supported a greater level of Dominion Department independence, and as such proposed it be granted its own ministerial department.[147] Over the course of October and November 1910, Baron Islington used Amery's and Curtis's proposals to prepare a number of issues which the New Zealand government wanted included in the agenda of the planned Imperial Conference. In his memorandum, Baron Islington was pursuing the objective of ensuring that the ministerial subcommission preparing for the Imperial Conference in the coming year paid sufficient attention to the Imperial situation and that certain topics did not fall by the wayside.[148]

In mid-November 1910, however, Philip Kerr was worried that their efforts could be thwarted during Conference discussions by the negative position of Liberal leader Herbert Henry Asquith and the Prime Ministers of Canada and South Africa, Wilfrid Laurier and Louis Botha. Kerr's main objective was to establish an Imperial government responsible to all voters in the Empire and symbolising Imperial union; he therefore decided to do all he could to campaign for it. He saw the opportunity to achieve his goal in promoting the idea of Imperial union within specially published books and influential periodicals, and also in supporting various steps moving towards Imperial consolidation, such as public talks on Imperial affairs.[149] Kerr's activities were supported by former Colonial Secretary Lyttelton, although in response to an article by Garvin published in the *Observer* newspaper in October 1910, Lyttelton warned against the hasty promotion of an overly radical plan.[150] Although Baron Islington's memorandum was subsequently modified, the final version presented to New Zealand in May 1911 had a significant Imperial dimension.

Alongside the activities of Round Table Movement members exerting an influence in particular on the position of the Pacific Dominions, and the Royal Colonial Institute,[151] Britain's Colonial Office was also preparing for the upcoming Imperial Conference. On 4 July 1910, an anonymous memorandum was produced which analysed Lyttelton's original proposals and the positions of Dominion prime ministers during the 1907 meeting and gave an overview of the steps the Office had taken in these matters. The memorandum recommended expanding the role of the Imperial Secretariat.[152] Ten days later, leading Secretariat figure Sir Hartmann Wolfgang Just submitted a proposal for reorganising the Colonial Office. Just accepted the division of the Office into two offices, of which one would administer Crown Colonies affairs and the second would focus on the Dominions. This was all to take place on condition that it would be of benefit for running the Empire, and not just the fervent wish of the Dominions.[153] The issue of eventual independence of the Dominion Department increased in importance when the head of the department, Sir Charles Prestwood Lucas, got involved in the debate. He was of the opinion that the state at the time was a half-compromise, and it was only a matter of time until the Colonial Office was split up. Lucas thought that in future it would be necessary to exclude all aspects from relations between the mother country and the Dominions which looked, even if only ostensibly, like any form of subordination, and as such he thought establishing three ministries (for India, for the Crown Colonies and for the Dominions) was the ideal solution reflecting the true nature of mutual relations.[154]

Although both memoranda represented two differing approaches to the issue of Imperial reorganisation, the cabinet committee did not take much account of them in preparing for the Imperial Conference, even though there were voices in the Dominions calling for reform of the Empire.[155] Summer 1910 was marked by domestic political unrest, and as such Imperial organisation was not a pressing topic,[156] although debate did take place on separating the Dominion Department from the Colonial

Office.[157] Despite all this, from early October 1910 until early May 1911, Dominion Department officers focused intensively on preparing a recommendation and resolution for the upcoming Conference.[158] They perceived New Zealand's proposal for establishing an Imperial Council as unworkable, instead focusing on the issue of the Colonial Office's status within the Imperial structure.[159] The arranged Conference agenda was significantly influenced by the arrival of new Colonial Secretary Lewis Vernon Harcourt, later Viscount Harcourt, who did not express much sympathy with the Dominions' aspirations.[160] As such, it was no surprise that during the height of preparations for the Imperial Conference, advocates of Imperial federation warned one another of his cynical and indifferent approach to the topics proposed.[161]

In early 1911, Imperial affairs become topical again when Prime Minister Asquith asked Secretary of State for War Richard Haldane, a former influential member of the Pollock Committee, for his position on the organisation of relations between Britain and its Dominions. Haldane utilised the Pollock Committee's original arguments, and as such the core of his plan was based on the importance and status of the Privy Council. He proposed appointing an Advisory Committee of the Privy Council, to be headed by the Prime Minister, in which the Secretaries of State for the Colonies, India and Foreign Affairs would sit alongside the prime ministers of the Dominion governments, and which would have a Permanent Secretary who would represent the main channel of communication between ministries. The Committee's status was to be independent to a similar degree to the Committee of Imperial Defence.[162]

The proposal to establish an Advisory Committee came at a time when the Colonial Office was dismayed by a request from the Union of South Africa that the Secretariat looking after preparations for the Imperial Conference and Dominion agenda be transferred to the responsibility of the British Prime Minister.[163] For these reasons, Secretariat head Hartmann Just produced a long memorandum in which he went through at length the possible impacts of the proposal by New Zealand, Australia and Haldane, and outlined three options for proceeding. The first option, based on Sir Charles Lucas's previous proposal, suggested that the Prime Minister become spokesman for the Dominions in the House of Commons, but this came up against the fact that his other roles meant he was too busy. The second suggestion was based on setting up some kind of committee which would look after Imperial Conferences, comprised of High Commissioners. The third proposal to a large extent matched Haldane's plan and considered setting up a committee within the Privy Council.[164]

Just's memorandum did not really convince the British Prime Minister, although he was not one to ignore any eventuality in the issue of Imperial reorganisation. As such, in March 1911 the Prime Minister asked the Parliamentary Under-Secretary of State for the Colonies, Colonel John

(Jack) Seely, future Baron Mottistone, to prepare another project looking at splitting up the Colonial Office. Seely submitted a memorandum in which he came to the conclusion that due to the Dominions' positions, it was essential to turn the Dominion Department into its own ministry and precisely define its territorial scope so it did not administer non-self-governing territories. Since in regard to the Secretariat, he primarily emphasised administrative stability and continuity, he did not recommend making any changes which might cause destabilisation.[165] As such, Seely was clearly against setting up an independent office and against leaving the Colonial Office to operate in an unchanged form. Asquith did not agree with his conclusions, however, and preferred Harcourt's cautious vision.

Alongside discussions on the reorganisation of the Colonial Office, in contrast to the original assumption of Dominion Department workers, the issue of expanding the role of High Commissioners was reopened. The original New Zealand plan was supported by the South African Prime Minister, General Louis Botha, who vacillated between extreme Imperialist and national positions in relations to the mother country, and who saw the establishment of an Imperial Council as an opportunity for the Union of South Africa to become more actively involved in Imperial matters.[166] At the time, however, the Colonial Office was highly sensitive to debate arguing over the existing form of the Empire, the role of High Commissioners and methods of communication between Dominions and the mother country, and as such it endeavoured to dampen the enthusiasm particularly shown by New Zealand and the Union of South Africa for direct communication with Britain's Foreign Office without the mediation of local Governors, or Governors-General.

In early April 1911, South Africa's High Commissioner in London, Sir Richard Solomon, submitted a compromise plan which aimed to help improve the system of Conferences, proposing the establishment of an Imperial Conference Council, which would comprise Britain's Colonial Secretary and his Under-Secretary, secretaries for state who came into contact with the Dominions, and High Commissioners or other representatives nominated by Dominion governments. The Council was to be nominally headed by the British Prime Minister and was to be based on the principle of equality of members. Although Solomon took many of his arguments from the previous Pollock Committee proposals and members of the Round Table Movement, the significance of his plan was in the fact that Harcourt used it in setting up his own proposal in regard to setting up the Standing Committee of Imperial Conference, which in June 1911 was submitted for discussion by delegates at the Imperial Conference.[167]

In the second half of April 1911, Harcourt began working in conjunction with Asquith on a proposal which would take account of previous memoranda, and suggested creating two Permanent Under-Secretary posts, one of which would take care of Dominions and the other Crown Colonies, and an Imperial Conference Standing Committee comprising

High Commissioners or other representatives nominated by Dominion cabinets.[168] Asquith and Harcourt sought to ensure there was no reorganisation of the Colonial Office, and as such they suggested this division, which complied with the British perspective. Although Harcourt personally preferred the establishment of a separate committee with an advisory rather than executive role to the parallel establishment of two Permanent Under-Secretaries, he made preparations for all possible eventualities which might result from discussions with overseas prime ministers. Mutual consultation between Dominion governments and the London cabinet was to continue to take place via the Governors-General of Canada, the Union of South Africa and the Commonwealth of Australia and the Governors of New Zealand and Newfoundland; however, the High Commissioner, whose status Harcourt did not precisely define, could provide information to their government freely.[169] Harcourt's proposal represented more of the *status quo* favoured by conservative figures in the Colonial Office, rather than a compromise between radical and moderate proponents of Imperial reorganisation.

In 1911 on the occasion of George V's coronation, delegates met in Westminster for the largest Imperial Conference prior to the First World War.[170] It was the first standard meeting (after four years) of its type. The growing number of Dominions and the level of their importance meant that the Conference represented an essential institution based on a system of consultation and co-operation with the mother country. Although at first sight it might seem that each of the Dominions had the same relationship with Great Britain, this was not actually the case. The individual needs, problems and, above all, nationalist and constitutional demands, alongside historical developments and geographic, economic, political and social conditions, had created unique relations between individual Dominions and London.[171]

During long discussions on current problems, the term "family of nations" was once again heard a number of times in the speeches of delegates, who believed that the phrase characterised – or rather, should characterise – the relations between the Dominions and Great Britain. Australian Prime Minister Andrew Fisher, for example, noted mutual historical interests and was quick to describe the Empire as, "a family of nations working in unity and amity under one Crown".[172] Canadian Prime Minister Wilfrid Laurier followed up these words with the realistic declaration that, "the British Empire is a family of nations ... [that] the greater burden it has carried on the shoulders of the Government of the United Kingdom".[173] The question remained, however, as to whether a "family of nations" could really exist when all its members did not have the same status and when the original "larger Colonies of the British Empire had become practically nations".[174]

Most Dominion statesmen did not come to the Conference with fundamental (Imperial) issues for discussion which went beyond regional significance.[175] The most significant part of the agenda was the plan by New Zealand Prime Minister Sir Joseph Ward, who proposed setting up an "Imperial Federal Parliament". Ward had identified with the proposals and vision[176] of influential Round Table Movement members[177] for many years, and he had therefore decided to exploit the strong domestic position he had acquired through a decisive election victory in 1908 to promote his ideas on the form of the Empire.[178] Other major points in the Conference included Harcourt's proposal for setting up an Imperial Conference Standing Committee, the reorganisation of Britain's Colonial Office, the so-called Declaration of London which looked at the level of consultation in Imperial foreign policy, the issue of immigrants from India in the Dominions, and other economic, trade and social issues.[179]

On 23 May 1911, British Prime Minister Asquith opened the Imperial Conference with a speech in which he called for a natural Imperial flexibility. He also stressed that even though Great Britain and the Dominions were part of a larger whole, each of them remained "masters of their own domain".[180] The evening of that day, a gala banquet was held in the Savoy Hotel, organised by the Pilgrims Club, in which Field Marshal Frederick Sleigh Roberts, 1st Earl Roberts, welcomed the representatives of "sister nations" present. Like Asquith, he called for unanimity of opinion, under the motto "united we stand, divided we fall", and surprisingly highlighted New Zealand's successful economic development and the courage, constructive approach and ardent Imperial patriotism of its Prime Minister, Sir Joseph Ward.[181]

Debate took place over the subsequent two days on Ward's proposal. The New Zealand Prime Minister argued:

> That the Empire has now reached a stage of Imperial development which renders it expedient that there should be an Imperial Council of State, with Representatives from all the self-governing parts of the Empire, in theory and in fact advisory to the Imperial Government on all questions affecting the interests of His Majesty's Dominions overseas.[182]

Ward perceived setting up an Imperial Council which would replace the system of Imperial Conferences and which would expand the power of the Dominions as affirmation of their true partnership in Imperial relations.[183] He also noted that former British Colonial Secretary of State for the Colonies Joseph Chamberlain had advocated a similar scheme. He also underscored the benefits it would bring: (1) strengthened Imperial unity; (2) better Imperial defence organisation; (3) equal division of costs and responsibilities in the defence of the Empire and (4) representation of Dominions in the Imperial Parliament of Defence with two chambers, so that at times of peace and war, Dominions could assist in matters of defending the Empire, foreign policy, etc.[184]

According to Ward's proposal, elections to the lower chamber of this parliament – the Imperial House of Representatives for Defence – were to take place once every five years with each elected official representing 200,000 citizens within the Dominions or mother country.[185] Subsequently, Great Britain, Newfoundland, New Zealand, the Commonwealth of Australia, Canada and the Union of South Africa were each to send two representatives to the Imperial Council of Defence, which would form the upper chamber carrying out an advisory and scrutiny role. The executive body was to comprise a maximum of fifteen members. This Imperial parliament was to be in charge of all matters affecting the Empire, in times of both peace and war.[186]

Ward's plan was significantly different from Curtis's original Green Memorandum of 1910, and at first sight it did not appear particularly comprehensive. Over two days of discussion, the New Zealand Prime Minister often mixed up or renamed the proposed institutions, which did not arouse much confidence in his project amongst those present, even if he did table it with good intent. Canadian Prime Minister Laurier and his Australian opposite number Fisher described it as impractical, while the Prime Minister of Newfoundland, Sir Edward Patrick Morris, later 1st Baron Morris, instead feared a loss in the function of the Imperial (British) government. Ward's proposal was naturally enough not appreciated by Britain's Prime Minister Asquith, who saw it as undermining the London government's authority, as an attempt at staking out the mother country's power and a highly damaging intervention in the existing system of government responsibility.[187] Some critics of Ward's proposal accused it of being overly nationalistic in nature.[188] Most critical was South African Prime Minister Botha, who said of the plan that he had, "never heard a more idiotic proposal".[189] Botha and Laurier were advocates of decentralisation and were thus of the opinion that "matters of Imperial unity are best served when each nation is able to run its own affairs alone," and that the system of Conferences would continue on a round-table basis.[190]

On 25 May 1911, Conference participants rejected Ward's plan for establishing an Imperial Council and focused their attention on another New Zealand proposal involving reorganising the British Colonial Office, which Round Table Movement members had again been involved in setting up. The New Zealand government proposed: (1) splitting the Colonial Office into one department for the Dominions and one for the Crown Colonies, with a Permanent Under-Secretary at the head of each; (2) renaming the Colonial Office the Imperial Office, (3) transferring officials of the Permanent Secretariat for Imperial Conferences to the Dominion Department; (4) securing communication between Dominion cabinets and London through High Commissioners who would take part in meetings where defence, foreign, trade and social matters affecting the Dominions were discussed; and (5) High Commissioners should be recognised as a parallel communication channel in addition to Governors and Governors-General. The South African cabinet subsequently added to the proposal with the suggestion that the Secretariat for Imperial Conferences be directly subordinate to Britain's Prime Minister.[191]

Secretary of State for the Colonies Harcourt responded to the points raised by outlining a counterproposal which was for the much part based on propositions he had agreed upon with Asquith before the start of the Conference. He thought transforming the Colonial Office into an Imperial Office was an inappropriate step, because India had its own ministry which might lead to disputes over competencies. He also noted that establishing direct communication between High Commissioners and the Dominion governments would contravene perceived ministerial responsibility. On the issue of splitting up the Colonial Office, he argued that it would be more practical to have one Permanent Under-Secretary of State with two Assistant Under-Secretaries, one of whom would take care of the Dominion agenda, and the other Crown Colonies issues. He did not think any kind of split of his ministry was positive, as it would be disadvantageous both for the Office itself and for the Dominions. In regard to transferring the Secretariat to the Dominion Department, he proposed establishing an Imperial Conference Standing Committee comprising the Colonial Secretary, Parliamentary Under-Secretary, Permanent Under-Secretary of State, High Commissioners and other representatives named by Dominions with a purely advisory role.[192]

Almost all the Dominion prime ministers, except for Laurier who opposed any kind of change, were not in favour of some kind of radical administrative division of the Colonial Office, and thus Ward failed again. Subsequent debate focused on the proposed role of High Commissioners. It was clear from the start that the British government did not want High Commissioners to act almost like British Ambassadors in the Dominions. At the same time, some Dominion politicians did not trust their competence. South Africa's Education Minister, François Stephanus Malan, for example, stated that the High Commissioners were "not selected as political agents in the first instance, but very largely as business men" and were thus insufficiently qualified to represent the Dominions at meetings with the Secretary of State for the Colonies or at Imperial Conferences.[193] Australian Prime Minister Fisher did not share either Malan's opinion or Harcourt's position. He thought the presence of High Commissioners in London to represent Dominion cabinets would be a beneficial channel of communication; due to the distance from the mother country and speed of mutual communication, he thought the Australian continent had previously been at a disadvantage; as such he complained that, "Canada is more fortunate than Australia in regard to distance".[194] Fisher also commented ironically about Laurier that Canada should take a more active position in regard to High Commissioners. Since most Dominions did not want major changes in the Imperial structure, and the Conference was still to discuss a plan for establishing an Imperial Conference Standing Committee in the coming days, Asquith ended discussions.[195]

On 8 June 1911, politicians restarted discussions on constitutional matters, specifically on the possible creation of an Imperial Conference Standing Committee. Although Colonial Office representatives did not want change because they held the opinion that the current system of consultation and levels of co-operation sufficed, Harcourt's proposal was meant to be a "government" alternative to Ward's plans. The Secretary of State for the Colonies proposed establishing a Standing Committee as an effective institutional addition to the Imperial Conference system with a purely advisory, and not executive, role. The benefits were meant to be that in contrast to the Conference, its members would be able to meet more frequently and look at more diverse issues. The Standing Committee was to comprise the Secretary of State for the Colonies, the relevant Parliamentary Under-Secretary, the Colonial Office Permanent Under-Secretary of State, the deputy Permanent Under-Secretary of State for the Dominions, the Secretary of the Imperial Conference Secretariat, and High Commissioners or other representatives named by the Dominion governments. The Committee would focus only on the agenda of previous Conferences, or make preparations for future meetings. It would consult with Dominion governments on all matters through Governors-General, Governors, High Commissioners or other Dominion representatives.[196] Laurier, Botha and Morris were against adopting the proposal, not wishing any administrative changes to the existing system. Fisher assessed the submitted proposal positively, while only Ward was in clear agreement with it. Due to the negative position of the majority, this point was withdrawn from further discussions.[197] Harcourt's lukewarm support for a Standing Committee was later criticised by the former Secretary of State for the Colonies, Alfred Lyttelton.[198]

The rejection of Ward's and Harcourt's proposals was an affirmation of the *status quo*, and a disappointment for Round Table Movement members, with both projects partially based on the ideas or original vision of this movement. The public failure of the idea of a closer Imperial union significantly hindered the private activities of Movement members striving to gain support from influential figures within the Empire. Over the coming years, none of the goals the Round Table Movement had set for itself when it was founded were achieved. The outbreak of war in 1914 definitively quashed all federalist plans. As in 1907, so four years later no transformation of the Imperial Conferences into an effective tool for dealing with the Empire's problems was achieved, because the Colonial Office did not want to lose any of its status, and because Dominion prime ministers did not accept the changes to the Imperial structure proposed fearing they might lose some of their recently acquired privileges from acquiring Dominion status. The inability to find a satisfactory solution to certain problems in defence and foreign policy was disadvantageous to the system of Conferences as a central Imperial forum on the eve of the First World War, while the Committee of Imperial Defence continued to evolve and operate effectively.[199]

2.3 The Committee of Imperial Defence and the Dominions, 1904–1911

Prior to the First World War, Great Britain had to confront major internal political problems and complications in the foreign policy field. In terms of the status, or position, of the island nation within the world, many Britons were fearful of the growing strength of the German navy in particular. The Dominions were not indifferent to this threat to the mother country and were willing to provide help in the event of any conflict. A costly naval programme was one of the reasons why Liberal Chancellor David Lloyd George submitted a state budget proposal in 1909,[200] which, however, the House of Lords, controlled by the Conservatives, later vetoed. This was followed by a general election and the attempt of the government and government ministers to break down the House of Lords' resistance, eventually culminating in the adoption of the so-called Act of Parliament (1911) which significantly restricted the House of Lords' powers. When participants in the Imperial Conference sat down for discussions in summer 1911, they found themselves in the midst of a whirlwind of significant events. On the one hand, the coronation of Kind George V was taking place, and on the other hand, the problem of Irish Home Rule had been reopened for the simple reason that Asquith's government depended on the votes of the Irish nationalists, headed by John Redmond, for whom Home Rule was of great importance.[201]

At the turn of the 20th century, the British government began to focus more intensively on matters of defence. The Defence Committee of the Cabinet had been in existence since 1895, but its members had played the role of passive observers of events more than active drivers. In December 1902 when the main battles in the south of Africa had subsided, British Prime Minister Sir Arthur James Balfour decided to reorganise this advisory body, newly renamed the Committee of Imperial Defence. Secretary of the State for War William St. John Brodrick, later 1st Earl of Midleton, and First Lord of the Admiralty, the Earl of Selborne, submitted an expansive memorandum on the form and role of the new Committee.[202] In 1902–1904, the new Committee found itself in a kind of transition period; it comprised permanent members – the Prime Minister, Secretary of the State for War and First Lord of the Admiralty – and other figures invited from outside the cabinet. Its principle objective was to deal comprehensively with the Empire's strategic military needs.[203] The new Committee structure allowed the Prime Minister flexibility in convening meetings, and he was able if needed to invite other experts or representatives of Self-Governing Colonies or Dominions to take part.[204]

The War Office (Reconstitution) Committee began operating in 1903, headed by Reginald Baliol Brett, 2nd Viscount Esher, with the job of modernising the institution. At the start of 1904, it submitted a report to the Prime Minister which supported organisational changes in the Committee of Imperial Defence.[205] Viscount Esher put a lot of work into the reconstitution committee, and as such he is perceived as the "godfather" of the innovated Committee of Imperial Defence.[206] In March of the same year, the Committee was more firmly embedded within the Imperial defence structure on the basis of Balfour's initiative.[207] Once it had received the promised funding in May 1904, it was established officially in its new form.[208]

Balfour had established the Committee to serve prime ministers as a consultative and advisory body at any time when the need to consider problems of Imperial defence within a wider context arose. As such, it did not have executive power, it was not meant to determine government policy and it was not meant to issue orders to the armed forces. It comprised one permanent member – the Prime Minister – and other persons invited by the Prime Minister, generally the relevant ministers, experts, and representatives of the army, navy, the Self-Governing Colonies and the Dominions. It also had its own permanent secretariat to take care of essential administration. From its beginning, its flexible structure and lack of other restrictive rules turned the Committee into a powerful body effectively dealing with Imperial defence matters.[209] Balfour was not a proponent of the ill-conceived increasing of Committee member numbers because he thought this would adversely reduce its effectiveness, which would be reflected in the "fragmentation" of its agenda amongst subcommittees.[210] The newly established Committee of Imperial Defence had aroused a certain level of mistrust amongst British members of parliament from its beginning. As such, in August 1904 Balfour had to again reassure them that the Committee would not interfere in any way in the authority of the armed services or the cabinet, and that it would not set up any "branches" in the Self-Governing Colonies and Dominions.[211]

Establishment of the Committee did not have an immediate impact on the Self-Governing Colonies or Dominions; in practice overseas matters were often discussed without their involvement.[212] Nevertheless, the self-governing overseas territories' relationship to the Committee became one of the key factors impacting its operation within the Imperial structure in subsequent years. To begin with, representatives of the Self-Governing Colonies and Dominions took part in Committee meetings in order to receive counsel on matters affecting their countries on the basis of information from their British colleagues. Nevertheless, they remained subject only to domestic governments.[213] Over time it was shown that mutual relations had to be more precisely defined. As early as during the 1907

Colonial Conference, the Australian delegation submitted a resolution allowing permanent, and not just *ad hoc*, representation within the Committee of Imperial Defence. Dominion representatives were always to take part when matters were discussed which affected them.[214] Asquith's position on the permanent presence of Dominion representatives at Committee of Imperial Defence meetings was the same as Balfour's previous recommendations. As such, until the Imperial Conference on Defence in 1909, the self-governing territories were unable to express their views on all matters, nor could they name a representative to take part in discussions.[215]

The increasing interest of the Self-Governing Colonies and Dominions in Imperial defence also led to debate on how to effectively secure the co-ordination of overseas land and naval forces in times of peace, how to train the forces and how to unify military equipment. Until 1904 when the Committee of Imperial Defence was established, individual armies were rather chaotic in their development.[216] The situation stabilised somewhat in subsequent years, with a solution definitively found in 1909 when the Imperial General Staff was set up on the basis of principles adopted at the 1907 Colonial Conference. This body brought order into defence efforts, even though its role was purely advisory.[217] A Dominions section was set up within the General Staff, whose members were in charge of co-ordinating Dominions' military efforts, and this resulted in a strategic document for the event of war – the War Book.[218]

A resolution of the 1907 Colonial Conference allowed for sub-meetings of Dominion statesmen and British representatives to convene in the event of urgent matters which required immediate attention. Thus, the British Prime Minister decided to call an Imperial Defence Conference for July and August 1909,[219] in response to growing fears of Germany's increasing arming of its navy[220] and in order to discuss joint defence and the recent proposals of the Australian and Canadian governments[221] and New Zealand's offer to help fund naval construction.[222]

When the Self-Governing Colonies had been created in the past, the idea of securing their own defence developed naturally within them. An 1862 House of Commons resolution confirmed that the self-governing territories should be mainly responsible for defending their own land territory and that only in the event of need would London help with an expeditionary force.[223] By the 1870s, most of the British land forces had withdrawn from these territories.[224] The mother country appreciated the help of the Self-Governing Colonies and Dominions at moments of threat, and as such supported the construction of local armed forces.[225] The fact that the Australian Self-Governing Colonies promised to contribute to maintaining the British fleet in its waters at the 1897 Colonial Conference can be considered a partial success.[226] Issues linked to the defence of distant Self-Governing Colonies in the Pacific, or the maintenance of coaling stations, had been actively dealt with since the 1880s;[227] however, the German arms policy gave it a new dimension.[228]

In June 1902, the British Admiralty expressed its fears of losing its superiority in the event of large naval battles, as it believed that it was losing the ability to undertake offensive action when the circumstances required it.[229] Leading Admiralty officers were of the opinion that the German fleet had been built up in order to confront Britain on the seas.[230] As such, the 1902 Colonial Conference confirmed a financial contribution towards maintaining the fleet in Australian waters[231] and establishing Laurier's proposed Canadian navy.[232] Although the British Admiralty, supported by New Zealand, had tried in practice to promote a single Imperial fleet as presented in the motto, "there is one sea, there is one Empire, and there is one Navy", Australia and Canada in particular were insistent in promoting the idea of building up territorial fleets.[233]

British representatives had long wished not to abandon the idea of one large Imperial army and navy. When in 1907 Canada's Minister of Militia and Defence, Sir Frederick William Borden, accommodatingly spoke of his country's readiness to get involved in wars in the interests of the Empire alongside Great Britain, British Prime Minister Asquith declared of the proposal: "That should the Dominions desire to assist in the defence of the Empire in a real emergency, their forces could be rapidly combined into one homogenous Imperial Army."[234] In January 1910, Canadian Prime Minister Laurier underscored his country's resolve by stating: "When Great Britain is at war, Canada is at War."[235] Laurier nevertheless differentiated between Canada's level of involvement in general war and in a "struggle-for-life-and-death", in which Canada would be eager to assist the mother country.[236]

The 1909 Imperial Conference on Defence was an important meeting, because its participants from Britain, the Self-Governing Colonies and Dominions agreed on joint action for the first time – the systematic build-up of defence. The strategy, based on the principle of equality and free collaboration, likely represented, besides cohesion during war years, the most effective project within the British Empire.[237] The memorandum submitted by the First Lord of the Admiralty, Reginald McKenna, affirmed the principle that the armed forces would not be built up on the principle of one Imperial army or navy under the control of the mother country,[238] but rather that the national character of the armed forces remain preserved, to be built up in co-ordination on the basis of a joint plan, and which in periods of war would co-operate closely in defending the Empire.[239]

Canada had long been of the opinion that the Empire's military weakness meant Canada was more vulnerable.[240] Implementing a more extensive build-up of the Canadian navy did not pass without domestic political debate. The Conservatives, headed by Robert Laird Borden, criticised Laurier's decision because of the anticipated significant costs, doubts over whether the fleet's parameters were wisely chosen, and a rejection of an Imperial navy.[241] It was subsequently expected of the Royal Canadian Navy that it would ease the Royal Navy's work in the Pacific so that it could fully focus on the threat from the German navy.[242]

The establishment of national naval forces in particular underscored the key importance of the Dominions in Imperial foreign and defence policy, and contributed to the process of their transformation from colonies with responsible governments to Dominions.[243] The principles of co-operation between British and Dominion armed forces were definitively laid down in a 1911 memorandum.[244] Despite the fact that the 1909 Conference had confirmed the growing influence of the Dominions, Asquith was not going to further concede in the issue of a shared Imperial foreign policy.[245] British politicians did not consider the Dominions to be mature or experienced enough, and thought they were too distant from Europe to be able to have a responsible say in complicated international relations; furthermore, just one authority was meant to promote Imperial foreign policy.[246] No Dominion statesmen wished to bear this responsibility. Canadian Prime Minister Laurier, for example, who held the reputation of being a "war hawk" domestically,[247] did not protest against the British government's desire to wield the reigns in Imperial foreign policy, because as the first francophone Canadian Prime Minister, he was satisfied with full autonomy in domestic matters and the right to make independent decisions.[248]

During the 1909 Imperial Conference on Defence, there was some dispute over competencies. Although then head of the Committee of Imperial Defence Secretariat, Rear-Admiral Sir Charles Langdale Ottley, and his deputy, Sir Maurice Pascal Alers Hankey, later 1st Baron Hankey, expressed the opinion in private discussion that the Conference on Defence should be run by the Committee, due to anticipated opposition from the Colonial Office, the proposal was not officially submitted. Both made it clear that the Committee of Imperial Defence should take on the co-ordination and management of Imperial forces and dealing with crucial Imperial defence issues from the Imperial Conference. They argued that, in contrast to the Conference, the Committee was in more frequent direct contact with the Dominions and the mother country.[249] Compared to the period prior to the previous Colonial Conference, the Committee's activities had intensified, and, as such since 1908, the Committee had been meeting regularly every other month, while standard Conferences were held once every four years.[250] The Secretariat's influence had also risen proportionally, its members no longer wishing to "only" prepare the agenda. They wanted to supervise various planning subcommittees and work more intensively with government officials as an executive administrative body. Since 1908, the number of Secretariat workers had increased to such an extent that Esher's vision of "a small Permanent Secretariat" was irretrievably in the past.[251] The number of members of the Committee itself had also risen in parallel,[252] which was in contrast to Balfour's original concept, and which was also reflected in the establishment of permanent and *ad hoc* subcommittees.[253]

In mid-November 1909, Hankey submitted a memorandum to Prime Minister Asquith entitled the "War Organisation of the British Empire", in which he explained at great length his position in regard to Imperial defence policy and the importance of the Committee of Imperial Defence.[254] Influential Round Table Movement member Lionel Curtis had also noted the Committee's growing influence, and had prepared a resolution alongside New Zealand Prime Minister Sir Joseph Ward for the planned 1911 Imperial Conference which would allow Dominion High Commissioners to take part in Committee meetings.[255] The New Zealand proposal induced Hankey and Ottley to prepare a new memorandum in which the Committee members explained their own perspective on the issue. They stated that the New Zealand demand for establishment of an Imperial Council was redundant because its proposed role was already generally filled by the Committee which with minor modifications could operate as a discussion forum in which Imperial countries could discuss mutual defence. On the issue of High Commissioners' participation in Committee meetings, they held the opinion that permanent Dominion representation would only partially contribute to effective co-ordination, and as such proposed that the Dominions set up their own defence committees which would then closely co-operate with the Committee.[256]

On 23 May 1911, British Prime Minister Asquith suggested on the basis of the 1909 precedent that issues of defence and foreign policy should be discussed not within the Imperial Conference but rather at a joint meeting of Dominion prime ministers and members of the Committee of Imperial Defence.[257] Although many explanations emerged as to why the British government had taken this step,[258] the most likely would seem to be that it wished to discuss sensitive defence and foreign policy matters in secret, something the form of Conference meetings did not permit.[259] During three joint meetings (26–30 May), a surprising level of mistrust was expressed by the British Foreign Office towards the Dominions.[260]

Then the Secretary of State for Foreign Affairs Sir Edward Grey, later 1st Viscount Grey of Fallodon, disagreeing with some Dominion positions, even decided to slight the overseas statesmen by declaring:

> It is possible to have separate Fleets in a united Empire, but it is not possible to have separate Fleets in a united Empire without having a common Foreign Policy which shall determine the action of the different Forces maintained in different parts of the Empire.[261]

Grey's comment was of deeper significance, because it presented a strong argument for maintaining the Anglo-Japanese Alliance. This 1902 alliance had significantly impacted the traditional interests of

Australia, Canada and New Zealand in the Pacific. When Japan became a great power, as affirmed by its military victory over Russia in 1905, the Dominions' objections grew in strength. The Dominions argued that signing the Alliance implied the Empire's economic, political and naval weakness. In 1911, Australia in particular vehemently opposed its renewal, making particular reference to the undesirable mass migration of Japanese people to the Australian continent and adjacent islands, and the haughty method by which Japan was expanding its influence in the Pacific, weakening the British, and Australian, position.[262] On the other hand, the alliance with Japan provided the Pacific Dominions with a certain level of security because ending the alliance would lead to a deterioration in the British Empire's strategic position in the Far East.[263]

At the first two joint meetings of London representatives, Dominion prime ministers and members of the Committee of Imperial Defence, issues of British Imperial foreign policy, the navy and ground forces were discussed. Britain's Secretary of State for Foreign Affairs, Edward Grey, brilliantly summarised the key aspects of European policy[264] and looked in great detail at the Anglo-Japanese Alliance, whose renewal he was advocating.[265] He also expressed the desire that he would welcome more intensive consultation between the mother country and the Dominions and the sharing of information in foreign and defence policy before any definitive decision was made. His call did not automatically represent an offer to take part in implementing Imperial foreign policy.[266] Participants of the joint meeting subsequently agreed to negotiations with the Japanese government beginning on extending the Alliance for a further ten years.[267] This was the first ever officially recorded joint decision which had also been jointly discussed on an important foreign policy issue.[268]

The First Lord of the Admiralty, Reginald McKenna, subsequently informed those present of the maritime strategy for civil and military ships in the event of war, alongside his request that Dominion navies be put under one command; a lack of organisation would, he believed, lead to chaos. The Dominions complied only partially with McKenna's request. They agreed that their fleets would be subject to the Admiralty's authority in international waters and that in times of war they would be available to the Empire.[269] They were responding in particular to Asquith's argument that if British were in war, then the whole Empire would be in war, i.e. all its possessions, and trading interests would suddenly be put in danger.[270] The Secretary of State for War Richard Haldane subsequently summarised the British ground forces' readiness in comparison to the German army.[271]

The 30 May 1911 discussions were likely the most important, because they included debate not just on British concessions towards the Dominions in the issue of Imperial maritime policy,[272] but in particular on the role and importance of the Committee of Imperial Defence in regard to the Dominions. Hankey and Ottley promised from the discussions that there would be a change in status of the Committee in its favour and away from the Imperial Conference, although this actually did not happen. During discussions, Asquith decided that he would invite Dominion representatives to the Committee, stressing in so doing that it would continue to have a purely advisory role. In regard to High Commissioners' involvement in Committee meetings, those present agreed that High Commissioners would only partially improve co-ordination, and as such they agreed to the original proposal of Hankey and Ottley that each Dominion, if it wanted, could establish its own defence committee which would co-operate with the Committee.[273] Although the Committee had become the highest advisory body in naval, military and foreign affairs for all Imperial cabinets and parliaments, it still lacked sufficient anchorage within the Imperial structure.[274]

After the joint meeting with the Committee of Imperial Defence had concluded, on 1 June 1911, discussion began on Australia's subproposal on a so-called London Declaration as submitted by the Australian government which was in regard to consultative procedures during negotiations on treaties between the mother country and other states. Discussion of this point was marked by the failure of Ward's proposal and the previous joint meeting with the Committee of Imperial Defence. Fisher began by complaining that it was a shame the Dominions had not been consulted by British delegates before the term "London Declaration" was accepted, which he did not consider particularly suitable due to the already-in-force London Declaration which had arisen from the second Hague Conference of 1909.[275] He noted that in concluding international conventions, the affected Dominions should be consulted.[276] Conference participants subsequently approved the resolution on the London Declaration as prepared by the Australian government.[277]

2.4 The Committee of Imperial Defence, or the Imperial Conference?

In the period prior to the First World War, three core topics relating to defence matters influenced relations between the Dominions and the mother country. First of all was the search for a response to the question of whether the Dominions should first secure their own defence in the event of war, and only then help Britain, or whether they should first assist the mother country and thus prevent its defeat, which could lead to the Dominions remaining isolated. The second problem was around organising Imperial defence, in which Dominion nationalism and the isolationism of the non-English-speaking citizens in Canada and South Africa on the one hand clashed with the demands of the Admiralty and Committee of Imperial Defence on the other. The third complication was found in the disparity between British defence commitments and Great Britain's own resources.[278]

Over the final decades of the 19th century, some overseas territories linked to Britain achieved marked political, economic and social development. At the same time as their importance rose, so their desire for greater autonomy also rose, which they saw as ideally expressed through constitutional changes in relation to the mother country, and a greater level of involvement in decision-making on Imperial foreign policy. This process was a result of the Imperial Conference system's weakness as an institution, because none of its resolutions were binding since the Conference did not have legislative or executive power. At the same time, the complicated international situation and problems linked to common Imperial defence had a negative impact on the system.[279] Furthermore, the previous three Colonial and Imperial Conferences had brought only disappointment for their "reformers" – Seddon (1902), Deakin (1907) and Ward (1911).[280] Despite all these shortcomings, the system of Imperial Conferences had still managed to contribute to the Empire's institutional and constitutional development and had significantly helped in the Empire's transformation into the British Commonwealth.[281]

In the final years of peace, the international situation underwent rapid changes, with one crisis following on from another, and the institutional "machinery" of the British Empire found that it was unable to adequately respond, with Prime Minister Asquith's rigid position further preventing a response from being found. The frequent criticism of Imperial Conference opponents that the system found itself in the unfortunate position of sitting idle in periods between conferences grew in intensity following the 1911 Conference.[282] Due to the fact that those at the Conference had been unable to find agreement in implementing necessary reforms, a number of foreign and defence policy problems remained unsolved.[283] The idea that the Conference's backlog should be transferred to the Committee of Imperial Defence to find an adequate solution became a generally acknowledged one. Some government officials furthermore openly prioritised the Committee over the Conference. The Committee represented a more flexible body because it was able to meet up more frequently than the Conference, while the British Prime Minister also had a direct influence on it, which could result in undue pressure on its members' "impartial" decisions.[284]

In 1911–1914, Imperial defence fell within the competence of two bodies: The Imperial General Staff and the Committee of Imperial Defence. Both held advisory roles, and representatives of the Dominions were able to take part in meetings of both, although the Committee did not have a firm membership structure.[285] Discussions in the Committee on foreign policy in 1911 had a large impact on Dominions' autonomy. Nevertheless, co-operation in foreign policy issues was not as effective as in the case of matters of defence.[286]

In 1911, the Round Table Movement saw its plans fail, unable to push through Ward's proposals. Nevertheless, its members did not become embittered, and they did not cease overnight in focusing on Imperial reorganisation. They intensified their efforts in promoting a strengthened common defence and foreign policy, because they felt threatened by the growing power of Wilhelmine Germany.[287] Not only had Lionel Curtis, Leopold Amery and other Round Table Movement members been long aware of the Committee's importance, but so had Dominion politicians, and as such they sought its evolution into a full-fledged Imperial institution.[288] As in 1907, Canada's position seemed key. As such, Lionel Curtis focused his attention on Canada's new Conservative Prime Minister, Sir Robert Laird Borden, who had held the office since October 1911.[289] Sir Robert had become Prime Minister with the vision as head of the executive that he should: (1) speak sincerely and truthfully; (2) remain dignified, honourable and decisive; (3) maintain a clear and smart mind, with sympathy for the peace-loving Britons and friendship with the Americans, and (4) above all, not to forget that he was Canadian.[290] In contrast to Laurier, Borden did not promote isolationist positions, and in regard to the mother country he based his positions on three principal interconnected factors: (1) Canadian autonomy; (2) a greater level of responsibility and (3) greater involvement in decision-making on Imperial foreign policy.[291]

In December 1911, Curtis sent Borden a copy of his Green Memorandum, requesting he read it with haste; he believed that the Empire's future wellbeing depended on Canada's steps. In March 1912, he even called on Borden to prioritise the Committee over the system of Imperial Conferences as a continual communication channel between the overseas governments and the British cabinet.[292] Curtis was also supported by the new First Lord of the Admiralty, Winston Churchill, who raised an appeal in the House of Commons on 20 March 1912 that the Committee for Imperial Defence should be granted a more important status in terms of relations between the Dominions and the mother country before the status of the self-governing territories within the Empire could be settled once and for all.[293] Curtis planned to exploit Borden's visit to London where he was to discuss maritime and defence affairs with his British opposite number, the Admiralty and Foreign Office;[294] during a number of meetings with members of the Round Table Movement, he was to convince him to place preference on the Committee over the Imperial Conference.[295] Borden travelled to England knowing he held an ace in his hands – Canada's contribution to Imperial naval defence.[296]

Although the Round Table Movement was considerably active in 1912, not all its members approved this approach. The Movement's Toronto branch, for example, did not share Curtis's enthusiasm, because they thought it was fruitless to call for something that would solve itself in the near future.[297] Leopold Amery instead held the opinion that instead of the Movement seeking an expanded authority and role for the Committee, it should instead focus on concluding discussions on reorganising the

British Colonial Office at the next Imperial Conference, planned for 1915. Specifically, Amery advocated transferring the Dominion agenda from the current department to a newly created British Office for Imperial Affairs; the Colonial Office would then administer only the affairs of the Crown Colonies. Local Ministries for Imperial Affairs would be set up within the Dominions which would communicate with the Committee and the Foreign Office in matters of defence and foreign policy.[298] Amery also accepted that the Committee was an effective and practical institution.[299] His ideas had been long based on the idea that the fundamental prerequisite for strong Imperial union was adopting a principle of equality in relations between the Dominions and the mother country.[300]

In summer 1912 during his trip to England, with the support of the Round Table Movement, Borden met a number of times with influential figures, who in time acquired the status of an unofficial group of experts on Imperial issues, but they were unable to make him take the bolder moves as Curtis had hoped.[301] Rather, the Committee of Imperial Defence's new Secretary, Maurice Hankey, was able to influence Borden, the British government and the Prime Minister himself. Hankey had consistently advocated the idea of Imperial defensive co-operation through the Committee.[302] Hankey's Imperial vision was based on creating a "quasi-federal organisation with common economy, common defence and common foreign policies".[303] At the end of July 1912, Asquith suggested a way that Dominions could influence foreign policy. During a debate on the tasks and significance of the Committee of Imperial Defence in the House of Commons, he admitted that Dominions' growing share of the Empire's commitments meant it was Britain's duty to take more account of their opinions; he thought the Committee could become an appropriate "mediator" in the exchange of opinions. Asquith also perceived the Committee as an "invaluable complement to constitutional ties" with the Dominions.[304]

In September 1912, the Round Table Movement launched a public campaign to replace the system of Conferences with the Committee of Imperial Defence, which it considered a forerunner of the Cabinet of the Empire. It did so through the article *Canada and the Navy* in the journal *The Round Table*. The anonymous author underscored the importance of Canada and the Commonwealth of Australia in particular, and called on both countries to become more thoroughly involved in forming Imperial foreign policy.[305] Some were of the opinion that since the Committee already held an important position within the Imperial structure, it could become a temporary, but not permanent, Imperial forum, since as an advisory body it was not sufficiently representative or independent for Dominion representatives, being indirectly influenced by the British Foreign Office.[306] At the end of 1912, Richard Jebb, renowned advocate of the Conference system and colonial nationalism, became involved in the discussions. Jebb firmly rejected the notion that the Committee of Imperial

Defence should replace Conference meetings. He also emphasised that the Imperial Conference was based on a principle of equality, whereas the nature of the Committee lay in British superiority over the self-governing territories. He thought that the fact that, in contrast to the Conference, the Committee was convened on the basis of a decision of the British Prime Minister was a symbol of the London government's dominance.[307]

Subsequent discussion in the autumn of 1912 on the pages of *The Times* eliminated any minor ambiguities in the relationship between the Committee of Imperial Defence and the system of Imperial Conferences. Over the course of November, on the request of Secretary of State for the Colonies Harcourt, and with Asquith's blessing, Hankey worked on a memorandum on the future activities and position of the Committee of Imperial Defence. On 25 November, Hankey submitted it to the British government, proposing that the Committee be expanded with two additional specialised subcommittees which would meet the demands of the Dominions for more frequent and more substantial discussion of defence and foreign policy problems.[308] Before the British government had made a final decision on Hankey's memorandum, Borden made a speech during a debate on Canadian naval policy in Canada's lower parliamentary chamber on 5 December 1912 in which he made scathing comments on how he had received a promise from British representatives during his London meetings that the advisory votes of Dominions would be given a weight in decisions of matters of Imperial foreign policy that they had never had before. Borden also stressed the important fact that in future, the Committee would not make any important decisions without Canada's representative having a say.[309]

The London government used Borden's public statement and sent a telegram to other overseas self-governing governments on 10 December 1912, asking them whether they wanted to participate in the Committee of Imperial Defence's decision-making process like the Canadians. Harcourt proposed that one minister could take part in discussions from each Dominion, having the status of a standard (permanent) Committee member. In contrast to before, this would result in increasing the level of the Dominions' shared responsibility in decision-making on Imperial affairs; the Dominion representatives would no longer find themselves in the role of mere specialist consultants. Britain's Secretary of State for the Colonies further stressed that the Committee would remain a purely advisory body which under no circumstances would become a political decision-maker; this prerogative was solely reserved for the British cabinet. During Committee meetings, Dominion representatives were to have free access to the British Prime Minister and Secretaries of State for the Colonies and Foreign Affairs if they needed more comprehensive information on any issues of Imperial policy.[310]

Harcourt's telegram was positively received by members of the Round Table Movement,[311] but none of the four Dominion governments who received it shared their enthusiasm. The South Africans questioned the practicality of the idea if control of foreign policy was to remain a privilege of the British government. Australian Prime Minister Fisher preferred more frequent meetings within the Imperial Conferences system to permanent membership of the Committee of Imperial Defence.[312] Prime Minister William Massey also expressed a certain "distaste" for permanent representation within the Committee, which he did not favour even purely in terms of New Zealand's great distance from Britain; Newfoundland representatives were of a similar feeling. Hankey and the Round Table Movement were disappointed by the opposition of the other Dominions; it was thus definitively confirmed that the Committee would not become the Empire's central advisory body for the foreseeable future. Newfoundland, New Zealand and the Union of South Africa accepted the fact that the mother country made decisions on foreign policy, while Canada and Australia continued to aspire for greater influence in Imperial policy, differing only in the method for achieving this objective. Borden preferred the Committee to the Imperial Conferences, while Fisher was of the opposite opinion.[313]

The Dominions' lukewarm attitude towards the Committee of Imperial Defence was also seen in the fact that until the outbreak of the First World War, Dominion representatives seldom took part in its meetings.[314] It wasn't until June 1914 that Borden sent Sir George Halsey Perley as Minister without Portfolio and High Commissioner to London to first represent Canada in meetings of the Committee as a permanent and regular member. Nevertheless, the Dominions did not ignore matters of defence and continued to use the Dominion defence committees as "communication channels" for discussions with the Committee of Imperial Defence, whose nature and importance was significantly transformed by the outbreak of the Great War.[315]

The years 1912–1914 saw no major[316] debate on transforming the Conference system. Only in December 1912 did Australian Governor-General Thomas Denman, 3rd Baron Denman, make a request that a minor Imperial Conference take place in Australia in January or February 1913 focused on current problems of naval defence. Denman supported this request with the surprising argument that it was not practical for the Australian ministers to travel overseas in 1913. Although Harcourt was initially taken aback by the proposed meeting, he subsequently rejected Denman's request because most of the other Dominion representatives did not have the time to visit Australia in early 1913. Instead, he proposed personal consultation in London if it was a matter of urgency.[317]

By 1914, the system of Imperial Conferences had evolved into an institution with a clear composition, regular meetings and proven procedures. During 1887–1911, all the Conferences had for the most part become an arena for exchanges of opinion where proponents and opponents of federalism came together.[318] It also frequently happened that the participation of Dominion prime ministers at Conference proceedings, and the opinions they upheld there, weakened their positions at home to such an extent that it contributed to their political downfall. Changes of Prime Minister also saw a break in the continuity of issues advocated, and as such debates had to start from scratch again. Britain's Colonial Office continued to provide the Secretariat organising the Conferences, although the vision of its independence was never achieved. The official method of communication remained as outdated as it always had been, i.e. through cablegrams and telegrams – from the British Secretary of State for the Colonies to Governors or Governors-General and the British Prime Minister and back. If the Dominions wanted to communicate with a third country, they had to use this clumsy mechanism based on a system of British mediators which was lengthy and inefficient and led to a number of bizarre misunderstandings. This system inevitably became a "brake" once the war broke out when rapid exchange of information was a strategic advantage. Change came following implementation of the principle of permanent cabinet consultation in 1917.[319]

Notes

1. Hall, Hessel Duncan, *Commonwealth: A History of the British Commonwealth of Nations*, London: Von Nostrand Reinhold Co, 1971, 8–9.
2. The existence of settlements of white people and their dominance were important factors forming Anglo-Dominion relations. Great Britain frequently supported the Dominions' policies of discrimination and approved white superiority in the interests of maintaining Commonwealth unity. There were even people of the opinion that if these principles could not be maintained, then the Empire would collapse. Cf. Holland, Robert F., *The Commonwealth in the British Official Mind: A Study in Anglo-Dominion Relations, 1925–37*, PhD Thesis, Oxford: University of Oxford, 17–19; University of Oxford: Bodleian Library (hereafter BLO), Curtis Papers (hereafter CP), Mss. Curtis 91, W. M. Macmillan to L. G. Curtis, High Wycombe, 16 May 1935 [251].
3. An essential role in terms of communication between Great Britain and the self-governing colonies was played, in addition to open transport routes, by undersea telegraph cables. See more in Boyce, Robert W. D., "Imperial Dreams and National Realities: Britain, Canada and the Struggle for a Pacific Telegraph Cable, 1879–1902", *The English Historical Review* 115, No. 460, 2000, 39–70; Kennedy, M., "Imperial Cable Communications and Strategy, 1870–1914", *The English Historical Review* 86, No. 341, 1971, 728–752.
4. Kendle, John Edward, *The Colonial and Imperial Conferences 1887–1911: A Study in Imperial Organizations*, London: Longmans 1967, 2.
5. Mehrotra, S. R., "On the Use of the Term 'Commonwealth'", *Journal of Commonwealth Political Studies* 2, No. 1, 1963, 5.
6. For more on the development of anti-imperialist sentiments in the colonies, see Schuyler, Robert Livingston, "The Rise of Anti-Imperialism in England", *Political Science Quarterly* 37, No. 3, 1922, 440–471.

7 Glazebrook, George Parkin de Twenebroker, *A History of Canadian External Relations*, London: Oxford University Press, 1950, 150–151.
8 E.g. Greater Britain, United States of Britain, British Commonwealth, Imperial Commonwealth. Mehrotra, *On the Use*, 5, 14.
9 Kendle, *The Colonial*, 3.
10 See more in Burgess, Michael, "'Forgotten Centenary': The Formation of the Imperial Federation League in the UK, 1884", *The Round Table* 73, No. 289, 1984, 76–85; Hind, R. J., *Henry Labouchere and the Empire 1880–1905*, London: Athlone Press, 213–214; Labillière, Francis Peter de, *Federal Britain: Or, Unity and Federation of the Empire*, London: S. Low & Co, 1894.
11 Froude, James Anthony, *Short Studies on Great Subjects*, Vol. 2, London: Longmans, Green & Co, 1898, 210.
12 The first federalists, with few exceptions, did not include India in their federalist plans because they perceived it from the outside as a "calm and safe" British possession, and also because their concept of Empire also took account of racial aspects. They were also afraid that the issue of Indian involvement in a federation was an unresolved issue which could quash their federalist projects if they were too hasty. Cf. Mehrotra, S. R., "Imperial Federation and India, 1868–1917", *Journal of Commonwealth Political Studies* 1, No. 1, 1961, 29–30; Studdert-Kennedy, Gerald, "Political Science and Political Theology: Lionel Curtis, Federalism, and India", *The Journal of Imperial and Commonwealth History* 24, No. 2, 1996, 197–217; Young, Frederick, *A Pioneer of Imperial Federation in Canada*, London: George Allen, 1902, 148–149.
13 Bosák, Tomáš, "Britské federalistické koncepce a pojetí Evropy v éře 'skvělé izolace'", *Mezinárodní vztahy* 45, No. 1, 2010, 85–86.
14 The conference was officially termed "Colonial" because the term they did not perceive the term "Imperial" to be appropriate if Indian representatives were not allowed to take part. Kendle, *The Colonial*, 8.
15 Ollivier, Maurice (Ed.), *The Colonial and Imperial Conferences from 1887 to 1937*, Vol. 1, Ottawa: Queen's Printer, 1954, 3.
16 Cd. 2785, *Colonial Conference: Correspondence Relating to the Future Organization of Colonial Conferences*, London: HMSO, 1906, 1–2.
17 Edward Stanhope to the Governors of Colonies under Responsible Government, Downing Street, 25 November 1886, C. 5091, *Colonial Conference, 1887: Proceedings of the Colonial Conference: 1887*, Vol. 1, London: HMSO, 1887, No. 1, vii–xiii.
18 Ibid., 5.
19 Hofmeyr's speech inspired Natal politician John Robinson to call on delegates at the subsequent debate to take a firm stand on Hofmeyr's statement. As was to be expected, Secretary of State for the Colonies Holland did not allow a resolution on this point. Ibid., 467–468, 473–474.
20 See Denison, George Taylor, *The Struggle for Imperial Unity: Recollections and Experiences*, New York: Macmillan & Co, 1909, 176–208.
21 Kendle, *The Colonial*, 13.
22 Bosák, 85–86; Kendle, *The Colonial*, 14–17.
23 For more on this issue, see Denison, 194–225.
24 Keith, Arthur Berriedale, *Responsible Government in the Dominions*, Vol. 3, Oxford: Oxford University Press, 1912, 1466.
25 See more in C. 7553, *Colonial Conference, 1894: Report by the Right Hon. the Earl of Jersey, G.M.G., on the Colonial Conference at Ottawa, with the Proceedings of the Conference and Certain Correspondence*, London: HMSO, 1894.

26 Keith, Arthur Berriedale, *The Governments of the British Empire*, London: Macmillan & Co, 1935, 180; Kendle, *The Colonial*, 18.
27 Canada, for instance, prioritised its links with Great Britain and the United States, and only to a lesser extent with European countries, for economic and geographic reasons. The fact that Canada was part of the Empire gave it economic and diplomatic advantages on the one hand, but on the other hand overly constrained it in certain matters. Glazebrook, 150–164.
28 Cf. Hall, *Commonwealth*, 13; Thierry, C. de, "The Colonial Office Myth", *Contemporary Review*, No. 78, 1900, 374.
29 Cf. Garvin, James Louis, *The Life of Joseph Chamberlain, 1895–1900: Empire and World Policy*, Vol. 3, London: Macmillan & Co., 1934, 5; Hall, *Commonwealth*, 20.
30 McInnis, Edgar, "The Imperial Problem in the Minds of Chamberlain and His Successors", *The Canadian Historical Review* 16, No. 3, 1935, 66.
31 Cf. Joseph Chamberlain, "Splendid Isolation", Whitehall Rooms, London, 21 January 1896, in: Boyd, Charles W. (Ed.), *Mr. Chamberlain's Speeches*, Vol. 1, London: Constable, 1914, 358–365; Joseph Chamberlain, "The Future of the British Empire", London, 6 November 1895, in: Chamberlain, Joseph, *Foreign and Colonial Speeches*, London: G. Routledge, 1897, 73–81; Joseph Chamberlain, "A Young Nation", Imperial Institute, London, 11 November 1895, in: Chamberlain, *Foreign*, 82–90; Joseph Chamberlain, "The First Step to Federation," London, 25 March 1896, in: Chamberlain, *Foreign*, 161–176.
32 Joseph Chamberlain, "Commercial Union of the Empire", Congress of Chambers of Commerce of the Empire, London, 6 June 1896, in: Boyd, Vol. 1, 365–372.
33 See more in Grimshaw, Charles, "Australian Nationalism and the Imperial Connection", *The Australian Journal of Politics and History* 3, No. 2, 1958, 161–183; Sinclair, Keith, *Imperial Federation: A Study of New Zealand Policy and Opinion, 1880–1914*, London: Athlone Press, 1955, 7–25.
34 Denison, 194–224.
35 C. 8485, *Correspondence between the Secretary of State for the Colonies and the Self-Governing Colonies Respecting the Celebration of the Sixtieth Anniversary of the Accession of Her Majesty the Queen*, London: HMSO, 1897, 3.
36 It was the Prime Ministers of Canada, New South Wales, Victoria, New Zealand, Queensland, Cape Colony, South Australia, Newfoundland, Tasmania, Western Australia and Natal. Ollivier, Vol. 1, 127.
37 C. 8596, *Proceedings of a Conference between the Secretary of State for the Colonies and the Premiers of the Self-Governing Colonies, at the Colonial Office, London, June and July 1897*, London: HMSO, 1897, 4–13.
38 Skelton, Oscar Douglas, *Life and Letters of Sir Wilfrid Laurier*, Vol. 2, Toronto: S. B. Gundy, 1921, 70–71.
39 Kendle, *The Colonial*, 27–28.
40 For more on Chamberlain's speech, see Keith, Arthur Berriedale (Ed.), *Selected Speeches and Documents on British Colonial Policy, 1763–1917*, Vol. 2, London: Oxford University Press, 1933, 212.
41 Hall, *Commonwealth*, 22.
42 Ollivier, Vol. 1, 154.
43 Cf. Hall, *Commonwealth*, 21; Kendle, *The Colonial*, 27.
44 Skelton, *Life*, 342.
45 C. 8596, 15.
46 Kendle, *The Colonial*, 28.

47 See more cf. Kendle, *The Colonial*, 34–38; Messamore, Barbara Jane, *The Governors General of Canada, 1888–1911: British Imperialists and Canadian "Nationalists"*, PhD Thesis, Burnaby: Simon Fraser University, 1991, 41; Wilde, Richard H., "Joseph Chamberlain's Proposal of an Imperial Council in March, 1900", *The Canadian Historical Review* 37, No. 3, 1956, 225–246.

48 Edward VII, by the Grace of God of the United Kingdom of Great Britain and Ireland and of the British Dominions beyond the Seas King, Defender of the Faith, Emperor of India. Cf. Baumgartl, Liselotte, *Empire and Commonwealth*, PhD Thesis, Wien: Universität Wien, 1950, 144; Hall, *Commonwealth*, 889.

49 See more in Cd. 708, *Colonies: Correspondence Relating to the Proposed Alteration of the Royal Style and Titles of the Crown*, London: HMSO, 1901, 3–5.

50 Hall, *Commonwealth*, 25.

51 Nicolson, Harold, Sir, *King George the Fifth: His Life and Reign*, 3rd Ed., London: Pan Piper, 1967, 106.

52 Also involved in discussion besides the prime ministers, for example, were the British Secretary of State for War, the Australian Minister for Defence, the Canadian Minister of Militia and Defence, Canada's Minister of Finance, and others. See more in Cd. 1299, *Colonial Conference, 1902: Papers Relating to a Conference between the Secretary of State for the Colonies and the Prime Ministers of Self-Governing Colonies; June to August, 1902*, London: HMSO, 1902, 1.

53 Cf. Cd. 1299, 4; Kendle, *The Colonial*, 49–50; Ollivier, Vol. 1, 153–154.

54 Cf. Hall, *Commonwealth*, 23; Alfred Milner, *The Two Empires*, Royal Colonial Institute, 16 June 1908, in: Milner, Alfred, *The Nation and the Empire: Being a Collection of Speeches and Addresses*, London: Constable, 1913, 299.

55 Fiddes, George Vandeleur, Sir, *The Dominions and Colonial Offices*, London: G. P. Putnam's Sons, 1926, 237–239.

56 For more on other plans for Imperial reorganisation, see Kendle, *The Colonial*, 46–49.

57 Joseph Chamberlain, "The True Conception of Empire", Royal Colonial Institute, 31 March 1897, in: Chamberlain, *Foreign*, 248.

58 Cf. Garvin, 581; "Speech of the Right Hon. Joseph Chamberlain, M. P., in the House of Commons, April 3, 1900", *The Edinburgh Review* 192, No. 393, 1900, 247–252.

59 Amery, Julian, *The Life of Joseph Chamberlain, 1901–1903: At the Height of His Power*, Vol. 4, London: Macmillan, 1951, 422.

60 Joseph Chamberlain, "As One Great Nation", Wanderers' Hall, Johannesburg, 17 January 1903, in: Boyd, Vol. 2, 108.

61 Mehrotra, *On the Use*, 5.

62 Cd. 1299, ix.

63 Kendle, *The Colonial*, 50.

64 Amery, *The Life*, 429–447.

65 In particular, this involved the Coefficients group, which was founded in November 1902 by Sidney and Beatrice Webb and whose members included Herbert George Wells, Sir Edward Grey and Sir Alfred Milner, as well as "The Compatriots", a group behind whose founding stood Leopold S. Amery. Cf. Amery, Leopold Stennett, *My Political Life: England before the Storm, 1896–1914*, Vol. 1, London: Hutchinson, 1953, 223–226; Halpérin, Vladimir, *Lord Milner and the Empire: The Evolution of British Imperialism*, London: Odhams Press, 1952, 155; Kendle, *The Colonial*, 55.

66 D'Egville, Howard, *Imperial Defence and Closer Union*, London: King, 1913, 221–222.
67 Drage, Geoffrey, *Imperial Organization of Trade*, London: Smith, Elder & Co, 1911, 3; Frederick Pollock, "Imperial Organisation", 11 April 1905, in: *Proceedings of the Royal Colonial Institute*, Vol. 36, London: [s. n.], 1905, 287–319.
68 Kendle, *The Colonial*, 57.
69 Holland, Bernard Henry, *Imperium et Libertas: A Study in History and Politics*, London: Edward Arnold, 1901, 308.
70 Cf. "Cabinet and Empire", *The Press* 60, No. 11637, 17 July 1903, 2; Richard Burdon Haldane, "The Cabinet and the Empire", 9 June 1903, in: *Proceedings of the Royal Colonial Institute*, Vol. 34, London: [s. n.], 1903, 325–352.
71 See Reeves, William Pember, "A Council of the Empire", *Journal of the Society of Comparative Legislation* 5, No. 2, 1904, 241–243.
72 For more details on aspects Britain's Colonial Office was interested in TNA, Colonial Office (hereafter CO) 323/511/10975, Sir F. Pollock's Scheme of "Imperial Organisation", 19 December 1904, [194–197].
73 The British Library (hereafter BL), Balfour Papers (hereafter BP), Add MS 49698, Vol. XVI, Proposed Draft of a Circular Despatch to the Governors of the Self-Governing Colonies, December 1904, [181–185]; BL, BP, Add MS 49775, Vol. XCIII, Lyttelton to Balfour, 30 December 1904, [20].
74 Cf. BL, BP, Add MS 49775, Vol. XCIII, Balfour to Lyttelton, 13 January 1905, [22–26]; BL, BP, Add MS 49775, Vol. XCIII, Lyttelton to Balfour, 1 February 1905, [31–40].
75 Mr. Lyttelton to the Governors of the Self-Governing Colonies, Downing Street, 20 April 1905, in: Cd. 2785, *Colonial Conference: Correspondence Relating to the Future Organization of Colonial Conferences*, London: HMSO, 1906, No. 1, 3.
76 TNA, CO 323/511, Circular Despatch to the Governors of the Self-Governing Colonies, Downing Street, 20 April 1905, 4–5.
77 Australian Prime Minister Alfred Deakin, for example, agreed with Lyttelton that the term "Colonial Conference" did not sufficiently express the importance of the meetings, and as such preferred the use of the term "Imperial Council". In regard to the permanent commission, however, he expressed the desire that the Commonwealth of Australia should have two representatives, one of which would be a High Commissioner. See more in Alfred Deakin [to] the Governor-General Lord Northcote, 19 August 1905, Cd. 2785, Encl. 2, No. 10, 11–12.
78 For more details on Canada's position report of the Secretary of the Privy Council John Joseph McGee. Cd. 2785, Encl., No. 14, 13–14.
79 Cf. Richard Jebb, "Some Aspects of Imperialism", Empire Club of Canada, 27 October 1905, in: Hopkins, J. Castell (Ed.), *Empire Club Speeches: Being Addresses Delivered before the Empire Club of Canada during Its Sessions of 1905–06*, Toronto: [s. n.], 1906, 22–30; Miller, John Donald Bruce, *Richard Jebb and the Problem of Empire*, London: Athlone Press, 1956, 15–16.
80 Only Cape representatives were against postponing the Conference to the first half of 1907. Cf. Mr. Lyttelton to the Governors of the Self-Governing Colonies, 29 November 1905, in: Cd. 2785, No. 15, 15; Thomas William Smartt [to the Governor Sir W. Hely-Hutchinson], 6 December 1905, in: Cd. 2975, *Colonial Conference: Correspondence Relating to a Proposed Colonial Conference in 1907*, London: HMSO, 1906, Encl., No. 4, 2.

81 The Earl of Elgin to the Governors of Self-Governing Colonies, Downing Street, 22 February 1906, in: Cd. 2975, No. 9, 4; TNA, CO 323/514/2854, Col[onial] Conference, 26 January 1906, [42–46].
82 The Secretary of State to the Governors-General of the Commonwealth of Australia, the Dominion of Canada, and the Governors of New Zealand, Cape Colony, Natal, and Newfoundland, Downing Street, 4 January 1907, in: Cd. 3337, *Colonial Conference, 1907: Despatch from the Secretary of State for the Colonies, with Enclosures, Respecting the Agenda of the Colonial Conference, 1907*, London: HMSO, 1907, 3–4.
83 In the event of establishment of an Imperial Council permanent secretariat, the Commonwealth of Australia was of the opinion that running costs should be calculated in proportion to population. Cf. Commonwealth of Australia, *Parliamentary Debates* (hereafter *APD*), *House of Representatives* (hereafter *HoR*), No. 8, 21 February 1907, 123; Resolution of Government of Commonwealth of Australia to be Submitted to Colonial Conference, in: Cd. 3337, Encl. No. 1, 6–7.
84 Resolution of Government of New Zealand for Submission to Colonial Conference, in: Cd. 3337, Encl. No. 2, 8.
85 Cape representatives believed that every self-governing colony should make a contribution to defence corresponding to their size and economic strength, and as such in 1907 they proposed that each autonomous territory be informed in advance exactly how many troops they needed to train and arm to defend the Empire. Resolution of Government of Cape Colony for Submission to Colonial Conference, 1907, in: Cd. 3337, 11.
86 Jebb, Richard, *The Imperial Conference: A History and the Study*, Vol. 2, London: Longmans & Co, 1911, 73–74.
87 Cf. Extract from a Report of the Committee of the Privy Council, Approved by the Governor-General on the 20th July 1906, in: Cd. 3340, *Colonial Conference, 1907: Correspondence Relating to the Colonial Conference, 1907*, London: HMSO, 1907, Encl. No. 5, 3–4; The Secretary of State to the Governor-General of Canada, Downing Street; 11 August 1906, in: Cd. 3340, No. 6, 4–5; Extract from a Report of the Committee of the Privy Council, Approved by the Governor-General on the 17th October 1906, in: Cd. 3340, Encl. No. 15, 11; The Secretary of State to the Governor-General of Canada, Downing Street, 29 November 1906, in: Cd. 3340, No. 17, 12.
88 TNA, Cabinet Papers (hereafter CAB) 17/77, Imperial Organization, *The Times*, 14 March 1907, [112].
89 Kendle, *The Colonial*, 80–82.
90 For more details on his attitudes cf. Alfred Milner, "The Imperialist Creed", Manchester, 14 December 1906, in: Milner, *The Nation*, 135–152; Milner, Alfred, "Some Reflections on the Coming Conference", *National Review* 49, 1907, 195–206; Gollin, Alfred Manuel, *Proconsul in Politics: A Study of Lord Milner in Opposition and in Power*, London: Anthony Blond, 1964, 132–135.
91 Kendle, *The Colonial*, 87.
92 Amery, Leopold Stennett, *Union and Strength: A Series of Papers on Imperial Questions*, London: Edward Arnold, 1912, 1–48.
93 Cross, J. A., "The Colonial Office and the Dominions before 1914", *Journal of Commonwealth Political Studies* 4, No. 2, 1966, 138.
94 Wilfrid Laurier, *Canadienne Gazette*, 3 July 1902, in: Jebb, Richard, *Studies in Colonial Nationalism*, London: Edward Arnold, 1905, 1.
95 Dafoe, John Wesley, *Laurier: A Study in Canadian Politics*, Toronto: Thomas Allen, 1922, 70.
96 Ollivier, Vol. 1, 213.

97 Cd. 3523, *Colonial Conference, 1907: Minutes of Proceedings of the Colonial Conference, 1907*, London: HMSO, 1907, 15–18, 55–56.
98 Cd. 3404, *Colonial Conference, 1907: Published Proceedings and Précis of the Colonial Conference, 15th to 26th April, 1907*, London: HMSO, 1907, 6; "The Conference and the Empire", *The Round Table* 1, No. 4, 1911, 392.
99 Kendle, *The Colonial*, 91.
100 Cd. 3523, 7–8; La Nauze, John Andrew, *Alfred Deakin*, Melbourne: Oxford University Press, 1968.
101 Cf. Grimshaw, 181; Gollin, *Proconsul*, 136; La Nauze, John Andrew, *Alfred Deakin: Two Lectures*, Brisbane: University of Queensland Press, 1960, 16.
102 Cf. Kendle, *The Colonial*, 92; La Nauze, John Andrew, *Alfred Deakin: A Biography*, Vol. 2, Melbourne: Melbourne University Press, 1962, 494.
103 Cf. Cd. 3523, 35–39; Cunningham, Alain MacAlpine, *Canadian Nationalism and the British Connection 1899–1919*, MA Thesis, Burnaby: Simon Fraser University, 1980, 79; Kendle, *The Colonial*, 92–93.
104 Dewey, Alexander Gordon, *The Dominion and Diplomacy: The Canadian Contribution*, Vol. 1, London: Longmans, Green & Co, 1929, 107–111.
105 Cf. *APD, HoR*, No. 8, 21 February 1907, 123; Cd. 3523, 26, 30–33, 52; Hall, *Commonwealth*, 26.
106 Cf. *APD, HoR*, No. 8, 21 February 1907, 124; Cd. 3523, 26–30, 33–35, 41–44, 56; Hancock, *Survey of British*, 48–49; La Nauze, *Alfred Deakin: A Biography*, 499–504.
107 Amery was deeply frustrated by Laurier's position, who maintained an entirely negative position over the whole Conference. He was also of the opinion that if Laurier acted "more fairly" in regard to a Secretariat, the resistance of Britain's Colonial Office could also be overcome, which would allow Canada and other Dominions to escape from its control in Imperial matters. CAC, AP, AMEL 1/2/16, L. S. A[mery] on 1907 Conference, [1907].
108 Kendle, John Edward, *The Round Table Movement and Imperial Union*, Toronto: University of Toronto Press, 1975, 48.
109 Richard Jebb, "Twelve Months of Imperial Evolution", in: *Proceedings of the Royal Colonial Institute*, Vol. 39, London: [s. n.], 1908, 4–37.
110 Cf. Cd. 5273, *Dominions No. 4: Further Correspondence Relating to the Imperial Conference*, London 1910, 1; Kendle, *The Colonial*, 105.
111 George E. Foster, "The Imperial Conference of 1907", in: Hopkins, J. Castell (Ed.), *Empire Club Speeches: Being Addresses Delivered before the Empire Club of Canada during Its Sessions of 1905–06*, Toronto: [s. n.], 1906, 11–14.
112 Cf. TNA, CO 323/534/29255A, H[opwood] to [Cortylyou], Draft to Treasury Submitting Proposals for the Colonial Office Reorganization, 15 August 1907, [511–529]; TNA, CO 885/8/12, Miscellaneous No. 154, Graham, Memorandum on the Colonial Office Establishment, March 1903, 1–12.
113 For more details on this issue, see Cross, J. A., "Whitehall and the Commonwealth: The Development of British Departmental Organisation for Commonwealth Affairs", *Journal of Commonwealth Political Studies* 2, No. 3, 1964, 191–193; Parkinson, Cosmo, *The Colonial Office from Within, 1909–45*, London: Faber & Faber, 1947, 24–51.
114 Despatch to the Governors of the Self-Governing Colonies Relative to the Reorganization of the Colonial Office, Downing Street, 21 September 1907, in: Cd. 3795, *Despatch to the Governors of the Self-Governing Colonies Relative to the Reorganization of the Colonial Office*, London: HMSO, 1907, 3–5.

115 For more on the activities and staff of the Dominion Department prior to the First World War, see Cross, "The Colonial Office", 139–148; Hyam, Ronald, "The Colonial Office Mind 1900–1914", *Journal of Imperial and Commonwealth History* 8, No. 1, 1979, 34–55.
116 Cf. Cd. 3523, v; Cd. 5273, 1; Ollivier, Vol. 1, 217–218.
117 The issue of the involvement of Indian representatives, and the validity of this point of the 1907 Colonial Conference resolution were again discussed during the Imperial War Conference of 1917. See more in Jebb, Richard, "Conference or Cabinet?" *United Empire: The Royal Colonial Institute Journal* 11, No. 4, 1920, 161.
118 Cf. Holland, Robert, "Britain, Commonwealth and the End of Empire", Bogdanor, Vernon (Ed.), *The British Constitution in the Twentieth Century*, Oxford: Oxford University Press, 2003, 633; Keith, *The Governments*, 180; Lucas, Charles, *Greater Rome and Greater Britain*, Oxford: Clarendon Press, 1912, 6–7.
119 For more on Canada's position on preferential tariffs, see Colvin, James A., "Sir Wilfrid Laurier and the British Preferential Tariff System", Neatby, H. Blair et al., *Imperial Relation in the Age of Laurier*, Toronto: University of Toronto Press, 1969, 34–44.
120 Amery, Leopold Stennett, *Thoughts on the Constitution*, London: Oxford University Press, 1964, 112.
121 CAC, AP, AMEL 1/3/40, [L. S. Amery] to Milner, 27 November 1906, 3.
122 Grayson, Richard S., "Imperialism in Conservative Defence and Foreign Policy: Leo Amery and the Chamberlains, 1903–39", *The Journal of Imperial and Commonwealth History* 34, No. 4, 2006, 509.
123 Not even the plan for the "revival" of the Imperial Federation (Defence) Committee was successful. See Loring, A. H., "The Imperial Federation (Defence) Committee: 1894–1906", *United Empire: The Royal Colonial Institute Journal* 6, 1915, 341–346. At the same time, the importance of the League of Empire, whose activities Frederick Pollock became actively involved in, did not have a major impact on discussions underway. See more in Greenlee, James G. C., "The A B C's of Imperial Unity", *Canadian Journal of History/Annales canadiennes d'histoire* 14, No. 1, 1979, 49–64.
124 Another significant Imperial grouping was the so-called Compatriots, founded in London in January 1904 by Leopold Amery, and whose members included, for example, geographer H. J. Mackinder, journalist James Louis Garvin, Joseph Chamberlain and Alfred Milner, who headed it. When the Compatriots expanded their activities overseas in 1907 through societies within the self-governing colonies, Amery began extensive communication with his Australian and Canadian branches – Alfred Deakin, William Morris Hughes, Robert Laird Borden and William Lyon Mackenzie King – on reform plans. Amery, *My Political*, Vol. 1, 265–269; Kendle, John Edward, "The Round Table Movement: Lionel Curtis and the Formation of the New Zealand Groups in 1910", *The New Zealand Journal of History* 1, No. 1, 1967, 36.
125 Kendle, *The Round Table Movement and*, 50–51; Reese, 74.
126 Cf. CAC, AP, AMEL 1/2/16, L. S. A[mery] on 1907 Conference, [1907]; Gollin, *Proconsul*, 143; Kendle, *The Colonial*, 125–128; Milner, Alfred, "Imperial Unity: External Advantages", Canadian Club, Vancouver, 9 October 1908, in: Milner, Alfred, *Speeches Delivered in Canada in the Autumn of 1908*, Toronto: William Tyrrell & Co, 1909, 1–12; Milner, Alfred, "Imperial Unity: Internal Benefits", Canadian Club, Winnipeg, 15 October 1908, in: Milner, *Speeches*, 13–26; Quigley, Carroll, "The Round Table Movement in Canada, 1909–38", *The Canadian Historical Review*

43, No. 3, 1962, 204–209; Thompson, J. Lee, *A Wider Patriotism: Alfred Milner and the British Empire*, London: Routledge, 2007, 123–125.
127 Bosák, 86; Cross, "The Colonial Office", 147; Geyser, O., "Jan Smuts and Alfred Milner", *The Round Table* 90, No. 360, 2001, 425.
128 Other influential members included Robert Brand, Patrick Duncan, Richard Feetham, Lionel Hichens and Dougal Malcolm. Major figures who worked with them included Frederick Scott Oliver, Reginald Coupland, Edward Grigg and Alfred Zimmern, who was not entirely on board with Curtis's positions. See May, Alex, "The Round Table and Imperial Federation, 1910–17", *The Round Table* 99, No. 410, 2010, 548–549; Peatling, G. K., "Globalism, Hegemonism and British Power: J. A. Hobson and Alfred Zimmern Reconsidered", *History* 89, No. 295, 2004, 386.
129 For more on the positions of members of the so-called Milner's Kindergarten in Imperial matters, see Nimocks, Walter, *Milner's Young Men: The 'Kindergarten' in Edwardian Imperial Affairs*, London: Hodder & Stoughton, 1970.
130 Cf. Amery, Leopold Stennett (Ed.), *The Times History of the War in South Africa, 1899–1902*, Vol. 6, London: Sampson, Low, Marsten & Co, 1909, 147; Louis, William Roger, *In the Name of God, Go!: Leo Amery and the British Empire in the Age of Churchill*, London: W. W. Norton, 1992, 40.
131 Beloff, Max, *Imperial Sunset: Britain's Liberal Empire 1897–1921*, Vol. 1, London: Macmillan, 1969, 129; Crankshaw, Edward, *The Forsaken Idea: A Study of Viscount Milner*, London: Longmans, Green & Co, 1952, 138–145.
132 Kendle, *The Colonial*, 133.
133 Cf. Campbell-Miller, Jill, "'Ex Unitate Vires': Elite Consolidation and the Union of South Africa, 1902–10", *Canadian Journal of History/Annales canadiennes d'histoire* 45, No. 1, 2010, 97–102; Cole, Douglas, "The Problem of 'Nationalism' and 'Imperialism' in British Settlement Colonies", *Journal of British Studies* 10, No. 2, 1971, 160–182.
134 May, 548–550.
135 Cf. Donnelly, Murray S., *J. W. Dafoe and Lionel Curtis: Two Concepts of the Commonwealth*, London: University of London, 1960; Donnelly, Murray S., "J. W. Dafoe and Lionel Curtis – Two Concepts of the Commonwealth", *Political Studies* 8, No. 2, 1960, 170–182; Potter, Simon J., "Richard Jebb, John S. Ewart and the Round Table, 1898–1926", *The English Historical Review* 122, No. 495, 2007, 105–132.
136 See Shaw, G. Bernard, *Fabianism and the Fiscal Question: An Alternative Policy*, London: Fabian Society, 1904.
137 Cf. Beloff, *Imperial*, Vol. 1, 138–140; MacDonald, James Ramsey, *Labour and Empire*, London: Labour Party, 1907; MacDonald, James Ramsey, *The Awakening of India*, London: Hodder & Stoughton, 1910; MacDonald, James Ramsey, *The Government of India*, New York: Swarthmore Press, 1920.
138 Cf. CAC, AP, AMEL 2/2/8, L. S. A[mery] to Deakin, 13 April 1911, 2; Gorman, Daniel, "Lionel Curtis, Imperial Citizenship, and the Quest for Unity", *The Historian* 66, No. 1, 2004, 68; Janitor [Lockhart, J. G.], *The Feet of the Young Men*, 2nd Ed., London: Duckworth, 1929, 177.
139 Butler, James Ramsey Montagu, *Lord Lothian (Philip Kerr) 1882–1940*, London: Macmillan, 1960, 36.
140 The so-called Green Memorandum was named after the colour of its cover. In confidential communication between Round Table Movement members, it was familiarly referred to as the Egg, or the Omelette. By the end of 1911, following the incorporation of a number of points of criticism from Round Table Movement members, the so-called Green Memorandum was ready for

printing as the Annotated Memorandum. Hodson, Harry, "The Round Table: Until the Early 1930s", *The Round Table* 88, No. 352, 1999, 679; Eayrs, John, "The Round Table Movement in Canada, 1909–1920", *The Canadian Historical Review* 38, No. 1, 1957, 3; Kenneth, Daniel, *Commonwealth: Imperialism and Internationalism, 1919–1939*, PhD Thesis, Austin: The University of Texas at Austin, 2012, 31–35; May, 551.
141 Cf. Kendle, *The Round Table Movement and*, 74–80; *Report on the Green Memorandum Prepared by the Oxford University Segment of the Round Table Society*, [Oxford: s. n., s. a.].
142 New Zealand was considered the Dominion most favourable towards an Imperial federation project. Eayrs, 2. For more on Curtis's journeys, see Kendle, *The Round Table Movement: Lionel*, 39–50.
143 Kendle, John Edward, "The Round Table Movement, New Zealand, and the Conference of 1911", *The Round Table* 84, No. 336, 1995, 496–497.
144 Cf. Amery, Leopold Stennett, "Some Practical Steps towards an Imperial Constitution", *United Empire: The Royal Colonial Institute Journal* 1, No. 7, 1910, 487–509; CAC, AP, AMEL 1/2/5; Kendle, *The Round Table Movement and*, 51.
145 Cf. CAC, AP, AMEL 1/2/16, [L. S. Amery] to Hordern, 2 July 1910, 1–4; CAC, AP, AMEL 2/2/8, L. S. A[mery] to Deakin, 7 August 1908, 1–[6]; CAC, AP, L. S. A[mery] to Haldane, 4 November 1910, [1–4].
146 Cf. CAC, AP, AMEL 1/2/16, [L. S. Amery] to Esher, 9 May 1910; Kendle, *The Colonial*, 138.
147 Cf. CAC, AP, AMEL 1/2/16, Curtis to Kerr, Auckland, 10 September 1910, 1–10.
148 Cf. CAC, AP, AMEL 1/2/16, Kerr to L. S. A[mery], London, 12 November 1910, [1]–2.
149 Cf. CAC, AP, AMEL 1/2/16, Kerr to L. S. A[mery], London, 11 November 1910, [1]; CAC, AP, AMEL 1/2/16, Kerr to L. S. A[mery], London, 12 November 1910, 2.
150 BL, BP, Add MS 49775, Vol. XCIII, Lyttelton to Balfour, 16 October 1910, [65–66].
151 The Royal Colonial Institute was a parallel group supporting constitutional reform, and partially co-operating with some Round Table Movement members. For more on its activities, see Greenlee, James G. C., "Imperial Studies and the Unity of the Empire", *The Journal of Imperial and Commonwealth History* 7, No. 3, 1979, 321–335; Reese, 75–79.
152 TNA, CO 886/4/5, Dominions No. 25, Imperial Conference 1911, 4 July 1910, [1]–8.
153 TNA, CO 886/4/7, Dominions No. 27, H. W. J[ust], Proposed Reorganization of the Colonial Conference, 14 July 1910, [1]–10.
154 TNA, CO 886/4/9, Dominions No. 29, C. P. L[ucas], Proposed Reorganization of the Colonial Conference, 23 July 1910, [1]–5.
155 South African politician General Jam Smuts, for example, also recommended setting up a separate Dominion Office. Kendle, *The Colonial*, 154.
156 See more in Gollin, Alfred Manuel, *The Observer and J. L. Garvin, 1908–1914: A Study in a Great Editorship*, London: Oxford University Press, 1960, 168–204.
157 Cross, "Whitehall", 193.
158 For more on preparations for the 1911 Imperial Conference, see TNA, CO 886/3/2, Dominions No. 19, Further Correspondence [July 7, 1909, to April 1911] Relating to the Imperial Conference, 1–397.
159 TNA, CO 886/4/12, Dominions No. 32, H. W. J[ust], Imperial Conference 1911: Reorganization of the Colonial Office and Position of High Commissioners, January 1911, [1]–6.

160 Kendle, *The Colonial*, 155.
161 CAC, AP, AMEL 1/2/16, Kerr to L. S. A[mery], London, 8 March 1911, [2].
162 Kendle, *The Colonial*, 158–159.
163 The [South African] Governor-General [Gladstone] to the Secretary of State [Harcourt], in: Cd. 5513, *Dominions No. 5: Imperial Conference: Correspondence Relating to the Imperial Conference*, No. 7, London: HMSO, 1911, 12–13.
164 TNA, CO 886/4/13, Dominions No. 33, H. W. J[ust], Imperial Conference 1911, 6 February 1911, [1]–4.
165 TNA, CAB 37/106/52, Suggested Reorganization of the Colonial Office, April 1911, [1]–8.
166 Spender, Harold, *General Botha: The Career and the Man*, Boston: Constable, 1916, 227–229.
167 See Kendle, *The Colonial*, 164–165.
168 TNA, CO 886/5A/2, Dominions No. 35, Reorganization of the Colonial Office, April 1911, [1]–8.
169 TNA, CAB 37/106 (CO 886/5A/3), Dominions No. 36, Imperial Conference, 1911: Statement Showing Proposed Action of His Majesty's Government on the Resolutions Submitted by the Dominion Governments, May 1911, [1]–16.
170 The newly used term "Imperial" more precisely reflected the growing importance of the Dominions and very soon supplanted the term "Colonial", much used until that time, with "Colonial" being used solely for matters of the Crown Colonies. For the first time, the term "Imperial" was used for the Imperial Defence Conference which was held in 1909. Hall, *Commonwealth*, 13.
171 Ibid.
172 Cd. 5745, *Dominions No. 7: Imperial Conference, 1911: Minutes of Proceedings of the Imperial Conference, 1911*, London: HMSO, 1911, 98.
173 TNA, CO 886/5B/1, Dominions No. 38, Imperial Conference, 1911: Minutes of Proceedings, June 1911, 116.
174 Borden, Robert Laird, *Canadian Constitutional Studies: The Marfleet Lectures, University of Toronto, October, 1921*, London: [s. n.], 1922, 127–128.
175 Australian representatives had focused for many years on Pacific affairs, i.e. issues which related to New Guinea and the New Hebrides. In contrast, Canadian representatives, who weren't concerned with anything particularly serious except defining the border with Alaska, took a laxer approach, and as such did not propose to include any major points for discussion in the Conference agenda. Representative of the India Office, Sir Herbert Risley, only took part in meetings at which "Indian" matters were dealt with, such as the migration of Indians to Dominions. Cf. Alport, Cuthbert James MacCall, *Kingdoms in Partnership: A Study of Political Change in the British Commonwealth*, London: Lovat Dickson, 1937, 28; Cd. 5745, 394–399; Brown, Robert Craig – Cook, Ramsay, *Canada 1896–1921: A Nation Transformed*, Toronto: McClelland and Stewart, 1974, 162; Hall, *Commonwealth*, 62–63; APD, *HoR*, No. 47, 25 November 1910, 6852–6880.
176 For more on the positions which prompted Joseph Ward to submit the proposal, see Findlay, John George, Sir, *The Imperial Conference of 1911 from Within*, London: Constable & Co, 1912, 61–175.
177 Philip Kerr in particular repeatedly noted that it was essential for the Imperial federation to gain support amongst influential figures across the Empire, because he believed that the populations in the Dominions were not entirely familiar with this complex process, or even directly feared it might

not be to their advantage. CAC, AP, AMEL 1/2/16, Kerr to L. S. A[mery], London, 24 January 1911, 3.
178 Gardner, W. J., "The Reform Party", Chapman, R. M. (Ed.), *Ends and Means in New Zealand Politics*, Auckland: Auckland University Press, 1961, 30.
179 See Cd. 5746-1, *Dominions No. 8: Imperial Conference, 1911: Papers Laid before the Conference*, London: HMSO, 1911.
180 Cd. 5745, 22–23.
181 Cf. CAC, AP, AMEL 1/2/18, At a Dinner given by "The Pilgrims" to the Prime Ministers of the Over-sea Dominions, London, 23 May 1911, [1–3]; "Pilgrims' Banquet: No Troubles in New Zealand", *Evening Post* 82, 5 July 1911, 15.
182 Ollivier, Vol. 2, 55.
183 Cf. Austin, Dennis, "In Memoriam: Legacies of Empire", *The Round Table* 87, No. 348, 1998, 432; Hancock, I. R., "The 1911 Imperial Conference", *Historical Studies: Australia and New Zealand* 12, No. 47, 1966, 357.
184 Cd. 5745, 37.
185 Numbers of representatives were as follows: Australia 25, Canada 37, South Africa 7, New Zealand 6, Newfoundland 2, and Great Britain 220. Ollivier, Vol. 2, 57.
186 Cd. 5745, 57–58.
187 Cf. Bastian, Peter, *Andrew Fisher: An Underestimated Man*, London: UNSW Press, 2009, 211; Cd. 5745, 67–72; Hancock, "The 1911", 360; Skelton, Oscar Douglas, *The Canadian Dominions: A Chronicle of Our Northern Neighbor*, New Haven: Yale University Press, 1919, 228.
188 Ewart, John Skirving, *The Kingdom Papers*, Vol. 1, Ottawa: [s. n.], 1912, 228–229.
189 Hancock, William Keith, *Smuts: The Sanguine Years, 1870–1919*, Vol. 1, Cambridge: Cambridge University Press, 1962, 351.
190 Cf. Botha to Smuts, London, 15 June 1911, in: Hancock, William Keith – Poel, Jean van der (Eds.), *Selections from the Smuts Papers: June 1910–November 1918*, Vol. 3, Cambridge: Cambridge University Press, 1966, Doc. Vol. 9, No. 4, 36; Hancock, "The 1911", 360.
191 Ollivier, Vol. 2, 59–60.
192 Kendle, *The Colonial*, 178–180.
193 Cd. 5745, 92.
194 Ibid., 86.
195 Cf. Findlay, 27; Kendle, *The Colonial*, 180–181.
196 Cf. Hancock, "The 1911", 363; Ollivier, Vol. 2, 72–74.
197 Cd. 5745, 174–193.
198 PD, HoC, 5th Series, Vol. 28, 20 July 1911, 1334–1335.
199 Cf. CAC, AP, AMEL 1/2/18, Imperial Mission: Mr. Amery on the Possibilities of an Imperial Council, Caxton Hall, Westminster, 21 November 1911, [1]–4; Kendle, *The Colonial*, 183–184; May, 553.
200 According to the Chancellor, the budget was called "Lloyd George's People's Budget" and although it was centred around social welfare legislation, income from increased taxes were also to go to a new naval arms programme. For more on this issue, see Lee, Geoffrey, *The People's Budget: An Edwardian Tragedy*, London: Shepheard-Walwyn, 2008.
201 Hall, *Commonwealth*, 33–34.
202 Johnson, Franklyn Arthur, *Defence by Committee: The British Committee of Imperial Defence 1885–1959*, London: Oxford University Press, 1960, 53–54.
203 PD, HoC, 4th Series, Vol. 118, 5 March 1903, 1579, 1582–1583.

204 Johnson, 57–58.
205 Cf. Cd. 1932, *Report of the War Office (Reconstitution) Committee*, Part 1, London: HMSO, 1904; Cd. 1968, *Report of the War Office (Reconstitution) Committee*, Part 2, London: HMSO, 1904; Cd. 2002, *Report of the War Office (Reconstitution) Committee*, Part 3, London: HSMO, 1904.
206 Hankey, Maurice Pascal Alers, *Diplomacy by Conference: Studies in Public Affairs, 1920–1946*, London: Ernest Benn, 1946, 87.
207 Dugdale, Blanche Elizabeth Campbell, *Arthur James Balfour: 1848–1905*, Vol. 1, London: Hutchinson & Co., 1939, 277; *PD, HoC*, 4th Series, Vol. 118, 5 March 1903, 1649.
208 See Cd. 2200, *Committee of Imperial Defence: Copy of Treasury Minute Dated 4th May 1904, as to Secretariat*, London: HMSO, 1904; MacKintosh, John P., "The Role of the Committee of Imperial Defence before 1914", *The English Historical Review* 77, No. 304, 1962, 493; TNA, CAB 17/77, *Treasury Minute Dated 4th May, 1904*, [111A].
209 Cf. Hankey, *Diplomacy*, 84–85; TNA, CAB 1/4/37, A. J. B[alfour], A Note on the Constitution of the Defence Committee, 29 February 1904, [1]–5.
210 Dugdale, Vol. 1, 276; Johnson, 93–105.
211 *PD, HoC*, 4th Series, Vol. 139, 2 August 1904, 618–619.
212 Cunningham, 71.
213 Cf. Dewey, Vol. 1, 295; Silburn, Percy Arthur Baxter, *The Colonies and Imperial Defence*, London: Longmans & Co, 1909, 166–167.
214 Cd. 3523, 83; TNA, CAB 17/77, Resolution of Commonwealth of Australia, [1]–3.
215 From the end of the 19th century, the Dominions had ordinarily been able to express their views on overseas defence matters through the Colonial Defence Committee, which was replaced by the Overseas Sub-Committee of the Committee of Imperial Defence in 1908, which was subsequently referred to in a shorter form, the Overseas Defence Committee. See more cf. Cd. 3524, *Colonial Conference, 1907: Papers Laid and before the Colonial Conference, 1907*, London: HMSO, 1907, 16; Hankey, Maurice Pascal Alers, *The Supreme Command, 1914–1918*, Vol. 2, London: George Allen & Unwin, 1961, 125; *PD, HoC*, 5th Series, Vol. 41, 25 July 1912, 1388; TNA, CAB 2/2, Committee of Imperial Defence: Minutes of the 110th Meeting, 4 May 1911, 6; TNA, CO 886/2/5, Dominions No. 12, M. Nathan, The Colonial Defence Committee, 11 June 1909, 45–48.
216 Hall, *Commonwealth*, 40.
217 For more on establishment of the Imperial General Staff, see Amery, Leopold Stennett, *The Problem of the Army*, London: Edward Arnold, 1903, 119–136; Cd. 3523, 94–121; Cd. 4475, *Imperial Conference: Correspondence Relating to the Proposed Formation of an Imperial General Staff*, London: HMSO, 1909; TNA, CO 886/2/7, Dominions No. 14, Further Correspondence Relating to Proposed Formation of an Imperial General Staff, July 1909, 45–48.
218 Borden, Robert Laird, *The War and the Future*, London: Hodder & Stoughton, 1917, 17–18; TNA, CO 886/3/2, Imperial General Staff, [Do] Nos. 92–102, [73–81].
219 See TNA, CO 886/2/8, Dominions No. 15, Imperial Conference on the Subject of the Defence of the Empire, 1909: Minutes and Proceedings, October 1909, [1]–93.
220 For more on the armament of the German navy, see Dufek, Pavel, *Německé námořní zbrojení a vztah Velké Británie a Německa do roku 1906*, PhD Thesis, Praha: Univerzita Karlova, 2002.

221 Cd. 4948, *Imperial Conference: Correspondence and Papers Relating to a Conference with Representatives of the Self-Governing Dominions on the Naval and Military Defence of the Empire*, London: HMSO, 1909, 18. On the issue of Canadian defence in more detail, see Gooch, John, "Great Britain and the Defence of Canada, 1896–1914", *The Journal of Imperial and Commonwealth History* 2, No. 2, 1974, 368–385.

222 New Zealand spontaneously offered funds for construction of another Dreadnought-type battleship for the British fleet. McCraw, David J., "The Zenith of Realism in New Zealand's Foreign Policy", *Australian Journal of Politics and History* 48, No. 3, 2002, 356; Sarty, Roger, "Canadian Maritime Defence 1892–1914", *The Canadian Historical Review* 71, No. 4, 1990, 479.

223 TNA, CO 886/2/9, Dominions No. 16, Defence Conference, 1909: Confidential Papers Laid Before of the Imperial Defence Conference, 1909, September 1909, 33.

224 Hall, *Commonwealth*, 35.

225 Cd. 1299, 3.

226 Skelton, *Life*, 75.

227 During the 1887 Colonial Conference, the self-governing colonies in the Pacific agreed on joint funding to support naval fleets in Australian waters. Gordon, Donald C., "The Admiralty and Dominion Navies, 1902–1914", *The Journal of Modern History* 33, No. 4, 1961, 408.

228 See more in Overlack, Peter, "German Assessments of the British-Australian Relations, 1901–1914", *The Australian Journal of Politics and History* 50, No. 2, 2004, 194–210; Overlack, Peter, "German Interest in Australian Defence, 1901–1914: New Insights into a Precarious Position in the Eve of War", *The Australian Journal of Politics and History* 40, No. 1, 1993, 36–51; Shields, R. A., "Australian Opinion and Defence of the Empire: A Study in Imperial Relations 1880–1890", *The Australian Journal of Politics and History* 10, No. 1, 1964, 41–53.

229 See Cd. 1597, *Colonial Conference, 1902: Memorandum on Sea Power and the Principles Involved in It*, London: HMSO, 1903, 4–6.

230 Marder, Arthur Jacob, *The Anatomy of British Sea Power*, New York: Putnam & Co., 1940, 464.

231 For more on the defensive importance of Australian waters, see Cd. 4325, *Australasia: Correspondence Relating to the Naval Defence of Australia and New Zealand*, London: HMSO, 1908.

232 Cd. 1299, 60; Ollivier, Vol. 1, 153–154; Preston, Richard A., *Canadian Defence Policy and the Development of the Canadian Nation 1867–1917*, Ottawa: Canadian Historical Association, 1970, 18.

233 Prime Minister Alfred Deakin, for example, accepted Australian financial support for the construction of warships on condition they would subsequently be deployed in Australian waters. Cf. Albertini, Rudolf von, "England als Weltmacht und der Strukturwandel des Commonwealth", *Historische Zeitschrift* 208, No. 1, 1969, 58–59; Gordon, 414; Hall, *Commonwealth*, 36, 37; McIntyre, W. David, *The Commonwealth of Nations: Origins and Impact, 1869–1971*, Minneapolis: University of Minnesota Press, 1977, 170.

234 Cunningham, 85.

235 Neatby, H. Blair, "Laurier and Imperialism", *Report of the Annual Meeting of the Canadian Historical Association/Rapports annuels de la Société historique du Canada* 34, No. 1, 1955, 30.

236 Canada, *Parliamentary Debates* (hereafter *CPD*), *House of Commons* (hereafter *HoC*), 5 February 1900, 64–72, Dawson, Robert MacGregor (Ed.),

The Development of Dominion Status, 1900–1936, London: Frank Cass & Co, 1965, 135.
237 Gordon, 412; Hall, *Commonwealth*, 34, 37.
238 Only in the event of extreme threat to the Empire would the creation of an Imperial army be accepted. Cd. 4948, 19.
239 See more in Cd. 4611, *Army: Memorandum by the Army Council on the Existing Army System and on the Present State of the Military Forces in the United Kingdom*, London: HMSO, 1909; Cd. 5135, *Dominions No. 2: Report of the Dominions Department of the Colonial Office for the Year 1909–1910*, London: HMSO, 1910, 3–4; Johnson, 107; Preston, Richard A., *Canada and 'Imperial Defence'*, Toronto: University of Toronto Press, 1967.
240 Berger, Carl, *The Sense of Power: Studies in the Ideas of Canadian Imperialism 1867–1914*, Toronto: University of Toronto Press, 1970, 233.
241 For more on this issue, see Borden, Robert Laird, *The Naval Question: Speech Delivered by Mr. R.L. Borden, M.P. 12th January, 1910*, [Ottawa: s. n., 1910]; Borden, Robert Laird, *The Naval Question: Speech Delivered by Mr. R.L. Borden, M.P. 3rd February, 1910*, [Ottawa: s. n., 1910]; *Canada and the Navy*, Ottawa: [s. n., 1909].
242 Sarty, 483.
243 Cf. Asquith, Herbert Henry, *The Genesis of the War*, London: Cassell & Co, 1923, 133–134; DeCelles, Alfred Duclos, *Laurier et son temps*, Montréal: Librairie Beauchemin, 1920, 77; Grimshaw, 176.
244 See more in Cd. 5746-2, *Dominions No. 9: Imperial Conference, 1911: Papers Laid before the Imperial Conference: Naval and Military Defence*, London: HMSO, 1911.
245 Asquith particularly appreciated consultation with the Dominions regarding Imperial defence policy, and as such did not rule out their future involvement in the Committee of Imperial Defence once it had greater executive powers. Cf. Dewey, Vol. 1, 283; *PD, HoC*, 5th Series, Vol. 8, 29 July 1909, 1395–1396.
246 Johnson, 107.
247 See Bourassa, Henri, *Le projet de loi navale: Sa nature, ses consequences: Discours prononce au Monument National le 20 janvier 1910*, [Montreal: s. n.], 1910.
248 Cf. Courtney, William Leonard – Courtney, J. E., *Pillars of the Empire: Studies & Impressions*, London: Jarrolds, [1918], 79–85; Hancock, "The 1911", 367–368; McArthur, Peter, *Sir Wilfrid Laurier*, London: J. M. Dent & Sons, 1919, 81–82.
249 Hankey, *The Supreme*, Vol. 1, 125–127.
250 MacKintosh, 496.
251 Johnson, 92.
252 *PD, HoC*, 5th Series, Vol. 19, 25 July 1910, 1895.
253 Some of the most significant included Oversea Defence Committee, or Home Ports Defence Committee. *PD, HoC*, 5th Series, Vol. 41, 25 July 1912, 1388–1390.
254 Hankey, *The Supreme*, Vol. 1, 85.
255 Kendle, *The Colonial*, 192.
256 Hankey, *The Supreme*, Vol. 1, 130; Kendle, *The Colonial*, 192–193.
257 Cd. 5745, 23.
258 Richard Jebb believed it was a cunning British government attempt at transferring the entire foreign relations and defence agenda away from the Conference and into the competency of the Committee of Imperial Defence. Jebb, Richard, *The Britannic Question: A Survey of Alternatives*, London: Longmans & Co, 1913, 41–50.

259 Nish, Ian H., "Australia and the Anglo-Japanese Alliance, 1901–1911", *The Australian Journal of Politics and History* 9, No. 2, 1963, 209.
260 Hancock, "The 1911", 365–366.
261 Gooch, George Peabody – Temperley, Harold (Eds.), *British Documents on the Origins of the War, 1898–1914: Anglo-German Tension: Armaments and Negotiation*, 1907–12, Vol. 6, London: HMSO, 1930, Appendix V, 781.
262 Cf. Gowen, Robert Joseph, "British Legerdemain at the 1911 Imperial Conference: The Dominions, Defense Planning, and the Renewal of the Anglo-Japanese Alliance", *The Journal of Modern History* 52, No. 3, 1980, 385–413; Hall, *Commonwealth*, 77; Delaquis, Danys R. X., *Une variante nationale du continentalisme le Canada et l'alliance anglo-japonaise, 1919 à 1921*, MA Thesis, Moncton: Université de Moncton, 1995, 49–54; Lowe, Peter, "The British Empire and the Anglo-Japanese Alliance, 1911–1915", *History* 54, No. 181, 1969, 213–214; Meaney, Neville K., "'A Proposition of the Highest International Importance': Alfred Deakin's Pacific Agreement Proposal and Its Significance for Australian-Imperial Relations", *Journal of Commonwealth Political Studies* 5, No. 3, 1967, 201; Meaney, Neville, *A History of Australian Defence and Foreign Policy 1901–23: The Search for Security in the Pacific, 1901–14*, Vol. 1, Sydney: Sydney University Press, 1976; Nish, *Australia*, 207–208.
263 TNA, CAB 1/4, No. 78–C, Australia and New Zealand: Strategic Situation in the Event of the Anglo-Japanese Alliance Being Determined: Memorandum by the Committee of Imperial Defence, Whitehall Gardens, 3 May 1911, 14–16 [242–243].
264 Lloyd George, David, *War Memoirs*, Vol. 2, London: Odhams Press, 1938, 28; TNA, CAB 2/2, Committee of Imperial Defence: Minutes of the 111th Meeting, 26 May 1911, 10–15.
265 TNA, CAB 2/2, Committee of Imperial Defence: Minutes of the 111th Meeting, 26 May 1911, 16–18.
266 Cf. Asquith, 122–127; Urtis, Lionel, *The Problem of the Commonwealth*, London: Macmillan, 1916, 108–114; Egerton, George W., "The Dominions and the Peace Settlement", *United Empire: The Royal Colonial Institute Journal* 6, No. 6, 1915, 426–427.
267 TNA, CAB 2/2, Committee of Imperial Defence: Minutes of the 111th Meeting, 26 May 1911, 36.
268 Cf. Bennett, Neville R., "Consultation or Information? Britain, the Dominions and the Renewal of the Anglo-Japanese Alliance, 1911", *The New Zealand Journal of History* 4, No. 2, 1970, 178–194; Hall, *Commonwealth*, 82.
269 Cf. Asquith, 128–131; CAC, Hankey Papers (hereafter HP), HNKY 7/6–7/7, Copy of Memo Sent to McKenna, 11 May 1911, [1]–15; CAC, HP, HNKY 7/6–7/7, Memorandum on the Officering of the Navies of the Dominions, [1]–3; Hancock, "The 1911", 369; TNA, CAB 2/2, Committee of Imperial Defence: Minutes of the 112th Meeting, 29 May 1911, 1–9; Tunstall, W. C. B., "Imperial Defence, 1897–1914", in: *The Cambridge History of the British Empire: The Empire-Commonwealth 1870–1919*, Vol. 3, Cambridge: Cambridge University Press, 1967, 595–596.
270 Hall, *Commonwealth*, 86.
271 Asquith, 131–134.
272 TNA, CAB 2/2, Committee of Imperial Defence: Minutes of the 113th Meeting, 30 May 1911, 1–15.
273 Cf. Johnson, 111–113; TNA, CAB 2/2, Committee of Imperial Defence: Minutes of the 113th Meeting, 30 May 1911, 16–17; TNA, CAB 5/3, [D.] 94–C, Proceedings of the Committee of Imperial Defence at the 113th Meeting, 30 May 1911, 2–3.

274 Borden, Robert Laird, Sir, *Splendid Record of the Borden Government Naval Policy Clearly Defined*, Ottawa: Federal Press Agency, 1913, 22.
275 Cd. 5745, 97–99.
276 For more on this issue, cf. Hall, *Commonwealth*, 93–96; Keith, Arthur Berriedale, *Imperial Unity and the Dominions*, Oxford: Clarendon Press, 1916, 288–289; Lauterpacht, H. – Jennings, R. Y., "International Law and Colonial Questions, 1870–1914", in: *The Cambridge History of the British Empire: The Empire-Commonwealth 1870–1919*, Vol. 3, Cambridge: Cambridge University Press, 1967, 707–710.
277 Ollivier, Vol. 2, 133.
278 Watt, Donald Cameron, "Imperial Defence Policy and Imperial Foreign Policy, 1911–1939 – A Neglected Paradox?" *Journal of Commonwealth Political Studies* 1, No. 1, 1963, 267.
279 Hancock, "The 1911", 357.
280 Dafoe, 57–58.
281 Dewey, Vol. 1, 147.
282 Cf. Hall, *Commonwealth*, 103; Hancock, William Keith, *Australia*, Melbourne: Jacaranda Press, 1966, 221.
283 Asquith, 120–121.
284 Kendle, *The Colonial*, 185–186.
285 Glazebrook, 273.
286 Jebb, *The Britannic*, 43–45; Dewey, Vol. 1, 294–295.
287 Kendle, *The Round Table Movement and*, 114.
288 Kendle, *The Colonial*, 198.
289 See more in MacQuarrie, Heath, "Robert Borden and the Election of 1911", *The Canadian Journal of Economics and Political Science/Revue canadienne d'Economique et de Science politique* 25, No. 3, 1959, 271–286.
290 Courtney – Courtney, 92.
291 Borden, *Splendid*, 18–23; Soward, Frederic H., "Sir Robert Borden and Canada's External Policy, 1911–1920", *Report of the Annual Meeting of the Canadian Historical Association/Rapports annuels de la Société historique du Canada* 20, No. 1, 1941, 65–82.
292 Kendle, *The Colonial*, 199–200.
293 PD, HoC, 5th Series, Vol. 35, 20 March 1912, 1946.
294 For more on Borden's meetings, cf. Borden, Robert Laird, *Bill relatif aux forces navales de l'empire: discours prononcé par le Très Hon. R.L. Borden, le 5 décembre 1912* (Ottawa: s. n., 1912); *Canada and the Navy: Reasons by the Rt Hon. R. L. Borden, M.P., in Favour of a Canadian Naval Service and Against a Contribution*, Ottawa: Central Information Office of the Canadian Liberal Party, 1913; Gordon, 414–417; Tucker, Gilbert Norman, "The Naval Policy of Sir Robert Borden, 1912–14", *The Canadian Historical Review* 28, No. 1, 1947, 1–30; Tunstall, *Imperial*, 596–597.
295 Kendle, *The Colonial*, 201.
296 Brown – Cook, 205.
297 Eayrs, 7.
298 For more on Amery's positions, see CAC, AP, AMEL 1/2/20, Some Suggestions on Imperial Policy, November 1912, [1]–14.
299 CAC, AP, AMEL 2/2/8, L. S. A[mery] to Deakin, 29 July 1912, 2.
300 CAC, AP, AMEL 1/2/18, Parliamentary Empire Tour: Meeting of the Imperial Mission Held at the Connaught Rooms, Great Queen St., London, 2 February 1914, 5.
301 The Canadian Prime Minister met up in England, for example, with Viscount Alfred Milner, Lionel Curtis, Sir Valentine Chirol, Sir James Meston and Viscount Waldorf Astor and his wife. Kendle, *The Colonial*, 201.

302 Cf. TNA, CAB 17/101, Hankey to Harcourt, 3 July 1912, [1–4]; TNA, CAB 17/101, Hankey to Grey, 29 July 1912, [5–7].
303 Watt, 268.
304 *PD, HoC,* 5th Series, Vol. 41, 22 July 1912, 872; *PD, HoC,* 5th Series, Vol. 41, 25 July 1912, 1386–1387.
305 Cf. "Canada and the Navy", *The Round Table* 2, No. 8, 1912, 634–637; Kendle, *The Colonial,* 205.
306 D'Egville, 210.
307 Kendle, *The Colonial,* 207–209.
308 Cf. CAC, HP, HNKY, 7/8, Future Work of the Committee of Imperial Defence, 22 November 1911, [1]–11; TNA, CAB 17/101, Hankey to Harcourt, Representation of the Dominions on the Committee of Imperial Defence, 5 November 1912, [11].
309 *CPD, HoC,* 5 December 1912, 676–693, Dawson, *The Development,* 161–165.
310 Cf. The Secretary of State [Harcourt] to the Governor-General of Australia, the Governor-General of the Union of South Africa, and the Governors of New Zealand and Newfoundland, Downing Street, 10 December 1912, in: Cd. 6560, *Dominions No. 13: Despatch from the Secretary of State for the Colonies As to the Representation of the Self-Governing Dominions on the Committee of Imperial Defence,* London: HMSO, 1913, No. 1, 2–3; Cd. 6863, *Dominions No. 14: Report for 1912–13 Relating to the Self-Governing Dominions: Prepared in the Dominions Department of the Colonial Office,* London: HMSO, 1913, 9–10.
311 "Policy and Sea Power", *The Round Table* 3, No. 10, 1913, 197–231.
312 TNA, CAB 5/3, [D.] 101–C, Committee of Imperial Defence: Representation of the Dominions on the Committee of Imperial Defence at the 113th Meeting, 5 April 1913, [64–70].
313 Kendle, *The Colonial,* 213–214.
314 Some who did take part were, e.g. Sir James Allen (New Zealand), Sir Edward Morris (Newfoundland) and others. Hankey, *Diplomacy,* 90.
315 Cf. Johnson, 124; Keith, Arthur Berriedale, *War Government of the British Dominions,* Oxford: Clarendon Press, 1921, 17.
316 Only partial constitutional discussions took place between Richard Jebb and Leopold Amery on whether it was better to use the term "alliance" or the term "union". CAC, AP, AMEL 1/2/18, Alliance or Union, January/February 1914, [1]–16.
317 Cf. The Governor-General [Denman] to the Secretary of State [Harcourt], 19 December 1912, in: Cd. 7347, *Dominions No. 15: Correspondence Relating to the Representation of the Self-Governing Dominions on the Committee of Imperial Defence,* London: HMSO, 1914, No. 2, 6; The Secretary of State [Harcourt] to the Governor-General [Denman], 10 January 1913, in: Cd. 7347, No. 5, 7.
318 Tunstall, W. B., "The Development of the Imperial Conference, 1887–1914", in: *The Cambridge History of the British Empire: The Empire-Commonwealth 1870–1919,* Vol. 3, Cambridge 1967, 436.
319 Hall, *Commonwealth,* 103–105.

3 The Empire During the War and Post-War Period

3.1 The Imperial War Cabinet and the Imperial War Conferences of 1917–1918

The First World War was the greatest test of the Empire's cohesion since the first Dominions were formed.[1] The British Empire joined the fights as one whole, even though the Dominions still formally had a subordinate status to the mother country. Australian Prime Minister Andrew Fisher noted: "Australia is part of the Empire. When the Empire is at war, so is Australia at War ... [and – J. V.] we will stand behind the Mother Country to hold and defend her to the last man and the last shilling."[2] Although it was up to the Dominions to decide on the extent of their involvement in the war effort, pre-war agreements meant that their fleets and expeditionary forces came under the command of the British Admiralty and the head of the Army.[3] Although the Dominions' military deployment was not to the same level as that of the mother country, they were of marked assistance.[4] The defeats and victories of the overseas territories, symbolised by the heroism of Australian and New Zealand forces during operations on the Gallipoli Peninsula, the Canadians at Passchendaele and Vimy Ridge and the South Africans in occupying German South West Africa and German East Africa, became deeply engraved in the collective memory of the Dominions, boosting nationalist feeling and weakening the populations' imperial patriotism, deepening the desire for policies of independence.[5]

At the start of the war, the Dominions were internally united and as such were able to fully focus on the war effort. Once losses began to mount and compulsory conscription into the army began, they were met with a groundswell of criticism from opposition ranks, and political unity was lost.[6] Canada saw its politics split into anglophone and francophone parts,[7] the Union of South Africa had to deal with disloyal Afrikaners and Australia had to hold a referendum on issues of war.[8] Over time, voices began to emerge overseas calling for more frequent consultation and extensive exchange of information between the Dominions and the mother country, because brief information and speculation in the daily papers was no longer satisfactory for Dominion statesmen. Over the course of 1915, Canada's Prime Minister Borden visited Britain's Secretary of State for the Colonies Andrew Bonar Law to find out more about events in the Empire. Over the course of discussions, it transpired that it was impractical for Dominion representatives to "have to travel" to London for information. Borden considered the war a conflict of the whole Empire, and not just Great Britain, and as such, in January 1916 he openly demanded the introduction of an appropriate system of consultation which would help to achieve better co-ordination of the war effort and also deepen relations between the self-governing territories and the mother country.[9]

During the first months of 1916, the new Australian Prime Minister, William Morris "Billy" Hughes, travelled to London to meet Asquith, whose coalition cabinet was slowly losing support amongst politicians. On the way, he visited William Massey in New Zealand and Borden in Canada, agreeing on Dominion priorities with them – to gain involvement in decision-making and to focus on the Empire's war policy. In March, Hughes took part in a meeting of the cabinet at Asquith's invitation, and subsequently in June he had the opportunity to defend Australian interests as a younger member of the British delegation at the Allied Powers' Economic Conference in Paris.[10] Asquith remained inflexible, however, and rejected any greater involvement of the Dominions in co-ordinating the war effort.

The Empire experienced a number of moments of tension during the war. As these critical moments grew in number, proposals for creating an effective imperial union which would accelerate co-operation between the Empire's nations were posited ever more frequently.[11] No actual steps could be made, however, until the fall of Asquith's cabinet.[12] Over the course of 1916, the British government's support weakened, and it was also facing more frequent criticisms about the incompetent and ineffective conduct of the war.[13] There was a cabinet reshuffle on 19 December 1916 with David Lloyd George coming in as Prime Minister, someone who did not hide his greater sympathy for Dominion demands. As such, he did not waste time, and in his first speech in the House of Commons as British Prime Minister, he invited the Dominions to take part in the Imperial Conference which was to take place in spring 1917.[14] He also called on the Dominions to choose delegates who could expand the previous five-member British War Cabinet, assuring them that he would fully respect their equal status and right to decide upon the conduct of the war.[15] In parallel, communication between Britain's Colonial Office and the overseas governments was improved.[16]

Due to the new composition of the war cabinet, Sir Maurice Hankey renamed it the Imperial War Cabinet.[17] With hindsight, Asquith determined that linking the Imperial Conference meeting in 1911 with the meeting of the Committee of Imperial Defence was a precedent which predetermined the future composition of the 1917 Imperial War Cabinet. While the system of conferences was based on formalities and discretion and their course and resolutions were made public, meetings of the Committee of Imperial Defence, in which serious issues of foreign and defence policy were discussed, were held behind closed doors. The fact that India did not have its representation at Imperial Conferences, and that it was not customary for standard conference discussions to take place in secret, played a part in the establishment of the Imperial War Cabinet,[18] headed by David Lloyd George and with its own executive secretariat. Australian Prime Minister Hughes was unable to take part in discussions due to a complicated domestic political situation, and as such, in 1917 Australia was not represented.[19]

The Imperial Cabinet met at the same time as the British War Cabinet, which had its own permanent Cabinet Secretariat from 1916,[20] headed for two decades by the influential figure Hankey, who also managed the Committee of Imperial Defence and from 1917 also the British Secretary of the Supreme War Council. Due to the extent of war co-operation, the original "British" secretariats gained an international character, as such becoming Imperial institutions co-ordinating the Empire's military and political affairs.[21] In early 1917, Hankey combined the role of Cabinet Secretary with the administrative parts of the Imperial War Cabinet, helping to achieve more extensive co-operation between British and Dominion officials, who accompanied "their" prime ministers at Imperial meetings.[22] The roles and posts which Hankey held gave him a detailed overview of all aspects of British war policy.[23] The Committee of Imperial Defence itself underwent significant changes during the war. Although until 1914 it had been a place where Dominion representatives had been able to generally discuss matters of defence,[24] it gradually lost influence to a number of smaller committees over which its competencies were divided up.[25] Although Haldane wanted it to move from being an advisory body to become an executive body, this did not happen.[26]

The Imperial War Cabinet first met on 20 March 1917.[27] Although two cabinets met in London headed by the British Prime Minister, they each had precisely defined competencies, and as such the Imperial Cabinet was not involved in Britain's conduct of the war, instead focusing "only" on the management of military operations and determining peace objectives from an imperial perspective.[28] Canadian Prime Minister Borden in particular perceived the establishment of the Imperial Cabinet as an important milestone in the Empire's constitutional development against the background of the war.[29] He particularly stressed the fact that the meetings were held under a principle of equality, even if the British Prime Minister had the status of *primus inter pares*, and that each Dominion was able to speak freely of matters which immediately affected them, as well as general problems.[30] He also perceived the establishment of the

Imperial Cabinet as that of a new type of Imperial institution.[31] Lloyd George did not share Borden's enthusiasm. He considered establishment of the Imperial Cabinet and a single Imperial foreign policy line as merely a strategic necessity as a result of the events of the war.[32] Despite all this, the Cabinet in 1917–1918 was the most representative forum at which overseas statesmen were able to discuss Imperial affairs.[33]

On the one hand, the creation and composition of the Imperial Cabinet was a satisfactory solution to the critical lack of information which the Dominions had felt themselves to have before its establishment; but on the other hand, the original expectation that it would comprise all Dominion prime ministers did not come to pass.[34] As such, on 17 May 1917, Lloyd George announced procedural changes to which cabinet members had already unanimously consented. He determined that for 1918, the Cabinet would hold its regular meeting once a year and that only in the event of unanticipated situations which had to be dealt with immediately would an extraordinary meeting take place, whose members would comprise the British Prime Minister and his Dominion counterparts, or their named representatives and a representative of India nominated by the Indian government. This step eliminated certain Dominions having double representation (such as Canada).[35]

Members of the Cabinet Secretariat did not consider this innovation to be sufficient and endeavoured to achieve bolder transformation. Leopold Stennett Amery, who assisted Hankey at the Imperial Cabinet Secretariat, perceived the establishment of the Imperial Cabinet as the "first acknowledgement of Dominions' equal political status to British statesmen", and as such he anticipated that it would fully satisfy the political demands of the self-governing territories since it was a "real cabinet". Therefore, in the interest of maintaining its effectiveness, he stressed keeping continuity of participants because he thought that overly frequent changes in members would not be beneficial. He also proposed that it would be best if the Dominions named permanent members, ideally ministers without portfolio, who would remain permanently in London so they would not have to travel back overseas for their duties. The permanent representatives would be able to take part in weekly meetings of the newly established Committee of Foreign Affairs, comprising the British Foreign Secretary as Chair alongside the Dominion representatives. Since the overseas ministers would thus partially "fill in for" the role of High Commissioners (such as Sir George Perley of Canada), Amery left the question open and entirely within the competencies of the relevant governments. In the second section of the memorandum, Amery looked at the issue of the Imperial Secretariat. He had been involved in developing the original Deakin Plan of 1907, a proposed independent secretariat for arranging the agenda for conferences, whose activities the British Colonial Office would be unable to affect. Amery proposed that during the war, the Secretariat be used as an administrative facility for Dominion ministers taking part in meetings not just at the Imperial War Conference, but also the Imperial War Cabinet.[36] He arranged his fundamental reform similarly carefully.[37]

The First World War moved "non-war" problems and issues to the back-burner only for a time. By 1916, the years-long dispute over reorganisation of the Colonial Office reopened. Contemporaries considered establishment of the Imperial War Cabinet as Lloyd George's greatest success because he had introduced the principles of direct communication on important matters of the Empire, thus recognising Dominion equality and indirectly contributing to a decline in the Colonial Office's prestige amongst the Dominions. The previously rigid system for sending messages from the Colonial Office via Governors, or Governors-General, did not correspond to the demands of the era, nor to the status of the Dominions within the Empire. As such, Amery proposed that communication between Dominion ministers and the mother country take place directly and that Governors or Governors-General be only copied in so they do not have to fulfil the role of "postmen" for the Colonial Office. Amery also "dusted off" the request made at the 1911 Imperial Conference and requested that Dominion affairs be moved from the Colonial Office, with establishment of a new Imperial Office or Dominion Office which would not be run by an ordinary official, but rather a statesman with an overview of complex Imperial affairs. Amery believed that separation of the Dominion agenda was a courtesy to the self-governing territories which would allow for peaceful development of relationships between the Dominions and the mother country.[38]

Over the course of 1917, Leopold Amery developed his thoughts on the Imperial system in further detail. Although he conceded that creation of the Imperial Cabinet did not necessarily have to mean the creation of an Imperial federation or another form of centralised Imperial government making decisions on executive, legislative and financial matters across the Empire, he was of the conviction that effective co-operation was possible on the basis of joint consultation, which he perceived as a condition for implementing a common policy. As such, he proposed establishing a Ministry for Imperial Affairs which would focus on general relations between the governments of the Empire's countries and wide Imperial topics; the administration of dependent territories would be left to the Colonial Office. The changes were not meant to impact on the Foreign Office. Amery also advocated the establishment of an Imperial Ministry of Defence and splitting what was then the single Imperial General Staff in accordance with the branch of the armed forces into the Imperial Military General Staff, the Admiralty War Staff and the smaller Air Staff. The Ministry of Imperial Trade and Communications was to take care of economic and transport policy, while finance was to be dealt with by the Imperial Treasury. The system of Imperial Conferences was to expand to become a conference of parliamentary delegations also including opposition members of parliament from the Dominions and representatives of India.³⁹

The war effort stopped all constitutional debate at an official level for a period of time. Members of the Round Table Movement, however, did not give up. They thought that a suitable moment would soon arrive for intensive discussion of Imperial affairs, although they accepted they could not expect immediate progress in constitutional matters.⁴⁰ When the war broke out, the British government had assumed it would be a good idea to move the ordinary Imperial Conference which was to have taken place in 1915 to a time after the war. Influential Canadian members of the Round Table Movement, however, had disagreed with this and had called upon the Canadian Prime Minister at the time, Sir Robert Borden, not to agree to the postponement.⁴¹ In December 1914, Australian Prime Minister Fisher also expressed his support for the Conference taking place during the war. As such, Britain's Secretary of State for the Colonies, Lewis Harcourt, announced that although the planned conference in 1915 would not go ahead, the British government intended in future to consult conditions for agreeing peace with the Dominions.⁴²

During the first two years of the war, Movement members focused on analysing Curtis's memoranda. Curtis was busy too, and in mid-1915 he submitted a document to his closest colleagues for internal assessment, called *The Project of the Commonwealth*.⁴³ In October 1915 it was published in book form and entitled *The Problem of the Commonwealth*. It was subsequently sent out to Dominion members of the Movement overseas, although it was not as yet made public. Curtis's publication comprised two sections. In the first section, the author gave a comprehensive description of the political, economic, social, institutional and constitutional problems surrounding the establishment and development of the Self-Governing Colonies, or Dominions. In the second section, he came to the conclusion that the Dominions must have greater control over Imperial foreign and defence policy. This was to be achieved by establishing an Imperial parliament responsible to all voters in self-governing parts of the Empire and having the right to declare war, agree peace and impose taxes. He consistently emphasised his financial proposals, including the principle of joint tax collection, as the key aspect of his proposed Imperial arrangement. Curtis did not preclude other dependent territories playing a part in decision-making, and as such the Dominions would have to accept that they would be sharing influence not just with the mother country. He proposed enshrining these changes within a treaty. He saw the collapse of the Empire as the only other alternative.⁴⁴

Movement supporters were not enthusiastic about Curtis's project.⁴⁵ Its Australian and Canadian members in particular openly criticised "Imperial" taxation and India's insufficiently defined status. Curtis was not inclined to make any changes; as such he decided to publish the book himself in spring 1916 and take full responsibility for its contents.⁴⁶

Although Milner gave significant support to Curtis in publishing his work and agreed with his ideas, he did not agree with the submitted project.[47] Despite all Curtis's attempts, commentators continued to link the book, which had caused significant criticism, to the political positions and thoughts of the Round Table Movement.[48]

From 21 March to 27 April 1917, the Imperial War Conference[49] took place at the same time as the closed meeting of the Imperial War Cabinet, which was exceptionally chaired by Secretary of State for the Colonies Walter Long, later 1st Viscount Long.[50] In contrast to the strictly confidential decisions of the Cabinet, the conclusions of the Conference discussions were partially made public.[51] Although the Imperial Cabinet and the Imperial Conference did not have executive powers, neither were they ordinary meetings of statesmen.[52] The course of the war was having a significant impact on events in the Empire, and as such it was essential that the conference take place on a similar basis to 1911 when Asquith had ensured a joint meeting of the Conference with the Committee of Imperial Defence. Indian representatives' special position next to British and Dominion representatives stressed the unusualness of the meeting.[53] As such, it is no surprise that questions of general co-operation and the post-war order dominated the meeting, and matters relating to constitutional relations, India's representation at future Imperial Conferences and Imperial preferences were dealt with only marginally.[54]

Dominion statesmen were very interested in the Empire's future, and as such placed their greatest hopes in discussions regarding the Empire's constitutional arrangements, which took place at the ninth conference session on 16 April 1917. The issue of the Dominions' equal status to the mother country most weighed on the mind of Canadian Prime Minister Borden, although he did not expressly advocate absolute equality. His New Zealand counterpart, William Massey, in contrast strived to achieve continuity for the Imperial War Cabinet.[55] South Africa's General Smuts perceived the issue being looked at within a wider context because he considered the British Empire to be "the most important and fascinating problem in political and constitutional government which the world has ever seen," and because he believed in its ability to transform itself on the basis of principles of "freedom and equality". Smuts was convinced that any idea of federalising the Empire, or of some form of Curtis's economic, fiscal and political "super-State" should be abandoned, as these were based on erroneous assumptions, because an "Empire is not just a state, but a system of nations".[56]

Although with hindsight it is not clear whether Smuts or Borden are due more credit for promoting a "constitutional" resolution, its adoption represented a milestone in the Commonwealth's development.[57] The outcome of discussion and informal talks between Conference participants resulted in adoption of Resolution IX demanding modification of constitutional relationships between different parts of the Empire. Due to the importance of the topic, participants in the Imperial War Conference decided to dedicate a special Imperial Conference to the entire matter, which was to meet after the end of the war. They considered it essential to have "full recognition of the Dominions as autonomous nations in the Imperial Commonwealth, with India as an important part of it," in order to "take account of the rights of the Dominions and India to make decisions about foreign policy and have a say in foreign relationship," and in order to "secure effective permanent consultation on all important issues of Imperial nature".[58] The definition according to which the Dominions would be autonomous nations within a Commonwealth was of great significance for the future constitutional development of the Empire, because it served as a basis for the Balfour Declaration of 1926. At the same time there was a strengthening in India's status, which from 1918 was represented at Imperial meetings not just by the Secretary of State for India, but also by Indian delegates.[59]

The Imperial War Cabinet and Conference in 1917 repeatedly firmly rejected the idea of an Imperial federation. Thus, the idea of federalisation of the Empire could not be promoted in a similar way as it was at the Imperial Conference in 1911. Conference participants adopted the constitutional resolution in which, as Smuts stressed, negated the vision of an Imperial federation and rejected constitutional nationalism.[60] It turned out that Curtis's plan, which had won public attention in 1916–1917 and which involved the establishment of an Imperial parliament, did not arouse the interest, never mind support of the Dominion representatives. South African Prime Minister Botha preferred, "the idea of increasing those rights and making the Self-Governing Colonies ... putting in fact the Dominions on an equal footing with the Mother Country".[61]

Smuts's participation in Imperial War Cabinet meetings was often emphasised. Looking back, the South African general stated that, "I have never worked so hard in my life".[62] Shortly after the Imperial War Cabinet meeting ended, a proposal was submitted that he be named a member of the British government. It was anticipated that this step would lead to the "smooth unofficial continuation" of the Imperial Cabinet at a time when it was not sitting. However, a convincing argument emerged that only a British politician could be a government member, and as such Lloyd George offered Smuts the post of a member of parliament "for ideal Anglicisation". In September 1917, Smuts rejected a seat in the House of Commons after consultation with Botha; he remained in London until June 1919 and, surprisingly, continued to operate in Imperial politics.[63] His position in Britain was unique. Although he was merely representing the government of the Union of South Africa, did not hold any British ministerial post and was not officially named a member of the British War Cabinet, he nevertheless took part in its meetings.[64]

On 11 June 1918, a ten-day meeting of the Imperial Cabinet began in its new make-up on the basis of changes made in May 1917.[65] As in

1917, cabinet members met in parallel with the Imperial War Conference taking place at the same time. Compared to the previous year, there was a marked improvement in how well-informed the Dominion representatives were, and furthermore Australian representatives were also involved in decision-making. Due to the speed of events taking place on the Western Front,[66] matters of strategy and military decisions dominated the agenda, and as such the delegates took part in the meeting of the Supreme War Council on 5 July in Versailles.[67] However, Britain's military decisions did not avoid criticism from the Dominions. Prime Minister Borden in particular spoke highly critically of Britain's supreme command, accusing it of a lack of operational preparation and unnecessary material and human losses due to the casualties suffered by Canadian forces[68] at Passchandaele. His New Zealand counterpart, William Massey, had similar concerns.[69] In response to this criticism, Lloyd George set up a special Committee of Prime Ministers in order to investigate the steps of military command in the past, and make proposals for the future. Due to the fact that Smuts's military experience stood out amongst the other members of this new committee, and the fact the committee members met regularly, it held an important role alongside the Imperial War Cabinet.[70]

Over the course of the first half of 1918, Amery consulted selected Dominion statesmen on current proposals for innovating the Imperial Cabinet system,[71] and subsequently included their suggestions in a coherent structure which he presented internally to Dominion prime ministers on 29 June 1918 in the form of an extensive memorandum. He based it on the assumption that the Imperial Cabinet had proven itself during the war and that it represented a true form of government because it directed Imperial military and foreign policies. As such, he advocated setting up meetings in the post-war period too, as long as three basic conditions were met: (1) meetings would take place on the basis of personal and confidential consultations within a medium-large cabinet; (2) Dominion and British representatives would take part, ideally prime ministers; (3) it would be a responsible government. The Imperial Cabinet met the first two conditions, but the third represented a problem. To whom and for what was it to be responsible? Amery was of the opinion that if the overseas self-governing territories were to have equal status with the mother country, then responsibility should be shared equally amongst all nations involved. He repeatedly proposed establishing a Ministry for Imperial Affairs, in order to strengthen Imperial relations, and reorganising the Colonial Office. He also proposed Imperial Conferences be transformed into meetings of parliaments, something he thought would boost the Imperial Cabinet system's coherent vision.[72] He later gave more detail on the proposal: the number of Imperial Cabinet members should be just six, and he considered Lord Milner to be the most appropriate Dominions Secretary.[73]

Amery also noted the negative aspects of the idea. The principle of an Imperial Cabinet was a serious threat to the authority and importance of the system of Imperial Conferences, since both bodies met in parallel and because Cabinet discussions took place in a more open and confidential atmosphere than Conference meetings. Amery thought that it would be a pity if Imperial Conferences, enjoying recognition across the Empire, were to lose the position they had acquired over the generations. As such, he proposed that future constitutional changes should also include a redefinition of the essence of the Conference system, and adjustments to their agenda.[74]

Amery's idea stood in opposition to Curtis's notion[75] based on a joint and strictly defined administrative and executive power of the Empire and shared funds.[76] Although Amery's memorandum did not immediately resonate, it aroused substantial discussion.[77] In terms of content, it corresponded to his long-term position that the Empire's future unity depended on to what extent the Dominions were to be persuaded that they were equal partners to the mother country.[78]

In parallel with the Imperial Cabinet meetings, the issue of how the British cabinet and Dominion governments communicate with each other was discussed at the Imperial War Conference.[79] Due to the approaching anticipated victory of the Allied armies, the post-war form of Imperial co-operation was becoming a more pressing issue. In this regard, Amery did not particularly trust Hankey,[80] and as such focused on convincing the Prime Ministers of Australia and Canada. Hankey similarly did not trust Amery, his activities often contrary to the official line, and as such he did not hesitate to call him, "a scheming little devil".[81] Amery based his argument on the idea that if an Imperial Cabinet is viewed as an Imperial institution, then the method of communication should correspond to this position. "As a member of the Imperial Cabinet you are a colleague not only of Walter Long's, but also of Lloyd George's, Milner's and Balfour's," Amery told Australian Prime Minister Hughes, "and it would obviously be absurd if you could not communicate direct with your colleagues on common business, but only through the intermediary of a particular colleague, namely Long".[82]

The issue of whether the British Colonial Office would continue to be the only official "mediator" for communication between Dominions and the mother country, or whether another specialist department should be set up, was looked into as a key factor in shaping mutual relations.[83] On 8 July 1918, Amery, who continued to advocate reorganisation of the Colonial Office and the establishment of an Imperial Affairs Department, expressed his full support for Dominion demands, and he advised Canadian Prime Minister Borden not to put off dealing with the matter and called on him to look into it before the Dominion statesmen left London.[84] On 18 July, Conference participants passed a resolution in which they agreed that relations between Britain and the Dominions had reached such a level that it was essential to communicate directly with each other. They also asked the Imperial War Cabinet to undertake the necessary administrative measures and implement rules for this method of communication.[85] The Dominion statesmen saw adoption of this principle as confirmation of the equality of "sister nations" within the Empire. Australian Prime Minister Hughes thought that daily communication between the London government and Dominion cabinets should occur directly between governments and not between Governors-General or Governors and Ministries as had previously been the case.[86]

Members of the Imperial War Cabinet expressed their views on the demand on 30 July 1918. Although Amery had convinced Hankey that the only way forward was to remove Dominion affairs from the hands of the Colonial Office and noted that there had not been unnecessary sending of encryption books outside Britain,[87] the Dominion prime ministers took a different position. They stated that members of the Imperial Cabinet were entitled to communicate with the British Prime Minister directly and, in contrast, in terms of content, communication is reserved for dealing with Cabinet matters and standard messages should be sent via the British Colonial Office, with direct communication with the British Prime Minister occurring only exceptionally. They also agreed that in order to preserve the continuity of the Imperial War Cabinet agenda discussed at times in between standard meetings, Dominion prime ministers should be able to nominate one minister to defend the interests of the domestic government as a resident in London.[88]

The statement of the Imperial Cabinet members on the method of communication can essentially be considered a non-committal resolution representing a weak compromise between Britain's rigid position and the Dominion demands in regard to their evermore important status within the Empire. British unwillingness to undertake a real step confirming the Dominions' equal status, and not merely just declare it, boosted overseas nationalist groups who held a more pronounced position in regard to the mother country.[89]

In mid-August 1918, the defining of peace objectives was discussed, representing another important topic in the agenda of the Imperial Cabinet and Committee of Prime Ministers. Most discussed were two points in the declaration of Britain's Foreign Secretary Balfour: (1) the future of enemy overseas territories; and (2) general conditions for peace. Balfour was of the opinion that Britain should not endeavour to acquire occupied German and Ottoman territories, because he thought that the United States should take responsibility for them. Canadian Prime Minister Borden had long advocated for convergence between American and British, or Canadian, interests, and as such he agreed with Balfour's position. Australia and New Zealand declared they were ready to claim these territories; Canada even proposed taking over administration of British possessions in the Caribbean.[90] General Smuts expressed his opposition to the idea of involving the Americans, something no one had consulted them about, in the annexation of German and Ottoman colonial possessions, proposing instead that the nascent League of Nations should be given responsibility for these territories, with New Zealand Prime Minister Massey in partial agreement with this idea.[91]

Following the end of the Imperial War Cabinet meeting, the Dominion statesmen, with the exception of Hughes and Smuts who sporadically took part in meetings of the British War Cabinet, left the country. Further developments were accelerated, however, by the collapse of Germany. At the end of October 1918, it was therefore decided that the next meeting of the Imperial War Cabinet should take place in the second half of November, although representatives of New Zealand and India and South African Prime Minister General Botha would be unable to attend due to time constraints. At these meetings, Cabinet members discussed some tentative issues and points in regard to the post-war peace settlement, and immediate measures against the defeated states.[92] On the basis of a meeting with France's Prime Minister Georges Clemenceau, Marshal Ferdinand Foch and Italian Prime Minister Vittorio Orlando, it was decided to transfer the main discussions to the planned Paris Conference.[93]

3.2 The 1919 Peace Talks and the Dominions' Position

The British government had assured the Dominions in 1915 that it would consult with them on the form of the post-war peace settlement.[94] They didn't always keep that promise, however. In mid-November 1918, for example, Australian Prime Minister Hughes complained that the British cabinet had adopted Wilson's Fourteen Points without consulting the Dominions.[95] Overseas statesmen felt particularly threatened by the American principles of an "open door policy" and "free seas" policy, principles he did not want to see applied, particularly in regard to former German colonies, as the policies were contrary to British Imperial policy which aimed for the gradual implementation of an Imperial preference system.[96]

Shortly after the armistice was signed, representatives of the British government and Dominions began discussing the Dominions' position at the peace conferences. From the beginning, Leopold Amery attempted to push through the idea that the Dominions and India should have direct representation at the conference, and that the overseas autonomous territories be perceived as equal partners of the mother country, partners who can express themselves freely on all matters of the peace settlement, and not just those which affect them directly.[97] Amery believed that if the Dominions were allowed to take effective part in the peace negotiations, this would affect their perspective on dealing with Imperial matters in future.[98]

David Lloyd George was sympathetic to the aspirations of the Dominions, but he nevertheless originally thought that the British Empire Delegation would need only five places. The Dominions, however, overtly demanded separate representation at a level of minor allies due to their war efforts. Hughes went further in this regard, and was not satisfied merely with the Dominions receiving representation comparable to some neutral state. He claimed that since Australia had sent more soldiers to fight than Belgium had, they deserved to have a more representative position at the conference. With Britain's support, the Dominions eventually received greater representation, even though French representatives, American President Woodrow Wilson and his Secretary of State, Robert Lansing, did not agree to this.[99]

As a consequence, double representation for the Dominions and India came into being, firstly as members of the British Empire delegation within one section, and also as members of warring parties which were able to send two delegates to the meeting because of their special interests.[100] India's representatives, however, did not agree to their level of representation and demanded this be expanded.[101] The Empire Delegation had a large secretariat available to it, headed by Sir Maurice Hankey, and including officials from the Dominions.[102] Hankey was also the unofficial secretary for the Council of Four.[103] Despite all this, the Dominions were subject to certain restrictions; they could not vote separately, for example, because the British Empire was to act from the outside as one "political entity" with a single view.[104] Great emphasis was also placed on the strict use of the term "British Empire" instead of "England" or "Great Britain" due to the separate representation of the Dominions.[105]

The dual representation of the Dominions raised the question of what the real position of the Dominions was at the Paris Peace Conference. The legal advisor to Canada's Foreign Minister, Loring Cheney Christie, believed that Canada should aspire to awaken nationalist feeling within the Imperial structure. As such, in an extensive confidential memorandum, he summarised the gradual development of Canada's status as an international conference member. He thought that the Dominions had now acquired dual status and that their involvement in decision-making about the peace settlement was not insignificant. He thus stressed the fact that compared to other European allies, Dominion representatives were at an advantage in that they had access to confidential materials and the conclusions reached by the Council of Ten and Council of Five as members of the British Empire Delegation, and as such they were able to have a say on all the fundamental issues discussed at the conference within the Empire Delegation. They were, moreover, actively involved in the work of various committees and commissions in which they frequently held an important position.[106] Leopold Amery, who became Permanent Under-Secretary for the Colonies in 1919, Australian Prime Minister William

Hughes and his British counterpart David Lloyd George all came to similar conclusions to Loring Christie.[107]

The Dominions' particular interests were expressed in particular in regard to the division of the former German colonies in Africa and the Pacific, and the related creation of the League of Nations mandate system. The Australians sought to annex the German Pacific islands, while the South Africans wanted to annex German Southwest Africa.[108] In this regard, New Zealand warned that meeting too many of Japan's demands might be a strategic error similar to that in 1899 when the fate of Samoa had been in the balance, and which resulted in Samoa becoming a base for the German navy.[109] Australia's representatives thought that annexing the former German islands would prevent the expansion of Japanese influence in the region and strengthen Imperial security.[110] Hughes also hoped that the dispute over the Anglo-French condominium on the New Hebrides might finally be solved. However, France was unwilling to discuss the matter at the conference.[111]

Even during the war, Australia had consistently warned of the necessity of defending the expansion of Japanese influence southwards,[112] and as such, in February 1917 an understanding was reached between Britain and Japan which dealt with the future organisation of the German territories in the Far East and Pacific.[113] Some Australian politicians proposed that it would be better for the future of German New Guinea and the Solomon Islands if the United States took over their administration.[114] In the end, Australian and New Zealand statesmen agreed that the former German territories in the Pacific should be taken over by Great Britain or another friendly country.[115]

On 29 January 1919, members of the British Empire Delegation discussed a draft resolution on the former German and Ottoman territories. Due to the fact that America's President Wilson rejected the principle of annexation, a compromise was reached in which the territories were to be divided into three categories (A, B and C) as trust territories of the League of Nations. During discussions on the proposal, Lloyd George stressed that he did not want the Japanese to participate in the administration of the trust territories. The proposed restrictions on the exercise of the mandate did not satisfy Australian Prime Minister Hughes, who was accustomed to a different degree of authority in the field of trade and immigration policy due to the administration of British New Guinea, and who felt considerable antipathy towards Japan.[116] Sir Maurice Hankey reassured Hughes that the purpose of establishing the Class C mandate territory was essentially to form a "lease for 999 years".[117] Lloyd George persuaded Hughes that, "the Class C mandate and outright annexion were virtually the same".[118] None of the British statesmen, however, shared the enthusiasm of their Dominion colleagues for expansion of the Empire;[119] some even doubted that a mandate system would be able to work.[120]

On 6 February 1919, Hughes submitted an important memorandum specifying Australia's position on the islands in the South Pacific. In it, Hughes restated his fear of the Japanese population supremacy, which he indirectly termed an "evil", and overtly raised racial issues and stated the necessity of continuing the "White Australia" policy, as in British New Guinea.[121] A few days later, he sent another memorandum in which he expressed his doubts over whether the League of Nations would have the power to deter Japan from its expansionist plans, and in which he criticised the proposed principles, in particular the mandate administration limits.[122] During a meeting on 20 February 1919, Australia's Minister for the Navy, Sir Joseph Cook, demanded that it should be forbidden to build armed forces within the mandate territories in the Pacific, because he feared Japan would exploit them as enemy bases.[123] The Australian demands raised fear amongst some British delegates that their uncompromising position could result in failure in the peace negotiations.[124] New Zealand's Prime Minister Massey, for a change, expressed significant frustration with Hughes's unwillingness to support New Zealand's endeavours to acquire control over Samoa and in the issue of the administration of Nauru,[125] where both Pacific Dominions had economic interests in particular.[126] Britain's Secretary of State for the Colonies, Lord Milner, nevertheless held the opinion that for practical reasons, it would be beneficial for Great Britain if Australia and New Zealand could be involved in the mandate administration in the Pacific.

On 13 March 1919, the British Empire Delegates discussed in detail Milner's memorandum of 8 March[127] containing notes on Article 19 of the Covenant of the League of Nations on mandate administration. The passages focused on Class C mandate administration were of most relevance to the Dominions (except Canada and Newfoundland), which,

> owing to the sparseness of their population, or their small size, or their remoteness from the centres of civilisation, or their geographical contiguity to the mandatory state ... can be best administered under the laws of the mandatory State as integral portions thereof, subject to the safeguards above-mentioned in the interests of the indigenous population.

Milner did not think their administration would be difficult, and as such they should have a small degree of independence. Coincidentally, the Class C mandate territory was located close to Australia, South Africa and New Zealand. Milner openly accepted Japan's involvement in administering the former German territories north of the equator and discussed the issue of the status of the island of Nauru.[128] He expressed some doubts over the effectiveness of Article 19, Paragraph 6, which enabled the mandate to be integrated into the territory of the mandate power. In this regard, he highlighted complications which might occur if the citizens of the administered territory were to want to become independent.[129] Since the Australians intended to continue implementing the "White policy" in New Guinea, Japan repeatedly demanded that the "open door" principle be respected within the mandate territories.[130]

The Dominions' new status at the Paris Peace Conference was first expressed during discussions on the form of a new international organisation – the League of Nations – although the Australian and New Zealand representatives were not overly concerned about the first American proposal for the Covenant which did not provide for Dominions membership.[131] Nevertheless, the Dominions did focus on the issue of the League of Nations during discussions at the Imperial War Cabinet,[132] although they did not discuss Canada's memorandum on its nature.[133] No "Dominion document" had a greater impact, however, than Smuts's pamphlet on the League of Nations of December 1918. Smuts himself considered it a short text which was written at the last minute; furthermore, it was produced under the pressure of other obligations he had related to preparation for the Peace Conference.[134]

During 1917, Smuts had spoken a number of times in support of establishing an international organisation that would replace the Great Powers in monitoring compliance of international law and general peace between nations in the post-war period.[135] The organisation was to take up the position of the global powers which had failed to ensure peace because they had allowed the outbreak of war. Winston Churchill pointed out that the League of Nations would be able to work effectively only if there was an understanding and agreement between Britain, France and the United States.[136] Milner also recommended co-ordinating steps with the Allies, and especially the Americans.[137]

On 20 March 1918, the Committee of Sir Walter Phillimore, 1st Baron Phillimore, with whom great advocate of the League of Nations and Under-Secretary of State for Foreign Affairs Robert Cecil, later 1st Viscount Cecil of Chelwood, collaborated, submitted an internal report to Britain's Secretary of State for Foreign Affairs, Arthur Balfour, on what the League of Nations' Covenant should look like.[138] The subsequent final report of early July was expanded to include a detailed analysis of historical and contemporary peace projects.[139]

At the same time, there was an official group in France led by León Bourgeois[140] which published its idea about the international organisation on 8 June 1918, an idea which Lord Phillimore was extremely critical of.[141] On 5 October that same year, Robert Cecil submitted a memorandum on the nature and status of the League of Nations to the British War Cabinet, having written it at the request of the Prime Minister. Cecil took a rather visionary perspective on the whole matter, and as such he did not submit a particularly realistic proposal which would include the exact structure of the organisation.[142] Lloyd George was not satisfied with either project,[143] and as such called on Smuts to prepare his own perspective on the matter.[144] Thus, the South African General submitted "one of the ablest state papers ... [Lloyd George] had read".[145]

On 16 December 1918, with support from the British government, Smuts published his own "practical suggestion" on the nature of the League of Nations, which was to represent the heir to the values of a devastated Europe.[146] Matters regarding the former territories of the Ottoman Empire, Russia and Austria-Hungary were to follow the basic principles of "No annexations, and self-determination of nations". In regard to Alsace and Lorraine, he acknowledged France's legitimate claim, and in regard to the German African and Pacific territories, "inhabited by barbarians, who ... cannot possibly govern themselves," and whose primitive barbaric regime was based solely on slavery, headhunting and cannibalism, he accepted that ideas of autonomy were impractical.[147] As such, from the outset Smuts was a firm advocate of establishing mandate administration.[148]

The principal benefit of Smuts's document was in his view on the future nature of relations between nations. Experience of the growth of the British Empire meant that Smuts held the opinion that relations between nations should be based on the principles of political freedom and equality, broad autonomy, political decentralisation, allowing the existence of small nations "and finally an institution like the League of Nations, which will give stability to that decentralisation and thereby guarantee the weak against the strong".[149] Smuts's vision of international relations aroused the interest of President Wilson, who took out of it the proposed structure of the organisation, making minor and larger modifications to some points.[150] Smuts believed that it would be advantageous for the British Empire if its opinions on the League and those of America could converge at the Conference, and this is what happened.[151] Borden held a similar position to Smuts, while Hughes viewed Wilson's plans with much suspicion.[152] The Australian Prime Minister ostentatiously noted that the general concept of the League of Nations created a deeper bond between Britain and foreign countries than between the Dominions and the mother country.[153] Smuts's plan led Lord Cecil to further specify his ideas on the international organisation and write a more sophisticated proposal.[154]

The American and British delegations began co-operating on preparing a final version of the League of Nations Covenant from early January 1919.[155] On 3 February 1919, British legal advisor Sir Cecil Hurst and his American counterpart David Hunter Miller submitted the compromise Hurst-Miller draft,[156] which largely relied on Smuts's previous proposals, and this became the source text for further debates in the Commission of the League of Nations. There was no further discussion of Léon Bourgeois's French proposal,[157] greatly annoying the French.[158]

The Hurst-Miller draft, containing 22 clauses, indirectly disadvantaged the British self-governing territories; according to Article 2, League of Nations members were to be represented by ambassadors or ministers, but Dominions were not to have separate diplomatic representation.[159] Miller subsequently changed his mind, however, and pushed through modifications to the working so that Dominions without diplomatic representation could also be members of the League of Nations.[160] Great Britain did not want the League of Nations to become some kind of "super state"; it rather endeavoured to ensure the Dominions had comparable rights to other countries,[161] and thus accepted the principle of separate Dominion representation within the League's bodies.[162] Subsequently, on 14 February 1919, the working of the Covenant of the League of Nations was adopted.[163]

Miller remained doubtful, however, as to whether the Dominions were true states, and as such rejected their involvement as potential non-permanent members of the Council of the League of Nations, as he believed that the Dominions and other dependent territories should not possess the privilege of representation.[164] The Dominions did not reflect[165] on this situation adequately until 21 April 1919, when Canadian Minister Arthur Sifton pointed out that according to Article 4 the Dominions could not be elected to the Council of the League of Nations, something Canada perceived as an unfortunate formulation. Hughes surprisingly had no objections and argued that if the British Empire was one state, then it should also have one representative. Nevertheless, Borden requested that the Dominions' right to be members of the Council be secured. Lord Robert Cecil subsequently assured the Dominions' statesmen that it was not Britain's intention to prevent the Dominions from being involved in the running of the League of Nations. As such, he also came to a compromise position with Sifton that the word "state" should be replaced in the text by the expression "members of the League", which included the Dominions.[166] Following discussions with the American delegation, the change was made, resulting in Dominions having the right to be elected members of the Council.[167]

The Canadians subsequently strived to ensure Article 10 of the Covenant, which dealt with those intruding on the territorial sovereignty of League of Nations members, was either modified or deleted, because they considered it too binding.[168] In practice, the Dominions would have greater obligations towards Poland and Czechoslovakia,[169] for example, than towards the British Isles. All the Dominions except Newfoundland subsequently became members of the new international organisation.[170] Thanks to the persistence of Robert Borden in this matter, they also acquired a new international status which they had not had before.[171]

On 4 February 1919, Japanese delegates Count Makino Nobuaki and Viscount Chinda Sutemi began negotiations with the American member of the Commission for the Preparation of the Covenant of the League of Nations, Edward Mandell House, known as Colonel House, over the best way to expand the Covenant with a passage on racial equality.[172]

In the end, they decided to insert one into the article on religion.[173] On 13 February 1919, the negotiators submitted their final draft text, in which Makino argued that equality of nations was the fundamental idea on which the League of Nations was based, and as such it should also include respect for other races and nationalities. Adoption of the declaration of racial equality aimed to produce a reduction in racial and religious animosities in the world.[174] Japan demanded that they be guaranteed equal status to the Europeans as a condition to them signing the League of Nations agreement. This particular clause aroused an ambivalent response. Representatives of smaller nations welcomed it, while representatives of the Dominions firmly rejected it. The representatives of Canada, Australia and New Zealand in particular felt threatened by Japan's expansive policy in the Pacific and Far East and as such did not want it to receive the same status as the Europeans. Although the British government stressed the importance of racial issues, they did not see adopting the Japanese demand, which would affect the sovereignty of future members of the League of Nations in the field of immigration policy, as a solution.[175]

In Hughes's eyes, the Japanese demand was a clear challenge to soften Australia's immigration laws and to change its "White policy".[176] Australia assumed that America and Canada, which practised similar restrictive immigration policies, would not support the Japanese proposal. The opposite proved to be the case. Within the British Empire Delegation, only Hughes and Massay vigorously rejected the clause; Smuts rejected it only partially. As such, at the meeting on the Covenant of the League of Nations on 11 April 1919, the Japanese proposal did not pass by a margin of 16 votes to 11.[177] The approved document looked at the mandate territories in Article 22. On 7 May, the Council selected four mandate powers that were to administer the former German and Ottoman territories, including the Dominions (except for Canada and Newfoundland). The Australians were to gain administration over the German part of New Guinea, the Bismarck Archipelago islands and areas south of the equator. New Zealand was to administer the former German Samoa, while Japan was to oversee islands north of the equator, i.e. the Marshall Islands and the Caroline Islands. Australia, Britain and New Zealand were to jointly administer the island of Nauru, renowned as being an important source of phosphates. The Union of South Africa was to receive the territory of the former German Southwest Africa. The mandate system, which gradually took shape and underwent modification until 1925, allowed the League of Nations to become the sole guarantor of peace, but not a colonial power.[178]

The Dominions' position at the Paris Peace Conference led to some theoretical (dis)advantages in the signing of treaties. Were authorised Dominion representatives to sign certain treaties, they would be doing so with the knowledge of their domestic governments, and as such the treaties would come into force automatically.[179] In contrast, British delegates did not affirm conventions merely on behalf of Britain, but on behalf of the whole Empire.[180] On 12 March 1919, Sir Robert Borden sent a memorandum to his Dominion colleagues, in which he stressed that all treaties and conventions should be written in such a manner that Dominions could be considered equal parties. Borden justified this approach by noting Resolution 9 of the 1917 Imperial War Conference which spoke of the equality of nations within the Empire.[181] He also proposed that names and signatures of British signatories should be followed by a list of Dominion signatories.[182] The Canadian Prime Minister sought to ensure that the Dominions signed treaties separately and that they could then ratify them in their domestic parliaments as evidence of their new post-war status, similarly to the Hague Convention of 1907.[183] Borden's stance was shared by the Indian representative, Britain's Secretary of State for India Edwin Samuel Montagu, who stressed that the new international status of the Dominions and India as founding members of the League of Nations could not be ignored.[184]

In April 1919, Canada's Privy Council drew up a precise procedure, but because of Borden's absence in Europe, the process could not be completed before signature of the peace treaty with Germany.[185] In early May, members of the British Empire Delegation received detailed instructions from Hankey on the circumstances of delivering the peace treaty to German representatives.[186] Although the official signature of the Treaty of Versailles took place in line with Borden's proposal, and the Dominions' delegates added their signatures on behalf of their own countries to those of Britain's five statesmen, the symbolic international recognition of the Dominions' new status which the Canadian Prime Minister had aimed to cement through these signatures was not fully achieved. From a legal perspective, and considering the existence of the British Empire Delegation in which the Dominions were represented, the signatures of the Dominion statesmen next to those of the British were unnecessary since Britain represented the whole Empire to the world.[187] For this reason, the Dominion statesmen insisted that the treaty did not place any obligation on the Dominions until they were adopted by their overseas parliaments.[188]

There was another controversy which arose in relation to ratification of the treaty. In a telegram on 4 July 1919, Lord Milner urged the Canadian government to ratify the treaty by the end of the month because from a political, but not legal, perspective the British Empire was perceived as a whole unit comprising a number of parts whose consent was essential to complete the ratification process.[189] Canada in particular, in contrast to the mother country, strived to ensure the treaty was first approved by the domestic parliament, and that only then should it be officially handed over to the King for ratification on behalf of Canada.[190] This Anglo-Canadian discussion, however, did not reach any conclusion leading to any kind of constitutional amendment.[191] Nevertheless, Borden saw partial success in another area. In early October 1919, he demanded of the British government that Ottawa be directly involved in its diplomatic representation in Washington due to the growing intensity and importance of Canadian-American trading relations. In March 1920, Britain's Secretary of State for the Colonies agreed.[192] In the matter of ratification of the peace treaty, in the end the deadline had to be repeatedly extended; it was eventually ratified in early January 1920.[193]

Although Borden's intention to use the signing of the peace treaty with Germany as symbolic international acknowledgement of the Dominions' independence did not entirely work out, the fact that the Dominions were entitled to make their own decision over whether to add their signatures to the treaty or not represented a certain level of acceptance of their new status by the mother country. Thus the Dominions indirectly acquired the opportunity to execute their own foreign policy. The overseas self-governing territories also gained in importance in terms of their membership of the League of Nations. Although alongside other dependent territories they made up the British Empire, they had acquired the right to individual representation within the League's Assembly, and they could be elected to its Council. Nevertheless, the international community continued to view them as an integral part of the British Empire, which represented them in many areas to the rest of the world.

Despite all the restrictions arising from the status of Dominion, the British representatives were fully aware that "they were no longer colonies, but nations intensely conscious of their nationhood".[194] Dominion representatives' participation in the peace discussions in Paris represented the start of a new era in the constitutional history of the British Empire's autonomous territories.[195] South Africa's General Smuts was well aware of this; on 5 August 1919 he declared:

> British statesmen had accepted this new view of the Empire, and thus it was that the most important document in the War had been signed by their representatives as equals, not only of the others parts of the Empire, but of the great Powers of the world.[196]

Although the Dominions gained a lot, Smuts was personally disappointed. He perceived involvement in the Paris Peace Conference as a "great failure", because he had been unable to push through many matters he thought were of great priority in regard to the establishment of the League of Nations and the policy of the victors towards the defeated Germany. As 1919 came to an end, he even declared that, "1919 will remain the year of the greatest and deepest disappointments of my life".[197]

3.3 The Post-War Constitutional Debate

Participants in the 1917 Imperial War Conference discussed the future form of Imperial relations. The adoption of Resolution IX, which declared full recognition of the Dominions and autonomous nations within the Imperial Commonwealth, and the right of Dominions to make foreign policy decisions and have a say in foreign relations, triggered a wave of optimism amongst overseas statesmen.[198] At a stroke, the "young" Dominions were seen as equivalents to some European states.[199] The First World War had accelerated the trend already begun after the 1911 Imperial Conference, i.e. the Dominions moving towards a wider concept of autonomy and more intensive co-operation within the Empire. The war had helped establish joint responsibility for foreign policy between the Dominions and Great Britain.[200] The post-war inclusion of the overseas autonomous territories within the administration of mandate territories was to some extent an affirmation of the trend of recent years. Although after the war the Dominions did not openly pursue a separate foreign policy, one can distinguish hints of one in the Australian and New Zealand positions during the Paris talks in 1919.[201]

Over the course of the war years, through participation in Imperial War Cabinet meetings, Dominion statesmen had acquired significant influence in the decision-making process on Imperial matters. As such, at the end of the war some Imperial politicians placed great hope in the idea that some form of Imperial Cabinet carrying on in the post-war period would help to generally develop relations between the mother country and the Dominions. Although no Imperial Conferences were planned in 1919, a number of formal and informal meetings were held between British and Dominion representatives when they were part of the British Empire delegation at the Paris Peace Conference. Although the Dominion statesmen perceived membership in the British Empire delegation as a modified continuation of the Imperial War Cabinet meetings, some British representatives were only partially satisfied by this status of Dominion politicians, and as such requested their position be strengthened within the Imperial structure.[202]

Leopold Amery, for example, had long been of the opinion that the Imperial Cabinet had acquired the status of a full-fledged Imperial institution during the war, since at standard meetings Dominion residents or ministers present in London were in charge of its agenda. As a result, there was no longer a temporary interruption in issues being discussed as had been previously common following publication of Imperial Conference resolutions. He now believed that the importance of the Imperial Cabinet had increased, becoming the "ideal" Imperial institution which could be the "missing link in the Imperial chain" and which could bridge the gap between Conferences, a suitable solution to the frequent criticism that the Imperial agenda was neglected during this intervening period. Amery saw this continuity of discussions amongst Imperial representatives as the affirmation of true equality between the governments of the Empire, and an opportunity for Dominion prime ministers to communicate with the British Prime Minister directly without having to observe the previously binding communication procedure via the British Colonial Office.[203]

Since he feared the collapse of Imperial unity as a result of the ineffectiveness of the former British War Cabinet, Amery advocated preserving some kind of modified form of both cabinets in the post-war period. He personally believed that the ideal composition would bring together a reconstructed British War Cabinet and the original Imperial War Cabinet, but he was able only to partially do this due to the composition of the British Empire delegation in Paris.[204] Amery also stressed the fact that the Imperial Cabinet system allowed the Empire to be made more effective on a more widespread basis than that envisaged in the standard constitutional idea of Round Table Movement proponents.[205]

Amery was not alone amongst British representatives in his positions.[206] During debate in the House of Lords on 17 June 1920, when a question was raised on the extent to which previous British government declarations on the method of permanent consultation in Imperial and foreign policy between the Dominions and India had been met, Lord Milner clarified a previous government declaration on the nature of the Empire. Like Amery, he saw the Dominions as equal partners, and thus placed hope in the authority of Imperial Conferences, which, because they met regularly, and had a Secretariat to ensure agenda continuity between regular meetings, he perceived as an indispensable institution within the Empire. He saw their fundamental disadvantage in the fact that Imperial Conference meetings did not take place particularly frequently and that adopted resolutions, or Secretariat activities, had scant influence on the implementation of Imperial policies. As such, he stressed the work of the Imperial War Cabinet during the war, and the British Empire delegation at the peace negotiations in Paris.[207] Milner considered it beneficial to continue joint meetings between British and Dominion representatives, allowing the Dominions to be more substantially involved in Imperial foreign policy decisions.[208] As such, he advocated establishment of a new institution – an Imperial government which would comprise representatives of the Empire's self-governing territories and whose discussions would go beyond just Imperial matters. Since Milner believed in its importance, the Imperial government was not "just" a formal representation of the Empire's autonomous parts, but rather a direct representation of the Empire's executive power.[209]

A few days later, South African Prime Minister Smuts responded to Milner's statement at the House of Lords, summarising his own position on the matter in a speech on 23 June 1920; he essentially wanted to explain Milner's positions to domestic politicians. The General relied on the assumption that the signatories to the Treaty of Versailles recognised the Dominions as equal and independent states.²¹⁰ He thought that, "it was imperatively necessary, if the British Empire was to continue in future, that the Dominion status should be entirely revised"²¹¹ and that the position of Governors-General, or Governors, within the autonomous territories should also be revised.²¹² Smuts held the opinion that the British Empire could continue to exist only as, "a league of free, equal, independent States ... bound by closer ties of common defence ... [because] the old principles of federation were unworkable, and would lead to the breakup of the Empire".²¹³ He did not place great hope in the idea of establishing a great Imperial parliament representing the various parliaments, because he feared great resistance from Britain, and as such he saw the British Commonwealth's future more in securing total freedom for all countries in the Empire.²¹⁴ Due to the nationalism rife in South African politics, he was not afraid to stress the fact that nations' freedom and independence could be achieved even within the Empire, and that secession leading to the declaration of a Republic would be a hollow gesture making little sense.²¹⁵ Despite the fact that the Afrikaners advocated Republican ideas, Smuts judged that he was strongly supported by the population of British origin, who he thought were more loyal to the Empire than the British in Great Britain were.²¹⁶

In his speech to the South African politicians, Smuts agreed with Milner in that the British Empire found itself in an awkward situation because the form of Imperial Conferences no longer corresponded to the requirements of the age. Smuts had long stressed the Dominions' activities at the Paris peace negotiations, and he saw the signature by the Dominion representatives of the peace treaty with Germany as a real watershed moment. As such, he was one of the strong supporters of close co-operation between Dominions and British representatives in Imperial foreign policy. In contrast to Milner, he did not see the implementation of Imperial government principles as essential, and as such was a strenuous advocate of requiring a more precise definition of the status of Dominions not just within the Empire, but also in relation to neighbouring countries. In Smuts's eyes, the official declaration of Dominions' international status and influence in formulating Imperial foreign policy played an important role, because on the one hand this represented a completion of the process of the formal recognition they were to have acquired in Paris in 1919, and on the other hand it was a symbol of achieving independence with disintegration of the Empire.²¹⁷

British representatives did not share Smuts's interpretation of the significance of the Dominions' activities at the Paris peace negotiations for the future. They did acknowledge, however, that besides Smuts, none of the Dominion statesmen who supported constitutional change on the basis of the Imperial War Conference resolution of 1917 knew what course the Empire should take, and what exactly it should require from the mother country.²¹⁸ Leopold Amery, for example, in a memorandum on the impact of war events and on the Imperial status of the Dominions over the course of the Paris Peace Conference, came to the conclusion that British and Dominion statesmen advocated Imperial interests, and as such these were successes of the Empire as a whole, and not specifically Australian Prime Minister Hughes and his South African counterpart Botha, or others. He did, however, admit that it was difficult to bring together both Dominion autonomy and the implementation of an effective Imperial policy and Imperial unity.[219]

The Secretary of the British Empire delegation, Sir Clement Jones, was similarly critical of the actions of Dominion representatives, particularly those from Australia, in certain important issues of Imperial foreign policy. He noted that from the start, foreign state representatives had not really understood why the Dominions had separate representation to Great Britain. Sir Clement co-operated closely with Australian Prime Minister Hughes at the Paris Peace Conference, and he considered Hughes a "playboy amongst delegates", coming out worst in his internal evaluation of the activities of Dominion representatives. Jones was particularly disappointed by Hughes's smug behaviour and frequent lack of appreciation of the severity of issues being discussed.[220] Another member of the British Empire delegation, Maurice Hankey, was more moderate in his assessment of the Dominion representatives. In contrast to Amery's slight criticism of Dominion statesmen, Hankey stressed in particular the actions of South African Prime Minister Botha, whom he referred to retrospectively in a BBC broadcast as "one of the greatest statesmen" to take part in the Paris conference.[221] He also saw General Smuts in a similarly positive light.[222]

Australian politicians who, once the euphoria of signing the peace treaty in Versailles had subsided, "suddenly" realised no visible transformation in relations between the mother country and the Dominions had occurred, held a similar opinion to Smuts in terms of the status and influence of the Dominions on formulating Imperial foreign policy. As such, in a July 1919 memorandum, Australian Prime Minister Hughes distanced himself from the existing limits which bound the freedom of the Dominions. He particularly criticised the fact that the overseas self-governing territories would still not have a voice in who would become their Governor-General or Governor. His perception of the problematic status of Dominions, as Smuts's was, was based on the assumption that the overseas territories should be equal partners to London in Imperial matters. However, Smuts was significantly more critical than Hughes. In particular, Smuts was not afraid to describe the method of communication between the mother country and the Dominions via the British Colonial Office, the status of the Governors-General and the lack of Dominions' diplomatic representation in third countries as anomalous and in need of swift redress. He saw the only solution for clarifying these matters in calling a Constitutional Conference based on the principle of equality of different parts of the Empire.²²³ In contrast, Hughes vigorously defended the "clear set-up of relations" between Britain and the Dominions.²²⁴

Milner's June 1920 speech was well-received in the Union of South Africa and by Australian politicians. Advocates of a conservative approach and the Round Table Movement saw in it a tendency for restoring federalist visions, and as such called for a Constitutional Conference redefining the Dominions' status to be convened soon. The Australian Labour Party took a hostile attitude towards the speech, because they feared it would lead to the end of the "White Australia" political principle. Australian Liberals also expressed their disagreement with the speech.²²⁵

The lack of consensus over the importance of the Imperial Conferences, or over the planned Constitutional Conference, foreshadowed further developments and highlighted problems in the post-war transformation of the Empire. Although Milner and Smuts had criticised the shortcomings of the system of Conferences, the South African general believed that the Conference remained irreplaceable as an Imperial institution.²²⁶ Canadian Prime Minister Borden held the opinion that in recent years the Dominions had seen great progress in the development of their relations to the mother country, because new methods and ways of consultation had been set up for the period between Imperial Conferences, which the Dominions participated in as sister nations to Great Britain. Like Smuts, however, he thought that the process had not been completed, because the Dominions were still viewed as dependent territories of His Majesty's government, and as such he sought the convening of a Constitutional Conference as soon as possible to deal with these unresolved issues.²²⁷

Overseas and British advocates of Imperialism placed significant hopes in the first post-war Imperial, or rather Constitutional, Conference where the focus was to be on constitutional matters. Most of them, with some minor differences, agreed with Milner's 1919 position that "the only possibility of a continuance of the British Empire ... is on a basis of absolute out-and-out equal partnership between the United Kingdom and the Dominions".²²⁸ Milner considered the demands placed by the Dominions on the mother country were the logical outcome of the events of the previous five years, because the Imperial War Cabinet and the Imperial delegation at the peace negotiations in Paris had fulfilled an executive role within the Empire only temporarily. As such, he hoped that the Conference would formulate a permanent Imperial constitution on a similar basis to that on which the League of Nations was founded.²²⁹ The faith then placed in the new international set-up, the principles of the international organisation and the idealised vision of the Commonwealth fuelled inaccurate, even fantastical, ideas of certain analogous features between them. In fact, claims were made that the Imperial structure represented a miniature model of the League of Nations, or even its prototype.²³⁰

Eventually, Milner lost faith in the meaning of the Constitutional Conference, which was originally planned for 1920, and referring to the alleged domestic problems of the overseas governments, he instead proposed postponing it for a year. He was not sure whether important constitutional issues should be dealt with directly at a special conference, and proposed a smaller Constituent Assembly be convened instead, as a more appropriate forum for discussing future relations between the Dominions and the mother country. In October 1920, he further clarified his position, stating that constitutional matters should be discussed and decided upon only within existing Imperial institutions, and the evolution of a "new Imperial constitution" should not be allowed.[231]

Milner subsequently proposed that a constitutional sub-conference could be held in Ottawa. His idea failed, because the new Canadian Prime Minister, Arthur Meighen, in contrast to his predecessor, was an opponent of further defining the Dominions' constitutional status. The Canadian representatives were also unsure whether they should fear more the mother country's intervention in the course of Imperial foreign policy, or a more active involvement in Imperial matters which meant significant commitments in the post-war international situation.[232] The Canadian rejection forced the British Prime Minister to announce, on the basis of Milner's recommendation and following consultation with other Dominion prime ministers, his decision to postpone all discussion on constitutional matters until the standard Imperial Conference which was to take place in mid-June 1921.[233] Milner welcomed the postponement of the Conference because he believed that the Dominion leaders would have more time to deal with Imperial matters in 1921.[234]

Since the agenda of the upcoming meeting between British and Dominion prime ministers was unclear, the British press instigated a debate on what politicians should discuss. From post-war constitutional discussions the journalists surmised that a system of Imperial government would be defined – an Imperial Peace Cabinet. This Peace Cabinet would represent the "peacetime" form of the Imperial War Cabinet and hold executive power. Imperial Conferences would fulfil a purely advisory role and would be somewhere where overseas and London representatives would meet up.[235] This speculation was fuelled in April 1921 by British Colonial Secretary Winston Churchill, who did not hesitate to characterise the upcoming meeting thus:

> This was a very important year in the life of the British Empire, for it would see the first peace meeting of the Imperial cabinet. It would not be like the old Imperial conferences, but a meeting of the regular Imperial cabinet.[236]

The form of the upcoming Imperial Conference was influenced more by Smuts's activities, however, than by journalistic speculation. The General's position had long been subject to mistrust amongst South African politicians, who perceived it as overly "obsequious to British policy".[237]

Smuts made no secret of his opinion that the Union of South Africa's interests and prosperity were best served through partnership with Great Britain.[238] The British were not particularly enthusiastic either, considering Smuts "dangerous for the British Empire" because they believed he did not understand it much. Some were even of the opinion that Smuts's "constitutional, political and military significance was zero".[239] However, despite all the doubters, Smuts did not lose faith in his concept for the Dominions. In the first half of 1921, he was the first to come up with the idea that Dominion status had to be defined due to growing nationalism in certain Dominions, and he attempted to use a long memorandum on the subject to help deal with constitutional problems.[240] He wanted to bring together the theoretically applicable relations and the current state within the Empire, which had transformed into a commonwealth of free and equal sister states.[241]

The General had assumed that following the First World War, the British Empire represented a heterogeneous whole made up of the self-governing territories, independent territories, protectorates and mandates. They were all formally linked by a collective loyalty to the Crown (except for the protectorates and mandates), and informally by history, shared interests and faith in the institute of parliament. He believed that fundamentally the Empire was moving towards fully responsible self-government, something the Dominions had already achieved, and that other areas such as Southern Rhodesia were aspiring towards. This diverse unity was to some extent also symbolised by the rare and complex intricacies of constitutional relations.[242]

In his memorandum entitled "The Constitution of the British Commonwealth", Smuts summarised developments so far and the current state, and outlined his vision of what course the British Commonwealth should take. He hoped that the war efforts expended by the Dominions meant that there would be no delay in precisely determining their status, and that the situation would not escalate to such an extent as it had in Ireland. On the one hand, the First World War had strengthened Imperial cohesion, but on the other hand it had helped to spread nationalist feelings which stressed the difference, uniqueness and size of the Empire's autonomous nations compared to other countries. In this regard, Smuts warned that "unless Dominion status is settled soon in a way which will satisfy the legitimate aspirations of these young nations, we must look for separatist movements in the Commonwealth".[243]

Smuts warned that merely opening the issue to discussion at the upcoming Imperial Conference was not enough, because experience of past Conference proceedings and policy discussions in the Union of South Africa showed that the whole matter could get "bogged down" in long academic debates, and this would not help to calm the situation in the Dominions. For this reason, he called on the British government to ensure Conference participants were able to discuss a specific, previously written proposal without having to create one.²⁴⁴ His Majesty's Government, however, did not want any constitutional debate prior to the Conference beginning.²⁴⁵

The General listed three basic areas for discussion: (1) the nature of Dominion status; (2) the relationship of the King, or the Crown, to the Dominions; (3) the form of Conference discussions and method of consultation. He noted that signature of the Treaty of Versailles was of great importance for the evolution of the Dominions' status and their membership of the League of Nations. His opinion was that the Dominions theoretically had status equal to other sovereign states and Great Britain, but that this had not been affirmed by any laws. Although each Dominion had its own constitution, Smuts though that it was essential that the 1865 Colonial Laws Validity Act, which put Dominion parliaments in a subsidiary position towards British (Imperial) legislative decrees and placed some restrictions on them, should no longer apply to the Dominions, in order to ensure constitutional equality. Smuts was convinced that expanding the power of the Dominions' representative parliaments, who would then be able to change their constitutions, was the right path to take.²⁴⁶

In regard to executive sovereignty, Smuts noted that there were certain constitutional limits in the relationship between the King and Dominion governments. In foreign affairs, for example, he consistently referred to the continuing forms of Dominion subordination. Although the overseas autonomous territories had received international status in 1919 and had also received their recognition, this was not seen in practice because Dominions' foreign relations with foreign states continued to remain under the sole control of the London government. Rarely was there any consultation between Britain and Dominion representatives, this generally taking place during *ad hoc* meetings in dealing with a particular international situation. Smuts thought the ties between the mother country and the Dominions were so complicated that he made no bones about stating that, "foreigners find it difficult to understand the unwritten British Constitution".²⁴⁷

He saw the problem in the ambiguous distinction between the "letter of the law" and established Imperial constitutional practice, and as such sought formal clarification through a "general declaration of constitutional rights", in which the Dominions' true position would be clarified. In this matter, he referred back to a demand previously made by leading theorist analysing Dominion status, Professor Hessel Duncan Hall.²⁴⁸ He therefore proposed that if the British parliament did not have legislative power over the Dominion parliaments, not even the King would have the right to veto laws voted on by the Dominions. Smuts also saw the Dominions' subordinate position in judicial matters. From a purely legal perspective, this particularly applied in regard to the issue of appeals to the Judicial Committee of the Privy Council.²⁴⁹

Smuts likewise saw a certain inequality in the King's relationship to the Dominions. He saw the complication here in the fact that the King, the official representative of the United Kingdom, named Governors or Governors-General on the recommendation of the British government to represent him in the Dominions. He also referred to what he described as a "relict of the past" – the practice that Dominion representatives did not have direct access to the sovereign, and that they could communicate with him only through the British government, or the British Colonial Secretary. He held the opinion that this unequal status could no longer be tolerated and as such submitted a proposal which was to fully demonstrate Dominions' equal status to the mother country within the Empire. As such, he proposed: (1) the Dominion agenda not be administered by the British Colonial Office or another department; (2) governments in the Dominions should have direct access to the King without having to go through the British government or a corresponding minister; (3) Governors-General should become Viceroys as sole representative of the sovereign within Dominion executives, not the British government, and they should be appointed on the basis of a consensus recommendation of British and Dominion representatives. Domition affairs should be moved to a newly established Dominions Committee, comprising the British Prime Minister and Dominion representatives acting *de facto* on behalf of the whole Commonwealth.[250]

In his memorandum, Smuts focused in detail on the form of Conference discussions and methods of consultation between Dominions and the mother country. On the basis of discussions which had taken place at the Imperial War Conference in 1917, he noted it was essential to ensure continuous consultation at three levels: (1) Imperial Conferences; (2) prime ministerial conferences; (3) Dominions Committee meetings. According to Smuts, Imperial Conferences (or Commonwealth Congresses) were to take place every four years and were to serve as a forum at which issues of general interest would be publicly discussed. As well as the "traditional" prime ministers taking part, he anticipated a larger number of participants being invited from amongst government and opposition Dominion legislators. Smuts thought the Dominions Committee, with its own secretariat, should serve as a "follow-up, or additional" institution and as a "link" between the Crown and Dominion cabinets at the same time, and as such should focus on debates around Imperial foreign policy and other important issues and problems with which the League of Nations would turn to the British Commonwealth.[251]

The third consultation method was during prime ministerial conferences, which were to replace current meetings of the British Prime Minister with his Dominion counterparts during meetings of the Imperial Cabinet. Since the term "cabinet" was imprecise because it did not hold any executive power or responsibilities to parliament, it often contended with misunderstandings or even open criticism from the Dominions.

Smuts held the opinion that prime ministerial conferences, which should take place once every two years and have a greater level of authority, should represent a broader form of the Dominions Committee. Last but not least, the General proposed that in ratifying this "landmark document", a new term for the British Empire should be adopted – the British Commonwealth of Nations – as a symbol of Dominions' freedom and equality. Introducing national flags in addition to the Union Jack was also meant to provide symbolic affirmation of the Dominions' new status.[252]

Shortly after arriving in London on 11 June 1921, Smuts met privately with the former Permanent Under-Secretary at the Colonial Office, Leopold Amery, who now held the post of Financial Secretary to the Admiralty, and with whom he had regularly corresponded on Imperial matters.[253] Amery's new post meant he would be unable to attend the planned conference, and thus the South African General decided to consult him on his memorandum proposal.[254] Amery was very well informed on Imperial matters, and as such from January to April 1921 was responsible for preparing the agenda at the upcoming Imperial Conference as chair of the interdepartmental committee. In his preliminary material, like Smuts, Amery had worked on a "rival" idea of a Declaration of General Constitutional Principles, which was likewise meant to define relations within the Empire on the basis of equal status of its members.[255]

For the future development of constitutional relations within the Empire, it was important that Smuts's memorandum proposal particularly impressed Amery, who also had his own vision of Imperial relationships. On 20 June 1921, he sent Smuts an extensive analysis of the document including his own perspective on the issue. On the one hand, this showed that although they had worked separately on concepts, they were of the same opinion on the main points; and on the other hand, they differed in the way to theoretically and practically achieve this. Both identified with the argument that adopting a fixed or written constitution was contrary to the nature and gradual process of the British Commonwealth's constitutional development. Amery agreed with the theoretical interpretation of Dominion sovereignty but proposed emphasising certain aspects on which Commonwealth unity was to rest, in particular the full independence and equality of its members and an inseparable link to all sovereigns and the Crown. Amery also supported Smuts in the method of consultation between Dominion governments and the mother country, direct access of Dominion statesmen to the King, and the anomalous status of Governors or Governors-General in the overseas self-governing territories. They also agreed that the Dominion agenda had to be removed from the authority of the British Colonial Office, something Amery had already suggested in 1911, and an alternative term for the British Empire – the British Commonwealth – should be put in place. Despite the fact that there was consensus in most points, Amery was not afraid to express some doubts, in particular over the effectiveness of expanding the system of Imperial Conferences to the level of a wider Imperial forum, and the terminological definition of the words "Cabinet" and "Imperial Cabinet".[256]

Although Amery had been interested in the issue for many years, he judged that the time was not yet right for opening public debate on these matters, and furthermore, the situation at the time was not favourable towards doing so. He saw a solution in naming a government commission which would look at these points and subsequently incorporate them into documents for the future Constitutional Conference.[257] Despite the fact that he complemented or agreed with Smuts on many points, with hindsight Amery determined that in June 1921 he should take up a more reserved position.[258] Until autumn 1926, leading British politicians had no idea of Amery's response to Smuts's memorandum.[259]

Smuts saw his prepared memorandum as a preliminary draft resolution on the future form of constitutional relationships within the Empire. Since in the end only a "standard" Imperial Conference was convened, his memorandum quickly became less topical. As such, Smuts decided not to send it officially to Imperial Conference participants, instead sending the text to Austen Chamberlain and Lord Balfour.[260] The public declarations of the Dominion prime ministers also show that none of them were willing to support it in public. Australian Prime Minister Hughes, for example, assured parliament before leaving for Europe that he was not going to agree to any constitutional changes which would disturb the unity of the Empire.[261] Thus Smuts was warned in advance to take a low profile in the matters his memorandum had looked at. This "public silence", however, did not give Smuts any advantages; quite the opposite.[262]

An unusually long Imperial Conference was held from 20 June to 5 August 1921, at which representatives of Great Britain, the Dominions and India met up.[263] The agenda for discussion was dominated by issues of Imperial defence, alongside common foreign policy, migration within the Empire and constitutional affairs. Besides official discussions, informal meetings and a number of Committee meetings also took place.[264] Even the introductory speeches demonstrated that none of the Dominion or British representatives favoured discussion of a declaration of constitutional rights, nor convening any other kind of constitutional forum. It is no surprise, then, that greatest attention was paid to foreign policy matters in regard to Upper Silesia, Egypt, the Ruhr, the League of Nations and the Anglo-Japanese Alliance; constitutional matters were very much downplayed.[265]

In his opening speech, on the one hand Lloyd George praised the Dominions' active approach at the Paris Peace Conference, their membership of the League of Nations and that, "they now stand beside the United Kingdom as equal partners in the dignities and the responsibilities of the British Empire". On the other hand, he admitted there may be differing interpretations of the status of overseas territories, and thus he expressed his readiness to discuss their status if such a request was made.[266] There was an opinion that, "the Empire must maintain its historic role of a moderating reconciling influence between the civilisations of East and West".[267] Due to events in Ireland, the British Prime Minister preferred dialogue with the Dominions' statesmen. He did not want the situation to culminate in the coming together of a nationalistic-minded opposition whose steps would be hard to predict. As such it was up to the positions of the Dominion prime ministers alone whether the Commonwealth would move towards autonomy of its members, or whether the current unity would be maintained. The dilemma was further complicated by the issue of implementing Imperial foreign policy, where Dominions were viewed as self-governing units at a theoretical level.[268]

Although the 1917 Imperial War Conference's Resolution IX stressed the necessity of discussing constitutional matters, nobody except Smuts supported convening a special Constitutional Conference. Australia's Prime Minister Hughes was a leading opponent of any changes or even requests for redefining Dominion status. During conference meetings, he even stated that he didn't understand the reasons why the holding of a Constitutional Conference in 1917 was proposed. He admitted that, "the difference between the status of the Dominions now and twenty-five years ago is very great", but he immediately added that the extent of progress the Dominions had achieved had been accompanied by a corresponding evolution in relations between them and the mother country, because in fact the Dominions "have all the rights of self-government enjoyed by independent nations". As such, he believed the course taken had been satisfactory and did not need to be corrected.[269] The only shortcomings he saw were in the methods of communication between different members of the British Commonwealth.[270] Despite all this, he was firmly convinced of Imperial unity because he expressed his belief to the delegates that they were almost all the same nation.[271]

His Canadian opposite number, Arthur Meighen, whose political position had been significantly weakened because his Liberal rival William Lyon Mackenzie King was expected to win the election,[272] supported William Hughes and vigorously opposed implementing any kind of "revolutionary changes in constitutional relations" in the name of Dominion autonomy. New Zealand Prime Minister Massey agreed. He held the opinion that the British Empire would be stronger if it was not bound by written rules, since the Commonwealth of Nations, regardless of nationality and country of origin, was bound together by patriotism.[273]

During his opening speech, Massey resorted to an anachronistic declaration in which he expressed his doubts over whether the Dominions should pursue an independent foreign policy and whether they should have separate membership of the League of Nations. He feared that they could turn against each other at moments of crisis.[274] One interesting part of his speech was his idea that the Imperial Conference did not always have to take place in London. He assumed that it would be difficult to "govern the Empire from the windows of Downing Street," and Conferences could be held during joint trips of the British Prime Minister and Colonial Secretary to the overseas self-governing territories. One reason behind this was the fact that the New Zealand Prime Minister had the furthest to travel of all his Dominion colleagues to get to London.[275]

At a time when David Lloyd George declared in his opening statement Britain's readiness to discuss constitutional matters, it was shown that Smuts had not chosen the right approach in not sending his memorandum to the other Dominion statesmen before the Conference began. William Hughes and other opponents of any kind of change took advantage of the absence of any detailed analyses of constitutional problems, giving them the lead in arguments. Although Smuts attempted to turn the situation around during Conference discussions, he had nothing to base his reformist positions on, and they were lost amongst Hughes's and Massey's counterarguments. Smuts had also unwittingly helped his successor James Hertzog in his political triumph at the 1926 Imperial Conference.[276]

On 11 July 1921, the 22nd Conference meeting took place, at which important debate took place on constitutional affairs. Until this moment, the South African Prime Minister had abstained from making any statements on constitutional changes. During this discussion, however, he decided to summarise what Dominion status meant. He essentially based his statement on the memorandum he had previously produced on constitutional matters and which he had consulted only with a small number of British politicians who all wanted Commonwealth reform.[277]

Smuts placed particular focus on the simple fact that the need to clarify the constitutional position of the overseas self-governing territories within the Empire was not just an academic issue, but also a vitally important step to complete international recognition of the Dominions, which had begun during the Paris peace negotiations. After a comprehensive analysis of the positions within South African politics, in which there were ever more frequent calls for breaking away from the British Empire, he came to the conclusion that a declaration on Imperial constitution should be adopted. He also clearly rejected the idea that this should be a written constitution along the lines of that of the United States. Smuts thought a different type would be more appropriate for the British Commonwealth, based on unwritten precedents which would occasionally evolve in accordance with the international situation. None of his counterparts supported him. New Zealand Prime Minister Massey was markedly distrustful of Smuts's statements because he feared that in fact, he sought a written Imperial constitution, even though Smuts had expressly denied it.[278]

Smuts also expressed his fear that entrusting the whole issue to some subcommittee wasn't the ideal solution, preferring unofficial discussion on a constitutional declaration.[279] His compromise draft declaration, seeking in its second article "that all surviving forms of inequality and subordination in their relations shall disappear",[280] was not particularly well received by prime ministers at an informal meeting on 27 July.[281] Hughes's firm stance put an end not just to considerations of convening a Constitutional Conference, but also Smuts's effort at adopting some form of constitutional declaration. Hughes perceived a Constitutional Conference as unnecessary and dangerous.[282] He also opposed any kind of declaration of constitutional rights, because he believed that the Dominions already had everything they needed and were self-governing nations. He remained of the opinion that in practice contentious issues could be dealt with more easily when no one was restricted by any written rules. He also feared that he would "never be able to explain" adopting a written constitution to domestic representatives.[283] Constitutional arguments were frequently accompanied by a marked lack of terminological clarity, a result of the fact that delegates frequently, wittingly or unwittingly, mixed up terms and phrases such as Imperial Cabinet, cabinet, special meeting of prime ministers and conference of prime ministers with the established term of Imperial Conference.[284]

During the discussions on constitutional relations, Canada's position did not play an important role. Canada's politicians did not agree with a Constitutional Conference being convened because they were satisfied with the level of autonomy they had already. If anything needed to be improved, then it was communication between the mother country and the overseas autonomous territories, and as such they supported Smuts's idea of establishing permanent ministers or liaison officers who would facilitate communication between British and Dominion representatives in London.[285] Although Arthur Meighen was positively disposed to the idea of a constitutional declaration, his position politically was so precarious that he was extremely reticent in expressing himself publicly.[286] Sir Robert Borden later regretted that no general declaration of constitutional rights had been adopted.[287] During the 27 July discussions, New Zealand Prime Minister Massey largely supported Hughes in his negative take on a written constitution. He thought that "America and Australia and New Zealand all had written Constitutions, but he did not want one for the Empire".[288] He also wanted to ensure Imperial unity was maintained and a common Imperial foreign policy was rigorously implemented.[289] Finally, those present at the discussion agreed on a draft final resolution submitted by Sir Maurice Hankey, which was adopted following minor modifications.[290]

In the end, the Dominion representatives had the impression that they were sufficiently equal, and as such they decided it was unnecessary to revise constitutional relations between the mother country and the Dominions, never mind calling a special conference. On the other hand, however, those present stressed the importance of timely consultation within the Empire and agreed that it was essential to continue to improve communication. For this reason they committed to meeting every year if circumstances allowed.[291] They also affirmed a continuation of the methods of direct communication between the prime ministers of Great Britain and the Dominions without going through Britain's Colonial Office, and the right of overseas governments to nominate a cabinet minister to represent them in consultations with the British Prime Minister.[292] Although Smuts's memorandum was not officially published at the Imperial Conference, it was nevertheless a document which the Balfour Declaration of 1926 was later built on, paving the way for the Statute of Westminster in 1931.

3.4 The Dominions and the Anglo-Japanese Alliance

Despite the fact that the Canadian delegates did not particularly intervene in discussions on constitutional relations, they had a marked influence on the issue of the renewal of the Anglo-Japanese Alliance.[293] Beginning at the end of January 1921, the British government advised the Dominions that a number of issues in regard to current Imperial defence problems had to be dealt with prior to the summer Imperial Conference meeting. Nevertheless, discussion on ending or extending the Anglo-Japanese Alliance completely overshadowed all other defence matters.[294]

Ottawa's politicians considered relations with Japan to be a matter of fundamental importance which could affect the course of Imperial foreign policy for a long time to come, and as such had a thorough analysis undertaken. On 1 February 1921, Loring Christie submitted a memorandum whose lengthy analysis of twenty years of Anglo-Japanese co-operation came out clearly against the automatic renewal of the Alliance, instead proposing an alternative be found.[295] In mid-February, the Canadian government expressed its opposition to the idea of extending the Alliance, because they feared a deterioration in Anglo-American relations, and the unforeseeable impacts on Canadian interests on the North American continent which further alliance with Japan would likely lead to. They also opposed the unnecessary creation of barriers between the English-speaking countries, who should be co-operating rather than competing.[296] The Canadian perspective was also influenced by fears of the outcome of any American-Japanese animosity in the Far East, where Ottawa had had trading interests since the Siberian Intervention, and where they had an active mission on the Korean peninsula. Another factor was Canada's unwillingness to take in Japanese immigrants.[297]

The other Dominions, except for the Union of South Africa, viewed the matter differently. The Prime Ministers of Australia and New Zealand especially saw alliance with Japan more as a security guarantee than a threat.[298] Hughes feared that after the war, the Pacific could become an area where another international crisis could erupt, because the Wars and the Panama Canal has shifted the world's stage from the Mediterranean and the Atlantic to the Pacific. ... The American Navy is now in those waters. Peace in the Pacific means peace for this Empire and for the world.[299]

Although Hughes and Meighen differed in their perspective, their countries had similar priorities. An appropriate balance of powers in the Pacific meant more to Canadian and Australian interests than the international situation within Europe.[300]

His Majesty's Government realised in early 1920 that it was in a tricky situation. The Foreign Office and War Office proposed continuing the alliance with Japan, but Britain had significant interests in China and Korea.[301] An extensive memorandum from the end of February 1920 written by an official at the Foreign Office's Far Eastern Department, Charles Henry Bentinck, which analysed the ambitions of the great powers and European powers involved in China and the Far East confirmed the fact that British and American interests in the Pacific were in fact the same, whereas British and Japanese interests there were diametrically opposed. Bentinck pointed out that Japan was seeking a weak central government in China, a closed economy there, and that it was aiming to be the hegemon in the Far East. This was in opposition to Britain's endeavour at achieving a united and strong China and maintaining the principle of an open-door policy and equal trading opportunities there. The Foreign Office perceived Tokyo's hegemonic tendencies as a threat to Britain's power base and economic status in Hong Kong, Singapore, the Pacific islands and the Yangtze Basin. Disagreements between the Dominions and Japan mainly centred around the practical execution of the Dominions' "White policy", limiting "coloured" immigration and contrary to Japan's expansionistic objectives in the Pacific. Bentinck also stressed that the opposing positions of Japan and America in the Far East and Pacific regions would likely one day result in conflict, and Great Britain had better be careful in choosing which side it was going to be on.[302]

Although the First World War had tested the alliance with Japan, which had provided a certain feeling of security to the Pacific Dominions,[303] the British Empire's post-war naval weakness in the Fear East and Pacific[304] led to a reassessment of the situation and the beginning of intensive cooperation with the United States in Pacific affairs.[305] As such, generally good relations with America eventually became axioms of Imperial foreign policy. Britain became almost squeamish in its attempts at maintaining apparent unity of Imperial opinion in regard to third countries, and thus feared the Canadian cabinet might take too much initiative and begin expressing its opposition to renewal of the Alliance too openly.[306] Thus, after the war the Pacific was transformed into a place where the economic and political influence of Britain and America in particular clashed, alongside latent racial overtones of whether the Pacific should be "yellow or white".[307]

Following the First World War, the Anglo-Japanese Alliance was highly unpopular in the United States, because Tokyo's policies had taken on a more clearly expansionist course. The Americans feared extension of the alliance would be linked to acknowledgement of "Japan's special interests in eastern Asia,"[308] which they viewed as, "treachery … [of] modern civilised ideals".[309] For this reason, American politicians from 1920 had held the opinion that if the Anglo-Japanese Alliance was to be accepted, it should be renewed with certain modifications. In particular, it should guarantee an open-door principle in China, and Japan's volatile foreign policy meant that it should be concluded for no longer than five years.[310]

The Anglo-Japanese Alliance had been agreed in 1902 as a purely British treaty, in which the Dominions were not party to the agreement, even if the terms of the agreement were closely concerned with them from the very start. Since the self-governing overseas territories and the mother country had decided together to extend the alliance in 1911 for a further ten years, they also consulted over all aspects of renewal of the alliance in 1921.[311] When Dominion and British representatives met in June 1921 at the Imperial Conference, the London government following a number of months' discussion with Canada was in favour of renewing the alliance treaty with modifications which would satisfy America's reservations and which would align the treaty with the principles of the Covenant of the League of Nations,[312] something the 1911 alliance treaty did not align with.[313] Leading advocates of extending co-operation and alliance with Japan in the British cabinet included Lloyd George, former Prime Minister Arthur Balfour, the Secretary of State for Foreign Affairs George Nathaniel Curzon, later 1st Marquess Curzon of Kedleston, and the Secretary of State for the Colonies, Sir Winston Churchill.[314]

At the start of conference proceedings, it appeared that the matter would have to be dealt with quickly, because the alliance was coming to an end on 13 July 1921.[315] Australian Prime Minister Hughes, who mostly supported the arguments of the New Zealand Prime Minister, advocated in favour of a renewal of the Alliance. Canadian Prime Minister Meighen was particularly vigorously opposed, arguing for the necessity of accepting the American observations about the treaty.[316] In debates on implementing Imperial foreign policy, Meighen pursued the principle that the voice of the Dominions should be given due weight in decisions made in affairs which particularly affected them. The Canadian Prime Minister was thereby indicating that Ottawa's position should be a crucial factor in whether to renew or end the alliance with Japan.[317] Dominion statesmen were fully aware that the issue of alliance with Japan was an important foreign policy decision which would determine not just the form of relations with the United States, but also the British Empire's status in the Far East and in the Pacific.[318] British Prime Minister Lloyd George warned in this regard that the Empire had to speak with one voice in foreign policy to the outside, and as such he was a strong advocate of communication to the world taking place solely via the British Foreign Office.[319]

Although the Australian Prime Minister realised that Japanese Far East and Pacific policies were arousing significant international controversy and had long not corresponded to Australian "White policy", he anticipated that extension of the Alliance would allow the British Empire to control it better, and even direct it. During Conference discussions, Hughes therefore presented himself as a leading advocate of co-operation with Japan.[320] Shortly after the Imperial Conference began, Tokyo's representatives assured Britain that they wanted the Alliance extended in a form which would satisfy the American demands, that there were no insurmountable difficulties in terms of Japanese immigration to the Dominions, and that the "indefinite fears" of Japan's policy towards China were unfounded. Japan *de facto* posed arguments which endeavoured to give the impression that there was no animosity between America and Japan which could not be overcome.[321]

Nevertheless, the other Dominion representatives consistently expressed their worries over a renewal of the Anglo-Japanese Alliance, stressing that some kind of compromise had to be arrived at in order to maintain a united Imperial policy.[322] South Africa's General Smuts in particular noted on 29 June 1921 that Japan represented more of a "potential danger" than a friendly country, and that if the British Empire wanted to, "look to world peace, we must do nothing to alienate Japan". Smuts, who perceived most matters within a wider international context, considered Japan a threat to the peace guaranteed by the League of Nations, and as such suggested that all powers concerned should act on Pacific matters together.[323] The South African general did not hide his opinion that close co-operation with the United States would ensure the British Empire's security for the future.[324]

Meighen had long held a similar position, and on the same day spoke on the floor with a proposal that a conference of the four powers with interests in the Pacific be immediately convened in order to deal with current problems. Through his request that the Americans, Chinese and Japanese be involved in discussions, the Canadian Prime Minster had thus openly launched a campaign against extending the Alliance. Hughes's objection stressing the necessity of the British Empire having a reliable friend in the Pacific was ignored.[325] Australia's Prime Minister was not one of those who categorically rejected co-operation with America, but he did fear the threats the Australian continent might find itself subjected to if the treaty with Japan was not extended. During the 29 June 1921 discussions, he even declared: "If Australia was asked whether she would prefer America or Japan as an Ally, her choice would be America. But that choice is not offered her. ... Our Young democracy in its remote isolation, there is no answer."[326] Thus the Imperial Conference found itself in deadlock.

The British government found itself in an awkward position, because America had implied to them on 23 June 1921 that they were not in favour of any form of extending the Anglo-Japanese Alliance.[327] Not particularly optimistic either was a confidential report from the Committee of Imperial Defence analysing the strategic situation in the Far East in the event of non-renewal of co-operation with Tokyo. It noted that such a step would likely arouse resentment from Japan, which might turn it against the British Empire.[328] The conclusions of the Imperial Conference meeting at the end of June 1921 did not preclude the possibility that consensus might soon be achieved between Hughes, Massey, Meighen and Smuts. There was also an unlikely possibility that the Americans could agree to replacing the Anglo-Japanese treaty with a tripartite agreement.[329] As such, on 30 June the London parliament weighed up all the arguments and decided to accept three basic points which its foreign Policy in the Far East and Pacific should be based on in the coming period: (1) avoiding disputes with the United States; (2) endeavouring not to offend Japan to ensure the friendship of past years is not overlooked; and (3) to invite China to discussions so it can take part in seeking a viable solution.[330] Thus, the position of the Dominion of Canada at the turn of June and July 1921 significantly reformulated Imperial foreign policy.[331]

When American President Warren Harding's invitation to a conference in Washington which was to look in detail at naval arms limits and Pacific affairs arrived in London on 8 July 1921,[332] Lloyd George used it to postpone discussion of Pacific affairs including issues regarding extending the Anglo-Japanese Alliance until that forum.[333] In subsequent weeks, intensive communications took place between Britain and America on Pacific matters. The British government's attempt at achieving a preliminary compromise agreement, or even a preliminary conference on the Pacific in London, however, was not positively received in Washington. America informed Britain that no preliminary conclusions could be reached because the agenda was neither properly defined nor prepared; Japanese and Chinese delegates would be unlikely to be able to participate. At the same time, they claimed that American "public opinion" did not share the British desire to extend its Alliance with Tokyo.[334] The Americans shunned repeated British pleas in this matter due to the time available to President Harding and the text of the invitation to the conference.[335] The subsequent attempt by Dominion and British politicians to move preliminary Anglo-American-Japanese "consultation" to US territory, in Bar Harbor, Maine, was also unsuccessful.[336]

On 18 August 1921, British Prime Minister Lloyd George summarised the events and positions of British and Dominion politicians of recent weeks for members of the House of Commons in such a manner that the Americans surmised that the alliance with Japan was going to continue and no end was being planned.[337] In the second half of September, discussion between America and Britain resulted in strong warning by American Secretary of State Charles Evans Hughes, stating that an alliance with Japan represented a serious obstacle to Anglo-American friendship and co-operation;[338] America preferred multilateral treaties in the Pacific rather than bilateral pacts.[339] Pressure on the British cabinet grew. Over the course of September, British public opinion gradually moved towards friendship with America and away from renewing the alliance with Japan.[340] Harding's administration also became tougher in its arguments, opening up the outstanding issue of Britain's war debts to ensure His Majesty's hesitant government finally made the definitive decision of prioritising American friendship over alliance with Japan.[341]

Tokyo naturally agreed to the Americans' invitation to discussions.[342] To begin with, Japan took an evasive, almost non-committal position to British reappraisal of Imperial foreign policy in the Far East and Pacific.[343] Eventually, Japanese politicians started to view the circumstances surrounding the convening of the conference, and Britain's decision to take part, with considerable mistrust; it was difficult for them not to get the impression that Britain and America were plotting against Japan. As such, they decided to endeavour to defend Japan's "special" interests in the Far East and Pacific at the upcoming conference in Washington as strongly as possible.[344] They considered maintaining the Anglo-Japanese Alliance to be essential in order to "keep peace and order" in the Far East.[345]

America's attitudes in preliminary discussions upset not just British but also Dominion representatives, and the feelings deepened when America refused to expand those states invited to include Dominion representatives who would sit separately from the British delegates, or even dually with Britain as had been the case in the Paris Peace Conference.[346] In so refusing, on the one hand, they were rejecting the "new" international status of the Dominions as autonomous parts of the British Empire after the First World War and, on the other hand, were ostentatiously ignoring the fact that Australia, Canada and New Zealand had a natural interest in the situation in the Pacific.[347] The fact that Portugal was invited to the first large international conference after the Paris negotiations, and the Dominions were not invited, though General Smuts considered them states with interests in the region, was something Smuts considered a "major step backwards for the status of the Dominions"; the situation was somewhat improved when Dominion representatives were included in the British Empire delegation.[348] In early November 1921, Smuts stated that his objection to the inadequate status of the Dominions at the Washington conference was widely shared in the Union of South Africa, and that, "Dominion status is a matter which is not only fundamental for the present critical Irish negotiations, but also for the future peace and welfare of the whole British Empire".[349]

The British Empire delegation in Washington was led by former British Prime Minister Arthur James Balfour, who formally represented the Union of South Africa which did not have its own representative due to strict delegate number limits; he was assisted by the First Lord of the Admiralty, Arthur Hamilton Lee, 1st Viscount Lee of Fareham, and the British Ambassador in Washington, Sir Auckland Geddes, formally representing the absent David Lloyd George who was busy with Irish matters. Canada was represented by Prime Minister-designate Robert Laird Borden, since Meighen was taking part in an election campaign, India by Srinivasa Sastri, New Zealand by Supreme Court Judge Sir John William Salmond, and Australia by Senator and Defence Minister George Foster Pearce. Sir Maurice Hankey was not just heading the British Empire delegation secretariat but was also responsible for political co-operation with the senior negotiators of states involved; when absent, Canadian Foreign Ministry legal advisor Loring Christie took his place.[350]

From the moment the conference in Washington was announced, Britain's Foreign Office prepared thoroughly for it. In the second half of August 1921, there was still uncertainty over what position the Americans would take in discussions of the Anglo-Japanese Alliance, and whether they would favour a modified form of the alliance or a tripartite agreement.[351] American representatives repeatedly indicated they were going to oppose both these possibilities. Even so, at the end of October, Britain declared the Imperial foreign policy priorities they would strive to achieve prior to the upcoming conference: (1) to sign a tripartite treaty or declaration between the United States, Japan and Britain; and (2) to agree a naval treaty for the Pacific region.[352] Britain's Foreign Office anticipated that the chances of a tripartite agreement being adopted would increase if it was purely declarative in nature without including any military commitments in the document.[353] Balfour set off for the conference without any detailed instructions on how exactly to approach certain points. Assuring Japan of Britain's continued friendship was a wider objective for the London cabinet; in other matters, Balfour's hands were free.[354]

On 12 November 1921, American President Warren Harding officially opened the Washington Disarmament Conference, promising that it would contribute to "minimising errors in international relations".[355] Although the Anglo-Japanese Alliance was not part of the conference's officially approved programme, Britain considered it of great importance. Since the Americans had openly informed Britain that the security of the Pacific Dominions and India fell solely within the competence of the three largest naval powers, i.e. the British Empire, United States and Japan,[356] Balfour, who internally hated the idea of ending the alliance with Japan which had been proven in times of war,[357] decided to propose signing a tripartite agreement. Despite America's previous reserved declaration, Balfour judged that if formulated appropriately and balanced in content, then the document might convince the Americans of the benefits of dealing with Pacific and Far East affairs trilaterally.[358]

On 11 November 1921, Balfour used a discussion with American Secretary of State Charles Hughes to outline a tripartite arrangement, much of which he had worked on himself without precise instructions from the British government.[359] According to the proposal, whose content was based on documents originally from Foreign Office officials,[360] the signatories would agree to respect each other, consult each other on matters of importance and not threaten each other. In the event of territorial demands, they were able to conclude military arrangements, but not military alliances.[361] This mention of defence agreements allowed the Anglo-Japanese alliance to be restored under appropriate circumstances. The fact that Balfour intended to deal with issues related to the policies of the great powers towards China separately, and that his document did not mention its status, was a major weakness in his plan.[362]

Although in discussions over the wording, Balfour incorporated some of Hughes's objections, he was unable to convince him even a little that Britain's steps and proposals were not hiding a latent attempt at keeping some form of the Anglo-Japanese Alliance alive.[363] Japanese representatives generally supported a tripartite arrangement which would allow some form of alliance with Britain.[364] The Japanese ambassador in Washington, Baron Kijūrō Shidehara, doubted Balfour's plan would be acceptable and instead proposed a compromise wording for a trilateral agreement between Britain, Japan and the United States; he was unable to turn around the Americans' reluctant attitude, however.[365] At the same time, the Pacific Dominions were gradually retreating from their previously uncompromising positions. On 24 November, the Australian delegate, Senator Pearce, declared that Australia would only pursue a form of Anglo-Japanese alliance which would be acceptable to the United States.[366]

During November 1921, intensive communication took place between American, British and Japanese representatives, resulting in significant modification of the Balfour plan. Once discussions between Balfour and American delegates Senator Henry Cabot Lodge and Elihu Root had taken place,[367] the head of the British delegation met with American Secretary of State Hughes, who agreed with Shidehara's formulations but proposed two key changes: (1) to expand the parties to the treaty to include France; and (2) the new four-party treaty should focus only on Pacific islands and leave out divisive issues relating to the Chinese mainland, in particular the province of Shandong.[368] Hughes's demands essentially ended ideas that an alliance between Britain and Japan might form under appropriate circumstances.[369] America's representatives were vigorous in pushing through this four-party treaty, because it corresponded better with their perspective on the power balance in the Pacific and because they had long had to face criticism from a domestic public opposed to concluding a tripartite treaty.[370]

The American position disappointed Japan's negotiators. Although they accepted a four-party arrangement, they had to give up hope not just of a restoration of the Anglo-Japanese Alliance, but also the opportunity of dealing with the issue of China[371] as part of the Four-Power Treaty.[372] In the end, Britain accepted Hughes's 7 December 1921 proposal when they were assured the treaty also applied to Australia and New Zealand.[373] The Dominion prime ministers agreed with the arrangement. The treaty's contents were a particular success for Canadian representatives, because it generally corresponded to Meighen's proposals and positions, as he had presented at the Imperial Conference in summer 1921; furthermore, differences of opinion between the Dominions had been overcome.[374] On 13 December, the Four-Party Treaty was signed, its fourth article ending the Anglo-Japanese Alliance. The treaty was to remain valid for a period of ten years.[375] One can conclude that the Four-Power Treaty satisfied American demands and did not expressly "offend" the Japanese.[376] At the same time, a trigger for potential future Anglo-American animosity was also eliminated.[377]

Conclusion of the four-party treaty was a great success for Washington, which had managed to push the "American view" on arrangements in the Pacific, and in particular prevent a renewal of the Anglo-Japanese Alliance. Nevertheless, London's representatives still believed the British position was not significantly weakened; on the contrary, they anticipated that the new circumstances would help bring discussions on further naval treaties to a successful conclusion. Despite all the troubles which came along with discussing extension of the alliance in 1921, Britain considered its relations with Japan to have remained friendly.[378] Balfour, for example, did not consider it a significant failure, as he did not perceive expanding the signatories from three to four to be a change in policy, but rather a necessary addition of another party with interests in the Pacific.[379] Nevertheless, the Four-Power Treaty confirmed a trend of many years: Great Britain was prioritising good relations with the United States over a closer alliance with Japan.[380]

From the first days of the conference in Washington, in addition to confidential meetings on the Four-Power Treaty, another key issue was discussed publicly at the same time – naval disarmament. From the beginning, America stuck firmly to the vision it presented.[381] Secretary of State Hughes proposed a ratio of battleships for the USA, British Empire and Japan of 5:5:3, and a ten-year "naval vacation" for the construction of new ships.[382] Balfour was dismayed by Hughes's proposal, although he admitted that the "statesmanlike and courageous"[383] American Secretary of State had apparently, "sunk in thirty-five minutes more ships than all the admirals of the world have destroyed in a cycle of centuries".[384]

Borden subsequently responded to Hughes's speech, wanting to minimise the anticipated negative reaction of Britain's navy,[385] by submitting an extensive memorandum. Although the Canadian navy had no battleships, and it could not be claimed that the proposed arms limits directly affected them, Borden supported the American plan. He also proposed using regular disarmament conferences to draw the United States into global events; he expected this would result in their soon joining the League of Nations.[386] Borden was supported in this matter by Australia's Senator Pearce.[387] Britain was more cautious.[388] In subsequent weeks, the issue of naval disarmament was discussed in detail and thorny issues were dealt with.[389] The Washington Naval Treaty was signed on 6 February 1922 by five powers – the United States of America, Great Britain, Japan, France and Italy – with arms limit ratios of 5:5:3:1.75:1.75. The issue of China's sovereignty and territorial integrity was dealt with in the Nine-Power Treaty which included, in addition to the aforementioned powers, countries with interests in the region, namely Belgium, China, the Netherlands and Portugal.[390] From the start, the treaties were viewed comprehensively as an interlinked system of treaties dealing with Pacific and Far East matters.

The Washington Naval Conference established a new balance of naval power in the Pacific in early 1922, preventing the renewal of the Anglo-Japanese Alliance.[391] The Four-Power Treaty was designed to serve as a sufficient guarantee of the *status quo* in the Pacific, while also helping to minimise Australia and New Zealand's fears of future developments. However, the opposite proved true.[392] Australia and New Zealand viewed the treaty as a painful compromise which provided only temporary security, not permanent security.[393] The Washington discussions represented the first great opportunity in which the Dominions were heavily involved in formulating Imperial foreign policy, although this did not mean they influenced British foreign policy.[394] Ottawa representatives in particular justifiably believed that their unshakable positions had helped to push through Canadian foreign policy priorities.[395] British Prime Minister David Lloyd George declared in this regard: "There was a time when Downing Street controlled the Empire; today the Empire gives orders to Downing Street."[396]

3.5 Irish Affairs and the Question of Accepting Dominion Status

The Irish question, linked to attempts at implementing Home Rule, dominated British politics from the late Victorian period until the signing of the Anglo-Irish Treaty in December 1921. It was of great importance for constitutional relations within the British Commonwealth of Nations, because for the first time the granting of Dominion status was laid down in a treaty without a previous gradual transformation from a Crown colony through self-governing colony to adoption of Dominion status.[397] Politicians in the other "white settlements" first sought autonomy, then endeavoured to restrict the mother country's authority, or directly demanded the specification or redefining of the country's status within the Empire. Ireland took a different path.[398] When the third Home Rule bill was submitted in 1912, no Dominion had the level of freedom in internal affairs which this bill gave Ireland.[399] Although shortly afterwards doubts arose about the financial, administrative and constitutional feasibility of Home Rule,[400] until 1921 when British politics became split over the issue of Ireland, Dominion status had never been offered to Irish officials.[401]

The 1916 Easter Rising and the revealing of Irish-German collaboration led to a growth in Anglo-Irish antagonism to such an extent that as the Great War was drawing to a close, Irish nationalists began seeking international recognition of an independent Ireland, and this led to a gradual weakening of relations with the British Empire.[402] The post-war general election at the end of December 1918 led to victory for the republican Sinn Féin party, which acquired a majority in the Irish Parliament (*Dáil Éireann*). At its first sitting on 21 January 1919, MPs voted to declare Ireland's independence, heralding a new and even more turbulent period in Anglo-Irish relations.[403]

From London's perspective, the 1919–1921 armed conflict which further exacerbated mutual animosity had only two solutions: (1) granting Ireland Dominion status within the British Empire; and (2) Irish independence and the creation of a Republic of Ireland. Until May 1921, British officials, in particularly members of the Irish Committee, did not wish to consider granting Ireland full Dominion status such as that enjoyed by Canada. As such, they spoke only using the vague term of Dominion Home Rule, which was markedly limited and in fact meant merely fiscal autonomy; it was *de facto* a scaled-back version of Dominion status. The fundamental idea behind the proposal for Dominion Home Rule was to expand the original 1914 bill to take account of the events of subsequent years. Until 1921, this proposal had the support of Asquith's Liberals, the Southern Irish Unionists, Sir Horace Plunkett and H. A. L. Fisher.[404] At the end of March 1921, Lloyd George used a debate in the House of Commons to pose the rhetorical question of whether the proposal was acceptable for the Irish. He answered that this was hardly likely.[405] Thus, Irish affairs became a thorny issue for Britain's Liberal government.[406]

In his address, the Prime Minister referred to the fact that there was no point in working on a plan which was *a priori* unacceptable for the Irish, or rather for their political representation. All interested parties agreed that it all depended on what Ireland's representatives were seeking. Labour advocated that the Irish perspective on self-determination be respected. John Robert Clynes, for example, believed that self-determination in the Irish context would lead towards a maximalist form of national government within a wider Imperial unit framework, i.e. *de facto* a form of government as seen in self-governing overseas territories.[407]

During debates on Irish self-determination and Dominion Home Rule, there was frequent overlap in terms and what those terms meant. Proponent of a strong Dominion status, Andrew Bonar Law, noted this in a speech on 30 March 1920 when he posed this question in the House of Commons: "What does Dominion status mean?" He immediately answered that for the Irish, it should mean the opportunity to have control of the destinies of their own country. He saw the difference between the status of the Dominions and the proposed Dominion Home Rule in the fact that Dominions could make their own free decisions, whereas Dominion Home Rule excluded that possibility. According to Bonar Law, the level of freedom in a Dominion's decision-making was such that, "if the self-governing Dominions, Australia, Canada, chose tomorrow to say, 'We will no longer make a part of the British Empire,' we would not try to force them. Dominion Home Rule means the right to decide their own destinies".[408] The Unionists trusted his interpretation, though he did not convince Sinn Féin supporters.[409] The Irish were already clearly seeking the establishment of a republic.[410]

On 23 July 1920, an extended meeting of the British government took place, at which they endeavoured to determine the most appropriate approach to the Irish question. A proposal for beginning discussions with Sinn Féin representatives was the key point, and this was debated for some time. Foreign Secretary Lord Curzon agreed with the position of British representatives in Dublin and endorsed the idea that the "scaled-back" Dominion Home Rule be expanded in line with Irish demands in return for an agreement that London would hold on to Ulster. The next day, the British Prime Minister received a summary report from cabinet officer Thomas Jones of previous discussions. Its conclusions clearly supported the acceptance of a Dominion principle in dealing with the Irish question. The conclusions also emphasised Britain's overall military weakness in Ireland and the fact that the British government found itself at a crossroads in which it would have to choose between a gradation of the conflict or beginning discussions with Irish representatives. Jones proposed that Lloyd George make a major speech offering a peace settlement through Dominion Home Rule for the south of Ireland alongside the principle of self-determination for Ulster. At the time, however, British politicians were not considering awarding Dominion status as meant in Law's March 1920 speech, but rather again just its limited form, i.e. fiscal autonomy without the ability to make decisions on defence matters.[411]

Over the subsequent months, especially after adoption of the Government of Ireland Act in December 1920, there was an escalation in conflict since the majority of the Irish population saw the new law as another act of British aggression intended to divide the island's unity and prevent it from becoming independent. Many British and Dominion officials, the press, members of the Round Table Movement who had been interested in Irish affairs for many years, and last but not least, even the King himself, began expressing their doubts over the justification for using military strength, which negated the principles on which British society was founded and which it should defend.[412]

At the start of summer 1921, the British Prime Minister found himself in an unenviable situation, facing a growing number of demands for radical change in the current course being taken in the Irish question. In particular, the well-known proponent of Irish independence Jan Smuts, who had arrived in England for a meeting of the Imperial Conference, demanded that he end this, "unmeasured calamity ... [tending to] poison both our Empire relations and our foreign relations" and give Ireland Dominion status.[413] Essentially overnight, Lloyd George decided to try to reach a compromise through political dialogue instead of continuing an approach of confrontation.[414] However, he did not definitively reject the possibility of military operations being restarted. Referring to this policy shift, Winston Churchill astutely noted:

> No British Government in modern times has ever appeared to make so complete and sudden a reversal of policy as that which ensued. In May ... [all means] were used to "hunt down the murder gang": in June the goal was "a lasting reconciliation with the Irish people".[415]

One reason the British Prime Minister did this was so that the conflict did not contribute to stoking revolutionary nationalism in India and Egypt and did not promote republicanism in South Africa.[416] After publication of the conditions for a ceasefire on 24 June 1921, Lloyd George officially invited the President of the Irish parliament, Éamon de Valera, and the Prime Minister of Northern Ireland, Sir James Craig, to a conference in London, where discussions were to be held with the objective of ending Anglo-Irish hostility.[417]

Most of the Empire's statespeople showed a keen interest in events in Ireland, but it was General Smuts whose opinion particularly stood out, as someone who lauded the principles of Dominion status. For many, Smuts was not just another Dominion Prime Minister, but rather a proponent of an "alternative vision for a Commonwealth of Nations" standing in opposition to advocates of Empire centralisation.[418] Since de Valera was hesitating in confirming his participation in the July conference in London,[419] at the request of the King, Smuts became directly involved in settling any disputes and accepted de Valera's invitation to hold preliminary discussions in Dublin.[420] George V believed that Smuts would be able to persuade de Valera to agree to Britain's peace initiative.[421]

On 5 July 1921, Smuts set out with the consent of the British Prime Minister as Mr Smith on his journey. Although he was not an official representative of the British government and he was not bearing a specific offer to the highly suspicious de Valera and his three fellow ministers, Eamonn J. Duggan, Arthur Griffith and Robert C. Barton, he tried to make use of his experience from the period of the Anglo-Boer conflict to ensure de Valera did not make what Smuts considered a fatal mistake, i.e. *a priori* rejecting Britain's proposal for peace without taking part in the planned London conference in mid-May and to once again reconsider the demand for a republic and instead see the advantages arising from Dominion status in Anglo-Irish relations.[422] Smuts was of the opinion that, "Dominions are happy in the Commonwealth", and as such he did not see why the Irish should not strive to achieve autonomy.[423] Smuts's journey was a success, with de Valera confirming his acceptance of the invitation a few days later.[424]

At the start of July 1921, David Lloyd George had just two solutions in mind: (1) allowing the Irish their independence, which would prevent a united island; or (2) allow them unification, which would rule out independence.[425] When he met Éamon de Valera in mid-July in Downing Street, he decided after a few days to propose something "new" – Dominion status.[426] He based this proposal on the idea that the British Empire represented the largest community of free fraternal nations in the world.[427] On 20 July, the British cabinet submitted a proposal for settling the conflict based on the idea that if the British and French in Canada had been able to overcome their rivalry of many years, and if the British and Boer colonists had been able to come together to form the Union of South Africa, then why could something similar not be possible in Ireland? The proposal included a promise of full autonomy in domestic affairs (the economy, judicial system, domestic security, etc.). Compared to some other Dominions, however, London reserved the right to use its air and naval bases there. The proposal also included the theoretical possibility of reunification of the island should representatives of Northern Ireland agree to the abolition of its current privileges.[428]

Although Éamon de Valera for himself rejected the proposal initially, he left the final decision to the Irish parliament.[429] The Irish leader had been mistrustful for many years of participation in various colonial and imperial projects, as he considered the Irish to be victims of British colonialism.[430] Smuts, who was aware of the limits of Britain's proposal, endeavoured to persuade de Valera to accept the submitted proposal. He called on him to consider above all the fact that Dominion status meant an offer of freedom, not the Home Rule on offer during the times of Gladstone and Asquith. He also stressed the Imperial Conferences aspect, which over time had helped to develop the British Empire. In the issue of Irish unity, he recommended greater patience since he believed that the dissenting position of Ulster representatives required more time for the island's unification to be achieved.[431] All his efforts, however, proved fruitless. On 10 August, de Valera sent Lloyd George his official response, in which he welcomed the recognition of Irish right to self-determination, but in which he also described the proposed Dominion status as insufficient for Irish freedom because he feared Ireland's geographical proximity meant Dominion status would not work in practice.[432]

De Valera was right to some degree. Ireland had not in fact undergone similar developments as the other self-governing overseas territories. Canada, the Union of South Africa, Australia, Newfoundland and New Zealand had strived for Dominion status because they perceived it as a certain type of reward, or advancement, for successful development, while Ireland saw it as something which politicians in London were forcing them into.[433] Although de Valera accepted that the essence of Dominion government was based on practical independence since Dominions had their own armed forces and navy and thus did not need to rely for defence on their mother country, he nevertheless determined that in Ireland's case, its short distance from Great Britain meant that this was independence only "on paper".[434]

Three days later, the British Prime Minister sent a response to de Valera, in which he warned that Dominion status was the maximum that His Majesty's Government was able to offer Ireland. He underscored his position, stating that, "no British Government can compromise, namely, the claim that we should acknowledge the right of Ireland to secede from her allegiance to the King".[435] A rather fruitless exchange of opinions through letters and telegrams continued until the end of September 1920.[436] Over time, both sides came to the conclusion that it would be more practical to meet at a conference which would be called, "with a view to ascertaining how the association of Ireland with the community of nations known as the British Empire may best be reconciled with Irish National Aspirations".[437] Both the Irish and British were weary of the conflict, and this increased hopes that an agreement could be achieved. British Secretary of State for the Colonies Winston Churchill, for example, believed that it was in the interests of the Empire that a permanent peace be agreed with Ireland.[438] In contrast, South African Prime Minister Smuts called on Lloyd George to offer Ireland Dominion status.[439]

On 11 October 1921, British and Irish officials met at a conference in London aiming to find a compromise, and they eventually succeeded in doing so on 6 December. Neither side could claim to be winners.[440] During prior discussions in the Irish parliament, it was decided that Éamon de Valera would not participate in the conference, and as such Arthur Griffith, the Foreign Affairs Minister, was to be head of the Irish delegation; Michael Collins, the Finance Minister, was to be one of his principal assistants.[441] However, the Irish delegates were at a disadvantage: although they had plenipotentiary status, in reality their hands were tied, and they often had to ask Dublin to approve their decisions.[442] Furthermore, de Valera did not hold back from repeatedly providing critical comments to the negotiators;[443] in contrast to them, he came from Sinn Féin's republican wing.[444]

The British side was represented by Prime Minister David Lloyd George, Lord Privy Seal and Leader of the House of Commons Austen Chamberlain, Secretary of State for the Colonies Winston Churchill and Lord Chancellor Frederick Edwin Smith, 1st Earl of Birkenhead.[445] Important roles at conference negotiations were held by British official Lionel Curtis, who was present as an authority in Dominion status, and who later helped ensure smooth incorporation of the treaty within the constitutional process underway within the Empire; and Thomas Jones, Deputy Secretary to the Cabinet of many years.[446] Since the British officials were also representing the British Empire, Dominion government officials were essentially not involved in discussions, although they did take part in the Imperial Conference in London in summer.

De Valera's correspondence with Lloyd George meant that there was an assumption from the beginning that the debate would be dominated by two key points: (1) Ireland's relationship to the Crown and Empire; and (2) Northern Ireland's position. The conference did, nevertheless, look at a wider range of issues, and as such the agenda was divided up through the appointment of three committees – the Committee on the Observance of the Truce, the Committee on Naval and Air Defence, and the Committee on Financial Relations.[447]

Britain's 20 July proposal also included a clause stating that Great Britain reserved the right to use its naval bases in Ireland to defend the British Isles, as specified in an Admiralty report.[448] The issue of defence at times of peace and war was discussed at a meeting of the Committee on Naval and Air Defence chaired by Churchill on 17 October 1921. However, an argument broke out between the chair and Childers regarding Dominion neutrality in a war. The dispute was about whether the principle of neutrality was compatible with Dominion status. Churchill stated the government's position that neutrality was incompatible with Dominion status, as a state of war was declared by the monarch on behalf of all entities in a constitutional relationship.[449]

A day later, the Irish negotiators submitted a memorandum to Britain in which they expressed their dissatisfaction with Churchill's concept of naval and air defence and armed forces recruitment. British presence at Irish ports was a particular thorn in their side, as Ireland planned to build up its own navy. Nor were British demands consistent with their objective of achieving Irish independence and neutrality. The Secretary to Ireland's delegation, Robert Erskine Childers, sought to achieve confirmation of Ireland's neutral status, and its subsequent guarantee from the international community. Childers was one of Ireland's experts on Dominion status, and as such he endeavoured to ensure Ireland received the same conditions as Canada, which he perceived as a "model Dominion" amongst the overseas self-governing territories.[450]

London's July proposal offered Dominion status, something which was meant to allow Ireland to find the ideal way that "the Irish people may find as worthy and as complete an expression of their political and spiritual ideals within the Empire as any of the numerous and varied nations united in allegiance to His Majesty's Throne".[451] Yet Dominion status certainly could not be perceived as merely a symbol of monarchy. In reality, it was more a clarification of relations between different parts of the Commonwealth, or the link between the Irish state and the mother country, rather than matters of international relations. Above all, the Irish wanted to clarify at the conference whether Dominion status was compatible with their aspirations, and whether it was the same model in practice that self-governing territories had overseas, in particular Canada.[452] Nevertheless, Irish politicians were not united in accepting Dominion status. Home Affairs Minister Austin Stack, for example, who was known for his extreme positions, vehemently rejected accepting any kind of compromise form of independence (including along the model of Canada); he was stubborn in his insistence on complete independence for Ireland.[453]

Since British representatives anticipated disagreement in this matter, during the first days of the conference they gave Lionel Curtis the task of producing a report in which he would try to define Dominion status on the basis of his personal experience and knowledge, as acquired over many years studying the issue and from living in self-governing overseas territories. On 17 October, Curtis submitted his memorandum summarising the rapid transformation of British-Dominion relations and changes which had taken place since 1914. He stressed the growing influence of Dominion representatives in the British Empire's decisions and foreign policies. Their new international position was meant to have become apparent in the division of the signature of the peace treaties at the Paris negotiations. Curtis acknowledged, however, that the practical completion of this change was in the competencies of the Imperial Conference, as Dominions now had an equal status with the mother country both in terms of representation within Imperial institutions and in domestic and foreign affairs. He admitted, however, that one could not precisely define relations between the Dominions and Great Britain because matters which were undefined did not have precise limits and allowed for more practical utilisation, contributing the strengthening of the union and power of the British Empire. He also highlighted the fact that even if the Empire looked united from the outside, there was free exchange of opinions between its members. According to Curtis, the Imperial system depended entirely on the willingness of its participants to refrain from acts which could threaten the other parts of the British Empire.[454]

Two days later, Britain received Ireland's position in response to Curtis's document, in which Erskine Childers expressed his dissatisfaction with the aspects of Dominion autonomy revealed. Childers was of the impression that Curtis had ignored certain specific facts in the memorandum, and as such he was critical of the British conclusions. He determined that the right of Dominions to freely leave the British Empire was only covert in Curtis's material, and that Bonar Law's well-known and clear March 1923 assertion that Dominions could leave the Empire at any time was not taken sufficient account of. Childers firmly rejected Curtis's reasoning for not being able to precisely define relations between the Dominions and Great Britain. He noted that if there were no defined constitutional relations, then every Dominion was entirely free in regard to other members of the British Empire, whom they were linked to only through bonds of friendship.[455]

The tense atmosphere and conclusions of previous discussions made Arthur Griffith form the opinion that the proposed form of Dominion status was unacceptable for Ireland. The Irish negotiators were using the definition as expressed by Bonar Law in the House of Commons in March 1920, and which allowed at a certain time for free withdrawal from the British Empire, something which would suit Ireland's demand for independence. The difficulty was in the fact that although in practice secession might take place in line with Bonar Law's assertion, there was no actual legislation in this regard. Neither were the British delegates able to dispel Irish fears over the geographic proximity of the mother country.[456]

On 24 October 1921, the Irish delegation submitted a document entitled Draft Treaty A, in which over the course of October it had laid down its own vision for Anglo-Irish relations and which was meant to represent a compromise between advocates of Dominion status and the Republican establishment.[457] Their ideas were based on the theory of "external association", which de Valera devised in July 1921 and in which the Irish vision was interpreted as absolute sovereignty in all domestic matters, and only an external connection to the British Commonwealth in order to defend shared foreign interests.[458] In contrast, Britain was basing its ideas on a concept of "free association".[459]

In this counterproposal, the Irish openly demanded recognition of Ireland as a sovereign independent state, associated in an external form with the British Commonwealth, which, along with the League of Nations and the United States, would guarantee the island's permanent neutrality. The question of Ulster was to be declared an Irish domestic matter. At meetings of the Imperial Conference, Ireland was to receive separate representation at the same level as Great Britain. However, the proposal did not touch upon the Republican or monarchist establishment. The absence of obligations towards the Crown prevented Britain from ever accepting it.[460] Although at first sight any differences between "external association" and membership of the Commonwealth appeared small, in fact the opposite was true.

After studying the Irish counterproposal, British officials came to the conclusion that the nature of the London negotiations had now changed, since the new proposed concept was materially different from their July proposal. Besides the principle of "external association", the Irish negotiators also aimed to prevent Ireland's permanent division into northern and southern parts. As such, they used of a number of informal meetings with Lloyd George and Churchill to express their willingness to make a trade with Britain. They suggested they could reassess their rejection of obligations towards the Crown and Dominion status in exchange for reunification of the island under Dublin's influence.[461] On 27 October 1921, an optimistic Griffith informed de Valera that good progress was being made.[462] In their subsequent memorandum, the Irish even retreated in the issue of naval and air defence, allowing their joint operation. They also confirmed their previous spoken promises in writing, i.e. their readiness to acknowledge the Crown's authority and join the British Commonwealth on condition that Ireland would be reunited.[463]

On 10 November 1921, Lloyd George informed his Northern Irish counterpart, Sir James Craig, of how discussions were going at the London conference. He suggested that Craig should accept Irish unity and recognise the establishment of an all-Ireland parliament which would respect the principle of a self-governing Irish state.[464] Craig refused to proceed on that basis, and as an Ulster Unionist he insisted on the rules and privileges which Northern Ireland had received through adoption of the Government of Ireland Act 1920.[465] He also expressed the wish that Ulster maintain closer ties with Great Britain and the Empire. If ties with London had to be severed, he asked for the granting of Dominion status.[466] In subsequent discussions between Lloyd George and Craig, the request was made that the often informal and vague assurances of Sinn Féin on the content of the agreement be clearly stated.[467]

For this reason, on 22 November 1921, the Irish delegates submitted a new memorandum written by Childers, Barton and Duffy which contained their proposals for maintaining Ireland's "essential unity". The Irish insisted on keeping Irish independence, sovereignty and integrity, and securing an equal status to Great Britain within the League of Nations, and they expressed their intention to be involved in defending the island. They were ready to consider the issue of naval bases for the British navy. In return, they offered close association with the British Empire in issues of shared interest, recognition of the Crown as a symbol and representation of fraternity, and adoption of friendly policies towards Great Britain. Part of their proposal was also to include an agreement for free trade of goods. They were prepared to incorporate the Northern Ireland Parliament's existing legislative positions with security guarantees defending its own interests into the national parliament.[468] For Ireland, this memorandum represented a concession on a number of points within the formerly submitted Draft Treaty A. Although this new document reopened the option of maintaining the republican apparatus, it entrusted foreign policy within the auspices of the British Commonwealth. Thus the Irish negotiators again confirmed that they wanted primarily to ensure the unity of Ireland; they did not want to be members of the British Empire, they did not accept the British sovereign as the King of Ireland and they continued to insist on republican status.[469]

The 22 November 1921 memorandum generated opposition from the British side, since Ireland's maximalist demands increased the likelihood conference negotiations would fail. Although Griffith attempted to allay uncertainties over the level of Ireland's association with the Commonwealth,[470] he was unable to affect British disappointment with the document. Britain accepted that there were two diametrically opposed perspectives on the method for coming to a solution, Irish and British, but it did not agree with the claim that Dominion status was a vague abstract concept. The British accused the Irish delegation of not submitting even one constructive proposal over six weeks of discussions, and as such they decided to bring discussions to a close and submit their final proposal.[471]

Ireland received the proposed treaty on 1 December 1921, which contained eighteen articles and one appendix specifying the military installations Britain required. Britain again offered Dominion status with the new name of the Irish Free State, excluding Ulster. This led to some unease amongst Irish delegates, since the proposal had little in common with October 1921's Draft Treaty A which they considered the basis for conference discussions.[472] Although the Irish cabinet was divided in opinion, there was a clear majority in favour of rejecting the submitted agreement.[473]

Three days later, Ireland submitted a counterproposal, which British representatives rejected after just ten minutes since its contents did not correspond to previous discussions.[474] The Irish delegation had a choice: (1) sign the proposed agreement; or (2) reject it, which would mean military operations restarting. The British Prime Minister had decided to take a final gamble.[475] Looking back, his position was a key factor which forced the Irish delegates to sign the agreement without consulting their government and waiting for instructions, as Dublin had rejected the same wording two days earlier.[476] Michael Collins aptly described the act of signing it as having essentially signed his own death warrant.[477]

On 6 December 1921, the treaty was signed, and on this basis the Irish Free State was formed, or rather recognised, as a part of the community of nations forming the British Commonwealth of Nations, with the same Dominion status as Canada, the Commonwealth of Australia, New Zealand, the Union of South Africa and Newfoundland.[478] In reality, however, Ireland became another Dominion with a Governor-General representing the Crown's interests. From the very time the treaty was signed, it faced criticism from many quarters. According to some, the very fact that Ireland's status was put down in a treaty was a *de facto* recognition of the Irish state's domestic sovereignty.[479]

Members of Ireland's cabinet who were not involved in negotiations in London discovered that the treaty had been signed, along with de Valera, from the morning papers, which had a detailed summary of the status of negotiations. As such, it is no wonder that they were opposed to the treaty terms from the beginning.[480] Some of them held the opinion that by signing the treaty, the delegates had disobeyed instructions, exceeded their powers and presented the government with a *fait accompli*.[481] On 8 December 1921, a meeting of Ireland's ministers took place, during which Arthur Griffith offered his unqualified support for the treaty, Michael Collins, Robert Barton, Thomas Cosgrave and Kevin O'Higgins supported it only because it was already signed, and Éamon de Valera, Cathal Brugha and Austin Stack refused to recommend it for ratification.[482]

Britain began meeting certain clauses in the treaty regardless of whether the Irish parliament was going to approve the treaty or not, although their implementation was not an easy task.[483] On 14 December 1921, a debate began in Westminster which ended with ratification of the Anglo-Irish Treaty. During its course, the issue of defining Dominion status re-emerged. David Lloyd George posed the question: "What does 'Dominion status' mean? It is difficult and dangerous to give a definition." Although he did not attempt to give a definition, he spoke of the pitfalls which accompanied it, and directly of what should not occur within a Dominion arrangement. Above all, he feared various restrictive measures and rigid procedures would have a negative impact on the development of relations between the mother country and Dominions. Lloyd George was adamant that Dominion status should not allow limits arising from the status of the "model Dominion", Canada, to be encroached.[484] As such, Canada closely followed the discussion around signature of the Anglo-Irish Treaty and establishment of the Irish Free State, because it had a special interest as the "model Dominion".[485]

On 14 December 1921, de Valera attempted to turn the unfavourable situation around by submitting an alternative agreement based on the concept of "external association", but without success.[486] He then promised members of parliament he would not give up,[487] and as such he reformulated previous conclusions to submit them with a new proposal called Document No. 2 on 3 January 1922, which was meant to represent a compromise over the agreed Anglo-Irish Treaty (sometimes also referred to as Document No. 1). The main difference between these documents was in the fact that the 6 December 1921 agreement had already been signed, while the new proposal was not.[488] De Valera spoke against the Anglo-Irish Treaty during a debate in a powerful speech in which he declared: "I am against this Treaty because it does not reconcile Irish national aspirations with association with the British Government. I am against this Treaty, not because I am a man of war, but a man of peace. I am against this Treaty because it will not end the centuries of conflict between the two nations of Great Britain and Ireland."[489] De

Valera's argument, however, fell on deaf ears, and the Irish parliament ratified the treaty with a majority of seven votes. On 10 January 1922, de Valera resigned from his post as President of the parliament, and members of parliament elected Arthur Griffith to take his place.[490] In the future, de Valera would call signature of the treaty "historic appeasement" which did, however "conserve" a final settlement between Britain and Ireland.[491]

During Anglo-Irish discussions in London in autumn 1921 and over the course of subsequent debates, a complication arose over the precise definition of Dominion status. Advocates of the Anglo-Irish Treaty reassured their sympathisers by claiming that freedom and equality arose directly from Dominion status. The absence of a precise definition of Dominions' rights and obligations, as Irish Republicans were zealous in pointing out, however, represented a marked drawback for proponents of the acceptance of the Anglo-Irish Treaty. Discussions which took place over signature of the treaty stressed the need to convince not just politicians, but also the public, of the form of freedom which Dominion status provided. As such in the resulting arguments, Irish premier William Thomas Cosgrave was inclined to reinterpretation of the exact nature of the Commonwealth which the Irish Free State was now a part of.[492] Ambiguities over the precise definition of the status and rights of Dominions towards the mother country were overcome only over the course of the Imperial Conference in 1926.

Notes

1 See more in Egerton, Hugh Edward, *The War and the British Dominions*, Oxford: Oxford University Press, [1914].
2 Barclay, Glen St. J., *The Empire Is Marching: A Study of the Military Effort of the British Empire 1800–1945*, London: Weidenfeld and Nicolson, 1976, 58; Carrington, C. E., "The Empire at War, 1914–1918", in: *The Cambridge History of the British Empire: The Empire-Commonwealth 1870–1919*, Vol. 3, Cambridge: Cambridge University Press, 1967, 605; Hall, Hessel Duncan, *Commonwealth: A History of the British Commonwealth of Nations*, London: Von Nostrand Reinhold Co, 1971, 128.
3 Mansergh, Nicholas, *The Commonwealth Experience*, London: Weidenfeld & Nicolson, 1969, 166.
4 The Dominions suffered extensive losses during the war. Although precise figures cannot be given since some Britons served in Dominion armies, there are the official figures of Britain's War Office. See more in Carrington, 641–642.
5 May, Alex, "The Round Table and Imperial Federation, 1910–17", *The Round Table* 99, No. 410, 2010, 553.
6 Carrington, 633–634; Portus, Garnet Vere, *Britain and Australia*, London: Longmans, Green and Co, 1946, 41.
7 See more cf. Borden, Robert Laird, *Canada at War: A Speech Delivered by Rt. Hon. Sir Robert Laird Borden in New York City*, [s. l.: s. n.], 1916; Bray, Matthew, "'Fighting as an Ally': The English-Canadian Patriotic Response to the Great War", *The Canadian Historical Review* 64, No. 2, 1980,

141–168; Skelton, Oscar Douglas, *Life and Letters of Sir Wilfrid Laurier*, Vol. 2, Toronto: S. B. Gundy, 1921, 437–462.

8   For more on this issue, see Cartwright, Albert, "The South African Situation", *Edinburgh Review* 221, No. 451, 1915, 65–85; Cd. 7874, *Union of South Africa: Report on the Outbreak of the Rebellion and the Policy of the Government with Regard to Its Suppression*, London: HMSO, 1915; Davenport, T. R. H., "The South African Rebellion, 1914", *The English Historical Review* 78, No. 306, 1963, 73–94; Hancock, William Keith, *Smuts: The Sanguine Years, 1870–1919*, Vol. 1, Cambridge: Cambridge University Press, 1962, 379–390.

9   Mansergh, *The Commonwealth Experience*, 170–171; Underhill, F. H., "Canada and the Last War", in: Martin, Chester (Ed.), *Canada in Peace and War: Eight Studies in National Trends since 1914*, London: Oxford University Press, 1941, 126.

10 Cf. Bridge, Carl, *William Hughes: Australia*, London: Haus, 2011, 38–39; Mansergh, *The Commonwealth Experience*, 171–172; Sladen, Douglas, *From Boundary-Rider to Prime Minister: Hughes of Australia: The Man of the Hour*, London: Hutchinson & Co, 1916, 11–14.

11 Hurd, Percy – Hurd, Archibald, *The New Empire Partnership: Defence – Commerce – Policy*, Toronto: John Murray, 1916; Worsfold, William Basil, *The Empire on the Anvil: Being Suggestions and Data for the Future Government of the British Empire*, London: Smith, Elder & Co, 1916.

12 Thompson, J. Lee, *A Wider Patriotism: Alfred Milner and the British Empire*, London: Routledge, 2007, 150.

13 Louis, William Roger, *In the Name of God, Go! Leo Amery and the British Empire in the Age of Churchill*, London: W. W. Norton, 1992, 61.

14 Cf. Lockwood, A., "Milner's Entry into the War Cabinet, December 1916", *The Historical Journal* 7, No. 1, 1964, 120–134; Packer, Ian, *Lloyd George*, London: Palgrave Macmillan, 1998, 53; PD, HoC, 5th Series, Vol. 88, 19 December 1916, 1355.

15 Amery, Leopold Stennett, *My Political Life: War and Peace 1914–1929*, Vol. 2, London: Hutchinson, 1953, 91; Dawson, Robert MacGregor, "Canadian and Imperial War Cabinets", in: Martin, Chester (Ed.), *Canada in Peace and War: Eight Studies in National Trends since 1914*, London: Oxford University Press, 1941, 179–181.

16 Long, Walter Hume, *Memories*, London: Hutchinson & Co., 1923, 237.

17 An alternative term used was The Imperial Cabinet. Hankey, Maurice Pascal Alers, *The Supreme Command, 1914–1918*, Vol. 2, London: George Allen & Unwin, 1961, 660.

18 In 1917, the Imperial War Cabinet operated with the following members: British Prime Minister David Lloyd George, Chancellor of the Exchequer Andrew Bonar Law, Lord President of the Council Marquess Curzon, Secretary of State for the Colonies Walter Long, Secretary of State for India Austen Chamberlain with three Indian experts (the Maharaja of Bikaner, Sir James Scorgie Meston and Sir Satyendra Prasanna Sinha), Canadian Prime Minister Sir Robert Borden with the High Commissioner Sir George Perley, New Zealand Prime Minister William Massey and his coalition partner Sir Joseph Ward, South African Minister of Defence General Jan Smuts and Newfoundland Prime Minister Sir Edward Patrick MorrNo. Cf. Asquith, Herbert Henry, *The Genesis of the War*, London: Cassell & Co, 1923, 138; Carrington, 632; Hankey, *The Supreme*, Vol. 2, 657.

19 Keith, Arthur Berriedale, *War Government of the British Dominions*, Oxford: Clarendon Press, 1921, 27–28.

20 The establishment of the Cabinet Secretariat in more detail is covered in Naylor, John F., *A Man and an Institution: Sir Maurice Hankey, the Cabinet Secretariat and the Custody of Cabinet Secrecy*, Cambridge: Cambridge University Press, 1984, 8–48.
21 Hall, *Commonwealth*, 150–151.
22 Although Dominion officials had accompanied their prime ministers at Imperial Conferences since 1911, they had not been members of the Imperial Conference Secretariat. Hankey, *The Supreme*, Vol. 2, 659.
23 Warman, Roberta M., "The Erosion of Foreign Office Influence in the Making of Foreign Policy, 1916–1918", *The Historical Journal* 15, No. 11, 1972, 138–139.
24 MacKintosh, John P., "The Role of the Committee of Imperial Defence before 1914", *The English Historical Review* 77, No. 304, 1962, 502.
25 First it was the War Council, the Dardanelles Committee and the War Committee. Hankey, Maurice Pascal Alers, *Diplomacy by Conference: Studies in Public Affairs, 1920–1946*, London: Ernest Benn, 1946, 93.
26 Haldane, Richard Burdon, *An Autobiography*, New York: Hodder & Stoughton, 1929, 251.
27 TNA, CAB 23/43/1, Procès-verbal of the First Meeting of the Imperial War Cabinet, 20 March 1917, [1]–13.
28 For more detail on the activities of the British War Cabinet, see Schuyler, Robert Livingston, "The British War Cabinet", *Political Science Quarterly* 33, No. 3, 1918, 378–395.
29 Wrong, George M., "Canada and the Imperial War Cabinet", *The Canadian Historical Review* 1, No. 1, 1920, 15.
30 Robert Borden, Empire Parliamentary Association, 3 April 1917, in: Dawson, Robert MacGregor (Ed.), *The Development of Dominion Status, 1900–1936*, London: Frank Cass & Co, 1965, 172–173; Cd. 9005, *War Cabinet: Report for the Year 1917*, London: HMSO, 1918, 8–9.
31 Wrong, 16.
32 Lloyd George, David, *War Memoirs*, Vol. 2, London: Odhams Press, 1938, 1047–1057.
33 Purcell, Hugh, *Maharajah of Bikaner: India*, London: Haus, 2010, 54.
34 TNA, CO 886/8/3, Dominions No. 66, D. 35269, Extracts from the Debates of the Canadian House of Commons, 18 May 1917, [Doc.] No. 2, 2–4 [72–73].
35 Cf. TNA, CAB 23/40/14, Minutes of a Meeting of the Imperial War Cabinet, [No.] 14, 2 May 1917, 2–4; TNA, CO 886/8/3, Dominions No. 66, D. 23399, Lloyd George, House of Commons, 17 May 1917, Encl. [Doc.] No. 1, [1]–2.
36 TNA, CAB 17/190, Memorandum upon the Development of the War Cabinet in Relation to an Imperial Executive, 22 June 1917, [1]–8; TNA, CAB 17/190, State of the War Cabinet, 29 July 1917, [1]–4.
37 TNA, CAB 17/190, State of the War Cabinet, 29 July 1917, [1]–4.
38 Cf. Pugh, R. B., "The Colonial Office, 1801–1925", in: *The Cambridge History of the British Empire: The Empire-Commonwealth 1870–1919*, Vol. 3, Cambridge: Cambridge University Press, 1967, 756–757; TNA, CAB 17/190, Case for Breaking Up the Present Colonial Office, [1917], [1]–[3]; TNA, CAB 17/190, Re-arrangement of Imperial Administrative Offices, [1917], [1]–5.
39 TNA, CAB 17/190, The New Imperial System, 8 July 1917, [1]–3.
40 Thompson, 151.
41 Eayrs, John, "The Round Table Movement in Canada, 1909–1920", *The Canadian Historical Review* 38, No. 1, 1957, 10–11. The attitudes of the

Toronto section of the Round Table Movement in more detail are in CAC, AP, AMEL 3/4, Address Delivered in the Senate House of the University to the "Round Table" Groups at Toronto, 18 November 1913, 1–31; *The Round Table Movement: Its Past and Future*, [s. l. 1913].

42 *PD, HoC*, 5th Series, Vol. 71, 14 April 1915, 16–17.
43 Kendle, John Edward, *The Round Table Movement and Imperial Union*, Toronto: University of Toronto Press, 1975, 185.
44 Cf. Curtis, Lionel, *The Problem of the Commonwealth*, London: Macmillan, 1916, 13–247; Kendle, *The Round Table Movement and Imperial Union*, 185–186.
45 Ellinwood, Dewitt Clinton, Jr., "The Round Table Movement and India, 1909–1920", *Journal of Commonwealth Political Studies* 9, No. 3, 1971, 185.
46 See more in Kendle, *The Round Table Movement and Imperial Union*, 186–195, 206.
47 Cf. Hall, Hessel Duncan, *The British Commonwealth of Nations: A Study of Its Past and Future Development*, London: Methuen, 1920, 162–167, 204–225; Milner, Alfred – Wells, Herbert George, *The Elements of Reconstruction: A Series of Articles Contributed in July and August 1916 to The Times*, London: Nisbet & Co, [1916], 95–105.
48 Kendle, *The Round Table Movement and Imperial Union*, 206.
49 Shortly after the war broke out, the first to promote the use of this name was Leopold Amery. TNA, CAB 17/190, Suggestions for an Imperial War Conference, 12 October 1914, [1]–2.
50 Hall, *Commonwealth*, 154; Ollivier, Maurice (Ed.), *The Colonial and Imperial Conferences from 1887 to 1937*, Vol. 2, Ottawa: Queen's Printer, 1954, 171.
51 Keith, *War*, 29.
52 Elliott, William Yandell – Hall, Hessel Duncan (Eds.), *The British Commonwealth at War*, New York: Alfred A. Knopf, 1943, 31.
53 Hall, *Commonwealth*, 149–150.
54 Cd. 8566, *The Imperial War Conference, 1917: Extracts from Minutes of Proceedings and Papers Laid before the Conference*, London: HMSO, 1917, 3; Sundaram, Lanka, "The International Status of India", *Journal of the Royal Institute of International Affairs* 9, No. 4, 1930, 454.
55 Cd. 8566, 41–42.
56 Cf. Hancock, *Smuts*, Vol. 1, 430; Jan Christian Smuts, "The Commonwealth Conception", 15 May 1917, in: Smuts, Jan Christian, *Plans for a Better World: Speeches of Field-Marshal*, London: Hodder & Stoughton, 1942, 37; Ollivier, Vol. 2, 200–202.
57 Cf. Amery, *My Political*, Vol. 2, 109; Dewey, Alexander Gordon, *The Dominion and Diplomacy: The Canadian Contribution*, Vol. 1, London: Longmans, Green & Co, 1929, 315; Hall, *Commonwealth*, 155, 907; Hancock, *Smuts*, Vol. 1, 429.
58 TNA, CO 886/7/11, Dominions No. 61, Resolution IX: Constitution of the Empire, 120.
59 Coupland, Reginald, *The Indian Problems 1833–1935: Report on the Constitutional Problem in India*, Part 1, London: Oxford University Press, 1935, 83.
60 Cf. Cd. 8566, 47; Hancock, *Smuts*, Vol. 1, 430; Thompson, 163–164.
61 Cf. Hall, *Commonwealth*, 146; Kendle, *The Round Table Movement and Imperial Union*, 221.
62 Lentin, Anthony, *General Smuts: South Africa*, London: Haus, 2010, 43.

63 Cf. Smuts to M[argaret] C[lark] Gillett, London, 29 September 1917, in: Hancock, William Keith – Poel, Jean van der (Eds.), *Selections from the Smuts Papers: June 1910–November 1918*, Vol. 3, Cambridge: Cambridge University Press, 1966, Doc. Vol. 18, No. 346, 553; [S. C. Buxton, 1st Viscount of] Buxton to Smuts, Pretoria, 12 October 1917, in: Hancock – Poel, Vol. 3, Doc. Vol. 15, No. 109A, 564; Hancock, *Smuts*, Vol. 1, 436; Millin, Sarah Gertrude, *General Smuts*, Vol. 1, London: Faber and Faber, 1936, 355.

64 Influential journalist James Louis Garvin even proposed that Smuts be nominated as the British Secretary of State for Foreign Affairs. A. G. G., "The Future of General Smuts", *Nation and Athenaeum* 34, No. 3, 20 October 1923, 112–113; Keith, *War*, 30.

65 The Prime Minister, Secretaries of State for the Colonies, Foreign Affairs, War and Air and First Lord of the Admiralty took part for Britain. Canada was represented by Robert L. Borden and head of the Privy Council Newton W. Rowell, Australia by William M. Hughes and Sir J. Cook, New Zealand as in 1917 by William Massey and Sir Joseph Ward, the Union of South Africa by Jan Smuts and J. Burton, Newfoundland by its Prime Minister W. F. Lloyd, and India by Britain's Secretary of State for India, member of the Executive Council of the Governor of Bengal S. P. Sinha and the Maharaja of Patiala representing India's native states. Keith, *War*, 30.

66 To discuss the events on the Western Front between the British Supreme Command and the War Cabinet, cf. Gooch, John, "The Maurice Debate 1918", *Journal of Contemporary History* 3, No. 4, 1968, 211–228.

67 Hall, *Commonwealth*, 173.

68 For more on the deployment of Canadian troops during the First World War see Vince, Donald M. A. R., "Development in the Legal Status of the Canadian Military Forces, 1914–19, as Related to Dominion Status", *The Canadian Journal of Economics and Political Science/Revue canadienne d'Economique et de Science politique* 20, No. 3, 1954, 357–370.

69 Cf. Cook, George L., "Sir Robert Borden, Lloyd George and British Military Policy, 1917–1918", *The Historical Journal* 14, No. 2, 1971, 380; Marlowe, John, *Milner: Apostle of Empire*, London: Hamilton, 1976, 310; Soward, Frederic H., "Sir Robert Borden and Canada's External Policy, 1911–1920", *Report of the Annual Meeting of the Canadian Historical Association/ Rapports annuels de la Société historique du Canada* 20, No. 1, 1941, 74; TNA, CAB 23/43/4, Shorthand Notes of the Sixteenth Meeting of the Imperial War Cabinet, 13 June 1918, [2]–13.

70 Hall, *Commonwealth*, 175.

71 Cf. CAC, AP, AMEL 2/1/1, L. S. A[mery] to W. M. Hughes, 17 June 1918, [1]–3; TNA, CAB 17/199, L. S. A[mery] to W. M. Hughes, 17 June 1918, [1]–3.

72 TNA, CAB 17/199, The Future of the Imperial Cabinet System, 29 June 1918, [1]–17.

73 CAC, AP, AMEL 2/1/1, L. S. A[mery] to Lloyd George, 27 December 1918, [1]–4.

74 CAC, AP, AMEL 1/3/55, L. S. A[mery], The Future of the Imperial Cabinet System, 29 June 1918, 14–17.

75 To Curtis's vision of Commonwealth, see Lavin, Deborah, "Lionel Curtis and the Idea of Commonwealth", in: Madden, A. Frederick – Fieldhouse, D. K. (Eds.), *Oxford and the Idea of Commonwealth: Essays Presented to Sir Edgar Williams*, London: Croom Helm, 1982, 97–121.

76 See CAC, AP, AMEL 2/1/1, L. S. A[mery] to Fisher, 6 November 1918, 2.

148 The Empire During the War and Post-War Period

77 Richard Jebb was particularly involved in debate. Cf. CAC, AP, AMEL 2/1/1, L. S. A[mery] to Jebb, 10 October 1918, [1]–2; CAC, AP, AMEL 2/1/1, Jebb to L. S. A[mery], 13 October 1918, [1]–7; CAC, AP, AMEL 2/1/1, L. S. A[mery] to Jebb, 22 October 1918, [1–2].
78 CAC, AP, AMEL 2/1/1, L. S. A[mery] to Garvin, 14 November 1918, 2.
79 Cd. 9177, *The Imperial War Conference, 1918: Extracts from Minutes of Proceedings and Papers Laid before the Conference*, London: HMSO, 1918, 155–165.
80 CAC, AP, AMEL 2/1/1, L. S. A[mery] to Jebb, 4 June 1918, [1].
81 LOUIS, *In the Name*, 63.
82 CAC, AP, AMEL 2/1/1, L. S. A[mery] to W. M. Hughes, 17 June 1918, [1]–2.
83 DEWEY, Vol. 1, 318.
84 CAC, AP, AMEL 2/1/1, L. S. A[mery] to Borden, 8 July 1918, [1]–3.
85 Cd. 9177, 165.
86 Dewey, Vol. 1, 318.
87 CAC, AP, AMEL 2/1/1, L. S. A[mery] to Hankey, 22 July 1918, [1]–3.
88 Cd. 9177, 165.
89 Cf. Dewey, Vol. 1, 319–320; Worsfold, Basil W., "The Administration of the Empire", *United Empire: The Royal Colonial Institute Journal* 11, No. 7, 1920, 362.
90 Cf. CAC, AP, AMEL 2/1/1, L. S. A[mery] to Borden, 19 August 1918, [1]–3; Hall, *Commonwealth*, 176; TNA, CAB 23/42/1, Imperial War Cabinet, [No.] 30: Minutes of a Meeting of the Prime Ministers of the United Kingdom and of the Overseas Dominions and the British War Cabinet, Downing Street, London, 13 August 1918, 3–5; TNA, CAB 23/42/2, Imperial War Cabinet, [No.] 31: Minutes of a Meeting of the Prime Ministers of the United Kingdom and of the Overseas Dominions and the British War Cabinet, Downing Street, London, 14 August 1918, 3–4; TNA, CAB 23/42/3, Imperial War Cabinet, [No.] 32: Minutes of a Meeting of the Prime Ministers of the United Kingdom and of the Overseas Dominions and the British War Cabinet, Downing Street, London, 15 August 1918, 3–6; TNA, CAB 23/43/11, Imperial War Cabinet, [No.] 30: Shorthand Notes of a Meeting of the Prime Ministers of the United Kingdom and of the Overseas Dominions and the British War Cabinet, Downing Street, London, 13 August 1918, [1]–19; TNA, CAB 23/43/12, Imperial War Cabinet, [No.] 31: Shorthand Notes of a Meeting of the Prime Ministers of the United Kingdom and of the Overseas Dominions and the British War Cabinet, Downing Street, London, 14 August 1918, 3–8; TNA, CAB 23/43/13, Imperial War Cabinet, [No.] 32: Shorthand Notes of a Meeting of the Prime Ministers of the United Kingdom and of the Overseas Dominions and the British War Cabinet, Downing Street, London, 15 August 1918, [1]–13.
91 Hancock, *Smuts*, Vol. 1, 491; TNA, CAB 23/43/12, Imperial War Cabinet, [No.] 31: Shorthand Notes of a Meeting of the Prime Ministers of the United Kingdom and of the Overseas Dominions and the British War Cabinet, Downing Street, London, 14 August 1918, 3–12.
92 Cf. Keith, *War*, 32; TNA, CAB 23/42/8, Imperial War Cabinet, [No.] 37: Minutes of a Meeting of the Imperial War Cabinet, Downing Street, London, 20 November 1918, 4–5; TNA, CAB 23/42/9, Imperial War Cabinet, [No.] 38: Minutes of a Meeting of the Imperial War Cabinet, Downing Street, London, 26 November 1918, 3–5; TNA, CAB 23/43/14, Imperial War Cabinet, [No.] 37: Shorthand Notes of the Meeting of the Imperial War Cabinet, Downing Street, London, 20 November 1918, [1]–12; TNA, CAB 23/43/15, Imperial War Cabinet, [No.] 38: Shorthand Notes of the Meeting

of the Imperial War Cabinet, Downing Street, London, 26 November 1918, [1]–12; TNA, CAB 23/43/16, Imperial War Cabinet, [No.] 39: Shorthand Notes of the Meeting of the Imperial War Cabinet, Downing Street, London, 28 November 1918, [1]–12.
93 TNA, CAB 23/42/12, [Imperial War Cabinet, No. 41]: Notes of an Allied Conversation Held in the Cabinet Room, Downing Street, London, 3 December 1918, [1]–8; TNA, CAB 23/42/13, [Imperial War Cabinet, No. 41–1]: Notes of an Allied Conversation Held in the Cabinet Room, Downing Street, London, 3 December 1918, [1]–5.
94 PD, HoC, 5th Series, Vol. 71, 14 April 1915, 16–17.
95 BL, BP, Add MS 49775, Vol. XCIII, L. S. Amery, Representation of the Dominion at the Peace Negotiations, 14 November 1918, [191–192].
96 TNA, CAB 23/42/19, Imperial War Cabinet, [No.] 47: Minutes of a Meeting of the Imperial War Cabinet, 30 December 1918, 2.
97 CAC, AP, AMEL 2/1/1, Representation of the Dominions at the Peace Negotiations, 14 November 1918, [s. p.].
98 BL, BP, Add MS 49775, Vol. XCIII, L. S. Amery, Representation of the Dominion at the Peace Negotiations, 14 November 1918, [191].
99 For more on this issue, cf. Borden, Robert Laird, *Canada and the Peace: A Speech on the Treaty of Peace, Delivered in the Canadian House of Commons on Tuesday, September 2, 1919* [Ottawa: s. n., 1919], 13; Fitzhardinge, L., "Hughes, Borden and Dominion Representation at the Paris Peace Conference", *The Canadian Historical Review* 49, No. 2, 1968, 163–169; Lloyd George, David, *The Truth about the Peace Treaties*, Vol. 1, London: Victor Gollancz, 1938, 205; Marston, Frank Swain, *The Peace Conference of 1919: Organisation and Procedure*, London: Oxford University Press, 1944, 37, 51; Stacey, Charles Perry, *Canada and the Age of Conflict: A History of Canadian External Policies: 1867–1921*, Vol. 1, Toronto: University of Toronto Press, 1984, 270–274; TNA, CAB 29/28, B. E. D. [No.] 1, Peace Conference: British Empire Delegation: Minutes of a Meeting of Members of the British Empire Delegation, Villa Majestic, Paris, 13 January 1919, [1].
100 Canada, Australia and South Africa were able to send two delegates, with India sending one for British India and another as a representative of the native states there. New Zealand could send one, while Newfoundland could not send any. Fitzhardinge, L. F., "W. M. Hughes and the Treaty of Versailles 1919", *Journal of Commonwealth Political Studies* 5, No. 2, 1967, 133; TNA, CAB 29/7, W. C. P. [No.] 5, British Empire Delegation: Note by the Secretary of the Imperial War Cabinet, 13 January 1919, [25].
101 For more details on the representation of native states in India cf. TNA, CAB 29/7, W. C. P. [No.] 14, E. S. M[ontagu], To the Members of the Imperial War Cabinet in Paris, 19 January 1919, [138–141]; TNA, CAB 29/7, W. C. P. [No.] 28, Tilak to Lloyd George, British Empire Delegation: Representation of India, Villa Majestic, Paris, 15 January 1919, [173].
102 Mansergh, *The Commonwealth Experience*, 178.
103 Glazebrook, George Parkin de Twenebroker, *Canada at the Paris Peace Conference*, Toronto: Oxford University Press, 1942, 48.
104 Cf. Keith, *War*, 151; TNA, CAB 29/28, B. E. D. [No.] 1, Peace Conference: British Empire Delegation: Minutes of a Meeting of Members of the British Empire Delegation, Villa Majestic, Paris, 13 January 1919, 3.
105 TNA, CAB 29/7, W. C. P. [No.] 7, Note by Sir Maurice Hankey, Villa Majestic, Paris, 14 January 1919, [33].
106 Cf. Bothwell, Robert, *Loring Christie: The Failure of Bureaucratic Imperialism*, New York: Garland Pub, 1988, 169–171; Dafoe, John Wesley, "Canada and

the Peace Conference of 1919", *The Canadian Historical Review* 24, No. 3, 1943, 237–240; Inglis, Alex I., "Loring C. Christie and the Imperial Idea: 1919–1926", *Journal of Canadian Studies/Revue d'études canadiennes* 7, No. 2, 1972, 21; Mansergh, *The Commonwealth Experience*, 179.
107 Cf. Amery, *My Political*, Vol. 2, 177–178; Bridge, 76–77; Lloyd George, *The Truth*, Vol. 1, 205–206.
108 Cf. Louis, William Roger, "Australia and the German Colonies in the Pacific, 1914–1919", *Journal of Modern History* 38, No. 4, 1966, 407–421; CAC, HP, HNKY 8/11, British Empire Interests, 23 March 1919, [1]; TNA, CAB 29/28, B. E. D. [No.] 4, Peace Conference: British Empire Delegation: Minutes of a Meeting of Members of the British Empire Delegation, Villa Majestic, Paris, 27 January 1919, [1]; TNA,CAB 29/1, 34, Peace Conference: Memorandum Respecting German Colonies, January 1919, [1]–20.
109 For more details on New Zealand's position on Samoa, see Boyd, Mary, "New Zealand's Attitude to Dominion Status 1919–1921: The Procedure for Enacting a Constitution in the Samoan Mandate", *Journal of Commonwealth Political Studies* 3, No. 1, 1965, 64–70; Lerner, Bruno, *Der Einfluß der Dominions auf die Außenpolitik Großbritanniens (einige Aspekte)*, PhD Thesis, Wien: Universität Wien, 1965, 46.
110 Cf. "Future of the Islands", *Evening Post* 97, No. 64, 18 March 1919, 6; Keith, *War*, 151–152.
111 TNA, CAB 29/9, W. C. P. [No.] 246, J. F. N. Green, New Hebrides, 12 March 1919, [362].
112 TNA, CAB 23/43/2, Procès-verbal of the Second Meeting of the Imperial War Cabinet, 22 March 1917, 3.
113 Cf. Andrews, Eric, *The Anzac Illusion: Anglo-Australian Relations during World War I*, Melbourne: Cambridge University Press, 1993, 133; Understanding between Great Britain and Japan Regarding Ultimate Disposal of German Rights, February [16], 1921, in: MacMurray, John Van Antwerp (Ed.), *Treaties and Agreements with and Concerning China, 1894–1919: Republican Period (1912–1919)*, Vol. 2, New York: Oxford University Press, 1921, 1167–1168.
114 Snelling, R. C., "Peacemaking 1919: Australia, New Zealand and the British Empire Delegation at Versailles", *The Journal of Imperial and Commonwealth History* 4, No. 1, 1975, 17–18.
115 Cf. "Administration of Samoa", *The New Zealand Herald* 55, No. 17073, 31 January 1919, 4; "Our Share", *Auckland Star* 50, No. 25, 29 January 1919, 4; Snelling, 18.
116 Fitzhardinge, W. M. *Hughes*, 136; Hankey, Maurice Pascal Alers, *The Supreme Control at the Paris Peace Conference*, London: George Allen & Unwin, 1963, 58–59; TNA, CAB 29/28, B. E. D. [No.] 6, Peace Conference: British Empire Delegation: Minutes of a Meeting of Members of the British Empire Delegation, Rue Nitot, Paris, 29 January 1919, [1].
117 Bridge, 80.
118 Jones, Dorsey D., "The Foreign Policy of William Morris Hughes of Australia", *Far Eastern Quarterly* 2, No. 2, 1943, 158.
119 Cf. BL, BP, Add MS 49748, Vol. LXVI, Montagu to Balfour, 20 December 1918, [300–305]; Kenneth, 83–84; TNA, CAB 29/1, 34, Peace Conference: Memorandum Respecting German Colonies, January 1919, 18.
120 More details on Balfour's position on the mandate power are found in TNA, CAB 29/7, W. C. P. [No.] 42, 27 January 1919, [301–303].
121 TNA, CAB 29/7, W. C. P. [No.] 71, W. M. Hughes, Australia and the Pacific Islands, 6 February 1919, 1–5, [584–588]. To the importance of "White Policy", see *APD, HoR*, No. 37, 10 September 1919, 12174–12176.

The Empire During the War and Post-War Period   151

122 TNA, CAB 29/8, W. C. P. [No.] 116, W. M. Hughes, Memorandum Regarding the Pacific Islands, 8 February 1919, 1–4.
123 TNA, CAB 29/28, B. E. D. [No.] 9, Peace Conference: British Empire Delegation: Minutes of a Meeting of Members of the British Empire Delegation, Villa Majestic, Paris, 20 February 1919, 2.
124 Fitzhardinge, W. M. Hughes, 137.
125 For more on Nauru, see TNA, CAB 29/9, W. C. P. [No.] 240, W. M. Hughes to Walter H. Long, 3 January 1919, [313]; TNA, CAB 29/7, W. C. P. [No.] 97, W. F. Massey, New Zealand and the Pacific Islands, 14 February 1919, 1–2, [761]; TNA, CAB 29/9, W. C. P. [No.] 240, W. M. Hughes, The Control of Nauru under the Mandatory System, 13 March 1919, [312]; TNA, CAB 29/10, W. C. P. [No.] 345, W. M. Hughes, The Control of Nauru, 21 March 1919, [173].
126 Snelling, 16, 20, 23.
127 TNA, CAB 29/9, W. C. P. [No.] 211, Lord Milner, Mandates: Under Clause XIX of the Draft "Covenant" of the League of Nations, 8 March 1919, [1]–13, [99–111].
128 TNA, CAB 29/28, B. E. D. [No.] 13, Peace Conference: British Empire Delegation: Minutes of a Meeting of Members of the British Empire Delegation, Hotel Majestic, Paris, 13 March 1919, 7–9.
129 Cf. TNA, CAB 29/9, W. C. P. [No.] 211, Lord Milner, Mandates: Under Clause XIX of the Draft "Covenant" of the League of Nations, 8 March 1919, 4, [102]; TNA, CAB 29/9, W. C. P. [No.] 211A, W. M. Hughes, Mandates: New Clause 6 for Typical Mandate Class "C", 14 March 1919, [112].
130 See more at BL, BP, Add MS 49734, Vol. LII, C. J. B. Hurst, 'B' and 'C' Mandates: Memorandum on the Present Position, 20 July 1920, [203–205].
131 Soward, 78.
132 Wheare, Kenneth Clinton, "The Empire and the Peace Treaties 1918–1921", in: The Cambridge History of the British Empire: The Empire-Commonwealth 1870–1919, Vol. 3, Cambridge: Cambridge University Press, 1967, 652.
133 Glazebrook, Canada, 60–61.
134 For more details on how Smuts's text came about, see Smuts, J. C., Jr., Jan Christian Smuts, London: Cassell, 1952, chapter 38.
135 Cf. Curry, George, "Woodrow Wilson, Jan Smuts, and the Versailles Settlement", The American Historical Review 66, No. 4, 1961, 969; Lentin, General, 52; TNA, CAB 23/40/12, Imperial War Cabinet, [No.] 46: Minutes of a Meeting of the Imperial War Cabinet, 26 April 1917, 9.
136 TNA, CAB 23/42/18, Imperial War Cabinet, [No.] 46: Minutes of a Meeting of the Imperial War Cabinet, 24 December 1918, 4–7.
137 TNA, CAB 29/1, 28, Report of Committee on Terms of Peace, 24 April 1917, 3.
138 See Cecil, Robert Gascoyne, A Great Experiment: An Autobiography, London: Jonathan Cape, 1941, 60; Raffo, Peter, "The League of Nations Philosophy of Lord Robert Cecil", Australian Journal of Politics and History 20, No. 2, 1974, 186–196; TNA, CAB 29/1, 26, The Committee on the League of Nations: Interim Report, 20 March 1918, [1]–7.
139 TNA, CAB 29/1, 26, The Committee on the League of Nations: Final Report, 3 July 1918, [1]–24.
140 León Bourgeois was dealing with international relations between nations for a long time. See more in Bourgeois, Léon Victor Auguste, Pour la Société des Nations, Paris: Bibliothèque-Charpentier, 1910.

152 The Empire During the War and Post-War Period

141 TNA, CAB 29/1, 28, Report of the Committee Appointed by the French Government, 9 August 1918, [1]–7.
142 TNA, CAB 29/1, 29, War Cabinet: League of Nations: Memorandum by Lord R. Cecil, 5 October 1918, [253–273].
143 On the French proposal and the report of Britain's Lord Phillimore Commission, which was not published at America's request, see cf. TNA, CAB 23/42/9, Imperial War Cabinet, [No.] 38: Minutes of a Meeting of the Imperial War Cabinet, Downing Street, London, 26 November 1918, 4–5; Zimmern, Alfred Eckhard, Sir, *The League of Nations and the Rule of Law 1918–1935*, London: Macmillan & Co, 1936, 180–189.
144 Curry, 969.
145 Lentin, *General* 53.
146 McKercher, Brian J. C., *The Golden Gleam, 1916–1920: Britain and the Origins of the League of Nations*, PhD Thesis, Edmonton: The University of Alberta, 1975, 48; Wheare, 653; Yearwood, Peter J., "'On the Safe and Right Lines': The Lloyd George Government and the Origins of the League of Nations, 1916–1918", *The Historical Journal* 3, No. 1, 1989, 150–155.
147 Cf. Smuts, Jan Christian, *The League of Nations: A Practical Suggestion*, London: Hodder & Stoughton, 1918, 12–15; "Windows of Freedom", *The Round Table* 9, No. 33, 1918, 29.
148 Miller, David Hunter, *The Drafting of Covenant*, Vol. 1, New York: G. P. Putnam's Sons, 1928, 38.
149 Cf. Smuts, *The League*, 27–28; Wheare, 653.
150 Baker, Ray Stannard, *Woodrow Wilson and World Settlement*, Vol. 1, New York: Heinemann, 1922, 225–228; University of Cambridge: Cambridge University Library (hereafter CUL), Smuts Papers (hereafter SP), Add MS 7917, Vol. 1, Sect. 2, Smuts to Mr. and Mrs. Gillet, Paris, 20 January 1919, Doc. No. 152, 78.
151 For more on Anglo-American co-operation, see Kerr, Philip Henry, "The British Empire, the League of Nations, and the United States", *The Round Table* 10, No. 38, 1920, 221–253.
152 Beloff, Max, *Imperial Sunset: Britain's Liberal Empire 1897–1921*, Vol. 1, London: Macmillan, 1969, 281.
153 TNA, CAB 23/42/18, Imperial War Cabinet, [No.] 46: Minutes of a Meeting of the Imperial War Cabinet, 24 December 1918, 12.
154 Cecil submitted his first Covenant proposal on 17 December 1918. He had it modified by 20 January 1919 and subsequently presented it with the modifications as Britain's proposal at joint Anglo-American discussions. Cf. BL, Cecil of Chelwood Papers (hereafter CCP), Add MS 51102, Vol. XXXII, League of Nations: Draft Convention, [17 December], 1918, [72–90]; League of Nation: Draft Convention, [20 January 1919], in: Baker, Vol. 3, Doc. No. 15, 130–143; Goldstein, Erik, *Winning the Peace: British Diplomatic Strategy, Peace Planning, and the Paris Peace Conference 1916–1920*, Oxford: Clarendon, 1991, 215; TNA, CAB 29/7, W. C. P. [No.] 23, League of Nation: Draft Convention, 20 January 1919, [160–166].
155 Curry, 975–981; Egerton, George W., *Great Britain and the Creation of the League of Nations: Strategy, Politics, and International Organization, 1914–1919*, Chapel Hill: University of North Carolina Press, 1979, 115–116.
156 Draft Covenant [3 February 1919], in: Baker, Vol. 3, Doc. No. 16, 144–151.
157 Draft Adopted by the French Ministerial Commission for the League of Nations [8 June 1919], in: Baker, Vol. 3, Doc. No. 17, 152–162.
158 Curry, 981–982.
159 Draft Covenant [3 February 1919], in: Baker, Vol. 3, Doc. No. 16, 145.

160 Miller, David Hunter, *My Diary at the Conference of Paris with Documents*, Vol. 4, New York: [s. n.], 1924, Doc. No. 236, 171.
161 Cf. Cecil, Robert Gascoyne, *The Moral Basis of the League of Nations: The Essex Hall Lecture, 1923*, London: Lindsey Press, 1923, 21; Henig, Ruth, "New Diplomacy and Old: A Reassessment of British Conceptions of a League of Nations, 1918–20", in: Dockrill, Michael L. – Fisher, John (Eds.), *The Paris Peace Conference, 1919: Peace without Victory?* London: Palgrave Macmillan, 2001, 169. To the criticism of the accepted form of the Covenant of the League of Nations in more detail, see TNA, CAB 29/14, W. C. P. [No.] 729, R. Jebb, The British Empire and the League of Nations, April 1919, [149–167].
162 BL, CCP, Add MS 51102, Vol. XXXII, R. Cecil, Memorandum, 12 June 1923, [91–93].
163 Covenant [14 February 1919], in: Baker, Vol. 3, Doc. No. 18, 163–173.
164 Miller, *The Drafting*, 480.
165 Although Hughes and Borden had previously analysed the draft Covenant of the League of Nations, they had not objected to Article 4. See more cf. TNA, CAB 29/10, W. C. P. [No.] 346, The League of Nations: W. M. Hughes, Notes on the Draft Covenant, 21 March 1919, [179–187]; TNA, CAB 29/9, R. L. Borden, The Covenant of the League of Nations, 13 March 1919, W. C. P. [No.] 245, 1–17 [345–361].
166 Brown, Robert Craig, *Robert Laird Borden: A Biography: 1914–1937*, Vol. 2, Toronto: Macmillan, 1980, 157; TNA, CAB 29/28, B. E. D. [No.] 26, Peace Conference: British Empire Delegation: Minutes of a Meeting of Members of the British Empire Delegation, Hotel Majestic, Paris, 21 April 1919, 3–4.
167 Miller, *The Drafting*, 477–483, 487–493.
168 Cf. Carter, Gwendolen M., "Some Aspects of Canadian Foreign Policy after Versailles", *Report of the Annual Meeting of the Canadian Historical Association/Rapports annuels de la Société historique du Canada* 22, No. 1, 1943, 99–103; Cecil, Robert, "The League of Nations and the Problem of Sovereignty", *History* 5, 1920/1921, 13.
169 "The British Empire, the League of Nations and the United States", *The Round Table* 10, No. 38, 1920, 238.
170 Hedges, R. York, "Australia and the Imperial Conference", *The Australian Quarterly* 9, No. 1, 1937, 81.
171 Laing, Lionel H., "In Memoriam: Sir Robert Borden", *The American Journal of International Law* 31, No. 4, 1937, 705.
172 Cf. Lauren, Paul Gordon, "Human Rights in History: Diplomacy and Racial Equality at the Paris Peace Conference", *Diplomatic History* 2, No. 3, 1978, 257–278; Seymour, Charles (Ed.), *The Intimate Papers of Colonel House: The Ending of the War*, Vol. 4, Boston: Houghton Mifflin Company, 1928, 309–313.
173 Purcell, Hugh, "Paris Peace Discord", *History Today* 59, No. 7, 2009, 38–40.
174 Baker, Vol. 2, 234; Fitzhardinge, *W. M. Hughes*, 138.
175 Allerfeldt, Kristofer, "Wilsonian Pragmatism? Woodrow Wilson, Japanese Immigration, and the Paris Peace Conference", *Diplomacy and Statecraft* 15, No. 3, 2004, 547–548.
176 Bridge, 83; Carter, Gwendolen Margaret, *The British Commonwealth and International Security: The Role of the Dominions 1919–1939*, Toronto: Ryerson Press, 1947, 4; Moore, William Harrison, "The Imperial and Foreign Relations of Australia", in: Hurst, Cecil J. B. – Smiddy, Timothy

A. – Dafoe, John Wesley et al., (Eds.), *Great Britain and the Dominions*, Chicago: University of Chicago Press, 1928, 298–301.
177 Cf. Allerfeldt, 565; Bridge, 84; Lauren, Paul Gordon, "Human Rights in History: Diplomacy and Racial Equality at the Paris Peace Conference", *Diplomatic History* 2, No. 3, 1978, 257–278; Snelling, 23.
178 See more in Crozier, Andrew J., "The Establishment of the Mandates System 1919–25: Some Problems Created by the Paris Peace Conference", *Journal of Contemporary History* 14, No. 3, 1979, 483–513; Ilsley, Lucretia L., "The Administration of Mandates by the British Dominions", *The American Political Science Review* 28, No. 2, 1934, 287–302; Sharp, Alan, *The Versailles Settlement: Peacemaking after the First World War, 1919–1923*, 2nd Ed., Basingstoke: Palgrave Macmillan, 2008, 173–174; TNA, CO 886/9/7, Dominions No. 80, Mandates, May 1921, [246–275].
179 Mansergh, *The Commonwealth Experience*, 180.
180 Hancock, William Keith, *Survey of British Commonwealth Affairs: Problems of Nationality 1918–1936*, Vol. 1, London: Oxford University Press, 1937, 67–68.
181 TNA, CAB 29/9, W. C. P. [No.] 242, R. L. Borden, The Dominions as Parties and Signatories to the Various Peace Treaties, 12 March 1919, [318–319].
182 Borden, Robert Laird, *Canada in the Commonwealth: From Conflict to Co-operation*, Oxford: Clarendon Press, 1929, 102–103.
183 TNA, CAB 29/9, W. C. P. [No.] 242, R. L. Borden, The Dominions as Parties and Signatories to the Various Peace Treaties, 12 March 1919, [319].
184 Cf. TNA, CAB 29/9, W. C. P. [No.] 257, Memorandum by E. S. M[ontagu], 12 March 1919, [443]; TNA, CAB 29/9, W. C. P. [No.] 287, Memorandum by the Indian Delegation, 17 March 1919, [589].
185 Soward, 79.
186 TNA, CAB 29/14, W. C. P. [No.] 727, M. P. A. Hankey, Arrangements for the Meeting with the Germans, 5 May 1919, [111–112].
187 Cf. Borden, *Canada in the Commonwealth*, 103; Glazebrook, *Canada*, 111; Noel Baker, Philip John, *The Present Juridical Status of the British Dominions in International Law*, London: Longmans & Co, 1929, 67–83; Wheare, 664.
188 Keith, *War*, 154; Wigley, Philip, *Canada and the Transition to Commonwealth: British-Canadian Relations, 1917–1926*, Cambridge: Cambridge University Press, 1977, 92.
189 Telegram from the Secretary of State for the Colonies [Milner] to the Governor-General [Duke of Devonshire], 4 July 1919, in: Dawson, *The Development*, 186.
190 Glazebrook, *Canada*, 113–117; Stacey, Vol. 1, 274–275.
191 Telegram from the Secretary of State for the Colonies [Milner] to and from the Governor-General [Duke of Devonshire], 9 July–19 September 1919, in: Dawson, *The Development*, 186–194.
192 Cf. Bothwell, Robert, "Canadian Representation at Washington: A Study in Colonial Responsibility", *The Canadian Historical Review* 53, No. 2, 1972, 125–148; TNA, CO 886/8/3, Dominions No. 66, D. 57047/S, The Governor-General to the Secretary of State, 4 October 1919, [Doc.] No. 63, 120–121 [131]; TNA, CO 886/8/3, Dominions No. 66, D. 11924/S, The Secretary of State to the Governor-General, 15 March 1920, [Doc.] No. 76, 127–128 [134–135].
193 Wheare, 665.
194 TNA, CO 886/8/3, Dominions No. 66, D. 22114, Extract from *The Times*, 11 April 1919, [Doc.] No. 8, 16 [79].

The Empire During the War and Post-War Period   155

195 Toynbee, Arnold J., *The Conduct of British Empire Foreign Relations since the Peace Settlement*, London: Oxford University Press, 1928, 83.
196 TNA, CO 886/8/3, Dominions No. 66, D. 52442, Extract from Rand Daily Mail, 5 August 1919, [Doc.] No. 10, 23 [82].
197 Cf. CAC, HP, HNKY 24/3, Hankey to Lloyd George, 19 March 1919, [1–7]; CUL, SP, Add MS 7917, Vol. 1, Smuts to Lloyd George, Paris, 26 March 1919, 94–97; CUL, SP, Add MS 7917, Vol. 1, Smuts to Mr. and Mrs. Gillet, Pretoria, 30 December 1919, Doc. No. 243, 162; Lentin, Anthony, *Quilt at Versailles: Lloyd George and the Pre-history of Appeasement*, London: Methuen, 1984, 129.
198 TNA, CO 886/7/11, Dominions No. 61, Resolution IX: Constitution of the Empire, 120.
199 Mansergh, *The Commonwealth Experience*, 181.
200 Watt, Donald Cameron, "Imperial Defence Policy and Imperial Foreign Policy, 1911–1939 – A Neglected Paradox?" *Journal of Commonwealth Political Studies* 1, No. 1, 1963, 269.
201 Borden, *Canada and the Peace*, 15.
202 Cf. Gilbert, Angus Duncan, *The Political Influence of Imperialist Thought in Canada, 1899–1923*, Toronto 1974, 323; TNA, CAB 29/7, W. C. P. [No.] 7, Note by Sir Maurice Hankey, Villa Majestic, Paris, 14 January 1919, [33].
203 CAC, AP, AMEL 2/1/1, [L. S. Amery] to Worsfold, 24 October 1918, [1].
204 Cf. CAC, AP, AMEL 2/1/1, Representation of the Dominions at the Peace Delegation, 14 November 1918, [s. p.]; CAC, AP, AMEL 2/1/1, [L. S. Amery] to Hankey, 20 November 1918, [1]–2; CAC, AP, AMEL 2/1/1, [L. S. Amery to Lloyd George], 27 December 1918, [1]–4.
205 CAC, AP, AMEL 2/1/2, [L. S. Amery] to Dawson, 2 January 1919, [1]–4.
206 CAC, AP, AMEL 2/1/2, Hankey to Milner, 14 January 1919, [1–3].
207 PD, *House of Lords* (hereafter HoL), 5th Series, Vol. 40, 17 June 1920, 675, 683–684.
208 TNA, CO 886/8/3, Dominions No. 66, D. 22114, Extract from *The Times*, 11 April 1919, No. 8, 16 [79].
209 PD, HoL, 5th Series, Vol. 40, 17 June 1920, 684–688.
210 TNA, CO 886/8/3, Dominions No. 66, D. 65056, Extract from *Cape Times*, 24 September 1919, No. 11, 24 [83].
211 TNA, CO 886/8/3, Dominions No. 66, D. 52442, Extract from *Rand Daily Mail*, 9 August 1919, No. 10, 23 [82].
212 TNA, CO 886/8/3, Dominions No. 66, D. 65056, Extract from *Rand Daily Mail*, 25 September 1919, No. 11, 25 [83].
213 TNA, CO 886/8/3, Dominions No. 66, D. 52442, Extract from *Rand Daily Mail*, 5 August 1919, No. 10, 22 [82].
214 TNA, CO 886/8/3, Dominions No. 66, D. 65056, Extract from *Cape Times*, 23 September 1919, No. 11, 24 [83].
215 TNA, CO 886/8/3, Dominions No. 66, D. 65056, Extract from *Rand Daily Mail*, 26 September 1919, No. 11, 25 [83].
216 CUL, SP Add MS 7917, Box No. 1, Smuts to Clark, Cape Town, 9 April 1920, Doc. No. 108, 98.
217 Cf. Keith, Arthur Berriedale, *Dominion Home Rule in Practice*, London: Oxford University Press, 1921, 37–39; TNA, CO 886/8/3, Dominions No. 66, D. 35173, Extract from the Speech of the Prime Minister of the Union of South Africa, House of Assembly, 23 June 1920, No. 12, 30 [86]; TNA, CO 886/8/3, Dominions No. 66, D. 63372, Extract from the Speech by General Smuts, Pretoria, 4 December 1920, No. 14, 34–35 [88].
218 TNA, Public Record Office (hereafter PRO) 30/30/22 [Sir H. Lambert, Memorandum on Imperial Constitution], 14 June 1920.

156 The Empire During the War and Post-War Period

219 Cf. CAC, AP, AMEL 2/1/2, L. S. A[mery], Influence of the War and of the Paris Peace Conference on the Imperial Position, [January–December 1920], [1]–5; Hall, Hessel Duncan, "The Imperial Crown and the Foreign Relations of the Dominions", *Journal of Comparative Legislation and International Law* 2, No. 3, 1920, 197–198.
220 Cf. "An Australian View of Mr. Hughes in Paris", *New Statesman* 14, No. 352, 10 January 1920, 399–401; CAC, HP, HNKY 24/2, C. Jones, W. M. Hughes at Paris Peace Conference 1919, 1–22; Fitzhardinge, *W. M. Hughes*, 139–140.
221 CAC, HP, HNKY 24/2, M. P. A. Hankey, General Botha, 27 November 1960, [1–5].
222 CAC, HP, HNKY 27/5, M. P. A. Hankey, General (Field-Marshall) Smuts, 29 August 1959, [1]–13.
223 Cf. TNA, CO 886/8/3, Dominions No. 66, D. 42086, Memorandum by the Prime Minister of the Commonwealth of Australia, Australia House, 2 July 1919, No. 6, 14–15 [78]; TNA, CO 886/8/3, Dominions No. 66, D. 35173, Extract from the Speech of the Prime Minister of the Union of South Africa, House of Assembly, 23 June 1920, No. 12, 30 [86].
224 Alport, Cuthbert James MacCall, *Kingdoms in Partnership: A Study of Political Change in the British Commonwealth*, London: Lovat Dickson, 1937, 49.
225 Biggs, L. V., "Does Australia Want Imperial Federation?" *New Statesman* 15, No. 384, 31 August 1920, 544–545.
226 TNA, CO 886/8/3, Dominions No. 66, D. 63372, Extract from the Speech by General Smuts, Pretoria, 4 December 1920, [Doc.] No. 14, 36 [89].
227 Cf. Borden, *Canada and the Peace*, 15; Hall, *Commonwealth*, 338; Rowell, N. W., "Canada and the Empire, 1884–1921", in: Rose, J. Holland – Newton, A. P. – Benians, E. A. (Eds.), *The Cambridge History of the British Empire: Canada and Newfoundland*, Vol. 6, Cambridge: Cambridge University Press, 1930, 711; TNA, CO 886/8/3, Dominions No. 66, D. 39026, Memorandum, Home Office, Whitehall, 6 August 1920, Encl. [Doc.] No. 25, 57 [99].
228 Hancock, *Survey of British*, 52; Kerr, Philip Henry, "From Empire to Commonwealth", *Foreign Affairs: An American Quarterly Review* 1, No. 2, 1922, 97.
229 Cf. Dewey, Vol. 1, 321; "Editorial Notes and Comments", *United Empire: The Royal Colonial Institute Journal* 11, No. 7, 1920, 351–352; "The Mansion House Meeting", *United Empire: The Royal Colonial Institute Journal* 11, No. 5, 1920, 256–257.
230 Ireland, *Parliamentary Debates* (hereafter IPD), *Dáil Éireann* (hereafter DÉ), Vol. T, No. 6, 19 December 1921, 45–46; Miller, John Donald Bruce, "The Commonwealth and World Order: The Zimmern Vision and After", *The Journal of Imperial and Commonwealth History* 8, No. 1, 1979, 160–164.
231 Cf. Milner to Lloyd George, 8 October 1920, in: Gollin, Alfred Manuel, *Proconsul in Politics: A Study of Lord Milner in Opposition and in Power*, London: Anthony Blond, 1964, 596; PD, HoL, 5th Series, Vol. 40, 17 June 1920, 686–688.
232 Cf. Beloff, *Imperial*, Vol. 1, 319; Dawson, Robert MacGregor, *William Lyon Mackenzie King: A Political Biography: 1874–1923*, Vol. 1, London: Methuen, 1958, 328–329, 333–335; Graham, Roger, *Arthur Meighen: A Biography: And Fortune Fled*, Vol. 2, Toronto: Clarke Irwin and Co, 1963, 61; Hall, *Commonwealth*, 338–339; Colonial Secretary [Milner] to Prime Minister [Meighen], London, 4 October 1920, in: *DCER*, Vol. 3, Doc. No. 205, 157–160.

233 Colonial Secretary [Milner] to Governor General [Devonshire], London, 13 October 1920, in: *DCER*, Vol. 3, Doc. No. 206, 161; *PD, HoC*, 5th Series, Vol. 134, 11 November 1920, 1361.
234 O'BRIEN, Terence H., *Milner: Viscount Milner of St James's and Cape Town, 1854–1925*, London: Constable, 1979, 349.
235 Cf. Hall, *Commonwealth*, 340–341; "Outcroppings from the Imperial Conference", *Advocate of Peace through Justice* 83, No. 7, 1921, 271–274; *The Times*, 18 November 1920, in: Dawson, *The Development*, 203–204; "The Imperial Conference", *Spectator* 126, No. 4850, 11 June 1921, 739–740.
236 John W. Dafoe, "Imperial Cabinet or Imperial Conference?", *Manitoba Press*, 6 July 1925, in: Dawson, *The Development*, 213.
237 Cf. Hancock, *Smuts*, Vol. 2, 41; Lambert, J., "South African British? Or Dominion South Africans? The Evolution of an Identity in the 1910s and 1920s", *South African Historical Journal*, Vol. 43, No. 1, 2000, 197–222.
238 William, B., "Botha and Smuts: *Par Nobile Fratrum*", *Contemporary Review*, Vol. 165, 1944, 217.
239 Hancock, William Keith, Sir, *Smuts: The Fields of Force, 1919–1950*, Vol. 2, Cambridge: Cambridge University Press, 1968, 41–42.
240 Ingham, Kenneth, *Jan Christian Smuts: The Conscience of a South African*, London: Weidenfeld and Nicolson, 1986, 126.
241 Hancock, *Smuts*, Vol. 2, 46.
242 Hall, Hessel Duncan, "The Genesis of the Balfour Declaration of 1926", *Journal of Commonwealth Political Studies* 1, No. 3, 1962, 173.
243 TNA, DO 117/33, D. 11047, Memorandum by General Smuts on Constitutional Relations, [June 1921], [5].
244 Ibidem, [6].
245 Walker, Eric Anderson, "South Africa and the Empire", in: Newton, A. P. – Benians, E. A. (Eds.), *The Cambridge History of the British Empire: South Africa, Rhodesia and the Protectorates*, Vol. 8, Cambridge: Cambridge University Press, 1936, 756.
246 Cf. Bernas, Vlastimil, *Politicko-geografické aspekty transformace Britského impéria na Společenství národů*, MA Thesis, Praha: Univerzita Karlova, 2013, 25; TNA, DO 117/33, D. 11047, Memorandum by General Smuts on Constitutional Relations, [June 1921], [6]; *Colonial Laws Validity Act, 1865,* [565]–567, [http://www.legislation.gov.uk/ukpga/1865/63/pdfs/ukpga 18650063_en.pdf; cit. 2014-07-25].
247 TNA, DO 117/33, D. 11047, Memorandum by General Smuts on Constitutional Relations, [June 1921], [7].
248 Cf. Hall, *The British Commonwealth of Nations: A Study*, 229–231; Hall, Hessel Duncan, "The British Commonwealth of Nations", *The American Political Science Review* 47, No. 4, 1953, 1005–1006; TNA, DO 117/33, D. 11047, Memorandum by General Smuts on Constitutional Relations, [June 1921], [7].
249 TNA, DO 117/33, D. 11047, Memorandum by General Smuts on Constitutional Relations, [June 1921], [7].
250 TNA, FO 372/2198, Memorandum by General Smuts on Constitutional Relations, [June 1921], 8–9 [293–294].
251 TNA, DO 117/33, D. 11047, Memorandum by General Smuts on Constitutional Relations, [June 1921], [9–10].
252 Ibidem.
253 Amery, *My Political*, Vol. 2, 214; Hancock, *Smuts*, Vol. 2, 48.
254 Cf. CAC, AP, AMEL 2/1/4, Smuts to L. S. A[mery], Cape Town, 8 March 1921, [1]–2; CAC, AP, AMEL 2/2/11, H. D. Hall to L. S. A[mery], 18 June [1953], [1–2].

158 The Empire During the War and Post-War Period

255 Hall, *Commonwealth*, 349–350.
256 BL, BP, Add MS 49775, Vol. XCIII, L. S. A[mery] to Smuts, 20 June 1921, [227–233].
257 TNA, DO 117/33, L. S. Amery to Smuts, 20 June 1921, 7 [36].
258 TNA, DO 117/33, L. S. Amery to A. Chamberlain, Downing Street, 19 October 1926, [37–39].
259 TNA, FO 372/2198, L. S. Amery to A. Chamberlain, Downing Street, 19 October 1926, [283–285].
260 CAC, AP, AMEL 2/2/11, H. D. Hall to L. S. A[mery], 18 June [1953], [1–2]; Ollivier, Vol. 2, 406; TNA, DO 117/33, L. S. Amery to Davis, 15 October 1926, [2].
261 Dewey, Vol. 1, 332.
262 Hall, *Commonwealth*, 369.
263 At the conference were delegates from Great Britain (Prime Minister David Lloyd George, Lord Privy Seal Austen Chamberlain, Lord President of Council Arthur Balfour, Secretary of State for Foreign Affairs Lord Curzon and Secretary of State for the Colonies Sir Winston Churchill), from Canada (Prime Minister Arthur Meighen, Minister of Marine and Fisheries Charles Ballantyne), from Australia (Prime Minister William M. Hughes), from New Zealand (Prime Minister William F. Massey), from South Africa (Prime Minister General Jan Smuts, Minister of Agriculture Sir Thomas Smartt, and Minister of Defense Colonel H. Mentz), and from India (Secretary of State for India Edwin S. Montagu, etc.). Cmd. 1474, *Conference of the Prime Ministers and Representatives of the United Kingdom, the Dominions and India, Held in June, July, and August 1921: Summary of Proceedings and Documents*, London: HMSO, 1921, 1.
264 Ollivier, Vol. 2, 397–407.
265 Hancock, *Survey of British*, 86.
266 "An Imperial Conference", *Advocate of Peace through Justice* 83, No. 7, 1921, 252; TNA, CAB 32/2, E. 1st Meeting, Stenographic Notes of a Meeting of Representatives of the United Kingdom, the Dominions and India, 20 June 1921, 5 [3].
267 "The Imperial Conference", *The Round Table* 11, No. 14, 1921, 739.
268 Hall, *Commonwealth*, 365–366.
269 Cmd. 1474, 9, 22–23; TNA, CAB 32/2, E. 2nd Meeting, Stenographic Notes of a Meeting of Representatives of the United Kingdom, the Dominions and India, 21 June 1921, 6–7, 9 [9–10].
270 Hall, *Commonwealth*, 367.
271 Britain's India Secretary, Edwin Montagu, did not entirely agree with Hughes's declaration, and as such he remarked ironically to Hankey that there still were some national differences: "Balfour and Smartt – Scots, Massey, Meighen and Chamberlain – Englishmen, Hughes and Lloyd George – Welshmen, Churchill – English, American and Indian, Smuts – Dutch, Montagu – Jew and Curzon – superhuman." Roskill, Stephen, *Hankey, Man of Secrets: 1919–1931*, Vol. 2, London: Collins, 1972, 232.
272 On Mackenzie King's political rise, see Ferns, Henry Stanley – Ostry, Bernard, *The Age of Mackenzie King: The Rise of the Leader*, London: William Heinemann, 1955, 283–322.
273 Cf. Hall, *Commonwealth*, 364; Ollivier, Vol. 2, 416, 430; TNA, CAB 32/2, E. 1st Meeting, Stenographic Notes of a Meeting of Representatives of the United Kingdom, the Dominions and India, 20 June 1921, 7 [4].
274 Beloff, *Imperial*, Vol. 1, 320; TNA, CAB 32/2, E. 20th Meeting, Stenographic Notes of a Meeting of Representatives of the United Kingdom, the Dominions and India, 8 July 1921, 9 [131].

275 TNA, CAB 32/2, E. 2nd Meeting, Stenographic Notes of a Meeting of Representatives of the United Kingdom, the Dominions and India, 21 June 1921, 15 [13].
276 Hall, *Commonwealth*, 369–370.
277 TNA, DO 117/33, [A Note by Mr. Dixon], 14 October 1926, [3].
278 For more on constitutional disputes cf. TNA, CAB 32/2, E. 22nd Meeting, Stenographic Notes of a Meeting of Representatives of the United Kingdom, the Dominions and India, 11 July 1921, 12–13 [149]; TNA, CAB 32/2, E. 23rd Meeting, Stenographic Notes of a Meeting of Representatives of the United Kingdom, the Dominions and India, 12 July 1921, 7–15 [157–161]; TNA, CAB 32/2, E. 24th Meeting, Stenographic Notes of a Meeting of Representatives of the United Kingdom, the Dominions and India, 12 July 1921, [1]–7 [163–165].
279 TNA, CAB 32/2, E. 22nd Meeting, Stenographic Notes of a Meeting of Representatives of the United Kingdom, the Dominions and India, 11 July 1921, 14 [150]; TNA, CAB 32/4, E–26 C., Notes of a Meeting of the Prime Ministers of the Empire, Downing Street, London, 22 July 1921, 4–5 [30–31].
280 NA CAB 32/4, E–31 B., Appendix I, Draft Resolution Submitted by General Smuts, [27 July 1921], 18 [63].
281 The British Prime Minister feared that the text presented might sound unfavourable to India. TNA, CAB 32/4, E–31 B., Notes of a Meeting of the Prime Ministers of the Empire, Downing Street, London, 27 July 1921, 1 [47].
282 Cf. *APD, HoR*, No. 39, 30 September 1921, 11643; TNA, CAB 32/4, E–26 C., Notes of a Meeting of the Prime Ministers of the Empire, Downing Street, London, 22 July 1921, 4–6 [30–32]; TNA, CAB 32/4, E–31 B., Notes of a Meeting of the Prime Ministers of the Empire, Downing Street, London, 27 July 1921, 1–3 [47–49]; TNA, CAB 32/4, E–31 B., Appendix IV, Memorandum Read by Mr. Hughes, [27 July 1921], 21–22 [66–67].
283 Hall, "The Genesis", 182; TNA, CAB 32/4, E–31 B., Notes of a Meeting of the Prime Ministers of the Empire, Downing Street, London, 27 July 1921, 3–5 [49–51].
284 Cf. Cmd. 1474, 1–5; Hall, *Commonwealth*, 346–348; Stacey, Vol. 1, 333.
285 Cf. Hall, "The Genesis", 182; Kennedy, William Paul McClure, "Canada and the Imperial Conference", *Contemporary Review*, No. 120, 1921, 61–64; TNA, CAB 32/4, E–31 B., Notes of a Meeting of the Prime Ministers of the Empire, Downing Street, London, 27 July 1921, 6–7 [52].
286 A general election was to be held in Canada, in which the Conservatives were expected to be defeated by Mackenzie King's Liberals. Hall, "The Genesis", 182; Thornton, Martin, *Sir Robert Borden: Canada*, London: Haus 2010, 105, 117.
287 Borden, *Canada in the Commonwealth*, 124.
288 TNA, CAB 32/4, E–31 B., Notes of a Meeting of the Prime Ministers of the Empire, Downing Street, London, 27 July 1921, 8 [53].
289 TNA, CAB 32/4, E–31 B., Appendix II: Sir Edward Grigg's Draft, as Revisited by Mr. Massey, [27 July 1921], 19 [64].
290 TNA, CAB 32/4, E–31 B., Appendix III: Draft Submitted by Sir Maurice Hankey, [27 July 1921], 20 [65].
291 Ollivier, Vol. 2, 406; TNA, CAB 32/4, E – 31 B., Notes of a Meeting of the Prime Ministers of the Empire, Downing Street, London, 27 July 1921, 11–13 [56–58].
292 Cf. TNA, CAB 17/190, L. S. A[mery] to Fiddes, Channels of Communication, 5 January 1920, [41–44]; TNA, CO 886/9/3, Dominions No. 76, 1510/S,

Part II: Channels of Communication, The Acting Secretary of State to the Governors-General, 22 January 1920, No. 27, 32.
293 Allin, Caphas Daniel, "Recent Developments in the Constitutional and International States of the British Dominions", *Minnesota Law Review*, No. 10, 1925/1926, 104–110.
294 Stacey, Vol. 1, 334.
295 See more Loring Christie, "The Anglo-Japanese Alliance", 1 February 1921, in: Lower, Arthur Reginald Marsden, "Loring Christie and the Genesis of the Washington Conference of 1921-1922", *The Canadian Historical Review* 47, No. 1, 1966, 42–48; Scheuer, Michael Frank, *Loring Christie and the North Atlantic Community, 1913–1941*, PhD Thesis, Winnipeg: University of Manitoba, 1986, 134–140.
296 Cf. Governor General to Colonial Secretary, Ottawa, 15 February 1921, in: *DCER*, Vol. 3, Doc. No. 209, 162–163; Fry, Michael G., *Illusions of Security: North Atlantic Diplomacy 1918-22*, Toronto: University of Toronto Press, 1972, 91–92; Nish, Ian H., *Alliance in Decline: A Study in Anglo-Japanese Relations, 1908-23*, London: Athlone Press, 1972, 325; TNA, CAB 1/4, 130–C, Committee of Imperial Defence: Memorandum by Sir B. Alston Respecting Suggestions for an Anglo-Saxon Policy for the Far East, 1 August 1920, [1]–5 [273–275]; TNA, CO 886/9/8, The Secretary of State to the Governor General, 26 February 1921, Doc. No. 140, 89–90.
297 Fry, Michael G., "The North Atlantic Triangle and the Abrogation of the Anglo-Japanese Alliance", *Journal of Modern History* 39, No. 1, 1967, 46–47; Woodsworth, Charles J., "Canada and the Far East", *Far Eastern Survey* 10, No. 14, 1941, 162–163.
298 To the attitudes of Australia and New Zealand in detail cf. Brebner, John Bartlet, "Canada, the Anglo-Japanese Alliance and the Washington Conference", *Political Science Quarterly* 40, No. 1, 1935, 51–52; Galbraith, J., "The Imperial Conference of 1921 and the Washington Conference", *The Canadian Historical Review* 29, No. 2, 1948, 147; Glazebrook, George Parkin de Twenebroker, "Canadian External Relations", in: Martin, Chester (Ed.), *Canada in Peace and War: Eight Studies in National Trends since 1914*, London: Oxford University Press, 1941, 164; Tate, Merze – Foy, Fidele, "More Light on the Abrogation of the Anglo-Japanese Alliance", *Political Science Quarterly* 74, No. 4, 1959, 536–537; Thornton, Robert, "Semblance of Security: Australia and the Washington Conference, 1921–22", *Australian Outlook* 32, No. 1, 1978, 66.
299 Cmd. 1474, 21.
300 Brebner, "Canada, the Anglo-Japanese", 53.
301 Cf. Boulger, Demetrius C., "The Anglo-Japanese Alliance", *Contemporary Review* 118, 1920, 326–333; Fry, "The North Atlantic", 48; PD, HoC, 5th Series, Vol. 130, 24 June 1920, 2365–2366; TNA, CAB 1/4, 126–C, Committee of Imperial Defence: Anglo-Japanese Alliance: Memoranda and Minutes Regarding the Renewal Anglo-Japanese Alliance Received from Foreign Office March 1920, 27 April 1920, [1]–6 [263–266].
302 See more cf. [F 199/199/23], Foreign Office Memorandum on Effect of Anglo-Japanese Alliance upon Foreign Relationships, Foreign Office, 28 February 1920, in: *DBFP: 1919*, 1st Series, Vol. 6, London 1956, Doc. No. 761, 1016–1023; Kerr, Philip Henry, "The Anglo-Japanese Alliance", *The Round Table* 11, No. 41, 1920, 93–96; Koehn, George L., "Menace of the Anglo-Japanese Alliance", *Current History* 14, No. 5, 1921, 738–739; Lowe, Peter, "The Round Table, the Dominions and the Anglo-Japanese Alliance, 1911–22", *The Round Table* 86, No. 341, 1997, 87; Northedge,

The Empire During the War and Post-War Period   161

Frederick Samuel, *The Troubled Giant: Britain among the Great Powers 1916–1939*, London: G. Bell & Sons, 1966, 286; TNA, CAB 24/97/102, C. P. 599, [M.] Ferguson, Paraphrase Telegram from the Governor General of the Commonwealth of Australia to the Secretary of State for the Colonies, 3 February 1920, 658.
303 Casson, Herbert N., "The Significance of the Imperial Conference", *Barron's* 1, No. 10, 11 July 1921, 5.
304 After the First World War, the British Admiralty had to make a decision due to the distribution of naval forces, as to whether it was going to maintain two naval bases in the Pacific – Singapore and Hong Kong – or not. For strategic and financial reasons, and taking account of the position of Australia and New Zealand, it eventually chose Singapore as its main base. Cf. Bell, Christopher Michael, *British Ideas of Sea Power, 1914–1941*, PhD Thesis, Calgary: The University of Calgary, 1998, 84–151; "Britain's Navy", *Evening Post* 101, No. 48, 25 February 1921, 2; Callahan, Raymond, "The Illusion of Security: Singapore 1919–42", *Journal of Contemporary History* 9, No. 2, 1974, 73–92; TNA, CAB 34/1, S. S. – 2, A. J. Balfour, Committee of Imperial Defence: Standing Sub-Committee: Naval and Military Situation in the Far East, 3 May 1921, [1]–5 [7–11]; TNA, CAB 34/1, S. S.–6, Committee of Imperial Defence: Standing Sub-Committee: Empire Naval Policy and Cooperation: Summary of Admiralty Recommendations in Regard to Dominions Naval Policy, 26 May 1921, [21–22]; TNA, CAB 34/1, S. S.–12, Committee of Imperial Defence: Standing Sub-Committee: Singapore – Development of as Naval Base: Draft Conclusion, 13 June 1921, [34–35].
305 TNA, CAB 1/4, 122–C, Committee of Imperial Defence: Anglo-Japanese Alliance: Effect of the Anglo-Japanese Alliance upon Foreign Relations, 28 February 1920, 4–5 [245].
306 Cf. Cmd. 1474, 13; [F 1579/63/23], Memorandum by Mr. Lampson on Correspondence with Canadian Government Relating to the Anglo-Japanese Alliance, Foreign Office, 8 April 1921, in: *DBFP: Far Eastern Affairs April 1920–February 1922*, 1st Series, Vol. 14, London 1966, Doc. No. 261, 271–276; Governor General to Colonial Secretary, Ottawa, 1 April 1921, in: *DCER*, Vol. 3, Doc. No. 213, 166–167; *PD, HoC*, 5th Series, Vol. 143, 17 June 1921, 792, 795–796; TNA, CO 886/9/8, The Secretary of State to the Governor General, 26 April 1921, Doc. No. 142, 91–92.
307 See more in Best, Anthony, "Race, Monarchy, and the Anglo-Japanese Alliance, 1902–1922", *Social Science Japan Journal* 9, No. 2, 2006, 171–186; Poynter, J. R., "The Yo-yo Variations: Initiative and Dependence in Australia's External Relations, 1918–1923", *Historical Studies* 14, No. 54, 1970, 233; [F 3823/2635/10], V. Wellesley, General Survey of Political Situation in Pacific and Far East with Reference to the Forthcoming Washington Conference, Foreign Office, 20 October 1921, in: *DBFP*, Vol. 14, Doc. No. 404, 438.
308 The Acting Secretary of State [Phillips] to the Ambassador in Great Britain (Davis), Washington, 2 October 1919, in: *FRUS*, 1920, Vol. 2, 679.
309 Eggleston, F. W., "The Imperial Conference", *New Statesman* 17, No. 426, 11 June 1921, 268.
310 The Acting Secretary of State [Polk] to the Ambassador in Great Britain (Davis), Washington, 10 May 1920, in: *FRUS*, 1920, Vol. 2, 680–681.
311 Hall, *Commonwealth*, 438–439; Hargreaves, J. D., "The Anglo-Japanese Alliance, 1902–1952", *History Today* 2, No. 4, 1952, 257–258; Spinks, Charles Nelson, "The Termination of the Anglo-Japanese Alliance", *Pacific Historical Review* 6, 1937, 322–323.

162   The Empire During the War and Post-War Period

312 Cf. Brebner, "Canada, the Anglo-Japanese", 51; Fry, "The North Atlantic", 53–55; Spinks, 325; TNA, CAB 1/4, 121–C, Committee of Imperial Defence: Anglo-Japanese Alliance: Correspondence Regarding Strategical and International Considerations Involved in the Continuance of the Alliance, Foreign Office, 5 March 1920, 2–10 [236–240]; TNA, CAB 1/4, 122–C, Committee of Imperial Defence: Anglo-Japanese Alliance: Anglo-Japanese Alliance as Affected by the Covenant of the League of Nations, 18 February 1920, 2–3 [244]; TNA, CAB 23/25/27, Cabinet 43 (21), Conclusions of a Meeting of the Cabinet, Downing Street, 30 May 1921, 2–17 [298–313].
313 The Chargé in Japan (Bell) to the Secretary of State, Tokyo, 26 July 1920, in: *FRUS*, 1920, Vol. 2, 685–686.
314 Nish, Ian H., "Britain and Japan: Long-Range Images, 1900–52", *Diplomacy and Statecraft* 15, No. 1, 2004, 153; Tate – Foy, 539.
315 The Alliance was able to continue formally for a further twelve months following the moment the Alliance was declared ended. See more cf. Carter, *The British Commonwealth*, 44; Louis, William Roger, *British Strategy in the Far East 1919–1939*, Oxford: Clarendon Press, 1971, 74; TNA, CO 886/9/8, House of Commons: Far Eastern and Pacific Policy: United States and British Empire Relations, 11 July 1921, Encl. No. 1 to Doc. No. 146, 95.
316 Cassidy, James Thomas, *Prelude to a New World Order: The Atlantic Triangle and Japan 1914–1921*, MA Thesis, Montreal: McGill University, 1974, 63–66; Cmd. 1474, 31; Spinks, 322–323.
317 TNA, CAB 32/2, E. 22nd Meeting, Stenographic Notes of a Meeting of Representatives of the United Kingdom, the Dominions and India, 11 July 1921, 8 [147].
318 "The Anglo-Japanese Alliance", *Spectator* 125, No. 4802, 10 July 1920, 39; Cmd. 1474, 13; Prang, M., "N. W. Rowell and Canada's External Policy, 1917–1921", *Report of the Annual Meeting of the Canadian Historical Association/Rapports annuels de la Société historique du Canada* 39, No. 1, 1960, 101.
319 TNA, CAB 32/2, E. 23rd Meeting, Stenographic Notes of a Meeting of Representatives of the United Kingdom, the Dominions and India, 12 July 1921, 2–4 [155–156].
320 Cf. *APD, HoR*, No. 14, 7 April 1920, 7265; *APD, HoR*, No. 37, 9 September 1921, 4387–4390; Cmd. 1474, 19; Brawley, Sean, *The White Peril: Foreign Relations and Asian Immigration to Australasia and North America, 1919–1978*, Sydney: UNSW Press, 1995, 73–74; Dignan, D. K., "Australia and British Relations with Japan, 1914–1921", *Australian Outlook* 21, No. 2, 1967, 135–150; Louis, *British Strategy*, 55; Piesse, E. L., "Japan and Australia", *Foreign Affairs: An American Quarterly Review* 4, No. 1/4, 1925/1926, 475–488; Poynter, 236–238; "The Anglo-Japanese Pact", *Evening Post* 101, No. 48, 25 February 1921, 6; TNA, CAB 32/2, E. 10th Meeting, Stenographic Notes of a Meeting of Representatives of the United Kingdom, the Dominions and India, 29 June 1921, 2–8 [70–73].
321 Okamoto, T., "American-Japanese Issues and the Anglo-Japanese Alliance", *Contemporary Review* 119, 1921, 354–360; TNA, CAB 24/125/49, C. P. 3048, W. S. C[hurchill], The Cabinet: The Anglo-Japanese Alliance: Memorandum by the Secretary of State for the Colonies, Colonial Office, 17 June 1921, 281.
322 Carrington, 890.
323 Influential members of the Round Table Movement held a similar opinion to Smuts. Cf. Kerr, *The Anglo-Japanese*, 96; TNA, CAB 32/2, E. 10th Meeting, Stenographic Notes of a Meeting of Representatives of the United Kingdom, the Dominions and India, 29 June 1921, 8–10 [73–74].

324 Cmd. 1474, 24; Galbraith, 147.
325 Cf. Galbraith, 147; Spinks, 330; Stacey, Vol. 1, 343; Tate – Foy, 543; TNA, CAB 32/2, E. 9th Meeting, Stenographic Notes of a Meeting of Representatives of the United Kingdom, the Dominions and India, 29 June 1921, 8 [65].
326 TNA, CAB 32/2, E. 9th Meeting, Stenographic Notes of a Meeting of Representatives of the United Kingdom, the Dominions and India, 29 June 1921, 14 [68].
327 Cf. Memorandum of a Conversation between the Secretary of State [C. E. Hughes] and the British Ambassador (Geddes), 23 June 1921, in: *FRUS*, 1921, Vol. 2, 314–316; TNA, CAB 32/2, E. 8th Meeting, Stenographic Notes of a Meeting of Representatives of the United Kingdom, the Dominions and India, 28 June 1921, 4–7 [55–56].
328 TNA, CAB 34/1, S. S.–16, Committee of Imperial Defence: Strategic Situation in the Event of the Anglo-Japanese Alliance Being Determined, Whitehall Gardens, 15 June 1921, [1]–6 [43–48].
329 A number of Anglo-American debates took place beginning 23 June 1921, looking at possible forms of trilateral co-operation. See more Memorandum of a Conversation between the Secretary of State [C. E. Hughes] and the British Ambassador (Geddes), 23 June 1921, in: *FRUS*, 1921, Vol. 2, 315; Fry, "The North Atlantic", 59–62; Vinson, J. Chal, "The Imperial Conference of 1921 and the Anglo-Japanese Alliance", *Pacific Historical Review* 31, No. 3, 1962, 262–264.
330 TNA, CAB 23/26/11, Cabinet 56 (21), Conclusions of a Meeting of the Cabinet, Downing Street, 30 June 1921, 2–6 [101–105].
331 For more on discussions of the Dominions' influence on changing British policy, see Klein, Ira, "Whitehall, Washington, and the Anglo-Japanese Alliance, 1919–1921", *Pacific Historical Review* 41, No. 4, 1972, 464–468.
332 Invitations to the Washington conference were received by the naval powers of the British Empire, the United States, Japan, France and Italy, alongside countries with interests in the Pacific such as China, the Netherlands, Belgium and Portugal.
333 "Fruits of the British Imperial Conference", *Current History* 14, No. 6, 1921, 1048; Spinks, 332–333; The Secretary of State [C. E. Hughes] to the Ambassador in Great Britain (Harvey), Washington, 8 July 1921, in: *FRUS*, 1921, Vol. 1, 18; Colonial Secretary to Governor General, Downing Street, 12 September 1921, in: *DCER*, Vol. 3, Doc. No. 429, 484–486.
334 Cf. [A 5169/18/45], The Marquess Curzon of Kedleston to Sir A. Geddes (Washington), Foreign Office, 14 July 1921, in: *DBFP*, Vol. 14, Doc. No. 335, 342–343; The Ambassador in Great Britain (Harvey) to the Secretary of State [C. E. Hughes], London, 11 July 1921, in: *FRUS*, 1921, Vol. 1, 26; The Secretary of State to the Ambassador in Great Britain (Harvey), Washington, 13 July 1921, in: *FRUS*, 1921, Vol. 1, 28–29.
335 Cf. [A 5489/18/45], Memorandum by the Marquess Curzon of Kedleston to the Situation Re-proposed Conference at Washington, Foreign Office, 24 July 1921, in: *DBFP*, Vol. 14, Doc. No. 337, 345–351; [A 5509/18/45], Sir A. Geddes (Washington) to the Marquess Curzon of Kedleston, Washington, 27 July 1921, in: *DBFP*, Vol. 14, Doc. No. 340, 353–354; The Ambassador in Great Britain (Harvey) to the Secretary of State, London, 15 July 1921, in: *FRUS*, 1921, Vol. 1, 33; The Ambassador in Great Britain (Harvey) to the Secretary of State, London, 19 July 1921, in: *FRUS*, 1921, Vol. 1, 36–37; The Secretary of State to the Ambassador in Great Britain (Harvey), Washington, 20 July 1921, in: *FRUS*, 1921, Vol. 1, 37–38.

336 Cf. [A 5551/18/45], Sir A. Geddes (Washington) to the Marquess Curzon of Kedleston, Washington, 30 July 1921, in: *DBFP*, Vol. 14, Doc. No. 345, 357–358; The Ambassador in Great Britain (Harvey) to the Secretary of State [C. E. Hughes], London, 27 July 1921, in: *FRUS*, 1921, Vol. 1, 46–47; The Secretary of State to the Ambassador in Great Britain (Harvey), Washington, 28 July 1921, in: *FRUS*, 1921, Vol. 1, 47–50.

337 [F 3078/63/23], Memorandum by Mr. Lampson as to Whether the Anglo-Japanese Alliance Should Be Directly Discussed at the Washington Conference, Foreign Office, 18 August 1921, in: *DBFP*, Vol. 14, Doc. No. 363, 380–382; [F 3099/63/23], Sir A. Geddes (Washington) to the Marquess Curzon of Kedleston, Washington, 20 August 1921, in: *DBFP*, Vol. 14, Doc. No. 364, 382; Tate – Foy, 546.

338 Memorandum by the Secretary of State of a Conversation with the British Ambassador (Geddes), 20 September 1921, in: *FRUS*, 1921, Vol. 1, 73.

339 Brebner, John Bartlet, *North Atlantic Triangle: The Interplay of Canada, the United States and Great Britain*, 3rd Ed., New Haven: Yale University Press, 1947, 282.

340 Best, Anthony, "The 'Ghost' of the Anglo-Japanese Alliance: An Examination into Historical Myth-Making", *The Historical Journal* 49, No. 3, 2006, 818.

341 For more on this issue, see Allbert Dayer, Roberta, "The British War Debts to the United States and the Anglo-Japanese Alliance, 1920–1923", *Pacific Historical Review* 45, 1976, 580–583; [A 6915/18/45], Sir A. Geddes (Washington) to the Marquess Curzon of Kedleston, Washington, 21 September 1921, in: *DBFP*, Vol. 14, Doc. No. 380, 401.

342 The Chargé in Japan (Bell) to the Secretary of State [C. E. Hughes], Tokyo, 13 July 1921, in: *FRUS*, 1921, Vol. 1, 31.

343 Tate – Foy, 544.

344 See more cf. Asada, Sadao, "Between the Old Diplomacy and the New, 1918–1922: The Washington System and the Origins of Japanese-American Rapprochement", *Diplomatic History* 30, No. 2, 2006, 211–230; Asada, Sadao, "Japan's 'Special Interests' and the Washington Conference, 1921–22", *The American Historical Review* 67, No. 1, 1961, 63; Louis, *British*, 94; Tate – Foy, 547–551; The Chargé in Great Britain (Wheeler) to the Secretary of State [C. E. Hughes], London, 6 August 1921, in: *FRUS*, 1921, Vol. 1, 52–53.

345 Katsuizumi, Sotokichi, *Critical Observation on the Washington Conference*, Ann Arbor: [s. n.], 1922, 16.

346 Cf. The Secretary of State to the Ambassador in Great Britain (Harvey), Washington, 23 August 1921, in: *FRUS*, 1921, Vol. 1, 60–61; The Ambassador in Great Britain (Harvey) to the Secretary of State, London, 26 August 1921, in: *FRUS*, 1921, Vol. 1, 63–64; Vinson, J. Chal, "The Problem of Australian Representation at the Washington Conference for the Limitation of Naval Armament", *The Australian Journal of Politics and History* 4, No. 2, 1958, 157–164.

347 Carter, *The British Commonwealth*, 49–50; Galbraith, 150–151; Stewart, Robert B., *Treaty Relations of the British Commonwealth of Nations*, New York: Macmillan, 1939, 159–160; Toynbee, 84–85.

348 Press Statement (1921), in: Hancock, William Keith – Poel, Jean van der (Eds.), *Selections from the Smuts Papers: September 1919–November 1934*, Vol. 5, Cambridge: Cambridge University Press, 1966, Doc. Box G, No. 7A, 107–109; Colonial Secretary to Governor General, London, 21 October 1921, in: *DCER*, Vol. 3, Doc. No. 435, 489; Smuts [to Meighen], 19 October 1921, Dawson, *The Development*, 219; TNA, CO 886/9/8, Union of South Africa: The Governor General to the Secretary of State, 26 October 1921, Doc. No. 304, 208.

349 TNA, CO 886/9/8, Union of South Africa: The Governor General to the Secretary of State, 2 November 1921, Encl. Doc. No. 311, 211–212.
350 Borden, Robert Laird, Sir, *Conference on the Limitation of Armament Held at Washington November 12, 1921, to February 6, 1922: Report of the Canadian Delegate Including Treaties and Resolutions*, Ottawa: F. A. Acland, 1922, 8; Stacey, Vol. 1, 348; TNA, CAB 30/1B, B. E. D. [No. 72], M. P. A. Hankey, The Washington Conference on the Limitation of Armaments: Provisional Organization of the British Empire Delegation, 21 October 1921, 1–[5] [7–11].
351 Fry, *Illusions*, 158; [F 3078/63/23], Memorandum by Mr. Lampson as to Whether the Anglo-Japanese Alliance Should be Directly Discussed at the Washington Conference, Foreign Office, 18 August 1921, in: *DBFP*, Vol. 14, Doc. No. 363, 380–382.
352 [F 3823/2635/10], V. Wellesley, General Survey of Political Situation in Pacific and Far East with Reference to the Forthcoming Washington Conference, Foreign Office, 20 October 1921, in: *DBFP*, Vol. 14, Doc. No. 404, 440.
353 Cf. TNA, Board of Trade Papers (hereafter BT), 11/19, D. 11769, [V. Wellesley], General Survey of Political Situation in Pacific and Far East with Reference to the Forthcoming Washington Conference, 20 October 1921, 5–8; [F 3930/2905/23], Foreign Office Memorandum Respecting a Tripartite Agreement, Foreign Office, 22 October 1921, in: *DBFP*, Vol. 14, Doc. No. 405, 448–450.
354 Stacey, Vol. 1, 349.
355 TNA, CAB 30/5, W. D. C. 1, Cabinet: Washington Disarmament Conference: President Harding's Opening Speech, Washington, 12 November [1921], 6.
356 Colonial Secretary to Governor General, London, 3 October 1921, in: *DCER*, Vol. 3, Doc. No. 433, 487–488.
357 Dugdale, Blanche Elizabeth Campbell, *Arthur James Balfour: 1906–1930*, Vol. 2, London: Hutchinson & Co., 1939, 235.
358 TNA, CAB 30/5, W. D. C. 13, Cabinet: Washington Conference on the Limitation of Armament: Copy of a Despatch (No. 1) from Mr. Balfour to the Prime Minister, 11 November 1921, 127.
359 TNA, CAB 30/27, S. W. 1, M. Hankey, Mr. Balfour's Interview with Mr. Hughes, 11 November 1921, 2; Memorandum, in Outline Form by the Secretary of State [C. E. Hughes] of a Conversation with Mr. Balfour, of the British Delegation, 11 November 1921, in: *FRUS*, 1922, Vol. 1, 1–2.
360 [F 3930/2905/23], Formula (Drafted by Sir J. Jordan) for a Tripartite Joint Declaration, Foreign Office, 22 October 1921, in: *DBFP*, Vol. 14, Appendix (B) to Doc. No. 405, 450.
361 Memorandum by Mr. Balfour, of the British Delegation, [11 November 1921], in: *FRUS*, 1922, Vol. 1, 2–3.
362 See more cf. TNA, CAB 30/5, W. D. C. 13, Cabinet: Washington Conference on the Limitation of Armament: Copy of a Despatch (No. 1) from Mr. Balfour to the Prime Minister, 11 November 1921, Encl. 1, 127; TNA, Admiralty Papers (hereafter ADM) 1/8630/142, B. E. D. [No. 52], British Empire Delegation: Fifth Conference of British Empire Delegation, Washington, Franklin Square Hotel, 18 November 1921, [1]–3 [8–9].
363 Cf. Fry, *Illusions*, 166; TNA, CAB 30/5, W. D. C. 14, Cabinet: Washington Conference on the Limitation of Armament: Copy of a Despatch (No. 2) from Mr. Balfour to the Prime Minister, 14 November 1921, [1]–2 [127–128]; TNA, CAB 30/5, W. D. C. 47, Cabinet: Washington Conference on the Limitation of Armament: Copy of a Despatch (No. 4) from Mr. Balfour to the Prime Minister, 24 November 1921, [1]–2 [110–111].
364 Sir M. Hankey to Mr. Balfour, 18 November 1921, in: *DBFP*, Vol. 14, Encl. [No.] 1 in Doc. No. 449, 508–511; TNA, CAB 30/27, S. W. 2, Mr. Balfour's

166   *The Empire During the War and Post-War Period*

Interview with Prince Tokugawa, Franklin Square Hotel, 12 November 1921, 3; TNA, CAB 30/27, S. W. 3, Conversation between Sir M. Hankey and M. Sabuki, 18 November 1921, 4–8.

365 Draft by Ambassador Shidehara, of the Japanese Delegation, of an Arrangement between Japan, the United States of America, and the British Empire, [Undated], in: *FRUS*, 1922, Vol. 1, 4; TNA, CAB 30/5, W. D. C. 38, Cabinet: Washington Conference on the Limitation of Armament: Propos D Tripartite Agreement, 28 November 1921, No. 2, 138.

366 "Far Eastern Problem: Quadruple Agreement Possible: Britain, America, Japan, China", *The Sydney Morning Herald*, No. 26174, 24 November 1921, 9. To the activities of the Australian delegate in Washington in more detail, see Thornton, "Semblance", 70–80.

367 TNA, CAB 30/27, S. W. 6, M. Hankey, Note of a Conversation between Mr. Balfour and Senator Lodge and Mr. Root, 26 November 1921, 13–15.

368 Hughes did not include the Kingdom of the Netherlands in the arrangement, because it was not a great power, nor did he include Italy since it did not own any territory in the Pacific. See TNA, CAB 30/5, W. D. C. 38, Cabinet: Washington Conference on the Limitation of Armament: Propos D Tripartite Agreement, 28 November 1921, No. 3, 139; [F 4413/ 2905/23], Mr. Balfour (Washington Delegation) to the Marquess Curzon of Kedleston, Washington, 29 November 1921, in: *DBFP*, Vol. 14, Doc. No. 458, 522–523.

369 To discuss the form of the Treaty of Four in more detail: Draft by the Secretary of State of an Agreement between the United States of America, the British Empire, France, and Japan, [December 1921], in: *FRUS*, 1922, Vol. 1, 7–8; Vinson, J. Chal, "The Drafting of the Four-Power Treaty of the Washington Conference", *Journal of Modern History* 25, No. 1, 1953, 44–47.

370 TNA, CAB 30/5, W. D. C. 13, Cabinet: Washington Conference on the Limitation of Armament: Copy of a Despatch (No. 1) from Mr. Balfour to the Prime Minister, 11 November 1921, 126; Vinson, "The Drafting", 43.

371 The word "China" in the Four-Power Treaty technically referred not just to China itself, but also Korea and other parts of the Asian continent. [F 4453/2905/23], Mr. Balfour (Washington Delegation) to the Marquess Curzon of Kedleston, Washington, 3 December 1921, in: *DBFP*, Vol. 14, Doc. No. 472, 535.

372 Cf. [F 4451/2905/23], Mr. Balfour (Washington Delegation) to the Marquess Curzon of Kedleston, Washington, 3 December 1921, in: *DBFP*, Vol. 14, Doc. No. 471, 535; Memorandum by the Secretary to the British Empire Delegation of a Conversation at the Department of State, 2 December 1921, in: *FRUS*, 1922, Vol. 1 p. 5; TNA, CAB 30/5, W. D. C. 50, Cabinet: Washington Conference on Limitation of Armament: Proposed Pacific Agreement, 7 December 1921, 258–259.

373 TNA, CAB 30/5, W. D. C. 52, Cabinet: Washington Conference on Limitation of Armament: Proposed Quadruple Agreement, 7 December 1921, No. 112, 265; TNA, CAB 30/1A, B. E. D. [No. 58], British Empire Delegation: Eleventh Conference of British Empire Delegation, Washington, Franklin Square Hotel, 7 December 1921, [1]–3 [41–42].

374 Carter, *The British Commonwealth*, 54; Canadian Delegate [R. L. Borden] to Prime Minister [A. Meighen], Washington, 10 December 1921, in: *DCER*, Vol. 3, Doc. No. 449, 505; TNA, CAB 30/1A, B. E. D. [No. 59], British Empire Delegation: Twelfth Conference of British Empire Delegation, Washington, Franklin Square Hotel, 9 December 1921, [1]–5 [44–47]; TNA, ADM 1/8630/142, B. E. D. [No. 60], British Empire Delegation: Thirteenth Conference of British Empire Delegation, Washington, Franklin Square Hotel, 10 December 1921, [1]–2 [8].

375 See Buell, Raymond Leslie, *The Washington Conference*, New York: D. Appleton & Co, 1922, 172–200; Spinks, 337; [F 4539/2905/23], Mr. Balfour (Washington Delegation) to the Marquess Curzon of Kedleston, Washington, 3 December 1921, in: *DBFP*, Vol. 14, Doc. No. 471, 541–542; The Secretary of State [C. E. Hughes] to Mr. Frank H. Simonds, Washington, 29 December 1921, in: *FRUS*, 1922, Vol. 1, 40; Treaty between the United States of America, the British Empire, France, and Japan, Signed at Washington, 13 December 1921, in: *FRUS*, 1922, Vol. 1, 33–36.
376 Sullivan, Mark, *The Great Adventure at Washington: The Story of the Conference*, New York: William Heinemann, 1922, 236.
377 Carter, *The British Commonwealth*, 55.
378 [F 4745/2905/23], Mr. Balfour (Washington Delegation) to the Marquess Curzon of Kedleston, Washington, 19 December 1921, in: *DBFP*, Vol. 14, Doc. No. 512, 566–567.
379 CAC, HP, HNKY 8/22, W. D. C.–226, Cabinet: Washington Conference on Limitation of Armament, Copy of Despatch (No. 27) from Mr. Balfour to the Prime Minister, Washington, 6 February 1922, [1].
380 Carter, *The British Commonwealth*, 54.
381 See [Hughes, Charles Evans], "Washington Agreement on Capital Ships", *A League of Nations* 4, No. 5, 1921, 373–393; TNA, CAB 30/5, W. D. C. 8, Cabinet: Conference on the Limitation of Armament: The Proposal of the United States for a Limitation of Naval Armament, 12 November 1921, 43–46.
382 Kodet, Roman, "The Imperial Japanese Navy and the Washington Conference", *Prague Papers on the History of International Relations*, 2009, 545; TNA, CAB 30/1B, B. E. D. [No. 76], The Proposal of the United States for a Limitation of Naval Armaments, [12 November] 1921, [54–65].
383 Carter, *The British Commonwealth*, 55; Riddell, George Allardice, Baron, *Lord Riddell's Intimate Diary of the Peace Conference and After, 1918–1923*, London: Victor Gollancz, 1933, 337.
384 Repington, Charles à Court, *After the War*, New York: Houghton Mifflin Co, 1922, 432.
385 Fry, *Illusions*, 179–180.
386 Cf. Carter, *The British Commonwealth*, 55–57; TNA, CAB 30/1B, B. E. D. [No. 77], British Empire Delegation: American Proposal for the Limitation of Armament: Memorandum by Sir Robert Borden, Washington, Franklin Square Hotel, 14 November 1921, [66–68]; Memorandum by Canadian Delegate [R. L. Borden], Washington, 14 November 1921, in: *DCER*, Vol. 3, Doc. No. 438, 493.
387 TNA, CAB 30/1B, B. E. D. [No. 80], British Empire Delegation: American Proposal for the Limitation of Armament: Note by Senator Pearce on Sir R. Borden's Memorandum, Washington, Franklin Square Hotel, 14 November 1921, [78].
388 TNA, CAB 30/1B, B. E. D. [No. 85], British Empire Delegation: American Proposal for the Limitation of Armament: Note by Foreign Office Section on Sir Robert Borden's Memorandum, Washington, Franklin Square Hotel, 16 November 1921, [108–109].
389 Although the British public considered the meeting in Washington a success, the French were not enthusiastic. See Birn, Donald S., "Open Diplomacy at the Washington Conference of 1921-2: The British and French Experience", *Comparative Studies and History* 12, No. 3, 1970, 297–319.
390 Louis, *British*, 104.
391 Williamson, James Alexander, *A Short History of British Expansion: The Modern Empire and Commonwealth*, 3rd Ed., London: Macmillan, 1947, 349–350.

168 The Empire During the War and Post-War Period

392 Marks, Sally, *The Illusion of Peace: International Relations in Europe 1918–1933*, London: Macmillan, 1976, 40–42.
393 Poynter, 246; Spencer, Alex M., *A Third Option: Imperial Air Defence and the Pacific Dominions, 1918–1939*, PhD Thesis, Auburn: Auburn University, 2008, 118–119.
394 Brebner, "Canada, the Anglo-Japanese", 57.
395 Borden, *Canada in the Commonwealth*, 118.
396 Glasgow, George, "The British View", in: Croly, Herbert David, *Roads to Peace: A Hand-book to the Washington Conference*, New York: New York Republic Pub. Co., 1921, 30–31.
397 For more on the development of Anglo-Irish relationships up to 1921, see Mansergh, Nicholas, *The Irish Question, 1840–1921*, London: George Allen & Unwin, 1965.
398 Mansergh, *The Commonwealth Experience*, 197.
399 See Campbell, James Henry Mussen, *A Guide to the Home Rule Bill*, London: Union Defence League and National Unionist Association, 1912.
400 Balfour, Arthur James, *Nationality and Home Rule*, London: Longmans & Co, 1913.
401 Mansergh, *The Commonwealth Experience*, 198; Oliver, Frederick Scott, *Ireland and the Imperial Conference: Is There a Way to Settlement?* London: Macmillan & Co, 1917.
402 See more in Nerad, Filip, *Německo a irské separatistické hnutí: Německo-irská spolupráce do vzniku Irského svobodného státu*, PhD Thesis, Praha: Univerzita Karlova, 2012, 118–231.
403 For more on this issue, see Macardle, Dorothy, *The Irish Republic: A Documented Chronicle of the Anglo-Irish Conflict and the Partitioning of Ireland, with a Detailed Account of the Period 1916–1923*, New York: Farrar, Straus and Giroux, 1965, 271–282.
404 Mansergh, Nicholas, *The Unresolved Question: The Anglo-Irish Settlement and Its Undoing 1912–72*, New Haven and London: Yale University Press, 1991, 146–147.
405 PD, HoC, 5th Series, Vol. 127, 31 March 1920, 1322–1332.
406 Peatling, G. K., *British Opinion and Irish Self-Government, 1865–1925: From Unionism to Liberal Commonwealth*, Dublin 2001, 90.
407 PD, HoC, 5th Series, Vol. 127, 29 March 1920, 944–956.
408 PD, HoC, 5th Series, Vol. 127, 30 March 1920, 1124–1125.
409 No discussions on Dominion status took place between the British government and Sinn Féin until 11 July 1921. Mansergh, *The Unresolved*, 146–147.
410 See more cf. *The Struggle of the Irish People: Address to the Congress of the United States Adopted at the January Session of Dail Eireann, 1921*, Washington: Government Printing Office, 1921, 1–31; Valera, Eamon de, *The Moral Basis of the Claim of the Republic of Ireland for Official Recognition: A Speech Delivered by Eamon de Valera at Worcester, Mass., February 6, 1920*, New York: Nation's Forum, [1920], [1–7].
411 Cf. Jones, Thomas, *Whitehall Diary: 1916–1925*, Vol. 1, London: Oxford University Press, 1969, 118; Mansergh, *The Unresolved*, 150–152.
412 See more cf. Geyser, O., "Irish Independence: Jan Smuts and Eamon de Valera", *The Round Table* 87, No. 348, 2008, 475–476; Kendle, John Edward, "The Round Table Movement and 'Home Rule All Round'", *The Historical Journal* 11, No. 2, 1968, 332–353; Nicolson, Harold, *King George the Fifth: His Life and Reign*, 3rd Ed., London: Pan Piper, 1967, 454–455; *Report of Labour Commission to Ireland*, London: [s. n., 1921], 1–119.
413 Smuts to Lloyd George, London, 14 June 1921, in: Hancock – Poel, Vol. 5, Doc. Vol. 24, No. 261, 89–91.

The Empire During the War and Post-War Period   169

414 Lawlor, S. M., "Ireland from Truce to Treaty: War or Peace? July to October 1921", *Irish Historical Studies* 22, No. 85, 1980, 51.
415 Churchill, Winston Spencer, Sir, *The World Crisis: The Aftermath*, Vol. 5, London: Thornton Butterworth Limited, 1929, 290.
416 Cf. Briollay, Sylvain, *Ireland in Rebellion*, Dublin: Talbot Press, 1922, 129; CUL, SP, Add MS 7917, Vol. 1, Smuts to A. Gillet, Pretoria, 11 November 1920, Doc. No. 263, 181; Gallagher, John, "Nationalisms and the Crisis of Empire, 1919–1922", *Modern Asian Studies* 15, No. 3, 1981, 1981, 355–368; Hancock, *Survey of British*, 126.
417 TNA, CAB 24/128/38, C. P. 3331 (Revise), Copies of Documents Relating to the Proposals of His Majesty's Government for an Irish Settlement: The Terms of the Armistice, 9 June 1921, No. 4, 3–4; TNA, CAB 24/128/38, C. P. 3331 (Revise), Letter from the Prime Minister to Sir James Craig and Mr. de Valera, Downing Street, London, 24 June 1921, No. 5, 4.
418 Some of the leading advocates of the concept of Irish membership in a Commonwealth were Irish journalist Stephen Gwynn and Sir Horace Plunkett and the Irish Dominion League. See Geyser, *Irish*, 475–476; Reid, Colin, "Stephen Gwynn and the Failure of Constitutional Nationalism in Ireland, 1919–1921", *The Historical Journal* 53, No. 3, 2010, 723–745.
419 TNA, CAB 21/243, C. P. 3331 (Revise), Copies of Documents Relating to the Proposals of His Majesty's Government for an Irish Settlement: Mr. de Valera's Reply to Sir James Craig, Dublin, 29 June 1921, [Doc.] No. 12, 6.
420 Cf. *IPD, DÉ*, Vol. S, No. 4, 22 August 1921, 27–28; Stamfordham to Smuts, Buckingham Palace, 1 July 1921, in: Hancock – Poel, Vol. 5, Doc. Vol. 24, No. 237A, 94; [Extract from the Stamfordham's Memorandum to the King], 29 June 1921, in: Hancock – Poel, Vol. 5, Doc. Vol. 24, Box G, No. 5A, 92.
421 Mansergh, Nicholas, "Ireland: From British Commonwealth towards European Community", *Historical Studies* 13, No. 51, 1968, 384.
422 Ingham, 128; Memorandum of a Conversation between the King and General Smuts at Buckingham Palace, London, 7 July 1921, in: Hancock – Poel, Vol. 5, Doc. Box G, No. 5B, 95–98; Hancock, *Smuts*, Vol. 2, 56–58.
423 Kraus, René, *Old Master: The Life of Jan Christian Smuts*, New York: E. P. Dutton & Co, 1944, 295.
424 TNA, CAB 21/243, C. P. 3331 (Revise), Copies of Documents Relating to the Proposals of His Majesty's Government for an Irish Settlement: Letter from Mr. de Valera to the Prime Minister, Mansion House, Dublin, 8 July 1921, [Doc.] No. 14, 7.
425 Mansergh, *The Unresolved*, 165.
426 MacManus, M. J., *Eamon de Valera*, Chicago – New York: Ziff-Davis, 1946, 97–99.
427 Aitken, William Maxwell, 1st Baron Beaverbrook, *The Decline and Fall of Lloyd George*, London: Collins, 1963, 86.
428 Proposals of the British Government for an Irish Settlement, Downing Street, London, 20 July 1921, in: Cmd. 1502, *Correspondence Relating to the Proposals of His Majesty's Government for an Irish Settlement*, London: HMSO, 1921, 2–3.
429 Bromage, Mary C., "De Valera's Plan", *University Review* 5, No. 1, 1968, 25.
430 Knirck, Jason, "The Dominion of Ireland: The Anglo-Irish Treaty in an Imperial Context", *Éire-Ireland* 42, No. 1/2, 2007, 234.
431 Cf. Éamon de Valera to Jan Christian Smuts, Mansion House, Dublin, 31 July 1921, in: *DIFP*, Doc. No. 145; TNA, CAB 21/243, C. P. 3331 (Revise), Copies of Documents Relating to the Proposals of His Majesty's Government for an Irish Settlement: Letter from General Smuts to Mr. de Valera, Savoy Hotel, London, 4 August 1921, [Doc.] No. 18, 10–13.

432 Cf. Reply from Mr. De Valera, Mansion House, Dublin, 10 August 1921, Cmd. 1502, 3–5; Memorandum by Erskine Childers on Irish Defence as Affected by the British Proposals of 20 July 1921, Dublin, July 1921, in: *DIFP*, Doc. No. 142.
433 McIntyre, W. David, "'A Formula May Have to Be Found': Ireland, India, and the Headship of the Commonwealth", *The Round Table* 91, No. 365, 2002, 392.
434 Knirck, 237.
435 The Prime Minister's Reply to Mr. De Valera's Letter, Downing Street, London, 13 August 1921, Cmd. 1502, 5.
436 See Cmd. 1539, *Further Correspondence Relating to the Proposals of His Majesty's Government for an Irish Settlement*, London: HMSO, 1921, [2]–11.
437 TNA, CAB 21/243, C. P. 3353, Cabinet: Ireland: De Valera to [Lloyd George], Dublin, 30 September 1921, 1.
438 Cf. TNA, CAB 21/243, [Intelligence Report]: Subject Sinn Fein: Internal Dissention, Cork, 12 October 1921, [1–4]; Toye, Richard, "'Phrases Make History Here': Churchill, Ireland and the Rhetoric Empire", *The Journal of Imperial and Commonwealth History* 38, No. 4, 2010, 558.
439 CUL, SP, Add MS 7917, Vol. 1, Smuts to M. Gillet, Doornkloof, 21 September 1921, Doc. No. 300, 213.
440 *IPD, DÉ*, Vol. T, No. 6, 19 December 1921, 32.
441 Besides Griffith and Collins, Members of Parliament Eamon Duggan and George Gavan Duffy, Ireland's Minister for the Economy Robert Barton and four assistant secretaries took part in negotiations. For more on this issue, see Lawlor, 54; *IPD, DÉ*, Vol. S, No. 10, 14 September 1921, 94–96.
442 Instructions to Plenipotentiaries from the Cabinet, Dublin, 7 October 1921, in: *DIFP*, Doc. No. 160.
443 *IPD, DÉ*, Vol. T, No. 2, 14 December 1921, 11; Laffan, Michael, *The Resurrection of Ireland 1916–1923: The Sinn Féin Party*, New York: Cambridge University Press, 1999, 349–350.
444 Mair, Peter, "The Break-up of the United Kingdom: The Irish Experience of Regime Change, 1918–1949", *The Journal of Commonwealth & Comparative Politics* 16, No. 3, 1978, 294.
445 Also taking part in negotiations were the Secretary of State for War Sir Laming Worthington-Evans, Sir Hamar Greenwooda, and Sir Gordon Hewart. Mansergh, Nicholas, *The Irish Free State: Its Government and Politics*, London: George Allen & Unwin, 1934, 30.
446 Mansergh, *The Unresolved*, 175.
447 TNA, CAB 21/243, S. F. C. 4, Conference on Ireland: Third Session: Aide-memoire, Whitehall Gardens, 13 October 1921.
448 For more on the admiralty's demands cf. TNA, CAB 21/243, S. F. C. 14, Conference on Ireland: British Proposals of July 20th 1921: Explanatory Additions Drafted by the Attorney General, Whitehall Gardens, 18 October 1921, [18]; TNA, CAB 21/243, C. P. 3409, Cabinet: Irish Settlement: Memorandum by the First Lord of Admiralty, 15 October 1921, [1]–2.
449 Knirck, 239; Mansergh, *The Unresolved*, 179–180; TNA, CAB 21/243, S. F. C. 10, Conference on Ireland: Committee of Naval and Air Defence: Draft Formula, [1921], [1]; TNA, CAB 21/243, S. F. C. 8, Conference on Ireland: Committee of Naval and Air Defence: Aide memoire, 17 October 1921, [1–2].
450 Hawkings, F. M. A., "Defence and the Role of Erskine Childers in the Treaty Negotiations of 1921", *Irish Historical Studies* 22, No. 87, 1981, 251–270;

TNA, CAB 21/243, S. F. C. 11, Committee of Naval and Air Defence: Memorandum by the Irish Representatives, 18 October 1921, 1–[8].
451 Proposals of the British Government for an Irish Settlement, Downing Street, London, 20 July 1921, Cmd. 1502, 2.
452 Cf. Mansergh, *The Unresolved*, 179; Mohr, Thomas, "British Imperial Statuses and Irish Law: Statutes Passed Before the Creation of the Irish Free State", *The Journal of Legal History* 31, No. 3, 2010, 299–321.
453 *IPD, DÉ*, Vol. T, No. 6, 19 December 1921, 27.
454 Cf. TNA, CAB 21/243, S. F. C. 13, Memorandum on Dominion Status: By Mr. Lionel Curtis, 17 October 1921, [1]–20; TNA, CAB 21/243, S. F. B. 3, Memorandum on Dominion Status with Special Reference to Recent Imperial Developments, [October 1921], 1–[16].
455 Memorandum by Erskine Childers Replying to the British Proposals of 18 October 1921, London, 20 October 1921, in: *DIFP*, Doc. No. 172.
456 Knirck, 240; Mansergh, *The Unresolved*, 180–181; Memorandum of the Proposals of the Irish Delegates to the British Representatives, London, 24 October 1921, in: *DIFP*, Doc. No. 175.
457 Draft Treaty Proposals Taken by the Irish Delegation to London, Dublin, 7 October 1921, in: *DIFP*, Doc. No. 159; Macardle, 529–530.
458 Cf. Bromage, 26; Mansergh, Nicholas, "The Implications of Eire's Relationship with the British Commonwealth of Nations", *International Affairs* 24, No. 1, 1948, 1–2; McIntyre, 394; O'Duffy, Brendan – Githens-Mazer, Jonathan, "Status and Statehood: Exchange Theory and British-Irish Relations, 1921–41", *Commonwealth & Comparative Politics* 40, No. 2, 2002, 129.
459 Bromage, 26.
460 Boyce, David George, *Englishmen and Irish Troubles 1918–1922*, Cambridge: Cape, 1972, 156–157; Macardle, 544–545, 937–939.
461 Cf. Griffith to de Valera, London, 24 October 1921, in: *DIFP*, Doc. No. 176; Jones, 174.
462 Griffith to de Valera, London, 27 October 1921, in: *DIFP*, Doc. No. 182.
463 Memorandum by the Irish Delegation in Reply to British Memorandum of 27 October, 29 October 1921, in: *DIFP*, Doc. No. 185; TNA, CAB 21/243, S. F. C. 21A, Conference on Ireland: Further Memorandum by the Irish Delegates, 29 October 1921, [1].
464 Boyce, 159.
465 Macardle, 560.
466 Boyce, 160.
467 Macardle, 565.
468 Memorandum by the Irish Representatives, 22 November 1921, in: *DIFP*, Doc. No. 199.
469 Memorandum by Erskine Childers, 23 November 1921, in: *DIFP*, Doc. No. 201.
470 Memorandum by the Irish Delegates on Their Proposals for the Association of Ireland with the British Commonwealth, 28 November 1921, in: *DIFP*, Doc. No. 204.
471 Cf. Griffith to de Valera, London, 29 November 1921, in: *DIFP*, Doc. No. 206; TNA, CAB 21/243, Draft Reply to the Irish Memorandum of November 28th, 1921, Whitehall Gardens, 29 November 1921, [1–6].
472 Cf. Macardle, 576–579, 946–950; TNA, CAB 21/243, S. F. B. 33, Conference on Ireland: Proposed Articles of Agreement, [1 December 1921], 1–[7]; TNA, CAB 23/27/16, Cabinet 89 (21), Conclusions of a Meeting of the Cabinet, Downing Street, 5 December 1921, 1–[5].

473 Copy of Secretary's Notes of Meeting of the Cabinet and Delegation, Dublin, 28 November 1921, in: DIFP, Doc. No. 209.
474 Cf. Amendments by the Irish Representatives to the Proposed Articles of Agreement, Dublin, 4 December 1921, in: DIFP, Doc. No. 210; Griffith to de Valera, London, 4 December 1921, in: DIFP, Doc. No. 211.
475 Boyce, 170; Gilbert, Martin (Ed.), Lloyd George, Englewood Cliffs: Prentice-Hall, 1968, 115.
476 Mansergh, The Unresolved, 188.
477 Merivirta, Raita, The Gun and Irish Politics: Examining National History in Neil Jordan's Michael Collins, Bern: Peter Lang, 2009, 103.
478 Cmd. 1560, Articles of Agreement for a Treaty between Great Britain and Ireland, London: HMSO, 1921; Kennedy, William Paul McClure, "Significance of the Irish Free State", North American Review, No. 218, 1923, 316.
479 Cf. Keith, Arthur Berriedale, "Notes on Imperial Constitutional Law", Journal of Comparative Legislation and International Law 4, No. 4, 1922, 233; Mansergh, The Irish, 32; Mohr, Thomas, "British Imperial Statuses and Irish Sovereignty: Statutes Passed after the Creation of the Irish Free State", The Journal of Legal History 32, No. 1, 2011, 63–64.
480 Martin, Ged W., "The Irish Free State and the Evolution of the Commonwealth, 1921–1949", in: Hyam, Robert – Martin, Ged W. (Ed.), Reappraisals in British Imperial History, London: Macmillan, 1975, 204; TNA, CAB 23/27/5, Cabinet 78 (21), Conclusions of a Meeting of the Cabinet, Downing Street, 10 October 1921, 4 [61].
481 Macardle, 592–593.
482 Minutes of a Cabinet Meeting, Dublin, 8 December 1921, in: DIFP, Doc. No. 215; IPD, DÉ, Vol. T, No. 2, 14 December 1921, 8–19.
483 On implementation issues in more detail, see McColgan, John, "Implementing the 1921 Treaty: Lionel Curtis and Constitutional Procedure", Irish Historical Studies 20, No. 79, 1977, 312–335.
484 Buell, Raymond Leslie, "Britain's Changing Empire", Current History 22, No. 1, 1925, 57; PD, HoC, 5th Series, Vol. 149, 14 December 1921, 27–28.
485 See more in Brady, Alexander, "The New Dominion", The Canadian Historical Review 4, No. 3, 1923, 198–216.
486 Proposed Alternative Treaty of Association between Ireland and the British Commonwealth Presented by Mr Éamon de Valera to a Secret Session of Dáil Éireann, Dublin, 13–14 December 1921, in: DIFP, Doc. No. 217.
487 IPD, DÉ, Vol. T, No. 6, 19 December 1921, 43–45.
488 To the Document No. 2, see Collins, Michael, The Path to Freedom, London: Talbot Press, 1922, 43–54; Macardle, 959–963; Mansergh, Nicholas, The Commonwealth of the Nation: Studies in British Commonwealth Relations, London: Royal Institute of International Affairs, 1948, 195–196; Mansergh, The Unresolved, 203–207.
489 IPD, DÉ, Vol. T, No. 6, 19 December 1921, 24–26.
490 IPD, DÉ, Vol. T, No. 15, 7 January 1922, 345–347.
491 Wilson, Robert R., "Anglo-Irish Accord", The American Journal of International Law 32, No. 3, 1938, 546.
492 Mansergh, Nicholas, Survey of British Commonwealth Affairs: Problems of External Policy 1931–1939, London: Oxford University Press, 1952, 9.

4 The New Constitutional Status for the Dominions?

4.1 From the Chanak Crisis to Lausanne

After the 1921 Imperial Conference had ended in 1921, two key issues remained outstanding: (1) redefining the relationships between the mother country and the Dominions, considering the current legal arrangement which was meant to base on the principle of equal status for the overseas self-governing territories; and (2) Dominions' position in international relations.[1] The problem over Dominions' international status had already cropped up during the Washington Disarmament Conference, but it became more pressing during the course of the Chanak Crisis, sometimes also called the Chanak Incident, in September 1922 when the rather slow response of the Canadian Prime Minister William Lyon Mackenzie King demonstrated that some Dominions held differing opinions on the running of Imperial foreign policy.

The Chanak Crisis erupted in the Middle East as a result of controversial provisions of the Treaty of Sèvres securing peace between the Allies and the Ottoman Empire. Although Dominion representatives had signed the treaty in August 1920, they had not taken part in discussions and negotiations in regard to conditions in the Middle East, such as the San Remo conference in April 1920, because they had little interest in the region.[2] According to the Treaty of Sèvres, an international neutral zone was to be established at Chanak (Çanakkale), on the eastern shore of the Dardanelles opposite the Gallipoli Peninsula, to be occupied by British, French and Italian troops. When Turkish troops defeated the Greeks in Anatolia and captured Smyrna (İzmir) in autumn 1922, Mustafa Kemal (Atatürk) decided to enter the neutral zone and demand the return of the occupied territory between the Bosphorus and the Dardanelles.[3]

British and overseas statesmen had discussed the issue of the Straits and heated Greco-Turkish relations at the Imperial Conference at the end of June 1921, but no agreement had been reached. Members of the British government differed in their assessment of the situation, the Canadian Prime Minister Arthur Meighen and his South African counterpart Jan Smuts held neutral positions because the countries had no direct interests in the region, and Australian Prime Minister William Hughes didn't express much support for Greek matters either.[4] Until autumn 1922, the complications around the Anglo-Japanese Alliance and participation in the Washington Disarmament Conference meant that no fundamental discussion took place on the Greco-Turkish conflict between British and Dominion politicians.

The threat of Kemal's troops invading the neutral zone at Chanak led to an unexpected crisis,[5] which members of the British government discussed on 15 September 1922. David Lloyd George, a passionate supporter of Greece, advocated taking a strong line against Turkey. The Secretary of State for Foreign Affairs Lord Curzon gave him total support considering the military situation in the region. Although not all ministers approved of the Prime Minister's pro-Greek policy,[6] the decision was made to stop Kemal's army out of fears that he might repeat the massacre of the Greek population in Thrace.[7] The British Secretary of State for the Colonies Winston Churchill therefore sent a telegram on behalf of the Prime Minister to the Dominion governments, in which he asked that he be privately informed:

> whether they desire to be represented by a contingent. Not only does the freedom of the Straits for which such immense sacrifices were made in the War involve vital Imperial and world interests, but we cannot forget that there are 20,000 British and Anzac graves in the Gallipoli Peninsula and that it would be an abiding source of grief to the Empire if these were to fall into the ruthless hands of the Kemalists.[8]

On 15 September 1922, the Chanak Crisis unexpectedly led to a deterioration in relations between the Dominions and the mother country. On the instruction of the British Prime Minister, Churchill issued a declaration to the press at midnight in which he warned of the danger of Turkish aggression in the Balkans, and issued an ultimatum to Kemal to withdraw his troops and urged the Dominions publicly to send their armies. In so doing, he was forcing the Dominions into a *fait accompli*, since he had moved beyond the original confidential request to send a contingent, making a public request for assistance. The situation was further aggravated by the fact that there had been an unfortunate timing in the sending of documents; the communiqué had been delivered to the press before the overseas prime ministers had received a decrypted telegram containing the Colonial Office's confidential message.[9]

The first to respond to events was New Zealand, who through Governor-General Admiral John Jellicoe immediately promised to send troops.[10] The Union of South Africa and Newfoundland were significantly more restrained in their responses, due to their interests in the Straits region. Nevertheless, they expressed their willingness to help, at least symbolically.[11] The Canadian Prime Minister's response was different. On 16 September 1922, Mackenzie King was visiting voters in the North York constituency, where he happened to find out about Churchill's telegram and the public request to send troops from a journalist there asking what Ottawa's response to Britain's request was.[12] He subsequently sent an indignant response to London. First of all, he complained that the London cabinet's intentions had been sent to the press before he and his government had been sent a telegram via the Canadian Governor-General. He added that this had put him in an awkward situation as Prime Minister in front of journalists. Mackenzie King asked Britain for its consent to freely publish on the matter and to be sent documents in regard to the Chanak Crisis.[13] Churchill sent him an explanation that the press statement had been sent because the wording of the original telegram had not been suitable for publishing, and that it was mainly military assistance from the Australian Commonwealth and New Zealand governments that was expected; with assistance from other Dominions only on the basis of Imperial solidarity.[14]

The Canadian government took a cautious approach, fearing that, "it is drafted designedly to play the imperial game, to test out centralization vs. autonomy as regards European wars".[15] Mackenzie King thus informed London that local public opinion was not generally supportive of sending troops, and therefore he was asking the Ottawa parliament for its consent before making such a decision; at the same time, he again requested he be sent all relevant documents.[16] On the same day, 18 September 1922, Churchill informed the British government of Canada's demand. Ministers agreed to send Canada all information on the situation, while also calling on Ottawa to issue a prior declaration supporting the Imperial foreign policy official line before the parliament issued its consent to deploying troops.[17] At the same time, some British Colonial Office officials were assigned the task of being in daily constant contact with Dominion representatives to inform them of the political and military situation.[18]

On 20 September 1922, the British Secretary of State for the Colonies sent Dominion prime ministers information on the current course of the Chanak Crisis. Although Churchill stated that the Greeks had completely evacuated Anatolia and the future of the Straits, the European part of Turkey and Constantinople remained to be dealt with, he stressed the British troops still needed to be boosted in the region. As such, he asked, "from this point view the moral support of the Dominions and the undertaking to send contingents should the necessity arise is of the utmost value". He nevertheless added that it was not essential this was immediately organised, except for a demonstration of Imperial solidarity, defending the outcome of the Great War on the eastern front.[19]

Australian Prime Minister William Hughes made an important declaration at this same time. In contrast to his Canadian counterpart, since the crisis his response to Britain's request was more moderate, and was limited to just a protest against the method of communication between the Dominions and the mother country through the Governor-General.[20] He did not send a formal response to Churchill's 15 September 1922 telegram; he instead issued a press release in which he affirmed Australia's willingness to help Britain, including through sending a military contingent to secure the Gallipoli Peninsula.[21] On 20 September 1922, Hughes sent Britain's Colonial Office an extensive telegram in which he criticised the possible escalation of the conflict in Turkey. He held the opinion that Australia, "should not be asked to join in an unnecessary or unjust war … [because it professes the values of] a peace-loving democracy". At the same time, he stressed that even though Australians were tired of war, they were ready to defend not just their own land, but the land of the whole of the Empire. Since he worried Imperial unity was at threat, he also warned that it was essential the Dominions were involved in decision-making on the Empire's foreign policy focus.[22]

Due to the severity of the situation, David Lloyd George repeatedly contacted the Canadian Prime Minister to ask for his definitive statement on whether Canada would stand alongside the Empire in this matter. On 21 September 1922, Mackenzie King repeated that the consent of the Ottawa parliament would be required in order to send a military contingent, but during the September crisis the parliament had not met even once. He once again assured him Canada was loyal to the mother country and that if required the Canadian people were fully aware of what their duties were. Like Hughes, Canada's Prime Minister had little desire to go to war, and expected that the government was likely to support an isolationist position and would take a more cautious approach to the requests of the mother country.[23]

That same day, 21 September 1922, the British Prime Minister sent Hughes a response in which he denied that British steps in the Straits region were sucking the Empire into war. Lloyd George was unable to placate his Australian counterpart, however.[24] The offer of being involved in determining the course of Imperial foreign policy came too late. Hughes ended up having to confront questions and anti-war objections from Senator Albert Gardiner of New South Wales, leader of the Labour opposition in Australia's Senate.[25] Even though Hughes received over 130 British telegrams during the two critical September weeks in regard to Middle East affairs, the pressure of Australian public opinion and interpellations by members of parliament only confirmed to him that he did not have enough information to be able to make a final decision.[26]

On 30 September 1922, he even complained to Churchill that there was undue delay in transferring information between the Foreign Office and Colonial Office, and subsequent decryption between London and Melbourne. He therefore proposed that at critical moments when there was a threat of war, direct communication should be implemented between the Dominions and British Secretary of State for Foreign Affairs Lord Curzon, or even the Prime Minister Lloyd George.[27] Churchill, who had been looking at the method of communication with the Dominions for a number of months,[28] made some concessions in this regard and ordered that key documents be marked "clear the line" in order to speed up communication, but he refused to implement direct correspondence between the Prime Minister and the Secretary of State for Foreign Affairs in London and their Dominion opposite numbers, because he held the opinion that this would not save any time, and it would not make communication more efficient.[29]

Hughes's proposal for a new system of Imperial communication failed because Churchill did not want to change proven procedures. The Australian politician accepted the Imperial level of foreign policy due to specific – economic and political – interests in different regions. Hughes's government was unsure whether to implement an independent policy, or whether to co-operate with the other Dominions and take a united position. Until 1924, when Australian Prime Minister Stanley Melbourne Bruce sent Major Richard Gardiner Casey as a "liaison officer" to London, the Australian government did not receive confidential information unless via a mediator. This step meant that Australians co-ordinated their political steps more with the mother country than they had in the past.[30]

Looking back at this time, Hughes claimed that during the Chanak Crisis, "Australia was prepared to go to war – not because the Treaty of Sèvres had been signed by her, but because she was part of the Empire. ... [Although the decision] had not previously been consulted".[31] The issue of timely consultation and thus the opportunity to take part in decision-making on Imperial and foreign policy issues was an important factor which influenced Australia's position in September 1922. The "nebulous" idea of a common Imperial foreign policy was shown to be impossible in practice. This was all underscored by Hughes's declaration:

> If [Empire] is only another name for Britain, and the Dominions are to be told that things are done after they have been done, and that Britain has decided upon war ... [the Dominions] have in fact no other alternative, then ... all talk about the Dominions having a real share in deciding foreign and Imperial policy is empty air.[32]

Mackenzie King reached a similar position to Hughes. The Canadians were not seeking joint responsibility for implementing Imperial policy, but rather that the foreign policy implemented by the various Dominions could be separate from the common Imperial line. The Canadians were not demanding equality so that they could make decisions on the general course of Imperial foreign policy, but rather so that they could carry out their own policy.[33] Although Mackenzie King was criticised for his position during the Chanak Crisis by the opposition Conservative leader Arthur Meighen, who believed that Canada should have clearly answered the mother country – "Ready, aye, ready; we stand by you"[34] – on the other hand, his intransigence strengthened his own political position and secured a more robust position for the minority cabinet.[35] The crisis also led to foreign Imperial policy being implemented more cautiously in future.[36] The Canadian Prime Minister, and in particular his close collaborator and unofficial advisor in foreign policy matters, Professor Oscar Douglas Skelton, viewed Canadian-British relations from a "North American perspective". As such, they sought the gradual elimination of real and perceived attributes or mere symbols of the mother country's Imperial dominance, alongside true broad autonomy permitting them to execute their own active foreign policy within the British Empire – particularly in regard to the United States.[37]

The Chanak Crisis, which resolved itself at the end of September,[38] was not conducive to the British Prime Minister's political career and contributed to his political downfall on 19 October 1922. His successor was Andrew Bonar Law. Influential Round Table Movement member Philip Kerr had judged in April 1920 that, "the only method upon which the Empire can be run at present is that Great Britain should be responsible for foreign policy, keeping the Dominions informed mostly after the events, and consulting them about matters directly affecting their interests".[39] The September crisis in relations between the Dominions and the mother country revealed that Kerr's words no longer applied. The British Empire was now in a phase of Imperial power decentralisation. Mere consultation, which the Dominions had previously been satisfied with, was no longer enough. It was also shown that previous enthusiastic endeavours at creating some form of single Imperial government, or setting up an Imperial cabinet, were less realistic, if not entirely impossible, following the Middle East crisis.[40]

A number of events followed the end of the Chanak Incident, all confirming the fact that overseas and London politicians did not have the same perception of Dominions' equal status to Britain. At the end of September 1922, the Middle East crisis was being dealt with peacefully, and thus in the first half of October an armistice was signed with the Kemalists.[41] On 26 October 1922, Britain, France and Italy decided to convene a conference in Lausanne, Switzerland, for 20 November 1922, where a new peace treaty was to be negotiated with Turkey replacing the now-superseded Sèvres arrangement. A day later, the Dominions received a message via Britain's Colonial Office stating that the powers had invited representatives of Japan, Romania, the Kingdom of Serbs, Croats and Slovenes, Greece and the Turkish governments in Constantinople and Ankara and Soviet Russia, Bulgaria and the United States to negotiate the status of the Traits. Thus, the Dominions were surprised to find that they were not officially invited to the conference, even though Britain

The New Constitutional Status for the Dominions? 179

had acknowledged that they had a special interest in finding a solution to the Chanak Crisis and as such were to add their signatures to the treaty. At the same time, the Dominions were to be regularly informed by British negotiators on the general policy and the current course of negotiations.[42] The telegram also came with a brief confidential explanation by the new British Colonial Secretary Victor Christian William Cavendish, 9th Duke of Devonshire, stating that the Dominions and India could not be invited because France would then have demanded Morocco and Tunisia also take part.[43]

The response to the fact that the British Empire would be represented only by two British delegates at the Conference of Lausanne, Foreign Secretary Lord Curzon and High Commissioner in Turkey Sir Horace Rumbold, and that France viewed the Dominions similarly to their North African protectorates, was immediate. The telegram from South African Prime Minister Smuts came first, and although he did not demand his own representative at the conference, he instead strongly objected to the words of French Prime Minister Raymond Poincaré, whom the General said had denigrated the status of the Dominions and who represented a real threat to Anglo-French friendship and co-operation.[44] Smuts's uncompromising position was the result of long-term suspicion of France's "chauvinist" policy in Europe.[45]

Australian Prime Minister Hughes was more emphatic in his response, laconically noting the fact that the Commonwealth of Australia had not received an invitation to Lausanne and taking account of the September 1922 crisis: "We are to go on in the same bad old way." He also criticised the British government for not keeping to the common Imperial foreign policy concept, and taking an overly pro-Greek course, something he perceived as the cause of the Chanak Crisis.[46] Hughes pointed out that during the days of crisis, Australia was ready to go to war alongside the mother country not just because they had signed the Sèvres peace treaty, but because they were part of the lands of the British Empire. Hughes felt extremely disappointed:

> Plain speaking between friends and blood relations is best. What you suggest may be ... quite satisfactory to Canada and South Africa; they were not prepared to fight. Australia was, and most emphatically it is not satisfactory to her. ... there is only one course open to us in practice, and that is to support Britain. ... In foreign affairs the Empire must speak with one voice.[47]

The Australian Prime Minister was also critical that Imperial foreign policy was poorly thought out, comparing it to "the footballs of British political parties".[48] Australian politicians were consistent in their belief that, "a true Empire foreign policy [must be] acceptable to all the Dominions".[49] Australia, New Zealand and to a lesser extent also the

Union of South Africa considered a joint foreign policy was feasible and domestically politically acceptable if it involved speedy consultation.[50]

In contrast, Canadian Prime Minister Mackenzie King continued to promote an independent foreign policy, as such rejecting a joint Imperial policy managed by London without due consultation with the Dominions.[51] He even considered it "bad from a moral perspective" for Canada to agree to matters which nobody had consulted it about.[52] In contrast to Wilfrid Laurier's time, he insisted on consultation even in matters which did not affect Canadian economic and political interests.[53] He therefore received the British decision that Dominion representatives would not take part in the Conference of Lausanne without public protest. It is conceivable that the Canadian cabinet welcomed the British step; in crafting his response to Britain on the sidelines of the debate, Minister of Agriculture William Richard Motherwell stated: "Thank God, we weren't [invited]."[54] Mackenzie King did not consider it advantageous for Canada to be involved in the conference,[55] and as such used the opportunity to avoid accepting any other Canadian commitments in Europe.[56] Since Canada did not have a representative at the peace negotiations in Lausanne, he qualified Canada's signing of the new treaty with Turkey on the Ottawa parliament giving its consent, with the Canadian government promising to give it full information on the course of discussions.[57] Mackenzie King perceived the discussions in Switzerland as a distant matter of some importance for the mother country, but none for Canada.[58]

In mid-November 1922, Andrew Bonar Law sent Canada Britain's response, in which he acknowledged their right to submit the agreed peace treaty to the Ottawa parliament for its approval before ratification by His Majesty.[59] On 25 November, however, the Canadians in an attempt at avoiding misunderstanding specified that members of parliament would judge the matter in accordance with documents supplied and on the basis of Canada's interests. He thus indirectly informed Mackenzie King that their vote would not necessarily be positive.[60] In early December, British Secretary of State for the Colonies Lord Devonshire attempted to moderate the Canadian Prime Minister's intransigence by calling for Imperial unity, stressing that, "any Treaty which may result from Lausanne Conference will, of course, replace the Treaty of Sèvres, and until it comes into force a state of war between the British Empire and Turkey will technically continue". For this reason, he proposed that its signing take place in a similar manner to that of the Treaty of Versailles, in which from a legal perspective the signature of the British representative was also on behalf of the Dominions. Concluding his telegram, Lord Devonshire called on Mackenzie King to make a concession and find a compromise so that the treaty could be binding for Canada even before it was approved by the Ottawa parliament.[61]

However, Canada's Prime Minister was not prepared to concede, preferring to run the risk of being viewed as a "destroyer" of joint Imperial foreign policy.[62] He therefore analysed the circumstances of signing the peace treaties with Germany, Austria and Bulgaria and the treaties during the Washington Disarmament Conference, stressing four linked yet strictly separate phases of peace negotiations: (1) Canada should have direct representation at conferences, and take part in composing treaties; (2) the Canadian representative should formally sign treaties on behalf of Canada; (3) treaties should be approved by the Ottawa parliament and (4) the Canadian government should officially express its consent to ratification by the Crown. Mackenzie King believed that if Canada had not been invited to Lausanne and if it was not taking part in peace negotiations either directly or indirectly, then it could not respect a treaty signed by a British delegate on Canada's behalf. He therefore insisted on the 1919 procedures being observed.[63] Since negotiations with Turkey were already taking place, his demands seemed both unfeasible and unrealistic.

In the meantime, Britain's Colonial Secretary Lord Devonshire and Canada's Governor-General, Field Marshal Julian Hedworth George Byng, 1st Viscount Byng of Vimy, had been discussing Mackenzie King's demands in secret. Viscount Byng was of the opinion that the Canadians would not want to get into a situation in which they would have to reject an explicit British request for signature of the treaty because they did not have a representative at the conference. He also thought that Mackenzie King would be able to agree to the British Secretary of State for Foreign Affairs signing the treaty on behalf of the Empire and that ratification would then be able to take place in the standard parliamentary manner.[64] Britain put off an official response until the end of January 1923 when the draft treaties were finalised. Without waiting for a response or otherwise responding to Canada's previous stance, the British Colonial Secretary informed the Ottawa government that, "any Treaties with Turkey resulting from Conference should be signed only by British plenipotentiaries who have negotiated them, if it is generally acceptable".[65] He also asked the Prime Ministers of Australia, New Zealand and the Union of South Africa whether they would agree to this approach.[66] Hughes and Massey responded positively.[67] Smuts, who was not entirely satisfied at first, eventually also agreed.[68] Devonshire had assumed that only the term "British Empire" would be included in the Lausanne peace treaty with Turkey and the convention on the Straits,[69] and that therefore the signature of Lord Curzon and Sir Horace would make the Crown's ratification binding for the whole Empire.[70]

Signature of the Treaty of Lausanne on 24 July 1923 triggered a further chain of misunderstandings between the Dominions and the mother country. The general election in Britain postponed its ratification in the second half of 1923, and thus in the first months of 1924, the Conservative opposition demanded the Labour government accelerate the slow process. On 21 March 1924, the new British Secretary of State for the Colonies James Henry Thomas informed the parliament in London that the process of approval of the agreements was coming to an end, and he asked the Governors and Governors-General whether the Dominion prime ministers were ready to express their consent to ratification.[71] Three days later, William Lyon Mackenzie King sent the following response:

> The Government of Canada not having been invited to send a representative to the Lausanne Conference and not having participated in the proceedings of the Conference either directly or indirectly, and not being for this reason a signatory to the Treaty on behalf of Canada ... my Ministers do not feel that they are in a position to recommend to Parliament the approval of the peace Treaty with Turkey and the Conventions thereto. Without the approval of Parliament, they feel they are not warranted in signifying concurrence in ratification of the Treaty and Conventions.[72]

During a debate on ratification on 1 April 1924 in the British House of Commons, the new Labour Prime Minister James Ramsay MacDonald responded to a question about Ottawa's position. He stated that their "Canadian friends" had raised "one or two" not particularly important "constitutional matters", and he was thus prepared to express his opinion: "Canada, I am perfectly certain, accepts the obligation, having been represented by Lord Curzon at Lausanne, with her full knowledge and consent."[73] It wasn't long before the Canadian Prime Minister responded. He immediately sent a lengthy telegram in which he summarised communication in regard to the Conference of Lausanne, and complained he had been totally misunderstood.[74] It was also demonstrated that Britain had mistakenly believed that Mackenzie King was aware of the content of the confidential telegram sent to the British Secretary of State for the Colonies Lord Devonshire by Canada's Governor-General Lord Byng at the end of 1922. However, the Canadian Prime Minister had had "no idea" of it and strongly rejected the idea that Canada had previously consented to the British Secretary of State for Foreign Affairs Lord Curzon signing on behalf of Canada.[75] This sharp exchange of opinions confirmed that the new British Prime Minister was oblivious to, or did not want to acknowledge, Canada's definition of foreign policy autonomy, which impacted the previously standard course of Imperial diplomacy.[76]

On 9 June 1924, the Ottawa parliament discussed the Lausanne affair, with the Canadian Prime Minister explaining government policy to MPs. Besides a comprehensive summary of the events of recent months, he expressed his opinion that although Canada was bound to the Treaty of Lausanne, in any future crisis legislators would decide on any expansion of its duties and commitments beyond those arrangements. During the debate, Mackenzie King faced criticism from the Conservative opposition headed by Arthur Meighen, who supported a joint Imperial foreign policy, that the Prime Minister was weakening the Empire by not accepting representation by Britain at the Conference of Lausanne and during the signature of agreements.[77] The political leader of the nationalist francophone Canadians, Henri Bourassa, summarised the different perspectives of Conservative and Liberal supporters on Canada's role as follows: "The Liberals ... believe in the autonomy of the Dominion and the maintenance of the unity of the Empire whereas the Conservatives believe in the unity of the Empire and the preservation of the autonomy of the Dominions."[78]

Mackenzie King concluded that from a legal perspective the situation was unclear, and so he ordered an expert analysis of the whole affair from unofficial government foreign relations advisor Oscar Skelton. This came up with four options of how to proceed: (1) remain at war with Turkey; (2) negotiate a separate peace treaty; (3) agree with ratification of the Lausanne agreements or (4) concede that George V's ratification as requested by His Majesty's Government is binding for Canada too. Although he personally did not want to accept any of these options, in the end he adopted the idea that the treaty was outwardly binding *de jure* for Ottawa, but not binding *de facto* in terms of the duties arising from it for the Empire.[79]

The Canadian representatives perceived the Anglo-Canadian differences of opinion which accompanied the Chanak Crisis and the Treaty of Lausanne as confirmation that their current course opposing "automatically accepting" commitments the mother country negotiated "for it" was the right one. They thus concluded that it remained essential to seek the ability to at least partially make decisions independently on certain foreign policy matters which they considered in Canada's eminent interests. In the end, Mackenzie King made some concessions, accepting that, "legally and technically Canada will be bound by the ratification of the Treaty; in other words, speaking internationally, the whole British Empire in relation to the rest of the world will stand as one [state] when this treaty is ratified".[80] In a personal letter he sent to the British Prime Minister on 23 April 1924, he gave a detailed analysis of Canada's perspective on what form relations within the Empire might take. He had a difference of opinion with Britain, however.[81] Like Amery and Smuts, he saw Dominions as equal nations within the Empire. He saw the presence of Dominion representatives as well as British representatives at the Paris peace negotiations as a precedent leading to their new international status, and that this status was not observed during the Conference of Lausanne. The Prime Minister repeated the argument already made that he refused to sign the submitted treaty, because his country was neither represented not sufficiently consulted during the negotiations with Turkey.[82]

4.2 The Halibut Treaty and the 1923 Imperial Conference

The circumstances surrounding the Chanak Crisis and signature of the Treaty of Lausanne strengthened Canada's Prime Minister Mackenzie King in his conviction that they had to break free from their obligations arising from common policies, and instead ensure that Ottawa enforce an independent, or at least autonomous, form of foreign policy.[83] As such, he used the completion of negotiations on the so-called Halibut Treaty (sometimes also called the Northern Pacific Halibut Fishery Convention) to demonstrate Canada's diplomatic independence.[84]

The beginnings of economic relations between the Self-Governing Colonies, or Dominions, and countries outside the British Empire date back to the 19th century when their long-term interests went beyond those of the mother country in some cases. Frequently, the British Secretary of State for Foreign Affairs would be pursuing a foreign policy in certain areas which was either contrary to the wishes or economic and political objectives of its Self-Governing Colonies or Dominions,[85] or in which the Dominions were not allowed to take part in negotiations, at least to some extent.[86] These blunders were unfortunate, and as such, beginning in the 1890s, voices began to be heard demanding the incorporation of the interests of overseas autonomous territories within Imperial foreign policy, and more intensive collaboration between Britain's Colonial Office and the Foreign Office.[87]

These tendencies were most noticeable within the oldest Dominion – Canada. The 1867 British North America Act meant that Canada was unable to conclude international treaties independently, as this remained the prerogative of the mother country. Beginning in 1870, Ottawa politicians endeavoured to gain the opportunity of communicating about commercial matters not just with the British Dominions, but also with foreign countries. Although by 1874 they were able to name Sir John A. MacDonald's successor, who held negotiations on a trade agreement with America, they were unable to approve the resulting document.[88] Nevertheless, contemporaries believed it was "the finest chapter in the history of Canadian diplomacy".[89] This principle was abandoned in the subsequent decade, and as such the 1884 trade agreement with Spain was signed in Madrid by Her Majesty's representative, Canadian High Commissioner Sir Charles Tupper.[90] The same approach was taken for an 1893 commercial agreement with France.[91] Subsequently, in 1895 Britain's Secretary of State for the Colonies, the Marquess of Ripon, made official the practice of allowing representatives of Dominions to take part in negotiating agreements affecting the Dominion's interests. However, if such conventions were to be considered an international document, only Her Majesty's Government would be able to conclude them with a foreign sovereign state.[92]

The New Constitutional Status for the Dominions? 185

The border dispute between the United States and Canada at the turn of the 20th century confirmed that Ottawa still did not have the means to pursue active independent policies in regard to its stronger neighbour, and that it continued to have to "rely" on the protection of the mother country.[93] Although there were discussions at the 1902 Colonial Conference on matters linked to agreements affecting how the independent colonies and Dominions worked, much of the debate focused on trade agreements, ignoring foreign policy issues. When Sir Wilfrid Laurier's government separately negotiated an additional trade agreement with France in 1907, it still had to be signed by the British ambassador and subsequently ratified by the British government. The Colonial Office's memorandum of 1911 confirmed the rule that Dominions could not separately agree upon any convention with a foreign country.[94]

In 1917, discussions began between the USA and Canada on treaties dealing with the issue of fishing in coastal waters and in the Pacific. These made up a significant part of the economy, and as such, both countries wanted to deal with contentious issues.[95] In 1919, two separate treaties were agreed regulating the rights to fish salmon and halibut in the area.[96] It was shown that in practice the treaty conditions did not apply to the rest of the Empire, and thus Canada's negotiator, Sir John Douglas Hazen, endeavoured to add some modifications.[97] Although the so-called Salmon Treaty did go into force, contradictions between the competencies of state and federal authorities in the United States meant that it was difficult to enforce.[98] As such, negotiations on the so-called Halibut Treaty were put on ice.[99] It wasn't until March 1922 when there were changes at government level in both countries that discussions resumed.[100] A document was produced for signing in early 1923.

Canada's prime minister judged that countersignature by Britain was not necessary, since Canada had negotiated the treaty's contents independently, and so he replaced "Great Britain" in the preamble with "the Dominion of Canada".[101] As such, in January 1923 Mackenzie King officially asked the Foreign Office through Britain's Colonial Office for their consent that Canadian minister, Ernest Lapointe, whose resort included Pacific fishing, sign the document alone.[102] Although Britain's Colonial Office did not have any objections, since it was a local and special interest relevant only to Canada which did not threaten the Empire's diplomatic unity, the Foreign Office was vigorously opposed, despite admitting that there was precedence in the matter in the form of the recently concluded trade convention between Canada and France.[103] Foreign Office representatives did not share Ottawa's position that the signature of the authorised Canadian minister sufficed and signature of Britain's ambassador in Washington, Sir Auckland Geddes, was unnecessary since he represented the United Kingdom and not Canada. As such, they instructed Geddes to order the preamble be changed so that in accordance with practice hitherto his signature would be first, with Lapointe merely attaching his signature on behalf of Canada.[104]

Despite the strong objection of Foreign Office officials and the Washington embassy, Mackenzie King was adamant. On 21 February 1923, he announced that Ernest Lapointe alone would sign the treaty since it was purely a Canadian-American matter. He threatened that were this not to occur, he would be forced to name an entirely independent Canadian diplomatic representative in Washington.[105] When Britain was told by America that the ratification process would begin on 4 March, they found themselves pressed for time.[106] As such, the British Foreign Office chose the "lesser evil". They agreed that the Canadian minister could formalise the treaty independently as Britain's authorised representative without the involvement of the British ambassador in Washington.[107] On 2 March 1923, Ernest Lapointe and America's Secretary of State for Foreign Affairs, Charles Evans Hughes, undertook the signing ceremony for the so-called Halibut Treaty.[108]

Shortly afterwards, the British Prime Minister found himself facing demands in the House of Commons that he submit the British-Canadian telegrams about the fishing treaties, and being asked whether a signature of the Ottawa minister had the same weight as that of a member of His Majesty's Government. Andrew Bonar Law refused to publish the correspondence and confirmed that Canada's representative had authorisation and as such was able to sign it on behalf of the King.[109] His Canadian opposite number had it no easier either; the Conservative opposition leader, Arthur Meighen, suspected him of secret cabinet diplomacy which was putting relations between Canada and Great Britain in danger. Mackenzie King was determined to defend himself against this accusation, and as such he asked Britain's Colonial Office to consent to the publication of the correspondence which it had had with Canada's Governor-General. Although he received a negative response from them, he used its ambiguous formulation as an excuse to submit the relevant telegrams to members of the Canadian parliament.[110] This did not go down well with Britain.[111]

In hindsight, Canada's March 1923 diplomatic success would seem to create momentum for further constitutional changes in relations between the Dominions and the mother country, although it seemed at first to be purely a formal and internal change in how treaties were concluded. It had been repeatedly demonstrated since the signing of the Treaty of Versailles that in practice the Dominions were acting more and more like independent states, although from a legal and constitutional perspective they still held a subordinate status towards London which allowed them to request and advise, but not to make decisions.[112] Ernest Lapointe saw the Canadian-American fishing treaty as purely a domestic matter, but he nevertheless believed it had far-reaching consequences since by concluding the treaty, the United States was recognising Canada's international standing.[113] He was drawn to this conviction because America had not ratified the Covenant of the League of Nations, and as such did not perceive membership of the Dominions within the League of Nations as evidence of their new status within the British Empire.[114]

Thus, the time came for Britain to reassess its Dominions policy. The Foreign Office viewed the circumstances around signature of the purely trade-focused Canadian-American treaty as a major threat for joint imperial diplomacy, since in signing it Lapointe had geographically unrestricted authorisation in representing not just an autonomous part of the British Empire, but also London itself. Thus, the opportunity was now there for Dominions to deal with foreign policy affairs themselves, breaking free from their role as "sleeping" partner to the Foreign Office. While Canadian Governor-General Lord Byng and the British Secretary of State for the Colonies preferred to put the incident behind them, Britain's Foreign Office was determined not to admit "defeat" or even mere retreat from established procedures.[115] This position was in line with Lord Curzon's persistent efforts to retrieve full control over foreign policy, about which more decisions were made during David Lloyd George's period in office amongst a small circle of people around the Prime Minister than within the Foreign Office.[116]

The British position that Mackenzie King should at least apologise to the Americans for the diplomatic confusion and clumsiness surrounding the completion and signature of the Halibut Treaty, or to Lord Byng for publishing the correspondence, was not realistic. Canada's Prime Minister went on the counter-attack and demanded that the issue of publishing communication between Dominions and the mother country be dealt with at the upcoming Imperial Conference.[117] At the same time, the ratification process was underway for agreements in other overseas parliaments, in which Dominion politicians held different opinions over the importance of these agreements. Australian Prime Minister Stanley Bruce considered them important and as such decided in autumn 1923 to discuss them at the planned Imperial Conference in London. His New Zealand opposite number was noticeably more cautious. South African nationalists, however, did not hide their enthusiasm for the idea of absolute equality with the mother country.[118]

Over the course of the summer of 1923, discussions were held in Whitehall which confirmed that the Foreign Office and Colonial Office had different perspectives on how to deal with the issue of whether Dominions could agree treaty arrangements "technically" without British involvement. Representatives of the British Foreign Office conceded that the Dominions had begun over "the last few years to regard themselves as members of a community of free nations" and as such came to the conclusion that it would be best to hold intensive discussions over the whole process of signing international agreements and clarify the situation at a meeting of Dominion and British leaders. As such they proposed in an August 1923 internal memorandum that each overseas autonomous government should be able to negotiate its own bilateral agreements with foreign states and sign it without British countersignature on condition that responsibility for any benefits and obligations arising from such agreements should be borne by that Dominion.[119]

In surprising contrast, the Colonial Office took an almost opposing position. In a September 1923 internal memorandum, officers there expressed the opinion that controversies arose only for multilateral agreements in which the Dominions did not negotiate alone, and which were generally signed by British negotiators in their name. As such, they came to the conclusion that there was no need for radical changes to the system of concluding agreements as long as the principle of properly consulting the Dominions about everything was strictly observed, and that Dominion and British representatives would subsequently sign such agreements. The Colonial Office nevertheless indirectly admitted from a diplomatic and legal perspective that it would be difficult to keep these conventions uniform.[120]

From 1 October to 8 November 1923, an Imperial Conference took place in the British capital. Although compared to the previous conference, its agenda did not include key constitutional topics, it played a significant part towards extending Dominion autonomy in matters of foreign affairs.[121] It substantially affected relations between the Dominions and the mother country because it opened up a path towards accepting separate Dominion responsibility for foreign relations.[122] As a result of the then incomplete ratification process of the Lausanne peace deal with Turkey and the British-Canadian disagreements over the American-Canadian fishing treaties, participants at the conference discussed foreign relations and issues regarding negotiating, signing and ratifying conventions, and other matters such as the status of High Commissioners, the running of the Imperial War Graves Commission and the New Hebrides Condominium, etc., were eclipsed.[123]

After British Prime Minister Stanley Baldwin welcomed the representatives of the Dominions and the new Irish Free State in his opening speech, he admitted about the Commonwealth that over the centuries, "our ever increasing control of natural forces has so knit the nations together that whatever affects one for good or ill affects them all." He stressed the necessity to continue to strengthen their common bond, because, "the British Empire cannot live for itself alone. Its strength [is] as a Commonwealth of Nations".[124] Unusually, Canada's Prime Minister stressed the benefit of Imperial Conferences. He perceived personal contact between the leaders as a major factor affecting relations between the Dominions and the mother country. The events of the preceding months made him again make the demand that conference discussions be published.[125] In this matter, however, there was agreement during the initial phases that any discussions regarding matters of foreign policy and defence would be strictly confidential, and as such any publication of their contents would only exceptionally occur.[126]

Due to the circumstances surrounding the Chanak Crisis and discussions in Lausanne, Mackenzie King arrived in London with a basic vision that the Dominions should have the right to pursue their own foreign policy to avoid unwanted shared obligations. He was also of the conviction that diplomatic independence was best demonstrated by the Dominions acquiring the opportunity to conclude treaties with foreign countries independently.[127] He based his arguments on the wording of a talk, called "Canada and the Control of Foreign Policy", given in early 1923 by his nationalist external affairs advisor Oscar Skelton, who conditioned the idea of an independent policy towards foreign countries on any measures taken not being allowed to have a negative impact on other parts of the Empire. As such, he stressed the fact that regular consultation should take place between the Dominions and the mother country in order to avoid different approaches in matters where the interests of participants overlapped or even diverged. Skelton had long held a negative view of a common imperial foreign policy, as he considered it disadvantageous for the Dominions since it included many obligations with little opportunity for influence.[128]

A third meeting between representatives of London and overseas representatives took place on 5 October 1923, at which Britain's Secretary of State for Foreign Affairs, Lord Curzon, gave an extensive analysis of developments in Imperial foreign policy since the last Imperial Conference of 1921, addressed current issues and called in particular for a common approach to be maintained in affairs in which the Dominions and the mother country had a shared interest.[129] In regard to a common Imperial foreign policy, he held the opinion that this should be implemented externally by Britain's Foreign Secretary, since Britain represented the whole Empire.[130]

Three days later at the next meeting, Canada's Prime Minister Mackenzie King responded to Curzon's declaration. He began by focusing on the genesis of Canadian-American relations; he then moved on to the issue of a common Imperial foreign policy. He noted a passage from a speech given in December 1921 in which British Prime Minister David Lloyd George had been convinced that the Dominions' position in foreign affairs had been entirely transformed over the previous four years,[131] and that

> the Dominions had been given equal rights with Great Britain in the control of the foreign policy of the Empire, that the instrument of this policy was, and must remain, the British Foreign Office, and that the advantage to Britain was that such joint control involved joint responsibility.

He then noted Sir Clifford Sifton's analysis, in which he controversially interpreted the section on Dominions' collective responsibility such that "the Dominions become jointly responsible for everything the British Foreign Policy does in every part of the world. ... I think it a complete abandonment of the theory of Dominion autonomy as it has developed for fifty years". Curzon's assumption that this was only Sifton's personal perspective proved then to be wrong, with Canada's Prime Minister stating that he endorsed Sifton's position.[132]

Mackenzie King then criticised the frequently used phase, "the foreign policy of the British Empire", noting that "it may be that in using phrases such as 'foreign policy' there are different things in the minds of each of us," and that each Dominion mainly focused on only those matters they were interested in. He further noted that Canada's foreign policy in regard to the United States was in line with the approved focus of British Empire foreign policy. He also expressed a willingness to accept the fact that "the policy of Great Britain is the policy of the British Empire, but we want to know how far the obligations arising out of that policy are material and how far they extend in reference to ourselves". He realised that a common foreign policy in all spheres of interest of the Dominions and the mother country was necessary, but he considered it to be unworkable in practice.[133]

Overall, the Canadian Prime Minister's position was a nationalist one, and as such he preferred full autonomy for the Dominions; he perceived the Imperial Conference as an institution with a purely consultative role without executive powers, and he rejected the vague idea of the Imperial Cabinet of 1917–1921.[134] He was of the opinion that the autonomous overseas territories were entitled to take control of domestic and geographically close foreign affairs which affected them directly, even where that would involve some part of Imperial policy already stated, and that the Dominion parliaments should have ultimate authority in these matters. He believed that

> if it is not possible or desirable that Great Britain or other Dominions should control these foreign affairs which are distinctly of primary concern to one Dominion, so it is equally impossible and undesirable for the Dominions to seek to control [over] foreign affairs which primarily affect Great Britain.

The problem here was that British leaders pursued a policy with the belief that this was the Empire's policy. Mackenzie King saw a certain difficulty in consultation too, since he was of the conviction that due to the Empire's geographic expanse, "it is possible to consult on matters of overwhelming and enduring common interest; [but] it is not possible to consult on the great range of matters of individual and shifting concern".[135]

The New Constitutional Status for the Dominions? 191

Other Dominion prime ministers did not offer Mackenzie King much support. His Australian opposite number, Stanley Bruce, feared Australia's isolation and possible threat from Japan, and as such he was one of the advocates for a common imperial policy and tariffs.[136] He did accept at the conference, however, that meetings between Dominion and British representatives on important issues of foreign policy should take place more frequently.[137] He even declared that "Australia would not be committed to any foreign policy decision of the British government without prior consultation".[138] New Zealand Prime Minister William Massey sympathised with Bruce's opinions, although he feared frequent consultation was difficult to implement in practice due to the urgency of some problems.[139] South African Prime Minister Jam Smuts rejected Canada's reasoning and supported a common policy, wishing for the Commonwealth to play an active role in international relations. He was guarded in what he said on the Commonwealth's automatic involvement in dealing with "all" European matters.[140] His Newfoundland opposite number, William Robertson Warren, Ireland's Kevin O'Higgins and India's representative were not particularly involved in the discussion, as they did not perceive foreign policy as an acute problem.[141] Although the pronouncements of some Dominion leaders sounded critical, they were not aimed at loosening the Dominions' relations with Great Britain; despite it all, Mackenzie King held the opinion that the British Empire was a great community of free nations with interests, obligations and responsibilities, and Canada, like other Dominions, acknowledged that.[142]

Due to the controversies which accompanied the Chanak Crisis, the Lausanne negotiations, etc., Britain anticipated criticism from the Dominion leaders regarding the methods and frequency of consultation from the mother country, and as such endeavoured to avoid such criticism by clarifying binding procedures. To make matters clearer, it divided up communication with Dominion governments on foreign affairs into five areas: (1) Imperial Conferences, (2) international conferences, (3) the League of Nations, (4) general issues of international relations and (5) trade agreements. The Foreign Office stated that when Imperial Conferences were taking place, overseas prime ministers would receive a copy of important telegrams and reports from British Ambassadors and other foreign representatives every day. At times when there were no discussions taking place in London, the Foreign Office took the position that sending out reports once a week was sufficient, with information on particularly important events, such as the Conference in Lausanne, being regularly supplied.[143]

According to the British Foreign Office, from the beginning a crucial factor in international conferences was whether the Dominions acted independently at them, or whether Britain represented them. In the event of overseas autonomous territories taking part in such meetings, then

British and Dominion members of the British Empire delegation should co-operate at meetings and in a common secretariat; treaties could then be signed separately on behalf of the Dominions. Where only the mother country was to represent overseas territories, then they would usually regularly inform Dominions on developments in discussions, with direct consultation taking place only on the final documents which would be signed separately either by Dominion representatives, or only by British negotiators. In regard to international conventions in which at least one Dominion had a special interest, then the ratification process was also to be consulted with them subsequently. Consultation with Dominions on matters falling within the competencies of the League of Nations were to take place regularly according to the gravity of points being looked at and during sessions of the Assembly through regular meetings between British and overseas delegates. In terms of general international issues which included, for example, customs tariffs with the United States and Spain, Britain promised to keep the Dominions regularly informed. For trade agreements, Foreign Office workers did not determine a precise procedure due to the extent of the issues, leaving the decision to Imperial Conference participants.[144]

On 10 October 1923, Lord President of the Council James Gascoyne-Cecil, 4th Marquess of Salisbury, a member of the British government, presented a memorandum which analysed discussions on foreign relations at the Imperial Conference, in which he came to the conclusion that it would not be easy to reconcile the positions of Mackenzie King and Bruce. According to Salisbury, they represented two opposing concepts, centralising and decentralising, which he characterised thus: "Australia will find how much common action is possible, and Canada will learn how much common action is desirable".[145] Surprisingly, Secretaries did not bear particular weight to the memorandum, determining that, "[at] the present stage, it would not be advisable for the British representatives at the Imperial Conference to take any initiative in suggesting any alteration in the present association of the Dominions with foreign affairs", but that they should await the proposals of the representatives of the Dominions and India.[146]

Britain's Secretary of State for Foreign Affairs, Lord Curzon, consistently rejected the idea that it was a good idea to give a precise definition of the principles for creating Imperial foreign policy over the course of the debate, stating he feared that this could restrict him in pursuing Britain's long-established policies.[147] The foreign policy debate did not come to any groundbreaking conclusions; rather, it exacerbated personal animosities between participants. Lord Curzon saw the Canadian Prime Minister as an obstacle in his way, and as such pulled no punches in his private correspondence, describing him as, "both obstinate, tiresome and stupid".[148] Mackenzie King's nationalist tactic, based on an endeavour to avoid any kind of obligations and do nothing, did not leave a great

The New Constitutional Status for the Dominions? 193

impression on Leopold Amery, who held the post of First Lord of the Admiralty, either.[149]

As such, the final resolution adopted focused only on a general assessment of European and world affairs at the time, such as the Occupation of the Ruhr,[150] relations with the United States and Japan, the activities of the League of Nations, etc. Ratification of the Lausanne Treaty was entirely disregarded. Only in the final passage was there a direct response to the requests made by Mackenzie King:

> This Conference is a conference of representatives of the several Governments of the Empire; its views and conclusions on Foreign Policy ... are necessarily subject to the action of the Governments and Parliaments of the various portions of the Empire, and it trusts that the results of its deliberations will meet with their approval.[151]

Although those involved did not find it was necessary to decentralise the operation of foreign policy, and thus confirmed standard practice, they did agree that the size of the agenda meant it would be a good idea to call a special conference to look at financial and economic issues.[152]

Conference participants also adopted a binding procedure for negotiating, signing and ratifying international agreements which have been signed by authorised representatives and which are subject to final approval. The Dominion representatives were able to negotiate conventions, but they had to look at the possible impacts on other autonomous governments, or on the Empire as a whole. Before beginning discussions on conventions, they were to ensure that other Dominions did not want to be regularly informed so they could decide whether to take part in negotiations or not. Where an agreement was to be negotiated at international conferences through a British Empire delegation, all involved were to receive information regularly. A local authorised negotiator was to be able to sign bilateral agreements which resulted in obligations for just one Dominion. Where the agreements resulted in obligations for a number of Dominions, the corresponding number of delegates from the overseas autonomous territories involved were to sign it. The ratification process was to remain the same.[153]

The adopted resolution on concluding agreements, formally acknowledging various precedents from previous years, allowed one of the problem areas in pursuing Imperial foreign policy to be resolved, and it went some way towards Dominions being partially recognised as independent states whose foreign policy was conducted by the mother country, and which had common obligations to the Crown.[154] Britain finally gave up its control over the conclusion of agreements, something which had come up against the aspirations and constitutional positions of the Dominions for many years, who now acquired the right to negotiate and sign agreements independently. Although there was also an acknowledgement of the supremacy of the British Empire delegation when international conferences were being held, Dominion representatives did not receive any guarantees that they would be adequately represented at such conferences. Some discussion arose on how to differentiate the obligations of one Dominion arising from a bilateral agreement from the obligations of other parts of the Empire.[155]

In 1923, the main difficulties in foreign policy issues were what form they were to take, and who was to implement them. When the Imperial Conference ended, no consensus on the roles of Dominion and British representatives could be found. Different positions remained in what the role of Imperial Conferences was, and the level of autonomy the Dominions should have in regard to Imperial matters from which substantial responsibilities and obligations arose. Discussions on Imperial foreign policy demonstrated that Dominion prime ministers, Mackenzie King and Bruce in particular, were not of one mind in their perspective on whether nationalist tendencies meant that the British Empire should decentralise or keep the traditional central role played by London.[156]

4.3 The Establishment of the Dominion office

The 1923 Imperial Conference was only a partial response to the newly forming relationships within the Empire. Apart from confirming the right of every Dominion to negotiate and sign treaties affecting their acknowledged interests, it did not result in much that was new.[157] It was demonstrated repeatedly that Canada and South Africa in particular opposed an Imperial foreign policy which was excessively focused on European matters, something they did not want to be particularly involved in due to the significant economic and military commitments it required. Australia and New Zealand in contrast preferred a common Imperial foreign policy and as such were willing to accept continental commitments under particular circumstances. Ireland was still formulating its stance on the working of the Empire and its foreign policy, and so it did not really engage in the issue as yet, focusing more on domestic issues.[158]

The 6 December 1921 Anglo-Irish Treaty gave Ireland the same rights the other Dominions had available to them. In March 1922, the London parliament passed the Irish Free State (Agreement) Act, on which basis the treaty provisions came into force, and an Irish provisional government was established.[159] From early 1922, a committee began meeting up in Dublin, chaired by Michael Collins, whose task was to prepare the new Irish constitution, the draft version of which was passed by the Irish assembly in October. Once it was affirmed by members of parliament in Westminster, the Irish Free State Constitution Act came into force on 6 December 1922. The discussion and circumstances around its adoption, however, made clear that Britain was not willing to grant the Irish full legal sovereignty.[160] Although London repeatedly assured Irish representatives that the Irish Free State had the same constitutional position in regard to the mother country institutions as the "pattern Dominion" of Canada, it was soon demonstrated that even this clause had its limits. British legal experts acknowledged that in the event of an expansion to the Canadian parliament's extraterritorial jurisdiction, Dublin would be unable to "reciprocally" claim the same constitutional status as Ottawa had attained. On the one hand, this was an objective complication bringing some level of mistrust into Anglo-Irish relations, and on the other hand, it gave Irish politicians the option of theoretically negotiating more since Dominion autonomy limits were not determined.[161]

Ireland took a bit of time to get used to its status as a Dominion, and as such was not particularly involved either in debates at the 1923 Imperial Conference or in the process of ratifying the Lausanne treaties in 1924. Despite having no direct interest in reparation payments, Ireland took part in the July 1924 London conference on the Dawes Plan.[162] Although the clause on the "pattern Dominion of Canada" represented a certain guide, they were still unclear what the Irish Free State's exact constitutional position was. As such, only in practice did they gain greater awareness of what being a Dominion brought them.[163] At the end of 1923, on the basis of previous Canadian precedent, the question arose over whether a separate diplomatic and consular representation in the United States could be set up for Ireland.[164] Although in May 1920 Canada had acquired the right to send its own Minister Plenipotentiary to the British Embassy in Washington,[165] it had not as yet done so because Canadian Prime Minister Mackenzie King was considering modifying the conditions of the agreement which had been negotiated by Borden.[166] The Foreign Office did not fundamentally contest the Irish request, although they did have some minor reservations.[167] In contrast, Britain's Colonial Office pointed out that diplomatic representation had been granted as a result of the special Canadian-American relationship.[168]

On 3 March 1924, Irish Prime Minister William Thomas Cosgrave officially called for the Irish Minister Plenipotentiary to be promptly named Special Envoy in Washington. He used Ireland's significant financial and trading interests to justify the request, as well as the "delicate" issue of Irish emigration to the United States.[169] British Prime Minister and the Secretary of State for Foreign Affairs Ramsay MacDonald and the Secretary of State for the Colonies James Henry Thomas came to the conclusion that for objective reasons, the request could not be denied.[170] On 22 April, Thomas asked the other Dominion governments to approve the decision because of the Irish Free State's "very considerable financial and commercial interests" to establish an Irish "virtually independent" diplomatic mission in Washington.[171] Canada and South Africa supported the British government's planned measure immediately.[172] Due to the fact that the Pacific Dominions had long prioritised a common Imperial foreign policy, they were in contrast strongly opposed. New Zealand feared that, "the present proposal is given effect to the first step towards disruption of the Empire ... [which] will have been taken".[173] Australia saw it as a threat to the fundamental principle of diplomatic unity, was openly sceptical of the special relationship or interests between Ireland and America, and pointed out that following this logic every Dominion would be able to request representation at all British embassies. Due to the severity of the matter, they proposed postponing a final decision until the next Imperial Conference.[174] Ireland naturally challenged these objections and instead called for the speedier approval of its request.[175]

However, Britain's Colonial Secretary was very sensitive about the diplomatic unity of the Empire, maintaining the view that it was best maintained when established procedures were strictly followed. This meant he considered it neither desirable nor possible in practice for the Irish envoy to operate independently of the British Ambassador, and as such he demanded that they co-operate closely. He further stressed that treaties between the Irish envoy and America would be signed in line with the relevant resolution of the 1923 Imperial Conference. He also rejected all doubts over the (non-)existence of special interests and relations between Ireland and the North American continent.[176] On 28 May, the British Foreign Office informed the United States that it would establish a separate diplomatic mission in Washington for the Irish Free State. Britain did not expect the Americans to be particularly interested in the appointment of an Irish envoy. They anticipated that the Irish republican propaganda in the country had not yet been entirely forgotten, and that the prospect of a "wave" of additional envoys from other Dominions would not be particularly appreciated.[177] Members of the House of Lords did not express enthusiasm either, and as such the Permanent Under-Secretary of State at the Colonial Office, Sydney Arnold, 1st Baron Arnold, was forced to defend the Labour government's decision.[178] Britain's Secretary of State for the Colonies, J. H. Thomas, had to do the same in the House of Commons.[179] At the end of June, America accepted Ireland's new envoy, professor and diplomat Timothy Aloysius Smiddy.[180]

The complications accompanying ratification of the Lausanne treaties and the Irish demand for a mission in Washington was confirmation for MacDonald's government that these were just the "tip of the iceberg", and the principal problem was in a lack of co-operation and consultation between the mother country and the Dominions. Britain's Colonial Secretary Thomas appealed to Resolution IX of the 1917 Imperial War Conference and called on the Dominion representatives to co-operate more deeply and more intensively in all affairs which involved common Imperial interest. He admitted that consultation was not effective when Imperial Conferences were not meeting, and that the frequent changes of government in the Dominions and in Britain made it very difficult to deal with controversial political and economic issues. Since he feared there might be a loss of faith in the system of Imperial Conferences, he urged the setting up of a new functional model for constitutional relationships within the Empire. Thomas was aware of the objective difficulty, and was thus unsure about how to arrive there because he did not really believe in restoring the idea of a Constitutional Conference or any other special meeting of the Imperial Conference. Despite it all, he determined that the outlined far-reaching changes had to be discussed in detail, and therefore asked that a meeting of Dominion prime ministers take place shortly.[181] The overseas prime ministers concurred with the Labour government conclusions but took a cautious approach to their plans. Although they did not *a priori* reject the idea of convening a conference, the proposed autumn timetable was not received positively because most were unable to travel at short notice due to complex domestic affairs.[182]

Discussions with Dominion statesmen on the form and date of a conference continued right into the autumn of 1924. By the beginning of November 1924 when the first MacDonald government collapsed due to a domestic political crisis,[183] however, nothing meaningful had been agreed. Leopold Stennett Amery, who had worked at the office under Lord Milner and who was an influential advocate of an evolution in Imperial relations in the 1920s, became the new Secretary of State for the Colonies. In contrast to Joseph Chamberlain's "human perspective", Amery sought, like others who had worked with Milner, to ensure any administrative changes were initiated by the Colonial Office. He had long been aware of Dominions' growing importance and, over time, had thus formed his own view on what course relationships between the overseas autonomous territories and the mother country should take, including constitutional issues. However, Amery's plans were opposed by many across Britain's political spectrum. Although he was cautious in his view of Dominion responsibility for implementing Imperial foreign policy, he decided to make his acceptance of the post of the Secretary of State for the Colonies in Baldwin's second Conservative government conditional on being allowed to create a distinct office administering Dominion affairs separately from other dependent Crown territories.[184]

When Amery took control of the Colonial Office in November 1924, he had to address the growing dissatisfaction of Dominion statesmen that British promises in terms of the level of consultation on important foreign policy issues had not been kept, and the lack of discussion on the issue initiated by his predecessor James Thomas.[185] Back in 1917, Amery had considered consolidating the self-governing parts of the Empire on the basis of common Imperial policy, and in June 1921 had spoken on Smuts's memorandum demanding a declaration of Dominion rights. Although he did not retreat from his basic premises, i.e. full independence and equality for the autonomous parts of the Empire and their inseparable link in the person of the sovereign and the Crown, in contrast to his predecessors as the Secretary of State for the Colonies, he had a greater understanding of Dominions' demands.[186] Conservative overseas politicians welcomed Amery's appointment, because they considered him the right person at the right time, due to his long-term interest in Imperial issues.[187] In December 1924, Amery ended floundering discussions on foreign policy consultation and common Imperial affairs by concluding that he did not really understand the timing or reasons which had led the Labour government to open up the whole matter. In contrast to his predecessors, he stressed the importance of personal consultation and contacts between British and overseas statesmen and repeatedly assured Dominion representatives that they would be fully informed on Imperial foreign policy implementation and other matters of common interest. He subsequently focused his efforts on making changes at the Colonial Office.[188]

There had already been some considerations made of reorganising Britain's Colonial Office. When Canada had attained Dominion status in 1867 and become an autonomous part of the Empire, the question of whether Canadian affairs should continue to be dealt with by the British Colonial Office, which had been formed by being split off from the Foreign Office in 1854, became a more pressing one. Numerous Imperialist organisations and overseas statesmen, in particular Alfred Deakin of Australia, held the opinion that Dominion affairs were so specific that they should be administered by a specific expert institution, and not automatically by the Colonial Office.[189] In early December 1907, Britain's Colonial Secretary Lord Elgin had thus proposed an internal reorganisation of the office and the establishment of a Dominion Department.[190] This, however, did not satisfy Leopold Amery and other advocates of equal partnership for autonomous parts of the Empire and the mother country, who demanded the complete separation of Colonial and Dominion affairs.[191] At the 1911 Imperial Conference, the British government did not support proposals for establishing an Imperial office dealing with a strictly Dominion agenda, although the Foreign Office and Imperial Defence Committee were not against the idea of limiting the rights of the Secretary of State for the Colonies.[192] In 1914, debate on competencies was ended by the outbreak of war. When Revolution IX was adopted at the 1917 Imperial War Conference, which fully recognised the Dominions as autonomous nations in the Imperial commonwealth and their right to make decisions on Imperial foreign policy,[193] the question of what competencies the Dominion agenda should fall within became pressing once again.

In November 1924, Amery opened up internal discussion and preparations for reorganising the Office.[194] At the start of December, he sent Stanley Baldwin a preliminary proposal in a memorandum in which he stressed that separation was essential for the smooth working of the office and maintaining Imperial unity, because the Dominions found themselves in latent undesirable "subservience" to the Colonial Office. He pointed out that although Dominion representatives had been seeking a change in the system since 1907, Britain had made only two concessions: (1) they had renamed Colonial Conferences Imperial Conferences; and (2) they had created a Dominion Department at the Colonial Office, managed by a deputy Permanent Under-Secretary of State. Amery also pointed out that after the First World War, the Colonial Office agenda had expanded to include administration of the League of Nations mandate territories, co-ordination of the economic development of African territories, and communication with a new Dominion – the Irish Free State – and the Self-Governing Colony of Southern Rhodesia.[195]

Amery considered the practice at that time of British Secretaries sending all correspondence in regard to Imperial foreign policy, the League of Nations and the Committee of Imperial Defence to Dominion governments via the Colonial Office to be an extremely complicated method of transferring information in terms of both time and personnel. He also thought it was a shortcoming that the Secretary of State for the Colonies barely had time once a year to visit the Dominions and maintain personal contacts with representatives there. He thus proposed two alternative administrative reorganisation models which he hoped would improve relations between the Dominions and the mother country. The first was more expensive and harder to organise because it involved establishing two new parliamentary Under-Secretaries, one of whom would be responsible for Dominion issues and the other for a transitional period would be involved in creating a separate Dominion Office, or Office of Imperial Affairs; each of whom would have their own Permanent Under-Secretary of State. The second alternative was vastly simpler, because this involved the immediate creation of a new Dominion Office, which would be managed by the Secretary of State for the Colonies for a fixed period of time. Another benefit of this second option was the almost-zero cost.[196]

Subsequent confidential discussion confirmed that the first option was problematic. There was a complication in finding people to fill the Parliamentary Under-Secretary posts, and wages costs, which the Chancellor of the Exchequer Winston Churchill claimed would be hard to defend to the opposition. Since he had previously held the post of Secretary of State for the Colonies and was an opponent of a separate Office for Dominion Affairs, Churchill did not agree with Amery's arguments about the over-capacity of his department. He held the surprising opinion that the Dominion agenda could be managed by "two or three carefully selected and experienced officials".[197]

On the basis of the wishes of Prime Minister Baldwin, taking account of Churchill's strong position in government and because of the ambiguity around Amery's draft proposal, the Secretary of State for the Colonies was required to establish the so-called Scott Commission, comprising three top Treasury officials, in order to analyse the situation and propose the best way to reorganise the Office.[198] On 20 February 1925, the Commission sent the Prime Minister a report in which it advised against the first option involving setting up two top representatives (Parliamentary Under-Secretaries) and their permanent Under-Secretaries of State at the new Office. This was because they feared administrative complications, chaos in competencies and the political uncertainty which could arise after every general election. Since no Dominion statesman had recently demanded Colonial Office reorganisation, the opinion was expressed that transformation of the Office should not be rushed, and as such the recommendation was to postpone a final decision until the matter could be thoroughly discussed at the next Imperial Conference.[199] Amery was disappointed with the report and disagreed with its conclusions, especially in regard to the position of the two Permanent Under-Secretaries of State.[200] The position of Secretary of State for the Colonies was also weakened because in contrast to the pre-war period, the overseas prime ministers were not openly demanding any changes in competencies at Dominion Office level; they were "merely" dissatisfied with the level of communication. Nevertheless, Amery considered it essential that a reorganisation be undertaken because he saw in the acts and steps of Canadian Prime Minister Mackenzie King a "purely historical 'complex' about the Colonial Office, they keenly resent the name as a badge of subordination".[201] Undeterred, Amery was determined to implement his plan, even though it was not supported by the Chancellor of the Exchequer Winston Churchill or the Secretary of State for Foreign Affairs Austen Chamberlain, who feared losing control over the Dominions' economic and foreign policies.[202]

In early March 1925, Amery sent his cabinet colleagues an official memorandum in which he proposed taking the Dominion Department out of the Colonial Office and subsequently establishing an Office for Dominion Affairs, as well as an Office for Imperial Affairs, which would be a new institution co-ordinating relations between the Dominions and the mother country. For administrative, personnel, space and financial reasons, he proposed that he should temporarily run both offices, which would be based in the Colonial Office building. Despite the objections raised in internal debates in recent months, he urged the immediate appointment of an additional Parliamentary Under-Secretary to administer solely Dominion affairs, since he thought the current Under-Secretary should focus on the Colonial agenda and co-ordinating emigration and immigration within the Empire. He also planned the naming of another Permanent Under-Secretary of State, who would focus on "political and diplomatic" co-operation with the Dominions.[203] The government met on 18 March and discussed the submitted proposal, which was approved after long debate. The ministers insisted, however, that there would only be one Permanent Under-Secretary of State at the Colonial Office, and the Dominion Office would only have a lower-level official available to it (Deputy Under-Secretary) with direct access to the Secretary.[204]

Amery subsequently sent a personal letter to the Dominion prime ministers informing them of the planned changes at the Colonial Office.[205] Australian Prime Minister Stanley Bruce was pleased by the plan, his New Zealand counterpart William Massey welcomed it and South Africa's General Hertzog described it as a step in the right direction. Canadian Prime Minister Mackenzie King, however, was late in responding.[206] Due to the positive response from Dominion representatives, Amery was not willing to accept a "defeat" and repeatedly attempted to persuade Baldwin that the new Office must have a Permanent Under-Secretary of State and that the lower-status official was insufficient, despite the counter-arguments of Permanent Secretary to the Treasury Sir Norman Fenwick Warren Fisher.[207] In the end, he was successful. On 10 June 1925, he sent overseas statesmen official notice of the establishment of an Office for Dominion Affairs with its own Parliamentary and Permanent Under-Secretaries of State. He also expressed the opinion that this step corresponded to Dominions' current constitutional status, and that it promised the evolution of relations between the, "self-governing partner nations of the British Commonwealth" and the mother country.[208] He subsequently defended the creation of a Dominion Office to members of the House of Commons.[209]

4.4 The Article X, the Geneva Protocol and the Locarno Conference

On the one hand, the League of Nations represented an interesting international organisation for the Dominions, through which Australia, New Zealand and the Union of South Africa became mandate powers on the basis of Article XXII of the Covenant of the League of Nations, while on the other hand membership meant a number of European commitments which, especially for Canada as a neighbour of the United States, resulted only in complications. Excessive focus on the European continent, so-called continentalism, led to fears amongst Ottawa politicians over the real opportunities for pursuing Canada's specific interests compared to Imperial interests.[210] In practice, the Dominions were meant to have, for example, greater commitments towards certain European countries than towards the British Isles.[211] In this regard, Article X of the Covenant of the League of Nations represented a fundamental complication, stating:

> The Members of the League undertake to respect and preserve as against external aggression the territorial integrity and existing political independence of all Members of the League. In case of any such aggression or in case of any threat or danger of such aggression the Council [of the League of Nations] shall advise upon the means by which this obligation shall be fulfilled.[212]

Starting in February 1919, Canadian delegates lodged their objections to this article at the Paris Peace Conference, because they feared military commitments and because they had little inclination for defending disputed territory.[213] They also argued that in the case of Canada, it was unlikely anybody would attack it (originally, the United States was to be a member), and as such they did not understand why they should defend everyone else.[214] As early as during the great internal debates amongst the British Empire delegation on 21 April 1919, Canada made it clear to those present that they would prefer that the article be removed. Since they were alone in their opinion with the other Dominion and British representatives not providing support, they were unable to take any steps to prevent the implementation of the approved Covenant within the peace treaties.[215] Their next opportunity came following the final ratification of the treaties and establishment of the League of Nations in early 1920.[216]

In practice, this was a highly controversial clause which did not suit a number of states (such as Great Britain and the United States), because in reality defending the geographically distant members of the League of Nations was difficult, or even impossible, to achieve. It was nevertheless a well-intentioned article which was designed to cause concern for any aggressor over the outcome of any military intervention by member states, thus discouraging them from attacking, essentially preventing war as one possible way to deal with disputes amongst nations.[217] President Wilson himself saw Article X as the "heart" of the Covenant of the League of Nations.[218] There was also some criticism of the interpretation of certain terms and expressions. For example, in the commentary on this founding document, the term "external" was explained by stating that the League was not going to act like some Holy Alliance as a major player in international relations, following the Vienna Congress which would suppress national or other movements within the boundaries of its member states, except in situations which would involve forcible seizure of power.[219] Another subject of criticism was the extent of the guarantees, which was one of the main arguments why America refused to ratify the Treaty of Versailles, despite all of President Wilson's efforts, which included the Covenant of the League of Nations. Thus, the USA did not become a member,[220] and not only Canada, but also the other autonomous overseas territories and Britain, perceived this as a change in the originally planned function of the newly emerging international organisation promoted by the powers. At once, confidence in its power and determination to prevent attackers from engaging with their neighbours faded. Britain and the Dominion representatives now saw it as another suitable platform in addition to the British Commonwealth of Nations for spreading understanding between nations and promoting good relationships between neighbouring countries.[221]

For these reasons, right from the very first meeting of the Assembly of the League of Nations in November 1920, Canadian representatives sought the complete expungement of Article X of the Covenant[222] which related to those disturbing the territorial integrity of members of the international organisation, as they thought it was overly binding from a military and political perspective, and because it provided extensive guarantees without any limits.[223] At the first meeting of the Assembly, the delegates agreed not to rush, and therefore nominated a special Committee No. 1 under the League Council, whose responsibility was to deal with legal and constitutional matters and which was headed for the British Empire by Arthur James Balfour, later 1st Earl of Balfour. This committee was tasked with investigating all possible options proposed by individual members.[224] Canada was alone in its efforts, since the other member countries in the British Empire did not actively support it.[225] Nevertheless, Canadian representatives did not give up and continued to make their criticism known.[226]

In this regard, Canadian Justice Minister Charles Joseph Doherty, who was Canada's delegate to the League of Nations between 1920 and 1922, submitted an extensive memorandum in which he summarised their objections in regard to the guarantee in the event of external aggression and threat to the territorial integrity of League of Nations member states. Due to the constancy of territorial disputes which often led to war, Doherty opposed the "absolute commitment of mutual defence". He therefore proposed that territorial guarantees apply only to the territorial integrity and political independence of newly created or newly formed states on the basis of the peace treaties and who had responsibility for the new order. Any decision on what way to respect the commitment and defence of territorial integrity and the existing political independence of member states should be implemented was to be made on the basis of thorough consultation with member states, and not merely on the basis of a decision of the permanent and non-permanent members of the Council of the League of Nations.[227] Thus this memorandum built on his previous critical memorandum of February 1919.[228]

At the second meeting of the Assembly of the League of Nations in 1921, a special committee recommended that Doherty's "radical" proposals reducing the power of the League as a notional "mover" of international collective security to abolish the clause not be adopted. Since in contrast to Canada, the general opinion of organisation members was not to annul Article X of the Covenant, committee members proposed the reinterpretation of the clause. Debate at the plenary session resulted in the resolution that another meeting of the Assembly would deal with the problem of amending the article, where its final form would be decided upon.[229] The French delegation, for example, defended Article X and wanted to leave it in its original form. Naturally, smaller member states anxiously followed the debate which could lead to limiting the guarantee of their territorial integrity and political independence. Since they had the majority vote at the Assembly, in contrast to the large powers, any proposal leading to lesser protections for them would not have realistically passed.²³⁰

The third meeting of the Assembly took place in 1922, with Canada represented by a new delegation due to the electoral victory of William Lyon Mackenzie King's Liberals, who no longer sought the annulment of Article X, rather focusing on limiting or determining formal commitment limits for individual member states.²³¹ Of the countries who did not like the wording, the ambitions of Canada's new government to undertake independent diplomatic steps where possible led them to take the initiative, and they decided to submit a new, and more compromising, draft article:

> The members of the League undertake to respect and preserve as against external aggression the territorial integrity and existing political independence of all members of the League. In case of any such aggression or in case of any threat or danger of such aggression, the Council shall advise upon the means by which this obligation shall be fulfilled, taking into account the political and geographical circumstances of each State. The opinion given by the Council in such cases shall be regarded as a matter of the highest importance, and shall be taken into consideration by all members of the League, which shall use their utmost endeavours to conform to the conclusions of the Council, but no member shall be under the obligation to engage in any act of war without the consent of its Parliament, legislature or other representative body.²³²

Canada's proposed amendment was essentially in line with American objections to Article X of the Covenant of the League of Nations.²³³ It was no secret that Ottawa politicians were disappointed that America was not participating, and they hoped a platform could be found where the United States would work closely with the League of Nations.²³⁴ They were also in part responding to the "bitter" experience in September 1922 during the Chanak Crisis when Great Britain had expected an immediate declaration of Canada's willingness to send its troops on the basis of post-war commitments to defend the international demilitarised zone in the Straits; Public opinion had already led Mackenzie King to demand consent be given by the Ottawa parliament before making such a decision. He did not want to be automatically drawn into a war without being able to have a say in the act.²³⁵

Over the course of discussions at the fourth meeting of the Assembly of the League of Nations in September 1923, a special committee of the League Council decided to postpone discussion on amendments to the Article text, due to preparations for the Treaty of Mutual Assistance,²³⁶ which was set up in response to Canada's continuing criticism of the ambiguity of commitments closely linked to the Covenant of the League of Nations' controversial Article X in particular, which dealt with the security guarantee, and naval and military sanctions.[237] In this regard, francophone Canadian politician and new principal delegate to the League of Nations, Sir Jean Lomer Gouin, made a speech in which he stressed the necessity of making a decision on the content of an amended Article X before moving on to other matters. At the very least, he demanded a resolution be voted on which would contain a binding interpretation of the clause for member states of the international organisation. In particular, Ottawa contended that it was not clear what its actual responsibility was and what commitments it had to observe. Many League members considered this proposal to be a concession and compromise made by Canada, as well as a better solution to the controversy around Article X. The British government, for example, preferred an explanatory resolution to an amendment to the article.[238] Furthermore, since debates in recent years had not led to any conclusions, Britain privately admitted that Article X could not be used to force member states into defence commitments.[239]

In a submitted draft resolution at the twelfth plenary session on 24 September 1923, a vote was made more on the moral dimension of commitments than on legal aspects. The draft resolution went as follows:

> It is conformity with the spirit of Article X that, in the event of the Council [of the League of Nations] considering it to be its duty to recommend the application of military measures in consequence of an aggression or danger or threat of aggression, the Council [of the League of Nations] shall be bound to take account, more particularly, of the geographical situation and of the special conditions of each State. It is for the constitutional authorities of each Member to decide, in reference to the obligation of preserving the independence and the integrity of the territory of Members, in what degree the Member is bound to assume to execution of its obligation by employment of its military forces.[240]

France advocated adopting the resolution; while delegates from Persia and Panama were *a priori* opposed, objecting to the weaker power of the clause in the context of the international policy of collective security. The final vote went as follows: Of the 43 present League of Nations member states, only Persia voted against, 13 members abstained and 29 were in support.[241]

Although this approval of the interpreting resolution represented a significant shift from Canada's original demand that the article be annulled, and later that it be reworded, Canada achieved two partial successes on two points. League of Nations member states had accepted Canada's argument that geographic position, which was significant for Canada due to its isolated position on the North American continent, and political situation represented crucial aspects as to whether the member state could take part in intervention or not against an aggressor or threat of attack on another member. Similarly, the reference to the fact that the opinion of constitutional authorities was fundamental in the use of military force, which in Canada's case meant the domestic parliament and government, confirmed that Canada was free to make its own decisions in this regard.[242] One should also note the important fact that when trust in the policy of collective security finally collapsed in 1936, the Scandinavian countries shared similar opinions to those of Canada in 1923.[243]

The wide scope of the League of Nations' agenda, which dealt with commitments arising from the Treaty of Versailles (the Free City of Danzig, Saarland, Eupen and Malmedy), general matters in terms of peace and justice (such as the status of minorities in Poland, Bulgaria, Austria and Greece, disputes between Sweden and Finland over Fasta Åland, and between Poland and Lithuania, etc.),[244] from the beginning strengthened Ottawa's politicians in their fear that sooner or later something would fail to be agreed amicably and Geneva would call on members to provide active assistance in line with Article X in defending the territorial integrity and political independence of member states against external aggression. Canada no longer wanted to automatically join a war just because Britain found itself in one, as had been the case in the past.[245] Now, a maximalist and somewhat extreme interpretation of Article X could mean that when the League was at war, all its members would be at war. The right, or at least some suggestion of an ability, to influence whether Canada would have to intervene or not in the context of an unwillingness to defend territorial situations, in places where they had little interest alongside other Dominions and lands of the British Empire, was a key factor in grasping Canada's position towards Article X of the Covenant of the League of Nations. Yet the Dominion of Canada's position did not automatically mean it would be unwilling to support the League of Nations Council in discussions or steps it took in order to maintain peace. Canada merely sought the right to assess the situation and make its own free decision accordingly. One should also note that in this matter, Canada's position was significantly influenced by the fact that the United States of America had refused to participate in the League of Nations as an international project, something which led many Ottawa politicians to conclude that supporting isolationist principles was the right policy to take. Despite their "justifiable" positions, their policy of annulling or amending Article X of the Covenant ultimately led to a weakening in trust in the international organisation and the willingness of its members to act on the basis of the principle of international collective security.[246]

The importance which Canada assigned the international organisation is also seen in its relationship to the Council of the League of Nations. Despite Canada's perspective on the commitments arising from the Covenant's Article X, its politicians endeavoured to act as "exemplary"

The New Constitutional Status for the Dominions? 207

members who took part in executive bodies. Thanks to the acts of former Prime Minister Sir Robert Borden at the Paris Peace Conference, the Canadian delegate was able to be elected to the Council of the League of Nations as a non-permanent member in 1927. Thus between 1927 and 1930, Canada represented the American continent in the Council alongside Great Britain, which was a permanent member. At the same time, due to its geographic position, it was viewed as a "neutral state". In fact, however, it favoured Anglo-Saxon, or North American positions in issues discussed, balancing out Latin American positions.[247]

Beginning in 1924, the issue of the general relations of Dominions and the mother country with the League of Nations came more to the forefront. Despite the "Canadian campaign" against Article X, many overseas representatives saw membership of the international organisation as a milestone, and tangible proof confirming their new post-war constitutional status in regard to the mother country, and externally in regard to the international community. In the first half of 1924, Dominion and British representatives discussed the draft Treaty of Mutual Assistance, based on the Covenant of the League of Nations, dealing with security guarantees and naval and military sanctions.[248] The British delegate to the League of Nations and one of its "architects", Robert Cecil, anticipated improved Anglo-French relations from it.[249] However, the overseas statesmen saw the proposed vision of collective security as a threat to the Empire, and thus in the end MacDonald's government rejected it in September 1924.[250] From early October 1924 to March 1925, the Protocol for the Pacific Settlement of International Disputes (also the Geneva Protocol) was similarly discussed, something continental European countries placed great hopes in. Implementing principles of arbitration, maintaining collective security and disarmament was designed to restore the League of Nations' faltering spirit. The protocol was designed to provide its signatories not just with security guarantees but also the duty of taking part in any declarations of sanctions against aggressors.[251] Although the Labour government initiated debate on the Protocol, this debate did not end with its collapse in November 1924; rather, it intensified.

Due to the importance of the issue, in December 1924 Britain's new Secretary of State for the Colonies, Leo Amery, originally considered calling a special meeting of the Imperial Conference for March of the following year, which was to look at its position on the Protocol.[252] At the end of December 1924, Canadian Prime Minister William Lyon Mackenzie King informed him that he did not consider the chosen date to be ideal due to the sitting of Canada's parliament, and said Ottawa would welcome it if similar conclusions were made on the Geneva Protocol as on the draft Treaty of Mutual Assistance. His Australian counterpart Stanley Bruce instead said that on this "difficult and delicate matter [the] Empire should have [a] single policy and speak with [a] single voice". The Prime Ministers of Australia, New Zealand, the Union of South Africa and

Newfoundland made similar statements to Mackenzie King, i.e. that time constraints meant they were unable to meet up, and as such it was decided that consultation should take place telegraphically. However, the Canadian Prime Minister had criticised this method of discussing important issues.[253] As such, Amery ensured all reports and memorandum were always sent to him.

In contrast to his Canadian counterpart, Australian Prime Minister Bruce proposed taking a more cautious approach and formulating an alternative political solution in the event of a rejection of the Protocol.[254] New Zealand's Prime Minister Massey considered the document wording to be of poor quality, a threat to domestic jurisdiction in immigration and overall dangerous for the British Empire, and as such he proposed that Britain oppose it.[255] South Africa's General Hertzog did not particularly believe in the League of Nations' international position since the United States, Germany and the Soviet Union were not members, and as such he feared the commitments which would arise from adopting the Geneva Protocol. He preferred to leave the final decision to the Committee of Imperial Defence.[256] The Irish representatives did not recommend adopting the document either.[257] Indian representatives shared the concern of the Dominion statesmen and pointed out that the Protocol was unusable in practice and as such should be limited geographically to just Europe.[258] Although all the Dominion prime ministers supported the League of Nations and shared its ideals, they wanted to avoid the guarantees which would bind them economically, politically and militarily. For these reasons in particular, they did not recommend adopting the Protocol.[259]

Amery's proposal to hold a conference on the Geneva Protocol in London did not get a positive response from Dominion representatives, and Britain had to undertake extensive communication with them. Britain's Colonial Secretary was not an advocate of ratifying the Protocol because he considered it controversial due to extreme isolationist objections and the almost-hostile attitude of the United States.[260] American Secretary of State Charles Evans Hughes even candidly admitted his hope that "the Protocol would die a natural death".[261] From Amery's perspective, there were more disadvantages for the Empire than advantages.[262] London politicians generally were mistrustful of the Protocol, and it might be claimed that there were clearly more opponents than proponents of it. Over the course of February 1925, expert debates were held analysing the impact of security commitments on Imperial foreign policy and defence, not just between cabinet members and their resorts[263] but also within the Committee of Imperial Defence, which even set up a special Sub-Committee[264] headed by Committee Secretary Sir Maurice Hankey and supervised by Lord Balfour at Baldwin's request. On 19 February, the head of the Committee of Imperial Defence, Marquess Curzon, sent the government a final memorandum in which he strongly recommended not adopting the Protocol.[265]

The British government met on 4 March 1925. The ministers assessed all the submitted memoranda, which were not favourable to the Geneva Protocol for political, economic and military reasons, coming to the "logical" conclusion that the League of Nations document could not be adopted even though the previous British Prime Minister, Ramsay MacDonald, had been personally involved in formulating it alongside his French counterpart Édouard Herriot. On 12 March, British Secretary of State for Foreign Affairs Austen Chamberlain informed the League of Nations of this fact on behalf of the Commonwealth.[266] He also expressed his readiness to sign an arrangement between Britain, France, Belgium and Germany in order to guarantee the borders in Western Europe.[267] There were four main reasons for Britain's rejection: (1) the Dominions' negative stance; (2) concerns about possible complications with the United States; (3) an unwillingness to guarantee the territorial arrangements in Central and Eastern Europe, and (4) the deeply rooted aversion of the British Secretary of State for Foreign Affairs to compulsory arbitration.[268]

Considering the course of the Chanak Crisis, the circumstances around the Canadian-American fishing treaty and negotiations in Lausanne, a cursory look might suggest that the Geneva Protocol marked an end to the period in which Britain came up against dissenting opinions from Dominion representatives, and the arrival of Leopold Amery at the Colonial Office marked the beginning of an era of "harmonious" relations between the mother country and the self-governing parts of the Commonwealth. In fact, the opposite was true. By declaring the new British principle of collective security, Chamberlain was setting out on a path which led to the signing of the Locarno Treaties, which shook the common Imperial foreign policy to its core.[269]

Over the course of March 1925, the British government was criticised by European countries for not adopting the Geneva Protocol, and as such, at a meeting on 20 March, it decided to use Germany's January proposal seeking a guarantee of the borders between Germany, Belgium and France as a basis for achieving a pact on European security. It also authorised Secretary of State for the Colonies Amery to inform Dominion prime ministers of the change in foreign policy.[270] However, Britain found itself pressed for time and thus only really superficially informed them rather than properly consulting them of the step,[271] even though former analyses of the Committee for Imperial Defence had implied that the British guarantee in Western Europe was possible only to the extent that the Dominions and India were in concurrence.[272]

Amery, who was a leading opponent of Chamberlain's "new foreign policy course", was sympathetic to the opposition of the Dominions, who feared additional binding economic, political and military commitments.[273] He held isolationist opinions, and as such he was strongly averse to the declared Foreign Office policy. On 11 March 1925, Chamberlain's opponents in the government met with Prime Minister Baldwin.

210   *The New Constitutional Status for the Dominions?*

Permanent Under-Secretary of State at the Foreign Office Sir Eyre Crowe was extremely unflattering in a confidential letter to Chamberlain on Amery's arguments:

> Mr. Amery, as usual, dilated on the impossibility of doing anything, because the Dominions would never agree to anything being done. All that was required was to avoid the danger of any talk of entanglements … I confess I have never heard even Mr. Ramsay MacDonald, in his most woolly-headed pronouncements, talk such utter rubbish as Mr. Amery poured forth.[274]

On 24 March 1925, discussion took place in the House of Commons on Britain's foreign policy, in which Secretary of State for Foreign Affairs Chamberlain defended the government's decision of recent weeks to the Labour opposition. A Conservative member of parliament for West Derbyshire, Edward William Spencer Cavendish, known as the Marquess of Hartington, asked in relation to the rejection of the Geneva Protocol and the announcement of the new foreign policy course, "do the Government intend to call an Imperial Conference or otherwise to take means at once to discuss this question with the Dominions?" He posed this question as he wanted to ensure a fatal mistake was not made if, "we were to enter into obligations without having the fullest consultation and agreement with the Dominions". Prime Minister Baldwin supported Chamberlain and assured the Marquess Hartington in regard to the British government and the Dominions that, "we are, and we shall throughout keep in the closest possible touch with them" and that "it may be possible to conduct negotiations by cable". In regard to the demand that an Imperial Conference be convened, the Prime Minister acknowledged that this would not be possible due to Dominion representatives' time constraints, and as such he would strive to ensure a meeting with their representatives during the autumn meeting of the General Assembly of the League of Nations.[275]

There were "warning signs" in early April 1925 suggesting the Dominions did not entirely agree to the discussions taking place on a European security pact, and that they might reject such a pact.[276] On 6 May, Leopold Amery received an extensive informal telegram from Australian Prime Minister Bruce commenting on the security proposals discussed as a replacement to the Geneva Protocol. He was of the opinion that the British Empire was in an unenviable position because it had rejected the protocol without having any specific counterproposal. He thought the security pact seemed to be an ideal alternative basis for rejecting the Protocol. He considered an agreement between Britain, France and Belgium alone was disadvantageous because public opinion in the mother country and in the overseas self-governing territories was not in favour. He saw the expansion of the arrangement to include Germany as a more logical step, but he was concerned it might all come to an end when it joined the League of Nations, and that it might then become a mere hollow gesture to pacify the French public. Although Bruce accepted ideas of a security arrangement in Western Europe, he doubted it would be effective. The Australian warned Britain to avoid signing a pact without Dominion support. If that were to happen, it would mark a fateful step which "would be a blow at the principle of an Empire foreign policy, and would inevitably lead to a discussion as to what was the position of the self-governing parts of the Empire", since the Dominions would suddenly be in the position they had been in before the First World War broke out. As such, Bruce came to the conclusion that a different alternative should be found to ensure Imperial unity, which would suit all the interested countries. He proposed accepting Germany into the League of Nations as a first step, which would make European security a purely continental issue, with Britain as an island state able to play the role of "honest broker" in subsequent discussions.[277]

Like his Australian counterpart, Canadian Prime Minister Mackenzie King expressed his doubts, declaring in the Ottawa House of Commons that "Canada was not a party to the proposed Security Pact".[278] South Africa's General Smuts also disagreed with implementing a collective security policy.[279] In mid-June 1925, Secretary of State for Dominion Affairs and Secretary of State for the Colonies Amery informed Prime Minister Baldwin and Secretary of State for Foreign Affairs Chamberlain of Bruce's telegram, which Amery said indicated the negative position of the overseas autonomous territories towards Britain's negotiations on the security pact. Since he perceived Bruce's words in the context of complicated Anglo-Dominion relations, and thus he considered it a warning, he assured Chamberlain that he would strive to ensure there was an improvement in the regular sending of reports and method of consultation with overseas territories to ensure Imperial unity was not breached. Finally, he expressed the opinion that he thought it would be useful to hold a limited meeting of the Imperial Conference.[280]

Dominion prime ministers thus received minutes of meetings and summaries of events of the previous day every night, collected in London by Foreign Office officials. On 19 June 1925, Chamberlain responded unusually uncompromisingly to Amery's letter.[281] He rejected the expressed considerations on the necessity of organising a meeting of Dominion representatives in London, and he refused to engage in any discussion on the direction of foreign policy. Britain's Foreign Secretary said of Bruce's thoughts on the "island state" and the continent that,

> all our history shows [that] the Channel and the Channel ports have a vital interest for us. Nay, more. It shows how difficult it is for a country situated within twenty miles of the coast of the Continent of Europe to remain untouched by any great conflict [that] breaks out

here. ... If we withdraw from Europe, I say without hesitation that the chance of permanent peace is gone.[282]

France and Belgium's eastern borders were now to be in Britain's vital interests, just as the ports in the English Channel had been in the past. The defence of the British Isles was also to be of equal Imperial importance as the protection awarded Australia against invasion, and the guarding of Canada's borders.[283] Chamberlain thus judged that, "if the Dominions would admit that Britain's defence was an imperial interest, then they must also understand that the first line of that defence was now on the Rhine".[284]

At the end of June 1925, Austen Chamberlain informed members of parliament of the course of negotiations on the Locarno pact, which was now taking starting to take form. Conservative member of parliament and naval officer Carlyon Bellairs warned the government in regard to Britain's European engagement that

> if one of our great Dominions objects, I think you are working towards the disunion of the Empire, if you go in without that Dominion. That, to my mind, is absolutely vital. The alliance of the nations of the British Commonwealth is infinitely more important to us than any Pact.[285]

Over the course of negotiations on a security agreement, Britain's Foreign Office gave only the overseas governments the main information through the Dominion Office. The Dominions had expected to be consulted, but this did not occur in reality due to the marked correspondence with European partners. The Foreign Office did not perceive this method of communication as breaching its March 1925 commitment that Dominion representatives would be duly consulted on aspects of Imperial foreign policy.[286]

Labour member of parliament Thomas Shaw asked Chamberlain in the context of the debate, "what was the position of our Colonies and Dominions with regard to this Pact? Have they been in any way consulted, and, if so, what are their answers?" Britain's Secretary of State for Foreign Affairs confirmed that

> the Dominions have been kept fully informed of all the proceedings of His Majesty's Government. With the exception of New Zealand, which has expressed its complete confidence in the policy of His Majesty's Government, and its readiness to leave the decision in their hands, they have not yet declared themselves.

He also stressed that no Dominion government could accept any commitments if these were not approved by its domestic parliament.[287]

The New Constitutional Status for the Dominions? 213

Chamberlain neglected to mention, however, that the Foreign Office could ask the Dominions to take a particular position on the security pact being discussed. Thus, he indirectly hinted at the future content of Article IX of the Treaty of Locarno, which imposed no obligations upon the Dominions or India unless they themselves agreed to accept such obligations. Britain believed that "New Zealand and Australia were standing by, waiting for the time to come in [Security Pact]; Canada, South Africa and the Irish Free State were standing far back with their faces turned away from any commitment in Europe".[288]

At a meeting of the Committee of Imperial Defence on 1 July 1925, the Foreign Secretary declared that, "the Dominions shall have the opportunity to freely choose whether to sign the document or not".[289] Chamberlain was of the opinion that since it was not possible to convene an Imperial Conference, to avoid any differences of opinion and misunderstandings, "all that we can do is to leave to the Dominions their full liberty of action".[290] This step also marked a breach of the previous common Imperial policy doctrine, and as such in this regard the Foreign Office came to the conclusion that according to international, British and domestic law there was not obligation on the Dominions to assist the mother country in the event of war; there was rather merely a moral obligation.[291] In mid-July, rumours about the negotiations underway appeared, stating that in future the former German colonies might be returned to them. The Dominions strongly objected to any such actions.[292]

The method of communication during debates on the Pact of Locarno and the presentation of foreign policy to Dominions "suited" Canadian Prime Minister Mackenzie King, who did not have to publicly admit what position on the security pact and British collective security policy Canada took until December 1925 when the Locarno Treaties were to be signed.[293] On 6 July of that year, Amery received the Union of South Africa's position, which anticipated not accepting any commitments and not becoming party to the treaties.[294] Australian and New Zealand politicians took a different position, as advocators of a common Imperial policy, as such willing to make concessions to the mother country by adopting the treaty arrangements.[295] Irish representatives exploited the circumstances surrounding the Pact of Locarno and decided to take a different approach to the mother country, and as such did not hesitate to express their criticism of the concluded agreement.[296]

At the end of August 1925, Britain, France and Germany agreed on the final proposal for the pact which was to guarantee the borders between Germany and France and between Germany and Belgium.[297] A conference was held from 5 to 16 October in Locarno, Switzerland, at which British, French, German, Belgian and Italian delegates discussed the security of Germany's western border and sought to find a solution to its eastern border too.[298] To some degree, the conference was similar to discussions in Lausanne, since similarly the delegates discussed a geographically defined agenda; the Dominions were not represented separately. Although Britain had promised to consult the Dominions on everything, in fact it only sent them reports *ad informandum*.[299] It was decided once the conference had ended that the official signature of the Locarno Treaties would take place on 1 December 1925 in London.[300]

On 14 November 1925, Amery sent government members a proposed telegram to Dominion prime ministers and a memorandum in which he analysed the positions of the Dominions towards the Locarno Treaty, as he was considering beginning the ratification process while also calling on the overseas representatives to join the pact in line with Article IX. He also needed to summarise current official information and any indirect suggestions of what position the Dominion statesmen would take. In a 6 July telegram, the Dominions Secretary stated he thought that the South Africans would be against and would not take on any responsibilities, while he thought New Zealand would not have any objections to taking on the agreed commitments.[301] Looking at Canada, he noted the unofficial message from its politicians – Liberal leader William Lyon Mackenzie King and his Conservative rival Arthur Meighen – of 27 October 1925 in the *Morning Post*, in which they both concurred that no request for stating their position had yet been received and that the complicated domestic political situation following the autumn general election in which no party had acquired a parliamentary majority meant that it was not the right time for looking at the controversies around the treaty clauses.[302] Canada's advisor on external relations, Professor Oscar Skelton and his predecessor Loring Christie viewed the Locarno Pact with merciless "nationalist logic". The issue of continental security guarantees would always be a delicate matter for traditional common Imperial diplomacy. Skelton and Christie held the opinion that by accepting such long-term strategic commitments, Britain would be undermining Imperial unity, which they thought would justify Canada's attempt at having the opportunity to pursue an independent foreign policy, which could sometimes be opposed to some of the mother country's actions.[303]

In terms of the Commonwealth of Australia, Amery pointed out that Prime Minister Bruce was not *a priori* rejecting joining the security pact, but his final position was conditional upon receiving consent from the domestic parliament.[304] Irish Prime Minister Cosgrave wanted to use the situation to reject the treaty arrangements so he could demonstrate Irish independence of the mother country to Britain and his domestic opponents.[305] Britain's Secretary of State for Dominion Affairs saw involvement by the Dominions and India as important, and as such proposed that conditions of the agreement be discussed with them at the Imperial Conference in the wider context of general defence and foreign policy.[306]

Concerns of the Dominions' response were justified. On 12 October 1925, the *Times* published the position of South Africa's General Smuts who, although no longer Prime Minister, was still taken seriously by

British and Dominion politicians, since his positions often reflected the actual opinions of the overseas self-governing territories. Smuts criticised the Pact of Locarno and considered signing it a foreign policy error; he thought Imperial foreign policy should not be automatically equated with Great Britain's foreign policy. He doubted the Dominions would accept the agreement. He strongly warned British politicians that "the day may come where the Dominions feel they have little in common with such a policy and they will choose to pursue their own foreign policy in their own interests".[307] At the end of October, Smuts sent Chamberlain a letter in which he congratulated him on his personal involvement in the "brilliant success of the Locarno Conference" and "for the Empire too the Pact will become a new departure". He also shared his concerns that "the Dominions will keep out of this Pact and will look upon this as a precedent to disinterest themselves in future more and more in the foreign policy of Great Britain".[308]

As a precaution, Amery asked Chamberlain whether he had any objections to his proposed telegram, memorandum and recommendations in regard to public speeches on collective security of 14 November; the Secretary of State for Foreign Affairs agreed for the most part with the submitted document.[309] Four days later, the British government met, looked at the document and approved sending the proposed telegram wording to Dominion statesmen. The Secretary of State for Foreign Affairs was assigned the task at the expected parliamentary debate of defending the general policy of His Majesty's Government discussing Imperial aspects of European security with the Dominions at the first opportunity. Amery subsequently sent a telegram to the overseas representatives informing them that the ratification process had begun in Westminster and calling upon them to adopt the pact in accordance with Article IX of the Treaties of Locarno. He also declared his willingness to discuss all aspects of the matter at the next Imperial Conference.[310]

That same day, 18 November 1925, a debate was held in Britain's House of Commons on the points of the proposed agreement. The Secretary of State for Foreign Affairs explained the treaty's clauses and returned to the issue of Dominion representatives not being involved in the formation of the pact. Chamberlain was sorry that circumstances had not allowed the Dominions and India to take part in all consultations and meetings and that they did not always receive detailed information on time. He also reiterated the conclusions of the government's morning session and pointed out that personal discussion with Dominion and Indian representatives on the level of guarantees would take place at the next Imperial Conference.[311]

It wasn't just Dominion representatives who had doubts over the level of commitments accepted; so did British Liberal and Labour members of parliament. Labour leader James Ramsay MacDonald was critical of Chamberlain's statement. He thought that following the failure of the Geneva Protocol, Baldwin's government had plenty of time and the adopted Imperial foreign policy course was disastrous. He also doubted whether it was right from a constitutional perspective to sign something which did not commit the Dominions to anything, in contrast to Britain itself. Liberal member of parliament David Lloyd George viewed the situation differently. Like MacDonald, he was critical of the government's approach to consultation with overseas representatives, whom he saw as equal partners to Britain in the implantation of Imperial foreign policy following the First World War. He thus believed that the Dominions would adopt the pact in the end;[312] the Dominions, however, took an uncompromising position.[313] Conservative member of parliament Sir Percy Angier Hurd was one of those who defended government policy on communication with the self-governing parts of the Empire. In assessing the statements of Australian, Canadian and South African politicians, he concluded that with the exception of New Zealand, the Dominions had not expressed much willingness to join the Pact of Locarno, considering domestic political and economic matters more important than continental security, something which mainly affected Great Britain itself.[314]

The Secretary of State for Dominion Affairs was disappointed with all the problems surrounding the Rhineland guarantee pact. On 24 November he sent Smuts a letter in which he stressed that "the rejection of the Protocol must involve some alternativ [sic] constructive proposals to promote European peace". He was of the opinion that the utmost had been done to ensure the Dominions' positive response; every day they had been informed of the course of discussions on the security agreement. He did admit that the system of consultation as set up and implemented at the 1919 Paris Peace Conference and meetings on naval disarmament in Washington at the turn of 1921 and 1922 had worked. He acknowledged that for Lausanne, their "imperfection" had been confirmed. He came to the conclusion that the Locarno discussions were not within the "traditional" concept of an international conference due to the large number of informal debates and discussions, and as such he felt that the chosen method for informing the Dominions was the best that could be achieved at the time to ensure a common Imperial policy. He thought it was best to consult fully on all matters prior to the ratification process at the Imperial Conference which was to take place, in contrast to conferences in prior periods, regularly like the General Assembly of the League of Nations.[315]

Although the House of Commons eventually approved the treaty and it came into force in December, the November discussion confirmed the long-term trend begun with the 1922 Chanak Crisis, i.e. that Dominion and British representatives frequently disagreed in matters which appeared to be subjects of shared interest. As such, a common Imperial foreign policy could not be effectively pursued and thoroughly implemented. That being the case, British politicians placed their hopes on the

1926 Imperial Conference, where they anticipated Imperial unity could be restored, having been shaken by the crises and disagreements between 1922 and 1925.

Notes

1 Mansergh, Nicholas, *The Commonwealth Experience: From British to Multiracial Commonwealth*, Vol. 2, London: Macmillan, 1982, 3.
2 Hall, Hessel Duncan, *Commonwealth: A History of the British Commonwealth of Nations*, London: Von Nostrand Reinhold Co, 1971, 476.
3 Hind, Joseph Winton, *Lloyd George and the Turkish Question: An Examination of Lloyd George's Turkish Policy, 1918–1922*, MA Thesis, Vancouver: The University of British Columbia, 1978, 78–80; Ross, Angus, "Reluctant Dominion or Dutiful Daughter? New Zealand and the Commonwealth in the Inter-War Years", *Journal of Commonwealth Political Studies* 10, No. 1, 1972, 31–32; Willmott, H. P., *The Last Century of Sea Power: From Port Arthur to Chanak, 1894–1922*, Vol. 1, Bloomington: Indiana University Press, 2009, 333.
4 TNA, CAB 32/2, E. 7th Meeting, Stenographic Notes of a Meeting of Representatives of the United Kingdom, the Dominions and India, 27 June 1921, 1–14 [44–51].
5 See more TNA, CAB 23/39/38, Conference No. 137: Notes of Conference held at Churt, 11 September 1922, 247–249.
6 Secretary of State for the Colonies, Winston Churchill, in particular did not agree with the Prime Minister's "unilateral" support for Greeks, because he thought the British Empire's Middle East policy should mainly focus on matters relating to the British mandates in Palestine and Mesopotamia. Morgan, Kenneth O., *Consensus and Disunity: The Lloyd George Coalition Government 1918–1922*, Oxford: Oxford University Press, 197, 322; Wigley, Philip, *Canada and the Transition to Commonwealth: British-Canadian Relations, 1917–1926*, Cambridge: Cambridge University Press, 1977, 161.
7 Cf. Sales, Peter M., "W. M. Hughes and the Chanak Crisis of 1922", *Australian Journal of History and Politics* 17, No. 3, 1971, 392–393; TNA, CAB 23/31/2, Cabinet 49 (22), Conclusions of a Meeting of the Cabinet, Downing Street, 15 September 1922, 24–58; TNA, CAB 23/39/40, Minutes of a Conference of Ministers, Downing Street, 18 September 1922, 265–279.
8 TNA, CAB 24/138/1, C. P. 4200, Cabinet: The Turco-Greek Situation: Co-operation of Dominions, 15 September 1922, 484; TNA, CO 886/10/1, 46342/S, The Secretary of State to the Governors-General, 15 September 1922, Doc. No. 304, 231–232.
9 Cf. Hall, *Commonwealth*, 482, 486–488; *The Times*, 18 September 1922, Dawson, Robert MacGregor (Ed.), *The Development of Dominion Status, 1900–1936*, London: Frank Cass & Co, 1965, 234.
10 TNA, CAB 24/138/94, C. P. 4195, Cabinet: The Turco-Greek Situation: Co-operation of Dominions, 16 September 1922, 476.
11 Allin, Caphas Daniel, "International Status of the British Dominions", *The American Political Science Review* 17, No. 4, 1923, 617–619; TNA, CO 886/10/1, 46342/S, Union of South Africa: The Secretary of State to the Governor-General, 17 September 1922, Doc. No. 306, 232–233; TNA, CO 886/10/1, 46342/S, Newfoundland: The Secretary of State to the Acting Governor, 17 September 1922, Doc. No. 307, 233.

218 *The New Constitutional Status for the Dominions?*

12 Dawson, Robert MacGregor, *William Lyon Mackenzie King: A Political Biography: 1874–1923*, Vol. 1, London: Methuen, 1958, 409; *Montreal Gazette*, 18 September 1922, in: Dawson, *The Development*, 234–235.
13 TNA, CO 886/10/1, 46517/S, Canada: The Governor-General to the Secretary of State, 17 September 1922, Doc. No. 308, 233.
14 TNA, CO 886/10/1, 46517/S, Canada: The Secretary of State to the Governor-General, 18 September 1922, Doc. No. 309, 234.
15 Dawson, *William*, 409; *CPD, HoC*, 1 February 1923, 30–33, in: Dawson, *The Development*, 239–244; Walder, David, *The Chanak Affair*, London: Hutchinson, 1969, 215–216.
16 Cf. Sifton to Dafoe, 18 September 1922, in: Cook, Ramsey (Ed.), *The Dafoe-Sifton Correspondence, 1919–1927*, Winnipeg: D. W. Friesen & Sons, 1966, 121–122; Sifton to Dafoe, 8 October 1922, in: Cook, *The Dafoe-Sifton*, 122–124; TNA, CO 886/10/1, 46642/S, Canada: The Governor-General to the Secretary of State, 18 September 1922, Doc. No. 313, 236.
17 Cf. TNA, CAB 23/39/41, Minutes of a Conference of Ministers, Downing Street, 19 September 1922, 288–289; TNA, CO 886/10/1, 46918/S, Canada: The Secretary of State to the Governor-General, 19 September 1922, Doc. No. 316, 237.
18 Hall, *Commonwealth*, 490.
19 TNA, CO 886/10/1, 46918/S, The Secretary of State to the Governors-General and Acting Governor, 20 September 1922, Doc. No. 317, 237–238.
20 Sales, 394–395.
21 Hall, *Commonwealth*, 491.
22 Arnold-Forster, Mark, "Chanak Rocks the Empire: The Anger of Billy Hughes", *The Round Table* 58, No. 230, 1968, 172–174; TNA, CO 886/10/1, 46974/S, Commonwealth of Australia: The Governor-General to the Secretary of State, 20 September 1922, Doc. No. 318, 238–241.
23 Dawson, *William*, 411–412; TNA, CO 886/10/1, 472594/S, Canada: The Governor-General to the Secretary of State, 21 September 1922, Doc. No. 322, 242.
24 Sales, 398–399.
25 *APD, Senate*, No. 38, 20 September 1922, 2396–2398.
26 Sales, 399–400.
27 Cf. Ferris, John, "'Far Too Dangerous a Gamble'? British Intelligence and Policy during the Chanak Crisis, September-October 1922", *Diplomacy and Statecraft* 14, No. 2, 2003, 142; TNA, CO 886/10/1, 48876/S, Commonwealth of Australia: The Governor-General to the Secretary of State, 30 September, 1922, Doc. No. 339, 250.
28 See TNA, CO 537/1035, GG 30395, Commonwealth Channels of Communication, March–May 1922, 1–15.
29 TNA, CO 886/10/1, 48878/S, The Secretary of State to the Governors-General, 30 September 1922, Doc. No. 341, 250–251.
30 Edwards, Cecil, *Bruce of Melbourne: Man of Two World*, London: Heinemann, 1965, 86; Sales, 401; TNA, CO 886/10/4, D. 54369, Commonwealth of Australia: The Governor-General to the Secretary of State, 20 November 1924, Doc. No. 113, 75.
31 TNA, CO 886/10/1, 54323/S, Commonwealth of Australia: The Governor-General to the Secretary of State, 2 November 1922, Doc. No. 359, 259–260.
32 TNA, CO 886/10/1, 46974/S, Commonwealth of Australia: The Governor-General to the Secretary of State, 20 September 1922, Doc. No. 318, 238–241.
33 Dawson, *William*, 407–416; Glazebrook, George Parkin de Twenebroker, *A History of Canadian External Relations*, London: Oxford University Press, 1950, 358–359; Wigley, *Canada*, 166.

34 Montreal Gazette, 23 September 1922, Dawson, The Development, 236–237.
35 Hall, Commonwealth, 495; McIntyre, W. David, The Commonwealth of Nations: Origins and Impact, 1869–1971, Minneapolis: University of Minnesota Press, 1977, 186.
36 Carter, Gwendolen Margaret, The British Commonwealth and International Security: The Role of the Dominions 1919–1939, Toronto: Ryerson Press, 1947, 89.
37 Hillmer, Norman, "O. D. Skelton and the North American Mind", International Journal 60, No. 1, 2004/2005, 100.
38 TNA, CAB 23/39/54, Minutes of a Conference of Ministers, Downing Street, 29 September 1922, 419–448.
39 Wigley, Canada, 104.
40 John W. Dafoe, Manitoba Free Press, 3 August 1925, in: Dawson, The Development, 236–237.
41 Šubrt, Martin, "Kanada a Chanacká krize", Historica Olomucensia 56, 2019, 208–209.
42 The Secretary of State for the Colonies to the Governor-General of Canada, 27 October 1922, in: Cmd. 2146, Correspondence with Canadian Government on the Subject of the Peace Settlement with Turkey, London: HMSO, 1924, Doc. No. 1, 3–4; TNA, CAB 24/139/98, C. P. 4298, The Dominions and the Lausanne Conference: The Secretary of State for the Colonies to the Governors-General of Canada, Australia, New Zealand and the Union of South Africa, 27 October 1922, 681; TNA, CO 886/10/1, 53440/S, The Secretary of State to the Governors-General, 27 October 1922, Doc. No. 355, 256.
43 TNA, CO 886/10/1, 53440/S, The Secretary of State to the Governors-General, 27 October 1922, Doc. No. 356, 257.
44 TNA, CAB 24/139/98, C. P. 4298, Governor-General [Arthur Frederick] of the Union of South Africa to the Secretary of State for Colonies, 31 October 1922, 681–682.
45 Cf. CUL, SP, Add MS 7917, Vol. 1, Smuts to Mr. and Mrs. Gillet, Pretoria, 20 December 1922, Doc. No. 342, 253; CUL, SP, Add MS 7917, Vol. 1, Smuts to Mr. and Mrs. Gillet, Pretoria, 2 January 1923, Doc. No. 345, 255.
46 TNA, CAB 24/139/98, C. P. 4298, Governor-General of the Commonwealth of Australia to the Secretary of State for Colonies, 2 November 1922, 682.
47 TNA, CO 886/10/1, 54553/S, Commonwealth of Australia: The Governor-General to the Secretary of State for the Colonies, 2 November 1922, Doc. No. 359, 259–260.
48 TNA, CAB 24/139/98, C. P. 4298, Governor-General of the Commonwealth of Australia to the Secretary of State for Colonies, 2 November 1922, 682.
49 APD, HoR, No. 30, 24 July 1923, 1183.
50 Hall, Commonwealth, 500.
51 Beloff, Max, Imperial Sunset: Dream of Commonwealth, Vol. 2, London: Macmillan, 1989, 82; Hall, Commonwealth, 500; Lloyd, C. M., "Canada and Lausanne", New Statesman 23, No. 582, 14 June 1924, 276; Mansergh, Nicholas, Survey of British Commonwealth Affairs: Problems of External Policy 1931–1939, London: Oxford University Press, 1952, 62–63; Wrench, John Evelyn, "Mr. Mackenzie King and Lausanne", Spectator 132, No. 5008, 21 June 1924, 993.
52 Gibson, James A., "Mr. Mackenzie King and Canadian Autonomy, 1921–1946", Report of the Annual Meeting of the Canadian Historical Association/Rapports annuels de la Société historique du Canada 30, No. 1, 1951, 13.

53 Wigley, *Canada*, 172.
54 Dawson, *William*, 423; Stacey, Charles Perry, *Canada and the Age of Conflict: A History of Canadian External Policies: 1921–1948: The Mackenzie King Era*, Vol. 2, Toronto: University of Toronto Press, 1981, 37.
55 Wigley, *Canada*, 169–170.
56 Graham, Roger, *Arthur Meighen: A Biography: And Fortune Fled*, Vol. 2, Toronto: Clarke Irwin and Co, 1963, 214–215.
57 The Governor-General of Canada to the Secretary of State for the Colonies, 1 November 1922, in: Cmd. 2146, Doc. No. 2, 4; TNA, CO 886/10/1, 54323/S, Canada: The Governor-General to the Secretary of State for the Colonies, 1 November 1922, Doc. No. 358, 258.
58 Hancock, William Keith, Sir, *Survey of British Commonwealth Affairs: Problems of Nationality 1918–1936*, Vol. 1, London: Oxford University Press, 1937, 254–255.
59 TNA, CO 886/10/1, 54323/S, Canada: The Secretary of State for the Colonies to the Governor-General, 16 November 1922, Doc. No. 362, 262.
60 The Governor-General of Canada to the Secretary of State for the Colonies, 25 November 1922, in: Cmd. 2146, Doc. No. 4, 5; TNA, CO 886/10/1, 58410/S, Canada: The Governor-General to the Secretary of State for the Colonies, 25 November 1922, Doc. No. 368, 266.
61 TNA, CO 886/10/1, 58410/S, Canada: The Secretary of State for the Colonies to the Governor-General, 8 December 1922, Doc. No. 369, 266.
62 Hall, *Commonwealth*, 502.
63 The Governor-General of Canada to the Secretary of State for the Colonies, 31 December 1922, in: Cmd. 2146, Doc. No. 6, 7–8.
64 TNA, CO 886/10/2, 228/S, Canada: The Governor-General to the Secretary of State for the Colonies, 1 January 1923, Doc. No. 395, 262.
65 The Secretary of State for the Colonies to the Governor-General of Canada, 27 January 1923, in: Cmd. 2146, Doc. No. 7, 8.
66 TNA, CO 886/10/2, 3134, The Secretary of State for the Colonies to the Governors-General, 27 January 1923, Doc. No. 396, 262–263; TNA, CO 886/10/2, 3134, Union of South Africa: The Secretary of State for the Colonies to the Governor-General, 27 January 1923, Doc. No. 397, 263.
67 Cf. TNA, CO 886/10/2, 5101, New Zealand: The Governor-General to the Secretary of State for the Colonies, 29 January 1923, Doc. No. 399, 264; TNA, CO 886/10/2, 5101, Commonwealth of Australia: The Governor-General to the Secretary of State for the Colonies, 2 February 1923, Doc. No. 401, 264.
68 Cf. CUL, SP, Add MS 7917, Vol. 2, Smuts to A. Gillet, Groote Schuur, Rondebosch, 9 February 1923, Doc. No. 349, 261; TNA, CO 886/10/2, 5101, Union of South Africa: The Governor-General to the Secretary of State for the Colonies, 1 February 1923, Doc. No. 400, 264; TNA, CO 886/10/2, 5101, Union of South Africa: The Governor-General to the Secretary of State for the Colonies, 7 February 1923, Doc. No. 404, 265.
69 See Cmd. 1814, *Turkey No. 1 (1923): Lausanne Conference on Near Eastern Affairs 1922–1923: Records of Proceedings and Draft Terms of Peace*, London 1923, 684–861; Cmd. 1929, *Treaty Series No. 16 (1923): Treaty of Peace with Turkey, and Other Instruments Signed at Lausanne on July 24, 1923, Together with Agreements between Greece and Turkey Signed on January 30, 1923, and Subsidiary Documents Forming Part of the Turkish Peace Settlement*, London: HMSO, 1923.
70 Hall, *Commonwealth*, 502–503.
71 Cf. Colonial Secretary to Governor General, London, 22 February 1924, in: *DCER*, Vol. 3, Doc. No. 136, 93–94; The Secretary of State for the Colonies

to the Governor-General of Canada, 22 February 1924, in: Cmd. 2146, Doc. No. 10, 9–10; The Secretary of State for the Colonies to the Governor-General of Canada, 21 March 1924, in: Cmd. 2146, Doc. No. 11, 10.
72 Governor General to Colonial Secretary, Ottawa, 24 March 1924, in: *DCER*, Vol. 3, Doc. No. 137, 94.
73 Cf. Hall, *Commonwealth*, 504; Stacey, Vol. 2, 40.
74 Governor General to Colonial Secretary, Ottawa, 3 April 1924, in: *DCER*, Vol. 3, Doc. No. 138, 94–97.
75 Cf. Colonial Secretary to Governor General, London, 7 April 1924, in: *DCER*, Vol. 3, Doc. No. 139, 97; Governor General to Colonial Secretary, Ottawa, 7 April 1924, in: *DCER*, Vol. 3, Doc. No. 140, 97; Stacey, Vol. 2, 40–41; TNA, CO 886/10/2, 228/S, Canada: The Governor-General to the Secretary of State for the Colonies, 1 January 1923, Doc. No. 395, 262.
76 Governor General to Colonial Secretary, Ottawa, 7 April 1924, in: *DCER*, Vol. 3, Doc. No. 142, 98; Governor General to Colonial Secretary, Ottawa, 10 April 1924, in: *DCER*, Vol. 3, Doc. No. 143, 98–99; Colonial Secretary to Governor General, London, 12 April 1924, in: *DCER*, Vol. 3, Doc. No. 144, 99–100; Governor General to Colonial Secretary, Ottawa, 23 April 1924, in: *DCER*, Vol. 3, Doc. No. 145, 101–102; Neatby, H. Blair, *William Lyon Mackenzie King: 1924–1932: The Lonely Heights*, Vol. 2, London: Methuen & Co, 1963, 34.
77 *CPD, HoC*, 9 June 1924, 2923–2934, Dawson, *The Development*, 258–269.
78 Allin, Caphas Daniel, "Canada's Treaty Making Power", *Michigan Law Review* 24, No. 3, 1926, 275.
79 Stacey, Vol. 2, 42.
80 Stevenson, J. A., "Canada and Downing Street", *Foreign Affairs: An American Quarterly Review* 3, No. 1/4, 1924–1925, 142.
81 Neatby, *William*, 34.
82 Dewey, Alexander Gordon, *The Dominion and Diplomacy: The Canadian Contribution*, Vol. 2, London: Longmans, Green & Co, 1929, 147–166.
83 Hall, *Commonwealth*, 500.
84 Wigley, *Canada*, 173.
85 Ollivier, Maurice (Ed.), *The Colonial and Imperial Conferences from 1887 to 1937*, Vol. 1, Ottawa: Queen's Printer, 1954, 187.
86 For example, Canadian representatives were unable to take part in negotiations on extending the Elgin-Marcy (Canadian-American) Reciprocity Treaty in 1864. Stevenson, J. A., "Canada's Halibut Treaty", *New Statesman* 21, No. 524, 28 April 1923, 72.
87 Lord Rosebery, "Commerce and Empire", Leeds, 11 October 1888, in: Beeman, Neville (Ed.), *Lord Rosebery's Speeches (1874–1896)*, London: N. Beeman, 1896, 51–52.
88 Tupper, C. Hibbert, "Treaty-Making Powers of the Dominions", *Journal of the Society of Comparative Legislation* 17, New Series, No. 1/2, 1917, 5–7.
89 Martin, Chester, *Empire and Commonwealth: Studies in Governance and Self-Government in Canada*, London: Longmans, Green, and Co, 1929, 337–338.
90 TNA, CAB 32/8, E ("B" Series) 5, Appendix: Commercial Negotiations with Regard to the Dominions, March 1911, 10 [13].
91 Keith, Arthur Berriedale, *The Governments of the British Empire*, London: Macmillan & Co, 1935, 125.
92 Mackenzie, N. A. M., "The Treaty Making Power in Canada", *The American Journal of International Law* 19, No. 3, 1925, 492; The Marquis of Ripon to the Governor-General of Canada, etc., Downing Street, 28 June 1895, in: Kennedy, William Paul McClure (Ed.), *Statutes, Treaties and Documents of*

the Canadian Constitution 1713–1929, 2nd Ed., Toronto: Oxford University Press, 1930, [Doc. No.] 188, 680–693.
93 Granatstein, J. L. – Hillmer, Norman, *For Better or for Worse: Canada and the United States to the 1990s*, Toronto: Copp Clark Pitman, 1991, 43–44; Wrong, George M., "The Evolution of the Foreign Relations of Canada", *The Canadian Historical Review* 5, No. 3, 1925, 9–11.
94 See Keith, Arthur Berriedale, *Imperial Unity and the Dominions*, Oxford: Clarendon Press, 1916, 269–277.
95 On the significance of Pacific halibut fishing, see Adams, John Q., "The Pacific Coast Halibut Fishery", *Economic Geography* 11, No. 3, 1935, 247–257.
96 Draft Treaty between the United States of America and Great Britain Concerning Port Privileges of Fishing Vessels, Lobster Fishing, Halibut Fishing, and Tariff on Fresh Fish, 24 October 1919, in: *DCER*, Vol. 3, Encl. Doc. No. 589, 624–628.
97 Cf. Ambassador in United States [Grey] to Governor General [Devonshire], Washington, 2 October 1919, in: *DCER*, Vol. 3, Doc. No. 590, 622; Wigley, *Canada*, 175.
98 Ambassador in United States [Grey] to Governor General [Devonshire], Washington, 30 December 1919, in: *DCER*, Vol. 3, Doc. No. 593, 628–629.
99 Wigley, *Canada*, 175.
100 The British Ambassador (Geddes) to the Secretary of State [C. E. Hughes], Washington, 16 March 1922, in: *FRUS*, 1922, Vol. 1, 669–670.
101 From His Majesty's Ambassador at Washington to the Governor-General, Washington, 12 February 1923, in: Dawson, *The Development*, 254; TNA, CO 886/10/2, 4825, Foreign Office to Colonial Office, 24 January 1923, Encl. to Doc. No. 440, 303.
102 TNA, CO 886/10/2, 3157, Canada: The Governor-General to the Secretary of State, 17 January 1923, Doc. No. 438, 302.
103 TNA, CO 886/10/2, 3157, Colonial Office to Foreign Office, 30 January 1923, Doc. No. 441, 304.
104 TNA, CO 886/10/2, 7583, Foreign Office to Colonial Office, 10 February 1923, Doc. No. 442, 304; Wigley, *Canada*, 176.
105 The issue of Canada's mission in Washington had already been looked at in 1920. Canada had received the position of permanent member at the British Embassy, but its unclear status meant that the post was never filled. TNA, CO 886/10/2, 9411, Canada: The Governor-General to the Secretary of State, 21 February 1923, Doc. No. 447, 306; Wigley, Philip, "Whitehall and the 1923 Imperial Conference", *The Journal of Imperial and Commonwealth History* 1, No. 2, 1973, 225.
106 Dewey, Vol. 2, 138; TNA, CO 886/10/2, 10738, Canada: The Governor-General to the Secretary of State, 28 February 1923, Doc. No. 449, 307.
107 Cf. TNA, CO 886/10/2, 11044, Foreign Office to Sir A. Geddes (Washington), 1 March 1923, Doc. No. 450, 308; TNA, CO 886/10/2, 11044, Foreign Office to Sir A. Geddes (Washington), 1 March 1923, Doc. No. 452, 308; TNA, CO 886/10/2, 11044, 12272, Sir A. Geddes (Washington) to Foreign Office, 2 March 1923, Doc. No. 454, 309.
108 Convention between the United States of America and Great Britain, Signed at Washington, 2 March 1923, in: *FRUS*, 1923, Vol. 1, 468–470.
109 TNA, CO 886/10/2, 11898, House of Commons: Fishery Treaty, Canada and United States, 8 March 1923, Doc. No. 455, 309.
110 See more Secretary [Sladen], Governor General [Byng], to Under-Secretary of State for External Affairs [Pope], Ottawa, 17 March 1923, in: *DCER*, Vol. 3, Encl. Doc. No. 630, 655; Memorandum from Under-Secretary of State

The New Constitutional Status for the Dominions? 223

for External Affairs [Pope] to Prime Minister [Mackenzie King] Ottawa, 20 March 1923, in: *DCER*, Vol. 3, Doc. No. 631, 655–656; Prime Minister [Mackenzie King] to Governor General [Byng], Ottawa, 21 March 1923, in: *DCER*, Vol. 3, Doc. No. 633, 657–659.

111 For more on this issue see Memorandum from Secretary [Sladen], Governor General [Byng], to Prime Minister [Mackenzie King], Ottawa, 12 April 1923, in: *DCER*, Vol. 3, Doc. No. 635, 660–662; Memorandum from Under-Secretary of State for External Affairs [Pope] to Prime Minister [Mackenzie King], Ottawa, 19 April 1923, in: *DCER*, Vol. 3, Doc. No. 636, 662–663; Memorandum from Under-Secretary of State for External Affairs [Pope] to Prime Minister [Mackenzie King], Ottawa, 20 April 1923, in: *DCER*, Vol. 3, Doc. No. 637, 663.

112 Stevenson, "Canada's Halibut Treaty", 73; Wilson, Philip W., "The Imperial Conference", *North American Review* 213, 1921, 730.

113 Allin, "Canada's Treaty Making Power", 255. For more on Lapointe's attitudes, see MacFarlane, John, *Ernest Lapointe: Quebec's Voice in Canadian Foreign Policy, 1921–1941*, PhD Thesis, Quebec: Université Laval, 1995, 154–161.

114 Lowell, A. Lawrence, "The Treaty Making Power of Canada", *Foreign Affairs: An American Quarterly Review* 2, No. 1/4, 1923/1924, 15.

115 Cf. TNA, CO 886/10/2, 15576, House of Commons: Fishery Treaty, Canada and United States, 28 March 1923, Encl. in Doc. No. 458, 311; Lowell, *The Treaty*, 20; Wigley, *Canada*, 178–179; Wrong, 14.

116 See more in Bennett, G. H., "Lloyd George, Curzon and the Control of the British Foreign Policy 1919–22", *The Australian Journal of Politics and History* 45, No. 4, 1999, 467–482; Maisel, Ephraim, *The Foreign Office and Foreign Policy, 1919–1926*, London: Sussex Academic Press, 1994, 60–88; Muir, Thomas Alexander, *Britain's Official Mind: Foreign Policy Decision-making under the Lloyd George Coalition, 1918–1922*, MA Thesis, Fredericton: University of New Brunswick, 2003, 30.

117 Wigley, *Canada*, 179; Wigley, *Whitehall*, 226.

118 Allin, *Canada's*, 253; Dewey, Vol. 2, 144–145; TNA, CO 886/10/5, D. 58204, The Secretary of State to the Governors-General and Governor, 29 November 1922, [Doc.] No. 135, 102–103 [590].

119 TNA, CAB 32/8, E ("B" Series) 3, Imperial Conference, 1923: Treaty-Signing Powers of the Dominions: Memorandum by the Foreign Office, 24 August 1923, [6–7].

120 TNA, CAB 32/8, E ("B" Series) 5, Imperial Conference, 1923: Treaty-Signing Powers of the Dominions: Memorandum by the Colonial Office, 11 September 1923, [1]–9 [9–13].

121 Ollivier, Vol. 3, 8–11; Wigley, *Whitehall*, 224.

122 Lowell, A. Lawrence, "The Imperial Conference", *Foreign Affairs: An American Quarterly Review* 5, No. 1/4, 1926/1927, 382–383.

123 Cmd. 1987, *Imperial Conference, 1923: Summary of Proceedings*, London: HMSO, 1923, 10–15.

124 Cmd. 1988, *Imperial Conference, 1923: Appendices to the Summary of Proceedings*, London: HMSO, 1923, 10–11.

125 TNA, CAB 32/9, Imperial Conference, 1923: Stenographic Notes of the First Meeting, Downing Street, 1 October 1923, 8–9 [6].

126 Cf. TNA, CAB 32/7 (CO 537/1043), C. P. 218 (23), Cabinet: Imperial Conference (Agenda) Committee: Report, 3 May 1923, 4; TNA, CAB 32/8, E ("B" Series) 7, Imperial Conference, 1923: Publication of Correspondence between His Majesty's Government and the Dominion Governments: Memorandum by the Colonial Office, 25 September 1923, [1]–5 [16–18].

127 Wigley, *Whitehall*, 225.
128 Hancock, *Survey of British*, 304; Stacey, Vol. 2, 66–67.
129 TNA, CAB 32/9, Imperial Conference, 1923: Stenographic Notes of the Third Meeting, Downing Street, 5 October 1923, 2–30 [25–40].
130 Dawson, *William*, 458.
131 Dafoe, John Wesley, "The Problems of Canada", Hurst, Cecil J. B. – Smiddy, Timothy A. – Dafoe, John Wesley et al., *Great Britain and the Dominions*, Chicago: University of Chicago Press, 1928, 211; Hall, *Commonwealth*, 519–520.
132 Cf. Sifton, Clifford, "Some Canadian Constitutional Problems", *The Canadian Historical Review* 3, No. 1, 1922, 3–23; Sifton, Clifford, *The Political Status of Canada: Address before the Canadian Club of Ottawa, April 8, 1922*, Ottawa: [s. n.], 1922; TNA, CAB 32/9, Imperial Conference, 1923: Stenographic Notes of the Fourth Meeting, Downing Street, 8 October 1923, 11–12 [46–47].
133 Foreign Relations: Statement by the Prime Minister [Mackenzie King], 8 October 1923, in: *DCER*, Vol. 3, Doc. No. 234, 240–243; TNA, CAB 32/9, Imperial Conference, 1923: Stenographic Notes of the Fourth Meeting, Downing Street, 8 October 1923, 12–15 [47–48].
134 The term "Imperial Cabinet" corresponded more to the process than a precise definition of the institution. Dawson, *William*, 464; Hall, Hessel Duncan, "The Genesis of the Balfour Declaration of 1926", *Journal of Commonwealth Political Studies* 1, No. 3, 1962, 192.
135 TNA, CAB 32/9, Imperial Conference, 1923: Stenographic Notes of the Fourth Meeting, Downing Street, 8 October 1923, 14–15 [48]; Wigley, *Canada*, 193.
136 Dawson, *William*, 462–463.
137 TNA, CAB 32/9, Imperial Conference, 1923: Stenographic Notes of the Fourth Meeting, Downing Street, 8 October 1923, 22 [52].
138 Tsokhas, Kosmas, "Tradition, Fantasy and Britishness: Four Australian Prime Ministers", *Journal of Contemporary Asia* 31, No. 1, 2001, 14.
139 TNA, CAB 32/9, Imperial Conference, 1923: Stenographic Notes of the Fourth Meeting, Downing Street, 8 October 1923, 34 [59].
140 Hall, *Commonwealth*, 525–527; Hancock, *Smuts*, Vol. 2, 133.
141 TNA, CAB 32/9, Imperial Conference, 1923: Stenographic Notes of the Fifth Meeting, Downing Street, 8 October 1923, 3–21 [60–69].
142 TNA, CAB 32/9, Imperial Conference, 1923: Stenographic Notes of the Ninth Meeting, Downing Street, 17 October 1923, 16 [108].
143 TNA, CO 886/10/2, 31326, Note on Present Procedure as Regards Communication with the Governments of the Self-Governing Dominions on Foreign Affairs, 22 June 1923, Doc. No. 122, 77 [239].
144 Ibid., 78 [240].
145 TNA, CAB 24/162/8, C. P. 408 (23), Cabinet: The Discussion on Foreign Relations in the Imperial Conference, 8 October 1923, 1–5 [69–73].
146 TNA, CAB 23/46/20, Cabinet 48 (23): Conclusion of a Meeting of the Cabinet, Downing Street, 15 October 1923, 9 [279].
147 Wigley, *Whitehall*, 232.
148 Hall, *Commonwealth*, 533.
149 Amery, Leopold Stennett, *My Political Life: War and Peace 1914–1929*, Vol. 2, London: Hutchinson, 1953, 273, 275; Brady, Alexander, *Canada*, London: Ernest Benn, 1932, 339.
150 See more in Soukup, Jaromír, *Britové v Porýní: Britská okupace Kolínské zóny v letech 1918–1926*, Praha: Filosofická fakulta Univerzity Karlovy, 2011, 124–169.

151 TNA, CAB 32/9, Imperial Conference, 1923: Stenographic Notes of the Sixteenth Meeting, Downing Street, 8 November 1923, 6–8 [204].
152 "Summary of Proceedings of the Imperial Conference and the Imperial Economic Conference", *The Round Table* 14, No. 53, 1923, 209.
153 TNA, CAB 32/22, E (T. C), Imperial Conference 1923: Committee on the Position of the Dominions and India in Relation to the Signature of Treaties and the Question of Territorial Waters: Conclusions of a Meeting of the above Committee, Foreign Office, 16 October 1923, i–iii.
154 "Afterthoughts on the Imperial Conference", *The Round Table* 14, No. 54, 1924, 228–229; Beloff, *Imperial*, Vol. 2, 85.
155 Dewey, Vol. 2, 171–174; Royal Institute of International Affairs, *The British Empire: A Report on Its Structure and Problems*, London: Oxford University Press, 1939, 217.
156 Wigley, *Canada*, 199.
157 Cf. Borden, Robert Laird, *Canada in the Commonwealth: From Conflict to Co-operation*, Oxford: Clarendon Press, 1929, 125; John W. Dafoe, MacLean's Magazine, 15 January 1923, in: Dawson, *The Development*, 277–283.
158 Lowell, A. Lawrence – Hall, Hessel Duncan, *The British Commonwealth of Nations*, Boston: World Peace Foundation, 1927, 607–609.
159 Towey, Thomas, "The Reaction of the British Government to the 1922 Collins-de Valera Pact", *Irish Historical Studies* 22, No. 85, 1980, 65–66.
160 Mohr, *British Imperial Statutes and Irish Sovereignty: Statutes Passed After*, 63–73.
161 Cf. TNA, CO 886/10/4, D. 17223, Colonial Office to Law Officers and Law Officers' Report, Downing Street, 29 June 1923, [Doc.] No. 4, 3 [420]; TNA, CO 886/10/4, D. 36590, Irish Free State: The Secretary of State to the Governor-General, Downing Street, 17 August 1923, [Doc.] No. 5, 5–6 [421–422]; TNA, CO 886/10/4, D. 18151, Colonial Office to Law Officers, Downing Street, 13 November 1923, [Doc.] No. 6, 6 [422]; TNA, CO 886/10/4, D. 530, Law Officers to Colonial Office, 31 December 1923, [Doc.] No. 7, 7 [422].
162 Wigley, *Canada*, 221.
163 See more in Harkness, David William, *The Restless Dominion: The Irish Free State and the British Commonwealth of Nations, 1921–1931*, London: Macmillan, 1969; Kenneth, Daniel, *Commonwealth: Imperialism and Internationalism, 1919–1939*, PhD Thesis, Austin: University of Texas at Austin, 2012, 192–193.
164 TNA, CO 886/10/4, D. 55155, Sir Mark Sturgis (Colonial Office) to Mr. C. H. Montgomery (Foreign Office), Colonial Office, 23 November 1923, [Doc.] No. 37, 25–26 [431–432].
165 Bothwell, Robert, "Canadian Representation at Washington: A Study in Colonial Responsibility", *The Canadian Historical Review* 53, No. 2, 1972, 145–147; Keenleyside, Hugh L., *Canada and the United States: Some Aspects of the History of the Republic and the Dominion*, New York: A. A. Knopf, 1929, 385–386; TNA, CO 886/8/3, D. 11924/S, The Secretary of State [Milner] to the Governor-General [Duke of Devonshire], 15 March 1920, [Doc.] No. 76, 127–128 [134–135].
166 Wigley, *Canada*, 224.
167 TNA, CO 886/10/4, D. 57922, Foreign Office [Montgomery] to Colonial Office [Sturgis], Foreign Office, 26 November 1923, [Doc.] No. 38, 26–27 [431].
168 TNA, CO 886/10/4, D. 58294, Sir Mark Sturgis (Colonial Office) to Mr. N. G. Loughnane (Dublin), 29 November 1923, [Doc.] No. 41, 28–29 [432].

169 TNA, CO 886/10/4, D. 9905, Irish Free State: The Governor-General [T. M. Healy] to the Secretary of State [Thomas], Vice Regal Lodge, Dublin, 3 March 1924, [Doc.] No. 45, 30–31 [434].
170 TNA, CO 886/10/4, D. 9905, Colonial Office [C. T. Davis] to Foreign Office [G. R. Warner], Downing Street, 11 March 1924, [Doc.] No. 46, 31–32 [434–435]; TNA, CO 886/10/4, Foreign Office [G. R. Warner] to Colonial Office [C. T. Davis], Foreign Office, 20 March 1924, [Doc.] No. 47, 32–33 [435].
171 TNA, CO 886/10/4, D. 13497, The Secretary of State to the Governors-General, 22 April 1924, [Doc.] No. 51, 34–35 [436].
172 TNA, CO 886/10/4, D. 20191, Canada: The Governor-General [Lord Byng of Vimy] to the Secretary of State, 26 April 1924, [Doc.] No. 53, 36 [437]; TNA, CO 886/10/4, D. 20356, Union of South Africa: The Governor-General [Lord Athlone] to the Secretary of State, 28 April 1924, [Doc.] No. 54, 36 [437].
173 TNA, CO 886/10/4, D. 20190, New Zealand: The Governor-General [J. R. Jellicoe] to the Secretary of State, 3 May 1924, [Doc.] No. 55, 36–37 [437].
174 TNA, CO 886/10/4, D. 22212, Commonwealth of Australia: The Governor-General [Lord Forster] to the Secretary of State, 3 May 1924, [Doc.] No. 56, 37 [437].
175 TNA, CO 886/10/4, D. 23548, Irish Free State: The Governor-General [Healy] to the Secretary of State, Vice Regal Lodge, Dublin, 16 May 1924, [Doc.] No. 57, 37 [437].
176 Cf. TNA, CO 886/10/4, D. 22212, Colonial Office [C. T. Davis] to Foreign Office [R. Vansittart], 17 May 1924, [Doc.] No. 58, 38 [438]; TNA, CO 886/10/4, Draft Telegram to Governor-General, Commonwealth of Australia, 9 May 1924, Encl. 1 in [Doc.] No. 59, 39 [438]; TNA, CO 886/10/4, Draft Despatch to Governor-General, Irish Free State, May 1924, Encl. 3 in [Doc.] No. 59, 40 [439]; TNA, CO 886/10/4, D. 29304, Commonwealth of Australia: The Secretary of State to the Governor-General, 19 June 1924, [Doc.] No. 66, 44–45 [441]; TNA, CO 886/10/4, D. 29304, Irish Free State: The Secretary of State to the Governor-General, 19 June 1924, [Doc.] No. 68, 46 [442]; TNA, CO 886/10/4, D. 30155, Telegram to Sir E[smé] Howard (Washington) from the Foreign Office, 23 June 1924, Encl. 2 in [Doc. No. 75], 52 [445].
177 TNA, CO 886/10/4, D. 25620, Separate Diplomatic Representation at Washington of the Irish Free State, Foreign Office, 28 May 1924, Encl. in [Doc.] No. 60, 41–42 [439–440].
178 PD, HoL, 5th Series, Vol. 57, 25 June 1924, 998–999.
179 PD, HoC, 5th Series, Vol. 175, 26 June 1924, 596–598.
180 TNA, CO 886/10/4, D. 30547, Telegram from Sir E[smé] Howard (Washington) to the Foreign Office, 26 June 1924, Encl. in [Doc.] No. 80, 56–57 [447].
181 Amery, Leopold Stennett, "Foreign Policy of the British Empire", *Advocate of Peace through Justice* 87, No. 2, 1925, 112–113; TNA, CO 886/10/4, D. 27567, The Secretary of State to the Governors-General, 23 June 1924, [Doc.] No. 10, 9 [423].
182 TNA, CO 886/10/4, D. 31143, Canada: The Governor-General to the Secretary of State, 25 June 1924, [Doc.]. No. 12, 11 [421]; TNA, CO 886/10/4, D. 30986, New Zealand: The Governor-General to the Secretary of State, 28 June 1924, [Doc.]. No. 13, 11 [421]; TNA, CO 886/10/4, D. 34006, Commonwealth of Australia: The Governor-General to the Secretary of State, 16 July 1924, [Doc.]. No. 16, 12–15 [421–422]; TNA, CO 886/10/4, D. 37810, Canada: The Governor-General to the Secretary of State, 8 August

1924, [Doc.]. No. 18, 15–16 [426–427]; TNA, CO 886/10/4, D. 39456, Newfoundland: The Governor [Sir William Allardyce] to the Secretary of State, 8 August 1924, [Doc.]. No. 18, 15–16 [426–427]; TNA, CO 886/10/4, D. 40036, Union of South Africa: The Governor-General to the Secretary of State, 21 August 1924, [Doc.]. No. 25, 20 [429].
183 These were the consequences of the so-called Zinoviev's letter. See more Novotný, Lukáš, "Der Sinowjew Brief", *Prague Papers on the History of International Relations*, 2006, 201–227; Novotný, Lukáš, "Zinověvův dopis a Campbellův případ: Příspěvek ke zkoumání působnosti první labouristické vlády", *Historický obzor* 18, No. 9/10, 2007, 218–226.
184 Cf. Amery, *My Political*, Vol. 2, 335; Holland, Robert F., *Britain and the Commonwealth Alliance, 1918–1939*, London: Macmillan, 1981, 42–43.
185 Stewart, Andrew, "The 'Bloody Post Office': The Life and Times of the Dominions Office", *Contemporary British History* Vol. 24, No. 1, 2010, 45.
186 Cf. Beloff, Max, "Leo Amery, the Last Imperialist", *History Today* 39, No. 1, 1989, 17; BL, BP, Add MS 49775, Vol. XCIII, L. S. A[mery] to Smuts, 20 June 1921, [227–233]; TNA, DO 117/33, D. 11047, Memorandum by General Smuts on Constitutional Relations, [June 1921], [9–7].
187 CAC, AP, AMEL 2/1/9, Borden to L. S. Amery, Ottawa, 24 November 1924, [1]–3.
188 Amery, "Foreign", 117–118; The Secretary of State for the Colonies [L. S. Amery] to the Governors-General of Canada, the Commonwealth of Australia, New Zealand, the Union of South Africa and the Irish Free State, and the Governor of Newfoundland, Downing Street, 2 December 1924, in: Cmd. 2301, *Consultation on Matters of Foreign Policy and General Imperial Interest: Correspondence with the Governments of the Self-Governing Dominions*, London: HMSO, 1925, [Doc.] No. 25, 24–25.
189 Stewart, "The 'Bloody Post Office'", 44.
190 Cross, J. A., "Whitehall and the Commonwealth: The Development of British Departmental Organisation for Commonwealth Affairs", *Journal of Commonwealth Political Studies* 2, No. 3, 1964, 191.
191 Cf. Hall, "The Genesis", 179; Holland, *Britain and*, 41.
192 Hurst, Cecil J. B., "The British Empire as a Political Unit", in: Hurst, Cecil J. B. – Smiddy, Timothy A. – Dafoe, John Wesley et al. (Eds.), *Great Britain and the Dominions*, Chicago: University of Chicago Press, 1928, 39–41.
193 TNA, CO 886/7/11, Dominions No. 61, Resolution IX: Constitution of the Empire, 120.
194 Barnes, John – Nicholson, David (Eds.), *The Leo Amery Diaries: 1869–1929*, Vol. 2, London: Hutchinson, 1980, 392; TNA, DO 121/1, [Memo. by Sir W. Fisher Ref. Call on S. of S. Regarding Successor to Sir H. Read], 25 November 1924, [184–186].
195 TNA, DO 121/1, [L. S. Amery] to Baldwin, 4 December 1924, [182–183, 187–188].
196 Ibid., [189–192].
197 TNA, DO 121/1, Churchill to L. S. Amery, 7 December 1924, [168–176].
198 Cf. Amery, *My Political*, Vol. 2, 240–241; Holland, *Britain and*, 43; TNA, DO 121/1, Fisher to L. S. Amery, 23 January 1925, [165–166].
199 TNA, DO 121/1, [Report by R. R. Scott, H. P. Hamilton and R. V. Nind-Hopkins] to Baldwin, 20 February 1925, [149–164].
200 Cf. TNA, DO 121/1, L. S. Amery to Scott, 26 February 1925, [144]; TNA, DO 121/1, L. S. Amery to Baldwin, 26 February 1925, [137–143]; TNA, DO 121/1, L. S. Amery to Fisher, 26 February 1925, [144]; TNA, DO 121/1, L. S. Amery to Baldwin, 26 February 1925, [134–135].

228   *The New Constitutional Status for the Dominions?*

201 Holland, *Britain and*, 44; TNA, CAB 24/172/48, C. P. 148 (25), Cabinet: The Dominions and the Colonial Office: Proposals for Reorganisation: Memorandum by the Secretary of State for Colonies, 9 March 1925, [1].
202 Cf. Barnes – Nicholson, 392; Holland, *Britain and*, 44.
203 TNA, CAB 24/172/48, C. P. 148 (25), Cabinet: The Dominions and the Colonial Office: Proposals for Reorganisation: Memorandum by the Secretary of State for Colonies, 9 March 1925, 2–3.
204 In connection with the establishment of a new Office, it has not yet been decided whether it will be called the Dominions Office or the Imperial Office. TNA, CAB 23/49/25, Cabinet 16 (25): Conclusions of a Meeting of the Cabinet, Downing Street, 18 March 1925, [347–349].
205 TNA, DO 121/1, L. S. Amery to Hertzog, Downing Street, 19 March 1925, [127–130]; TNA, DO 121/1, L. S. Amery to Mackenzie King, Downing Street, 19 March 1925, [124–126]; TNA, DO 121/1, L. S. Amery to Bruce, Downing Street, 19 March 1925, [120–122]; TNA, DO 121/1, L. S. Amery to Massey, Downing Street, 19 March 1925, [117–119].
206 TNA, DO 121/1, The Prime Minister of Australia to the Secretary of State for Colonies, 4 April 1925, [108]; TNA, DO 121/1, The Governor-General of Canada to the Secretary of State for Colonies, 3 April 1925, [100]; TNA, DO 121/1, The Governor-General of the Union of South Africa to the Secretary of State for Colonies, 9 April 1925, [103]; TNA, DO 121/1, The Governor-General of New Zealand to the Secretary of State for Colonies, 30 April 1925, [106].
207 Cf. TNA, DO 121/1, L. S. Amery to Baldwin, 23 May 1925, [82–89]; TNA, Foreign Office (hereafter FO) 800/257, L. S. Amery to Fisher, 12 May 1925, [644–645]; TNA, FO 800/258, Fisher to L. S. Amery, 15 May 1925, [10–11]; TNA, FO 800/258, Fisher to L. S. Amery, 20 May 1925, [26–27]; TNA, FO 800/258, L. S. Amery to Fisher, [20] May 1925, [28–29].
208 George Villiers, 6th Earl of Clarendon, became the new Parliamentary Under-Secretary of State for Dominion Affairs, and Sir Charles Davis held the post of Under-Secretary of State. Cf. CAC, AP, AMEL 2/1/10, L. S. Amery to the Prince of Wales, 8 July 1925, 3–4; TNA, CO 886/10/4, D. 26476, The Secretary of State to the Governors-General and Governor, 10 June 1925, 76–77 [457]; TNA, DO 121/1, Fisher to L. S. Amery, 11 June 1925, [53–54].
209 PD, HoC, 5th Series, Vol. 187, 27 July 1925, 65–92.
210 Dewey, Vol. 2, 217.
211 "The British Empire, the League of Nations and the United States", *The Round Table* 10, No. 38, 1920, 238.
212 Cmd. 151, *The Covenant of the League of Nations with a Commentary Thereon*, London: HMSO, 1919, 5.
213 Cf. Glazebrook, *A History*, 311–312; Stacey, Charles Perry, *Canada and the Age of Conflict: A History of Canadian External Policies: 1867–1921*, Vol. 1, Toronto: University of Toronto Press, 1984, 261–265.
214 Hillmer, Norman – Granatstein, J. L., *Empire to Umpire: Canada and the World to the 1990s*, Toronto: Copp Clark Longman, 1994, 75.
215 Hall, *Commonwealth*, 282–283.
216 Despite Canadian objections, the Covenant of the League of Nations was accepted without reservations by the Ottawa Parliament. Dawson, *William*, 427.
217 Cf. Cmd. 195, *League of Nations: Return to an order of the Honourable the House of Commons, dated 19 July, 1921;– for: Copy "of Speech to the Imperial Conference of the Lord President of the Council on the League of Nations"*, London: HMSO, 1921, 6; White, Thomas Raeburn, "The Amended Covenant of the League of Nations", *The Annals of the American Academy of Political and Social Science* 84, No. 1, 1919, 181–182.

218 Johnson, Gregory Allan – Lenarcic, David A., "The Decade of Transition: The North Atlantic Triangle during the 1920s", McKercher, Brian J. C. – Aronsen, Lawrence (Eds.), *The North Atlantic Triangle in a Changing World: Anglo-American-Canadian Relations, 1902–1956,* Toronto: University of Toronto Press, 1996, 86; Soward, Frederic Hubert, *Canada and the League of Nations,* Ottawa: The League of Nations Society in Canada, [1931], 14.
219 Cmd. 151, 15.
220 See more cf. Cmd. 1807, *League of Nations: Third Assembly: Report of British Delegates,* London: HMSO, 1923, 7–8; Marshall, Thomas R., "America, the Nations and the League", *The Annals of the American Academy of Political and Social Science* 84, 1919, 194–200; Mathews, J. M., "The League of Nations and the Constitution", *Michigan Law Review* 18, No. 5, 1920, 383–384.
221 Carter, *The British Commonwealth,* 101; MacLaren, Roy, *Mackenzie King in the Age of the Dictators: Canada's Imperial and Foreign Policies,* Montreal – Kingston: McGill-Queen's University Press, 2019, 56–57.
222 Beloff, *Imperial,* Vol. 2, 82; Beloff, Max, "Britain and Canada between Two World Wars: A British View", in: Lyon, Peter (Ed.), *Britain and Canada: Survey of a Changing Relationship,* London: Frank Cass, 1976, 54.
223 Cf. Brady, Alexander, "Dominion Nationalism and the Commonwealth", *The Canadian Journal of Economics and Political Science/Revue canadienne d'Economique et de Science politique* 10, No. 1, 1944, 11; Miller, David Hunter, *The Drafting of Covenant,* Vol. 1, New York: G. P. Putnam's Sons, 1928, 354; Toynbee, Arnold J., *The Conduct of British Empire Foreign Relations since the Peace Settlement,* London: Oxford University Press, 1928, 56–58.
224 Dewey, Vol. 2, 220.
225 Carter, *The British Commonwealth,* 106.
226 Brebner, John Bartlet, *Canada: A Modern History,* Ann Arbor: University of Michigan Press, 1960, 416–417.
227 Cf. Forbes, Frederic J., *Canada in the League of Nations,* PhD Thesis, Montreal: McGill University, 1927, 122–125; C. J. Doherty, "Article 10 of the Covenant – Guarantees against External Aggression of the Territorial Integrity of All States Members of the League", in: Glazebrook, George Parkin de Twenebroker (Eds.), *Canada at the Paris Peace Conference,* Toronto: Oxford University Press, 1942, Appendix C, 140–149; L. C. Christie, Amendments to Article 10 of the Covenant of the League of Nations, Ottawa, 20 July 1922, in: *DCER,* Vol. 3, Doc. No. 385, 448.
228 See more in Brown, Robert Craig, *Robert Laird Borden: A Biography: 1914–1937,* Vol. 2, Toronto: Macmillan, 1980, 155; Extracts from Memorandum by Minister of Justice on Article X on Draft Covenant of League of Nations, [Paris, 22 February 1919], in: *DCER,* Vol. 2, Doc. No. 61, 58–63.
229 L. C. Christie, Amendments to Article 10 of the Covenant of the League of Nations, Ottawa, 20 July 1922, in: *DCER,* Vol. 3, Doc. No. 385, 446–447.
230 Cmd. 1807, 8.
231 Wigley, *Canada,* 237.
232 Cmd. 2015, *League of Nations: Fourth Assembly: Report of British Delegates,* London: HMSO, 1923, 6; Glazebrook, *A History,* 371.
233 Dewey, Vol. 2, 221.
234 Thornton, Martin, *Sir Robert Borden: Canada,* London: Haus 2010, 111.
235 Cf. Manning, Charles Anthony Woodward, *The Policies of the British Dominions in the League of Nations,* Oxford: Oxford University Press, 1932, 32; Sifton to Dafoe, 18 September 1922, in: Cook, Ramsey (Ed.), *The Dafoe-Sifton Correspondence, 1919–1927,* Winnipeg: D. W. Friesen & Sons, 1966, 121–122; Sifton to Dafoe, 8 October 1922, in: Cook, *The*

Dafoe-Sifton, 122–124; TNA, CAB 24/138/1, C. P. 4200, Cabinet: The Turco-Greek Situation: Co-operation of Dominions, 15 September 1922, 484; TNA, CO 886/10/1, 46342/S, The Secretary of State to the Governors-General, 15 September 1922, Doc. No. 304, 231–232; TNA, CO 886/10/1, 46642/S, Canada: The Governor-General to the Secretary of State, 18 September 1922, Doc. No. 313, 236.
236 The British delegation to the League of Nations promised to improve British-French relations. Unlike the British, however, dominated politicians perceived the proposed vision of collective security as a threat to the Empire and sovereign Imperial interests, and it eventually rejected the government of James Ramsay MacDonald in September 1924. For more on this issue, see Moore, William Harrison, "The Dominions of the British Commonwealth in the League of Nations", International Affairs 10, No. 3, 1931, 383; Novotný, Lukáš, "Postoj britských dominií k Locarnskému paktu", Acta Fakulty filozofické Západočeské univerzity v Plzni 3, No. 2, 2011, 20–21; Novotný, Lukáš, "Die Britischen Dominions und der Vertrag von Locarno: Der Prüfstein für eine einheitliche Außenpolitik des Empire in der Zwischenkriegszeit", Jahrbuch für Europäische Überseegeschichte 10, 2010, 170–171; Yearwood, Peter J., Guarantee of Peace: The League of Nations in British Policy 1914–1925, Oxford: Oxford University Press, 2009, 282–303; Yearwood, Peter J., "'A Genuine and Energetic League of Nations Policy': Lord Curzon and the New Diplomacy, 1918–1925", Diplomacy and Statecraft 21, No. 2, 2010, 167.
237 Cmd. 2015, 6; Dewey, Vol. 2, 221.
238 Cmd. 2015, 6; Henig, Ruth, The League of Nations, London: Haus, 2010, 80–81; Report of the Canadian Delegates [Lomer Gouin, G. P. Graham] to the Fourth Assembly of the League of Nations, Ottawa, 1 December 1923, in: Dawson, The Development, 251–254.
239 TNA, CAB 32/8, E ("B" Series) 3, Imperial Conference, 1923: Treaty-Signing Powers of the Dominions: Memorandum by the Foreign Office, 24 August 1923, [1]–3 [6–7].
240 Dewey, Vol. 2, 221; Glazebrook, A History, 372.
241 Cmd. 2015, 7–8.
242 Carter, The British Commonwealth, 105.
243 Ginneken, Anique H. M. van, Historical Dictionary of the League of Nations, Lanham: Scarecrow Press, 2006, 54.
244 Cmd. 1022, League of Nations: Report by the Secretary-General to the First Assembly of the League on the Work of the Council, London: HMSO, 1920, 2.
245 Neatby, H. Blair, "Laurier and Imperialism", Report of the Annual Meeting of the Canadian Historical Association/Rapports annuels de la Société historique du Canada 34, No. 1, 1955, 30.
246 Carter, The British Commonwealth, 105–106.
247 For more on this issue Lloyd, Lorna, "'Another National Milestone': Canada's 1927 Election to the Council of the League of Nations", Diplomacy & Statecraft 21, No. 4, 2010, 650–668; Soward, Frederic H., "The Election of Canada to the League of Nations Council in 1927", The American Journal of International Law 23, No. 4, 1929, 759–765.
248 Moore, 383.
249 Yearwood, "A Genuine", 167.
250 Novotný, "Postoj", 20–21; Yearwood, Guarantee, 282–303.
251 Henig, The League, 98–100; Novotný, Lukáš, "Konzervativní vláda Stanleyho Baldwina a její odmítnutí Ženevského protokolu: Příspěvek k

pokusům o vytvoření kolektivní bezpečnosti ve dvacátých letech 20. století", *Dvacáté století*, 2006, 117–153; Orde, Anne, *Great Britain and International Security 1920–1926*, London: Royal Historical Society, 1978, 68–69.

252 The Secretary of State for the Colonies [L. S. Amery] to the Governors-General of Canada, the Commonwealth of Australia, New Zealand, the Union of South Africa, and the Governor of Newfoundland, 19 December 1924, in: Cmd. 2458, *Protocol for the Pacific Settlement of International Disputes: Correspondence Relating to the Position of the Dominions*, London: HMSO, 1925, [Doc.] No. 2, 5–6.

253 The Secretary of State for the Colonies to the Governors-General of Canada, the Commonwealth of Australia, New Zealand, the Union of South Africa, and the Governor of Newfoundland, 15 January 1925, in: Ibid., [Doc.] No. 4, 7–8.

254 The Secretary of State for the Colonies to the Governors-General of Canada, the Commonwealth of Australia, New Zealand, the Union of South Africa, and the Governor of Newfoundland, 15 January 1925, in: Ibid., [Doc.] No. 5, 9–10.

255 Cf. Chaudron, Gerald, *New Zealand in the League of Nations*, PhD Thesis, Canterbury: University of Canterbury, 1989, 91–93; Chaudron, Gerald, "The League of Nations and Imperial Dissent: New Zealand and the British Labour Government, 1924–31", *The Journal of Imperial and Commonwealth History* 39, No. 1, 2011, 53–71; W. F. Massey, Memorandum on the Protocol for Pacific Settlement of International Disputes, Wellington, 6 January 1925, in: Cmd. 2458, Encl. in [Doc.] No. 8, 13–16.

256 The Governors-General of the Union of South Africa to the Secretary of State for the Colonies, 26 January 1925, in: Cmd. 2458, [Doc.] No. 7, 11–12.

257 *IPD, DÉ*, Vol. 11, No. 13, 13 May 1925, 1417–1419. For the Irish position on the Geneva Protocol in more detail, see Kennedy, Michael, "Chicanery and Candour: The Irish Free State and the Geneva Protocol, 1924–5", *Irish Historical Studies* 29, No. 115, 1995, 371–384.

258 TNA, CAB 24/172/11, C. P. 111 (25) / C. I. D. 592-B, Protocol for the Pacific Settlement of International Disputes: Telegram from Government of India, Foreign and Political Department, 18 February 1925, [99].

259 "British Dominions and the Protocol", *Advocate of Peace through Justice* 87, No. 9, 1925, 559–562; Moore, 384; The Governors-General of Canada to the Secretary of State for the Colonies, 4 March 1925, in: Cmd. 2458, [Doc.] No. 11, 18; The Governors-General of the Union of South Africa to the Secretary of State for the Colonies, 5 March 1925, Cmd. 2458, [Doc.] No. 12, 19–23.

260 See more cf. Burks, David D., "The United States and the Geneva Protocol of 1924: 'A New Holy Alliance'?" *The American Historical Review* 64, No. 4, 1959, 891–905; Memorandum by the Secretary of State [C. E. Hughes] of a Conversation with the British Ambassador (Howard), 5 January 1925, in: *FRUS*, 1925, Vol. 1, 16–18; TNA, CO 537/1061, Telegram from the Secretary of State for the Colonies to the Governors General of Canada, the Commonwealth of Australia, New Zealand, and the Union of South Africa and the Governor of Newfoundland, 5 February 1925, [12–13]; TNA, CO 537/1061, [C. I. D.] 573-B, Committee of Imperial Defence: United States and the Geneva Protocol: Memorandum by the Secretary of State for Foreign Affairs [A. Chamberlain], 27 January 1925, [8]

261 TNA, FO 800/257, Howard to A. Chamberlain, 9 January 1925, [55–60].
262 Hall, *Commonwealth*, 550.

263 See more TNA, CAB 24/172/5, C. P. 106 (25), British Policy Considered in Relation to the European Situation: Memorandum by Mr. Harold Nicolson, of the Foreign Office, 20 February 1925, [1]-6 [73–75]; TNA, CAB 24/172/12, C. P. 112 (25), Cabinet: Reduction of Armaments: Protocol for the Pacific Settlement of International Disputes: French and Belgian Security: Memorandum by the Right Hon. Viscount Cecil of Chelwood, 23 February 1925, [1]-3 [100–101]; TNA, CAB 24/172/16, C. P. 116 (25)/C. I. D. 597-B, Cabinet: French Security: Memorandum by the Secretary of State for War [L. Worthington-Evans], War Office, 26 February 1925, [1]-3 [109–110]; TNA, CAB 24/172/18, C. P. 118 (25) / [C. I. D.] 590-B, Committee of Imperial Defence: French and Belgian Security: Memorandum by the Chancellor of the Exchequers [W. Churchill], 24 February 1925, [1]-3 [115–116]; TNA, CAB 24/172/21, C. P. 121 (25), Cabinet: Reduction of Armaments: Protocol for the Pacific Settlement of International Disputes: French and Belgian Security: Memorandum by the Secretary of State for Air [S. Hoare], 27 February 1925, [1]-3 [121–122]; TNA, CAB 24/172/22, C. P. 122 (25), Cabinet: British Foreign Policy and the Problem of Security: [Memorandum by the Secretary of State for Foreign Affairs], 26 February 1925, [1]-2 [123].

264 TNA, CAB 24/172/5, [C. I. D.] 559-B, Committee of Imperial Defence: Report of the Sub-Committee on the Geneva Protocol, January 1925, [1]–29 [26–39].

265 TNA, CAB 24/172/5, C. P. 105 (25), Cabinet: The Geneva Protocol and Security: Memorandum by the Chairman [Curzon] of the Committee of Imperial Defence, 19 February 1925, [1]-3 [24–25].

266 TNA, CAB 24/172/36, C. P. 136 (25), Cabinet: Protocol for the Pacific Settlement of International Disputes: Draft Communication to the Secretary-General of the League of Nations, Foreign Office, [4] March 1925, [1]–6; The Secretary of State for the Colonies to the Governors-General of Canada, the Commonwealth of Australia, New Zealand, the Union of South Africa, and the Irish Free State, and the Governor of Newfoundland, 3 March 1925, in: Cmd. 2458, [Doc.] No. 9, 17.

267 TNA, CAB 23/49/23, Cabinet 14 (25), Conclusions of a Meeting of the Cabinet, House of Commons, 4 March 1925, 1 [320].

268 Cf. *PD, HoC*, 5th Series, Vol. 182, 24 March 1925, 323–327; Walters, Francis Paul, *A History of the League of Nations*, Vol. 1, Oxford: Oxford University Press, 1952, 284.

269 Wigley, *Canada*, 240.

270 TNA, CAB 23/49/26, Cabinet 16 (25), Conclusions of a Meeting of the Cabinet, House of Commons, 20 March 1925, 2–3 [369–370]. The genesis of the German proposal is described in more detail in Stambrook, F. G., "'Das Kind' – Lord D'Abernon and the Origins of the Locarno Pact", *Central European History* 1, No. 3, 1968, 233–263.

271 Novotný – Kodet, 199.

272 CAC, AP, AMEL 2/4/1, L. S. Amery to Bruce, 16 March 1925, [1]–7; TNA, CAB 24/172/5, [C. I. D.] 559-B, Committee of Imperial Defence: Report of the Sub-Committee on the Geneva Protocol, January 1925, 20.

273 Other opponents included the Chancellor of the Exchequer Sir Winston Churchill, the Secretary of State for Air Sir Samuel Hoare, delegate to the League of Nations Lord Cecil, the Secretary of State for India Lord Birkenhead, the First Lord of Admiralty William Clive Bridgeman, the Secretary of State for War Sir Laming Wothington-Evans, and the Lord Privy Seal Lord Salisbury. Middlemas, Keith – Barnes, John, *Baldwin: A Biography*, London: Weidenfeld & Nicolson, 1969, 353–354.

The New Constitutional Status for the Dominions? 233

274 Wigley, *Canada*, 241.
275 *PD, HoC*, 5th Series, Vol. 182, 24 March 1925, 327–328, 405.
276 CAC, AP, AMEL 2/1/10, Lambert to L. S. Amery, 2 April 1925, [s. p.].
277 TNA, FO 800/258, Bruce to L. S. Amery, 6 May 1925, [151–158].
278 TNA, CAB 23/50/8, Cabinet 28 (25): Conclusions of a Meeting of the Cabinet, Downing Street, 10 June 1925, 4 [123].
279 TNA, FO 800/258, A. Chamberlain to L. S. Amery, 6 August 1925, [407–411].
280 Cf. CAC, AP, AMEL 2/4/1, L. S. Amery to Bruce, 24 June 1925, [1]–6; ta CAC, AP, AMEL 2/4/1, L. S. Amery to [Baldwin], 15 June 1925, [1]–3; TNA, FO 800/258, L. S. Amery to A. Chamberlain, Downing Street, 16 June 1925, [149–150].
281 Hall, *Commonwealth*, 556.
282 TNA, FO 800/258, A. Chamberlain to L. S. Amery, 19 June 1925, [180–184].
283 TNA, FO 800/257, A. Chamberlain to Kerr, 6 April 1925, [497–498].
284 Wigley, *Canada*, 243.
285 *PD, HoC*, 5th Series, Vol. 185, 24 June 1925, 1639.
286 Holland, *Britain and*, 47.
287 New Zealand's position was partly due to the fact that Prime Minister William Massry was seriously ill at the time and was effectively disabled. Cf. CAC, AP, AMEL 2/1/10, Lambert to L. S. Amery, 2 April 1925, [s. p.]; *PD, HoC*, 5th Series, Vol. 185, 24 June 1925, c. 1667.
288 Hall, *Commonwealth*, 556
289 Novotný – Kodet, 201–202.
290 CAC, AP, AMEL 2/1/10, A. Chamberlain to L. S. Amery, 6 August 1925, [s. p.].
291 Holland, *Britain and*, 48.
292 TNA, FO 800/258, L. S. Amery to A. Chamberlain, 10 July 1925, [298–299].
293 Hall, *Commonwealth*, 557–558.
294 TNA, CAB 24/175/73, C. P. 473 (25), Cabinet: Position of the Dominions in Relations to the Locarno Treaty: Note by the Secretary of State for Dominion Affairs, 14 November 1925, 2–3 [398–399].
295 Hall, *Commonwealth*, 557–558.
296 Gwynn, Denis, *The Irish Free State 1922–1927*, London: Macmillan & Co, 1928, 94–97; Wigley, *Canada*, 245.
297 For more on the course of discussions on the security pact, see Novotný, Lukáš, "On the Journey to the Rhineland Pact: Contribution to the Study of British Perception of the Problem of Collective Security in the 1920's", *Öt kontinens: Az Új- és Jelenkori Egyetemes Történeti Tanszék közleményei/ Cinq Continents: Les cahiers du Département d'Histoire moderne et contemporaine*, No. 1, 2009, 369–383.
298 For more on the special conference discussions, see Novotný, Lukáš, "Velká Británie a konference v Locarnu", *Moderní dějiny: Sborník k dějinám 19. a 20. století* 18, No. 2, 2010, 23–49.
299 Glasgow, George, *From Dawes to Locarno: Being a Critical Record of an Important Achievement in European Diplomacy 1924–1925*, London: Ernest Benn, 1926, 11.
300 Maisel, 181.
301 Cf. Cmd. 2525, *Final Protocol of the Locarno Conference, 1925 (and Annexes): Together with Treaties between France and Poland and France and Czechoslovakia, Locarno, October 16, 1925*, London: HMSO, 1925, 13; TNA, CAB 24/175/73, C. P. 473 (25), Cabinet: Position of the Dominions in Relations to the Locarno Treaty: Draft Memorandum for Circulation to the Cabinet, 14 November 1925, 3 [399].

302 Cf. Novotný, "Postoj", 30; Novotný, "Die Britischen", 181; Stevenson, J. A., "Canadian Nationalism", *Edinburgh Review* 244, No. 497, 1926, 25; TNA, FO 800/258, Draft Memorandum for Circulation to the Cabinet, 14 November 1925, [707]; TNA, DO 117/4, Byng to L. S. Amery, Ottawa, 18 January 1926, [8–12].
303 Hillmer, Norman, "The Anglo-Canadian Neurosis: The Case of O. D. Skelton", in: Lyon, Peter (Ed.), *Britain and Canada: Survey of a Changing Relationship*, London: Frank Cass, 1976, 76; Stacey, Vol. 2, 79; Wigley, *Canada*, 246–247.
304 TNA, CAB 24/175/73, C. P. 473 (25), Cabinet: Position of the Dominions in Relations to the Locarno Treaty: Draft Memorandum for Circulation to the Cabinet, 14 November 1925, 3–4 [399–401].
305 Wigley, *Canada*, 245.
306 See more in TNA, CAB 24/175/73, C. P. 473 (25), Cabinet: Position of the Dominions in Relations to the Locarno Treaty: Draft Memorandum for Circulation to the Cabinet, 14 November 1925, 3–4 [399–401]; TNA, FO 372/2198, The Question of India's Accession to the Locarno Pact, [June 1926], [397–402].
307 Novotný – Kodet, 204.
308 Cf. CAC, AP, AMEL 2/2/24, Smuts to L. S. Amery, Irene, 21 October 1925, [s. p.]; CAC, AP, AMEL 2/2/24, Smuts to A. Chamberlain, Irene, 21 October 1925, [1]–3; TNA, FO 800/258, Smuts to A. Chamberlain, Irene, 21 October 1925, [588–589].
309 TNA, FO 800/258, Selby to Edgcumbe, 13 November 1925, [704]; TNA, FO 800/258, Leigh to Edgcumbe, 16 November 1925, [718].
310 TNA, CAB 23/51/7, Cabinet 53 (25): Conclusions of a Meeting of the Cabinet, Downing Street, 18 November 1925, [93–94].
311 *PD, HoC*, 5th Series, Vol. 188, 18 November 1925, 432.
312 Ibid., 444, 454–455.
313 On 8 January 1926, Canada sent a telegram in which it made clear its opposition to the commitments arising from the Pact of Locarno. Stacey, Vol. 2, 79–80.
314 *PD, HoC*, 5th Series, Vol. 188, 18 November 1925, 480–484.
315 CAC, AP, AMEL 2/2/24, L. S. Amery to Smuts, 24 November 1925, [1]–8.

5 The Road to the Statute of Westminster

5.1 The Balfour Declaration

Considering the course of the Chanak Crisis, the circumstances around the Canadian-American fishing treaty and discussions in Lausanne, it might appear that Canada's position was a key factor in the subsequent development of relations between the Dominions and Great Britain. In fact, this was not the case. As a result of his dispute with the Governor-General, 1st Viscount Byng of Vimy, Canada's Prime Minister William Lyon Mackenzie King played a large role in ensuring a precise definition of the institutional status of Governors-General rather than in fundamental constitutional issues which were the *raison d'être* for South African Prime Minister James Hertzog.

When Mackenzie King entered politics, he wanted to be a principled and moral politician of strong character like his grandfather.[1] From December 1921 when he became Prime Minister, he was heavily reliant on the votes of liberal francophone Quebec voters, who gave him a solid parliamentary majority.[2] In mid-1925, he came to the conclusion that it was essential a cabinet reshuffle take place to ensure support, and as such he called on the Governor-General to dissolve the House of Commons. Viscount Byng of Vimy consented. The general federal election took place at the end of October, and the campaign was mainly dominated by economic topics. Mackenzie King thought he would win easily;[3] he relied on the publicity the media surrounded him with.[4] The electoral results, however, represented a personal loss for the Liberal leader as he had failed to defend his mandate in his home constituency of North York. Liberals got only 101 of their previous 116 seats, while the Conservatives were boosted by 67 members of parliament to a total of 116. The Progressive Party managed to defend just 24 of their 63 seats.[5]

The Liberal loss shifted the balance of power within Canadian politics. The Prime Minister held confidential consultations with the Governor-General on his next step, who recommended he resign. Initially, Mackenzie King saw no alternative and agreed. Subsequently, however, he decided to remain in office for the time being, even though he did not have a majority in the House of Commons. During subsequent meetings, Viscount Byng allegedly made it clear that he did not see another dissolution of parliament and another election as a solution. However, he preferred the parliamentary crisis be dealt with quickly, and as such in the end he supported the Prime Minister's proposal that the members of parliament elected convene quickly. On the one hand, Canada's Governor-General did not want to extend the "post-electoral agony" indefinitely, and on the other hand he made it clear he was ready to act if needed.[6]

On 4 November 1925, Mackenzie King spoke publicly, acknowledging that no party had received a majority in parliament. He stated the cabinet had made "careful consideration of the constitutional precedents and their bearing upon the situation" and all eventualities, and that therefore, "the Cabinet decided unanimously this afternoon that it was their constitutional duty to meet Parliament at the earliest possible moment". Until the time it convened, Mackenzie King intended to govern the country along with his government even without confidence, thus postponing his resignation.[7] The fact that he was in clear disagreement with Byng on how to deal with the situation and that he did not mention this to the public was the bone of contention during the crisis of summer 1926. In the end, in mid-January 1926 Mackenzie King acquired limited support from the Progressive Party, gaining a parliamentary majority of three seats.[8]

A controversial government decision over customs tariffs led to conflict with Progressive Party members of parliament at the end of May 1926. The minority government's difficulties came to a climax on the weekend of 26 and 27 June, when Mackenzie King refused to make any concessions, instead asking Viscount Byng to dissolve the House of Commons and call a new election. He thought the Conservative opposition leader Arthur Meighen would be unable to set up a government and as such the Governor-General would have to accede to his request.[9] Byng rejected his request on the basis of similar precedents in New South Wales,[10] without waiting to hear the stance of Britain's Secretary of State for Dominion Affairs Leopold Amery, and on 28 June, Mackenzie King resigned.[11] The Governor-General believed that if he had acceded, he would have given the Liberals unfair advantage in the election campaign, and therefore concluded that Meighen should also reciprocally get the chance to set up a government, and Meighen gratefully accepted the opportunity.[12] On 2 July the newly formed cabinet appeared before the parliament to ask for its confidence, which in rather dramatic circumstances it did not receive. As such, Meighen was forced to ask the Governor-General that the parliament be dissolved, and the Governor-General acceded.[13]

From the start, Mackenzie King had considered Byng a confidential advisor, close friend and political partner who held the same status as he did hierarchically; in no way did he consider him senior.[14] Since the Canadian constitution did not have a clear interpretation in this matter,

Mackenzie King criticised the fact that Byng had not asked for precise instructions from London. Amery did not make any statement, because he thought "that in my view it would not be proper for the Secretary of State to issue instructions with regard to the exercise of his constitutional duties to a Governor".[15] Byng's position on dissolving the lower house at once confirmed to the Liberals that the Governor-General favoured the Conservatives, and as such they ran the election campaign as a battle for Canadian autonomy.[16] On 14 September 1926, the Liberal Party won, and Mackenzie King was happy to consider this proof that his request for dissolution of parliament had been justified. In contrast, Viscount Byng perceived it as a personal disappointment.[17]

Byng's decision really did seem to be mistaken rather than constructive, and was more attune to the acts of colonial governors during the Victorian era than during the 1920s. He had thought the Governor-General had the absolute right to dissolve parliament or choose not to.[18] Britain's Secretary of State for Dominion Affairs Amery had been critical for some time of Canada's Governor-General. Viscount Byng sent fewer reports to London, for example, than other Governors-General,[19] and as such Amery had to prompt him to send him more detailed information from time to time on the situation in Canada, which was "a matter of general Imperial interest".[20] In contrast, former Canadian Prime Minister Sir Robert Laird Borden said that during the autumn 1925 and summer 1926 crises, Byng had kept a cool head and despite the complexity of both situations was shown to have acted, "not only by perfect constitutional propriety, but by rare good judgment".[21]

As a result of the parliamentary crisis, Canada's Prime Minister publicly opened the issue of the royal prerogative and the status of the Governor-General. He perceived the dispute with Viscount Byng as clear evidence of the subordination and unequal status of the Dominions considering that in Britain no request for dissolution of parliament had been rejected for centuries.[22] Mackenzie King held a different opinion and interpretation of the Governor-General's status as an institutional tool of Crown power. For this reason, it was decided to ask the participants of the planned Imperial Conference to state their opinion on the position of Governors-General in Dominions and the request to dissolve the lower parliament in June 1926. The nub of the problem was in the ambiguous "technical status" of the Governor-General during government crises. It was shown that in these situations, a rigidly determined procedure would be better than an approach based on "trust" in the Governor-General's ambiguously defined constitutional role. As such, during 1926 the Canadian Prime Minister clearly supported the demand for the equal status of Dominions, as South African Prime Minister James Barry Munnik Hertzog had begun to seek.[23] The conflict between Mackenzie King and Byng struck a chord within nationalist-minded South African politics, which was sensitive about the "inadequate constitutional measures" taken by Britain, and the Governor-General in regard to the Dominions, and thus sympathised with Canada.[24]

Amery found himself in a difficult situation from early 1925. Besides the complications around the division of Britain's Colonial Office, he had to contend with the arrival of the new nationalist-minded South African Prime Minister, who was a close supporter of Canada's decentralising position and who demanded greater influence for the Dominions in pursuing Imperial foreign policy.[25] In June 1924, an election had taken place in the Union of South Africa, in which the National Party, led by former Boer General James Hertzog, had won a tight victory over Smuts; Smuts had to go into opposition.[26] It appeared that the South Africans were tired of Smuts's global, European and Imperial policies, and preferred domestic solutions, in particular of their economic problems.[27] There was great antagonism between the two generals and their political supporters,[28] and as such Hertzog's "political survival" depended entirely on support from the South African Labour Party, which was against South Africa's secession from the British Empire.[29] In contrast to Mackenzie King, the new South African Prime Minister had to contend with "radical" nationalist tendencies, openly demanding an independent republic, and he thus perceived various aspects more sensitively, including even mere suggestions of limits to the Union of South Africa's formal or informal level of independence within the British Empire. During the first session of the South African parliament, he tried to disarm the Republicans by giving a charismatic speech in strong support of maintaining warm relations with Britain and the Commonwealth.[30]

Shortly after arriving in office, Hertzog took over his predecessor's study, where he found Smuts's 1921 memorandum on the British Commonwealth Constitution and Amery's subsequent response which he likely did not realise was not official.[31] Leopold Amery and Jan Smuts agreed on the main points, but differed in how they should be achieved. They agreed on a theoretical definition of Dominion sovereignty, and Amery particularly stressed the necessity of acknowledging the full independence and equal status of Commonwealth territories. Due to the nationalist opposition.[32] Hertzog took on much of Smuts's concept of the relations between Dominions and the mother country, "borrowed" some of Smuts's phrases and arguments and began seeking "confirmation" from Britain in the form of a general declaration of constitutional rights that all constitutional anachronisms and anomalies had been eliminated and South Africa now had equal status within the Empire.[33] Nevertheless, the South African Prime Minister conceded that although he agreed with Smuts in Imperial matters, they still disagreed in matters of nationalism.[34]

Hertzog was quite hopeful about a British declaration, as he was convinced that it would "take the wind from the sails" of the advocates of radical political solutions. He believed that the system of consultation on Imperial foreign policy was inadequate, and responded positively to MacDonald's government's call to deepen and intensify co-operation in all matters falling within common Imperial interest. In January 1925, he sent Amery a personal letter in which he conceded that,

> every member of the Commonwealth by itself constitutes a distinct national entity with equal status ... [I] accede whole-heartedly to this view and have formed it the basis for joint consultation and common action in relation to foreign affairs and common interests.

In contrast to Irish representatives seeking their country's precise constitutional position, the South African Prime Minister came to the conclusion that the Dominions already had a corresponding and equal status to the mother country. He nevertheless saw the principal shortcoming in the fact that outside states had not yet acknowledged this fact. In this regard, he pointed out that any attempts at improving co-operation in foreign policy matters were pointless unless Britain secured recognition of the Dominions' new status abroad. Hertzog held the opinion that this step would significantly improve the method of consultation and implementation of Imperial foreign policy.[35] In contrast, Canadian Prime Minister Mackenzie King continued to insist on the principle that only Dominion parliaments and Imperial Conferences should make decisions on Imperial policy.[36]

Although Australian representatives were supporters of a common Imperial foreign policy, because they had their own special economic and political interests in various matters, from 1923 they sought a minimisation of the commitments arising from British policy in Europe, rather than them being deepened further. Australia clung to the old concept of Imperial foreign and defence policy based on an isolationist position, and as such did not take part in attempts at revising relations to the mother country and defining Dominions' constitutional status in 1923 or later.[37]

Australian Prime Minister Stanley Melbourne Bruce considered the method of communication and co-ordination of political measures with Britain to be a fundamental aspect of the common Imperial foreign policy, and as such decided at the end of November 1924 to go his own way. On the basis of conversations with the Labour government,[38] he named Major Richard Gardiner Casey "liaison officer" at Britain's Foreign Office. Casey was to ensure full exchange of information and, if needed, help by providing advice to officers there. Neither Baldwin nor Amery objected to this, as they wanted to see in practice how this step would affect the system of consultation between the Commonwealth of Australia and Britain. Thus, Casey was given an office at the Committee of Imperial Defence with direct access to Cabinet Secretary Hankey and Foreign Office and Colonial Office correspondence.[39] It was Maurice Hankey and his spouse Adeline who were like "mother and father" for Casey, without whose kind approach Bruce's intention to acquire a "liaison officer" would have ended in failure.[40]

Although Australia and New Zealand preferred to keep out of constitutional debates, the Irish Free State held a similar opinion to the Union of South Africa. Ireland disagreed with Hertzog in all details around redefining the relations and equality of Dominions within the Commonwealth, even though it generally supported South Africa overall. During discussions, although Canada began by trying to carry out the role of impartial mediator, as a result of the 1926 parliamentary crisis, it began to openly seek precise rules to specify the system of communication between London and Dominion statesmen which would clarify the ambivalent position of Dominion Governors-General as the sovereign representatives of the King yet also mere "postmen" for Britain's Dominion Office.[41]

Hertzog was not going to be put off by the lack of interest of the other Dominion prime ministers, because he hadn't lost sight of the declaration by Labour's Secretary of State for the Colonies Thomas that acknowledged the Union of South Africa's important position within the British Commonwealth.[42] Over the course of 1925, he continued his communication with Amery over constitutional rights, the status of the Dominions and a common Imperial foreign policy.[43] In regard to the signing of the Treaties of Locarno, Hertzog conceded in December that it represented a great success for Austen Chamberlain;[44] he continued to have reservations about the agreement, however.[45] The South African Prime Minister also used the circumstances around its negotiation to justify his arguments demanding the opening of the issue of international recognition of the individual Dominion nations. He thought that the criticism the British government received due to the absence of their representatives' signature was partially a result of the fact that foreign states had still not fully recognised the Dominions' independent status. The South African Prime Minister believed that their international status should be dealt with at the next Imperial Conference.[46] Amery was in full agreement, as he was of the opinion that the Dominions should also look at Imperial foreign policy from a "psychological perspective" and that they should realise what or who represented the greatest threat to the Empire.[47]

From early 1926, Hertzog worked hard doing groundwork for the upcoming meeting of Dominion statesmen, taking into account documents from previous Imperial Conferences and Smuts's memorandum. He did not criticise the level of Dominion autonomy which had been reached, and as such sought to ensure the Union of South Africa received confirmation and subsequently also international recognition of its equal status. He wanted to continue with Smuts's efforts which had failed in 1921. He continued to face republican opposition in parliament, and as such in a speech on 22 April 1926, he summarised the prevailing situation and expressed his support for continuing co-operation with the mother country:

South Africa had secured a complete international independent status equal to any other Dominion or any other part of the British Empire. ... We are as free and as independent as England itself. ... It would be foolish for us to appoint our own Ambassadors and have our own Embassies all over.[48]

On 15 May 1926, the South African Prime Minister made a public speech in which he repeated his previous position in regard to international recognition of the Dominions' status, and stressed that autonomy meant that each Dominion was as sovereign and as free a country as Great Britain itself. He believed there was no form of legal or constitutional subordination of the Dominions towards the mother country, and thus except for personal ties through shared sovereignty, there should be no other connections between them unless agreed otherwise. The South African general urged that adoption of the declaration of constitutional rights be accelerated, as this would clarify the Dominions' international status so that some "smaller independent states" such as Portugal no longer considered South Africa, "a Colony with large autonomy, but dependent on British Sovereignty".[49]

Hertzog's stance that the Empire was a mere personal union concerned Amery, but he did not wish to initiate any changes. He thought their importance went beyond the Dominion Office's standard agenda, and therefore urged his government colleagues to pay sufficient attention to the issue at the upcoming Imperial Conference.[50] Although General Smuts was an opponent of Hertzog, he did not doubt the magnitude of his Stellenbosch speech. He was worried that the Prime Minister was thinking of publicly declaring the Union of South Africa's external sovereignty. Hertzog rejected these considerations and repeatedly stressed that he was merely seeking recognition from other countries, and he was in no way encouraging the collapse of the Empire.[51] In contrast to his predecessor, the South African Prime Minister, like Lionel Curtis, conceded that the Dominions and the mother country did form a kind of "fictitious superstate".[52] Hertzog's speech had a significant impact on South African politics.[53]

From the end of 1925, the London government began intensive preparations for the upcoming Imperial Conference, although in the first half of 1926 it would have to cope with significant domestic political difficulties. The date of the Conference was changed a number of times, and eventually set for October 1926.[54] Amery realised the importance of the Conference, and as such communicated intensively with Dominion statesmen and also endeavoured to develop personal contacts with them too. In mid-December 1925, members of the British government submitted an extensive memorandum in which they defined the range of issues regarding Imperial foreign policy, defence and constitutional matters which was to be discussed at the Conference.[55] Considering the large agenda, the

British government set up a special interdepartmental committee – the Imperial Conference (Agenda) Committee – at the end of February 1926. Its chairman, Sir Maurice Hankey, co-ordinated the measures taken by individual ministries such that the preparation and organisation of the Conference enabled it to run smoothly.[56]

During March 1926, Committee members came to the conclusion that it would be necessary to set up three separate preparatory committees dealing separately with foreign and defence matters, economic issues and relations within the Empire (Inter-Imperial Relations).[57] In regard to constitutional issues, the committee believed there would be a revision in the system of communication and method of consultation between the Dominions and the mother country and that a decision would be made on how often and under what circumstances meetings of Dominion and London representatives would take place. It also agreed with Amery that it would be a good idea for Conference participants to discuss and specify: (1) British Empire representation at international conferences; (2) the issue of separate Dominion membership of the League of Nations in the context of the Imperial unity principle; (3) the Empire's diplomatic missions in foreign countries; and (4) the status of foreign consuls in the Dominions. The committee did not preclude the possibility that for some Dominions, this would open the issue of their international status.[58] On 31 March 1926, the British government approved the general outline of the committee's conclusions.[59]

One of these three committees was the Committee on Questions Affecting Inter-Imperial Relations, headed by Assistant Under-Secretary of State for Foreign Affairs Hubert Montgomery, which dealt with constitutional issues. The preparatory committee's thorough reports focused on the political and technical perspective of most points Britain was planning to discuss at the October Imperial Conference. Most of the material corresponded to Amery's long-term objective of a preference for decentralising the British Commonwealth of Nations, rather than centralising it, and as such was based on the principle of equal status and full autonomy for the Dominions in all matters of Imperial foreign policy which would not breach the Commonwealth's Imperial unity.[60] The sensitivity of some topics led British representatives to agree that documents relating to relations within the Empire would not be sent as standard to Dominion and Indian representatives.[61]

Britain focused on the system of communication and method of consultation between Dominions and the mother country at two basic levels – on the period between Imperial Conferences, and during Conference sessions.[62] Although it was anticipated that Dominion representatives would have their own proposals, Britain prepared its own. Committee members recommended carefully adhering to the principle that governments interested in discussions on foreign affairs should receive all information and that closer personal contacts should be developed with Dominion representatives as had happened in the appointment of Australia's "liaison officer" Major Casey in 1924. A complication arose in regard to the organisation and frequency of Imperial Conference meetings in that Amery wanted a "smaller conference" of British and Dominion representatives to take place in parallel with the General Assembly of the League of Nations each year in October, which would be expanded once every three years to include prime ministers. The fixed date for this change did not suit the Dominion prime ministers due to the frequent complexities of domestic affairs.[63] Australian Prime Minister Bruce, for example, proposed that regular Imperial Conferences held in the Dominions would be an appropriate demonstration of the Empire's solidarity.[64]

In regard to the British Empire's representation at international conferences, Dominion Office and Foreign Office officials proposed making a sharp distinction depending on the convenor, i.e. for conferences organised by the League of Nations, and others, which were then sorted on the basis of the issues being discussed into political (the Paris Peace Conference in 1919, the 1921–1922 Washington Conference, etc.) and technical (looking for example at tropical agriculture, or the operation of motor vehicles).[65] Britain also proposed this "analogously logical" division for issues relating to the negotiation, signature and ratification of conventions.[66] In regard to the publication of documents, it aimed for similar practice as in the previous 1923 Imperial Conference.[67] Members of the Inter-Imperial Relations Committee also acknowledged that the status of Dominions within the League of Nations Council went beyond the established limits of Dominion autonomy.[68]

Over the course of July, Hertzog sent Amery a letter in which he again stressed that recognition of the Dominions' status by the international community was in the Empire's interest. In contrast to the past, the South African Prime Minister openly compared his arguments with the content of Smuts's June 1921 memorandum on the Constitution of the British Commonwealth and Amery's comments in response.[69] It is highly likely that Hertzog thought that Amery's personal opinions were an official statement of British representatives, or maybe even the position of Britain's Colonial or Dominion Office. On 4 October 1926, Amery informed the British government of Hertzog's positions. He mentioned the British Colonial Secretary's March 1921 memorandum which conceded that Dominions had equal status and therefore were entitled to be recognised as independent states, but he said this was a position given in the interest of maintaining the principle of Imperial unity. The Dominions Secretary noted that in fact the Dominions and the mother country had a different level of relations to other countries, and therefore, "the 'independence' of the various States of the Empire was incompatible with their interdependence as parts of a whole [Commonwealth]".[70] Amery also showed the ministers that Hertzog had not fully grasped the essential nature of Dominions' international position, as arising from membership of the League of Nations, and that he had erroneously interpreted the debate in Portugal's upper parliamentary chamber which he had referred to in his May speech in Stellenbosch.[71]

In autumn 1926, the South African Prime Minister travelled to the Imperial Conference with two political options which were mutually exclusive: (1) to co-operate with the British Commonwealth of Nations on the basis of a definition of full equality for Dominions' status; or, if this was rejected, then (2) to assert the Union of South Africa's secession from the British Empire.[72] In early October 1926 during an informal discussion with Amery, Hertzog again based his arguments on Smuts's 1921 memorandum.[73] On 19 October 1926, considering the anticipated discussion on the international recognition of the Dominions' status, Amery officially sent Chamberlain and Balfour an analysis of Smuts's memorandum, his responses to it, and a clear summary of constitutional discussions between Dominion and British representatives since 1921 to ensure complete supporting documentation.[74]

On 19 October 1926, British Prime Minister Stanley Baldwin officially opened the Imperial Conference with a speech which on the one hand summarised the successes of the previous meeting between British and overseas representatives, and on the other hand outlined the future direction of the Empire.[75] The meeting was held at a time when common Imperial foreign policy had clearly come up against its limits. Most Dominions rejected the Treaty of Locarno due to inadequate consultation and the method of communication between British and overseas representatives.[76] Thus, the need had arisen to clarify the current ambiguous legal and constitutional status of the Dominions. Although the institutional reorganisation of Britain's Colonial Office and the establishment of the Dominion Office in 1925 had brought the principle of equality into relations between the Dominions and the mother country, in the summer of 1926 these changes seemed to be more "cosmetic" administrative measures with little impact on the constitutional situation within the Empire. As such, Britain anticipated that the Prime Ministers of the Union of South Africa, Canada and the Irish Free State would demand constitutional reforms at the Conference.[77] In contrast, New Zealand would view these efforts with extreme scepticism.[78] Despite all this, the "old maxim" applied that, "if we are imperialists, we must look at the Empire as a single state, separate in some sense from the rest of the world".[79]

In contrast to his constitutionally focused counterparts, Australian Prime Minister Bruce was a leading advocate of Imperial unity, which he did not want to breach under any circumstances. Like other Australians, he did not see the constitutional issue as a priority.[80] In 1921, William Morris Hughes asked: "What more could Dominions do as independent states that they cannot do already?" In 1926, Bruce declared that he did not want a written constitution. Four years later, his Labour successor James Henry Scullin, who wasn't excited about introducing new things,[81] declared: "I do not want the relations of myself and my children to be determined by rules written in a book, to which each of us must refer to discover who is right and who is wrong."[82] As such, in 1926 Bruce considered discussion of adopting the Treaty of Locarno to be the most important point the Conference should focus on.[83] In summer 1926, he declared that:

> Australia's aspiration must be a closer linking together of all the self-governing portions of the Empire, with as full a recognition of the independent status of all the Self-Governing Dominions as is compatible with the recognition of our mutual British nationality, and the maintenance of the closest possible relations between the English-speaking peoples.[84]

In contrast to the Australian Prime Minister, former South African Prime Minister Jan Smuts questioned the usefulness of the security pacts and whether the direction of British foreign policy in Europe was the right one.[85] In the mid-1930s, however, he changed his mind and revised his position on the Rhineland guarantee pact to such an extent that he declared of himself: "So now I am a Locarno man."[86]

On 25 October 1926, the prime ministers agreed that issues related to relations within the Empire, such as the system of communication, method of consultation, British Empire representation at international conferences, Dominions' memberships and activities within the League of Nations and the procedure for concluding treaties, which were considered the most complicated part of the agenda, would be the responsibility of a committee comprised of Prime Ministers and other important Dominion and British delegates. This committee would have the task of investigating all contentious issues and aspects of relations within the Empire, and subsequently present an extensive report to the Conference which would become an underlying instrument for the further development of the British Empire.[87] Lord Balfour was appointed chair of the Committee on Inter-Imperial Relations on Amery's suggestion, someone who was highly respected by Conference participants and who had the trust of all present as a result of his political career. The Secretary of State for Dominion Affairs put him there because he was an advocate for a new concept of the British Commonwealth based on the equality of its autonomous members.[88]

Frequent considerations were made of what direction the Commonwealth was going to, or should, take. Advocates of a centralised Empire, for example, expressed the opinion a few months before the Imperial Conference opened that Dominions should not in fact choose between a dependent and subordinate status in regard to the mother country and an independent national position, but rather between, "a nationalism which sees its fulfilment in isolation and a nationalism which sees it in an active participation in the world's affairs".[89] In the end, supporters of decentralisation prevailed over proponents of Imperial centralisation within the Dominions and at Britain's Dominion Office.

There remain today a number of stories told about the adoption of the Balfour Declaration of 1926. For example, while the Earl of Balfour was listening to the discussions of his Dominion colleagues, it is alleged he spontaneously wrote down the main phrases on the back of an envelope, and these then became known as the definition of the position of the Empire's autonomous parts.[90] There is another legend, based on a claim by Balfour's niece Blanche, that the "famous text" which later included the final report was written on a piece of paper torn out of a notebook during a meeting with the Secretary of the Committee on Inter-Imperial Relations, Sir Maurice Hankey. The truth is somewhat different from the myth of the Balfour Declaration's adoption. Most of the text was written during official and unofficial discussions and during informal meetings over the course of the Conference's large additional programme. The Declaration's final form represents a compromise between the proposals discussed at the meetings of the Committee on Inter-Imperial Relations, or which had already been suggested during confidential discussions between Dominion prime ministers and British representatives.[91]

On 27 October 1926, the Committee had its first meeting, which Chairman Lord Balfour opened with a statement containing the ideas and phrases which Balfour subsequently used as a basis for a number of passages in his Declaration. In response to this, Canadian Prime Minister Mackenzie King recommended also focusing on the status of Governors-General. His South African counterpart, whose arguments were based on Smuts's 1921 memorandum, proposed expanding the range of points to include adoption of a general declaration of constitutional rights, which would then receive international recognition. Hertzog did not outline his vision of what this should look like more specifically, however. Over the course of discussions, Amery repeatedly had to explain the circumstances of Smuts's memorandum being written, and his view of the document. He also warned that the issue of proposing a general declaration of constitutional rights was inextricably linked to the issue of the authority of the Imperial Conferences system. British Secretary of State for Foreign Affairs Sir Austen Chamberlain was not a great supporter of adopting such a declaration, as he was concerned it would introduce undesirable rigid principles into relations between the Dominions and the mother country. Irish Justice Minister Kevin O'Higgins criticised the fact that Hertzog was not dealing with the anomalies and anachronisms disputing their equal status within the Empire that were already there. Committee members came to the conclusion that Hertzog should submit more detailed material which could then be discussed further.[92]

Further discussions on the nature of relations had a major impact on Hertzog's clarifying proposal, which contributed significantly to the future definition of relationships within the Empire. In his memorandum of 28 October 1926, the South African general demanded the fact be accepted that Dominions were "independent States, equal in status and separately entitled to international recognition, with Governments and Parliaments independent of one another; united by the common bond of allegiance to the Crown and freely associated as members of the British Commonwealth of Nations". He also wanted those present to agree that, "whatever surviving forms of inequality or subordination" there were should not occur at any level of relations with the mother country. He also thought that "it is desirable that the constitutional relationship between Great Britain and the Dominions be properly known and recognised, and that the necessary steps be taken that the equal status of the associated States and their relations as above set forth be formally and authoritatively intimated to their own communities and to the world at large".[93]

Over the subsequent days, a number of informal meetings were held, of which there were no official minutes. The Dominion and British representatives debated not just Hertzog's proposal but also documents prepared by Balfour, Amery and Birkenhead. The new proposals contained various minor modifications or more cautiously formed associations. Although those at the meetings tried to reach a compromise, they were not particularly successful in doing so.[94] Although superficially, Hertzog's proposal appeared ponderous, it did contain valid arguments.[95] Kevin O'Higgins was nevertheless heavily critical of it, objecting that the memorandum gave no direct explanations, rather masking the true state of affairs.[96] Despite this Irish criticism, the South African Prime Minister was certain about what he wanted to achieve and how he wanted to do so.[97] According to O'Higgins, Hertzog's proposal continued to ignore the anomalies and anachronisms which remained, and as such the Irish delegation submitted its own text on 2 November 1926, entitled "Existing Anomalies of the British Commonwealth of Nations", in which they especially pointed out the fact that there should be, "the principle of the absolute equality of status and the legislative, judicial and constitutional independence of the members of the British Commonwealth of Nations". This opened up discussion of other issues such as the Dominions' relationship to the Crown, the status and powers of Governors-General and appeals to the Privy Council's Judiciary Committee,[98] which often had to resolve controversial cases.[99]

Discussion of the proposals for a general declaration of constitutional rights was temporarily interrupted by other important points such as adopting the Pact of Locarno, the status of Governors-General, the method of communication between governments, changing the Royal title and establishing a system of British Commissioners in the Dominions.[100] On 11 November, the debate continued with criticism from Amery of some passages of the Irish memorandum, and a presentation of his own analyses of the issue.[101] In the meantime, a number of brief meetings were held which led to the final formulation of the Balfour Declaration.[102] It was only thanks to Balfour that a compromise proposal was achieved which represented one of the most extraordinary constitutional documents of the British Empire.

On 18 November 1926, the Committee for Inter-Imperial Relations submitted its final report. Right at the beginning, the report states that "our discussions on these questions have been long and intricate", but that nevertheless they had found "fundamental principles affecting the relations of the various parts of the British Empire *inter se*" and their relations to external countries. In the second article, entitled "Status of Great Britain and the Dominions", the Committee came to the conclusion that adopting a traditional type of constitution would not make sense for the British Empire, because its different parts had very different histories and had developed markedly separately. Committee members nevertheless conceded that the Dominions' rapid development over the previous fifty years meant that some prevailing relations inevitably needed to be transformed. Since geography and other reasons did not allow for considerations of implementing a federal structure, the only real alternative was to grant autonomy, in which each separate member of the Empire would become responsible for its own future.[103]

The Balfour Declaration defined the status of the autonomous overseas territories and relations between the Dominions and the mother country as follows:

> They are autonomous Communities within the British empire, equal in status, in no way subordinate one to another in any aspect of their domestic or external affairs, though united by a common allegiance to the Crown, and freely associated as members of the British Commonwealth of Nations.

The equal status of Great Britain and the Dominions was highlighted by the fact that the mother country was one of seven "self-governing communities" which were part of the Empire.[104] Committee members held the opinion that the Declaration meant the Commonwealth had acquired not just a flexible tool allowing for adequate responses to a changing world, but also the opportunity to show foreign countries the "true character of the British Empire".[105] Others perceived it as, "the British Commonwealth's Charter of Freedom",[106] the start of a new era in relations between the mother country and Dominions,[107] the culmination of a long process which had started with Resolution IX at the Imperial War Conference in 1917,[108] or the gradual transition of the Commonwealth into an international organisation.[109] The importance of the Balfour Declaration was often compared to the importance of the Magna Carta or the Declaration of Rights.[110]

On 25 October 1926, the eighth meeting of the Imperial Conference was held, where Imperial foreign policy and the Pact of Locarno were discussed. Debate took place on whether a common foreign policy should continue to be strictly adhered to, or whether it was more appropriate to introduce the principle of local external relations as an additional aspect of Imperial foreign policy. Although in the end Australia and New Zealand decided to ratify the Treaties of Locarno after certain aspects were clarified, South Africa, Ireland and Canada were unyielding.[111] The fact was once again confirmed, as frequently seen in the post-war period, that the Union of South Africa and Canada especially no longer wanted to be tied up in British policy on the European continent, instead preferring political isolationism, while in contrast the Pacific Dominions expressed their willingness to support the mother country in its policies and accept the guarantees and commitments arising from the Rhineland guarantee pact. Nevertheless, business, financial and military ties represented such as strong bond that no Dominion came out in open opposition to British foreign policy, or Imperial foreign policy.[112] Despite all this, Britain's Dominions Secretary Amery believed that the Conference had helped strengthen the Empire's unity, and the equality of its members.[113] Between 1926 and 1939, Dominion representatives gradually came to recognise that Imperial foreign policy also included Britain's foreign policy towards Europe.[114]

Small adjustments were made in the formulation of the Balfour Declaration in terms of the procedure for concluding treaties. Although the relevant resolution from the 1923 Imperial Conference still applied, Dominion status now defined and confirmed that the negotiation, signature and ratification of treaties would take place exclusively on behalf of the whole British Empire with the Dominions holding a special relationship towards the Crown. Dominion negotiators, authorised by domestic governments, also had full authorisation to sign negotiated international agreements.[115]

The system of communication and method of consultation between the Dominions and the mother country and the position of the Governors-General was another important issue alongside defining the position of the autonomous overseas territories which was discussed at the Imperial Conference. As early as in 1921, General Smuts and Amery had considered it essential to further clarify the institutional role of Governors, or Governors-General in the Dominions; the new demand was made in particular by Canadian Prime Minister Mackenzie King. He thought that Governors-General should from now on represent the Crown, but not the London government. This change would give Dominion governments direct access to the King. Previously, Governors-General in the Dominions had been viewed more as "communication intermediaries" between Britain and local representatives rather than direct representatives of the King. The Committee on Inter-Imperial Relations therefore thoroughly discussed the role of Governors-General, their position in official communication and other matters.[116]

The final report included two articles focused on communication and the method of consultation within the Empire, entitled "System of Communication and Consultation", and "Position of Governors-General". Committee members came to the conclusion that "the Governor-General is no longer the representative of His Majesty's Government in Great Britain; there is no one therefore in the Dominion capitals in a position to represent with authority the views of His Majesty's Government in Great Britain".[117] This was a wider consensual concept to which Dominion statesmen agreed.[118] According to the report, this state was "an essential consequence of the equality of status existing among the members of the British Commonwealth of Nations that the Governor-General of a Dominion is the representative of the Crown, ... and that he is not representative or agent of His Majesty's Government in Great Britain or of any Department of that Government". As such, Committee members were of the opinion that although Governors-General had previously formally represented a mediator between London and Dominion statesmen, this did not correspond to their constitutional position, and as such in future, direct communication should take place between British and Dominion representatives.[119] In practice, Governors-General continued to represent the Crown where the sovereign was not present in the country in person, and corresponded directly with him.

The compact system of communication and method of consultation via High Commissioners represented a new challenge in the period in between Imperial Conferences not just for the Dominions, but also the mother country. The Committee on Inter-Imperial Relations preparing the agenda for the Conference conceded in June 1926 that it was desirable for closer personal contacts with Dominion representatives to develop to a form as established by Australia's "liaison officer", Major Casey, in 1924.[120] The 1926 idea of the system of High Commissioners was based on every Dominion having one British High Commissioner in its capital city, who would fulfil a quasi-diplomatic role and consult on current issues at a bilateral level.[121] The system of communication through High Commissioners who represented their government and not the King began to develop fully from the end of the 1920s, and it was expected that it would be more effective than the previous method of delivering messages through Governors-General.[122]

Although the representatives of the Union of South Africa and the Irish Free State were most active in debates, their influence was limited. Canada exploited its informal privileged position as the oldest Dominion and the strongest in political and economic terms, allowing them to have a major impact on discussions on the Commonwealth's future constitutional nature. Its position in between the mainly Imperialist-minded

Britain, Australia and New Zealand on the one hand and the nationalistic Ireland and South Africa on the other facilitated the adoption of compromise formulations in thorny issues. As such, not only could an open conflict between two opposing stances within the Empire be avoided, but also most doubts over the unity of the British Commonwealth could be dispelled for a relatively long time. Despite all this, the remnants of Dominion subordination to the mother country continued to be removed over the coming years.[123]

The 1926 Imperial Conference "resolved" the definition of Dominion status, and various longstanding anomalies and inequalities from the period when Dominions were perceived as subordinate territories. In some regards, the Balfour Declaration rectified these aspects of institutional and constitutional relations within the Empire, even though in fact it merely formally acknowledged current practice. In place of the original idea of a general declaration of Dominion constitutional rights and equalities, a series of partial definitions were adopted in response to the diverse demands of the Dominion governments. It might appear superficially that the whole process of Dominion autonomy was highly revolutionary in nature, but this was not the case because a constructive "spirit" dominated in discussions. Nevertheless, the Conference both covertly and overtly marked the beginning of a long road to extensive revisions and evaluations of the forms, measures and procedures within the Commonwealth. However, the Balfour Declaration did not come into force immediately. It took another five years for the legislative process, agreed at the 1930 Imperial Conference, to conclude in the form of the Statute of Westminster.[124]

5.2 1930 Imperial Conference

The Secretary of State for Dominion Affairs and the Colonies, Leopold Amery, perceived the writing and adoption of much of the Balfour Committee report on the status of the Dominions as the greatest success of his life.[125] Even his contemporaries concede he played a great personal role in the adoption of the Declaration.[126] He considered the implementation of two basic principles in relations between the Dominions and the mother country – the full equal status of the autonomous territories within the Empire, and the unity symbolised by the Crown – to be key. He attributed the Conference's successful course to the fact that discussions took place on the basis of personal, almost familiar, contacts and relations between British and Dominion representatives. He also accepted that Great Britain must from a long-term perspective play the main role in forming a common Imperial foreign policy.[127] The Earl of Balfour also expressed his satisfaction with the work of the Committee. He perceived its conclusions as a step required for the age. On 8 December 1926 in a speech to the House of Lords, he stressed that the British Empire is now a more united organism than it has ever been before, that that organism is held together far more effectually by the broad loyalties, by the common feelings and interests – in many cases, of history – and by devotion to great world ideals of peace and freedom. A common interest in loyalty, in freedom, in ideals – that is the bond of Empire. If that is not enough, nothing else is enough.[128]

Looking back on it, British Prime Minister Stanley Baldwin assessed the significance of the Balfour Declaration on a visit to Ottawa on 2 August 1927 when he highlighted the fact that "every self-governing member of the Empire is now the master of its destiny".[129] Almost every Dominion perceived the Imperial Conference as a successful meeting from their own perspective, with mainly representatives of the Irish Free State holding the opposite opinion.[130]

Although the Balfour Declaration "revived" the use of the term Commonwealth, this was not formally announced to foreign powers. Nevertheless, South African Prime Minister Hertzog was entirely satisfied, "that excellent results have been obtained from the Imperial Conference".[131] General Smuts saw the London meeting similarly. At the end of November 1926, he anticipated that since "the Imperial Conference has formulated Dominion Status in the way I have always stated it", some politicians would stop campaigning for South Africa to secede from the British Empire,[132] as he considered nationalism was a great danger which threatened Imperial unity.[133] Amery had similar expectations.[134] Despite the circumstances around discussion at the Imperial Conference, the British Dominion Secretary believed that it was South African General Smuts who deserved the most credit for the development of the new concept of the Commonwealth.[135] Similarly, the South African Governor-General, Major-General Alexander Cambridge, anticipated that the Union of South Africa's "new and acknowledged" constitutional position would satisfy the radical Afrikaners and that they would not view all political difficulties solely from a "racial perspective".[136]

Although the Foreign Office remained responsible for implementing Imperial foreign policy, the Dominions played a significant role in deciding on its focus. Not infrequently, politicians or expert advisors held positions within Dominions' foreign ministries who made no secret of their anti-British, nationalist or even pro-decentralisation positions.[137] Occasionally, Dominion interests even affected British foreign policy, or complicated relations between neighbouring states.[138] Canada, for example, was critical of the signature of the 1928 Anglo-French naval treaty because the United States had reservations over it, something Canadian politicians took great account of due to the specific nature of American-Canadian relations.[139]

Nevertheless, not all Dominion prime ministers entirely identified with the formulation regarding foreign policy as stated in the Balfour Declaration, and as such, frequently interpretations differed on the level of joint responsibility between the "autonomous communities" for implementing Imperial foreign policy, and the actual nature of their independent status and decision-making.[140] General Hertzog, for example, with his motto of "South Africa First",[141] generally perceived the Balfour Declaration as confirmation of the sovereign independent status, and *de facto* independence, of South Africa within the Empire,[142] and providing the option of secession or withdrawal from the Empire.[143] This led him to emphasise the importance of the Balfour Declaration in a number of speeches by stating that under certain circumstances it allowed the Union of South Africa to declare its neutrality in the event of war, i.e. avoiding joint commitments in Imperial foreign policy.[144] General Smuts often opposed him in this position,[145] because he held the opinion that in the end the British Empire would not collapse.[146] There were also more radical responses to Hertzog's declaration. Professor Fremantle, for example, in conversation with Leo Amery, stated that he considered Hertzog's steps and idea of secession so detrimental that he proposed to Amery that he "should get a taxi-driver to run him down when he is crossing Piccadilly".[147] In contrast, Australian representatives criticised the incompatibility of the principles of equal status of the members of the British Commonwealth of Nations with common loyalty.[148] Nevertheless, the British government did not indicate to foreign countries that Dominions now had the right to declare neutrality, and did not determine the process under which circumstances this would be possible, despite the various interpretations given by politicians in South Africa and Ireland.[149] There was essentially no explicit legal basis for these ideas of the future development of mutual relations.[150]

Despite the fact that the Committee on Inter-Imperial Relations did not come to any "ground-breaking conclusions", merely confirming the prevailing state, the Empire as a whole experienced a flood of enthusiasm.[151] Only Canadian politicians took a more cautious approach in assessing the constitutional status of the country.[152] The leader of the opposition Conservatives, Richard Bedford Bennett, later 1st Viscount Bennett, was a restraint on Mackenzie King's enthusiasm about the "national success", noting some of the still prevailing aspects of Canada's dependent position on Great Britain.[153]

After 1926, the Dominions' "new" equal status in regard to the mother country was reflected in a number of constitutional issues. Much debate was given over to the issue of ensuring British Empire diplomatic unity on the basis of special relations based on an *inter se* doctrine. This essentially involved relations between independent Commonwealth entities not having the nature of relations between foreign countries on the basis of international law, and this significantly affected the form of multilateral government agreements.[154] Application of the *inter se* doctrine, indisputably based on a common commitment to the Crown, nevertheless led to certain legal ambiguities in practice, and as such from the 1940s onwards it came to lose its justification.[155]

Further complications arose in establishing diplomatic missions for the Dominions in foreign states, and vice versa. In particular, this occurred in the naming of representatives of Canada (the United States, France, Japan), the Union of South Africa (the Netherlands, the United States and Italy) and the Irish Free State (France, Germany, the United States, the Holy See), because the question arose of whether they should have the status of Ambassador,[156] and how they should act in the event, for example, of the severance of diplomatic relations between Canada and Japan.[157] British Secretary of State for Foreign Affairs Sir Austen Chamberlain in this regard expressed his conviction that, "the British Empire was the first League of Nations", and as such, "we rejoice in the increasing part the Dominions are taking in world affairs". He was not afraid to also express his fears as a result of the fact that "several Ministers, in several different countries, speak for the British Commonwealth".[158] This was a procedural complication as to whether Dominion missions should act in line with the "Washington formula", i.e. the appointed representative should work as part of the British Embassy, or in line with the "Tokyo formula", i.e. independent diplomatic representation at the British Embassy.[159] Also being looked at was the issue of Dominion governments' representation in London.[160] Reciprocally, British representatives were also being sent overseas.[161] Limits were also being placed on the scope of consuls, and consul generals in the Dominions, and the process of sending and clarifying the scope of Dominion consular representatives in third countries was also being clarified.[162]

It is probable that the development of Dominion diplomacy helped strengthen advocates of isolationist tendencies in British foreign policy and Dominion influence not just as a result of the presence of their representatives in third countries, but also though a more active pursuance of the overseas autonomous territories' interests. The influence of Dominion politicians, and thus also the Dominion Office on the implementation of Imperial foreign policy, grew to such an extent that opinions were expressed that there was a danger of "Dominion liberum veto in Foreign Affairs", because the overseas representatives wanted to be heard more on the international scene in order to affirm the Dominions' new international status. For this reason, they also became more actively involved in matters discussed at the League of Nations.[163]

The 1926 Imperial Conference advised the British government to set up a committee of experts who would investigate the impacts of the conclusions of the Committee on Inter-Imperial Relations report on Dominion legislation.[164] Due to a complex agenda, it took a relatively long time to prepare, but the Dominion representatives nevertheless agreed that this should be finished before the planned Imperial Conference in 1930.[165] If any of the Dominion governments were to disagree with its conclusions, they would be able to reject them or insist on modifications, something which happened in the case of Canada.[166] Canada's original proposal that the meeting be held in Ottawa was rejected for practical reasons,[167] and as such, from 8 October to 4 December, the Conference on the Operation of Dominion Legislation and Merchant Shipping Legislation,[168] was held in London, with the objective of expertly assessing and proposing the best ways to incorporate the 1926 political conclusions of Dominion and British representatives into the British Commonwealth of Nations legislative framework.[169] Ministerial officials and legal experts had an internal British inter-departmental committee memorandum available to them (the so-called Schuster Committee),[170] which had prepared background documents from February 1927 to December 1928 and which had defined three basic types of issues: (1) disallowance and reservation, (2) the extraterritorial validity of Dominion legislation and (3) the 1865 Colonial Laws Validity Act.[171]

Disallowance meant the old Crown prerogative, on which basis and on the recommendation of British Secretaries of State, laws adopted in Dominions and Colonies could be annulled. This was not often used, and as such Conference participants recommended abolishing it for Dominions. There was a reservation over the right of the Governor-General or Governor to withhold approval of a submitted law in order that he could procedurally tender it directly to the sovereign who would make the final decision. The ministerial officials and legal experts agreed that this should no longer be the case because "it would not be in accordance with constitutional practice for advice to be tendered to His Majesty by His Majesty's Government in the United Kingdom against the views of the Government of the Dominion concerned". In regard to the validity of laws enacted by Dominions, they conceded there was a great difference between laws adopted by British and those adopted by Dominion legislators. As such, they recommended issuing a declaration on the basis of which laws adopted by Dominions would have full extraterritorial validity. For centuries, laws in the Colonies had been drawn up on the basis of the principles of the mother country's own laws. The 1865 Colonial Laws Validity Act put British (Imperial) legislation above laws adopted by Dominion parliaments. The Conference participants accepted that the equal status of the Commonwealth's autonomous members meant that this practice should end in order to deepen current co-operation.[172] Over the course of discussions, it was demonstrated that the representatives of the Union of South Africa and the Irish Free State were not predisposed to the vague or general formulations proposed by British head Sir Maurice Gwyer in regard to constitutional matters.[173] The Conference on the Operation of Dominion Legislation and Merchant Shipping Legislation's 1929 final report served as one background document in regard to the issue of relations within the Empire at the upcoming Imperial Conference.

At the beginning of January 1930, the British Secretary of State for Dominion Affairs, Sidney James Webb, 1st Baron Passfield, proposed in light of the planned special economic conference in Ottawa (1932) that London and overseas representatives could also discuss the Empire's economic affairs at the same time as the 1930 meetings in order to avoid convening a special Imperial Economic Conference as had happened in 1923. This was the first and also last meeting at which Dominion and British representatives did not more widely discuss the direction of Imperial foreign and defence policy and constitutional problems, and at which due to the Great Depression most time was spent debating economic issues and measures which should be taken to ensure the Commonwealth's economic recovery.[174] Since no conclusions could be reached on economic matters, especially in terms of Imperial preferences, never mind closer economic Imperial union, it is considered less successful.[175] It was the first meeting in a long time of British and overseas statesmen in a new form, because it was the first meeting at this level for almost all prime ministers in their new roles; as such, caution in certain matters was appropriate.[176] The British government adopted Passfield's proposal, including his recommendation that smaller expert committees be established on the basis of the 1926 precedent to ensure smoother discussion of the points.[177]

The British Secretary of State for Foreign Affairs Ramsay MacDonald opened the Imperial Conference, held from 1 October to 14 November 1930, with a speech in which he called on the British and Dominion representatives present to overcome their differences in spite of differing political positions and responsibly evaluate the report issued by the conference on the validity of Dominion legislation.[178] In contrast to the 1926 Imperial Conference, constitutional issues were not the principal part of the agenda and were only marginally discussed. In many regards, in terms of content, they copied the final report of the committee looking at Dominion legislation validity. Dominion statesmen in particular held the opinion that the essence of the 1926 Balfour Declaration was that there should be a balance between the principle of a common Imperial foreign policy and co-operation within the Empire on the one hand, and equal status and autonomy on the other hand. South Africa and Ireland preferred equality to self-government, while Australia in particular insisted on the importance of maintaining Imperial unity.[179] New Zealand seemed to be the only one who did not want anything to change in regard to relations within the Empire.[180] In contrast, the public were most interested in an answer to the entirely openly posited question of whether Dominions really did have equal status, and whether they had the right to make up their own mind on seceding from the British Commonwealth of Nations.[181] Despite all the circumstances, Australia held firm in its position, because it was convinced that it already had the equality and independence that it wished to have in constitutional matters.[182]

A key debate on relations within the Empire was held on 3 November 1930, with Irish Minister for Foreign Affairs Patrick McGilligan in particular considering the conclusions reached in constitutional matters only temporarily sufficient.[183] As a member of the special Committee on Inter-Imperial Relations headed by the Lord High Chancellor John Sankey, 1st Viscount Sankey, he had already disagreed with the practical use of the term "British subject" in concluding commercial agreements and in the issue of citizenship, since he believed the British Commonwealth of Nations was not a sovereign state; however he was not supported in his opinion by other delegates.[184] In reality, Dominion Office representatives were not particularly enthusiastic about the continuing constitutional discussions, because the previous decade had been a "difficult" period in terms of constitutional issues, and as such they would have welcomed their definitive closure with a once-and-for-all solution to the status of Dominions. They certainly did not welcome any "improvements" in the status of the autonomous territories as some overseas politicians and British academics were considering.[185]

Similarly, a clearer definition of "technical" phraseology in official documents was reached during discussions of British and overseas politicians, in particular in the field of foreign relations. The term "Member of the British Commonwealth of Nations" in line with a recently signed London agreement on restricting naval arms meant a state which was fully autonomous and which had Dominion status, had appropriated the principles of democratic government and had the privilege of separate representation at Imperial Conferences.[186] According to the recommendations and conclusions of the 1926 Imperial Conference, and considering India's specific constitutional status on the basis of the 1917 Resolution IX and the Government of India Act 1919, India was also viewed as a member of the British Commonwealth of Nations, even though it did not have Dominion status and the rights associated with it; in political and economic importance it frequently overshadowed some smaller Dominions.[187]

There was also discussion on use of the adjective "Britannic", which was most commonly used in relation to the name of a particular Dominion government, such as "His Britannic Majesty's Government in the Union of South Africa", etc. The objections of some nationalist Dominion politicians that the adjective "Britannic" evoked a form of subordination were taken into account, and the term "His Britannic Majesty" was henceforth to he used in documents where the full title of the sovereign was not intended to be used. From the perspective of British officials, the adjective "Britannic" had the advantage of not having precise geographic boundaries compared to the term "United Kingdom".[188] Time would show that the Dominion representatives would continue in their conventions, and they would not accept, or appreciate, the London politicians' ideas, because they continued to use the term "Britannic" in relation to the United Kingdom.[189] The adjective "British",[190] which had previously been used freely for various parts of the British Empire, was now not to refer to the term "Great Britain", as criticised, e.g., by Irish politicians, or the "British Government", but only in the terms "British Empire" and "British Commonwealth of Nations".[191]

In regard to the system of communication and consultation regarding Imperial foreign policy, the previous 1926 Imperial Conference set a number of recommendations, especially in regard to information transmission and co-ordinating steps in negotiating agreements, and implementing foreign policy. Conference participants stressed that current recommendations had to continue with greater mutual information-sharing at a governmental level in discussions of issues in which other autonomous parts of the British Empire may have an interest. At the same time, Dominion and British representatives highlighted the well-working system for appointing His Majesty's diplomatic representatives, who represented the interests of the British Commonwealth in foreign countries.[192] They gave a similarly positive appraisal of the operation and development of communication within the Empire on matters not just within foreign policy, but also the regular agenda, through liaison officers or High Commissioners in London as well as the traditional expansion of personal contacts amongst representatives of the British cabinet and Dominion governments.[193] Despite the fact that they could personally get together at meetings of ministers and officials at Imperial Conferences or special meetings, develop contacts during visits with Dominion High Commissioners in London and have diplomatic representatives from other parts of the Empire in foreign cities and with representatives in Geneva at international conferences, the British government thought that none of that could fully replace a system of official communication between governments.[194]

Imperial Conference participants also spoke on the method of communication between Dominion and foreign governments, a topical issue following adoption of the Balfour Declaration in 1926. The Irish delegation in particular was critical of a number of practical communication steps.[195] Although the circumstances and rules of accreditation for Dominion envoys in third countries had been determined in a 1926 resolution, this was further clarified, in particular for regions where autonomous governments had specific interests and which did not affect general Imperial policy.[196] However, the British government had to be informed in parallel of everything and receive a copy of negotiated documents.[197] It was stated that Dominions were responsible for negotiating commercial agreements with foreign countries, the issue of courtesy telegrams (congratulations, condolences, etc.) involvement in non-political conferences and other matters of a civil nature.[198]

Another important point discussed at the Conference was the position of High Commissioners.[199] The vision of the High Commissioners system of 1926 was that every Dominion would send one High Commissioner to London, who would have "diplomatic" status (although in the interwar period, they were not true diplomats) and would consult on current issues affecting Imperial policy on a bilateral basis.[200] Leopold Amery placed great hope in successfully creating a High Commissioner structure, and had wanted one since 1924 because it would present a certain form of Imperial unity.[201] Austen Chamberlain was somewhat hopeful, viewing the appointment of Richard Casey as "Australian liaison officer" in London in a positive light.[202] Initially, Chamberlain had been somewhat reserved about Amery's plans, because he was not particularly thrilled about the idea of the quasi-diplomatic status of Dominion High Commissioners.[203] Nevertheless, he was not particularly concerned that, for example, the United States would send a diplomatic representative to Ottawa (which actually happened in 1927) or Dublin, and that Great Britain would not have anyone there who would properly represent its interests, and as such he agreed in the end.[204]

Experience in the year gone had shown that the status of High Commissioners compared to the position of diplomatic representatives of third countries appeared to be inadequate considering the importance of overseas territories within the Commonwealth, and as such there was discussion of whether Dominion representatives should be prioritised over representatives of foreign countries.[205] Thus in regard to the status of High Commissioners in London, the British government concluded considering the importance and uniqueness of Dominion representatives' position in Great Britain that their status should be emphasised in a number of cases such that in ceremonies they were at a level immediately above Secretaries of State and below Cabinet Ministers. Only on visits of Dominion ministers would they have a higher status than High Commissioners.[206] Thus, as representatives of British Commonwealth members, High Commissioners were prioritised over the envoys and ambassadors of foreign countries, as demanded by the Dominions.[207]

In regard to the position of Governors-General, or the Governor-General, who according to the conclusions of the 1926 Imperial Conference were no longer representatives of His Majesty's government in Great Britain, but now representatives of the Crown, their status and the process of their appointment were clarified. Now, overseas politicians were to be consulted in advance on the suitability of the chosen candidate, something which was often already happening at a semi-official level between the British Prime Minister and his Dominion counterparts.[208] The importance of Governors-General as a communication channel between the Dominions and the mother country fell in comparison to the position of High Commissioners.

At the turn of the 1920s and 1930s, Imperial foreign policy focused on four main problem areas: (1) To finally resolve the political, financial and other problems associated with the Great War and the subsequent peace settlement; (2) disputes between the nations were to be dealt with on the basis of security, mutual assistance, the Covenant of the League of Nations and other tools preventing the outbreak of war; (3) to support endeavours at reducing or limiting arms and (4) to protect British interests abroad and develop friendly and fruitful relations with foreign countries. From a British perspective, diplomacy around reducing customs barriers was less successful, because most European countries and the United States continued to espouse strict protectionist policies. British Foreign Office representatives also submitted an important memorandum at the conference in which they noted that the countries of the British Commonwealth had a significant number of regional commitments arising from special relations with Egypt, Sudan, Iraq and mandate territories, from post-war 1919–1923 peace treaties, the Treaties of Locarno and the Four-Power Treaty from the 1921 Washington Conference relating to islands of the Pacific, in addition to their obligations as members of the League of Nations.[209] In many regards, these were older treaty commitments, and they numbered a total of twenty-one.[210] Many Dominions had no interest in European commitments;[211] for example, the Dominions did not accept the system of commitments arising from the Treaties of Locarno.[212] Despite all the steps of the British Foreign Office and the conclusions of the Imperial Conference, doubts over whether there really was a common Imperial foreign policy or whether it was instead co-operation and a certain level of co-ordination between the foreign policies of the mother country and the Dominions could not be dispelled.[213]

The final resolution of the Imperial Conference stated that the British and overseas representatives had discussed and subsequently approved the report of the Conference on the Operation of Dominion Legislation and that on the basis of Canada's wishes, due to the effectiveness of the 1865 Colonial Laws Validity Act, an appropriate regulation would be issued by the British Parliament – the Statute of Westminster. The delegates agreed to the important clause that, "no Act of Parliament of the United Kingdom passed after the commencement of this Act shall extend, or be deemed to extend, to a Dominion unless it is expressly declared in that Act that that Dominion has requested, and consented to, the enactment thereof". It further laid down a binding list of proposed legislation and recommended that the Statute be adopted by 1 December 1931 so that it could apply to all Dominion laws adopted after 1 August 1931 and so it could be extended to include further points should Dominion representatives request this.[214]

Despite the fact that the resolution of the 1930 Imperial Conference *de facto* represented an explicit draft law, the legislative process proceeded very slowly, due to lengthy discussions by the Dominions and because

Canada, Australia and Newfoundland demanded that it be extended to include additional clauses.[215] Discussions showed that the most problematic areas included the position of the Irish Free State, Australia, New Zealand and a number of smaller criticisms.[216] It wasn't until 4 September 1931 that Britain's Dominion Secretary, James Henry Thomas, finished a memorandum containing the final version of the Statute.[217] Five days later, it was approved by His Majesty's government. The political situation in Ireland led to it being agreed that the procedure be accelerated so that the law could be discussed in early December 1931 and come into force by the end of that month.[218] On 2 November, Thomas officially sent its final version to legislators.[219] The Statute of Westminster, which was adopted after significant debate on 11 December 1931,[220] removed all remaining constitutional inequalities between the mother country and the Dominions by setting forth their legislative independence within the British Empire.[221]

The Statute comprised twelve sections. The preamble referred to the conclusions of the Imperial Conferences of 1926 and 1930, according to which, "the Crown is the symbol of the free association of the members of the British Commonwealth of Nations, and as they are united by a common allegiance to the Crown". Their constitutional position prevented any act of the British parliament from applying within Dominion territory without the consent of the Dominion parliament. It also stated that the succession to the throne and any alteration in the Royal Style and Titles would require not just Westminster's consent, but also the consent of Dominion legislators.[222] The first section, considering the bias against India's position, defined that the term "Dominion" could only relate to "the Dominion of Canada, the Commonwealth of Australia, the Dominion of New Zealand, the Union of South Africa, the Irish Free State and Newfoundland".[223] The expression "dominion", meaning estate or possessions, could continue to be used in practice to refer to all territory where the British monarch was sovereign, i.e. specifically the United Kingdom and the Colonies in particular.[224]

The second clause determined that the 1865 Colonial Laws Validity Act would no longer apply after issuance of the Statute, and that "no law and no provision of any law made after the commencement of this Act by the Parliament of a Dominion shall be void or inoperative on the ground that it is repugnant to the law of England". The third section guaranteed that the laws enacted by Dominion parliaments had full extra-territorial force, something Britain considered useful in terms of Imperial interests.[225] The fourth section made clear that no Westminster law would apply in the Dominions after adoption of the Statute unless the Dominions express their consent to it. This procedure was formerly agreed at the 1926 Imperial Conference.[226]

The fifth section regulated the 1894 Merchant Shipping Act in regard to Dominion legislatures. The sixth section dealt with rights of Dominion parliaments in regard to the Colonial Courts of Admiralty Act of 1890. At the request of Canada, Section 7 expanded its legislative power in the provinces there. Section 8 assured the constancy of Australia and New Zealand's constitutions. The ninth section stressed the authority of the Parliament of the Commonwealth of Australia over other Australian legislative bodies. The tenth clause contained a provision that the second to sixth sections would not come into force until Australia, New Zealand and Newfoundland expressly adopt them. Australia, New Zealand and Newfoundland, however, took some time to adopt the legislation.[227] The eleventh section defined the use of the term "Colony" in line with the 1889 Interpretation Act, which was not to apply to Dominions and their provinces, or to any other part of their territories. The final, twelfth, section clarified the name of the law as the Statute of Westminster.[228]

The Statute of Westminster was not a universal or natural panacea to the Commonwealth's ailments, even if the overseas autonomous territories theoretically became sovereign states.[229] From a political perspective, the Pacific Dominions did not welcome the adoption of the Statute, although in the past they had not resisted closer co-operation with the mother country. Within the Empire, there was a strengthening of "centrifugal tendencies", something which had begun in 1926. On the one hand, the Balfour Declaration symbolised a stronger Commonwealth integrity, but on the other hand it marked the beginning of a new era in relations between London and the Dominion governments.[230] The economic and foreign policy challenges which the Empire had to confront in the early 1930s were a test of its unity, ability to come to agreements and effective co-operation.

Notes

1. Esberey, J. E., "Personality and Politics: A New Look at the King-Byng Dispute", *Canadian Journal of Political Science/Revue canadienne de science politique* 6, No. 1, 1973, 41.
2. Stacey, Charles Perry, *Canada and the Age of Conflict: A History of Canadian External Policies: 1921–1948: The Mackenzie King Era*, Vol. 2, Toronto: University of Toronto Press, 1981, 73.
3. Neatby, H. Blair, *William Lyon Mackenzie King: 1924–1932: The Lonely Heights*, Vol. 2, London: Methuen & Co, 1963, 60–73.
4. See Bourrie, Mark, "The Myth of the "Gagged Clam": William Lyon Mackenzie King's Press Relations", *Global Media Journal: Canadian Edition* 3, No. 2, 2010, 13–30.
5. Also elected to the parliament of 245 seats were one independent and three Labour candidates. Neatby, 75.
6. Esberey, 47; TNA, DO 117/4, [Memorandum by] A. F. Sladen, 18 January 1926, 1–4 [9–12].
7. Mackenzie King did not believe opposition leader Arthur Meighen would be able to get the support to set up a government, and dissolution of parliament and calling a new election would resolve the deadlock. TNA, DO 117/24, [Statement Issued by Mackenzie King], 4 December [sic] 1925, [9–10].

The Road to the Statute of Westminster 263

8 Neatby, 82, 111.
9 Esberey, 49.
10 TNA, CO 886/10/4, D. 7104, Canada: The Governor General to the Secretary of State, 30 June 1926, Doc. No. 146, 145 [491]; TNA, CO 886/10/4, D. 7104, Canada: The Governor General to the Secretary of State, 30 June 1926, Doc. No. 147, 146 [492].
11 CAC, AP, AMEL 2/4/4, Larkin to L. S. Amery, 29 June 1926, [s. p.].
12 Cf. Graham, Roger (Ed.), *The King-Byng Affair, 1926: A Question of Responsible Government*, Toronto: Copp Clark Publishing Co., 1967, 23–24; TNA, CAB 24/180/82, Mackenzie King to Byng, 3 July 1926, [79]; TNA, DO 117/24, Mackenzie King to L. S. Amery, 17 July 1926, [6–8]; TNA, CAB 24/180/64, C. P. 263 (26), Paraphrase Telegram from the Secretary of State of Dominion Affairs to the Governor General of Canada, 1 July 1926, 7; TNA, CO 886/10/4, D. 7104, Canada: The Governor General to the Secretary of State, 30 June 1926, Doc. No. 145, 144–145 [491]; TNA, DO 117/20, Note, [July 1926], [5]; TNA, CAB 24/180/64, C. P. 263 (26), Paraphrase Telegram from the Secretary of State of Dominion Affairs to the Governor General of Canada, 1 July 1926, 7.
13 Stacey, Vol. 2, 76.
14 Esberey, 44, 48; TNA, DO 117/20, *The Times*, 1 July 1926, [37].
15 TNA, DO 117/20, Telegram from the Secretary of State of Dominion Affairs to the Governor General of Canada, 1 July 1926, [30].
16 Stacey, Vol. 2, 76–77.
17 CAC, AP, AMEL 2/4/4, Byng to L. S. Amery, 18 September 1926, [1]–3.
18 Cf. CAC, AP, AMEL 2/4/4, Byng to L. S. Amery, 17 July 1926, [1]–2; TNA, CAB 24/180/64, C. P. 263 (26), Paraphrase Telegram from the Governor General of Canada to the Secretary of State of Dominion Affairs, 30 June 1926, 2; TNA, DO 121/60, Canada: Private Letters Addressed to Lord Byng of Vimy, Governor-General, June–July 1926, 1–15.
19 TNA, DO 117/4, C. P. D. to L. S. Amery, 2 January 1926, [4].
20 TNA, DO 117/4, L. S. Amery to Byng, 12 February 1926, [13–14].
21 CAC, AP, AMEL 2/1/11, Borden to Byng, Ottawa, 6 July 1926, [ff. 1–2]; CAC, AP, AMEL 2/1/11, Borden to L. S. Amery, Ottawa, 18 September 1926, [ff. 1–4]; CAC, AP, AMEL 2/1/11, L. S. Amery to Borden, 4 October 1926, [s. f.].
22 TNA, DO 117/20, *The Times*, 2 July 1926, [40–41].
23 Mansergh, Nicholas, *The Commonwealth Experience: From British to Multiracial Commonwealth*, Vol. 2, London: Macmillan, 1982, 22–23; Stevenson, J. A., "The Byng-King Controversy", *New Statesman* 28, No. 724, 12 March 1927, 659–660.
24 CAC, AP, AMEL 2/4/7, Die Burger: Our Also Concern, 5 July 1926, [1]–3; CAC, AP, AMEL 2/4/7, Our Vaderland: Canada's Lead, 13 July 1926, [1]–3; CAC, AP, AMEL 2/4/7, Die Burger: Allied Matters, 12 July 1926, [1]–4.
25 Wigley, Philip, *Canada and the Transition to Commonwealth: British-Canadian Relations, 1917–1926*, Cambridge: Cambridge University Press, 1977, 208.
26 CUL, SP, Add MS 7917, Vol. 2, Smuts to Mr. and Mrs. Gillet, Irene, 9 July 1924, Doc. No. 471, 284; William, Basil, *Botha, Smuts, and South Africa*, London: Hodder & Stoughton, 1946, 130.
27 Armstrong, Harold Courtenay, *Grey Steel (J. C. Smuts): A Study in Arrogance*, London: Methuen, 1946, 263.
28 Friedman, Bernard, *Smuts: A Reappraisal*, London: George Allen & Unwin, 1975, 82; Kiernan, R. H., *General Smuts*, London: George G. Harrap & Co, 1944, 147.

29 Crafford, F. S., *Jan Smuts*, Cape Town: George Allen & Unwin, 1945, 230–231; Judd, Denis – Slinn, Peter, *The Evolution of the Modern Commonwealth, 1902–80*, London: Macmillan, 1982, 62; Nicholls, George Heaton, *South Africa in My Time*, London: George Allen & Unwin, 1961, 163.

30 Cf. Brookes, Edgar H., "The Secession Movement in South Africa", *Foreign Affairs; an American Quarterly Review* 11, No. 1/4, 1932/1933, 347–354; Hall, Hessel Duncan, "The Genesis of the Balfour Declaration of 1926", *Journal of Commonwealth Political Studies* 1, No. 3, 1962, 183.

31 Pirow, Oswald, *James Barry Munnik Hertzog*, London: George Allen & Unwin, 1957, 105

32 TNA, FO 372/2198, L. S. Amery to Smuts, 20 June 1921, [303–309].

33 Hall, Hessel Duncan, *Commonwealth: A History of the British Commonwealth of Nations*, London: Von Nostrand Reinhold Co, 1971, 616.

34 Heever, C. M. van den, *General J. B. M. Hertzog*, Johannesburg: A. P. B. Bookstore, 1946, 211–212.

35 TNA, CAB 24/181/41, C. P. 341 (26), Cabinet: Status of the Union of South Africa: Annex B: Minute of the Union Government, Pretoria, 22 January 1925, 3–4 [328–329].

36 TNA, CO 886/10/4, D. 37810, Canada: The Governor-General to the Secretary of State, 8 August 1924, [Doc.] No. 18, 15–16 [426–427].

37 Latham, John Greig, *Australia and the British Commonwealth*, London: Macmillan & Co, 1929, 10–11; Poynter, J. R., "The Yo-yo Variations: Initiative and Dependence in Australia's External Relations, 1918–1923", *Historical Studies* 14, No. 54, 1970, 248.

38 TNA, CO 886/10/4, D. 37810, Commonwealth of Australia: The Governor-General to the Secretary of State, 16 July 1924, [Doc.] No. 16, 12–14 [425–426].

39 Barnes, John – Nicholson, David (eds.), *The Leo Amery Diaries: 1869–1929*, Vol. 2, London: Hutchinson, 1980, 392–393; TNA, CO 886/10/4, D. 54369, Commonwealth of Australia: The Governor-General to the Secretary of State, 20 November 1924, Doc. No. 113, 75; TNA, CO 886/10/4, D. 54369, Commonwealth of Australia: The Secretary of State to the Governor-General, 1 January 1925, Doc. No. 114, 76; TNA, CO 886/10/4, D. 54369, Commonwealth of Australia: The Secretary of State to the Governor-General, 1 January 1925, Doc. No. 115, 76.

40 CAC, HP, HNKY 5/7, Casey to Hankey, Melbourne, 10 February 1960, [100].

41 Dawson, R. MacGregor, "The Imperial Conference", *The Canadian Journal of Economics and Political Science/Revue canadienne d'Economique et de Science politique* 3, No. 1, 1937, 32.

42 Neame, Lawrence Elwin, *General Hertzog*, London: Hurst & Blackett, 1930, 244.

43 CAC, AP, AMEL 2/4/7, L. S. Amery to Hertzog, 30 July 1925, [1]–7.

44 TNA, FO 800/258, Hertzog to L. S. Amery, 9 December 1925, [829–831].

45 CAC, AP, AMEL 2/4/7, L. S. Amery to Hertzog, 25 November 1925, [s. p.].

46 Cf. TNA, FO 800/258, Hertzog to L. S. Amery, 18 December 1925, [823]; TNA, FO 800/259, L. S. Amery to A. Chamberlain, Pontresina, 3 January 1926, [2]; TNA, FO 800/259, [Extract from *The Daily Telegraph*], Imperial Conference: The Locarno Pact: General Hertzog's Hint, 30 January 1926, [35].

47 CAC, AP, AMEL 2/4/7, L. S. Amery to Hertzog, 4 March 1926, [s. p.].

48 Cf. CAC, AP AMEL 2/4/7, Die Burger: The Imperial Conference, 16 January 1926, [1]–3; CAC, AP AMEL 2/4/7, The South African Nation: The Right

Spirit, 23 January 1926, [s. p.]; TNA, CO 886/10/4, D. 6254, Union of South Africa: Extract from the Cape Times of Friday, 23 April 1926, Doc. No. 129, 92–95 [465–466]; TNA, FO 372/2197, Extract from the Cape Times: Statement by Prime Minister, 23 April 1926, [168–175].
49 TNA, CAB 24/181/6, C. P. 306 (26): Cabinet: Status of the Union of South Africa: Speech by General Hertzog at Stellenbosch, [15 May 1926], 2–8; TNA, CO 886/10/4, D. 6093/26, Union of South Africa: Extract from the Cape Times of Monday, 17 May 1926, Doc. No. 130, 95–101 [466–469].
50 TNA, CAB 24/181/6, C. P. 306 (26): Cabinet: Status of the Union of South Africa: Note by the Secretary of State for Dominion Affairs, 27 July 1926, [45].
51 TNA, FO 372/2197, Extract from the Cape Times: House of Assembly Debates, 29 May 1926, [190–192].
52 TNA, DO 117/32, C. P. 306 (26): Cabinet: Status of the Union of South Africa: Speech by General Hertzog at Stellenbosch, [15 May 1926], 4.
53 Cf. TNA, FO 372/2197, Die Burger: Our International Status, 17 May 1926, [177–181]; TNA, FO 372/2197, Die Burger: Through South African Classes, 18 May 1926, [182–184]; TNA, FO 372/2197, Die Burger: Capers, 20 May 1926, [185–188].
54 Cf. TNA, CO 537/1113, The Secretary of State to the Governors-General and Governor, 21 December 1926, [41]; TNA, CAB 23/51/14, Cabinet 60 (25), Conclusions of Meeting of the Cabinet, 18 December 1925, 7 [189]; TNA, FO 800/259, [Memorandum by Amery], January 1926, [29–34].
55 TNA, CAB 24/176/31, C. P. 532 (25), Next Imperial Conference: Memorandum by the Secretary of State for Dominion Affairs, 17 December 1925, [178–186].
56 TNA, CAB 23/52/8, Cabinet 8 (26), Conclusions of Meeting of the Cabinet, 26 February 1926, [132].
57 TNA, CAB 24/179/24 (DO 117/10), C. P. 124 (26), Cabinet: Imperial Conference (Agenda) Committee: Report, 24 March 1926, 1–8.
58 TNA, CAB 32/38, I. A (26), Cabinet: Imperial Conference (Agenda) Committee: Draft Report, 20 March 1926, 12–13 [45–46].
59 His Majesty's Government deleted from the telegram text to Dominion Prime Ministers the paragraphs concerning the problems of the diplomatic representation of the Empire in foreign countries and the status of foreign consuls in Dominions. TNA, CAB 23/52/14, Cabinet 14 (26), Conclusions of Meeting of the Cabinet, 31 March 1926, 6–7 [132–133].
60 Hall, "The Genesis", 186.
61 Cf. TNA, CAB 24/180/24, C. P. 224 (26), Cabinet: Imperial Conference, 1926: Documents Committee: Report, 4 June 1926, 2 [95].
62 TNA, CAB 32/39, E (B) 13, Cabinet: Imperial Conference, 1926: Appendix 5: The Present System of Communication and Consultation with the Dominion Governments, 5–7 [25–26].
63 TNA, CAB 24/180/77, C. P. 276 (26), Cabinet: Imperial Conference, 1926 (Documents) Committee: Second Report, 20 July 1926, 3–4 [456–457]; TNA, CAB 24/180/77, E (B) 13, Cabinet: Imperial Conference, 1926: Report No. 3 of Committee on Questions Affecting Inter-Imperial Relations, 22 June 1926, 1–4 [461–462].
64 CAC, AP, AMEL 2/1/11, Bruce to L. S. Amery, Melbourne, 28 August 1926, [s. f.].
65 TNA, CAB 32/39, E (B) 14, Cabinet: Imperial Conference, 1926: Report No. 4 of Committee on Questions Affecting Inter-Imperial Relations, 30 June 1926 ff. 1–3 [27–28].
66 Britain proposed a division into treaties linked to the League of Nations, other treaty arrangements, and government agreements. At the same time,

the standard practice of Dominions being able to sign international treaties according to geography was to continue. Cf. TNA, CAB 24/181/4, C. P. 304 (26), Cabinet: Imperial Conference 1926 (Documents) Committee: Sub-Committee on the Form of Preamble and Signature of Treaties: Report, 30 July 1926, [13–14]; TNA, CAB 32/42 (DO 117/22), E. 84, Imperial Conference, 1926: Form of Preamble and Signature of Treaties, July 1926, [4–8].

67 TNA, CAB 32/45, I. C., Imperial Conference, 1926: Notes of an Informal Meeting of British, Dominion and Indian Secretariats, 18 October 1926, 4.

68 TNA, DO 117/21, (B.) 15, Cabinet: Imperial Conference, 1926: Amended Report No. 5 of Inter-Departmental Committee on Questions Affecting Inter-Imperial Relations, 18 October 1926, [1]–9 [5–9].

69 TNA, DO 117/32, Hertzog to L. A. Amery, Pretoria, 26 July 1926, [1]–5.

70 TNA, DO 117/32, C. P. 341 (26), Cabinet: Status of the Union of South Africa: Note by the Secretary of State for Dominions Affairs, Dominions Office, 4 October 1926, [1]–2.

71 Cf. TNA, CAB 24/181/41, C. P. 341 (26), Cabinet: Status of the Union of South Africa: Annex C: Note a Conversation at Geneva between Mr. Batterbee, Dominions Office, and the High Commissioner for the Union of South Africa, Geneva, 13 September 1926, 4–6 [329]; TNA, CAB 24/181/41, C. P. 341 (26), Despatch from His Majesty's Representative [H. A. Grant Watson] at Lisbon, Lisbon, 2 September 1926, 6–7 [330].

72 Mansergh, Nicholas, *Survey of British Commonwealth Affairs: Problems of External Policy 1931–1939*, London: Oxford University Press, 1952, 11.

73 TNA, DO 117/33, [Letter to] Edgcumbe, 7 October 1926, [11].

74 TNA, DO 117/33, L. S. Amery to A. Chamberlain, Downing Street, 19 October 1926, [37–39]; TNA, DO 117/33, L. S. Amery to Balfour, Downing Street, 19 October 1926, [40–43].

75 Cmd. 2769, *Imperial Conference, 1926: Appendices to the Summary of Proceedings*, London: HMSO, 1927, 5–14; Cumpston, I. M. (Ed.), *The Growth of the British Commonwealth 1880–1932*, London: Edward Arnold, 1973, 57; TNA, CAB 32/46, E. (1926), Imperial Conference, 1926: Stenographic Notes of the First Meeting, Downing Street, 19 October 1926, [2–6].

76 For more on the system of communication and method of communication between Great Britain and the Dominions TNA, FO 372/2197, A. Koppel, Memorandum on Consultation with and Communication to the British Dominions on Foreign Policy, 16 January 1926, [1]–12; TNA, FO 372/2197, Memorandum on the Existing Arrangements for Communication of Information Regarding Foreign Affairs to the Governments of the Dominions, 8 February 1926, [42–47].

77 Oliver, Peter C., *The Constitution of Independence: The Development of Constitutional Theory in Australia, Canada, and New Zealand*, Oxford: Oxford University Press, 2005, 45–47; PD, HoL, 5th Series, Vol. 65, 27 July 1926, 285–287; TNA, CO 886/10/4, D. 7185/26, Irish Free State: Extract from Dail Eireann Debates, 2 June 1926, Doc. No. 132, 105–106 [471–472]; TNA, CO 886/10/4, D. 7185/26, Irish Free State: Extract from Dail Eireann Debates, 3 June 1926, Doc. No. 133, 106–107 [472]; TNA, CO 886/10/4, D. 7213/26, Canada: Extract from Canadian Debates, 21 June 1926, Doc. No. 134, 107–109 [472–473].

78 Ross, Angus, "Reluctant Dominion or Dutiful Daughter? New Zealand and the Commonwealth in the Inter-War Years", *Journal of Commonwealth Political Studies* 10, No. 1, 1972, 33.

79 CAC, AP, AMEL 1/3/40, [L. S. Amery] to Milner, 27 November 1906, 3.
80 TNA, FO 372/2198, Le Quitidien: Les Dominions Anglais sont en désaccord sur l'organisation de l'Empire, 2 septembre, 1926, [194].
81 Robertson, John, J. S. *Scullin: A Political Biography*, Nedlands: University of Western Australia Press, 1974, 274.
82 Hancock, William Keith, Sir, *Survey of British Commonwealth Affairs: Problems of Nationality 1918–1936*, Vol. 1, London: Oxford University Press, 1937, 52.
83 TNA, DO 117/9, Bruce to Casey, 10 March 1926, [22–24].
84 TNA, FO 426/1, T 13849/5885/384, Deputy Governor-General of the Commonwealth of Australia [Somers] to Mr. Amery, Melbourne, 18 August 1926, 13.
85 CUL, SP, Add MS 7917, Vol. 2, Smuts to Mr. and Mrs. Gillet, Cape Town, 11 June 1925, 325.
86 Cf. CUL, SP, Add MS 7917, Vol. 6, Smuts to Mr. and Mrs. Gillet, Tsalta, 23 February 1935, Doc. No. 903, 824–824a; Smuts, Jan Christiaan, "The Present International Outlook", *International Affairs* 14, No. 1, 1935, 9.
87 Cf. BL, BP, Add MS 49704, Hankey to Balfour, 12 October 1926, [110]; Cmd. 2768, *Imperial Conference, 1926: Summary of Proceedings*, London: HMSO, 1926, 12; Marshall, Peter, "The Balfour Formula and the Evolution of the Commonwealth", *The Round Table* 90, No. 361, 2001, 543; TNA, CAB 32/46, E. (1926), Imperial Conference, 1926: Stenographic Notes of the Eight Meeting, Downing Street, 25 October 1926, [84–85].
88 Zebel, Sydney, *Balfour: A Political Biography*, Cambridge: Cambridge University Press, 1973, 287.
89 "The Next Imperial Conference", *The Round Table* 16, No. 62, 1926, 231.
90 Mansergh, *Survey*, 11.
91 Cf. Adams, Ralph James Q., *Balfour: The Last Grandee*, London: John Murray, 2008, 372; CAC, AP, AMEL 5/39, Birmingham Post: Dominions Prime Ministers at Rugby Wireless Station, 8 November 1926, [1]; CAC, AP, AMEL 5/39, The Illustrated London News: [Statesmen of the British Empire during the Great Silence on Armistice Day], 20 November 1926, [17]; CAC, AP, AMEL 5/39, The Daily Telegraph: Kruger's Wagon, 20 November 1926, [19]; CAC, HP, HNKY 24/5, M. Hankey, Inter-Imperial Relations: The Balfour Formula, 1926, [October 1951], 7; Dugdale, Blanche Elizabeth Campbell, *Arthur James Balfour: 1906–1930*, Vol. 2, London: Hutchinson & Co., 1939, 379–380; TNA, DO 35/10, Edinburgh + Glasgow, 24 November 1926, [138–178]; TNA, DO 35/10, Manchester, 5 and 6 November 1926, [206–253].
92 Cf. TNA, CAB 32/56, E. (I. R.–26), Imperial Conference, 1926: Committee of Inter-Imperial Relations: Minutes of the First Meeting of the Committee, 27 October 1926, 2–11 [8–13]; White, Terence de Vere, *Kevin O'Higgins*, Dublin: Anvil Books, 1986, 221–222.
93 TNA, CAB 32/56, E. (I. R.–26) 1, Imperial Conference, 1926: Committee of Inter-Imperial Relations: Draft Declaration Prepared by General Hertzog, 28 October 1926, [49].
94 Cf. BL, BP, Add MS 49704, Hankey to Balfour, 1 November 1926, [141]; BL, BP, Add MS 49704, Harding to Hankey, 1 November 1926, [146]; TNA, CAB 32/56, Draft Prepared on 29 October 1926 [by L. S. Amery], 1 November 1926, [104–106]; TNA, DO 117/48, Hankey to Baldwin, 29 October 1926, [4–14]; TNA, DO 117/48, Appendix II: Lord Balfour's Draft, [29 October 1926], [22]; TNA, DO 117/48, L. S. Amery to Hankey, 29 October 1926, [24–26]; TNA, DO 117/48, Hankey to Baldwin, 1 November

1926, [27–35]; TNA, DO 117/48, Appendix III: Mr Amery's Draft, 1 November 1926, [38]; Wigley, Philip – Hillmer, Norman, "Defining the First British Commonwealth: The Hankey Memoranda on the 1926 Imperial Conference", *The Journal of Imperial and Commonwealth History* 8, No. 1, 1979, 107–116.

95 BL, BP, Add MS 49704, Hankey to Balfour, 1 November 1926, [141–145].
96 Mansergh, *The Commonwealth Experience*, Vol. 2, 26.
97 Mansergh, *Survey*, 12.
98 Cf. TNA, CAB 32/56, E. (I. R.–26) 3, Imperial Conference, 1926: Memorandum about Existing Anomalies of the British Commonwealth of Nation, Hotel Cecil, London, 2 November 1926, [52–53]; TNA, DO 35/10, E. 115, Imperial Conference, 1926: Appeals to the Judicial Committee of the Privy Council: Memorandum by the Irish Free State Delegation, Hotel Cecil, 18 October 1926, [596–597].
99 See more in Krikorian, Jacqueline D., "British Imperial Politics and Judicial Independence: The Judicial Committee's Decision in the Canadian Case Nadan v. The King", *Canadian Journal of Political Science/Revue canadienne de science politique* 33, No. 2, 2000, 291–332.
100 TNA, CAB 32/56, E. (I. R.–26), Imperial Conference, 1926: Committee of Inter-Imperial Relations: Minutes of the Fourth to Tenth Meetings of the Committee, 2–9 November 1926, [16–41]; TNA, CAB 32/56, E. (I. R.–26) 4, Imperial Conference, 1926: Conduct of Foreign Policy: Consultation and Communication: Memorandum by the Prime Minister of New Zealand, Hotel Cecil, 4 November 1926, [54–55].
101 TNA, CAB 32/56, E. (I. R.–26), Imperial Conference, 1926: Committee of Inter-Imperial Relations: Minutes of the Eleventh Meeting of the Committee, 11 November 1926, [41–42]; TNA, CAB 32/56, E. (I. R.–26) 3A, Cabinet: Imperial Conference, 1926: Existing Anomalies in the British Commonwealth of Nation: Memorandum by the Secretary of State for Dominion Affairs, 10 November 1926, [94–95]; TNA, CAB 32/56, E. (I. R.–26) 3B, Cabinet: Imperial Conference, 1926: Existing Anomalies in the British Commonwealth of Nation: Note by the Foreign Office on the Irish Free State Memorandum, 10 November 1926, [96–97].
102 TNA, DO 117/48, L. S. Amery, Definition of Status, 9 November 1926, [41].
103 TNA, CAB 32/56, Doc. E 129, Imperial Conference, 1926: Inter-Imperial Relations Committee: Report, 18 November 1926, 1–2 [2].
104 Great Britain and Northern Ireland, Canada, Australia, New Zealand, South Africa, the Irish Free State, and Newfoundland. TNA, CAB 32/46, E. (1926), Imperial Conference, 1926: Committee of Inter-Imperial Relations: Minutes of the First Meeting of the Committee, 27 October 1926, 2 [8].
105 TNA, CAB 32/56, Doc. E 129, Imperial Conference, 1926: Inter-Imperial Relations Committee: Report, 18 November 1926, 1–2 [2].
106 "The British Commonwealth's Charter of Freedom", *Spectator* 137, No. 5135, 27 November 1926, 948–949.
107 CAC, AP, AMEL 5/39, Glasgow Herald: Empire Unity, 17 December 1926, [47].
108 Cotton, James, "W. K. Hancock and International Relations in Australia: The Commonwealth as a Model of World Government", *Australian Journal of Politics and History* 55, No. 4, 2009, 480.
109 Kenneth, Daniel, *Commonwealth: Imperialism and Internationalism, 1919–1939*, PhD Thesis, Austin: The University of Texas at Austin, 2012, 143.
110 Amery, Leopold Stennett, *The Forward View*, London: Geoffrey Bles, 1935, 179.

The Road to the Statute of Westminster   269

111 Cf. TNA, CAB 32/46, E. (1926), Imperial Conference, 1926: Stenographic Notes of the Eight Meeting, Downing Street, 25 October 1926, [84–97]; TNA, DO 35/12, C 7332/1/18, Memorandum [March, 1926], [293–304].
112 *BDEEP*, xxxiii; CAC, AP, AMEL 5/39, The Times: Cooperation in the Empire: Mr. Bruce on Future Problems, 22 December 1926, [51].
113 CAC, AP, AMEL 5/39, The Times: Results of the Imperial Conference: Unity Strengthened, 20 November 1926, [29]; CAC, AP, AMEL 5/39, Canada: Equality and Unity, 4 December 1926, [35].
114 Mansergh, *Survey*, 67.
115 Stewart, Robert B., "Treaty-Making Procedure in the British Dominions", *The American Journal of International Law* 32, No. 3, 193, 468; TNA, CAB 32/57, E. (I. R./26) 10, Imperial Conference, 1926: Inter-Imperial Relations Committee: Treaty Procedure Sub-Committee: Report, 16 November 1926, [1]–4.
116 Cf. Hall, *Commonwealth*, 575–576; Miller, John Donald Bruce, *Britain and the Old Dominions*, London: Chatto & Windus, 1966, 105–107; Troop, William H., *The Political and Constitutional Implications of the 1926 Imperial Conference*, MA Thesis, Montreal, McGill University, 1929, 35–43.
117 TNA, CAB 32/56, Doc. E 129, Imperial Conference, 1926: Inter-Imperial Relations Committee: Report, 18 November 1926, 10.
118 Borden, Robert Laird, *Canada in the Commonwealth: From Conflict to Co-operation*, Oxford: Clarendon Press, 1929, 125–126; Borden, Robert Laird, Sir, "The Imperial Conference", *Journal of the Royal Institute of International Affairs* 6, No. 4, 1927, 204–205; CAC, AP, AMEL 2/4/2, Bruce to L. S. Amery, 11 November 1926, [1]–4; CAC, AP, AMEL 2/4/2, Bruce to L. S. Amery, 23 November 1926, [1]–4; CAC, AP, AMEL 2/4/7, Athlone to L. S. Amery, Pretoria, 9 November 1926, 3–4; Dawson, R. M., *The Government of Canada*, 5th Ed., Toronto 1970, 144–145; TNA, CO 886/10/4, D. 53845, New Zealand: House of Representatives: Dominions' Status in Foreign Policy of Empire, 1 September 1925, Doc. No. 128, 92 [465]; TNA, CO 886/10/4, D. 430/27, Extracts from a Speech Made by the Right Honourable W. L. Mackenzie King, 13 December 1926, Doc. No. 140, 113–117 [475–477].
119 TNA, CAB 32/56, Doc. E 129, Imperial Conference, 1926: Inter-Imperial Relations Committee: Report, 18 November 1926, 3.
120 CAC, AP, AMEL 2/4/6, [L. S. Amery] to Coates, 10 March 1926, 4; TNA, CAB 24/180/77, E (B) 13, Cabinet: Imperial Conference, 1926: Report No. 3 of Committee on Questions Affecting Inter-Imperial Relations, 22 June 1926, 1–4 [461–462].
121 Beloff, Max, *Imperial Sunset: Dream of Commonwealth*, Vol. 2, London: Macmillan, 1989, 95; Hall, *Commonwealth*, 589–590, 596–597; Skilling, Harold Gordon, *Canadian Representation Abroad: From Agency to Embassy*, Toronto: The Ryerson Press, 1945, 115–116.
122 See more in Hillmer, Norman, "A British High Commissioner for Canada, 1927–1928", *The Journal of Imperial and Commonwealth History* 1, No. 3, 1973, 339–356.
123 Cf. Mansergh, *Survey*, 14–15; Cook, Ramsay – Macrae, D. B., "A Canadian Account of the 1926 Imperial Conference", *Journal of Commonwealth Political Studies* 3, No. 1, 1965, 50–53; Wigley, *Canada*, 271.
124 Hyam, Ronald M., *Britain's Declining Empire: The Road to Decolonisation 1918–1968*, London: Cambridge University Press, 2006, 70; TNA, CO 886/10/4, D. 12913/26/S, Mr. E. J. Harding (Dominions Office) to Sir Maurice Hankey (Cabinet Office), 4 December 1926, Doc. No. 151, 148–149 [492].

125 Barnes – Nicholson, 482; CAC, AP, AMEL 2/1/13, L. S. Amery to Davis, 26 January 1927, [5].
126 TNA, DO 35/20, [Sir Sidney] Low to L. S. Amery, Kensington, 4 December 1926, [329].
127 Cf. Amery, Leopold Stennett, "Some Aspects of the Imperial Conference", *Journal of the Royal Institute of International Affairs* 6, No. 1, 1927, 4–5; CAC, AP, AMEL 2/4/2, *The West Australian*, 22 November 1926, [s. p.]; CAC, AP, AMEL 5/39, The Scotsman: What the Empire Is: Union of Mutual Help: Mr. Amery on Conference, 17 December 1926, [45].
128 *PD, HoL*, 5th Series, Vol. 65, 8 December 1926, 1334.
129 Baldwin, Stanley, *Our Inheritance: Speeches and Addresses*, London: Hodder & Stoughton, 97.
130 Cf. CAC, AP, AMEL 2/4/2, Bruce to [Johnny], 30 November 1926, [1]; CAC, AP, AMEL 2/4/6, L. S. Amery to [General Sir Charles] Fergusson [Governor-General of New Zealand], 1 December 1926, [1]–5; CAC, AP, AMEL 2/4/9, Allardyce to L. S. Amery, 27 December 1926, [1]; TNA, CO 886/10/4, D. 228/27, Irish Free State: Extracts from Dail Debates, 15 and 16 December 1926, Doc. No. 143, 121–139 [479–488].
131 Cmd. 2769, 411; TNA, CO 886/10/4, D. 384/27, Extracts from a Speech Made by General Hertzog at Dinner Given in his Honour, Cape Town, 13 December 1926, Doc. No. 141, 117–118 [477–478]; TNA, CO 886/10/4, D. 384/27, Extracts from a Speech Made by General Hertzog at Luncheon Given in His Honour, Cape Town, 13 December 1926, Doc. No. 142, 118–121 [478–479].
132 CUL, SP, Add MS 7917, Vol. 3, Smuts to Mr. and Mrs. Gillet, Irene, 25 November 1926, Doc. No. 471, 384.
133 "General Smuts on the British Empire", *Spectator* 144, No. 5298, 11 January 1930, 38; "General Smuts and the Empire", *Spectator* 144, No. 5299, 18 January 1930, 77.
134 CAC, AP, AMEL 2/2/24, L. S. Amery to Smuts, 24 January 1927, [1]–3.
135 Amery, Leopold Stennett, "Jan Christiaan Smuts", *Spectator* 184, No. 6360, 19 May 1950, 676.
136 CAC, AP, AMEL 2/4/7, Athlone to L. S. Amery, Pretoria, 22 December 1926, [1]–5.
137 These included, e.g. Canadian Professor Oscar Douglas Skelton, and South African minister Helgard Dewald Johannes Bodenstein.
138 The Anglo-Portuguese alliance, for example, made Hertzog's position on the Portuguese colonies, which neighboured Union of South Africa territory, more difficult. TNA, FO 800/261, A. Chamberlain to Balfour, 7 November 1927, [534–535].
139 Cf. Holland, Robert F., *The Commonwealth in the British Official Mind: A Study in Anglo-Dominion Relations, 1925–37*, PhD Thesis, Oxford: University of Oxford, 1977, 116; TNA, CAB 24/197/19, C. P. 270 (28), League of Nation: Mr. Chilton to Lord Cushendun, London, 28 September 1928, [164–165]; TNA, CAB 24/197/32, C. P. 283 (28), League of Nation: Mr. Houghton to Lord Cushendun, Beverly Farms, 16 August 1928, [161]; TNA, DO 35/47, Clark to L. S. Amery, 6 December 1928, [474–478].
140 TNA, CO 886/10/4, D. 12913/26/S, Stamfordham to Hankey, 29 November 1926, Encl. in Doc. No. 149, 147 [492]; TNA, CO 886/10/4, D. 12913/26/S, Mr. L. S. Amery (Dominions Office) to Sir Sidney Low, 29 November 1926, Doc. No. 150, 148 [493]; TNA, CO 886/10/4, D. 13330/26, Sir Sidney Low to Mr. L. S. Amery (Dominions Office), 4 December 1926, Doc. No. 152, 150 [494]; TNA, CO 886/10/4, D. 13330/26, Mr. L. S. Amery (Dominions

Office) to Sir Sidney Low, 15 December 1926, Doc. No. 154, 151–152 [494–495]; TNA, CO 886/10/4, D. 13330/26, Sir Sidney Low to Mr. L. S. Amery (Dominions Office), 17 December 1926, Doc. No. 155, 152–153 [495]; Young, Kenneth, *Arthur James Balfour: The Happy Life of the Politician Prime Minister, Statesman and Philosopher 1848–1930*, London: G. Bell & Sons, 1963, 450–451; Wheare, Kenneth Clinton, *The Statute of Westminster and Dominion Status*, 4th Ed., Oxford: Oxford University Press, 1949, 28.

141 TNA, DO 35/25, D. 384/27, Extract from a Speech Made by General Hertzog at Pretoria on 20 December 1926, As Reported in the *Rand Daily Mail* of 21 December 1926, [31].

142 Cf. "General Hertzog", *Spectator* 145, No. 5345, 6 December 1930, 867; CUL, SP, Add MS 7917, Vol. 3, Smuts to Mr. and Mrs. Gillet, Irene, 30 November 1926, Doc. No. 472, 386; CUL, SP, Add MS 7917, Vol. 3, Smuts to Mr. and Mrs. Gillet, Irene, 13 December 1926, Doc. No. 475, 388; TNA, DO 35/25, D. 387/27, Extract from a Speech Made by General Hertzog at a Luncheon Given in His Honour at Cape Town on 13 December 1926, as Reported in the *Cape Times* of 14 December 1926, [35].

143 Cf. "General Hertzog and the Imperial Conference", *Spectator* 145, No. 5331, 30 August 1930, 265; "The Crown and the Dominions", *The Round Table* 21, No. 81, 1930, 104–105; TNA, DO 35/92/1, Reuters: South Africa's Right to Secede from British Empire, Capetown, 20 May [1930], [15–16]; TNA, DO 35/92/1, Reuters: South Africa's "Right to Secede", Capetown, 22 May [1930], [13–14].

144 See more in Clokie, Hugh MacDowall, "International Affairs: The British Dominions and Neutrality", *The American Political Science Review* 34, No. 4, 1940, 737–749; Elliott, William Yandell, "The Riddle of the British Commonwealth", *Foreign Affairs* 8, No. 1/4, 1929/1930, 444; Hancock, William Keith, Sir, *Smuts: The Fields of Force, 1919–1950*, Vol. 2, Cambridge: Cambridge University Press, 1968, 205–206; TNA, DO 114/22, D. 3177/28, Union of South Africa: Speech by the Prime Minister (General J. B. Hertzog) in the House of Assembly, 8 March 1928, Doc. No. 429, ff. 323–330; TNA, DO 114/22, D. 3492/28, Union of South Africa: Speech by the Minister of Defence (Mr. F. H. P. Creswell) in the House of Assembly, 15 March 1928, Doc. No. 431, 338–341; TNA, DO 114/22, D. 3909/28, Union of South Africa: Speech by Prime Minister (General J. B. Hertzog) in the House of Assembly, 19 and 26 March 1928, Doc. No. 432, ff. 341–352.

145 TNA, DO 35/49, B. E. H. Clifford [Imperial Secretary] to L. S. Amery, Cape Town, 16 March 1928, [538–541]; TNA, DO 114/22, Union of South Africa: Speech by the General J. C. Smuts in the House of Assembly, 8 and 15 March 1928, Doc. No. 430, 331–338.

146 TNA, FO 426/2, U 142/43/750, Sir W. Clark to Lord Passfield, Ottawa, 23 January 1930, [1].

147 In contrast, Amery argued that it all depended on the interpretation of the word "right". Cf. CAC, AP, AMEL 2/1/19, Fremantle to L. S. Amery, Cape Town, 1 August 1930, [s. f.]; CAC, AP, AMEL 2/1/19, L. S. Amery, 11 September 1930, [s. f.].

148 TNA, 32/81, Imperial Conference, 1930: Committee on Certain Aspects of Inter-Imperial Relations: Memorandum Prepared by His Majesty's Government in the Commonwealth of Australia, 24 October 1930, [1].

149 Elliott, 445; Keith, Arthur Berriedale, "The Imperial Conference of 1930", *Journal of Comparative Legislation and International Law* 13, Third Series, No. 1, 1931, 26–42.

150 For more on the issue of Dominion neutrality during war cf. TNA, CAB 21/311, Dominion Neutrality, 13 November 1928, [1]–4; TNA, CAB 21/311, Hankey to Madden, 23 November 1928, 1–3
151 Wigley, *Canada*, 278.
152 Cf. Adams, Eric E., *The Idea of Constitutional Rights and the Transformation of Canadian Constitutional Law, 1930–1960*, PhD Thesis, Toronto: University of Toronto, 2009, 36; TNA, DO 35/105/6, [Sir William] Clark to Passfield, 23 January 1930, 6–7.
153 Holland, *The Commonwealth*, 61; TNA, CAB 24/192/46, C. P. 46 (28), Canada and the Empire: Memorandum by the Secretary of State for Dominion Affairs, Dominion Office, Downing Street, 13 February 1928, [263].
154 See more cf. Fawcett, James Edmund Sandford, *The Inter se Doctrine of Commonwealth Relations*, London: Athlone Press, 1958, 5–48; Lloyd, Lorna, "Loosening the Apron Strings: The Dominions and Britain in the Interwar Years", *The Round Table* 92, No. 369, 2003, 283–291; TNA, 32/83, E. (B) (30) 2, Cabinet: Imperial Conference, 1930: First Report of the Inter-Departmental Committee on Inter-Imperial Relations: Memorandum No. II: *Inter se* Applications of Multilateral Governal Agreements, Encl. No. 2, 4 June 1930, 17–20.
155 Cf. Hall, *Commonwealth*, 662; Miller, John Donald Bruce, "The Decline of 'Inter Se'", *International Journal* 24, No. 4, 1969, 765–775; Phillips, D., "The British Commonwealth of Nations: The Latest Phase", *Pacific Affairs* 3, No. 5, 1930, 481–482.
156 For more on this issue, see TNA, DO 114/22, Constitutional Relations of the Empire: Diplomatic Representation of the Dominions in Foreign Countries and of Foreign Countries in the Dominions, 1928–1929, [1]–172; TNA, CAB 24/192/46, C. P. 46 (28), Canada and the Empire: Memorandum by the Secretary of State for Dominion Affairs, Dominion Office, Downing Street, 13 February 1928, [263–265]; TNA, CAB 24/201/22, C. P. 22 (29): Cabinet: Functions of Dominion Ministers, February 1929, [286–289]; TNA, DO 35/55, C. R. Price to H. F. Batterbee [Assistant Permanent Under-Secretary of State for Dominion Affairs], Hotel Beau Rivage, 22 September 1928, [362–367]; DO 35/77,O./D/527/29, Appointments of Dominion Ministers to Foreign Countries Recently Made or Proposed, [January 1929], [95–97]; TNA, DO 35/51, Memorandum, [September 1928], [379–389]; TNA, DO 35/77, Circular to His Majesty's Ambassadors, July 1929, [714–723].
157 For more on this issue TNA, DO 114/22, Constitutional Relations of the Empire: Diplomatic Representation of the Dominions in Foreign Countries and of Foreign Countries in the Dominions, 1928–1929, [1]–172; TNA, CAB 24/192/46, C. P. 46 (28), Canada and the Empire: Memorandum by the Secretary of State for Dominion Affairs, Dominion Office, Downing Street, 13 February 1928, [263–265]; TNA, CAB 24/201/22, C. P. 22 (29): Cabinet: Functions of Dominion Ministers, February 1929, [286–289]; TNA, DO 35/55, C. R. Price to H. F. Batterbee [Assistant Permanent Undersecretary of State for Dominion Affairs], Hotel Beau Rivage, 22 September 1928, [362–367]; DO 35/77,O./D/527/29, Appointments of Dominion Ministers to Foreign Countries Recently Made or Proposed, [January 1929], [95–97]; TNA, DO 35/51, Memorandum, [September 1928], [379–389]; TNA, DO 35/77, Circular to His Majesty's Ambassadors, July 1929, [714–723].
158 TNA, DO 35/79, A. Henderson, Relations between Representatives of His Majesty's Different Governments Abroad, Foreign Office, 14 August 1929, [617–618].

The Road to the Statute of Westminster 273

159 CAC, AP, AMEL, 2/1/17, Harding to L. S. Amery, 14 January 1929, [f. 7].
160 TNA, CAB 24/186/39, C. P. 140 (27), Cabinet: Representation in the Dominions of His Majesty's Government in Great Britain: Memorandum Circulated by the Lord President of the Council, the Secretary of State for Foreign Affairs, and the Secretary of State for Dominion Affairs, 3 May 1927, [1]–3; TNA, DO 114/22, Constitutional Relations of the Empire: Representation of Great Britain in the Dominions and of the Dominions in Great Britain and Liaison Arrangements, 1928–1929, 259–292.
161 McManus, Mary Kathleen, *The End of Imperial Diplomatic Unity, 1919–1928: Anglo-Canadian Relations from the British Perspective*, PhD Thesis, London: University of London, 1992, 300–303; TNA, CAB 24/199/36, C. P. 386 (28), Cabinet: Appointment of the High Commissioner for Great Britain in Canada, December 1928, [120–126].
162 TNA, DO 114/22, Constitutional Relations of the Empire: Consular Representation of the Dominions in Foreign Countries, 1928–1929, 191–202; TNA, DO 114/22, Constitutional Relations of the Empire: Questions Relating to Foreign Consuls in the Dominions, 1928–1929, 202–241.
163 Cf. Holland, *The Commonwealth*, 97; TNA, FO 371/14104, R. C[ecil], Optional Clause, 19 August 1929, [211]; TNA, FO 371/14104, Draft Telegram, [August 1929], [177–179]; TNA, FO 371/14104, H. W. Malkin to C. Hurst, Foreign Office, 14 August 1929, [180–183].
164 "British Imperial Conference", *Advocate of Peace through Justice* 89, No. 1, 1927, 16.
165 TNA, DO 114/21, D. 10760/28, Telegram to [Canadian, Commonwealth, New Zealand, Union and Newfoundland Governments], 16 November 1928, 59 [33]; TNA, DO 114/26, D. 680/29, Telegram from Canadian Government, 16 January 1929, Doc. No. 129, 68–69; TNA, D. 2593/29, Telegram from Commonwealth Government, 28 February 1929, Doc. No. 131, 69; TNA, D. 3441/29, Telegram from New Zealand Government, 19 March 1929, Doc. No. 132, 69; TNA, D. 2638/29, Telegram to [Canadian, Commonwealth, New Zealand, Union and Newfoundland Governments], 23 March 1929, Doc. No. 133, 70.
166 CAB 24/198/29, C. P. 329 (28), Cabinet: Proposed Expert Committee on the Operation of Dominion Legislation and Sub-Conference on Merchant Shipping Legislation: Memorandum by the Secretary of State for Dominion Affairs, 1 November 1928, 2; CAB 24/199/10, C. P. 360 (28), Cabinet: Proposed Expert Committee on the Operation of Dominion Legislation and Sub-Conference on Merchant Shipping Legislation: Clark to L. S. Amery, Ottawa, 31 October 1928, [1]–2.
167 TNA, DO 35/56, Cabinet 53 (28): Extract from Conclusions of a Meeting held on Wednesday, 28 November 1928, [29–31].
168 For more on the content of conference discussions, see TNA, CAB 32/69, Conference on the Operation of Dominion Legislation: Minutes of Meetings and Reports and Committees, 8 October–4 December 1929.
169 TNA, CAB 24/204/43, C. P. 196 (29), The Operation of Dominion Legislation: Merchant Shipping Legislation: Memorandum by the Secretary of State for Dominion Affairs, 6 July 1929, [1]–3 [339–340].
170 TNA, Prime Minister's Office (PREM) 1/68, Passfield to MacDonald, Dominions Office, Downing Street, 26 September 1929, 24–25.
171 Report of the Conference on the Operation of Dominion Legislation and Merchant Shipping Legislation, Dawson, Robert MacGregor (Ed.), *The Development of Dominion Status, 1900–1936*, London: Frank Cass & Co, 1965, 373–374; TNA, DO 117/165, Expert Conference on the Operation of Dominion Legislation, 6 September 1929, [36–56].

274   The Road to the Statute of Westminster

172 Cmd. 3479, *Report of the Conference on the Operation of Dominion Legislation and Merchant Shipping Legislation, 1929*, London: HMSO, 1930, 10–41.
173 TNA, CAB 24/207/6, C. P. 316 (29), Cabinet: The Conference on the Operation of Dominion Legislation: Memorandum by the Secretary of State for Dominion Affairs, 11 November 1929, [1]–3 [44–45].
174 TNA, CAB 24/209/9, C. P. 9 (30), Cabinet: Imperial Conference and Economic Conference: Memorandum by the Secretary of State for Dominions Affairs, 9 January 1930, [1]–3 [45–46]. On the economic difficulties of the time, cf. Boyce, Robert W. D., "The Significance of 1931 for British Imperial and International History", *Histoire@Politique: Politique, culture, société*, No. 11, 2010, 1–17.
175 Cf. CAC, AMEL 1/5/3, L. S. Amery, *Imperial Conference Ends is Failure: Socialist Rebuff to the Dominions*, Home and Empire, December 1930, 5; CAC, AMEL 1/5/3, Hints for Speakers, 11 December 1930, 19–20.
176 Great Britain was represented by the Labour Prime Minister Ramsay MacDonald, Australia by the Labour Prime Minister James Henry Scullin, Canada by the Conservative Prime Minister and the Minister for Foreign Affairs Richard Bedford Bennett, New Zealand by the Prime Minister George William Forbes, Newfoundland by the Prime Minister Sir Richard Squires, Ireland by the Minister for Foreign Affairs Patrick McGilligan and India by the British Secretary of State for India William Wedgwood Benn, later 1st Viscount Stansgate. Cmd. 3717, *Imperial Conference 1930: Summary of Proceedings*, London 1930, 3–4.
177 TNA, CAB 23/63/2, Cabinet 2 (30), Conclusions of a Meeting of the Cabinet, Downing Street, 15 January 1930, 5–7 [23–25]; TNA, CAB 24/209/27 (DO 35/90/1), C. P. 28 (30), Cabinet: Imperial Conference and Economic Conference: Memorandum by the Secretary of State for Dominions Affairs, 27 January 1930, [s. p.].
178 Cmd. 3718, *Imperial Conference, 1930: Appendices to the Summary of Proceedings*, London: HMSO, 1930, 6–7.
179 Cf. Hall, *Commonwealth*, 696; Holland, Robert F., *Britain and the Commonwealth Alliance, 1918–1939*, London: Macmillan, 1981, 116–117; Ollivier, Maurice (Ed.), *The Colonial and Imperial Conferences from 1887 to 1937*, Vol. 3, Ottawa: Queen's Printer, 1954, 295.
180 Williams, Priscilla, "New Zealand at the 1930 Imperial Conference", *New Zealand Journal of History* 5, No. 1, 1971, 39.
181 "The Imperial Conference", *Spectator* 145, No. 5343, 22 November 1930, 760.
182 Wood, F. L. W., "Australia and the Imperial Conference", *The Australian Quarterly* 2, No. 8, 1930, 68.
183 TNA, CAB 32/79, M. (30) 14, Imperial Conference, 1930: Minutes of a Meeting of Prime Ministers and Heads of Delegations, Downing Street, 3 November 1930, 4–5 [52].
184 Cf. Elliott, 445; TNA, CAB 32/88, E. (I. R.) (30), Imperial Conference, 1930: Committee on Inter-Imperial Relations: Conclusions of the Third Meeting, 10 October 1930, [1]–5; TNA, CAB 32/88, E. (I. R.) (30), Imperial Conference, 1930: Committee on Inter-Imperial Relations: Conclusions of the Fourth Meeting, 14 October 1930, [1]–7; TNA, CAB 32/88, E. (I. R.) (30), Imperial Conference, 1930: Committee on Inter-Imperial Relations: Conclusions of the Fifth Meeting, 17 October 1930, [1]–9.
185 Holland, *The Commonwealth*, 73–75.
186 TNA, CAB 32/72, E. I. C. (30), Cabinet: Imperial Conference and Economic Conference (1930) Policy Committee: First Report of the Inter-Departmental Committee on Inter-Imperial Relations: Appendix B, [4 June 1930], 1–2.

187 Geographically defined, there were (1) Great Britain and Northern Ireland and all parts of the British Empire which are not separate members of the League of Nations, (2) the Dominion of Canada, (3) the Commonwealth of Australia, (4) the Dominion of New Zealand, (5) the Union of South Africa, (6) the Irish Free State and (7) India. Although Newfoundland had Dominion status, not being a member of the League of Nations limited it. TNA, 32/83, E. (B) (30) 2, Cabinet: Imperial Conference, 1930: First Report of the Inter-Departmental Committee on Inter-Imperial Relations: Memorandum No. V: Technical Phraseology in Official Documents, Appendix A to Encl. No. 5, 4 June 1930, 25–26.

188 TNA, CAB 32/72, E. I. C. (30), Cabinet: Imperial Conference and Economic Conference (1930) Policy Committee: First Report of the Inter-Departmental Committee on Inter-Imperial Relations: Memorandum No. V: Technical Phraseology in Official Documents, [4 June 1930], 2–3; TNA, CAB 32/88, E. (I. R.) (30), Imperial Conference, 1930: Committee on Inter-Imperial Relations: Conclusions of the Fifth Meeting, 17 October 1930, 9.

189 TNA, DO 35/104/3, Inter-Departmental Committee on Inter-Imperial Relations: Note of a Meeting Held in the Foreign Office, 13 March 1931, [4–5]; TNA, DO 35/104/3, Use of the Word "Britannic", [1931], [11–17].

190 The original proposal of the members of the Inter Imperial Relations Committee was to use the term "Britannic" as an adjective for all parts of the Empire and the term "British" to refer to the United Kingdom and its dependent territories; there was no understanding of the Secretary of State for Dominion Affairs, Lord Passfield. Cf. TNA, DO 35/104/3, Inter Imperial Relations Committee: Note of Meeting Held in the Foreign Office, 29 April 1930, [29–32]; TNA, DO 35/104/3, Inter Imperial Relations Committee: Note of Meeting Held in the Foreign Office, 8 April 1930, [35–38].

191 TNA, 32/83, E. (B) (30) 2, Cabinet: Imperial Conference, 1930: First Report of the Inter-Departmental Committee on Inter-Imperial Relations: Memorandum No. V: Technical Phraseology in Official Documents, Appendix A to Encl. No. 5, 4 June 1930, 28.

192 Cmd. 3717, 27–29; TNA, 32/83, E. (B) (30) 2, Cabinet: Imperial Conference, 1930: First Report of the Inter-Departmental Committee on Inter-Imperial Relations: Memorandum No. IV: Channels of Communication between Dominion Governments and Foreign Countries, Encl. No. 4, 4 June 1930, 21–24; TNA, DO 35/55, The Present System of Communication and Consultation with the Dominion Governments on Foreign Affairs, [September 1928], [350–355]; TNA, DO 114/22, Constitutional Relations of the Empire: Channels of Communication between Dominion Governments and Foreign Countries, 1928–1929, 241–257; TNA, DO 114/22, Constitutional Relations of the Empire: Official Channel of Communication between His Majesty's Government in the United Kingdom and in the Dominions, 1928–1929, 292–294.

193 TNA, CAB 32/88, E. (I. R.) (30), Imperial Conference, 1930: Committee on Inter-Imperial Relations: Conclusions of the 7th Meeting of the Committee, House of Lords, 20 October 1930, 6.

194 TNA, CAB 32/83 (DO 35/90/2), E. (B) (30) 13, Cabinet: Imperial Conference, 1930: G. Mounsey, The System of Communication and Consultation between His Majesty's Governments: Report of the Inter-Departmental Committee on Inter-Imperial Relations, 17 July 1930, 3.

195 TNA, 32/81, Imperial Conference, 1930: Certain Questions Raised by the Irish Free State, 12 September 1930, [1]–2.

196 Cmd. 3717, 29–30; TNA, CAB 32/88, Imperial Conference, 1930: Committee on Inter-Imperial Relations: Conclusions of the Fourth Meeting of the Committee, House of Lords, 14 October 1930, 6.

197 TNA, CAB 32/88, Imperial Conference, 1930: Committee on Inter-Imperial Relations: Conclusions of the 7th Meeting of the Committee, House of Lords, 20 October 1930, 2.
198 TNA, 32/81, Imperial Conference, 1930: Status of High Commissioners: Memorandum Prepared by His Majesty's Government in the Union of South Africa, Pretoria, 14 July 1930, [1].
199 Britain's representative in Canada was a High Commissioner, in the Union of South Africa he was an Imperial Secretary, while Australia and New Zealand had chosen the model of "junior liaison office" in the context of Richard Casey's position. For the Irish Free State, in contrast to the other Dominions, geographical proximity played a large role, alongside the fact that although the Irish agreed with the idea of High Commissioners, they were later critical of them because they saw them as an attempt by London to establish firm control over Dublin. Cf. TNA, CAB 24/188/2, C. P. 202 (27), Cabinet: Committee on the Representation in the Dominions of His Majesty's Government in Great Britain: Report, Whitehall Gardens, 18 July 1927, [1]–9 [20–27]; TNA, CAB 27/347, B. R. D. (27) – 3, Cabinet: Committee on the Representation in the Dominions of His Majesty's Government in Great Britain: Memorandum by the Secretary of State for Dominion Affairs, Dominions Office, 2 July 1927, 6–7; TNA, DO 35/52, Minutes of Discussion between the Secretary of State for Dominion Affairs and the New Zealand Government at Parliament House, Wellington, 14 December 1927, [379–385].
200 Although since 1918 Dominion prime ministers had been able to communicate directly with their British counterpart, in general they communicated via High Commissioners. Cf. Beloff, *Imperial*, Vol. 2, 95; Hall, *Commonwealth*, 589–590, 596–597; Lloyd, Lorna, *Diplomacy with a Difference: The Commonwealth Office of High Commissioner, 1880–2006*, Leiden: Martinus Nijhoff, 2007, 33–46; Skilling, 115–116; TNA, CAB 24/203/8, C. P. 108 (29), Cabinet: Position of the High Commissioner for the Union of South Africa in London: Memorandum by the Secretary of State for Dominion Affairs, Dominion Office, Downing Street, 10 April 1929, [116]; TNA, DO 114/22, D. 12518/28, Memorandum Dated 15th November, 1928, By Sir William Clark, High Commissioner for Great Britain in Canada, [Doc.] No. 376, 15 November 1928, 265.
201 McManus, 230.
202 Holland, *The Commonwealth*, 78–81; TNA, FO 800/259, L. S. Amery to A. Chamberlain, Dominion Office, Downing Street, 23 December 1926, [988–993]; TNA, FO 800/259, A. Chamberlain to L. S. Amery, Twitts Ghyll, 26 December 1926, [999–1003].
203 McManus, 232.
204 Hillmer, Norman – Granatstein, J. L., *Empire to Umpire: Canada and the World to the 1990s*, Toronto: Copp Clark Longman, 1994, 104–107; TNA, FO 800/259, A. Chamberlain to L. S. Amery, Twitts Ghyll, 26 December 1926, [1003].
205 TNA, DO 35/76, [Note of a Conversation between Bodenstein and Batterbee, 12 October 1929], [137–141].
206 Cmd. 3717, 29–31; TNA, 32/81, Imperial Conference, 1930: Status of Dominion High Commissioners: Memorandum by the Secretary of State for Dominion Affairs, Dominions Office, 15 October 1930, [1]–2; TNA, 32/83, E. (B) (30) 21, Cabinet: Imperial Conference, 1930: Status of Dominion High Commissioners, Dominions Office, August 1930, [1]–4.

207 TNA, 32/81, Imperial Conference, 1930: The Channel of Communication between Dominion Governments and Foreign Governments: J[ames] H[enry] T[homas], Note by the Secretary of State for Dominion Affairs, 13 October 1930, [1]–2.
208 Cf. Cmd. 3717, 26–27; Crisp, L. F., "The Appointment of Sir Isaac Isaacs as Governor-General of Australia, 1930: J. H. Scullin's Account of the Buckingham Palace Interviews", *Historical Studies: Australia and New Zealand* 11, No. 42, 1964, 253–257; *The Imperial Conference*, The Round Table: The Commonwealth Journal of International Affairs, Vol. 21, No. 81, 1930, 230–231; "The Imperial Conference and Governors-General", *Spectator* 145, No. 5341, 8 November 1930, 655; TNA, 32/83, E. (B) (30) 14, Cabinet: Imperial Conference, 1930: The Appointment of Dominion Governor-Generals, Dominions Office, June, 1930, [1]–4; TNA, 32/83, E. (B) (30) 14, Cabinet: Imperial Conference, 1930: Appendix II to Memorandum B: Memorandum as to Procedure with regard to the Appointment of Governor-General of the Union of South Africa, [July 1930], 8–10.
209 Cf. TNA, 32/81, Imperial Conference, 1930: The Foreign Policy of His Majesty's Government in the United Kingdom Together with a List of Commitments Arising out of the Policy or the Foreign Policy of Other Nations, Foreign Office, 22 September 1930, 3–5; CAB 24/221/25, C. P. 125 (31), Cabinet: [Robert Vansittart], An Aspect of International Relations in 1931, 14 May 1931, [1]–35 [231–248].
210 Hall, *Commonwealth*, 693.
211 Gibbs, Philip, "Britain and Her Dominions: A New Problem of Empire", *New York Times*, 23 November 1930, 131.
212 Holland, *The Commonwealth*, 172.
213 Zimmern, Alfred Eckhard, "Is There an Empire Foreign Policy?" *International Affairs* 13, No. 3, 1934, 303–304.
214 Cmd. 3717, 17–19.
215 See more in TNA, DO 114/33, Discussions on the Summary of Proceedings of the Imperial Conference, 1930 (Cmd. 3717), June 1930–July 1931, Doc. Nos. 620–624, 540–610 [106–141]; TNA, DO 127/10, [Canada]: Statute of Westminster, [1930–1931], 1–187.
216 TNA, DO 127/11, Statute of Westminster, [December 1931], 4–32.
217 TNA, CAB 24/223/8, C. P. 212 (31), Cabinet: The Statute of Westminster: Memorandum by the Secretary of State for Dominion Affairs, 4 September 1931, 3–6.
218 Cf. TNA, CAB 23/68/8, Cabinet 55 (31), Conclusions of Meeting of the Cabinet, 9 September 1931, 7–8 [139–140]; TNA, CAB 23/69/1, Cabinet 72 (31), Conclusions of Meeting of the Cabinet, 29 October 1931, 2, 4 [3, 5].
219 TNA, LCO 2/1190, H. A. 34/31, Cabinet: Home Affairs Committee: Statute of Westminster: Memorandum by the Secretary of State for Dominion Affairs, 2 November 1931, [1].
220 See more in TNA, DO 114/33, Discussions on the Statute of Westminster, November–December 1931, Doc. No. 625, 610–669 [141–170].
221 Burt, Alfred Leroy, *The Evolution of the British Empire and Commonwealth*, London: Harrap, 1956, 758.
222 Cf. *Statute of Westminster, 1931* [22 Geo. 5, Ch. 4], 1–2, [http://www.legislation.gov.uk/ukpga/1931/4/pdfs/ukpga_19310004_en.pdf; cit. 2019-08-29]; *Royal and Parliamentary Titles Act, 1927,* [17 Geo. 5, Ch. 4], 1–2, [http://www.legislation.gov.uk/ukpga/1927/4/pdfs/ukpga_19270004_en.pdf; cit. 2019-08-27]; *The Proclamation Altering the Royal Style and Titles*, 13 May 1927, Keith, *Speeches*, 171–172.

223 TNA, LCO 2/1234, Appendix II: Notes on Clauses of Bill: Clause 1, [November 1931], 6.
224 TNA, DO 35/104/3, [Sir] H[erbert] J[ames] Stanley, [High Commissioner for the United Kingdom in the Union of South Africa], to H[elgard] D[ewald] J[ohannes] Bodenstein, [Secretary of External Affairs], Cape Town, 30 January, 1930, [6–9].
225 TNA, DO 114/33, 4020/247, VI. Notes on Clauses: [Sections 2, 3], February 1932, 692–694 [182–183].
226 TNA, LCO 2/1234, [D.] 6591/7, Dominions Office [C. V. Dixon] to Law Officers of the Crown, Downing Street, 18 August 1932, [1].
227 Cf. TNA, LCO 2/1234, [D.] 6591/7, Dominions Office [C. V. Dixon] to Law Officers of the Crowns, Downing Street, 18 August 1932, [1]–2; TNA, LCO 2/1234, [D.] 6591/7, Law Officers of the Crowns [T. W. H. Inskip–F. B. Merriman] to Dominions Office, Downing Street, 18 August 1932, [1]; The Statute of Westminster, 1931, Dawson, *The Development*, 413–414.
228 The Statute of Westminster, 1931, in: Mansergh, Nicholas (Ed.), *Documents and Speeches on British Commonwealth Affairs 1931–1952*, Vol. 1, London: Oxford University Press, 1953, 3; TNA, DO 114/33, 4020/247, VI. Notes on Clauses: [Sections 11, 12], February 1932, 698.
229 Knaplund, Paul, *Britain, Commonwealth and Empire, 1901–1955*, New York: Harper & Brothers 1956, 301.
230 Carrington, C. E., "A New Theory of the Commonwealth", *International Affairs* 31, No. 2, 1955, 138.

Conclusion

Constitutional relations between the mother country and the Dominions, in addition to Imperial foreign and economic policy, were one of the most important and most fascinating chapters of British Imperial history in the first three decades of the 20th century. As such, most contemporaries perceived 1931 not just as the fulfilment of almost all Dominion demands of previous decades, but also as the start of a new era in relations within the Commonwealth, and also as the transformation of the British Empire into the British Commonwealth of Nations. Although the Statute of Westminster was merely a legal definition of what had already been stated in the Balfour Declaration in 1926, it was a watershed moment because the definition of Dominion status gave overseas representatives clear evidence that Dominion countries were equal in status to Britain, that they were not subordinate and that they were bound together in their shared commitments to the Crown and membership of the British Commonwealth of Nations. Although externally the Dominions had become independent states, there was still a long road ahead to achieve full emancipation at the international level.

The transformation in Dominions' constitutional position in regard to the mother country was accompanied by a gradual change in standard Imperial terminology. Over time, and in particular following the First World War, the term "Commonwealth", the use of which suggested freer relations with the mother country for overseas politicians, began to overshadow the term "Empire", which was used by advocates to give them an air of traditionalism and conservatism. It is true that overuse of the term "Empire" evoked an impression of the subordination of overseas territories to London. Although both terms coexisted next to each other, they should not be considered equivalents; in a certain sense they were synonyms loosely describing a wider concept of Great Britain's imperial structure. However, a more precise definition of the term "British Commonwealth" more accurately characterises the complex ties between the Empire's autonomous nations and Britain in the context of dynamically developing constitutional relations than the term "British Empire" does. Despite the fact that there had been ongoing debate on the substance of the terms for decades, it wasn't until the start of the 1930s that the conclusion was reached that "British Empire" should be used for the geographical boundaries of the Empire, and "Commonwealth" to characterise relations between its self-governing territories.

The establishment of the first Dominions through the coming together of previously geographically linked Self-Governing Colonies opened up the question of what the Dominions' new position was in regard to the mother country and other parts of the Empire. As such, academic and political debate was initiated on various concepts for the British Empire's future organisational structure. To begin with, it was not clear whether advocates of decentralisation (autonomists) or supporters of centralisation (federalists) would gain the upper hand. Before the First World War, matters related to Dominion status were discussed at a number of Colonial Conferences, then Imperial Conferences from 1907, without British and Dominion politicians agreeing on any kind of comprehensive solution. Only partial conclusions were made. A number of foreign policy problems, and in particular concern over German naval arms, affected discussions to such an extent that the importance of another influential Imperial institution grew – the Committee of Imperial Defence. Although the system of Imperial Conferences as a forum where key issues of Imperial foreign, defence and economic policy were decided had been institutionalised and firmly enshrined within the Imperial structure prior to the Great War, it had to compete with the powerful Committee for Imperial Defence.

Although by 1914 both these institutions were fully integrated within the Imperial system, the First World War brought this institutional confusion to an end. Despite the fact that the system of Imperial Conferences emerged "victorious", becoming an institution with a clear composition, regular meetings and proven procedural approaches, the situation remained far from ideal. Relations between the Dominions and the mother country were suffering in that during the interim period when no Conference meetings were being held, the Empire found itself in undesirable passivity, because the Dominions' ability to influence the direction of Imperial foreign policy and other measures taken by the mother country was reduced.

The First World War represented the greatest challenge and test of the cohesion of the Empire's various parts since the first Dominions were created. The course of fighting and the significant contribution made by Dominions to the war efforts induced the British government from 1917 to temporarily implement the principle of permanent cabinet consultation through the newly installed Imperial War Cabinet and hold an Imperial War Conference, where a constitutional resolution was adopted which definitively rejected the vision of federalisation of the Empire, and which launched discussions on a modification of constitutional relations between individual autonomous countries of the Commonwealth.

There was now to be full recognition of the Dominions as self-governing nations within the Imperial community. Dominions' participation in the Paris Peace Conference and the topics discussed there affected Dominions' status not just with regard to the mother country, but also externally with regard to foreign countries. All the Dominions except Newfoundland were members of the new international organisation, the League of Nations. Dominion delegates also attached their signatures to the Treaty of Versailles, and this led the overseas representatives to conclude that their formal independence from Britain had been recognised. However, in spite of the Dominion representatives' expectations, there was no symbolic international acknowledgement of the Dominions' new status, and thus the world continued to view them as integral parts of the British Empire, meaning Britain continued to represent them externally in many regards.

Nevertheless, the course of the conference confirmed that Dominions could no longer be viewed merely as ordinary "colonies" or dependent territories. The First World War generally boosted the Dominions' shift towards a broader concept of autonomy, and more intensive co-operation within the Empire. The Great War and participation in Imperial War Cabinet meetings helped ensure that the Dominions and the mother country shared responsibility for Imperial foreign policy, and the Dominions "became" nations which began to seek *de jure* affirmation of their new constitutional position. The vision of an Imperial Cabinet becoming the "ideal" Imperial institution which might represent the "missing link" in the Imperial chain which could "fill in" during periods the Conference was not being held,[1] did not gain ground in post-war constitutional debates.

Although South Africa's General Smuts's endeavours to adopt a general declaration of constitutional rights at the 1921 Imperial Conference were not positively received, discussion of constitutional matters shifted to what level of involvement Dominions should have in deciding the direction of Imperial foreign policy. During meetings on extending the Anglo-Japanese Alliance and at the Naval Disarmament Conference in Washington in 1921–1922, overseas and London representatives often held different positions. During this time, agreement was always eventually reached, maintaining Imperial unity in key foreign policy issues. Ireland's adoption of Dominion status at the end of 1921 led to a new phase of constitutional debate. Discussions around adoption of the Anglo-Irish Treaty resulted in ambiguity over what the actual definition of Dominions' status within the Imperial structure was, since a precise definition of their rights and responsibilities had never been written down.

Conflicts of opinion between the Dominions and mother country continued in later years, when a number of events occurred impinging on matters of international relations. The circumstances and debate around the Chanak Incident, the Conference of Lausanne, the so-called Halibut

Treaty, the 1923 Imperial Conference, the Geneva Protocol and the Pact of Locarno were significantly reflected in a clearer determination of Dominions' constitutional position. A secondary phenomenon of these events was the fact that the Dominions gradually began to split into two groups, one of which (especially New Zealand and the Commonwealth of Australia) sought a continuance of common Imperial policy substantially influenced by the mother country, while the second (the Dominion of Canada, the Union of South Africa) sought to ensure Dominions represented a formally independent partner to Britain in discussions. Although the second Baldwin government responded to the constitutional issue by taking Dominion matters out of the hands of the Colonial Office and creating a new distinct ministry for Dominion affairs, this was more of an administrative measure which did not really affect the Dominions' desire for a definition of their status within the Empire.

The Imperial Conference of 1926 marked a new phase in the constitutional relations between the Dominions and the mother country. Conflicts of opinion between the Canadian Prime Minister William Lyon Mackenzie King and the Canadian Governor-General Viscount Byng, and political changes within the Union of South Africa, affected the agenda of relations within the Empire over the course of 1926. A key constitutional declaration was adopted during the conference (sometimes called the Balfour Declaration), which defined Dominions' status within the Empire. In the report issued by the Committee on Inter-Imperial Relations, British and Dominion representatives agreed that:

> They are autonomous Communities within the British empire, equal in status, in no way subordinate one to another in any aspect of their domestic or external affairs, though united by a common allegiance to the Crown, and freely associated as members of the British Commonwealth of Nations.[2]

Although the definition of Dominion status eliminated various persistent inequalities and anomalies from the period when Dominions were viewed as subsidiary territories, the Balfour Declaration of itself was just the start of a five-year legislative process which had at the end to be "blessed" by the British parliament. A committee of legal experts assessed the impact of the Committee on Inter-Imperial Relations conclusions on Dominion legislation, and after incorporation of their recommendations, the procedure culminated in issuance of the Statute of Westminster, which confirmed the constitutional equality of Dominions and the mother country. On the one hand, 1931 marked the end of discussions on Dominions' position. However, this did not represent a universal solution to all the problems of the Commonwealth, which found itself in a difficult international and economic situation in the early 1930s. Conflicts in regard to Imperial foreign policy could not be overcome. In general, a disintegrating tendency began to rise within the Empire, linked to Dominions' caution in the mother country's commitments towards Europe.

The Dominions responded in different ways to their newly affirmed sovereign international status of *de facto* independence. The Pacific Dominions delayed application of the Statute of Westminster. The Commonwealth of Australia did not adopt the law until during the war in 1942, with the whole process finally coming to a definitive end with adoption of the Australia Act in 1986. New Zealand was in no hurry to adopt the law, accepting it in 1947; the remaining powers of the British government were not removed until the its new constitution in 1986. Although the Canadian parliament adopted the Statute of Westminster, following consultation with its provinces, amendments to the Canadian constitution were excluded, this only coming to an end in 1982. After minor discussion, the Union of South Africa confirmed its new status with two 1934 acts. For domestic political and economic reasons, Newfoundland never ratified the Statute, instead relinquishing its privilege to autonomous government in 1934 and joining Canada as one of its provinces after the Second World War. The Irish Free State never formally adopted the Statute of Westminster. Éamon de Valera's political victory in the 1932 general election led to Ireland deciding the country's future would not be bound up with Britain, and gradually its remaining ties were cut. In 1937 it adopted a controversial constitution, it declared neutrality in the Second World War, and subsequently in 1949 it declared independence and left the British Commonwealth of Nations.

Notes

1 CAC, AP, AMEL 2/1/1, [L. S. Amery] to Worsfold, 24 October 1918, [1].
2 These included Great Britain and Northern Ireland, Canada, Australia, New Zealand, South Africa, the Irish Free State and Newfoundland. TNA, CAB 32/46, E. (1926), Imperial Conference, 1926; Committee of Inter-Imperial Relations: Minutes of the First Meeting of the Committee, 27 October 1926, 2 [8].

Bibliography

1) **Primary Sources**

I) The National Archives (TNA)

a) Admiralty Papers (ADM)

ADM 1 – Admiralty, and Ministry of Defence, Navy Department: Correspondence and Papers
ADM 1/8630/142 – British Empire Delegation to the Washington Conference: Minutes of Meetings, 13 November 1921 to 31 January 1922.

b) Board of Trade Papers (BT)

BT 11 – Board of Trade and Successors: Commercial Relations and Exports Department and Predecessors
BT 11/19 – Washington Conference 1921–1922.

c) Cabinet Office Papers (CAB)

CAB 1 – Cabinet Office: Miscellaneous Records
    CAB 1/4 – Miscellaneous Records.
CAB 2 – Committee of Imperial Defence and Standing Defence Sub-Committee: Minutes
    CAB 2/2 – Meetings: Nos. 83–119.
CAB 5 – Committee of Imperial Defence: Colonial Defence Memoranda (C Series)
    CAB 5/3 – Memoranda – Series C. Nos. 90–130.
CAB 17 – Committee of Imperial Defence: Miscellaneous Correspondence and Memoranda
    CAB 17/77 – Colonial Conference, 1907: Papers Prepared for Conference: Colonial Preferential Tariffs: Naval and Military Subjects.
    CAB 17/101 – Dominions Representation on the Committee of Imperial Defence.
    CAB 17/190 – Imperial Co-Operation: Memoranda, etc., by L. S. Amery.
    CAB 17/199 – Imperial Co-operation: Memoranda, etc., by L. S. Amery.
CAB 21 – Cabinet Office and Predecessors: Registered Files (1916 to 1965)
    CAB 21/243 – Irish Settlement: Negotiations between HM Government and Irish Leaders.

Bibliography 285

CAB 21/311 – Great Britain and the Dominions, Mutual Support in Time of War; and Dominion Neutrality.
CAB 23 – War Cabinet and Cabinet: Minutes
  CAB 23/25/27 – Cabinet: Conclusions: CC 43 (21).
  CAB 23/26/11 – Cabinet: Conclusions: CC 56 (21).
  CAB 23/27/5 – Cabinet: Conclusions: CC 78 (21).
  CAB 23/27/16 – Cabinet: Conclusions: CC 89 (21).
  CAB 23/31/2 – Cabinet: Conclusions: CC 49 (22).
  CAB 23/39/38 – Conferences of Ministers: Conclusions: Ministerial Conference 137.
  CAB 23/39/54 – Conferences of Ministers: Conclusions: Ministerial Conference 153.
  CAB 23/40/12 – Imperial War Cabinet: Minutes of Meetings: IWC 12.
  CAB 23/40/14 – Imperial War Cabinet: Minutes of Meetings: IWC 14.
  CAB 23/42/1 – Imperial War Cabinet: Minutes of Meetings: IWC 1.
  CAB 23/42/2 – Imperial War Cabinet: Minutes of Meetings: IWC 31.
  CAB 23/42/3 – Imperial War Cabinet: Minutes of Meetings: IWC 32.
  CAB 23/42/8 – Imperial War Cabinet: Minutes of Meetings: IWC 37.
  CAB 23/42/9 – Imperial War Cabinet: Minutes of Meetings: IWC 38.
  CAB 23/42/12 – Imperial War Cabinet: Minutes of Meetings: IWC 41.
  CAB 23/42/13 – Imperial War Cabinet: Minutes of Meetings: IWC 41 (1).
  CAB 23/42/18 – Imperial War Cabinet: Minutes of Meetings: IWC 46.
  CAB 23/42/19 – Imperial War Cabinet: Minutes of Meetings: IWC 47.
  CAB 23/43/1 – Imperial War Cabinet: Minutes of Meetings: IWC 1.
  CAB 23/43/4 – Imperial War Cabinet: Minutes of Meetings: IWC 16.
  CAB 23/43/11 – Imperial War Cabinet: Minutes of Meetings: IWC 30.
  CAB 23/43/12 – Imperial War Cabinet: Minutes of Meetings: IWC 31.
  CAB 23/43/13 – Imperial War Cabinet: Minutes of Meetings: IWC 32.
  CAB 23/43/14 – Imperial War Cabinet: Minutes of Meetings: IWC 37.
  CAB 23/43/15 – Imperial War Cabinet: Minutes of Meetings: IWC 38.
  CAB 23/46/20 – Cabinet: Conclusions: CC 48 (23).
  CAB 23/49/23 – Cabinet: Conclusions: CC 14 (25).
  CAB 23/49/25 – Cabinet: Conclusions: CC 16 (25).
  CAB 23/49/26 – Cabinet: Conclusions: CC 17 (25).
  CAB 23/50/8 – Cabinet: Conclusions: CC 18 (25).
  CAB 23/51/7 – Cabinet: Conclusions: CC 53 (25).
  CAB 23/51/14 – Cabinet: Conclusions: CC 60 (25).
  CAB 23/52/8 – Cabinet: Conclusions: CC 8 (26).
  CAB 23/52/14 – Cabinet: Conclusions: CC 14 (26).
  CAB 23/63/2 – Cabinet: Conclusions: CC 2 (30).
  CAB 23/68/8 – Cabinet: Conclusions: CC 55 (31).
  CAB 23/69/1 – Cabinet: Conclusions: CC 72 (31).
CAB 24 – War Cabinet and Cabinet: Memoranda (GT, CP and G War Series)
  CAB 24/97/102 – C. P. 599: Mandates.
  CAB 24/125/49 – C. P. 3048: The Anglo-Japanese Alliance.
  CAB 24/128/30 – C. P. 3331: Copies of Documents Relating to the Proposals of His Majesty's Government for an Irish Settlement.
  CAB 24/138/1 – C. P. 4101: Report by General Officer Commanding-in-Chief on the Situation in Ireland for Week Ending July 8th, 1922.

CAB 24/138/94 – C. P. 4195: The Turco-Greek Situation: Co-operation of Dominions.
CAB 24/162/8 – C. P. 408 (23): The Discussion on Foreign Relations in the Imperial Conference, October 8th, 1923.
CAB 24/172/5 – C. P. 105 (25): The Geneva Protocol and Security.
CAB 24/172/6 – C. P. 106 (25): The British Policy Considered in Relation to European Situation.
CAB 24/172/11 – C. P. 111 (25): Protocol for the Pacific Settlement of International Disputes.
CAB 24/172/12 – C. P. 112 (25): Reduction of Armaments: Protocol for the Pacific Settlement of International Disputes: French and Belgian Security.
CAB 24/172/16 – C. P. 116 (25): French Security.
CAB 24/172/18 – C. P. 118 (25): French and Belgian Security.
CAB 24/172/21 – C. P. 121 (25): Reduction of Armaments: Protocol for the Pacific Settlement of International Disputes: French and Belgian Security.
CAB 24/172/22 – C. P. 122 (25): British Foreign Policy and the Problem of Security.
CAB 24/172/36 – C. P. 136 (25): Protocol for the Pacific Settlement of International Disputes.
CAB 24/172/48 – C. P. 148 (25): The Dominions and the Colonial Office: Proposals for Reorganisation.
CAB 24/175/73 – C. P. 473 (25): Position of the Dominions in Relation to the Locarno Treaty.
CAB 24/176/31 – C. P. 532 (25): Next Imperial Conference.
CAB 24/179/24 – C. P. 124 (26): Imperial Conference (Agenda) Committee 1926.
CAB 24/180/24 – C. P. 224 (26): Imperial Conference, 1926: Documents Committee.
CAB 24/180/64 – C. P. 263 (26): Canadian Political Crisis.
CAB 24/180/77 – C. P. 276 (26): Imperial Conference 1926 (Documents) Committee.
CAB 24/180/82 – C. P. 381 (26): Canadian Political Crisis.
CAB 24/181/4 – C. P. 304 (26): Imperial Conference 1926 (Documents) Committee: Sub-Committee on the Form of Preamble and Signature of Treaties.
CAB 24/181/6 – C. P. 306 (26): Status of the Union of South Africa.
CAB 24/181/41 – C. P. 341 (26): Status of the Union of South Africa.
CAB 24/186/39 – C. P. 140 (27): Representation in the Dominions of His Majesty's Government in Great Britain.
CAB 24/188/2 – C. P. 202 (27): Committee on the Representation in the Dominions of His Majesty's Government in Great Britain.
CAB 24/192/46 – C. P. 46 (28): Canada and the Empire.
CAB 24/193/36 – C. P. 87 (28): Situation that would be created by the Rupture of Diplomatic Relations between a Dominion and a Foreign County [sic] (e.g., Canada and Japan).
CAB 24/197/19 – C. P. 270 (28): League of Nations: United States Opinion on Anglo-French Naval Agreement.
CAB 24/197/32 – C. P. 283 (28): League of Nations: Anglo-French Naval Agreement. Despatch from Mr Houghton to Lord Cushendun.

CAB 24/198/29 – C. P. 329 (28): Proposed Expert Committee on the Operation of Dominion Legislation and Sub-Conference on Merchant Shipping Legislation.
CAB 24/199/10 – C. P. 360 (28): Proposed Expert Committee on the Operation of Dominion Legislation and Sub-Conference on Merchant Shipping Legislation.
CAB 24/199/36 – C. P. 386 (28): Appointment of the High Commissioner for Great Britain in Canada.
CAB 24/201/22 – C. P. 22 (29): Functions of Dominion Ministers.
CAB 24/204/43 – C. P. 196 (29): The Operation of Dominion Legislation: Merchant Shipping Legislation.
CAB 24/207/6 – C. P. 316 (29): The Conference on the Operation of Dominion Legislation.
CAB 24/208/3 – C. P. 108 (29): Position of the High Commissioner for the Union of South Africa in London.
CAB 24/209/9 – C. P. 9 (30): Imperial Conference and Economic Conference.
CAB 24/209/27 – C. P. 28 (30): Imperial Conference and Economic Conference.
CAB 24/221/25 – C. P. 125 (31): An Aspect of International Relations in 1931.
CAB 24/223/8 – C. P. 212 (31): The Statute of Westminster.
CAB 27 – Cabinet Office: War Cabinet and Cabinet: Miscellaneous Committees: Records (General Series)
    CAB 27/347 – British Representation in the Dominions.
CAB 29 – Cabinet Office: International Conferences: Minutes and Papers
    CAB 29/1 – Memoranda 1–34A.
    CAB 29/7 – Memoranda 1–100.
    CAB 29/8 – Memoranda 101–200.
    CAB 29/9 – Memoranda 201–300.
    CAB 29/10 – Memoranda 301–400.
    CAB 29/14 – Memoranda 701–800.
    CAB 29/28 – Peace Conference: British Empire Delegation: Minutes of Meetings B. E. D. 1–80.
CAB 30 – Cabinet Office: Washington (Disarmament) Conference, Minutes and Memoranda
    CAB 30/1A – British Empire Delegation Conference: Minutes 48–73.
    CAB 30/4 – British Empire Delegation Conference: Index to Plenary Sessions 1–7.
    CAB 30/5 – British Empire Delegation Conference: Minutes of Meetings and Memoranda, W. D. C. 1–80.
    CAB 30/27 – Notes of Conversations between the British Empire Delegation and Foreign Delegation, S.W. 1–51.
CAB 32 – Cabinet Office: Imperial and Imperial War Conferences: Minutes and Memoranda
    CAB 32/2 – Imperial Conferences: Stenographic Notes of Meetings: E. 1–E. 34.
    CAB 32/4 – Notes of Informal Talks between Prime Ministers and Representatives etc. of the Empire and Dominions, etc.
    CAB 32/7 – Imperial Conference London 1923: Preparatory arrangements: Agenda committee: Report and conclusions IA (23) Series.
    CAB 32/9 – Imperial Conference London 1923: Conference Documents: Stenographic Notes of Conference Meetings E (1923) 1–16.

288 Bibliography

CAB 32/22 – Imperial Conference London 1923: Conference Committees: The Position of the Dominions and India in Relation to the Signature of Treaties and the Question of Territorial Waters.
CAB 32/38 – Imperial Economic Conference London 1926: Preparatory Arrangements: Cabinet Agenda Committee.
CAB 32/39 – Imperial Economic Conference London 1926: Cabinet Documents Committee: Cabinet Documents Committee: Report and Proceedings.
CAB 32/42 – Imperial Economic Conference London 1926: Cabinet Documents Committee: Sub-Committee No. 1 of Cabinet Documents Committee.
CAB 32/45 – Imperial Economic Conference London 1926: Cabinet Documents Committee: Informal Meeting of British, Dominion and Indian Secretariats.
CAB 32/46 – Imperial Economic Conference London 1926: Conference Documents: Stenographic Notes of Meetings E (1926) 1–16.
CAB 32/56 – Imperial Economic Conference London 1926: Conference Committees: General Subjects: Certain Aspects of Inter-Imperial Relations.
CAB 32/57 – Imperial Economic Conference London 1926: Conference Committees: General Subjects: Sub-Committee on Treaty Procedure.
CAB 32/69 – Conference on the Operation of Dominion Legislation London, 1929.
CAB 32/72 – Imperial Conference London 1930: Preparatory Arrangements: Cabinet Committee on Policy: Memoranda 15–33.
CAB 32/79 – Imperial Conference London 1930: Conference Documents: Meetings of Prime Ministers and Heads of Delegations.
CAB 32/81 – Imperial Conference London 1930: Conference Documents: Memoranda: General 1–41.
CAB 32/83 – Imperial Conference London 1930: Briefs for British Ministers: General Subjects 1–31.
CAB 32/88 – Imperial Conference London 1930: Committees of the Conferences: Certain Aspects of Inter-Imperial Relations.
CAB 34 – Committee of Imperial Defence, Standing Defence Sub-Committee
CAB 34/1 – Memoranda (SS Series).
CAB 37 – Cabinet Office: Photographic Copies of Cabinet Papers
CAB 37/106/58 – Imperial Conference, 1911: Statement Showing Proposed Action of His Majesty's Government on the Resolutions Submitted by the Dominions Governments.

d) Colonial Office Papers (CO)

CO 323 – Colonies, General: Original Correspondence
CO 323/511 – Correspondence, Original – Secretary of State: Offices: Miscellaneous.
CO 323/514 – Correspondence, Original – Secretary of State: Offices: Despatches.
CO 323/534 – Correspondence, Original – Secretary of State: Offices: Miscellaneous.
CO 537 – Colonial Office and Predecessors: Confidential General and Confidential Original Correspondence: Dominions
CO 537/1029 – League of Nations, Voting Power of British Empire.

CO 537/1035 – Commonwealth Channels of Communication.
CO 537/1043 – Imperial Conference, Report on Agenda.
CO 537/1058 – Protocol for the Pacific Settlement of International Disputes.
CO 537/1061 – United States and the Geneva Protocol.
CO 537/1113 – Imperial Conference, Memorandum (DO 55357).
CO 885 – War and Colonial Department and Colonial Office: Subjects Affecting Colonies Generally, Confidential Print
CO 885/8/12 – Memorandum on the Colonial Office Establishment.
CO 886 – Colonial Office: Dominions, Confidential Print
   CO 886/2/5 – Extracts from Proceedings of Colonial Conferences [1887, 1897, 1902 and 1907] Relating to Defence.
   CO 886/2/7 – Further Correspondence Relating to the Proposed Formation of an Imperial General Staff.
   CO 886/2/8 – Imperial Conference on the Subject of the Defence of the Empire: 1909: Minutes of Proceedings.
   CO 886/2/9 – Defence Conference 1909: Confidential Papers Laid Before the Imperial Defence Conference 1909.
   CO 886/3/2 – Further Correspondence [July 7, 1909 to April 1911] Relating to the Imperial Conference.
   CO 886/4/5 – Imperial Conference 1911.
   CO 886/4/7 – Proposed Reorganisation of the Colonial Office.
   CO 886/4/9 – Proposed Reorganisation of the Colonial Office.
   CO 886/4/12 – Imperial Conference 1911: Reorganisation of the Colonial Office and Position of the High Commissioner: New Zealand Resolution 3.
   CO 886/4/13 – Imperial Conference 1911: Resolution (No. 1) of Union of South Africa.
   CO 886/5A/2 – Reorganisation of the Colonial Office.
   CO 886/5A/3 – Imperial Conference, 1911: Statement Showing Proposed Action of His Majesty's Government on the Resolutions Submitted by the Dominions Governments.
   CO 886/5B/1 – Imperial Conference 1911: Minutes of Proceedings.
   CO 886/7/11 – Correspondence [1917, 1918, and 1919 (Nos. 276, 286, and 289–293)] Relating to the Imperial Conference 1911 and the Imperial War Conferences of 1917 and 1918.
   CO 886/8/3 – Constitutional Relations of the Empire: Correspondence and Papers 1917–1921.
   CO 886/9/3 – (A) Representation on Council and Votes in Assembly: (B) Channels of Communication: Correspondence with the Self-Governing Dominions: 1919 & 1920.
   CO 886/9/7 – Mandates: I. Position of Mandatory Powers; II. Procedure Necessary to Enable Dominion Governments Legally to Exercise Powers Conferred upon Them by Mandates: Correspondence with Self-Governing Dominions, 1919–1920.
   CO 886/9/8 – International Arrangements and Treaty Relations: Position of the Self-Governing Dominions: Correspondence 1917–1920 (Nos. 147 to 150) 1921.
   CO 886/10/1 – International Arrangements and Treaty Relations: Position of the Self-Governing Dominions: Correspondence 1922.

CO 886/10/2 – International Arrangements and Treaty Relations: Position of the Self-Governing Dominions and Southern Rhodesia: Correspondence 1923.

CO 886/10/4 – Constitutional Relations of the Empire: Correspondence and Papers 1923–1926.

CO 886/10/5 – Correspondence [1923–1926] Relating to the Imperial Conference 1911, Imperial War Conferences of 1917 and 1918, Imperial Meetings, 1921, Imperial Conference 1923, and the Imperial Economic Conference, 1923.

e) Dominion Office Papers (DO)

DO 35 – Dominions Office and Commonwealth Relations Office: Original Correspondence
DO 35/10 – Vol. 10.
DO 35/12 – Vol. 12: Foreign Office.
DO 35/20 – Vol. 20: Individuals.
DO 35/25 – Vol. 5: Union of South Africa.
DO 35/47 – Vol. 4: Canada; Canadian Representative.
DO 35/49 – Vol. 6: Union of South Africa; Union Representative.
DO 35/51 – Vol. 8: Irish Free State.
DO 35/52 – Vol. 9: Admiralty; Air Ministry; Privy Council; Dominions Office.
DO 35/55 – Vol. 12: Dominions Office.
DO 35/56 – Vol. 13: Dominions Office.
DO 35/76 – Vol. 11: Dominions Office Department of Overseas Trade.
DO 35/77 – Vol. 12.
DO 35/79 – Vol. 14.
DO 35/90/1 – Imperial Conference, 1930.
DO 35/90/2 – Imperial Conference, 1930.
DO 35/92/1 – Operation of Dominions Legislation.
DO 35/104/3 – Inter-Imperial Relations: Phraseology.
DO 35/105/6 – Inter-Imperial Relations: Speech by General Smuts.
DO 35/538/5 – Dispatches: Inter-Imperial Relations: Phraseology.

DO 114 – Confidential Print Dominions
DO 114/21 – Imperial Conferences: Further Correspondence.
DO 114/22 – Constitutional Relations of the Empire: Further Correspondence and Papers.
DO 114/26 – Imperial Conferences: Further Correspondence.
DO 114/32 – Constitutional Relations of the Empire (Including Defence): Further Correspondence and Papers I.
DO 114/33 – Constitutional Relations of the Empire (Including Defence): Further Correspondence and Papers II.

DO 117 – Dominion Office: Supplementary Original Correspondence
DO 117/4 – Canadian General Election.
DO 117/9 – Treaty of Locarno.
DO 117/10 – Agenda & Organisation of Imperial Conference.
DO 117/20 – Canadian Political Crisis.
DO 117/21 – Position of Representative of the British Empire on the Council of the League of Nations, Imperial Conference Agenda.

DO 117/22 – Conclusions of Meeting of Sub Committee on the Form and Preamble and Signature of Treaties, Imperial Conference Agenda.
DO 117/24 – Canadian Political Crisis.
DO 117/32 – Inter-Imperial Relations, Status of South Africa.
DO 117/33 – Constitutional Position of the Dominions.
DO 117/48 – Inter-Imperial Relations, Meetings of Committee of Heads of Delegations.
DO 117/165 – Conference on the Operation of Dominion Legislation.
DO 121 – Dominions Office and Commonwealth Relations Office: Private Office Papers
  DO 121/1 – Setting-Up of Dominions Office: Report of Committee and Correspondence between Warren Fisher, Winston Churchill, L. S. Amery, etc.
  DO 121/60 – Canada: Private Letters Addressed to Lord Byng of Vimy, Governor-General, When He Declined to Dissolve Parliament at the Request of the Canadian Prime Minister, Mr Mackenzie King.
DO 127 – Dominions Office and Successors: High Commission and Consular Archives, Canada: Registered Files
DO 127/10 – Statute of Westminster.
DO 127/11 – Statute of Westminster.

f) Foreign Office Papers (FO)

FO 371 – Foreign Office: Political Departments: General Correspondence from 1906 to 1966
FO 371/14104 – League of Nations: Code 98 File 21 (Papers 5062–8135).
FO 372 – Foreign Office: Treaty Department and Successors: General Correspondence from 1906
FO 372/2197 – Empire Foreign Policy: Code 384 Files 5885 (to Paper 10764).
FO 372/2198 – Empire Foreign Policy: Code 384 Files 5885 (Papers 11267 – End) – End.
FO 426 – Foreign Office: Confidential Print Inter-Imperial Relations
FO 426/1 – Correspondence: Part 1.
FO 426/2 – Further Correspondence: Part 2. FO 800 – Foreign Office, Private Offices: Various Ministers' and Officials' Papers
FO 800/257 – Chamberlain, Sir Austen: Miscellaneous Correspondence: Volume 2.
FO 800/258 – Chamberlain, Sir Austen: Miscellaneous Correspondence: Volume 3.
FO 800/259 – Chamberlain, Sir Austen: Miscellaneous Correspondence: Volume 4.
FO 800/261 – Chamberlain, Sir Austen: Miscellaneous Correspondence: Volume 6.

g) Lord Chancellor's Office Papers (LCO)

LCO 2 – Lord Chancellor's Office and Lord Chancellor's Department: Registered Files
  LCO 2/1190 – Status of Westminster Bill, 1931: Giving Effect to Certain Resolutions Passed at the Imperial Conferences, 1926 and 1930.

LCO 2/1234 – Colonial and Dominion Matters, Including India and Eire: Statute of Westminster, 1931: Law Officers' Opinion on a Point Arising in Connection with the Interpretation of.

h) Public Record Office Papers (PRO)

PRO 30/30 – Viscount Alfred Milner: Papers
PRO 30/30/22 – Memorandum on Imperial Constitution by Sir H. Lambert.

i) Prime Minister's Office Papers (PREM)

PREM 1 – Prime Minister's Office: Correspondence and Papers, 1916–1940
PREM 1/68 – Dominion Legislation: Report of Interdepartmental Committee. Secretary of State for Dominion's Views.

II) University of Cambridge: Cambridge University Library (CUL)

a) Smuts Papers (SP)

Add. MS 7917 – Jan Christian Smuts: Correspondence
Add. MS 7917, Box No. 1 – Letters to Alice Clark, 1906–1933.
Add. MS 7917 1 – Letters to Margaret Clark Gillett and Arthur B. Gillett: 1906–1919.
Add. MS 7917 2 – Letters to Margaret Clark Gillett and Arthur B. Gillett: 1920–1925.
Add. MS 7917 3 – Letters to Margaret Clark Gillett and Arthur B. Gillett: 1926–1930.
Add. MS 7917 6 – Letters to Margaret Clark Gillett and Arthur B. Gillett: 1935–1936.

III) University of Cambridge: Churchill College: Churchill Archives Centre (CAC)

a) Amery Papers (AP)

AMEL 1/2 – Political, up to First World War
    AMEL 1/2/5 – General Articles.
    AMEL 1/2/16 – Colonial and Imperial Conferences.
    AMEL 1/2/18 – Speeches.
    AMEL 1/2/20 – General Articles.
AMEL 1/3 – First World War, Colonial Office and Admiralty
    AMEL 1/3/40 – Correspondence with 1st Lord Milner.
    AMEL 1/3/55 – The Future of the Imperial Cabinet System.
AMEL 1/5 – General political, 1930s
    AMEL 1/5/3 – Imperial Conference 1930.
AMEL 2/1 – Correspondence Year Files
    AMEL 2/1/1 – Correspondence A–Z [January 1918–December 1918].
    AMEL 2/1/2 – Correspondence A–Z [January 1919–January 1920].
    AMEL 2/1/3 – Correspondence A–Z [January 1920–December 1920].
    AMEL 2/1/4 – Correspondence A–Z [January 1921–December 1921].
    AMEL 2/1/9 – Correspondence A–Z [January 1924–December 1924].

AMEL 2/1/10 – Correspondence A–Z [January 1925–December 1925].
AMEL 2/1/11 – Correspondence A–K [January 1926–February 1927].
AMEL 2/1/13 – Correspondence A–L [December 1926–December 1927].
AMEL 2/1/17 – Correspondence A–Z [December 1928–June 1929].
AMEL 2/1/19 – Correspondence A–Z [December 1929–December 1930].
AMEL 2/2 – Special Correspondence
  AMEL 2/2/11 – Special Correspondence: Professor H. Duncan Hall.
  AMEL 2/2/24 – Special Correspondence: Jan Smuts.
AMEL 2/4 – Private and Personal Correspondence with Governors General, State Governors and Colonial Governors
  AMEL 2/4/1 – Australia.
  AMEL 2/4/2 – Australia.
  AMEL 2/4/4 – Canada.
  AMEL 2/4/6 – New Zealand.
  AMEL 2/4/7 – South Africa.
  AMEL 2/4/9 – Newfoundland, Southern Rhodesia and the Irish Free State.
AMEL 3 – Constituency
  AMEL 3/4 – Birmingham Constituency Correspondence M–Z.
AMEL 5 – Press Cuttings
  AMEL 5/39 – The Imperial Conference.

b) Hankey Papers (HP)

HNKY 5 – Correspondence – Special
  HNKY 5/7 – Correspondence with R. G. Casey.
HNKY 7 – Papers – C. I. D.
  HNKY 7/6 – Papers for the Imperial Conference.
  HNKY 7/7 – Co-ordination of Departmental Action on the Outbreak of War.
  HNKY 7/8 – Future Work of the Committee of Imperial Defence.
HNKY 8 – Papers – Cabinet Office
  HNKY 8/11 – British Empire Interests.
  HNKY 8/22 – Washington Conference – Reports to Lloyd George.
HNKY 24 – Historical
  HNKY 24/2 – Versailles Conference, 1919.
  HNKY 24/3 – Versailles Conference – Smuts.
  HNKY 24/5 – Imperial Conference, 1926.
HNKY 27 – Literary – Broadcasts
  HNKY 27/5 – General Smuts.

IV) The British Library (BL)

a) Balfour Papers (BP)

Add MS 49698 XVI – Confidential Correspondence with Members of the Cabinet, and the Committee of Imperial Defence.
Add MS 49704 XXII – [Correspondence with Sir Maurice Hankey]: 1916–1927.
Add MS 49734 LII – [Correspondence with Marquis Curzon of Keddleston]: 1915–1923.
Add MS 49748 LXVI – Papers Relating to Foreign Affairs: 1914–1918.
Add MS 49775 XCIII – [Correspondence with Alfred Lyttelton]: 1888–1912; Leopold Stennett Amery: 1903–1926.

b) Cecil of Chelwood Papers (CCP)

Add MS 51102 XXXII – Cabinet Memoranda and Other Papers Concerning Foreign and Home Affairs, Mostly Headed or Annotated 'War Cabinet', 'Cabinet', or 'For Cabinet': 1916–1927.

V) University of Oxford: Bodleian Library (BLO)

a) Curtis Papers (CP)

Mss. Curtis 91 – Correspondence and Papers Relating to South Africa, 1931–1954: South Africa, 1931–1935.

1) Published Sources

I) Parliamentary Papers

a) Command Papers

C. – S*econd* S*eries* *(1870–1899)*

C. 5091, *Colonial Conference, 1887: Proceedings of the Colonial Conference: 1887 I*, London: HMSO, 1887.
C. 7553, *Colonial Conference, 1894: Report by the Right Hon. the Earl of Jersey, G.C.M.G., on the Colonial Conference at Ottawa, with the Proceedings of the Conference and Certain Correspondence*, London: HMSO, 1894.
C. 8485, *Correspondence between the Secretary of State for the Colonies and the Self-Governing Colonies Respecting the Celebration of the Sixtieth Anniversary of the Accession of Her Majesty the Queen*, London: HMSO, 1897.
C. 8596, *Proceedings of a Conference between the Secretary of State for the Colonies and the Premiers of the Self-Governing Colonies, at the Colonial Office*, London, June and July 1897, London: HMSO, 1897.

C*d*. – T*hird* S*eries* *(1900–1918)*

Cd. 708, *Colonies: Correspondence Relating to the Proposed Alteration of the Royal Style and Titles of the Crown*, London: HMSO, 1901.
Cd. 1299, *Colonial Conference, 1902: Papers Relating to a Conference between the Secretary of State for the Colonies and the Prime Ministers of Self-Governing Colonies; June to August, 1902*, London: HMSO, 1902.
Cd. 1597, *Colonial Conference, 1902: Memorandum on Sea Power and the Principles Involved in It*, London: HMSO, 1903.
Cd. 1932, *Report of the War Office (Reconstitution) Committee, Part I*, London: HMSO, 1904.
Cd. 1968, *Report of the War Office (Reconstitution) Committee, Part II*, London: HMSO, 1904.
Cd. 2002, *Report of the War Office (Reconstitution) Committee, Part III*, London: HMSO, 1904.
Cd. 2200, *Committee of Imperial Defence: Copy of Treasury Minute Dated 4th May 1904, as to Secretariat*, London: HMSO, 1904.
Cd. 2785, *Colonial Conference: Correspondence Relating to the Future Organization of Colonial Conferences*, London: HMSO, 1906.
Cd. 2975, *Colonial Conference: Correspondence Relating to a Proposed Colonial Conference in 1907*, London: HMSO, 1906.

Cd. 3337, *Colonial Conference, 1907: Despatch from the Secretary of State for the Colonies, with Enclosures, Respecting the Agenda of the Colonial Conference, 1907*, London: HMSO, 1907.
Cd. 3340, *Colonial Conference, 1907: Correspondence Relating to the Colonial Conference, 1907*, London: HMSO, 1907.
Cd. 3404, *Colonial Conference, 1907: Published Proceedings and Précis of the Colonial Conference, 15th to 26th April, 1907*, London: HMSO, 1907.
Cd. 3406, *Colonial Conference, 1907: Published Proceedings and Précis of the Colonial Conference, 30h April to 14th May, 1907*, London: HMSO, 1907.
Cd. 3523, *Colonial Conference, 1907: Minutes of Proceedings of the Colonial Conference, 1907*, London: HMSO, 1907.
Cd. 3524, *Colonial Conference, 1907: Papers Laid and before the Colonial Conference, 1907*, London: HMSO, 1907.
Cd. 3795, *Despatch to the Governors of the Self-Governing Colonies Relative to the Reorganization of the Colonial Office*, London: HMSO, 1907.
Cd. 4325, *Australasia: Correspondence Relating to the Naval Defence of Australia and New Zealand*, London: HMSO, 1908.
Cd. 4475, *Imperial Conference: Correspondence Relating to the Proposed Formation of an Imperial General Staff*, London: HMSO, 1909.
Cd. 4611, *Army: Memorandum by the Army Council on the Existing Army System and on the Present State of the Military Forces in the United Kingdom*, London: HMSO, 1909.
Cd. 4948, *Imperial Conference: Correspondence and Papers Relating to a Conference with Representatives of the Self-Governing Dominions on the Naval and Military Defence of the Empire*, London: HMSO, 1909.
Cd. 5135, *Dominions No. 2: Report of the Dominions Department of the Colonial Office for the Year 1909–1910*, London: HMSO, 1910.
Cd. 5273, *Dominions No. 4: Further Correspondence Relating to the Imperial Conference*, London: HMSO, 1910.
Cd. 5513, *Dominions No. 5: Imperial Conference: Correspondence Relating to the Imperial Conference*, London: HMSO, 1911.
Cd. 5745, *Dominions No. 7: Imperial Conference, 1911: Minutes of Proceedings of the Imperial Conference, 1911*, London: HMSO, 1911.
Cd. 5746–1, *Dominions No. 8: Imperial Conference, 1911: Papers Laid before the Conference*, London: HMSO, 1911.
Cd. 5746–2, *Dominions No. 9: Imperial Conference, 1911: Papers Laid before the Imperial Conference: Naval and Military Defence*, London: HMSO, 1911.
Cd. 6560, *Dominions No. 13: Despatch from the Secretary of State for the Colonies as to the Representation of the Self-Governing Dominions on the Committee of Imperial Defence*, London: HMSO, 1913.
Cd. 6863, *Dominions No. 14: Report for 1912–13 Relating to the Self-Governing Dominions: Prepared in the Dominions Department of the Colonial Office*, London: HMSO, 1913.
Cd. 7347, *Dominions No. 15: Correspondence Relating to the Representation of the Self-Governing Dominions on the Committee of Imperial Defence*, London: HMSO, 1914.
Cd. 7874, *Union of South Africa: Report on the Outbreak of the Rebellion and the Policy of the Government with Regard to Its Suppression*, London: HMSO, 1915.
Cd. 8566, *The Imperial War Conference 1917: Extracts from Minutes of Proceedings and Papers Laid before the Conference*, London: HMSO, 1917.

Cd. 9005, *War Cabinet: Report for the Year 1917*, London: HMSO, 1918.
Cd. 9177, *The Imperial War Conference, 1918: Extracts from Minutes of Proceedings and Papers Laid before the Conference*, London: HMSO, 1918.

CMD. – FOURTH SERIES (1919–1956)

ftCmd. 151, *The Covenant of the League of Nations with a Commentary Thereon*, London: HMSO, 1919.
Cmd. 195, *League of Nations: Return to an Order of the Honourable the House of Commons, dated 19 July, 1921;– for: Copy "of Speech to the Imperial Conference of the Lord President of the Council on the League of Nations"*, London: HMSO, 1921.
Cmd. 1022, *League of Nations: Report by the Secretary-General to the First Assembly of the League on the Work of the Council*, London: HMSO, 1920.
Cmd. 1474, *Conference of the Prime Ministers and Representatives of the United Kingdom, the Dominions and India, Held in June, July, and August 1921: Summary of Proceedings and Documents*, London: HMSO, 1921.
Cmd. 1502, *Correspondence Relating to the Proposals of His Majesty's Government for an Irish Settlement*, London: HMSO, 1921.
Cmd. 1539, *Further Correspondence Relating to the Proposals of His Majesty's Government for an Irish Settlement*, London: HMSO, 1921.
Cmd. 1560, *Articles of Agreement for a Treaty between Great Britain and Ireland*, London: HMSO, 1921.
Cmd. 1807, *League of Nations: Third Assembly: Report of British Delegates*, London 1923.
Cmd. 1814, *Turkey No. 1 (1923): Lausanne Conference on Near Eastern Affairs 1922–1923: Records of Proceedings and Draft Terms of Peace*, London: HMSO, 1923.
Cmd. 1929, *Treaty Series No. 16 (1923): Treaty of Peace with Turkey, and Other Instruments Signed at Lausanne on July 24, 1923, Together with Agreements between Greece and Turkey Signed on January 30, 1923, and Subsidiary Documents Forming Part of the Turkish Peace Settlement*, London: HMSO, 1923.
Cmd. 1987, *Imperial Conference, 1923: Summary of Proceedings*, London: HMSO, 1923.
Cmd. 1988, *Imperial Conference, 1923: Appendices to the Summary of Proceedings*, London: HMSO, 1923.
Cmd. 2015, *League of Nations: Fourth Assembly: Report of British Delegates*, London: HMSO, 1923.
Cmd. 2146, *Correspondence with Canadian Government on the Subject of the Peace Settlement with Turkey*, London: HMSO, 1924.
Cmd. 2301, *Consultation on Matters of Foreign Policy and General Imperial Interest: Correspondence with the Governments of the Self-Governing Dominions*, London: HMSO, 1925.
Cmd. 2458, *Protocol for the Pacific Settlement of International Disputes: Correspondence Relating to the Position of the Dominions*, London: HMSO, 1925.

Cmd. 2525, *Final Protocol of the Locarno Conference, 1925 (and Annexes): Together with Treaties between France and Poland and France and Czechoslovakia, Locarno, October 16, 1925*, London: HMSO, 1925.
Cmd. 2768 *Imperial Conference, 1926: Summary of Proceedings*, London: HMSO, 1926.
Cmd. 2769, *Imperial Conference, 1926: Appendices to the Summary of Proceedings*, London: HMSO, 1927.
Cmd. 3479, *Report of the Conference on the Operation of Dominion Legislation and Merchant Shipping Legislation, 1929*, London: HMSO, 1930.
Cmd. 3717, *Imperial Conference 1930: Summary of Proceedings*, London: HMSO, 1930.
Cmd. 3718, *Imperial Conference, 1930: Appendices to the Summary of Proceedings*, London: HMSO, 1930.

b) Parliamentary Debates (Hansard)

UNITED KINGDOM (PD)

House of Commons, 4th Series
  Vol. 118, 5 March 1903.
  Vol. 139, 2 August 1904.
House of Commons (HoC), 5th Series
  Vol. 8, 29 July 1909.
  Vol. 19, 25 July 1910.
  Vol. 28, 20 July 1911.
  Vol. 35, 20 March 1912.
  Vol. 41, 22 July 1912.
  Vol. 41, 25 July 1912.
  Vol. 71, 14 April 1915.
  Vol. 88, 19 December 1916.
  Vol. 127, 29 March 1920.
  Vol. 127, 30 March 1920.
  Vol. 127, 31 March 1920.
  Vol. 130, 24 June 1920.
  Vol. 134, 11 November 1920.
  Vol. 143, 17 June 1921.
  Vol. 149, 14 December 1921.
  Vol. 159, 27 November 1922.
  Vol. 175, 26 June 1924.
  Vol. 182, 24 March 1925.
  Vol. 185, 24 June 1925.
  Vol. 187, 27 July 1925.
  Vol. 188, 18 November 1925.
House of Lords (HoL), 5th Series
  Vol. 40, 17 June 1920.
  Vol. 57, 25 June 1924.
  Vol. 65, 27 July 1926.
  Vol. 65, 8 December 1926.

Bibliography

Australia (APD)

House of Representatives (HoR)
  No. 8, 21 February 1907.
  No. 47, 25 November 1910.
  No. 37, 10 September 1919.
  No. 14, 7 April 1920.
  No. 37, 9 September 1921.
  No. 39, 30 September 1921.
  No. 30, 24 July 1923.
Senate
  No. 38, 20 September 1922.

Canada (CPD)

House of Commons (HoC)
  5 February 1900.
  5 December 1912.
  1 February 1923.
  9 June 1924.

Ireland (IPD)

Dáil Éireann
  Vol. S, No. 4, 22 August 1921.
  Vol. S, No. 10, 14 September 1921.
  Vol. T, No. 2, 14 December 1921.
  Vol. T, No. 6, 19 December 1921.
  Vol. T, No. 15, 7 January 1922.
  Vol. 11, No. 13, 13 May 1925.

II) Collected Documents

Ashton, S. R. – Stockwell, S. E. (Eds.), *British Documents on the End of Empire: Imperial Policy and Colonial Practice, 1925–45*, Series A, Vol. 1, London: HMSO, 1997.

Barton, G. B. (Ed.), *The Draft Bill to Constitute the Commonwealth of Australia, As Adopted by the Convention of 1891*, Sydney: N.S.W., 1891.

Butler, Rohan, – Bury, J. P. T. – Lambert, M. E. (Eds.), *Documents on British Foreign Policy 1919–1939: Far Eastern Affairs April 1920–February 1922*, 1st Series, Vol. 14, London: HMSO, 1966.

Butler, Rohan – Woodward, E. L. (Eds.), *Documents on British Foreign Policy 1919–1939: 1919*, 1st Series, Vol. 6, London: HMSO, 1956.

Clark, Lowell C. (Ed.), *Documents on Canadian External Relations: 1919–1925*, Vol. 3, Ottawa: Information Canada, 1970.

Cumpston, I. M. (Ed.), *The Growth of the British Commonwealth 1880–1932*, London: Edward Arnold, 1973.

Dawson, Robert MacGregor (Ed.), *The Development of Dominion Status, 1900–1936*, London: Frank Cass & Co, 1965.

Bibliography 299

Gooch, George Peabody – Temperley, Harold (Eds.), *British Documents on the Origins of the War, 1898–1914: Anglo-German Tension: Armaments and Negotiation, 1907–12*, Vol. 6, London: HMSO, 1930.

Hancock, William Keith – Poel, Jean van der (Eds.), *Selections from the Smuts Papers: June 1902–May 1910*, Vol. 2, Cambridge: Cambridge University Press, 1966.

Hancock, William Keith – Poel, Jean van der (Eds.), *Selections from the Smuts Papers: June 1910–November 1918*, Vol. 3, Cambridge: Cambridge University Press, 1966.

Hancock, William Keith – Poel, Jean van der (Eds.), *Selections from the Smuts Papers: September 1919–November 1934*, Vol. 5, Cambridge: Cambridge University Press, 1966.

Keith, Arthur Berriedale (Ed.), *Selected Speeches and Documents on British Colonial Policy, 1763–1917*, Vol. 2, London: Oxford University Press, 1933.

Keith, Arthur Berriedale (Ed.), *Speeches and Documents on the British Dominions, 1918–1931: From Self-Government to National Sovereignty*, Oxford: Oxford University Press, 1948.

Kennedy, William Paul McClure (Ed.), *Statutes, Treaties and Documents of the Canadian Constitution 1713–1929*, 2nd Ed., Toronto: Oxford University Press, 1930.

MacKay, R. A. (Ed.), *Documents on Canadian External Relations: The Paris Peace Conference of 1919*, Vol. 2, Ottawa: Queen's Printer, 1969.

MacMurray, John Van Antwerp (Ed.), *Treaties and Agreements with and Concerning China, 1894–1919: Republican Period (1912–1919)*, Vol. 2, New York: Oxford University Press, 1921.

Mansergh, Nicholas (Ed.), *Documents and Speeches on British Commonwealth Affairs 1931–1952*, Vol. 1, London: Oxford University Press, 1953.

Ollivier, Maurice (Ed.), *The Colonial and Imperial Conferences from 1887 to 1937*, 3 Vols., Ottawa: Queen's Printer, 1954.

United States Department of State, *Papers Relating to the Foreign Relations of the United States, 1920*, Vol. 2, Washington: Government Printing Office, 1936.

United States Department of State, *Papers Relating to the Foreign Relations of the United States, 1921*, 2 Vols., Washington: Government Printing Office, 1936.

United States Department of State, *Papers Relating to the Foreign Relations of the United States, 1922*, Vol. 1, Washington: Government Printing Office, 1938.

United States Department of State, *Papers Relating to the Foreign Relations of the United States, 1923*, Vol. 1, Washington: Government Printing Office, 1938.

United States Department of State, *Papers Relating to the Foreign Relations of the United States, 1925*, Vol. 1, Washington: Government Printing Office, 1940.

III) Newspapers and Periodicals

"Administration of Samoa", *The New Zealand Herald* 55, No. 17073, 31 January 1919, 4.

A. G. G., "The Future of General Smuts", *Nation and Athenaeum* 34, No. 3, 20 October 1923, 112–113.

Amery, Leopold Stennett, "Jan Christiaan Smuts", *Spectator* 184, No. 6360, 19 May 1950, 676–677.

"An Australian View of Mr. Hughes in Paris", *New Statesman* 14, No. 352, 10 January 1920, 399–401.

Biggs, L. V., "Does Australia Want Imperial Federation?" *New Statesman* 15, No. 384, 31 August 1920, 544–545.

Biggs, L. V., "Britain's Navy", *Evening Post* 101, No. 48, 25 February 1921, 2.

Biggs, L. V., "Cabinet and Empire", *The Press* 60, No. 11637, 17 July 1903, 2.

Casson, Herbert N., "The Significance of the Imperial Conference", *Barron's* 1, No. 10, 11 July 1921, 5.

Eggleston, F. W., "The Imperial Conference", *New Statesman* 17, No. 426, 11 June 1921, 267–269.

Eggleston, F. W., "Empire or Commonwealth?", *Spectator* 147, No. 5396, 28 November 1931, 723.

Eggleston, F. W., "Far Eastern Problem: Quadruple Agreement Possible: Britain, America, Japan, China", *The Sydney Morning Herald*, No. 26174, 24 November 1921, 9.

Eggleston, F. W., "Future of the Islands", *Evening Post* 97, No. 64, 18 March 1919, 6.

Eggleston, F. W., "General Hertzog", *Spectator* 145, No. 5345, 6 December 1930, 867–868.

Eggleston, F. W., "General Hertzog and the Imperial Conference", *Spectator* 145, No. 5331, 30 August 1930, 265.

Eggleston, F. W., "General Smuts", *Spectator*, No. 4638, 19 May 1917, 557–558.

Eggleston, F. W., "General Smuts on the British Empire", *Spectator* 144, No. 5298, 11 January 1930, 38.

Eggleston, F. W., "General Smuts and the Empire", *Spectator* 144, No. 5299, 18 January 1930, 77–78.

Gibbs, Philip, Sir, "Britain and Her Dominions: A New Problem of Empire", *New York Times*, 23 November 1930, 131.

Lloyd, C. M., "Canada and Lausanne", *New Statesman* 23, No. 582, 14 June 1924, 276.

Lloyd, C. M., "Pilgrims' Banquet: No Troubles in New Zealand", *Evening Post* 82, 5 July 1911, 15.

Lloyd, C. M., "Our Share", *Auckland Star* 50, No. 25, 29 January 1919, 4.

Stevenson, J. A., "Canada's Halibut Treaty", *New Statesman* 21, No. 524, 28 April 1923, 72–73.

Stevenson, J. A., "The Byng-King Controversy", *New Statesman* 28, No. 724, 12 March 1927, 659–660.

Stevenson, J. A., "The Anglo-Japanese Alliance", *Spectator* 125, No. 4802, 10 July 1920, 38–39.

Stevenson, J. A., "The Anglo-Japanese Pact", *Evening Post* 101, No. 48, 25 February 1921, 6.

Stevenson, J. A., "The British Commonwealth's Charter of Freedom", *Spectator* 137, No. 5135, 27 November 1926, 948–949.

Stevenson, J. A., "The Imperial Conference", *Spectator* 126, No. 4850, 11 June 1921, 739–740.

Stevenson, J. A., "The Imperial Conference", *Spectator* 145, No. 5343, 22 November 1930, 759–760.

Stevenson, J. A., "The Imperial Conference and Governors-General", *Spectator* 145, No. 5341, 8 November 1930, 655.

Stevenson, J. A., "The League of Nations", *Spectator* 141, No. 5233, 13 October 1928, 484.
Wrench, John Evelyn, "Mr. Mackenzie King and Lausanne", *Spectator* 132, No. 5008, 21 June 1924, 993.

IV) Internet Sources

Crowe, Catriona – Fanning, Ronan – Kennedy, Michael et al. (Eds.), *Documents on Irish Foreign Policy: The Anglo-Irish Treaty December 1920 – December 1921*, [https://www.difp.ie/documents/1921treaty.pdf].
Colonial Laws Validity Act, 1865, [http://www.legislation.gov.uk/ukpga/1865/63/pdfs/ukpga_18650063_en.pdf].
Royal and Parliamentary Titles Act, 1927, [17 Geo. 5, Ch. 4], [http://www.legislation.gov.uk/ukpga/1927/4/pdfs/ukpga_19270004_en.pdf].
Statute of Westminster, 1931, [22 Geo. 5, Ch. 4], [http://www.legislation.gov.uk/ukpga/1931/4/pdfs/ukpga_19310004_en.pdf].

V) Memoirs, Diaries, Autobiographies, and Speeches

Amery, Leopold Stennett, *My Political Life: England before the Storm, 1896–1914*, Vol. 1, London: Hutchinson, 1953.
Amery, Leopold Stennett, *My Political Life: War and Peace 1914–1929*, Vol. 2, London: Hutchinson, 1953.
Amery, Leopold Stennett (Ed.), *The Times History of the War in South Africa, 1899–1902*, Vol. 6, London: Sampson, Low, Marsten & Co, 1909.
Baldwin, Stanley, *Our Inheritance: Speeches and Addresses*, London: Hodder & Stoughton, 1928.
Barnes, John – Nicholson, David (Eds.), *The Leo Amery Diaries: 1869–1929*, Vol. 2, London: Hutchinson, 1980.
Beeman, Neville (Ed.), *Lord Rosebery's Speeches (1874–1896)*, London: N. Beeman, 1896.
Borden, Robert Laird, Sir, *Canada and the Peace: A Speech on the Treaty of Peace, Delivered in the Canadian House of Commons on Tuesday, September 2, 1919*, Ottawa: [s. n.], 1919.
Borden, Robert Laird, Sir, *Canada at War: A Speech Delivered by Rt. Hon. Sir Robert Laird Borden in New York City*, [s. l.: s. n.], 1916.
Borden, Robert Laird, Sir, *Canadian Constitutional Studies: The Marfleet Lectures, University of Toronto, October, 1921*, London: [s. n.], 1922.
Borden, Robert Laird, Sir, *Splendid Record of the Borden Government Naval Policy Clearly Defined*, Ottawa: Federal Press Agency, 1913.
Borden, Robert Laird, Sir, *Bill relatif aux forces navales de l'empire: discours prononcé par le Très Hon. R.L. Borden, le 5 décembre 1912*, Ottawa: [s. n.], 1912.
Borden, Robert Laird, Sir, *Canada in the Commonwealth: From Conflict to Co-operation*, Oxford: Clarendon Press, 1929.
Borden, Robert Laird, Sir, *The Naval Question: Speech Delivered by Mr. R.L. Borden, M.P. 12th January, 1910*, Ottawa: [s. n.], 1910.
Borden, Robert Laird, Sir, *The Naval Question: Speech Delivered by Mr. R.L. Borden, M.P. 3rd February, 1910*, Ottawa: [s. n.], 1910.
Borden, Robert Laird, Sir, *The War and the Future*, London: Hodder & Stoughton, 1917.

Bourassa, Henri, *Le projet de loi navale: Sa nature, ses consequences: Discours prononce au Monument National le 20 janvier 1910*, Montreal: [s. n.], 1910.
Boyd, Charles W. (Ed.), *Mr. Chamberlain's Speeches*, 2 Vols., London: Constable, 1914.
Cecil, Robert Gascoyne, Viscount of Chelwood, *A Great Experiment: An Autobiography*, London: Jonathan Cape, 1941.
Cecil, Robert Gascoyne, Viscount of Chelwood, *The Moral Basis of the League of Nations: The Essex Hall Lecture, 1923*, London: Lindsey Press, 1923.
Collins, Michael, *The Path to Freedom*, London: Talbot Press, 1922.
Cook, Ramsey (Ed.), *The Dafoe-Sifton Correspondence, 1919–1927*, Winnipeg: D. W. Friesen & Sons, 1966.
Gilbert, Martin (Ed.), *Lloyd George*, Englewood Cliffs: Prentice-Hall, 1968.
Haldane, Richard Burdon, 1st Viscount of Haldane, *An Autobiography*, New York: Hodder & Stoughton, 1929.
Hopkins, J. Castell (Ed.), *Empire Club Speeches: Being Addresses Delivered before the Empire Club of Canada during Its Sessions of 1905–06*, Toronto: [s. n.], 1906.
Hopkins, J. Castell (Ed.), *Empire Club Speeches: Being Addresses Delivered before the Empire Club of Canada during Its Sessions of 1907–1908*, Toronto: [s. n.], 1910.
Chamberlain, Joseph, *Foreign & Colonial Speeches*, London: G. Routledge, 1897.
Jones, Thomas, *Whitehall Diary: 1916–1925*, Vol. 1, London: Oxford University Press, 1969.
Lloyd George, David, *The Truth about the Peace Treaties*, 2 Vols., London: Victor Gollancz, 1938.
Lloyd George, David, *War Memoirs*, 2 Vols., London: Odhams Press, 1938.
Long, Walter Hume, 1st Viscount of Wraxall, *Memories*, London: Hutchinson & Co., 1923.
Miller, David Hunter, *My Diary at the Conference of Paris with Documents*, Vol. 4, New York: [s. n.], 1924.
Milner, Alfred, 1st Viscount of Milner, *Speeches Delivered in Canada in the Autumn of 1908*, Toronto: William Tyrrell & Co, 1909.
Milner, Alfred, 1st Viscount of Milner, *The Nation and the Empire: Being a Collection of Speeches and Addresses*, London: Constable, 1913.
Milner, Alfred, *Report of Labour Commission to Ireland*, London: [s. n., 1921].
Riddell, George Allardice, Baron, *Lord Riddell's Intimate Diary of the Peace Conference and After, 1918–1923*, London: Victor Gollancz, 1933.
Seymour, Charles (Ed.), *The Intimate Papers of Colonel House: The Ending of the War*, Vol. 4, Boston: Houghton Mifflin Company, 1928.
Shaw, George Bernard (Ed.), *Fabianism and Empire: A Manifesto by the Fabian Society*, London: G. Richards, 1900.
Shaw, George Bernard, *Fabianism and the Fiscal Question: An Alternative Policy*, London: Fabian Society, 1904.
Smuts, Jan Christian, *The British Commonwealth of Nations: A Speech Made by General Smuts on May 15th, 1917*, London: Hodder & Stoughton, 1917.
Smuts, Jan Christian, *Plans for a Better World: Speeches of Field-Marshal*, London: Hodder & Stoughton, 1942.
Smuts, Jan Christian, *War-time Speeches: A Compilation of Public Utterances in Great Britain*, London: Hodder & Stoughton, 1917.

Smuts, Jan Christian, *The League of Nations: A Practical Suggestion*, London: Hodder & Stoughton, 1918.

Smuts, Jan Christian, *The Struggle of the Irish People: Address to the Congress of the United States Adopted at the January Session of Dail Eireann, 1921*, Washington: Government Printing Office, 1921.

Valera, Éamon de, *The Moral Basis of the Claim of the Republic of Ireland for Official Recognition: A Speech Delivered by Eamon de Valera at Worcester, Mass., February 6, 1920*, New York: Nation's Forum, [1920].

VI) Contemporary Books

Amery, Leopold Stennett, *The Forward View*, London: Geoffrey Bles, 1935.

Amery, Leopold Stennett, *The Problem of the Army*, London: Edward Arnold, 1903.

Amery, Leopold Stennett, *Thoughts on the Constitution*, London: Oxford University Press, 1964.

Amery, Leopold Stennett, *Union and Strength: A Series of Papers on Imperial Questions*, London: Edward Arnold, 1912.

Asquith, Herbert Henry, *The Genesis of the War*, London: Cassell & Co, 1923.

Balfour, Arthur James, *Nationality and Home Rule*, London: Longmans & Co, 1913.

Baker, Ray Stannard, *Woodrow Wilson and World Settlement*, 3 Vols., New York: Heinemann, 1922.

Baring, Evelyn, 1st Earl of Cromer, *Political and Literary Essays, 1908–1913*, London: Macmillan, 1913.

Borden, Robert Laird, Sir, *Conference on the Limitation of Armament Held at Washington November 12, 1921, to February 6, 1922: Report of the Canadian Delegate Including Treaties and Resolutions*, Ottawa: F. A. Acland, 1922.

Bourgeois, Léon Victor Auguste, *Pour la Société des Nations*, Paris: Bibliothèque-Charpentier, 1910.

Briollay, Sylvain, *Ireland in Rebellion*, Dublin: Talbot Press, 1922.

Buell, Raymond Leslie, *The Washington Conference*, New York: D. Appleton & Co, 1922.

Campbell, James Henry Mussen, *A Guide to the Home Rule Bill*, London: Union Defence League and National Unionist Association, 1912.

Campbell, James Henry Mussen, *Canada and the Navy*, Ottawa: Central Information Office of the Canadian Liberal Party, 1909.

Campbell, James Henry Mussen, *Canada and the Navy: Reasons by the Rt Hon. R. L. Borden, M.P., in Favour of a Canadian Naval Service and Against a Contribution*, Ottawa: Central Information Office of the Canadian Liberal Party, 1913.

Churchill, Winston Spencer, Sir, *The World Crisis: The Aftermath*, Vol. 5, London: Thornton Butterworth Limited, 1929.

Courtney, William Leonard – Courtney, J. E., *Pillars of the Empire: Studies & Impressions*, London: Jarrolds, [1918].

Crewe-Milnes, Robert Offley Ashburton, 1st Marquis of Crewe, *Questions of Empire*, New York: Arthur L. Humphreys, 1901.

Curtis, Lionel (Ed.), *The Commonwealth of Nations: An Inquiry into the Nature of Citizenship in the British Empire, and into the Mutual Relations of the Several Communities Thereof*, Part 1, London: Macmillan, 1916.

Curtis, Lionel, *The Problem of the Commonwealth*, London: Macmillan, 1916.
Dafoe, John Wesley, *Laurier: A Study in Canadian Politics*, Toronto: Thomas Allen, 1922.
DeCelles, Alfred Duclos, *Laurier et son temps*, Montréal: Librairie Beauchemin, 1920.
D'Egville, Howard, *Imperial Defence and Closer Union*, London: King, 1913.
Denison, George Taylor, *The Struggle for Imperial Unity: Recollections and Experiences*, New York: Macmillan & Co, 1909.
Dewey, Alexander Gordon, *The Dominion and Diplomacy: The Canadian Contribution*, 2 Vols., London: Longmans, Green & Co, 1929.
Drage, Geoffrey, *Imperial Organization of Trade*, London: Smith, Elder & Co, 1911.
Egerton, Hugh Edward, *The War and the British Dominions*, Oxford: Oxford University Press, [1914].
Enock, Charles Reginald, *An Imperial Commonwealth: Being a Discussion of the Conditions and Possibilities Underlying the Unity of the British Empire, and a Plan for the Greater Conservation, Development, and Enjoyment of Its Resources in the Interests of the British People, and for the Advancement of Their Civilization*, London: Grant Richards, 1910.
Ewart, John Skirving, *The Kingdom Papers*, Vol. 1, Ottawa: [s. n.], 1912.
Fiddes, George Vandeleur, Sir, *The Dominions and Colonial Offices*, London: G. P. Putnam's Sons, 1926.
Findlay, John George, Sir, *The Imperial Conference of 1911 from Within*, London: Constable & Co, 1912.
Froude, James Anthony, *Short Studies on Great Subjects*, Vol. 2, London: Longmans, Green & Co, 1898.
Glasgow, George, *From Dawes to Locarno: Being a Critical Record of an Important Achievement in European Diplomacy 1924–1925*, London: Ernest Benn, 1926.
Gwynn, Denis, *The Irish Free State 1922–1927*, London: Macmillan & Co, 1928.
Hall, Hessel Duncan, *The British Commonwealth of Nations: A Study of Its Past and Future Development*, London: Methuen, 1920.
Hall, Hessel Duncan, *The Government of the British Commonwealth of Nations*, London: Labour Party, 1922.
Holland, Bernard Henry, *Imperium et Libertas: A Study in History and Politics*, London: Edward Arnold, 1901.
Hurd, Percy – Hurd, Archibald, *The New Empire Partnership: Defence – Commerce – Policy*, Toronto: John Murray, 1916.
Janitor [Lockhart, J. G.], *The Feet of the Young Men*, 2nd Ed., London: Duckworth, 1929.
Jebb, Richard, *Studies in Colonial Nationalism*, London: Edward Arnold, 1905.
Jebb, Richard, *The Britannic Question: A Survey of Alternatives*, London: Longmans & Co, 1913.
Jebb, Richard, *The Imperial Conference: A History and the Study*, 2 Vols., London: Longmans & Co, 1911.
Jose, Arthur Wilberforce, *The Growth of the Empire: A Handbook to the History of Greater Britain*, London: John Murray, 1901.
Katsuizumi, Sotokichi, *Critical Observation on the Washington Conference*, Ann Arbor: [s. n.], 1922.

Keenleyside, Hugh L., *Canada and the United States: Some Aspects of the History of the Republic and the Dominion*, New York: A. A. Knopf, 1929.
Keith, Arthur Berriedale, *Imperial Unity and the Dominions*, Oxford: Clarendon Press, 1916.
Keith, Arthur Berriedale, *Responsible Government in the Dominions*, 3 Vols., Oxford: Oxford University Press, 1912.
Keith, Arthur Berriedale, *War Government of the British Dominions*, Oxford: Clarendon Press, 1921.
Kerr, Philip Henry, 11th Marquess of Lothian. In Kerr, A. C. (Ed.), *The Growth of the British Empire*, London: Longmans & Co, 1911.
Labillière, Francis Peter de, *Federal Britain: Or, Unity and Federation of the Empire*, London: S. Low & Co, 1894.
Latham, John Greig, Sir, *Australia and the British Commonwealth*, London: Macmillan & Co, 1929.
Little, James Stanley, *Progress of the British Empire in the Century*, Toronto: Linscott Publishing Co., 1903.
Lowell, A. Lawrence – Hall, Hessel Duncan, *The British Commonwealth of Nations*, Boston: World Peace Foundation, 1927.
Lucas, Charles, Sir, *Greater Rome and Greater Britain*, Oxford: Clarendon Press, 1912.
MacDonald, James Ramsey, *Labour and Empire*, London: Labour Party, 1907.
MacDonald, James Ramsey, *The Awakening of India*, London: Hodder & Stoughton, 1910.
MacDonald, James Ramsey, *The Government of India*, New York: Swarthmore Press, 1920.
Martin, Chester, *Empire and Commonwealth: Studies in Governance and Self-Government in Canada*, London: Longmans, Green, and Co, 1929.
McArthur, Peter, *Sir Wilfrid Laurier*, London: J. M. Dent & Sons, 1919.
Miller, David Hunter, *The Drafting of Covenant*, 2 Vols., New York: G. P. Putnam's Sons, 1928.
Milner, Alfred, 1st Viscount of Milner – Wells, Herbert George, *The Elements of Reconstruction: A Series of Articles Contributed in July and August 1916 to The Times*, London: Nisbet & Co, [1916].
Neame, Lawrence Elwin, *General Hertzog*, London: Hurst & Blackett, 1930.
Noel Baker, Philip John, *The Present Juridical Status of the British Dominions in International Law*, London: Longmans & Co, 1929.
Oliver, Frederick Scott, *Ireland and the Imperial Conference: Is There a Way to Settlement?*, London: Macmillan & Co, 1917.
Pollard, Albert Frederick, Sir, *The British Empire: Its Past, Its Present, and Its Future*, London: League of the Empire, 1909.
Pollard, Albert Frederick, Sir, *The Commonwealth at War*, London: Longmans & Co, 1917.
Pollard, Albert Frederick, Sir, *Proceedings of the Royal Colonial Institute*, Vol. 34, London: [s. n.], 1903.
Pollard, Albert Frederick, Sir, *Proceedings of the Royal Colonial Institute*, Vol. 36, London: [s. n.], 1905.
Pollard, Albert Frederick, Sir, *Proceedings of the Royal Colonial Institute*, Vol. 39, London: [s. n.], 1908.

Repington, Charles à Court, *After the War*, New York: Houghton Mifflin Co, 1922.
Report on the Green Memorandum Prepared by the Oxford University Segment of the Round Table Society, [Oxford: s. n., s. a.].
Seeley, John Robert, Sir, *The Expansion of England: Two Courses of Lectures*, London: Macmillan and Co, 1883.
Sifton, Clifford, Sir, *The Political Status of Canada: Address before the Canadian Club of Ottawa, April 8, 1922*, Ottawa: [s. n.], 1922.
Silburn, Percy Arthur Baxter, *The Colonies and Imperial Defence*, London: Longmans & Co, 1909.
Skelton, Oscar Douglas, *Life and Letters of Sir Wilfrid Laurier*, Vol. 2, Toronto: S. B. Gundy, 1921.
Skelton, Oscar Douglas, *The Canadian Dominions: A Chronicle of Our Northern Neighbor*, New Haven: Yale University Press, 1919.
Sladen, Douglas, *From Boundary-Rider to Prime Minister: Hughes of Australia: The Man of the Hour*, London: Hutchinson & Co, 1916.
Smith, Goldwin, *Commonwealth or Empire: A Bystander's View of the Question*, New York: Macmillan Co, 1902.
Soward, Frederic Hubert, *Canada and the League of Nations*, Ottawa: The League of Nations Society in Canada, [1931].
Spender, Harold, *General Botha: The Career and the Man*, Boston: Constable, 1916.
Spender, John Alfred, *The Life of the Right Hon. Sir Henry Campbell-Bannerman*, London: Hodder & Stoughton, 1923.
Sullivan, Mark, *The Great Adventure at Washington: The Story of the Conference*, New York: William Heinemann, 1922.
Sullivan, Mark, *The Round Table Movement: Its Past and Future*, [s. l.]: Round Table Movement, [1913].
Toynbee, Arnold J., *The Conduct of British Empire Foreign Relations since the Peace Settlement*, London: Oxford University Press, 1928.
Worsfold, William Basil, *The Empire on the Anvil: Being Suggestions and Data for the Future Government of the British Empire*, London: Smith, Elder & Co, 1916.
Young, Frederick, Sir, *A Pioneer of Imperial Federation in Canada*, London: George Allen, 1902.
Zimmern, Alfred Eckhard, Sir, *The Third British Empire: Being a Course of Lectures Delivered at Columbia University New York*, London: Humphrey Milford, 1926.

VII) Monographs

Adams, Ralph James Q., *Balfour: The Last Grandee*, London: John Murray, 2008.
Aitken, William Maxwell, 1st Baron Beaverbrook, *The Decline and Fall of Lloyd George*, London: Collins, 1963.
Alport, Cuthbert James MacCall, *Kingdoms in Partnership: A Study of Political Change in the British Commonwealth*, London: Lovat Dickson, 1937.
Amery, Julian, *The Life of Joseph Chamberlain, 1901–1903: At the Height of His Power*, Vol. 4, London: Macmillan, 1951.

Bibliography

Andrews, Eric, *The Anzac Illusion: Anglo-Australian Relations during World War I*, Melbourne: Cambridge University Press, 1993.
Armstrongm Harold Courtenay, *Grey Steel (J. C. Smuts): A Study in Arrogance*, London: Methuen, 1946.
Barclay, Glen St. J., *The Empire Is Marching: A Study of the Military Effort of the British Empire 1800–1945*, London: Weidenfeld and Nicolson, 1976.
Bastian, Peter, *Andrew Fisher: An Underestimated Man*, London: UNSW Press, 2009.
Beloff, Max, *Imperial Sunset: Britain's Liberal Empire 1897–1921*, Vol. 1, London: Macmillan, 1969.
Beloff, Max, *Imperial Sunset: Dream of Commonwealth*, Vol. 2, London: Macmillan, 1989.
Berger, Carl, *The Sense of Power: Studies in the Ideas of Canadian Imperialism 1867–1914*, Toronto: University of Toronto Press, 1970.
Bothwell, Robert, *Loring Christie: The Failure of Bureaucratic Imperialism*, New York: Garland Pub, 1988
Boyce, David George, *Englishmen and Irish Troubles 1918–1922*, Cambridge: Cape, 1972.
Brady, Alexander, *Canada*, London: Ernest Benn, 1932.
Brawley, Sean, *The White Peril: Foreign Relations and Asian Immigration to Australasia and North America, 1919–1978*, Sydney: UNSW Press, 1995.
Brebner, John Bartlet, *Canada: A Modern History*, Ann Arbor: University of Michigan Press, 1960.
Brebner, John Bartlet, *North Atlantic Triangle: The Interplay of Canada, the United States and Great Britain*, 3rd Ed., New Haven: Yale University Press, 1947.
Bridge, Carl, *William Hughes: Australia*, London: Haus, 2011.
Brown, Robert Craig, *Robert Laird Borden: A Biography: 1914–1937*, Vol. 2, Toronto: Macmillan, 1980.
Brown, Robert Craig – Cook, Ramsay, *Canada 1896–1921: A Nation Transformed*, Toronto: McClelland and Stewart, 1974.
Burt, Alfred Leroy, *The Evolution of the British Empire and Commonwealth*, London: Harrap, 1956.
Butler, James Ramsey Montagu, *Lord Lothian (Philip Kerr) 1882–1940*, London: Macmillan, 1960.
Carter, Gwendolen Margaret, *The British Commonwealth and International Security: The Role of the Dominions 1919–1939*, Toronto: Ryerson Press, 1947.
Coupland, Reginald, Sir, *The Indian Problems 1833–1935: Report on the Constitutional Problem in India*, Part 1, London: Oxford University Press, 1935.
Crafford, F. S., *Jan Smuts*, Cape Town: George Allen & Unwin, 1945.
Crankshaw, Edward, *The Forsaken Idea: A Study of Viscount Milner*, London: Longmans, Green & Co, 1952.
Crewe-Milnes, Robert Offley Ashburton, 1st Marquis of Crewe, *Lord Rosebery*, Vol. 1, London: John Murray, 1931.
Dawson, Robert MacGregor, *The Government of Canada*, 5th Ed., Toronto: University of Toronto Press, 1970.

Dawson, Robert MacGregor, *William Lyon Mackenzie King: A Political Biography: 1874–1923*, Vol. 1, London: Methuen, 1958.
Donnelly, Murray S., J. W. *Dafoe and Lionel Curtis: Two Concepts of the Commonwealth*, London: University of London, 1960.
Dugdale, Blanche Elizabeth Campbell, *Arthur James Balfour: 1848–1905*, Vol. 1, London: Hutchinson & Co., 1939.
Dugdale, Blanche Elizabeth Campbell, *Arthur James Balfour: 1906–1930*, Vol. 2, London: Hutchinson & Co., 1939.
Edwards, Cecil, *Bruce of Melbourne: Man of Two Worlds*, London: Heinemann, 1965.
Egerton, George W., *Great Britain and the Creation of the League of Nations: Strategy, Politics, and International Organization, 1914–1919*, Chapel Hill: University of North Carolina Press, 1979.
Elliott, William Yandell, *The New British Empire*, New York: McGraw-Hill Book Co, 1932.
Elliott, William Yandell – Hall, Hessel Duncan (Eds.), *The British Commonwealth at War*, New York: Alfred A. Knopf, 1943.
Fawcett, James Edmund Sandford, *The Inter se Doctrine of Commonwealth Relations*, London: Athlone Press, 1958.
Ferns, Henry Stanley – Ostry, Bernard, *The Age of Mackenzie King: The Rise of the Leader*, London: William Heinemann, 1955.
Fiřtová, Magdalena, *Kanada*, Praha: Libri, 2014.
Frank, Jan, *Irsko*, Praha: Libri, 2006.
Friedman, Bernard, *Smuts: A Reappraisal*, London: George Allen & Unwin, 1975.
Fry, Michael G., *Illusions of Security: North Atlantic Diplomacy 1918–22*, Toronto: University of Toronto Press, 1972.
Garvin, James Louis, *The Life of Joseph Chamberlain, 1895–1900: Empire and World Policy*, Vol. 3, London: Macmillan & Co., 1934.
Ginneken, Anique H. M. van, *Historical Dictionary of the League of Nations*, Lanham: Scarecrow Press, 2006.
Glazebrook, George Parkin de Twenebroker, *A History of Canadian External Relations*, London: Oxford University Press, 1950.
Glazebrook, George Parkin de Twenebroker, *Canada at the Paris Peace Conference*, Toronto: Oxford University Press, 1942.
Goldstein, Erik, *Winning the Peace: British Diplomatic Strategy, Peace Planning, and the Paris Peace Conference 1916–1920*, Oxford: Clarendon, 1991.
Gollin, Alfred Manuel, *Proconsul in Politics: A Study of Lord Milner in Opposition and in Power*, London: Anthony Blond, 1964.
Gollin, Alfred Manuel, *The Observer and J. L. Garvin, 1908–1914: A Study in a Great Editorship,* London: Oxford University Press, 1960.
Graham, Roger, *Arthur Meighen: A Biography: And Fortune Fled*, Vol. 2, Toronto: Clarke Irwin and Co, 1963.
Graham, Roger (Ed.), *The King-Byng Affair, 1926: A Question of Responsible Government* Toronto: Copp Clark Publishing Co., 1967.
Granatstein, J. L. – Hillmer, Norman, *For Better or for Worse: Canada and the United States to the 1990s*, Toronto: Copp Clark Pitman, 1991.
Hall, Hessel Duncan, *Commonwealth: A History of the British Commonwealth of Nations*, London: Von Nostrand Reinhold Co, 1971.

Halpérin, Vladimir, *Lord Milner and the Empire: The Evolution of British Imperialism*, London: Odhams Press, 1952.
Hancock, William Keith, Sir, *Australia*, Melbourne: Jacaranda Press, 1966.
Hancock, William Keith, Sir, *Smuts: The Sanguine Years, 1870–1919*, Vol. 1, Cambridge: Cambridge University Press, 1962.
Hancock, William Keith, Sir, *Smuts: The Fields of Force, 1919–1950*, Vol. 2, Cambridge: Cambridge University Press, 1968.
Hancock, William Keith, Sir, *Survey of British Commonwealth Affairs: Problems of Nationality 1918–1936*, Vol. 1, London: Oxford University Press, 1937.
Hankey, Maurice Pascal Alers, 1st Baron Hankey, *Diplomacy by Conference: Studies in Public Affairs, 1920–1946*, London: Ernest Benn, 1946.
Hankey, Maurice Pascal Alers, 1st Baron Hankey, *The Supreme Command, 1914–1918*, 2 Vols., London: George Allen & Unwin, 1961.
Hankey, Maurice Pascal Alers, 1st Baron Hankey, *The Supreme Control at the Paris Peace Conference*, London: George Allen & Unwin, 1963.
Harkness, David William, *The Restless Dominion: The Irish Free State and the British Commonwealth of Nations, 1921–1931*, London: Macmillan, 1969.
Heever, C. M. van den, *General J. B. M. Hertzog*, Johannesburg: A. P. B. Bookstore, 1946.
Henig, Ruth, *The League of Nations*, London: Haus, 2010.
Hillmer, Norman – Granatstein, J. L., *Empire to Umpire: Canada and the World to the 1990s*, Toronto: Copp Clark Longman, 1994.
Hind, R. J., *Henry Labouchere and the Empire 1880–1905*, London: Athlone Press, 1972.
Holland, Robert F., *Britain and the Commonwealth Alliance, 1918–1939*, London: Macmillan, 1981.
Hyam, Ronald M., *Britain's Declining Empire: The Road to Decolonisation 1918–1968*, London: Cambridge University Press, 2006.
Ingham, Kenneth, *Jan Christian Smuts: The Conscience of a South African*, London: Weidenfeld and Nicolson, 1986.
Jennings, William Ivor, Sir, *Cabinet Britain*, 3rd Ed., New London: Cambridge University Press, 1959.
Johnson, Franklyn Arthur, *Defence by Committee: The British Committee of Imperial Defence 1885–1959*, London: Oxford University Press, 1960.
Judd, Denis – Slinn, Peter, *The Evolution of the Modern Commonwealth, 1902–80*, London: Macmillan, 1982.
Keith, Arthur Berriedale, *The Governments of the British Empire*, London: Macmillan & Co, 1935.
Kendle, John Edward, *The Colonial and Imperial Conferences 1887–1911: A Study in Imperial Organizations*, London: Longmans 1967.
Kendle, John Edward, *The Round Table Movement and Imperial Union*, Toronto: University of Toronto Press, 1975.
Kiernan, R. H., *General Smuts*, London: George G. Harrap & Co, 1944.
Koebner, Richard, *Empire*, New York: Cambridge University Press, 1961.
Koebner, Richard – Schmidt, H. D., *Imperialism: The Story and Significance of a Political Word, 1840–1960*, Cambridge: Cambridge University Press, 1964.
Knaplund, Paul, *Britain, Commonwealth and Empire, 1901–1955*, New York: Harper & Brothers 1956.

Kraus, René, *Old Master: The Life of Jan Christian Smuts*, New York: E. P. Dutton & Co, 1944.

Laffan, Michael, *The Resurrection of Ireland 1916–1923: The Sinn Féin Party*, New York: Cambridge University Press, 1999.

La Nauze, John Andrew, *Alfred Deakin*, Melbourne: Oxford University Press, 1968.

La Nauze, John Andrew, *Alfred Deakin: A Biography*, Vol. 2, Melbourne: Melbourne University Press, 1962.

La Nauze, John Andrew, *Alfred Deakin: Two Lectures*, Brisbane: University of Queensland Press, 1960.

Lee, Geoffrey, *The People's Budget: An Edwardian Tragedy*, London: Shepheard-Walwyn, 2008.

Lentin, Anthony, *General Smuts: South Africa*, London: Haus, 2010.

Lentin, Anthony, *Guilt at Versailles: Lloyd George and the Pre-history of Appeasement*, London: Methuen, 1984.

Lloyd, Lorna, *Diplomacy with a Difference: The Commonwealth Office of High Commissioner, 1880–2006*, Leiden: Martinus Nijhoff, 2007.

Louis, William Roger, *British Strategy in the Far East 1919–1939*, Oxford: Clarendon Press, 1971.

Louis, William Roger, *In the Name of God, Go! Leo Amery and the British Empire in the Age of Churchill*, London: W. W. Norton, 1992.

Macardle, Dorothy, *The Irish Republic: A Documented Chronicle of the Anglo-Irish Conflict and the Partitioning of Ireland, With a Detailed Account of the Period 1916–1923*, New York: Farrar, Straus and Giroux, 1965.

MacLaren, Roy, *Mackenzie King in the Age of the Dictators: Canada's Imperial and Foreign Policies*, Montreal – Kingston: McGill-Queen's University Press, 2019.

MacManus, M. J., *Eamon de Valera*, Chicago – New York: Ziff-Davis, 1946.

Maisel, Ephraim, *The Foreign Office and Foreign Policy, 1919–1926*, London: Sussex Academic Press, 1994.

Manning, Charles Anthony Woodward, *The Policies of the British Dominions in the League of Nations*, Oxford: Oxford University Press, 1932.

Mansergh, Nicholas, *Survey of British Commonwealth Affairs: Problems of External Policy 1931–1939*, London: Oxford University Press, 1952.

Mansergh, Nicholas, *The Commonwealth Experience*, London: Weidenfeld & Nicolson, 1969.

Mansergh, Nicholas, *The Commonwealth Experience: From British to Multiracial Commonwealth*, Vol. 2, London: Macmillan, 1982.

Mansergh, Nicholas, *The Commonwealth of the Nation: Studies in British Commonwealth Relations*, London: Royal Institute of International Affairs, 1948.

Mansergh, Nicholas, *The Irish Free State: Its Government and Politics*, London: George Allen & Unwin, 1934.

Mansergh, Nicholas, *The Irish Question, 1840–1921*, London: George Allen & Unwin, 1965.

Mansergh, Nicholas, *The Unresolved Question: The Anglo-Irish Settlement and Its Undoing 1912–72*, New Haven – London: Yale University Press, 1991.

Marder, Arthur Jacob, *The Anatomy of British Sea Power*, New York: Putnam & Co., 1940.

Marks, Sally, *The Illusion of Peace: International Relations in Europe 1918–1933*, London: Macmillan, 1976.
Marlowe, John, *Milner: Apostle of Empire*, London: Hamilton, 1976.
Marston, Frank Swain, *The Peace Conference of 1919: Organisation and Procedure*, London: Oxford University Press, 1944.
McIntyre, W. David, *The Commonwealth of Nations: Origins and Impact, 1869–1971*, Minneapolis: University of Minnesota Press, 1977.
Meaney, Neville, *A History of Australian Defence and Foreign Policy 1901–23: The Search for Security in the Pacific, 1901–14*, Vol. 1, Sydney: Sydney University Press, 1976.
Merivirta, Raita, *The Gun and Irish Politics: Examining National History in Neil Jordan's Michael Collins*, Bern: Peter Lang, 2009.
Middlemas, Keith – Barnes, John, *Baldwin: A Biography*, London: Weidenfeld & Nicolson, 1969.
Miller, John Donald Bruce, *Britain and the Old Dominions*, London: Chatto & Windus, 1966.
Miller, John Donald Bruce, *Richard Jebb and the Problem of Empire*, London: Athlone Press, 1956.
Millin, Sarah Gertrude, *General Smuts*, 2 Vols., London: Faber and Faber, 1936.
Morgan, Kenneth O., *Consensus and Disunity: The Lloyd George Coalition Government 1918–1922*, Oxford: Oxford University Press, 1979.
Naylor, John F., *A Man and an Institution: Sir Maurice Hankey, the Cabinet Secretariat and the Custody of Cabinet Secrecy*, Cambridge: Cambridge University Press, 1984.
Neatby, H. Blair, *William Lyon Mackenzie King: 1924–1932: The Lonely Heights*, Vol. 2, London: Methuen & Co, 1963.
Nicholls, George Heaton, *South Africa in My Time*, London: George Allen & Unwin, 1961.
Nicolson, Harold, Sir, *King George the Fifth: His Life and Reign*, 3rd Ed., London: Pan Piper, 1967.
Nimocks, Walter, *Milner's Young Men: The 'Kindergarten' in Edwardian Imperial Affairs*, London: Hodder & Stoughton, 1970.
Nish, Ian H., *Alliance in Decline: A Study in Anglo-Japanese Relations, 1908–23*, London: Athlone Press, 1972.
Northedge, Frederick Samuel, *The Troubled Giant: Britain among the Great Powers 1916–1939*, London: G. Bell & Sons, 1966.
Novotný, Lukáš – Kodet, Roman, *Velká Británie a konference v Locarnu: Příspěvek ke studiu kolektivní bezpečnosti ve 20. letech 20. století*, Plzeň: Západočeská univerzita v Plzni, 2013.
O'Brien, Terence H., *Milner: Viscount Milner of St James's and Cape Town, 1854–1925*, London: Constable, 1979.
Oliver, Peter C., *The Constitution of Independence: The Development of Constitutional Theory in Australia, Canada, and New Zealand*, Oxford: Oxford University Press, 2005.
Orde, Anne, *Great Britain and International Security 1920–1926*, London: Royal Historical Society, 1978.
Packer, Ian, *Lloyd George*, London: Palgrave Macmillan, 1998.
Parkinson, Cosmo, Sir, *The Colonial Office from Within, 1909–45*, London: Faber & Faber, 1947.

Peatling, Gary K., *British Opinion and Irish Self-government, 1865–1925: From Unionism to Liberal Commonwealth*, Dublin: Irish Academic Press, 2001.
Pirow, Oswald, *James Barry Munnik Hertzog*, London: George Allen & Unwin, 1957.
Portus, Garnet Vere, *Britain and Australia*, London: Longmans, Green and Co, 1946.
Preston, Richard A., *Canada and 'Imperial Defence'*, Toronto: University of Toronto Press, 1967.
Preston, Richard A., *Canadian Defence Policy and the Development of the Canadian Nation 1867–1917*, Ottawa: Canadian Historical Association, 1970.
Purcell, Hugh, *Maharajah of Bikaner: India*, London: Haus, 2010.
Rau, Benegal Narsinga, Sir, *India's Constitution in the Making*, Bombay: Orient Longmans, 1963.
Reese, Trevor R., *The History of the Royal Commonwealth Society 1868–1968*, London: Oxford University Press, 1968.
Robertson, John, *J. S. Scullin: A Political Biography*, Nedlands: University of Western Australia Press, 1974.
Roskill, Stephen, *Hankey, Man of Secrets: 1919–1931*, Vol. 2, London: Collins, 1972.
Royal Institute of International Affairs, *The British Empire: A Report on Its Structure and Problems*, London: Oxford University Press, 1939.
Sinclair, Keith, *Imperial Federation: A Study of New Zealand Policy and Opinion, 1880–1914*, London: Athlone Press, 1955.
Sharp, Alan, *The Versailles Settlement: Peacemaking after the First World War, 1919–1923*, 2 nd Ed., Basingstoke: Palgrave Macmillan, 2008.
Skilling, Harold Gordon, *Canadian Representation Abroad: From Agency to Embassy*, Toronto: The Ryerson Press, 1945.
Smuts, J. C., Jr., *Jan Christian Smuts*, London: Cassell, 1952.
Soukup, Jaromír, *Britové v Porýní: Britská okupace Kolínské zóny v letech 1918–1926*, Praha: Filosofická fakulta Univerzity Karlovy, 2011.
Stacey, Charles Perry, *Canada and the Age of Conflict: A History of Canadian External Policies: 1867–1921*, Vol. 1, Toronto: University of Toronto Press, 1984.
Stacey, Charles Perry, *Canada and the Age of Conflict: A History of Canadian External Policies: 1921–1948: The Mackenzie King Era*, Vol. 2, Toronto: University of Toronto Press, 1981.
Stewart, Robert B., *Treaty Relations of the British Commonwealth of Nations*, New York: Macmillan, 1939.
Thompson, J. Lee, *A Wider Patriotism: Alfred Milner and the British Empire*, London: Routledge, 2007.
Thornton, Martin, *Sir Robert Borden: Canada*, London: Haus 2010.
Walder, David, *The Chanak Affair*, London: Hutchinson, 1969.
Walters, Francis Paul, *A History of the League of Nations*, Vol. 1, Oxford: Oxford University Press, 1952.
Wheare, Kenneth Clinton, *The Statute of Westminster and Dominion Status*, 4th Ed., Oxford: Oxford University Press, 1949.
White, Terence de Vere, *Kevin O'Higgins*, Dublin: Anvil Books, 1986.
Wigley, Philip, *Canada and the Transition to Commonwealth: British-Canadian Relations, 1917–1926*, Cambridge: Cambridge University Press, 1977.

William, Basil, *Botha, Smuts, and South Africa*, London: Hodder & Stoughton, 1946.
Williamson, James Alexander, *A Short History of British Expansion: The Modern Empire and Commonwealth*, 3rd Ed., London: Macmillan, 1947.
Willmott, H. P., *The Last Century of Sea Power: From Port Arthur to Chanak, 1894–1922* 1, Bloomington: Indiana University Press, 2009.
Yearwood, Peter J., *Guarantee of Peace: The League of Nations in British Policy 1914–1925*, Oxford: Oxford University Press 2009.
Young, Kenneth, *Arthur James Balfour: The Happy Life of the Politician Prime Minister, Statesman and Philosopher 1848–1930*, London: G. Bell & Sons, 1963.
Zebel, Sydney, *Balfour: A Political Biography*, Cambridge: Cambridge University Press, 1973.
Zimmern, Alfred Eckhard, Sir, *The League of Nations and the Rule of Law 1918–1935*, London: Macmillan & Co, 1936.

VIII) Articles and Studies

Adams, James Truslow, "On the Term 'British Empire'", *The American Historical Review* 27, No. 3, 1922, 485–489.
Adams, John Q., "The Pacific Coast Halibut Fishery", *Economic Geography* 11, No. 3, 1935, 247–257.
Adams, John Q., "Afterthoughts on the Imperial Conference", *The Round Table* 14, No. 54, 1924, 225–241.
Albertini, Rudolf von, "England als Weltmacht und der Strukturwandel des Commonwealth", *Historische Zeitschrift* 208, No. 1, 1969, 52–80.
Allbert Dayer, Roberta, "The British War Debts to the United States and the Anglo-Japanese Alliance, 1920–1923", *Pacific Historical Review* 45, 1976, 569–595.
Allerfeldt, Kristofer, "Wilsonian Pragmatism? Woodrow Wilson, Japanese Immigration, and the Paris Peace Conference", *Diplomacy and Statecraft* 15, No. 3, 2004, 545–572.
Allin, Caphas Daniel, "Canada's Treaty Making Power", *Michigan Law Review* 24, No. 3, 1926, 249–276.
Allin, Caphas Daniel, "International Status of the British Dominions", *The American Political Science Review* 17, No. 4, 1923, 612–622.
Allin, Caphas Daniel, "Recent Developments in the Constitutional and International States of the British Dominions", *Minnesota Law Review*, No. 10, 1925/1926, 100–122.
Amery, Leopold Stennett, "Foreign Policy of the British Empire", *Advocate of Peace through Justice* 87, No. 2, 1925, 112–118.
Amery, Leopold Stennett, "Some Aspects of the Imperial Conference", *Journal of the Royal Institute of International Affairs* 6, No. 1, 1927, 2–24.
Amery, Leopold Stennett, "Some Practical Steps towards an Imperial Constitution", *United Empire: The Royal Colonial Institute Journal* 1, No. 7, 1910, 487–509.
Amery, Leopold Stennett, "An Imperial Conference", *Advocate of Peace through Justice* 83, No. 7, 1921, 251–252.
Arnold-Forster, Mark, "Chanak Rocks the Empire: The Anger of Billy Hughes", *The Round Table* 58 No. 230, 1968, 169–177.

Asada, Sadao, "Between the Old Diplomacy and the New, 1918–1922: The Washington System and the Origins of Japanese-American Rapprochement", *Diplomatic History* 30, No. 2, 2006, 211–230.

Asada, Sadao, "Japan's "Special Interests" and the Washington Conference, 1921–22", *The American Historical Review* 67, No. 1, 1961, 62–70.

Austin, Dennis, "In Memoriam: Legacies of Empire", *The Round Table* 87, No. 348, 1998, 427–439.

Baker, Andrew, "Divided Sovereignty: Empire and Nation in the Making of Modern Britain", *International Politics* 46, No. 6, 2009, 691–711.

Beloff, Max, "Britain and Canada between Two World Wars: A British View", in: Lyon, Peter (Ed.), *Britain and Canada: Survey of a Changing Relationship*, London: Frank Cass, 1976, 50–60.

Beloff, Max, "Leo Amery, the Last Imperialist", *History Today* 39, No. 1, 1989, 13–18.

Bennett, G. H., "Lloyd George, Curzon and the Control of the British Foreign Policy 1919–22", *The Australian Journal of Politics and History* 45, No. 4, 1999, 467–482.

Bennett, Neville R., "Consultation or Information? Britain, the Dominions and the Renewal of the Anglo-Japanese Alliance, 1911", *The New Zealand Journal of History* 4, No. 2, 1970, 178–194.

Best, Anthony, "Race, Monarchy, and the Anglo-Japanese Alliance, 1902–1922", *Social Science Japan Journal* 9, No. 2, 2006, 171–186.

Best, Anthony, "The 'Ghost' of the Anglo-Japanese Alliance: An Examination into Historical Myth-Making", *The Historical Journal* 49, No. 3, 2006, 811–831.

Birn, Donald S., "Open Diplomacy at the Washington Conference of 1921-2: The British and French Experience", *Comparative Studies and History* 12, No. 3, 1970, 297–319.

Borden, Robert Laird, Sir, "The Imperial Conference", *Journal of the Royal Institute of International Affairs* 6, No. 4, 1927, 197–213.

Bosák, Tomáš, "Britské federalistické koncepce a pojetí Evropy v éře 'skvělé izolace'", *Mezinárodní vztahy* 45, No. 1, 2010, 77–98.

Bothwell, Robert, "Canadian Representation at Washington: A Study in Colonial Responsibility", *The Canadian Historical Review* 53, No. 2, 1972, 125–148.

Boulger, Demetrius C., "The Anglo-Japanese Alliance", *Contemporary Review* 118, 1920, 326–333.

Bourrie, Mark, "The Myth of the "Gagged Clam": William Lyon Mackenzie King's Press Relations", *Global Media Journal: Canadian Edition* 3, No. 2, 2010, 13–30.

Boyce, Robert W. D., "Imperial Dreams and National Realities: Britain, Canada and the Struggle for a Pacific Telegraph Cable, 1879–1902", *The English Historical Review* 115, No. 460, 2000, 39–70.

Boyce, Robert W. D., "The Significance of 1931 for British Imperial and International History", *Histoire@Politique: Politique, culture, société*, No. 11, 2010, 1–17.

Boyd, Mary, "New Zealand's Attitude to Dominion Status 1919–1921: The Procedure for Enacting a Constitution in the Samoan Mandate", *Journal of Commonwealth Political Studies* 3, No. 1, 1965, 64–70.

Brady, Alexander, "Dominion Nationalism and the Commonwealth", *The Canadian Journal of Economics and Political Science/Revue canadienne d'Economique et de Science politique* 10, No. 1, 1944, 1–17.

Brady, Alexander, "The New Dominion", *The Canadian Historical Review* 4, No. 3, 1923, 198–216.
Bray, Matthew, "'Fighting as an Ally': The English-Canadian Patriotic Response to the Great War", *The Canadian Historical Review* 64, No. 2, 1980, 141–168.
Brebner, John Bartlet, "Canada, the Anglo-Japanese Alliance and the Washington Conference", *Political Science Quarterly* 40, No. 1, 1935, 45–58.
Brebner, John Bartlet, "British Dominions and the Protocol", *Advocate of Peace through Justice* 87, No. 9, 1925, 559–562.
Brebner, John Bartlet, "British Imperial Conference", *Advocate of Peace through Justice* 89, No. 1, 1927, 16–18.
Bromage, Mary C., "De Valera's Plan", *University Review* 5, No. 1, 1968, 23–50.
Brookes, Edgar H., "A Far-seeing International Statesman", in: Friedlander, Zelda (Ed.), *Jan Smuts Remembered: A Centennial Tribute*, London: Allan Wingate, 1970, 19–22.
Brookes, Edgar H., "The Secession Movement in South Africa", *Foreign Affairs: An American Quarterly Review* 11, No. 1/4, 1932/1933, 347–354.
Buell, Raymond Leslie, "Britain's Changing Empire", *Current History* 22, No. 1, 1925, 50–57.
Burgess, Michael, "'Forgotten Centenary': The Formation of the Imperial Federation League in the UK, 1884", *The Round Table* 73, No. 289, 1984, 76–85.
Burks, David D., "The United States and the Geneva Protocol of 1924: 'A New Holy Alliance'?" *The American Historical Review* 64, No. 4, 1959, 891–905.
Burroughs, Peter, "John Robert Seeley and British Imperial History", *The Journal of Imperial and Commonwealth History* 1, No. 2, 1973, 191–211.
Callahan, Raymond, "The Illusion of Security: Singapore 1919–42", *Journal of Contemporary History* 9, No. 2, 1974, 73–92.
Campbell-Miller, Jill, "'Ex Unitate Vires': Elite Consolidation and the Union of South Africa, 1902–10", *Canadian Journal of History/Annales canadiennes d'histoire* 45, No, 1, 2010, 83–103.
Campbell-Miller, Jill,"Canada and the Navy", *The Round Table* 2, No. 8, 1912, 627–656.
Carrington, C. E., "A New Theory of the Commonwealth", *International Affairs* 31, No. 2, 1955, 137–148.
Carrington, C. E., "The Empire at War, 1914–1918", in: *The Cambridge History of the British Empire: The Empire-Commonwealth 1870–1919*, Vol. 3, Cambridge: Cambridge University Press, 1967, 605–644.
Carter, Gwendolen M.,"Some Aspects of Canadian Foreign Policy after Versailles", *Report of the Annual Meeting of the Canadian Historical Association/Rapports annuels de la Société historique du Canada* 22, No. 1, 1943, 94–103.
Cartwright, Albert, "The South African Situation", *Edinburgh Review* 221, No. 451, 1915, 65–85.
Cecil, Robert, Viscount of Chelwood, "The League of Nations and the Problem of Sovereignty", *History* 5, 1920/1921, 11–14.
Chaudron, Gerald, "The League of Nations and Imperial Dissent: New Zealand and the British Labour Government, 1924–31", *The Journal of Imperial and Commonwealth History* 39, No. 1, 2011, 47–71.
Clokie, Hugh MacDowall, "International Affairs: The British Dominions and Neutrality", *The American Political Science Review* 34, No. 4, 1940, 737–749.

Cole, Douglas, "The Problem of 'Nationalism' and 'Imperialism' in British Settlement Colonies", *Journal of British Studies* 10, No. 2, 1971, 160–182.

Colvin, James A., "Sir Wilfrid Laurier and the British Preferential Tariff System", in: Neatby, H. Blair et al. (Eds.), *Imperial Relation in the Age of Laurier*, Toronto: University of Toronto Press, 1969, 34–44.

Cook, George L., "Sir Robert Borden, Lloyd George and British Military Policy, 1917–1918", *The Historical Journal* 14, No. 2, 1971, 371–395.

Cook, Ramsay – Macrae, D. B., "A Canadian Account of the 1926 Imperial Conference", *Journal of Commonwealth Political Studies* 3, No. 1, 1965, 50–63.

Cotton, James, "W. K. Hancock and International Relations in Australia: The Commonwealth as a Model of World Government", *Australian Journal of Politics and History* 55, No. 4, 2009, 475–495.

Crisp, L. F., "The Appointment of Sir Isaac Isaacs as Governor-General of Australia, 1930: J. H. Scullin's Account of the Buckingham Palace Interviews", *Historical Studies: Australia and New Zealand* 11, No. 42, 1964, 253–257.

Cross, J. A., "The Colonial Office and the Dominions before 1914", *Journal of Commonwealth Political Studies* 4, No. 2, 1966, 138–148.

Cross, J. A., "Whitehall and the Commonwealth: The Development of British Departmental Organisation for Commonwealth Affairs", *Journal of Commonwealth Political Studies* 2, No. 3, 1964, 189–206.

Crozier, Andrew J., "The Establishment of the Mandates System 1919–25: Some Problems Created by the Paris Peace Conference", *Journal of Contemporary History* 14, No. 3, 1979, 483–513.

Curry, George, "Woodrow Wilson, Jan Smuts, and the Versailles Settlement", *The American Historical Review* 66, No. 4, 1961, 968–986.

Dafoe, John Wesley, "Canada and the Peace Conference of 1919", *The Canadian Historical Review* 24, No. 3, 1943, 233–248.

Dafoe, John Wesley, "The Problems of Canada", in: Hurst, Cecil J. B., Sir – Smiddy, Timothy A. – Dafoe, John Wesley et al. (Eds.), *Great Britain and the Dominions*, Chicago: University of Chicago Press, 1928, 133–260.

Davenport, T. R. H., "The South African Rebellion, 1914", *The English Historical Review* 78, No. 306, 1963, 73–94.

Dawson, R. MacGregor, "The Imperial Conference", *The Canadian Journal of Economics and Political Science/Revue canadienne d'Economique et de Science politique* 3, No. 1, 1937, 23–39.

Dawson, Robert MacGregor, "Canadian and Imperial War Cabinets", in: Martin, Chester (Ed.), *Canada in Peace and War: Eight Studies in National Trends since 1914*, London: Oxford University Press, 1941, 176–211.

Dennis, Alfred L. P., "British Foreign Policy and the Dominions", *The American Political Science Review* 16, No. 4, 1922, 584–599.

Dignan, D. K., "Australia and British Relations with Japan, 1914–1921", *Australian Outlook* 21, No. 2, 1967, 135–150.

Donnelly, Murray S., "J. W. Dafoe and Lionel Curtis – Two Concepts of the Commonwealth", *Political Studies* 8, No. 2, 1960, 170–182.

Eayrs, John, "The Round Table Movement in Canada, 1909–1920", *The Canadian Historical Review* 38, No. 1, 1957, 1–20.

Eayrs, John, "Editorial Notes and Comments", *United Empire: The Royal Colonial Institute Journal* 11, No. 7, 1920, 349–356.

Egerton, George W., "The Dominions and the Peace Settlement", *United Empire: The Royal Colonial Institute Journal* 6, No. 6, 1915, 425–431.
Ellinwood, Dewitt Clinton, Jr., "The Round Table Movement and India, 1909–1920", *Journal of Commonwealth Political Studies* 9, No. 3, 1971, 183–209.
Elliott, William Yandell, "The Riddle of the British Commonwealth", *Foreign Affairs* 8, No. 1/4, 1929/1930, 442–464.
Esberey, J. E., "Personality and Politics: A New Look at the King-Byng Dispute", *Canadian Journal of Political Science/Revue canadienne de science politique* 6, No. 1, 1973, 37–55.
Ferris, John, "'Far Too Dangerous a Gamble'? British Intelligence and Policy during the Chanak Crisis, September–October 1922", *Diplomacy and Statecraft* 14, No. 2, 2003, 139–184.
Fieldhouse, David Kenneth, "Autochthonous Elements in the Evolution of Dominion Status: The Case of New Zealand", *Journal of Commonwealth Political Studies* 1, No. 2, 1962, 85–111.
Fitzhardinge, L., "Hughes, Borden and Dominion Representation at the Paris Peace Conference", *The Canadian Historical Review* 49, No. 2, 1968, 160–169.
Fitzhardinge, L. F., "W. M. Hughes and the Treaty of Versailles 1919", *Journal of Commonwealth Political Studies* 5, No. 2, 1967, 130–142.
Fitzhardinge, L. F., ""Fruits of the British Imperial Conference", *Current History* 14, No. 6, 1921, 1047–1048.
Fry, Michael G., "The North Atlantic Triangle and the Abrogation of the Anglo-Japanese Alliance", *Journal of Modern History* 39, No. 1, 1967, 46–64.
Galbraith, J., "The Imperial Conference of 1921 and the Washington Conference", *The Canadian Historical Review* 29, No. 2, 1948, 143–152.
Gallagher, John, "Nationalisms and the Crisis of Empire, 1919–1922", *Modern Asian Studies* 15, No. 3, 1981, 355–368.
Gardner, W. J., "The Reform Party", Chapman, R. M. (Ed.), *Ends and Means in New Zealand Politics*, Auckland: Auckland University Press, 1961, 27–35.
Geyser, O., "Irish Independence: Jan Smuts and Eamon de Valera", *The Round Table* 87, No. 348, 2008, 473–484.
Geyser, O., "Jan Smuts and Alfred Milner", *The Round Table* 90, No. 360, 2001, 415–432.
Gibson, James A., "Mr. Mackenzie King and Canadian Autonomy, 1921–1946", *Report of the Annual Meeting of the Canadian Historical Association/Rapports annuels de la Société historique du Canada* 30, No. 1, 1951, 12–21.
Glasgow, George, "The British View", in: Croly, Herbert David (Ed.), *Roads to Peace: A Hand-book to the Washington Conference*, New York: New York Republic Pub. Co., 1921, 29–34.
Glazebrook, George Parkin de Twenebroker, "Canadian External Relations", in: Martin, Chester (Ed.), *Canada in Peace and War: Eight Studies in National Trends since 1914*, London: Oxford University Press, 1941, 150–175.
Gooch, John, "Great Britain and the Defence of Canada, 1896–1914", *The Journal of Imperial and Commonwealth History* 2, No. 2, 1974, 368–385.
Gooch, John, "The Maurice Debate 1918", *Journal of Contemporary History* 3, No. 4, 1968, 211–228.
Gordon, Donald C., "The Admiralty and Dominion Navies, 1902–1914", *The Journal of Modern History* 33, No. 4, 1961, 407–422.

Gorman, Daniel, "Lionel Curtis, Imperial Citizenship, and the Quest for Unity", *The Historian* 66, No. 1, 2004, 67–96.

Gowen, Robert Joseph, "British Legerdemain at the 1911 Imperial Conference: The Dominions, Defense Planning, and the Renewal of the Anglo-Japanese Alliance", *The Journal of Modern History* 52, No. 3, 1980, 385–413.

Grayson, Richard S., "Imperialism in Conservative Defence and Foreign Policy: Leo Amery and the Chamberlains, 1903–39", *The Journal of Imperial and Commonwealth History* 34, No. 4, 2006, 505–527.

Greenlee, James G. C., "Imperial Studies and the Unity of the Empire", *The Journal of Imperial and Commonwealth History* 7, No. 3, 1979, 321–335.

Greenlee, James G. C., "The A B C's of Imperial Unity", *Canadian Journal of History/Annales canadiennes d'histoire* 14, No. 1, 1979, 49–64.

Grimshaw, Charles, "Australian Nationalism and the Imperial Connection", *The Australian Journal of Politics and History* 3, No. 2, 1958, 161–183.

Hall, Hessel Duncan, "The British Commonwealth of Nations", *The American Political Science Review* 47, No. 4, 1953, 997–1015.

Hall, Hessel Duncan, "The Genesis of the Balfour Declaration of 1926", *Journal of Commonwealth Political Studies* 1, No. 3, 1962, 169–193.

Hall, Hessel Duncan, "The Imperial Crown and the Foreign Relations of the Dominions", *Journal of Comparative Legislation and International Law* 2, No. 3, 1920, 196–205.

Hammond, J. L., "Colonial and Foreign Policy", in: Hammond, J. L. – Hirst, Francis W. – Murray, Gilbert (Eds.), *Liberalism and the Empire*, London: R. Brimley Johnson, 1900, 158–211.

Hancock, I. R., "The 1911 Imperial Conference", *Historical Studies: Australia and New Zealand* 12, No. 47, 1966, 356–372.

Hancock, William Keith, "Empire, Commonwealth, Cosmos and His Own Place: The Smutsian Philosophy", *The Round Table* 60, No. 240, 1970, 443–448.

Hargreaves, J. D., "The Anglo-Japanese Alliance, 1902–1952", *History Today* 2, No. 4, 1952, 252–258.

Hawkings, F. M. A., "Defence and the Role of Erskine Childers in the Treaty Negotiations of 1921", *Irish Historical Studies* 22, No. 87, 1981, 251–270.

Hedges, R. York, "Australia and the Imperial Conference", *The Australian Quarterly* 9, No. 1, 1937, 80–82.

Henig, Ruth, "New Diplomacy and Old: A Reassessment of British Conceptions of a League of Nations, 1918–20", in: Dockrill, Michael L. – Fisher, John (Eds.), *The Paris Peace Conference, 1919: Peace without Victory?* London: Palgrave Macmillan, 2001, 157–174.

Hillmer, Norman, "O. D. Skelton and the North American Mind", *International Journal* 60, No. 1, 2004/2005, 93–110.

Hillmer, Norman, "A British High Commissioner for Canada, 1927–1928", *The Journal of Imperial and Commonwealth History* 1, No. 3, 1973, 339–356.

Hillmer, Norman, "The Anglo-Canadian Neurosis: The Case of O. D. Skelton", in: Lyon, Peter (Ed.), *Britain and Canada: Survey of a Changing Relationship*, London: Frank Cass, 1976, 61–84.

Hirst, Francis W., "Imperialism and Finance", in: Hammond, J. L. – Hirst, Francis W. – Murray, Gilbert (Eds.), *Liberalism and the Empire*, London: R. Brimley Johnson, 1900, 1–117.

Hodson, Harry, "The Round Table: Until the Early 1930s", *The Round Table* 88, No. 352, 1999, 677–694.
Holland, Robert, "Britain, Commonwealth and the End of Empire", in: Bogdanor, Vernon (Ed.), *The British Constitution in the Twentieth Century*, Oxford: Oxford University Press, 2003, 631–661.
[Hughes, Charles Evans], "Washington Agreement on Capital Ships", *A League of Nations* 4, No. 5, 1921, 373–393.
Hurst, Cecil J. B., Sir, "The British Empire as a Political Unit", in: Hurst, Cecil J. B., Sir – Smiddy, Timothy A. – Dafoe, John Wesley et al. (Eds.), *Great Britain and the Dominions*, Chicago: University of Chicago Press, 1928, 3–103.
Hyam, Ronald, "The Colonial Office Mind 1900–1914", *Journal of Imperial and Commonwealth History* 8, No. 1, 1979, 30–55.
Ilsley, Lucretia L., "The Administration of Mandates by the British Dominions", *The American Political Science Review* 28, No. 2, 1934, 287–302.
Inglis, Alex I., "Loring C. Christie and the Imperial Idea: 1919–1926", *Journal of Canadian Studies/Revue d'études canadiennes* 7, No. 2, 1972, 19–27.
Jebb, Richard, "Conference or Cabinet?", *United Empire: The Royal Colonial Institute Journal* 11, No. 4, 1920, 160–168.
Johnson, Gregory Allan – Lenarcic, David A., "The Decade of Transition: The North Atlantic Triangle during the 1920s", in: McKercher, Brian J. C. – Aronsen, Lawrence (Eds.), *The North Atlantic Triangle in a Changing World: Anglo-American-Canadian Relations, 1902–1956*, Toronto: University of Toronto Press, 1996, 81–109.
Jones, Dorsey D., "The Foreign Policy of William Morris Hughes of Australia", *Far Eastern Quarterly* 2, No. 2, 1943, 153–162.
Keith, Arthur Berriedale, "Notes on Imperial Constitutional Law", *Journal of Comparative Legislation and International Law* 4, No. 4, 1922, 233–241.
Keith, Arthur Berriedale, "The Imperial Conference of 1930", *Journal of Comparative Legislation and International Law* 13, Third Series, No. 1, 1931, 26–42.
Kendle, John Edward, "The Round Table Movement and 'Home Rule All Round'", *The Historical Journal* 11, No. 2, 1968, 332–353.
Kendle, John Edward, "The Round Table Movement: Lionel Curtis and the Formation of the New Zealand Groups in 1910", *The New Zealand Journal of History* 1, No. 1, 1967, 33–50.
Kendle, John Edward, "The Round Table Movement, New Zealand, and the Conference of 1911", *The Round Table* 84, No. 336, 1995, 495–508.
Kennedy, M., "Imperial Cable Communications and Strategy, 1870–1914", *The English Historical Review* 86, No. 341, 1971, 728–752.
Kennedy, Michael, "Chicanery and Candour: The Irish Free State and the Geneva Protocol, 1924–5", *Irish Historical Studies* 29, No. 115, 1995, 371–384.
Kennedy, William Paul McClure, "Canada and the Imperial Conference", *Contemporary Review*, No. 120, 1921, 61–64.
Kennedy, William Paul McClure, "Significance of the Irish Free State", *North American Review*, No. 218, 1923, 316–324.
Kerr, Philip Henry, "Commonwealth and Empire", in: Newton, Arthur Percival (Ed.), *The Empire and the Future: A Series of Imperial Studies Lectures Delivered in the University of London, King's College*, London: Macmillan, 1916, 69–89.

Kerr, Philip Henry, 11th Marquis of Lothian, "From Empire to Commonwealth", *Foreign Affairs: An American Quarterly Review* 1, No. 2, 1922, 83–98.

Kerr, Philip Henry, 11th Marquis of Lothian, "The Anglo-Japanese Alliance", *The Round Table* 11, No. 41, 1920, 87–97.

Kerr, Philip Henry, 11th Marquis of Lothian, "The British Empire, the League of Nations, and the United States", *The Round Table* 10, No. 38, 1920, 221–253.

Klein, Ira, "Whitehall, Washington, and the Anglo-Japanese Alliance, 1919–1921", *Pacific Historical Review* 41, No. 4, 1972, 460–483.

Knirck, Jason, "The Dominion of Ireland: The Anglo-Irish Treaty in an Imperial Context", *Éire-Ireland* 42, No. 1/2, 2007, 229–255.

Kodet, Roman, "The Imperial Japanese Navy and the Washington Conference", *Prague Papers on the History of International Relations*, 2009, 543–548.

Koehn, George L., "Menace of the Anglo-Japanese Alliance", *Current History* 14, No. 5, 1921, 738–741.

Krikorian, Jacqueline D., "British Imperial Politics and Judicial Independence: The Judicial Committee's Decision in the Canadian Case *Nadan v. The King*", *Canadian Journal of Political Science/Revue canadienne de science politique* 33, No. 2, 2000, 291–332.

Laing, Lionel H., "In Memoriam: Sir Robert Borden", *The American Journal of International Law* 31, No. 4, 1937, 704–705.

Lambert, John, "South African British? Or Dominion South Africans? The Evolution of an Identity in the 1910s and 1920s", *South African Historical Journal* 43, No. 1, 2000, 197–222.

Lauren, Paul Gordon, "Human Rights in History: Diplomacy and Racial Equality at the Paris Peace Conference", *Diplomatic History* 2, No. 3, 1978, 257–278.

Lauterpacht, H., Sir – Jennings, R. Y., "International Law and Colonial Questions, 1870–1914", in: *The Cambridge History of the British Empire: The Empire-Commonwealth 1870–1919*, Vol. 3, Cambridge: Cambridge University Press, 1967, 667–710.

Lavin, Deborah, "Lionel Curtis and the Idea of Commonwealth", in: Madden, A. Frederick – Fieldhouse, D. K. (Eds.), *Oxford and the Idea of Commonwealth: Essays Presented to Sir Edgar Williams*, London: Croom Helm, 1982, 97–121.

Lawlor, S. M., "Ireland from Truce to Treaty: War or Peace? July to October 1921", *Irish Historical Studies* 22, No. 85, 1980, 49–64.

Lloyd, Lorna, "'Another National Milestone': Canada's 1927 Election to the Council of the League of Nations", *Diplomacy and Statecraft* 21, No. 4, 2010, 650–668.

Lloyd, Lorna, "Loosening the Apron Strings: The Dominions and Britain in the Interwar Years", *The Round Table* 92, No. 369, 2003, 279–303.

Lockwood, A., "Milner's Entry into the War Cabinet, December 1916", *The Historical Journal* 7, No. 1, 1964, 120–134.

Loring, A. H., "The Imperial Federation (Defence) Committee: 1894–1906", *United Empire: The Royal Colonial Institute Journal* 6, 1915, 341–346.

Louis, William Roger, "Australia and the German Colonies in the Pacific, 1914–1919", *Journal of Modern History* 38, No. 4, 1966, 407–421.

Lowe, Peter, "The British Empire and the Anglo-Japanese Alliance, 1911–1915", *History* 54, No. 181, 1969, 212–225.

Lowe, Peter, "The Round Table, the Dominions and the Anglo-Japanese Alliance, 1911–22", *The Round Table* 86, No. 341, 1997, 81–93.

Lowell, A. Lawrence, "The Imperial Conference", *Foreign Affairs: An American Quarterly Review* 5, No. 1/4, 1926-1927, 379-392.

Lowell, A. Lawrence, "The Treaty Making Power of Canada", *Foreign Affairs: An American Quarterly Review* 2, No. 1/4, 1923-1924, 12-22.

Lower, Arthur Reginald Marsden, "Loring Christie and the Genesis of the Washington Conference of 1921-1922", *The Canadian Historical Review* 47, No. 1, 1966, 38-48.

MacKenzie, N. A. M., "The Treaty Making Power in Canada", *The American Journal of International Law* 19, No. 3, 1925, 489-504.

MacKintosh, John P., "The Role of the Committee of Imperial Defence before 1914", *The English Historical Review* 77, No. 304, 1962, 490-503.

MacQuarrie, Heath, "Robert Borden and the Election of 1911", *The Canadian Journal of Economics and Political Science/Revue canadienne d'Economique et de Science politique* 25, No. 3, 1959, 271-286.

Mair, Peter, "The Break-up of the United Kingdom: The Irish Experience of Regime Change, 1918-1949", *The Journal of Commonwealth & Comparative Politics* 16, No. 3, 1978, 288-302.

Mansergh, Nicholas, "Ireland: From British Commonwealth towards European Community", *Historical Studies* 13, No. 51, 1968, 381-395.

Mansergh, Nicholas, "The Implications of Eire's Relationship with the British Commonwealth of Nations", *International Affairs* 24, No. 1, 1948, 1-18.

Marshall, Peter, "The Balfour Formula and the Evolution of the Commonwealth", *The Round Table* 90, No. 361, 2001, 541-553.

Marshall, Thomas R., "America, the Nations and the League", *The Annals of the American Academy of Political and Social Science* 84, 1919, 194-200.

Martin, Ged W., "The Irish Free State and the Evolution of the Commonwealth, 1921-1949", in: Hyam, Robert – Martin, Ged W. (Eds.), *Reappraisals in British Imperial History*, London: Macmillan, 1975, 201-223.

Mathews, J. M., "The League of Nations and the Constitution", *Michigan Law Review* 18, No. 5, 1920, 378-389.

May, Alex, "The Round Table and Imperial Federation, 1910-17", *The Round Table* 99, No. 410, 2010, 547-556.

McColgan, John, "Implementing the 1921 Treaty: Lionel Curtis and Constitutional Procedure", *Irish Historical Studies* 20, No. 79, 1977, 312-335.

McCraw, David J., "The Zenith of Realism in New Zealand's Foreign Policy", *Australian Journal of Politics and History* 48, No. 3, 2002, 353-368.

McInnis, Edgar, "The Imperial Problem in the Minds of Chamberlain and His Successors", *The Canadian Historical Review* 16, No. 3, 1935, 65-70.

McIntyre, W. David, "'A Formula May Have to Be Found': Ireland, India, and the Headship of the Commonwealth", *The Round Table* 91, No. 365, 2002, 391-413.

McIntyre, W. David, "Clio and Britannia's Lost Dream: Historians and the British Commonwealth of Nations in the First Half of the 20th Century", *The Round Table* 93, No. 376, 2004, 517-532.

Meaney, Neville K., "'A Proposition of the Highest International Importance': Alfred Deakin's Pacific Agreement Proposal and Its Significance for Australian-Imperial Relations", *Journal of Commonwealth Political Studies* 5, No. 3, 1967, 200-213.

Mehrotra, S. R., "Imperial Federation and India, 1868–1917", *Journal of Commonwealth Political Studies* 1, No. 1, 1961, 29–40.
Mehrotra, S. R., "On the Use of the Term 'Commonwealth'", *Journal of Commonwealth Political Studies* 2, No. 1, 1963, 1–16.
Miller, John Donald Bruce, "The Commonwealth and World Order: The Zimmern Vision and After", *The Journal of Imperial and Commonwealth History* 8, No. 1, 1979, 159–174.
Miller, John Donald Bruce, "The Decline of 'Inter Se'", *International Journal* 24, No. 4, 1969, 765–775.
Milner, Alfred, 1st Viscount of Milner, "Some Reflections on the Coming Conference", *National Review* 49, 1907, 195–206.
Mohr, Thomas, "British Imperial Statuses and Irish Law: Statutes Passed before the Creation of the Irish Free State", *The Journal of Legal History* 31, No. 3, 2010, 299–321.
Mohr, Thomas, "British Imperial Statuses and Irish Sovereignty: Statutes Passed after the Creation of the Irish Free State", *The Journal of Legal History* 32, No. 1, 2011, 61–85.
Moore, William Harrison, Sir, "The Dominions of the British Commonwealth in the League of Nations", *International Affairs* 10, No. 3, 1931, 372–391.
Moore, William Harrison, Sir, "The Imperial and Foreign Relations of Australia", in: Hurst, Cecil J. B., Sir – Smiddy, Timothy A. – Dafoe, John Wesley et al. (Eds.), *Great Britain and the Dominions*, Chicago: University of Chicago Press, 1928, 263–355.
Neatby, H. Blair, "Laurier and Imperialism", *Report of the Annual Meeting of the Canadian Historical Association/Rapports annuels de la Société historique du Canada* 34, No. 1, 1955, 24–32.
Nish, Ian H., "Australia and the Anglo-Japanese Alliance, 1901–1911", *The Australian Journal of Politics and History* 9, No. 2, 1963, 201–212.
Nish, Ian H., "Britain and Japan: Long-Range Images, 1900–52", *Diplomacy and Statecraft* 15, No. 1, 2004, 149–161.
Novotný, Lukáš, "Der Sinowjew Brief", *Prague Papers on the History of International Relations*, 2006, 201–227.
Novotný, Lukáš, "Die Britischen Dominions und der Vertrag von Locarno: Der Prüfstein für eine einheitliche Außenpolitik des Empire in der Zwischenkriegszeit", *Jahrbuch für Europäische Überseegeschichte* 10, 2010, 163–188.
Novotný, Lukáš, "Konzervativní vláda Stanleyho Baldwina a její odmítnutí Ženevského protokolu: Příspěvek k pokusům o vytvoření kolektivní bezpečnosti ve dvacátých letech 20. století", *Dvacáté století*, 2006, 117–153.
Novotný, Lukáš, "On the Journey to the Rhineland Pact: Contribution to the Study of British Perception of the Problem of Collective Security in the 1920's", *Öt kontinens: Az Új- és Jelenkori Egyetemes Történeti Tanszék közleményei/ Cinq Continents: Les cahiers du Département d'Histoire moderne et contemporaine*, No. 1, 2009, 369–383.
Novotný, Lukáš, "Postoj britských dominií k Locarnskému paktu", *Acta Fakulty filozofické Západočeské univerzity v Plzni* 3, No. 2, 2011, 15–36.
Novotný, Lukáš, "Velká Británie a konference v Locarnu", *Moderní dějiny: Sborník k dějinám 19. a 20. století* 18, No. 2, 2010, 23–49.

Novotný, Lukáš, "Zinověvův dopis a Campbellův případ: Příspěvek ke zkoumání působnosti první labouristické vlády", *Historický obzor* 18, No. 9/10, 2007, 218–226.
O'Duffy, Brendan – Githens-Mazer, Jonathan, "Status and Statehood: Exchange Theory and British-Irish Relations, 1921–41", *Commonwealth & Comparative Politics* 40, No. 2, 2002, 120–145.
Okamoto, T., "American-Japanese Issues and the Anglo-Japanese Alliance", *Contemporary Review* 119, 1921, 354–360.
Okamoto, T., ", "Outcroppings from the Imperial Conference", *Advocate of Peace through Justice* 83, No. 7, 1921, 271–274.
Overlack, Peter, "German Assessments of the British-Australian Relations, 1901–1914", *The Australian Journal of Politics and History* 50, No. 2, 2004, 194–210.
Overlack, Peter, "German Interest in Australian Defence, 1901–1914: New Insights into a Precarious Position in the Eve of War", *The Australian Journal of Politics and History* 40, No. 1, 1993, 36–51.
Parmoor, Charles Alfred Cripps, 1st Baron of, "The Imperial Conference and the League of Nations", *Contemporary Review* 131, 1927, 1–6.
Parry, Glyn, "John Dee and the Elizabethan British Empire in Its European Context", *The Historical Journal* 49, No. 3, 2006, 643–675.
Peatling, G. K., "Globalism, Hegemonism and British Power: J. A. Hobson and Alfred Zimmern Reconsidered", *History* 89, No. 295, 2004, 381–398.
Phillips, D., "The British Commonwealth of Nations: The Latest Phase", *Pacific Affairs* 3, No. 5, 1930, 476–482.
Piesse, E. L., "Japan and Australia", *Foreign Affairs: An American Quarterly Review* 4, No. 1/4, 1925/1926, 475–488.
Piesse, E. L., "Policy and Sea Power", *The Round Table* 3, No. 10, 1913, 197–231.
Potter, Simon J., "Richard Jebb, John S. Ewart and the Round Table, 1898–1926", *The English Historical Review* 122, No. 495, 2007, 105–132.
Poynter, J. R., "The Yo-yo Variations: Initiative and Dependence in Australia's External Relations, 1918–1923", *Historical Studies* 14, No. 54, 1970, 231–249.
Prang, M., "N. W. Rowell and Canada's External Policy, 1917–1921", *Report of the Annual Meeting of the Canadian Historical Association/Rapports annuels de la Société historique du Canada* 39, No. 1, 1960, 83–103.
Pugh, R. B., "The Colonial Office, 1801–1925", in: *The Cambridge History of the British Empire: The Empire-Commonwealth 1870–1919*, Vol. 3, Cambridge: Cambridge University Press, 1967, 711–768.
Purcell, Hugh, "Paris Peace Discord", *History Today* 59, No. 7, 2009, 38–40.
Quigley, Carroll, "The Round Table Movement in Canada, 1909–38", *The Canadian Historical Review* 43, No. 3, 1962, 204–224.
Raffo, Peter, "The League of Nations Philosophy of Lord Robert Cecil", *Australian Journal of Politics & History* 20, No. 2, 1974, 186–196.
Reeves, William Pember, "A Council of the Empire", *Journal of the Society of Comparative Legislation* 5, No. 2, 1904, 241–243.
Reid, Colin, "Stephen Gwynn and the Failure of Constitutional Nationalism in Ireland, 1919–1921", *The Historical Journal* 53, No. 3, 2010, 723–745.
Romancov, Michael, "Commonwealth – vznik a vývoj", in: Šanc, David – Ženíšek, Marek (Eds.), *Commonwealth: Z perspektivy politické vědy*, Plzeň: Aleš Čeněk, 2008, 7–37.

Ross, Angus, "Reluctant Dominion or Dutiful Daughter? New Zealand and the Commonwealth in the Inter-War Years", *Journal of Commonwealth Political Studies* 10, No. 1, 1972, 28–44.

Rowell, N. W., "Canada and the Empire, 1884–1921", in: Rose, J. Holland – Newton, A. P. – Benians, E. A. (Eds.), *The Cambridge History of the British Empire: Canada and Newfoundland*, Vol. 6, Cambridge: Cambridge University Press, 1930, 704–737.

Sales, Peter M., "W. M. Hughes and the Chanak Crisis of 1922", *Australian Journal of History and Politics* 17, No. 3, 1971, 392–405.

Sarty, Roger, "Canadian Maritime Defence 1892–1914", *The Canadian Historical Review* 71, No. 4, 1990, 462–490.

Schuyler, Robert Livingston, "The British War Cabinet", *Political Science Quarterly* 33, No. 3, 1918, 378–395.

Schuyler, Robert Livingston, "The Rise of Anti-Imperialism in England", *Political Science Quarterly* 37, No. 3, 1922, 440–471.

Shields, R. A., "Australian Opinion and Defence of the Empire: A Study in Imperial Relations 1880–1890", *The Australian Journal of Politics and History* 10, No. 1, 1964, 41–53.

Sifton, Clifford, Sir, "Some Canadian Constitutional Problems", *The Canadian Historical Review* 3, No. 1, 1922, 3–23.

Smuts, Jan Christiaan, "The Present International Outlook", *International Affairs* 14, No. 1, 1935, 3–19.

Snelling, R. C., "Peacemaking 1919: Australia, New Zealand and the British Empire Delegation at Versailles", *The Journal of Imperial and Commonwealth History* 4, No. 1, 1975, 15–28.

Soward, Frederic H., "Sir Robert Borden and Canada's External Policy, 1911–1920", *Report of the Annual Meeting of the Canadian Historical Association/Rapports annuels de la Société historique du Canada* 20, No. 1, 1941, 65–82.

Soward, Frederic H., "The Election of Canada to the League of Nations Council in 1927", *The American Journal of International Law* 23, No. 4, 1929, 753–765.

Soward, Frederic H., "Speech of the Right Hon. Joseph Chamberlain, M. P., in the House of Commons, April 3, 1900", *The Edinburgh Review* 192, No. 393, 1900, 247–270.

Spinks, Charles Nelson, "The Termination of the Anglo-Japanese Alliance", *Pacific Historical Review* 6, 1937, 321–340.

Stambrook, F. G., "'Das Kind' – Lord D'Abernon and the Origins of the Locarno Pact", *Central European History* 1, No. 3, 1968, 233–263.

Stevenson, J. A., "Canada and Downing Street", *Foreign Affairs: An American Quarterly Review* 3, No. 1/4, 1924–1925, 135–146.

Stevenson, J. A., "Canadian Nationalism", *Edinburgh Review* 244, No. 497, 1926, 18–31.

Stewart, Andrew, "The 'Bloody Post Office': The Life and Times of the Dominions Office", *Contemporary British History* Vol. 24, No. 1, 2010, 43–66.

Stewart, Robert B., "Treaty-Making Procedure in the British Dominions", *The American Journal of International Law* 32, No. 3, 1938, 467–487.

Studdert-Kennedy, Gerald, "Political Science and Political Theology: Lionel Curtis, Federalism, and India", *The Journal of Imperial and Commonwealth History* 24, No. 2, 1996, 197–217.

Studdert-Kennedy, Gerald, "Summary of Proceedings of the Imperial Conference and the Imperial Economic Conference", *The Round Table* 14, No. 53, 1923, 205–224.
Sundaram, Lanka, "The International Status of India", *Journal of the Royal Institute of International Affairs* 9, No. 4, 1930, 452–466.
Šubrt, Martin, "Kanada a Chanacká krize", *Historica Olomucensia* 56, 2019, 199–214.
Tate, Merze – Foy, Fidele, "More Light on the Abrogation of the Anglo-Japanese Alliance", *Political Science Quarterly* 74, No. 4, 1959, 532–554.
"The British Empire, the League of Nations and the United States", *The Round Table* 10, No. 38, 1920, 221–253.
"The Conference and the Empire", *The Round Table* 1, No. 4, 1911, 371–425.
"The Crown and the Dominions", *The Round Table* 21, No. 81, 1930, 96–105.
"The Imperial Conference", *The Round Table* 11, No. 14, 1921, 735–758.
"The Imperial Conference', *The Round Table* 21, No. 81, 1930, 229–238.
"The Mansion House Meeting", *United Empire: The Royal Colonial Institute Journal* 11, No. 5, 1920, 254–261.
"The Next Imperial Conference", *The Round Table* 16, No. 62, 1926, 227–255.
Thierry, C. de, "The Colonial Office Myth", *Contemporary Review*, No. 78, 1900, 365–380.
Thornton, Robert, "Semblance of Security: Australia and the Washington Conference, 1921–22", *Australian Outlook* 32, No. 1, 1978, 65–83.
Towey, Thomas, "The Reaction of the British Government to the 1922 Collins-de Valera Pact", *Irish Historical Studies* 22, No. 85, 1980, 65–76.
Toye, Richard, "'Phrases Make History Here': Churchill, Ireland and the Rhetoric Empire", *The Journal of Imperial and Commonwealth History* 38, No. 4, 2010, 549–570.
Tsokhas, Kosmas, "Tradition, Fantasy and Britishness: Four Australian Prime Ministers", *Journal of Contemporary Asia* 31, No. 1, 2001, 3–30.
Tucker, Gilbert Norman, "The Naval Policy of Sir Robert Borden, 1912–14", *The Canadian Historical Review* 28, No. 1, 1947, 1–30.
Tunstall, W. C. B., "Imperial Defence, 1897–1914", in: *The Cambridge History of the British Empire: The Empire-Commonwealth 1870–1919*, Vol. 3, Cambridge: Cambridge University Press, 1967, 563–604.
Tunstall, W. C. B., "The Development of the Imperial Conference, 1887–1914", in: *The Cambridge History of the British Empire: The Empire-Commonwealth 1870–1919*, Vol. 3, Cambridge: Cambridge University Press, 1967 406–437.
Tupper, C. Hibbert, "Treaty-Making Powers of the Dominions", *Journal of the Society of Comparative Legislation* 17, New Series, No. 1/2, 1917, 5–18.
Underhill, F. H., "Canada and the Last War", in: Martin, Chester (Ed.), *Canada in Peace and War: Eight Studies in National Trends since 1914*, London: Oxford University Press, 1941, 120–149.
Valkoun, Jaroslav – Urban, Martin, "Kanada ve Společnosti národů a její postoj k článku 10 Paktu Společnosti národů", *Acta Historica Universitatis Silesianae Opaviensis* 11, 2018, 69–80.
Vince, Donald M. A. R., "Development in the Legal Status of the Canadian Military Forces, 1914–19, as Related to Dominion Status", *The Canadian Journal of Economics and Political Science/Revue canadienne d'Economique et de Science politique* 20, No. 3, 1954, 357–370.

Vinson, J. Chal, "The Drafting of the Four-Power Treaty of the Washington Conference", *Journal of Modern History* 25, No. 1, 1953, 40–47.

Vinson, J. Chal, "The Imperial Conference of 1921 and the Anglo-Japanese Alliance", *Pacific Historical Review* 31, No. 3, 1962, 257–266.

Vinson, J. Chal, "The Problem of Australian Representation at the Washington Conference for the Limitation of Naval Armament", *The Australian Journal of Politics and History* 4, No. 2, 1958, 155–164.

Walker, Eric Anderson, "South Africa and the Empire", in: Newton, A. P. – Benians, E. A. (Eds.), *The Cambridge History of the British Empire: South Africa, Rhodesia and the Protectorates*, Vol. 8, Cambridge: Cambridge University Press, 1936, 734–758.

Warman, Roberta M., "The Erosion of Foreign Office Influence in the Making of Foreign Policy, 1916–1918", *The Historical Journal* 15, No. 11, 1972, 133–159.

Watt, Donald Cameron, "Imperial Defence Policy and Imperial Foreign Policy, 1911–1939 – A Neglected Paradox?", *Journal of Commonwealth Political Studies* 1, No. 1, 1963, 266–281.

Wheare, Kenneth Clinton, "The Empire and the Peace Treaties 1918–1921", in: *The Cambridge History of the British Empire: The Empire-Commonwealth 1870–1919*, Vol. 3, Cambridge: Cambridge University Press, 1967, 645–666.

White, Thomas Raeburn, "The Amended Covenant of the League of Nations", *The Annals of the American Academy of Political and Social Science* 84, No. 1, 1919, 177–193.

Wigley, Philip, "Whitehall and the 1923 Imperial Conference", *The Journal of Imperial and Commonwealth History* 1, No. 2, 1973, 223–235.

Wigley, Philip, Hillmer, Norman, "Defining the First British Commonwealth: The Hankey Memoranda on the 1926 Imperial Conference", *The Journal of Imperial and Commonwealth History* 8, No. 1, 1979, 105–116.

Wilde, Richard H., "Joseph Chamberlain's Proposal of an Imperial Council in March, 1900", *The Canadian Historical Review* 37, No. 3, 1956, 225–246.

William, Basil, "Botha and Smuts: Par Nobile Fratrum", *Contemporary Review* 165, 1944, 212–220.

Williams, Priscilla, "New Zealand at the 1930 Imperial Conference", *New Zealand Journal of History* 5, No. 1, 1971, 31–48.

Wilson, Philip W., "The Imperial Conference", *North American Review* 213, 1921, 725–735.

Wilson, Robert R., "Anglo-Irish Accord", *The American Journal of International Law* 32, No. 3, 1938, 545–547.

Wilson, Robert R., "Windows of Freedom", *The Round Table* 9, No. 33, 1918, 1–47.

Wood, F. L. W., "Australia and the Imperial Conference", *The Australian Quarterly* 2, No. 8, 1930, 68–74.

Woodsworth, Charles J., "Canada and the Far East", *Far Eastern Survey* 10, No. 14, 1941, 159–164.

Worsfold, Basil W., "The Administration of the Empire", *United Empire: The Royal Colonial Institute Journal* 11, No. 7, 1920, 357–363.

Wrong, George M., "Canada and the Imperial War Cabinet", *The Canadian Historical Review* 1, No. 1, 1920, 3–25.

Wrong, George M., "The Evolution of the Foreign Relations of Canada", *The Canadian Historical Review* 5, No. 3, 1925, 4–14.
Yearwood, Peter J., "'A Genuine and Energetic League of Nations Policy': Lord Curzon and the New Diplomacy, 1918–1925", *Diplomacy and Statecraft* 21, No. 2, 2010, 159–174.
Yearwood, Peter J., "'On the Safe and Right Lines': The Lloyd George Government and the Origins of the League of Nations, 1916–1918", *The Historical Journal* 3, No. 1, 1989, 131–155.
Young, Robert, "The Anglo-Japanese Alliance", *Contemporary Review* 120, 1921, 8–19.
Zimmern, Alfred Eckhard, Sir, 'German Culture and British Commonwealth," in: Seton-Watson, Robert William et al. (Eds.), *The War and Democracy*, London: Macmillan, 1915, 348–383.
Zimmern, Alfred Eckhard, Sir, "Is There an Empire Foreign Policy?", *International Affairs* 13, No. 3, 1934, 303–324.
Zimmern, Alfred Eckhard, Sir, "The Commonwealth Today", in: Bailey, Sydney Dawson (Ed.), *Parliamentary Government in the Commonwealth*, London: Hansard Society, 1951, 9–13.

IX) Unpublished MA Theses

Bernas, Vlastimil, *Politicko-geografické aspekty transformace Britského impéria na Společenství národů*, Praha: Univerzita Karlova, 2013.
Cassidy, James Thomas, *Prelude to a New World Order: The Atlantic Triangle and Japan 1914–1921*, Montreal: McGill University, 1974.
Cunningham, Alain MacAlpine, *Canadian Nationalism and the British Connection 1899–1919*, Burnaby: Simon Fraser University, 1980.
Delaquis, Danys R. X., *Une variante nationale du continentalisme le Canada et l'alliance anglo-japonaise, 1919 à 1921*, Moncton: Université de Moncton, 1995.
Hind, Joseph Winton, *Lloyd George and the Turkish Question: An Examination of Lloyd George's Turkish Policy, 1918–1922*, Vancouver: The University of British Columbia, 1978.
Muir, Thomas Alexander, *Britain's Official Mind: Foreign Policy Decision-making under the Lloyd George Coalition, 1918–1922*, Fredericton: University of New Brunswick, 2003.
Troop, William H., *The Political and Constitutional Implications of the 1926 Imperial Conference*, Montreal, McGill University, 1929.

X) Unpublished PhD Theses

Adams, Eric E., *The Idea of Constitutional Rights and the Transformation of Canadian Constitutional Law, 1930–1960*, Toronto: University of Toronto, 2009.
Baumgartl, Liselotte, *Empire and Commonwealth*, Wien: Universität Wien, 1950.
Bell, Christopher Michael, *British Ideas of Sea Power, 1914–1941*, Calgary: The University of Calgary, 1998.
Chaudron, Gerald, *New Zealand in the League of Nations*, Canterbury: University of Canterbury, 1989.

Dufek, Pavel, *Německé námořní zbrojení a vztah Velké Británie a Německa do roku 1906*, Praha: Univerzita Karlova, 2002.

Forbes, Frederic J., *Canada in the League of Nations*, Montreal: McGill University, 1927.

Gilbert, Angus Duncan, *The Political Influence of Imperialist Thought in Canada, 1899–1923*, Toronto: University of Toronto, 1974.

Holland, Robert F., *The Commonwealth in the British Official Mind: A Study in Anglo-Dominion Relations, 1925–37*, Oxford: University of Oxford, 1977.

Kenneth, Daniel, *Commonwealth: Imperialism and Internationalism, 1919–1939*, Austin: The University of Texas at Austin, 2012.

Lerner, Bruno, *Der Einfluß der Dominions auf die Außenpolitik Großbritanniens (einige Aspekte)*, Wien: Universität Wien, 1965.

MacFarlane, John, *Ernest Lapointe: Quebec's Voice in Canadian Foreign Policy, 1921–1941*, Quebec: Université Laval, 1995.

McKercher, Brian J. C., *The Golden Gleam, 1916–1920: Britain and the Origins of the League of Nations*, Edmonton: The University of Alberta, 1975.

McManus, Mary Kathleen, *The End of Imperial Diplomatic Unity, 1919–1928: Anglo-Canadian Relations from the British Perspective*, London: University of London, 1992.

Messamore, Barbara Jane, *The Governors General of Canada, 1888–1911: British Imperialists and Canadian "Nationalists"*, Burnaby: Simon Fraser University, 1991.

Nerad, Filip, *Německo a irské separatistické hnutí: Německo-irská spolupráce do vzniku Irského svobodného státu*, Praha: Univerzita Karlova, 2012.

Scheuer, Michael Frank, *Loring Christie and the North Atlantic Community, 1913–1941*, Winnipeg: University of Manitoba, 1986.

Spencer, Alex M., *A Third Option: Imperial Air Defence and the Pacific Dominions, 1918–1939*, Auburn: Auburn University, 2008.

Author Index

Amery, Leopold Stennett (1873–1955) 1, 4–5, 7–8, 18, 39–40, 42, 44–47, 65–66, 90–91, 95–99, 108–111, 117–118, 183, 193, 197–201, 207–211, 213–215, 236–247, 249, 251–253, 259

Arnold, Sydney, 1st Baron Arnold (1878–1945) 196

Asquith, Herbert Henry, 1st Earl of Oxford and Asquith (1852–1928) 47, 49–56, 58–64, 66–67, 88, 93, 132, 135

Atatürk, Mustafa Kemal (1881–1938) 173–174

Baldwin, Stanley, 1st Earl Baldwin of Bewdley (1867–1947) 188, 198–199, 201, 209–211, 239, 244, 252, 282

Balfour, Arthur James, 1st Earl of Balfour (1848–1930) 7, 37, 56–57, 97, 102, 118, 124, 128–130, 203, 208, 244–247, 251

Barton, Robert Childers (1881–1975) 140, 142

Bellairs, Carlyon Wilfroy (1871–1955) 212

Bennett, Richard Bedford, 1st Viscount Bennett (1870–1947) 253

Bentinck, Charles Henry, Sir (1879–1955) 123

Bonar Law, Andrew (1858–1923) 88, 133, 139, 178, 180, 186

Botha, Louis (1862–1919) 42, 48, 50, 53, 55, 94, 98, 111

Borden, Frederick William, Sir (1847–1917) 59

Borden, Robert Laird, Sir (1854–1937) 8, 17–18, 59, 65–68, 88–89, 92–93, 95–97, 104, 106–107, 112, 121, 128, 131, 195, 207, 237

Bourassa, Joseph Napoléon Henri (1868–1952) 183

Bourgeois, Victor Auguste Léon (1851–1925) 102–103

Braddon, Edward Nicholas, Sir (1829–1904) 32

Brett, Reginald Baliol, 2nd Viscount Esher (1852–1930) 57

Brodrick, William St. John Fremantle, 1st Earl of Midleton (1856–1942) 56

Bruce, Stanley Melbourne, 1st Viscount Bruce of Melbourne (1883–1867) 177, 187, 191–192, 194, 201, 207–208, 210–211, 214, 239, 243–245

Bruce, Victor Alexander, 9th Earl of Elgin, 13th Earl of Kincardine (1849–1917) 38

Brugha, Cathal (1874–1922) 142

Byng, Julian Hedworth George, 1st Viscount Byng of Vimy (1862–1935) 5, 181–182, 187, 235–237, 282

Cambridge, Alexander Augustus, 1st Earl of Athlone (1874–1957) 252

Campbell-Bannerman, Henry, Sir (1836–1908) 15, 41

Casey, Richard Gardiner, Baron Casey (1890–1976) 177, 239–240, 243, 250, 259

Cavendish, Edward William Spencer, 10th Duke of Devonshire (1895–1950) 210

Author Index

Cavendish, Victor Christian William, 9th Duke of Devonshire (1868–1938) 179
Cecil, Edgar Algernon Robert Gascoyne, 1st Viscount Cecil of Chelwood (1864–1958) 7–8, 102
Cecil, James Edward Hubert Gascoyne, 4th Marquess of Salisbury (1861–1947) 192
Cecil, Robert Arthur Talbot Gascoyne, 3rd Marquess of Salisbury (1830–1903) 29, 32–33
Chamberlain, Austen, Sir (1863–1937) 118, 137, 200, 209–213, 215, 240, 244, 246, 254, 259
Chamberlain, Joseph (1836–1914) 8, 14–15, 30–37, 44, 52
Childers, Robert Erskine (1870–1922) 137–140
Chinda, Sutemi, Count (1857–1929) 104
Christie, Loring Cheney (1885–1941) 99–100, 122, 128, 214
Churchill, Winston Spencer Leonard, Sir (1874–1965) 65, 102, 113, 124, 134, 136–137, 140, 174–177, 199–200
Clemenceau, Georges Benjamin (1841–1929) 98
Clynes, John Robert (1869–1949) 132
Collins, Michael (1890–1922) 136, 141–142, 194
Cook, Joseph, Sir (1860–1947) 101
Cosgrave, William Thomas (1880–1965) 142–143, 195, 214
Craig, James, 1st Viscount Craigavon (1871–1940) 134, 140
Crowe, Eyre Alexander, Sir (1864–1925) 210
Curtis, Lionel George (1872–1955) 16, 45–47, 61, 65–66, 92–93, 137–138, 241
Curzon, George Nathaniel, 1st Marquess Curzon of Kedleston (1859–1925) 124, 133, 174, 177, 179, 181–182, 189, 192, 208

Dafoe, John Wesley (1866–1944) 46
Dawson, George Geoffrey (1874–1944) 45
Deakin, Alfred (1856–1919) 41–42, 64, 198

Denman, Thomas, 3rd Baron Denman (1874–1954) 68
Dickson-Poynder, John Poynder, 1st Baron Islington (1866–1936) 46–47
Doherty, Charles Joseph (1855–1931) 203
Drage, Geoffrey (1860–1955) 39
Duggan, Eamonn (Edmund) S. (1874–1936) 135
Duffy, George Gavan (1882–1951) 140

Edward VII (1841–1910) 33
Ewart, John Skirving (1849–1933) 46

Fisher, Andrew (1862–1928) 51, 53–55, 63, 68, 87, 92
Fisher, Herbert Albert Laurens (1865–1940) 132
Fisher, Norman Fenwick Warren, Sir (1879–1948) 201
Foch, Ferdinand (1851–1929) 98
Foster, George Eulas, Sir (1847–1931) 43, 128

Gardiner, Albert (1867–1952) 176
Garvin, James Louis (1868–1947) 48
Geddes, Auckland, 1st Baron Geddes (1879–1954) 19–20, 128, 185
George V (1865–1936) 56, 134
Gladstone, William Ewart (1809–1898) 29, 135
Glazebrook, Arthur James (1861–1940) 45
Gouin, Jean Lomer, Sir (1861–1929) 205
Grey, Edward, 1st Viscount Grey of Fallodon (1862–1933) 61–62
Griffith, Arthur (1872–1922) 135–136, 139–143
Gwyer, Maurice Linford, Sir (1878–1952) 255

Haldane, Richard Burdon, 1st Viscount Haldane (1856–1928) 36, 49, 62, 89
Hall, Hessel Duncan (1891–1976) 8, 115
Hamilton, George Francis, Lord (1845–1927) 35

Author Index 331

Hancock, William Keith, Sir (1898–1988) 9
Hankey, Maurice Pascal Alers, 1st Baron Hankey (1877–1963) 7, 60–63, 66–68, 88–90, 96–97, 99–100, 106, 111, 121, 128, 208, 239, 242, 246
Harcourt, Lewis Vernon, 1st Viscount Harcourt (1863–1922) 49–51, 54, 67–68, 92
Harding, Warren Gamaliel (1865–1923) 126, 128
Hazen, John Douglas, Sir (1860–1937) 185
Henry VIII (1491–1547) 13
Herriot, Éduard Marie (1872–1957) 209
Hertzog, James Barry Munnik (1866–1942) 20, 120, 201, 208, 235, 237–241, 243–244, 246, 252–253
Hofmeyr, Jan Hendrick (1845–1909) 29
Holland, Bernard Henry (1856–1926) 36
Holland, Henry Thurstan, 1st Viscount Knutsford (1825–1914) 29
Hopwood, Francis John Stephens, 1st Baron Southborough (1860–1947) 43
House, Edward Mandell (1858–1938) 104
Hughes, Charles Evans, Sr. (1862–1948) 19–20, 127, 129–130, 186, 208
Hughes, William, "Billy" Morris (1862–1952) 88–89, 96–101, 103–105, 111–112, 118–126, 174–177, 179, 181, 244
Hurd, Percy Angier, Sir (1865–1950) 216
Hurst, Cecil James, Sir (1870–1963) 103

Jameson, Leander Starr, Sir, 1st Baronet (1853–1917) 42
Jebb, Richard (1874–1953) 42, 46, 66
Jellicoe, John Rushworth, 1st Earl Jellicoe (1859–1935) 174
Jones, Clement Wakefield, Sir (1880–1863) 111
Jones, Thomas (1870–1955) 133, 137
Just, Hartmann Wolfgang, Sir (1854–1929) 48–49

Keith, Arthur Berriedale (1879–1944) 8–9
Kerr, Philip Henry, 11th Marquess of Lothian (1882–1940) 16–17, 45, 47–48, 178

Lansing, Robert (1864–1928) 99
Lapointe, Ernest (1876–1941) 185–187
Laurier, Henri Charles Wilfrid, Sir (1841–1919) 31, 34, 39–42, 48, 51, 53–55, 59–60, 65
Lee, Arthur Hamilton, 1st Viscount Lee of Fareham (1868–1947) 128
Little, James Stanley (1856–1940) 14
Lloyd George, David (1863–1945) 8, 17, 56, 88–90, 94–95, 99–100, 102–103, 118, 120, 124, 126, 128, 131–137, 140, 142, 174, 176–177, 189, 216
Lodge, Henry Cabot (1850–1924) 129
Long, Walter Hume, 1st Viscount Long (1854–1924) 93, 96
Lucas, Charles Prestwood, Sir (1853–1931) 48
Lyttelton, Alfred (1857–1913) 15, 37–39, 48, 55
MacDonald, James Ramsay (1866–1937) 182, 195–197, 207, 209–210, 215–216, 239, 256
Macdonald, John Alexander, Sir (1815–1891) 184
Mackay, James Lyle, 1st Earl of Inchcape (1852–1932) 40
Mackenzie King, William Lyon (1874–1950) 5, 119, 173, 175–177, 180–187, 189–195, 200–201, 204, 207–208, 211, 213–214, 235–239, 246, 249, 282
Makino, Nobuaki, Count (1861–1949) 104–105
Malan, François Stephanus (1871–1941) 54
Mansergh, Philip Nicholas Seton (1910–1991) 9
Massey, William Ferguson (1856–1925) 17, 19, 68, 88, 93, 95, 98, 101, 119–121, 126, 181, 191, 201, 208

McGilligan, Patrick (1889–1979) 257
McKenna, Reginald (1863–1943) 59, 62
Meighen, Arthur (1874–1960) 113, 119, 121, 123–126, 128, 173, 178, 183, 186, 214, 236
Merriman, John Xavier (1841–1926) 15–16
Miller, David Hunter (1875–1961) 8, 103–104
Milner, Alfred, 1st Viscount Milner (1854–1925) 8, 15–16, 19, 35, 39, 45, 93, 95, 101–102, 106, 109–110, 112–113, 197
Montagu, Edwin Samuel (1879–1924) 106
Montgomery, Hubert Charles, Sir (1876–1942) 242
Morris, Edward Patrick, 1st Baron Morris (1859–1935) 53, 55
Motherwell, William Richard (1860–1943) 180

O'Higgins, Kevin Christopher (1892–1927) 142, 191, 246–247
Orlando, Vittorio Emanuele (1860–1952) 98
Ottley, Charles Langdale, Sir (1858–1932) 60–63

Palmer, William Waldergrave, 2nd Earl of Selborne (1859–1942) 45
Pearce, George Foster, Sir (1870–1952) 128–129, 131
Perley, George Halsey, Sir (1857–1938) 68, 90
Phillimore, Walter George Frank, 1st Baron Phillimore (1845–1929) 102
Plunkett, Horace Curzon, Sir (1854–1932) 132
Poincaré, Raymond (1860–1934) 179
Pollard, Albert Frederick, Sir (1869–1948) 16
Pollock, Frederick, Sir, 3rd Baronet (1845–1937) 36, 38, 45
Powell, Ellis Thomas (1869–1922) 15

Reeves, William Pember (1857–1932) 36
Roberts, Frederick Sleigh, 1st Earl Roberts (1832–1914) 52

Robinson, George Frederick Samuel, 1st Marquess of Ripon (1827–1909) 29, 184
Root, Elihu (1845–1937) 129
Rosebery, Archibald Philip Primrose, 5th Earl of Rosebery, 1st Earl of Midlothian (1847–1929) 8, 13
Rumbold, Horace George Montagu, 9th Baronet of Woodhall (1869–1941) 179

Sankey, John, 1st Viscount Sankey (1866–1948) 257
Scullin, James Henry (1876–1953) 244
Seddon, Richard John (1845–1906) 32, 64
Seeley, John Robert, Sir (1834–1895) 14
Seely, John Edward Bernard, 1st Baron Mottistone (1868–1947) 50
Shaw, George Bernard (1856–1950) 14
Shaw, Thomas (1872–1938) 212
Sifton, Arthur Lewis Watkins (1858–1921) 104
Sifton, Clifford, Sir (1861–1929) 190
Skelton, Oscar Douglas (1878–1941) 20, 178, 183, 189, 214
Smiddy, Timothy Aloysius "Audo" (1875–1962) 196
Smith, Frederick Edwin, 1st Earl of Birkenhead (1872–1930) 137, 247
Smuts, Jan Christiaan (1870–1950) 5, 7–8, 17–19, 93–94, 97–98, 102–103, 105, 107, 109–112, 114–120, 125–127, 134–136, 173, 179, 181, 183, 191, 211, 214–216, 238, 241, 245, 249, 252–253
Solomon, Richard, Sir (1850–1913) 50
Stack, Austin (1879–1929) 138, 142
Stanhope, Edward (1840–1893) 29
Shidehara, Kijūrō, Baron (1872–1951) 129

Thomas, James Henry (1874–1949) 182, 196–197
Tupper, Charles, 1st Baronet of Armdale (1821–1915) 184

Valera, Éamon de (1882–1975) 134–136, 139–140, 142–143
Victoria (1819–1901) 29, 31

Ward, Joseph George, 1st Baronet, of Wellington (1856–1930)
Warren, William Robertson (1879–1937) 42, 52, 54–55, 61, 64

Webb, Sidney James, 1st Baron Passfield (1859–1947) 256
Wilson, Thomas Woodrow (1856–1924) 99–100, 103, 202

Zimmern, Alfred Eckhard, Sir (1879–1957) 18

Subject Index

Anglo-Irish Agreement 4, 6, 19, 131, 142–143, 194, 281
Anglo-Japanese Alliance 5, 61–62, 118, 122, 124–131, 174, 281
Article X 5, 201–207

Balfour Declaration 5, 20–21, 94, 122, 235, 246, 248–249, 251–253, 256, 258, 262, 279, 282

Chanak Crisis 5, 9, 173–175, 177–179, 183–184, 189, 191, 204, 209, 216, 235, 281
Colonial Conference 1887 28–29
Colonial Conference 1897 31–32
Colonial Conference 1902 34–37
Colonial (Imperial) Conference 1907 42–44
Committee of Imperial Defence 6–7, 49, 56–64, 66–68, 88–89, 93, 126, 199, 208, 213, 239, 280

Dominion Office 3, 6–7, 20, 47, 91, 194, 199–201, 212, 240, 243–244, 246, 254, 257

Geneva Protocol 5, 201, 207–210, 216, 282

Halibut Treaty 5, 184–187

Imperial Conference 1911 45–56, 61, 64, 91, 94, 108, 198
Imperial Conference 1921 113–114, 118–122, 124–126, 130, 134, 137, 139, 173, 281
Imperial Conference 1923 184, 187–190, 192, 194–195, 282

Imperial Conference 1926 20–21, 120, 143, 217, 237, 240–245, 249, 251–252, 254, 259, 261, 282
Imperial Conference 1930 255–257, 260
Imperial Conference on Defence 1909 58–60
Imperial Council 14, 31–39, 42, 49–50, 52–53, 61
Imperial Federation League 28, 31, 36
Imperial War Cabinet 4, 87–89, 91, 93–95, 97–98, 102, 108–109, 112–113, 281
Imperial War Conference 1917 4, 17–18, 21, 87–88, 91, 93–96, 106, 108, 110, 116, 119, 196, 198, 248, 280
Inter-Imperial Relations Committee 5, 243–251, 253–257

King-Byng Affair 235–237

Lausanne Conference 5, 173, 178–184, 188–191, 193, 195–196, 209, 213, 216, 235, 281
League of Nations 8, 98, 100–107, 112, 115–116, 118–119, 124–125, 131, 139–140, 187, 191–193, 199, 201–211, 216, 242–245, 254, 260, 281
Locarno Conference 5, 201, 209, 212–216, 240, 244–245, 247, 249, 260, 282

Pollock Committee 36–39, 41–42, 45, 49–50

Resolution IX 4, 21, 93, 108, 119, 196, 248, 257
Round Table Movement 4, 16, 45–48, 50, 52–53, 55, 61, 64–68, 92–93, 109, 112, 134, 178

Statute of Westminster 1, 5–6, 21, 122, 235, 251, 260–262, 279, 282–283

Washington Disarmament Conference 6, 128, 174, 181